Canadian Perspectives in Sexualities Studies

Canadian Perspectives
in Sexualities Studies

Identities, Experiences, and the Contexts of Change

edited by
Diane Naugler

OXFORD
UNIVERSITY PRESS

Oxford University Press is a department of the University of Oxford.
It furthers the University's objective of excellence in research, scholarship, and education by publishing worldwide.
Oxford is a registered trade mark of Oxford University Press in the UK and in certain other countries.

Published in Canada by
Oxford University Press
8 Sampson Mews, Suite 204,
Don Mills, Ontario M3C 0H5 Canada
www.oupcanada.com

Library and Archives Canada Cataloguing in Publication

Canadian perspectives in sexualities studies : identities, experiences,
and the contexts of change / edited by Diane Naugler.

Includes bibliographical references.
ISBN 978-0-19-543973-1

1. Sex—Canada.   2. Sex customs—Canada.   3. Gender identity—Canada.
I. Naugler, Diane

HQ18.C3C36 2012   306.70971   C2012-900063-9

Cover image: Nikolai Larin/Getty Images

This book is printed on permanent acid-free paper ∞.

Printed and bound in Canada.

1 2 3 4 — 15 14 13 12

Contents

Part II   Sexual Identities in Changing Social Contexts   107

Part III Status and Stigma: Sex and Sexualities in Social Institutions 255

6   Health, Illness, and Sexualities   259

7   Sex Information and Educational Council of Canada   298

Part IV   Mutually Constructing Knowledges: Sex, Gender, and Sexualities   379

Preface

Canadian Perspectives in Sexualities Studies: Experiences and Identities in the Context of Change is a collection of influential previously published work in sexualities studies in the social sciences. This anthology combines international examples of the founding texts in the field with a sustained exploration of how Canadian scholars have challenged and further developed these founding inquiries.

In the last 30 years in particular Canadian scholars have put forward a wide variety of internationally recognized scholarship that attends to and participates in the popular and academic dialogues concerned with the meanings and experiences of sexualities and sexual identities. This anthology fills a specific need in undergraduate programs for an accessible, Canadian text that presents the richness of the interrelated fields of sexualities studies (sociology, gender studies, queer studies, women's studies, etc.) in the social sciences.

Canadian Perspectives in Sexualities Studies is designed for use in second- or third-year social sciences courses in sexuality. The chosen chapter selections are accessible and engaging for students and substantive and rich enough to provide instructors with both flexibility and depth in the design of these courses. The anthology is organized through four two- to three-chapter parts. Each part begins with several 'Starting Points Questions'. Through these questions students are encouraged to consider their existing knowledge about chapter topics and how they have come to hold these knowledges. These Starting Points questions are followed by a part introduction that explains the organization of the part, identifies its main themes, and provides brief introductions to each article. Each chapter contains four to five individual articles, primarily written by Canadian scholars. Article bibliographies are included as resources for further student research. Each part concludes with 'Critical Considerations: Discussion Questions', questions designed to reinforce students' engagements with the readings and encourage them to think across the presented articles to generate new understandings. In order to help develop students' conceptual and theoretical competencies, each part concludes with a glossary of key terms drawn from the readings.

Canadian Perspectives in Sexualities Studies brings together a selection of Canadian scholarship in the interdisciplinary field of sexualities studies. The collection is an invitation for students, and all readers, to take part in the vibrant debates and discussions herein. The collected authors produce a dialogue about sexuality and society that offers students conceptual and theoretical tools, historical perspectives, and timely information to encourage them to reconsider their knowledge, experiences, and opinions about sexuality and sexual orientation, and hopefully participate in the development of a thoughtful and progressive sexual social order.

Diane Naugler

Acknowledgements

Many people have had a hand in the development of this collection and, to each, I offer my heartfelt thanks. For lively discussions that convinced me of the merits of this project, I'd like to thank my colleagues at Acadia University and Kwantlen Polytechnic University. For helpful suggestions about possible articles and authors my thanks go to Ailsa Craig, Kate Campbell, and Fiona Wittington-Walsh. The careful considerations and comments of the five anonymous reviewers throughout the development of this volume were essential to the development of a useful and thought-provoking collection. In addition, I want to especially thank the editors at Oxford University Press: Nancy Reilly, who first championed the idea of a Canadian collection; and Mary Wat, who helped me stay on track throughout the process of bringing it to press. I would like to especially thank my 'at home' editor Kate Campbell whose careful eye and thoughtful feedback infuse and enliven this volume.

Introduction

'There's no place for the state in the bedrooms of the nation.' Those unforgettable words made famous by Pierre Trudeau in 1967 caused a tidal wave of controversy that rippled across the entire nation. Trudeau's Omnibus Bill brought issues like abortion, homosexuality, and divorce law to the forefront for the first time, changing the political and social landscape in Canada forever. (Canadian Broadcasting Corporation Archives, 2009)

With the introduction of his proposed changes to the federal Criminal Code in December 1967, then Justice Minister Pierre Trudeau helped shift the public discourses of sex and sexuality to an arguably more tolerant and pluralist understanding of people's relationships and desires. This set the stage for important changes in the Canadian legal system's treatment of abortion, divorce, and sexuality that are still being felt today. It may come as a surprise to many contemporary readers that sexual activities (private, personal, and 'Nobody's business but my own!') are a focus of state regulation. In a nation of YouTube nudity, explicitly sexual music lyrics and videos, and municipally sanctioned Gay Pride parades it may be hard to imagine what all the fuss was about. But, if we think things through a bit further, aren't we still a nation of communities and individuals whose ideas about sex and sexuality offer different, and often outright competing, perspectives?

The word sex has many diverse and related meanings. Sex is at once a category of human existence, a variously purposed activity, and an orientation or aspect of individual and/or group identity. It is a very busy word. In some ways, its variant sexuality only gets busier! Isn't it interesting that you don't have to have had sex to have a sexual orientation? Is everyone on the planet straight, gay, or bi? Do we all think that these distinctions mean the same thing? Is sexuality a biological given, a social construction, a bit of both? As meanings of sexuality change within a given society, do people's experiences of sexuality change as well? What role does sexuality play in everyday people's lives anyway? These are deliberately provocative questions, and the answers are no less so. These and many other questions have been asked by educators, clergy, doctors, politicians, parents, teens, and other individuals and groups—all of us at one time or another. Understandably, social scientists and other academics have also been captivated by these kinds of questions.

In this anthology, you will be introduced to some answers Canadian sexualities studies scholars have developed in response to these questions.

Their works will challenge, inspire, and perhaps even infuriate. Much like our politicians, Canadian academics have been centrally involved in the discussions about sexuality that shape the fabric of our own sexual lives. The volume is divided into four related parts: Introduction to Sexualities Studies; Sexual Identities in Changing Social Contexts; Status and Stigma: Sex and Sexualities in Social Institutions; and Mutually Constructing Knowledges: Sex, Gender, and Sexualities. Each part comprises two or three thematically organized chapters that present students with some of the most influential and original Canadian scholarship related to the section's theme.

There are many potential starting points when discussing the field of sexualities studies. Certainly the European sexologists, including Havelock Ellis and others, have had a lasting impact on both public and academic discourses of sexuality. Another undeniable influence on the development of this field is the work of psychiatrists and psychoanalysts such as Sigmund Freud (1905). Early psychological and scientific considerations of sexuality, such as those by Richard Von Krafft-Ebing (1886), sought to legitimize 'natural' male/female sexual relations. According to scholars such as Canadian sociologist Gary Kinsman and American anthropologist Gayle Rubin (in this volume), this focus concretized definitions about modern sexual 'deviants' and minorities and aided in their stigmatization. In the last 30 or so years, the field of sexualities studies has encouraged much less judgmental work by sexologists such as Alfred Kinsey (1948, 1953) and others. The field has also been invigorated by academic and social movements such as feminism, anti-racism, and gay and transgender rights.

Part I, 'Introduction to Sexualities Studies', introduces readers to some of the founding authors, questions, debates, and theoretical traditions of sexualities studies within the social sciences. In terms of Canadian scholarship in this field, Marxist, feminist, and post-structural thought and movements have been particularly influential. Indeed, many of the authors assembled within this collection work from these perspectives. Chapter 1, 'Shaking the Foundations: Early Inquiries in Sexualities Studies', presents an overview of how theorists working within these traditions have helped us understand a range of sex-related phenomena, such as the relationships between the economy, the nuclear family, and sexuality; the social, rather than strictly biological, construction of sexuality; and society's regulation of sexual expression through the creation of social, political and legal boundaries. Chapter 2, 'Contemporary Approaches and Applications', offers a bridge between the classical offerings of chapter 1 and the rest of this collection through examples of how Canadian scholars in this field have taken up these inquiries and, in doing so, challenged and expanded their insights.

Often in everyday conversation our sexual desires and experiences are discussed as if they are completely natural, timeless, and unchanging elements of human behaviour and society (e.g., 'Women have always been less interested in sex than men'). Part II, 'Sexual Identities in Changing Social Contexts', considers various changes in constructions and regulations of sexualities within Canadian society. The section begins with a historical exploration of changing meanings of sexuality and sexual activity in Canadian society. The focus then shifts to meanings we make of sexual activity for a particular social group: youth. What is it about young people having sex that seems to generate controversy and excitement? The section concludes with an examination of the changes and trends in long-term (sexual) relationships in Canadian society.

As we know, not all sexual orientations, activities, and desires are equally encouraged or respected in society. Articles in Part III, 'Status and Stigma: Sex and Sexualities in Social Institutions', use the sociological concepts of status, stigma, and social institution to explore how meanings about our experiences of sexuality are made. Specifically, the authors in this section explore the construction of sexuality through our health care system, public education system, and the mass media. In these chapters, we are reminded how social institutions serve important societal needs (such as public health, the creation of a capable workforce, and an informed citizenry) and but also how they reinforce particular values and expectations about sexuality.

In Part IV, 'Mutually Constructing Knowledges: Sex, Gender, and Sexualities', we return to some of the ideas and issues that opened the collection. In Part I, scholars such as Friedrich Engels and Simone de Beauvoir helped us understand that what we understand as 'normal' sexuality in any given society is dependent upon other norms and social arrangements such as family structure, the economic system, and gender. Specifically, the chapters in this section explore how our experiences of sexuality are also organized through societal configurations of gender, race, and other socialized differences. Authors in this section reveal these constructions through analyses of contemporary social issues such as homophobia, bullying, immigration, citizenship, and gender harassment.

To encourage students to consider and reconsider their understandings of their own and others' sexualities, each part within this anthology begins with a few 'Starting Points Questions'. The goal of these is to get readers to articulate what they already know about section themes, reflect upon where this knowledge comes from, and consider how this knowledge is used in daily life. Starting Points questions are followed by a brief introduction through which readers are introduced to the chapter articles, themes, and insights. Included at the end of each part are 'Dialogue Boxes': images and new stories to promote reflection and discussion. Each section concludes with 'Critical Conversations: Discussion Questions' to help reinforce readers' engagements with the readings and encourage them to think across the presented texts to generate new understandings. The volume also includes article bibliographies (as potential aids to further student research), a glossary of key terms to facilitate the development of strong analytical connections across the sections of the anthology and an index for easy reference.

At its heart, the field of sexualities studies questions the production of common-sense understandings of sex and sexuality. Canadian Perspectives in Sexualities Studies is organized to highlight this questioning and to facilitate further inquiries. Across the diversity and complexity of this scholarship in the field of sexualities studies one thing is certain: whatever sex is, human societies organize it. We organize sex through the meanings we create about it (what counts as sex, what doesn't; who is sexually appealing; when, where, why, and what sex is acceptable and from whom . . .). In turn, our meanings about sex, and the categories and boundaries through which these meanings are formed, inform (and sometimes change) our sexual experiences.

Reference

Canadian Broadcasting Corporation. 'Trudeau's Omnibus Bill: Challenging Canadian Taboos'. http://archives.cbc.ca/politics/rights_freedoms/topics/538/# as accessed 10 May 2010.

PART I

Introduction to Sexualities Studies

Starting Points

1. What is sex? Make a list of all the ways the word *sex* is used in your everyday world (what does the word describe, or what kinds of comments do you hear or make?).
2. What is sexuality? Where does your understanding of sexuality come from?
3. Has there always been 'homosexuality' and 'heterosexuality'? When was sexuality invented?
4. Make a list of the topics you expect to learn about in this textbook and in this course. [Editor's Note: This would be a great list to make now and revisit toward the end of the course.]

Introduction

While perhaps not the out-of-bounds or taboo subject that it arguably was even 20 years ago, sex is still a topic that unsettles people and is often considered private or personal. However, challenging common-sense ideas about human relations is a central goal of the social sciences, and, accordingly, the articles in this collection challenge the traditional notion of sex and sexuality as private. The field of sexualities studies explores the identities, cultures, acts, and desires we have come to understand as sexual as well as the processes through which societies develop these understandings. By investigating established knowledge about sexuality, scholars help us think more critically about the social, political, economic, scientific, religious, and other traditions that condition our experiences and desires. Sexualities studies situate our sexual identities within the historical and contemporary contexts of our society, and encourage us to appreciate how and why our cultural standards for sexual conduct change. Indeed, it is difficult to engage with the field of sexualities studies without learning something new about ourselves, our communities, and the traditions that shape and change our collective understandings of sexuality.

This collection explores some of the contemporary issues that are frequently examined by Canadian scholars, such as questions surrounding same-sex marriage and sexual education in public schools. By exploring contemporary Canadian scholarship, we gain a sense of the theoretical traditions, methodologies, and individual scholars that have been prominent in the interdisciplinary landscape of sexualities studies in Canada. As this reader is both an introduction to the field in general and to Canadian scholarship within this field, our open-ing section is influenced by both international and Canadian interests. This collection begins with the work of both international and Canadian scholars whose articles illustrate some of the important starting places for subsequent Canadian inquiries in the field. Though there are many approaches to the study of sexualities throughout the social sciences, Marxism, feminism, and post-structuralism are prominent within this field in Canada. Scholarship from these traditions has influenced Canadian public and private life through its influence on the reform of sexual assault laws, the legislation of obscenity, and the expansion of the defini-tion of marriage to include same-sex couples. Chapter 1, 'Shaking the Foundation: Early Inqui-ries in Sexualities Studies', introduces each of these approaches. These five articles represent some of the central contentions and questions that arise through each theoretical approach. Friedrich Engels (1820–1895), most often remembered as Karl Marx's principal collaborator, offers a historical Marxist analysis of the emergence of the standard of monogamy within the institution of marriage. Engels was one of the earliest writers to assert that the apparent differ-ences between males and females was a product of social relations—in this case the capitalist need for the accumulation of private property—rather than innately biological. Writing over 100 years later, Canadian sociologist Gary Kinsman extends this Marxist analysis to a consider-ation of sexual orientation in 'The Creation of Homosexuality as a "Social Problem"'. Kinsman considers the 'discovery' of homosexuality and the political and economic structures that produced the categories of 'homo' and 'hetero' that are so familiar to us today. In so doing, he challenges readers to reconsider the supposed 'naturalness' of our common-sense under-standing of these categories of sexual identity.

The second theoretical tradition presented in chapter 1 is feminism, as represented in articles by the French philosopher Simone de Beauvoir (1908–1986) and American cultural anthropologist Gayle Rubin. This perspective helps us appreciate that many of the social arrangements we take for granted today (such as women's participation in post-secondary education and previously restricted aspects of the paid labour force) were the result of sus-tained scholarship and activism. De Beauvoir presents and ultimately refutes claims that the 'natures' of women and men are determined by biology. Though her language may feel a bit dated to the contemporary reader, her classic point-counterpoint argument is as provocative today as when it was first published in 1949. By questioning social beliefs about the biological basis of sexuality, scholars like Engels and de Beauvoir paved the way for the later explosion of writing in this field in the 1980s and beyond. In this collection, this more contemporary work is exemplified by Gayle Rubin's work. In a manner similar to Kinsman's contemporary extension of Engels, Rubin's work represents some of the incredible productivity that was instantiated by de Beauvoir and feminist movements of the late twentieth century. In this influential article, Rubin outlines a 'domino theory' of sexuality whereby the sexual activity of any individual will meet disapproval from another individual given the specifics of ideological and social context. When first published, Rubin's argument was extremely controversial; over time, her critique has gained significant credibility, particularly as her use of the post-structural insights of Michel Foucault pointed the way for a variety of future scholars (including Mary Louise Adams, in this collection).

The third theoretical approach profiled in this chapter is post-structuralism. Rubin's work provides a bridge between the feminist and post-structuralist traditions. French philosopher Michel Foucault (1926–1984) argues that, far from being a 'natural' phenomenon, the considerable attention to, and codes of conduct surrounding, sexuality in modern societies demonstrates both its importance and its changeability.

In addition to profiling these influential perspectives, this first section brings forward some of the issues that have been prominent in Canadian scholarship sexualities studies. Chapter 2, 'Contemporary Approaches and Applications', marks the transition in the collection from international to Canadian scholarship. Authors included in this chapter have helped establish some of the most productive considerations of sexuality by Canadian scholars in recent years. Authors included in subsequent chapters were chosen based on their elaborations of and challenges to the work of the authors presented in these first two chapters.

Questions about the relationships between sex, sexualities, and bodies permeate the field of sexualities studies. The selected essays in chapter 2 demonstrate the breadth of these related considerations in Canadian scholarship. Sociologist Sandy Welsh reviews 20 years of scholarship on sexual harassment, and outlines its political, methodological, and theoretical changes and trends. Specifically, Welsh highlights the emerging importance of approaches to sexual harassment that consider the implications of gendered organizational cultures. That social structures such as employment have gendered cultures also points to the role expectations of sexuality within these cultures. Social and legal theorist Marianna Valverde challenges the established social knowledge that 'deep down' everyone is either heterosexual or homosexual. Drawing on first-person accounts as well as Freudian and lesbian feminist theories, Valverde argues that this belief reveals a deep societal discomfort with sexual ambiguity. Societal anxieties about sex, bodies, and identities and the very categories of sexual experience and identity are further challenged in Clarice Kuhling and Gary Kinsman's 2003 interview with activist and educator Vivian Namaste. In this interview, Namaste asserts that there is widespread misunderstanding about the lives of transsexuals and connects these misunderstandings to the political, economic, medical, and other traditions that routinely organize all our experiences of sexuality. In the final article in this chapter, Martin Cannon explores how colonial knowledges, such as those embodied in Canada's *Indian Act,* have worked to regulate the gendered and erotic diversity of First Nations communities.

1 Shaking the Foundations: Early Inquiries in Sexualities Studies

The Monogamous Family

Friedrich Engels

II. The Family

4. The Monogamous Family

It develops out of the pairing family, in the transitional period between the upper and middle stages of barbarism; its decisive victory is one of the signs that civilization is beginning. It is based on the supremacy of the man, the express purpose being to produce children of undisputed paternity; such paternity is demanded because these children are later to come into their father's property as his natural heirs. It is distinguished from pairing marriage by the much greater strength of the marriage tie, which can no longer be dissolved at either partner's wish. As a rule, it is now only the man who can dissolve it, and put away his wife. The right of conjugal infidelity also remains secured to him, at any rate by custom (the Code Napoleon explicitly accords it to the husband as long as he does not bring his concubine into the house), and as social life develops he exercises his right more and more; should the wife recall the old form of sexual life and attempt to revive it, she is punished more severely than ever.

We meet this new form of the family in all its severity among the Greeks. While the position of the goddesses in their mythology, as Marx points out, brings before us an earlier period when the position of women was freer and more respected, in the heroic age we find the woman already being humiliated by the domination of the man and by competition from girl slaves. Note how Telemachus in the *Odyssey* silences his mother. [The reference is to a passage where Telemachus, son of Odysseus and Penelope, tells his mother to get on with her weaving and leave the men to mind their own business – Ed.] In Homer young women are booty and are handed over to the pleasure of the conquerors, the handsomest being picked by the commanders in order of rank; the entire *Iliad*, it will be remembered, turns on the quarrel of Achilles and Agamemnon over one of these slaves. If a hero is of any importance, Homer also mentions the captive girl with whom he shares his tent and his bed. These girls were also taken back to Greece and brought under the same roof as the wife, as Cassandra was brought by Agamemnon in Aeschylus; the sons begotten of them received a small share of the paternal inheritance and had the full status of freemen. The legitimate wife was expected to put up with all this, but herself to remain strictly chaste and faithful. In the heroic age a Greek woman is, indeed, more respected than in the period of civilization, but to her husband she is after all nothing but the mother of his legitimate children and heirs, his chief housekeeper and the supervisor of his female slaves, whom he can and does take as concubines if he so fancies. It is the existence of slavery side by side with monogamy, the presence of young, beautiful slaves belonging unreservedly to the man, that stamps monogamy from the very beginning with its specific character of monogamy for the woman only, but not for the man. And that is the character it still has today.

[. . .]

This is the origin of monogamy as far as we can trace it back among the most civilized and highly developed people of antiquity. It was not in any way the fruit of individual sex-love, with which it had nothing whatever to do; marriages remained as before marriages of convenience. It was the first form of the family to be based, not on natural, but on economic conditions—on the victory of private property over primitive, natural communal property. The Greeks themselves put the matter quite frankly: the sole exclusive aims of monogamous marriage were to make the man supreme in the family, and to propagate, as the future heirs to his wealth, children indisputably his own. Otherwise, marriage was a burden, a duty which had to be performed, whether one liked it or not, to gods, state, and one's ancestors. In Athens the law exacted from the man not only marriage but also the performance of a minimum of so-called conjugal duties.

Thus when monogamous marriage first makes its appearance in history, it is not as the reconciliation of man and woman, still less as the highest

form of such a reconciliation. Quite the contrary. Monogamous marriage comes on the scene as the subjugation of the one sex by the other; it announces a struggle between the sexes unknown throughout the whole previous prehistoric period. [. . .] Monogamous marriage was a great historical step forward; nevertheless, together with slavery and private wealth, it opens the period that has lasted until today in which every step forward is also relatively a step backward, in which prosperity and development for some is won through the misery and frustration of others. It is the cellular form of civilized society, in which the nature of the oppositions and contradictions fully active in that society can be already studied.

The old comparative freedom of sexual intercourse by no means disappeared with the victory of pairing marriage or even of monogamous marriage:

> The old conjugal system, now reduced to narrower limits by the gradual disappearance of the punaluan groups, still environed the advancing family, which it was to follow to the verge of civilization . . . It finally disappeared in the new form of hetaerism, which still follows mankind in civilization as a dark shadow upon the family. [Lewis H. Morgan, *Ancient Society*. London: MacMillan & Company, 1877, p. 511 – Ed.]

By 'hetaerism' Morgan understands the practice, coexistent with monogamous marriage, of sexual intercourse between men and unmarried women outside marriage, which, as we know, flourishes in the most varied forms throughout the whole period of civilization and develops more and more into open prostitution. This hetaerism derives quite directly from group marriage, from the ceremonial surrender by which women purchased the right of chastity. Surrender for money was at first a religious act; it took place in the temple of the goddess of love, and the money originally went into the temple treasury. The temple slaves of Anaitis in Armenia and of Aphrodite in Corinth, like the sacred dancing-girls attached to the temples of India, the so-called bayaderes (the word is a corruption of the Portuguese word *bailadeira*, meaning female dancer), were the first prostitutes. Originally the duty of every woman, this surrender was later performed by these priestesses alone as representatives of all other women. Among other peoples, hetaerism derives from the sexual freedom allowed to girls before marriage—again, therefore, a relic of group marriage, but handed down in a different way. With the rise of the inequality of property—already at the upper stage of barbarism, therefore—wage-labour appears sporadically side by side with slave labour, and at the same time, as its necessary correlate, the professional prostitution of free women side by side with the forced surrender of the slave. [. . .] For hetaerism is as much a social institution as any other; it continues the old sexual freedom—to the advantage of the men. Actually not merely tolerated, but gaily practised, by the ruling classes particularly, it is condemned in words. But in reality this condemnation never falls on the men concerned, but only on the women; they are despised and outcast, in order that the unconditional supremacy of men over the female sex may be once more proclaimed as a fundamental law of society.

But a second contradiction thus develops within monogamous marriage itself. At the side of the husband who embellishes his existence with hetaerism stands the neglected wife. And one cannot have one side of this contradiction without the other, any more than a man has a whole apple in his hand after eating half. But that seems to have been the husbands' notion, until

their wives taught them better. With monogamous marriage, two constant social types, unknown hitherto, make their appearance on the scene—the wife's attendant lover and the cuckold husband. The husbands had won the victory over the wives, but the vanquished magnanimously provided the crown. Together with monogamous marriage and hetaerism, adultery became an unavoidable social institution—denounced, severely penalized, but impossible to suppress. At best, the certain paternity of the children rested on moral conviction as before, and to solve the insoluble contradiction the Code Napoleon, Art-312, decreed: 'L'enfant confu pendant le marriage a pour père le mari', the father of a child conceived during marriage is the husband. Such is the final result of three thousand years of monogamous marriage.

[. . .]

However, monogamous marriage did not by any means appear always and everywhere in the classically harsh form it took among the Greeks. Among the Romans, who, as future world-conquerors, had a larger, if a less fine, vision than the Greeks, women were freer and more respected. A Roman considered that his power of life and death over his wife sufficiently guaranteed her conjugal fidelity. Here, moreover, the wife equally with the husband could dissolve the marriage at will. But the greatest progress in the development of individual marriage certainly came with the entry of the Germans into history, and for the reason that the Germans—on account of their poverty, very probably—were still at a stage where monogamy seems not yet to have become perfectly distinct from pairing marriage. We infer this from three facts mentioned by Tacitus. First, though marriage was held in great reverence—'they content themselves with one wife, the women live hedged round with chastity'—polygamy was the rule for the distinguished members and the leaders of the tribe, a condition of things similar to that among the Americans, where pairing marriage was the rule. Secondly, the transition from mother-right to father-right could only have been made a short time previously, for the brother on the mother's side—the nearest gentile male relation according to mother-right—was still considered almost closer of kin than the father, corresponding again to the standpoint of the American Indians, among whom Marx, as he often said, found the key to the understanding of our own primitive age. And, thirdly, women were greatly respected among the Germans, and also influential in public affairs, which is in direct contradiction to the supremacy of men in monogamy. [. . .]

But if monogamy was the only one of all the known forms of the family through which modern sex-love could develop, that does not mean that within monogamy modern sexual love developed exclusively or even chiefly as the love of husband and wife for each other. That was precluded by the very nature of strictly monogamous marriage under the rule of the man. Among all historically active classes—that is, among all ruling classes—matrimony remained what it had been since the pairing marriage, a matter of convenience which was arranged by the parents. The first historical form of sexual love as passion, a passion recognized as natural to all human beings (at least if they belonged to the ruling classes), and as the highest form of the sexual impulse—and that is what constitutes its specific character—this first form of individual sexual love, the chivalrous love of the Middle Ages, was by no means conjugal. Quite the contrary. In its classic form among the Provençals, it heads straight for adultery, and the poets of love celebrated adultery. The flower of Provençal love poetry are the Albas (aubades, songs of dawn). They describe in glowing colours how the knight lies in bed beside his love—the wife of another man—while outside stands the watchman who

calls to him as soon as the first grey of dawn (alba) appears, so that he can get away unobserved; the parting scene then forms the climax of the poem. [. . .]

Nowadays there are two ways of concluding a bourgeois marriage. In Catholic countries the parents, as before, procure a suitable wife for their young bourgeois son, and the consequence is, of course, the fullest development of the contradiction inherent in monogamy: the husband abandons himself to hetaerism and the wife to adultery. Probably the only reason why the Catholic Church abolished divorce was because it had convinced itself that there is no more a cure for adultery than there is for death. In Protestant countries, on the other hand, the rule is that the son of a bourgeois family is allowed to choose a wife from his own class with more or less freedom; hence there may be a certain element of love in the marriage, as, indeed, in accordance with Protestant hypocrisy, is always assumed, for decency's sake. Here the husband's hetaerism is a more sleepy kind of business, and adultery by the wife is less the rule. [. . .]

In both cases, however, the marriage is conditioned by the class position of the parties and is to that extent always a marriage of convenience. In both cases this marriage of convenience turns often enough into crassest prostitution—sometimes of both partners, but far more commonly of the woman, who only differs from the ordinary courtesan in that she does not let out her body on piece-work as a wage-worker, but sells it once and for all into slavery. And of all marriages of convenience Fourier's words hold true: 'As in grammar two negatives make an affirmative, so in matrimonial morality two prostitutions pass for a virtue.' [Charles Fourier, *Théorie de l'Uniti Universelle*. Paris, 1841–45, Vol. III, p. 120. – Ed.] Sex-love in the relationship with a woman becomes, and can only become, the real rule among the oppressed classes, which means today among the proletariat—whether this relation is officially sanctioned or not. But here all the foundations of typical monogamy are cleared away. Here there is no property, for the preservation and inheritance of which monogamy and male supremacy were established; hence there is no incentive to make this male supremacy effective. What is more, there are no means of making it so. Bourgeois law, which protects this supremacy, exists only for the possessing class and their dealings with the proletarians. The law costs money and, on account of the worker's poverty, it has no validity for his relation to his wife. Here quite other personal and social conditions decide. And now that large-scale industry has taken the wife out of the home onto the labour market and into the factory, and made her often the breadwinner of the family, no basis for any kind of male supremacy is left in the proletarian household—except, perhaps, for something of the brutality toward women that has spread since the introduction of monogamy. The proletarian family is therefore no longer monogamous in the strict sense, even where there is passionate love and firmest loyalty on both sides, and maybe all the blessings of religious and civil authority. Here, therefore, the eternal attendants of monogamy, hetaerism, and adultery, play only an almost vanishing part. The wife has in fact regained the right to dissolve the marriage, and if two people cannot get on with one another, they prefer to separate. In short, proletarian marriage is monogamous in the etymological sense of the word, but not at all in its historical sense.

Our jurists, of course, find that progress in legislation is leaving women with no further ground of complaint. Modern civilized systems of law increasingly acknowledge, first, that for a marriage to be legal, it must be a contract freely entered into by both partners, and, secondly, that also in the married state both partners must stand on a common footing of equal rights and duties. If both these demands are consistently carried out, say the jurists, women have all they can ask.

This typically legalist method of argument is exactly the same as that which the radical republican bourgeois uses to put the proletarian in his place. The labour contract is to be freely entered into by both partners. But it is considered to have been freely entered into as soon as the law makes both parties equal on paper. The power conferred on the one party by the difference of class position, the pressure thereby brought to bear on the other party—the real economic position of both—that is not the law's business. Again, for the duration of the labour contract both parties are to have equal rights, insofar as one or the other does not expressly surrender them. That economic relations compel the worker to surrender even the last semblance of equal rights—here again, that is no concern of the law.

In regard to marriage, the law, even the most advanced, is fully satisfied as soon as the partners have formally recorded that they are entering into the marriage of their own free consent. What goes on in real life behind the juridical scenes—how this free consent comes about—that is not the business of the law and the jurist. And yet the most elementary comparative jurisprudence should show the jurist what this free consent really amounts to. In the countries where an obligatory share of the paternal inheritance is secured to the children by law and they cannot therefore be disinherited—in Germany, in the countries with French law and elsewhere—the children are obliged to obtain their parents' consent to their marriage. In the countries with English law, where parental consent to a marriage is not legally required, the parents on their side have full freedom in the testamentary disposal of their property and can disinherit their children at their pleasure. It is obvious that, in spite and precisely because of this fact, freedom of marriage among the classes with something to inherit is in reality not a whit greater in England and America than it is in France and Germany.

As regards the legal equality of husband and wife in marriage, the position is no better. The legal inequality of the two partners, bequeathed to us from earlier social conditions, is not the cause but the effect of the economic oppression of the woman. In the old communistic household, which comprised many couples and their children, the task entrusted to the women of managing the household was as much a public and socially necessary industry as the procuring of food by the men. With the patriarchal family, and still more with the single monogamous family, a change came. Household management lost its public character. It no longer concerned society. It became a private service; the wife became the head servant, excluded from all participation in social production. Not until the coming of modern large-scale industry was the road to social production opened to her again— and then only to the proletarian wife. But it was opened in such a manner that, if she carries out her duties in the private service of her family, she remains excluded from public production and unable to earn; and if she wants to take part in public production and earn independently, she cannot carry out family duties. And the wife's position in the factory is the position of women in all branches of business, right up to medicine and the law. The modern individual family is founded on the open or concealed domestic slavery of the wife, and modern society is a mass composed of these individual families as its molecules.

In the great majority of cases today, at least in the possessing classes, the husband is obliged to earn a living and support his family, and that in itself gives him a position of supremacy, without any need for special legal titles and privileges. Within the family he is the bourgeois and the wife represents the proletariat. In the industrial world, the specific character of the economic oppression burdening the proletariat is visible in all its sharpness only when all special legal privileges of the capitalist class have been abolished and complete legal equality of both classes established. The democratic republic does not do away with the opposition of the two classes; on the contrary, it provides the clear field on which the fight can be fought out. And in the same way, the peculiar character of the supremacy of the husband over the wife in the modern family, the necessity of creating real social equality between them, and the way to do it, will only be seen in the clear light of day when both possess legally complete equality of rights. Then it will be plain that the first condition for the liberation of the wife is to bring the whole female sex back into public industry, and that this in turn demands the abolition of the monogamous family as the economic unit of society.

[. . .]

We are now approaching a social revolution in which the economic foundations of monogamy as they have existed hitherto will disappear just as surely as those of its complement—prostitution. Monogamy arose from the concentration of considerable wealth in the hands of a single individual man—and from the need to bequeath this wealth to the children of that man and of no other. For this purpose, the monogamy of the woman was required, not that of the man, so this monogamy of the woman did not in any way interfere with open or concealed polygamy on the part of the man. But by transforming by far the greater portion, at any rate, of permanent, heritable wealth—the means of production— into social property, the coming social revolution will reduce to a minimum all this anxiety about bequeathing and inheriting. Having arisen from economic causes, will monogamy then disappear when these causes disappear?

One might answer, not without reason: far from disappearing, it will, on the contrary, be realized completely. For with the transformation of the means of production into social property there will disappear also wage-labour, the proletariat, and therefore, the necessity for a certain—statistically calculable—number of women to surrender themselves for money. Prostitution disappears; monogamy, instead of collapsing, at last becomes a reality—also for men.

In any case, therefore, the position of men will be very much altered. But the position of women, of all women, also undergoes significant change. With the transfer of the means of production into common ownership, the single family ceases to be the economic unit of society. Private housekeeping is transformed into a social industry. The care and education of the children becomes a public affair; society looks after all children alike, whether they are legitimate or not. This removes all the anxiety about the 'consequences', which today is the most essential social—moral as well as economic—factor that prevents a girl from giving herself completely to the man she loves. Will not that suffice to bring about the gradual growth of unconstrained sexual intercourse and with it a more tolerant public opinion in regard to a maiden's honour and a woman's shame? And, finally, have we not seen that in the modern world monogamy and prostitution are indeed contradictions, but inseparable contradictions, poles of the same state of society? Can prostitution disappear without dragging monogamy with it into the abyss?

Here a new element comes into play, an element which, at the time when monogamy was developing, existed at most in germ: individual sex-love.

Before the Middle Ages we cannot speak of individual sex-love. That personal beauty, close intimacy, similarity of tastes and so forth awakened in people of opposite sex the desire for sexual intercourse, that men and women were not totally indifferent regarding the partner with whom they entered into this most intimate relationship—that goes without saying. But it is still a very long way to our sexual love. Throughout the whole of antiquity, marriages were arranged by the parents, and the partners calmly accepted their choice. What little love there was between husband and wife in antiquity is not so much subjective inclination as objective duty, not the cause of the marriage, but its corollary. Love relationships in the modern sense only occur in antiquity outside official society. [. . .]

Our sexual love differs essentially from the simple sexual desire, the Eros, of the ancients. In the first place, it assumes that the person loved returns the love; to this extent the woman is on an equal footing with the man, whereas in the Eros of antiquity she was often not even asked. Secondly, our sexual love has a degree of intensity and duration which makes both lovers feel that non-possession and separation are a great, if not the greatest, calamity; to possess one another, they risk high stakes, even life itself. In the ancient world this happened only, if at all, in adultery. And, finally, there arises a new moral standard in the judgment of a sexual relationship. We do not only ask, was it within or outside marriage? But also, did it spring from love and reciprocated love or not? Of course, this new standard has fared no better in feudal or bourgeois practice than all the other standards of morality—it is ignored. But neither does it fare any worse. It is recognized just as much as they are—in theory, on paper. And for the present it cannot ask anything more.

[. . .]

In the vast majority of cases, therefore, marriage remained, up to the close of the middle ages, what it had been from the start—a matter which was not decided by the partners. In the beginning, people were already born married—

married to an entire group of the opposite sex. In the later forms of group marriage similar relations probably existed, but with the group continually contracting. In the pairing marriage it was customary for the mothers to settle the marriages of their children; here, too, the decisive considerations are the new ties of kinship, which are to give the young pair a stronger position in the gens and tribe. And when, with the preponderance of private over communal property and the interest in its bequeathal, father-right and monogamy gained supremacy, the dependence of marriages on economic considerations became complete. The form of marriage by purchase disappears, the actual practice is steadily extended until not only the woman but also the man acquires a price—not according to his personal qualities, but according to his property. That the mutual affection of the people concerned should be the one paramount reason for marriage, outweighing everything else, was and always had been absolutely unheard of in the practice of the ruling classes; that sort of thing only happened in romance—or among the oppressed classes, who did not count.

Such was the state of things encountered by capitalist production when it began to prepare itself, after the epoch of geographical discoveries, to win world power by world trade and manufacture. One would suppose that this manner of marriage exactly suited it, and so it did. And yet—there are no limits to the irony of history—capitalist production itself was to make the decisive breach in it. By changing all things into commodities, it dissolved all inherited and traditional relationships, and in place of time-honoured custom and historic right, it set up purchase and sale, 'free' contract. And the English jurist, H.S. Maine, thought he had made a tremendous discovery when he said that our whole progress in comparison with former epochs consisted in the fact that we had passed 'from status to contract',

from inherited to freely contracted conditions—which, in so far as it is correct, was already in *The Communist Manifesto* [Chapter II].

But a contract requires people who can dispose freely of their persons, actions, and possessions, and meet each other on the footing of equal rights. To create these 'free' and 'equal' people was one of the main tasks of capitalist production. Even though at the start it was carried out only half-consciously, and under a religious disguise at that, from the time of the Lutheran and Calvinist Reformation the principle was established that man is only fully responsible for his actions when he acts with complete freedom of will, and that it is a moral duty to resist all coercion to an immoral act. But how did this fit in with the hitherto existing practice in the arrangement of marriages? Marriage, according to the bourgeois conception, was a contract, a legal transaction, and the most important one of all, because it disposed of two human beings, body and mind, for life. Formally, it is true, the contract at that time was entered into voluntarily: without the assent of the persons concerned, nothing could be done. But everyone knew only too well how this assent was obtained and who were the real contracting parties in the marriage. But if real freedom of decision was required for all other contracts, then why not for this? Had not the two young people to be coupled also the right to dispose freely of themselves, of their bodies and organs? Had not chivalry brought sex-love into fashion, and was not its proper bourgeois form, in contrast to chivalry's adulterous love, the love of husband and wife? And if it was the duty of married people to love each other, was it not equally the duty of lovers to marry each other and nobody else? Did not this right of the lovers stand higher than the right of parents, relations, and other traditional marriage-brokers and matchmakers? If the right of free, personal discrimination broke boldly into the Church and religion, how should it halt before the intolerable claim of the older generation to dispose of the body, soul, property, happiness, and unhappiness of the younger generation?

These questions inevitably arose at a time which was loosening all the old ties of society and undermining all traditional conceptions. The world had suddenly grown almost ten times bigger; instead of one quadrant of a hemisphere, the whole globe lay before the gaze of the West Europeans, who hastened to take the other seven quadrants into their possession. And with the old narrow barriers of their homeland fell also the thousand-year-old barriers of the prescribed medieval way of thought. To the outward and the inward eye of man opened an infinitely wider horizon. What did a young man care about the approval of respectability, or honourable guild privileges handed down for generations, when the wealth of India beckoned to him, the gold and the silver mines of Mexico and Potosi? For the bourgeoisie, it was the time of knight-errantry; they, too, had their romance and their raptures of love, but on a bourgeois footing and, in the last analysis, with bourgeois aims.

So it came about that the rising bourgeoisie, especially in Protestant countries, where existing conditions had been most severely shaken, increasingly recognized freedom of contract also in marriage, and carried it into effect in the manner described. Marriage remained class marriage, but within the class the partners were conceded a certain degree of freedom of choice. And on paper, in ethical theory and in poetic description, nothing was more immutably established than that every marriage is immoral which does not rest on mutual sexual love and really free agreement of husband and wife. In short, the love marriage was proclaimed as a human right, and indeed not only as a droit de l'homme, one of the rights of man, but also, for once in a way, as droit de la femme, one of the rights of woman.

This human right, however, differed in one respect from all other so-called human rights. While the latter, in practice, remain restricted to the ruling class (the bourgeoisie), and are directly or indirectly curtailed for the oppressed class (the proletariat), in the case of the former the irony of history plays another of its tricks. The ruling class remains dominated by the familiar economic influences and therefore only in exceptional cases does it provide instances of really freely contracted marriages, while among the oppressed class, as we have seen, these marriages are the rule.

Full freedom of marriage can therefore only be generally established when the abolition of capitalist production and of the property relations created by it has removed all the accompanying economic considerations which still exert such a powerful influence on the choice of a marriage partner. For then there is no other motive left except mutual inclination.

[. . .]

But what will quite certainly disappear from monogamy are all the features stamped upon it through its origin in property relations; these are, in the first place, supremacy of the man, and, secondly, indissolubility. The supremacy of the man in marriage is the simple consequence of his economic supremacy, and with the abolition of the latter will disappear of itself. The indissolubility of marriage is partly a consequence of the economic situation in which monogamy arose, partly tradition from the period when the connection between this economic situation and monogamy was not yet fully understood and was carried to extremes under a religious form. Today it is already broken through at a thousand points. If only the marriage based on love is moral, then also only the marriage in which love continues. But the intense emotion of individual sex-love varies very much in duration from one individual to another, especially among men, and if affection definitely comes to an end or is supplanted by a new passionate love, separation is a benefit for both partners as well as for society—only people will then be spared having to wade through the useless mire of a divorce case.

What we can now conjecture about the way in which sexual relations will be ordered after the impending overthrow of capitalist production is mainly of a negative character, limited for the most part to what will disappear. But what will there be new? That will be answered when a new generation has grown up: a generation of men who never in their lives have known what

it is to buy a woman's surrender with money or any other social instrument of power; a generation of women who have never known what it is to give themselves to a man from any other considerations than real love, or to refuse to give themselves to their lover from fear of the economic consequences. When these people are in the world, they will care precious little what anybody today thinks they ought to do; they will make their own practice and their corresponding public opinion about the practice of each individual—and that will be the end of it.

The Creation of Homosexuality as a 'Social Problem'

Gary Kinsman

Why Historical Materialism?

My method of exploration is a historical materialist one: that is, a perspective that views historical transformation as central to understanding our lives and that sees social relations and practices, rather than ideas or discourse separate from these,[1] as the primary elements in social change. Discourse both organizes and is organized through social relations. I am using 'materialism' here in a broad sense, including eroticism and sexualities, as sensuous human practices. I do not view class as separate from other societal relations and struggles, or as simply 'economic' in character. Rather than displacing class relations and struggles, we need new ways of viewing class— not as a reified concept—but as lived historical, social experience and practice.[2] Sexual relations have been an important part of the formation of class relations and struggles; and class relations have shaped sexual relations and struggles.[3]

We can learn a great deal from the method of historical materialism. But to do this, we cannot read historical materialism—as a critical method of analysis—as a form of economic determinism in which 'the economy' determines everything. This is unfortunately the main reading in current postmodernism and queer theory.[4] This is also a major problem with the 'political economy' tradition that has been the hegemonic intellectual interpretation of Marxism in Canada until recently and that has not engaged seriously with critical work on gender, and especially with sexual regulation.[5] Unfortunately, it is this very reading of Marxism that has provided part of the basis for the growth of a 'queer theory' divorced from and often antagonistic to the insights of historical materialism.

While Marx's and Engels' public and private writings on sex, and same-gender sex in particular, are an instance of 'unthinking sex', as Andrew Parker[6] suggests, this was in part because in the context of the times in which they lived and of their own gender and sexual practices they were unable to apply their revolutionary method to this arena. Their critical social method that contested naturalism in other spheres of social life accepted a form of sexual naturalism. The 'founding fathers' of Marxism relegated sex and eroticism to a historically insignificant terrain. Marx remained a prisoner of hegemonic social ideologies and practices, taking for granted the hegemonic forms of sexuality (and to some extent gender and race) he lived and found around himself as 'natural'. At the same time his critical method can be extended to these areas if it is taken up and transformed from the standpoint of women, gays, people of colour, and others who face oppression and marginalization.

Marx's critique of capitalist political economy shattered the 'natural' and ahistorical character of capitalist social relations and provided a way of moving beyond the appearance of 'fair' exchange between capitalist and worker to disclose the underlying relations of exploitation upon which this rested. He was able to go beyond the equal and ahistorical appearance of the exchange between capitalist and worker to reveal the underlying appropriation of surplus value by the capitalist, which defined the exploitation of the worker during the process of production; yet he proved unable to move beyond the 'natural' appearance of the existing and developing heterosexual social forms of sexual life to reveal how these, too, were historical and social creations. In the sphere of commodity production, exchange, and circulation, Marx and Engels were able to analyze commodity fetishism as the mystified surface appearance of capitalist social relations in which social relationships appear to be relations between products.[7] They could therefore reveal in the realm of commodities the relation between this phenomenal form, or the ways in which the everyday accepted phenomena of the world present themselves, and the underlying social relations organizing this experience.[8] Marx and Engels could not, however, go beyond the surface appearance of sexual relations to reveal the process of fetishism that obscures the social relations in which our sexuality is made. Insofar as they considered the matter, they were prisoners of a naturalist and essentialist view.

[. . .]

Historical materialism *for* queers, as I develop here, shatters the natural and ahistorical character of heterosexual hegemony, discloses the oppressions lying beneath the 'natural' appearance of this hegemony, points to the socially and historically made character of sexualities, and puts heterosexual hegemony in question. It directs our attention to the ideological practices through which heterosexual hegemonic relations are constructed. This points toward the possibilities of overturning heterosexual hegemony and transforming erotic relations, and would link this to the transformation of State, class, gender, and race relations. Marx's work and method still have a lot to tell us about the dynamics of capitalist social relations and how these shape the lives of lesbians and gay men as well as others. This approach also sharpens our focus of attention on class relations and struggles within gay, lesbian, and other communities.

[. . .]

If analysis can be rooted in the social relations that have organized these experiences, then a much better understanding of how sexuality has been defined, organized, and regulated in capitalist and patriarchal societies will be possible. Capitalism is a dynamic social system that is constantly 'transforming the "ground" on which we stand so that we are always . . . experiencing changing historical process'.[9] History does not stand still, and it is this very undermining of previous forms of sex and gender regulations that has created the basis for gay liberation and feminist movements.

Sexuality, History, and Social Organization

Contrary to 'common sense', sexuality is not natural nor innate. Cross-cultural and historical studies have unearthed the diverse ways in which eroticism has been organized in various social settings. Sexuality is not simply biologically defined; it is socially created, building on physiological potentialities.

> Biological sexuality is the necessary precondition for human sexuality. But biological sexuality is only a set of potentialities, which is never unmediated by human reality, and which becomes transformed in qualitatively new ways in human society.[10]

The various possible erotic zones of the human body provide the preconditions for the social and cultural forms of activity and meaning that come to compose human sexual practices. It is in this transition from 'biological'[11] to historical and social that the definitions and regulations of sexuality have emerged. Physiological capacities are transformed to create sexuality as a social need, and, in turn, to produce new erotic needs.

Our various forms of sexuality and the social identities built around them are organized through the sex and gender relations that have existed in different societies.[12] Sex is fundamentally a social activity. A history of sexuality *is* a history of social relations. Human sexual practice is composed of thoughts (eroticized images, socially learned courses of action, or 'sexual scripts'[13]) and physical/sensual activities themselves. [. . .]

In making sense of sexuality as a social practice, a historical materialist method is very useful.

At the most general level, erotic activity, in all its diversity and meanings, can be seen as a human universal similar to the way in which Marx saw human production. Sexual activity, like production in general, has existed in all human societies.[14] However, what can be said about sexual practice in this general sense is extremely limited. It provides us with no basis from which to explore sexuality in the historical sense. What organizes and comprises sexual relations in each period is therefore a historical and empirical question—a topic for exploration.[15] We need historically rooted concepts, and we must reject transhistorical categorizations—for instance, the notion that the homosexual, the lesbian, or the heterosexual have been around for all time (or, for some, since Sodom and Gomorrah). Both same-sex and different-sex sexual practices have existed throughout human history, but they have differed radically in their social organization.

[. . .]

Contemporary 'heterosexuality' and 'homosexuality' are historically and socially specific organizations of different-gender and same-gender desires and pleasures. For instance, male same-gender erotic activities have ranged from structured 'educational' relationships between men and boys in particular class, family, and State relations, to acts surrounding puberty or masculinity rituals, to cross-dressing and gender activity reversals.[16] These had different social meanings in different social/cultural contexts and were different social practices. Among the Sambia of Papua, for instance, same-gender sex for males between seven and nineteen was mandatory. Boys fellated men on a daily basis, so that they would grow into masculine adults. According to this culture males cannot produce sperm on their own; they can only recycle it from one generation to another. In their adult lives, these males engage in sex with women.[17] Our contemporary notions of the heterosexual/homosexual dichotomy make no sense in a culture like this. It is impossible to hold onto any transhistorical notion of homosexuality or homosexual behaviour—or transhistorical heterosexuality, for that matter—in the face of these diverse practices and social meanings.

Much critical understanding of the social organization of sexuality comes from how we see the social organization of gender. Sexuality, like gender, is a product of social interaction—a continuous social accomplishment.[18] Gender is assigned in our society at birth by doctors and nurses based on apparent genital features. It then takes on many social features that have nothing to do with physiology, even though biological determinist approaches argue that biology determines gender, whether it be through genes or hormones.[19] Tied in with this social organization of gender is an associated sexuality and sexual 'identity'. Through this social process a 'natural' attitude toward sexuality and gender is created.[20]

In patriarchal and capitalist societies, sexuality and sexual identities connect a number of needs—emotional contact, friendship, sensual closeness, bodily pleasure, and genital sex—with notions of biology, gender, and reproductive capacity. This formation of sexuality implants naturalized constructs of masculinity and femininity within our very social and sexual beings, making it very difficult to disentangle our various needs grouped together as sexuality from biology, reproduction, and gender. Sexuality can be seen as a collecting category that groups together diverse needs, capacities, and desires.[21] Our sexuality has come to be defined by naturalist notions to such a degree that the process of social organization is rendered invisible (or unconscious).[22] We tend to 'reify sex as a thing-in-itself'.[23] We see our sexualities as a personal essence defining who we are rather than as constituted through the social practices that we ourselves have been active in through which our

sexualities have been made. To critically investigate sexuality, we must put in question this 'natural attitude' to recover the social practices and relations through which sexualities are made.

[. . .]

Sexual practice and 'identity' is formed through a process of social interaction and encounters with social discourse, significant others, and bodily based pleasures.[24] There is no 'natural' or 'unitary' sexuality. No situation is inherently sexual, but many situations are capable of being eroticized. Sexuality is subject to 'socio-cultural moulding to a degree surpassed by few other forms of human behaviour'.[25] Sexuality is not simply individual or 'private', and the individual is only an individual in a social context. Social individuals come to take part in and take up particular sexual practices and identities. 'Proper' gender is associated with 'normal' sexuality, since gender shapes sexual conduct. Part of this process of normalization 'derives from organs being placed in legitimate orifices'.[26] 'Identities' such as heterosexual, homosexual, lesbian, and bisexual are socially created.

[. . .]

The Social Organization of Sexual Knowledge

This [article] proposes a shift of focus in the study of same-gender and different-gender desire and pleasure and sexual regulation: a shift away from homosexuality and lesbianism as a 'problem' and toward a historical and social account of the emergence of sexual life, including heterosexuality. The 'traditions' of religion, psychology, medicine, criminology, sexology, history, sociology, and anthropology have created the 'problem', defining us as sick, deviant, abnormal—even criminal—and defining heterosexuality as 'normal'. These socially organized forms of knowledge have been crucial to the construction of heterosexual hegemony. In these forms of knowledge production that have also been forms of social power (what Foucault describes as 'power/knowledge'[27]), lesbians and gay men have been treated as objects of study to be researched. It has always been homosexuality and lesbianism and not heterosexuality that stands in need of explanation. The 'problematization' of homosexuality has been a crucial part of the normalization[28] of heterosexuality. Four examples help clarify this social process.

Anthropology in the eighteenth and nineteenth centuries was engaged in setting sexual and social norms. Classification of the races was a main preoccupation,[29] integral to which was the classification of sexual behaviour. 'Savages' came to be defined as more primitive with regard to sexual behaviour than 'civilized' peoples, although sometimes the savages were romanticized as acting more 'naturally'. Anthropologists carried their own cultural values with them, displaying an acute ethnocentric and Eurocentric[30] bias but, at the same time supplying much of the data upon which the work of the sex psychologists and sexologists in the metropolitan countries relied.[31] Anthropology as a profession was very much involved in the organization of colonial, class, racial, gender, and sexual relations.

Perhaps this process can best be seen through an examination of Bronislaw Malinowski's classic study of the Trobriand Islanders. The villagers described their villages from ground view as a number of bumps. Malinowski saw them as a series of concentric circles, describing them from above using a mapping representation. This disparity in descriptions was socially rooted. Malinowski came from a vigorously class-divided society, and he was a member of the academic discipline of anthropology. His account was addressed to a specialized intelligentsia in the metropolitan countries. There was no position within Trobriand culture from which their

villages could be seen thus, but Malinowski, located as he was outside and 'above' their society, could so describe them. Malinowski's anthropological work embodied the developing social relations of imperialism.[32]

Malinowski's work also embodied a developing heterosexual hegemony. Among the Trobriand Islanders, they did not see different-gender sexual intercourse and reproduction as linked. In one book, Malinowski included homosexuality, masturbation, and fellatio in a section entitled 'The Censure of Sexual Aberrations'.[33] Despite accounts of widespread same-gender sex in Melanesian societies, he argued that homosexuality was not prevalent and that it was treated with contempt and derision.[34] His work embodied the imposition of sexual norms on indigenous populations. Malinowski saw things from the standpoint of the missionaries, the administrators, and a developing heterosexual hegemony.

The work of nineteenth-century forensic psychiatrists and sex psychologists—who classified and categorized sexualities and sexual practices—also reveals the social relations that their work embodied and helped organize. Dr. Richard Von Krafft-Ebing, the foremost forensic psychiatrist of the last century who addressed sexual pathologies (and the 'grand-daddy' of sexology), felt that sexual relations outside heterosexual marriage represented not only a degeneration to an earlier, lower stage of evolution, but that they threatened Western civilization itself. For example:

> Every expression of the sex-drive . . . which does not comply with the goals of nature, i.e., procreation, must be declared perverse . . . Episodes of moral decline in the life of peoples fall regularly together with times of effeminacy, voluptuousness, and luxury . . . Rapidly growing nervousness results in an increase in sensuality and by leading to the dissipation among the masses of

people, undermines the pillars of society: morality and purity of family life. If this is undermined through dissipation, adultery, and luxury, then the fall of the state is inevitable.[35]

Krafft-Ebing's work expresses not only the standpoint of State agencies, but also middle-class assumptions about the class character of sexual morality.

Mainstream psychiatry and psychology in the twentieth century have generally viewed homosexuality as a symptom of 'infantile regression' or some other pathological disorder and have developed various strategies to cure, regulate, or adjust patients to the heterosexual norm.[36] This has included various forms of aversion therapy, as well as partial lobotomies. Psychiatrists and psychologists rarely treated lesbians and gay men as individuals with our own unique biographies and experiences. Instead we are slotted into clinical and abstract categories of 'homosexuality' and produced as 'cases'. We were already cut out of 'normal' social interaction by this diagnosis.[37] Before we even enter a psychiatrist's or a psychologist's office, a homosexual or lesbian 'typology' has often already defined us as 'deviant', laying out a particular course of 'treatment'.

Homosexual 'deviance' is investigated with the aim of our elimination, containment, or control. Knowledge has been produced so that ruling institutions can formulate legal codes, policing policies, and social policies. According to Magnus Hirschfeld, an early sex psychologist and homosexual-rights reformer, most of the thousand or so works on homosexuality that appeared between 1898 and 1908 were addressed to the legal profession.[38] Many early works by medical and legal experts

were chiefly concerned with whether the disgusting breed of perverts could

be physically identified for the courts, and whether they should be held legally responsible for their acts.[39]

The men and women engaged in same-gender love have thus been labelled 'deviants', 'perverts', 'gender inverts', 'gender non-conformists', 'sexual psychopaths', 'dangerous sex offenders', 'promiscuous', guilty of committing 'gross indecency', engaging in 'anonymous' sex, and have been the subjects of the distinction between 'public' and 'private' sex.

Official knowledge about homosexuals and lesbians came chiefly from studies of imprisoned or 'psychologically disturbed' homosexuals.[40] Much of this work relies on data such as the legal codification of offences, court and police records, and sexological, medical, and psychological discourse,[41] and often incorporates features of the power relations of the legal and prison systems and the psychiatric and medical professions. A great deal of official knowledge about homosexuality and lesbianism has been produced so that social agencies can 'understand', classify, police, and regulate our sexual lives.

This knowledge has in turn shaped popular cultures and 'common-sense' notions of how society is organized, through the mass media, the schools, government policies, the Criminal Code, police action, and the social organization of intended 'moral panics'[42] on sexual questions.

During the last part of the nineteenth century, homosexuality was often seen by the scientific disciplines as a form of congenital inversion rooted in biological degeneration or anomaly. These approaches reduced homosexuality to a biological cause. More recently, given the challenge presented by lesbian and gay liberation to psychological theories of homosexuality and lesbianism as a mental illness, there has been a certain return to these types of approaches by some researchers. Initial results of some of this research has been magnified and intensified by mass-media coverage. The research usually starts off by assuming the 'normality' of heterosexuality and that it is (usually male) homosexuality that stands in need of explanation. It assumes that there are only two rigidly dichotomous sexualities (heterosexuality and homosexuality), and these are based in biological difference. Men and women who are interested in both men and women undermine the basis of this research.

[. . .]

The resurgence of biological determinist explanations of homosexuality is occurring in the context of a new popularity for biological explanations of human behaviours and differences. This is also related to a resurgence of biological explanations of gender and gender inequality and in some circles of race and racial inequality.[43] For instance, some researchers now suggest that women's math and spatial skills really are biologically inferior to men's. Therefore, the social equality that feminism has demanded is seen to go against 'nature'.[44] This is part of a broader social organization of a 'backlash' to feminism, and not the first time biological explanations have been used to buttress social inequality. 'Biology' has long been invoked to justify the social subordination of blacks, women and lesbians, and gay men.

[. . .]

Until recently, heterosexuals rarely encountered visible gays, lesbians, or bisexuals. Most images were those projected by the mass media and those circulating in popular cultures, which generally came from psychology, sexology, the churches, and the courts and police. Dorothy E. Smith describes the 'ideological circle', through which the world is interpreted by the media and other agencies;[45] this is one of the ways heterosexual hegemony operates. The world is interpreted through the schemas of 'expert sources' (police, policy analysts, government bureaucrats), and hegemonic cultural narratives to confirm the dominant interpretation of same-gender sexuality. 'Scientific' theories of homosexual deviance, criminality, or sickness thereby enter public discussion.

Shifting Standpoints

In suggesting that the basis of sexual inquiry be reoriented, I draw upon what can be called a standpoint approach, which, as formulated by Dorothy E. Smith, calls for a change in vantage point from that of hegemonic ruling relations to that of women and other oppressed groups.[46] Ruling relations and regimes are the agencies involved in the management of contemporary capitalist patriarchal societies. Ruling relations are broader than those of State agencies, and include the mass media, various professional groups, and the forms of bureaucracy that have emerged over the last century.[47]

In 'A Sociology for Women', Smith analyzes how ruling relations produce knowledge from the standpoint of a male-dominated ruling class.[48] A sociology *for* women entails a reorientation of inquiry starting from the social experiences of individual women or groups of women. Smith's analysis provides insights into how ruling knowledge is produced and how it rules—bringing into view the social relations through which women are subordinated.

> As we explored the world from this place in it, we became aware that this rupture in experience, and between experience and the social forms of its expression, was located in a relation of power between women and men, in which men dominated over women.[49]

[. . .] This web of relations shapes gender identifications, gender dichotomies, sexualities, and patriarchal social organization.[50]

Making the everyday world problematic moves analysis from 'experience' itself to the specific social relations that organize it. This helps to make people's social practices visible. There is no pure unmediated 'telling of experience', as this is always affected by social discourse, but starting with the experiences of the oppressed and marginalized and then making it problematic locates our investigation in a very different place, at least partially outside of or in rupture with ruling regimes and discourse. This allows us to see the workings of ruling relations from the standpoint of the oppressed. As Smith notes:

> It is not individual social behaviour which is our interest but the social determinations of our everyday experience. The object of inquiry is the historical processes and development of social relations which organize, shape, and determine our directly experienced worlds.[51]

I apply this method of inquiry to the historical and social situations of lesbians and gay men. A history and sociology for lesbians and gay men involves both a critique of official knowledge and a reorientation of inquiry to begin from the experiences of those who have engaged in same-gender sex and others who have been oppressed by ruling sexual regulation. The purpose is not to interrogate the experiences of lesbians and gay men but instead to learn from their experiences about the social organization of heterosexual hegemony and oppressive sexual regulation so that these ruling practices can be interrogated and transformed.[52]

The contemporary lesbian and gay experience of a rupture between our lives as 'deviants' or outsiders and the heterosexual norm serves as the beginning of inquiry. This rupture is lived differently by people on the basis of class, race, and gender. How this tension has come about is one of the key questions to be explored. By making our everyday experiences problematic and locating them in emerging social relations, we can reveal aspects of our oppression and of heterosexual hegemony that are not visible from the vantage point of ruling relations. This process exposes not only the work of the agencies who have labelled us 'perverts' and 'criminals', but also the activities of those engaged in same-gender sex ourselves. We have been able to construct a certain 'naturalness' and 'normalness' for ourselves in opposition to heterosexual hegemony. If we start from here—the experiences of lesbians, gays, and others who engage in queer sex of the ruptures we feel between hegemonic heterosexuality and the actualities of our lives—then the problem is no longer homosexuality, but rather heterosexual hegemony and sexual rule more generally.

From this socially and historically grounded standpoint, the absolute distinction between homosexuality and heterosexuality is rooted in the work of the ruling regime and relations. This distinction is not as clearly expressed in our individual erotic lives, however. The actual relationship between social categories, identity construction and formation, and sexual activity is not as clear-cut as official discourse contends.

Sexual preferences and 'identities' are not fixed in stone. They develop unevenly, are often contradictory, and are potentially fluid. Kinsey's statistics suggested that a majority of men involved in reported homosexual acts did not see their experiences as defining them as homosexual.[53] Many are able to engage in occasional erotic delights with males while maintaining a heterosexual and masculine gender 'identity'. Prison inmates and hustlers often managed their identities so that they were not tainted by the stigma of homosexuality. For instance, in prison, the 'masculine' man who plays the 'active' role in anal intercourse but never plays the 'passive' position in anal intercourse and who gets his penis fellated but never sucks another penis, may be able to escape the label of 'queer' and preserve his 'heterosexual' identity. Some hustlers manage their identities by claiming they have sex only for the money, or that they engage only in acts that don't define them as homosexual. John Rechy in *City of Night* quotes Pete, a hustler:

> Whatever a guy does with other guys, if he does it for money that don't make him queer. You're still straight. It's when you start doing it for free, with other young guys, that you start growing wings.[54]

[. . .]

Ruling concepts cannot simply be stretched to cover our experiences. We must step outside ruling discourses—as we must as women, people of colour, and other oppressed groups—if we are to create knowledge to help us in our struggles.[55]

This perspective starts from our own experiences and practices.[56] We must become the subjects of our work rather than its objects. We must move beyond this starting point, however, to view everyday life as problematic; to see the struggles between ruling institutions and lesbians and gays over the meanings, images, and definitions of sexual regulation. We must move beyond our immediate experiences and the assumed 'naturalness' of our existence by uncovering the social relations in which homosexuality and heterosexuality have emerged historically.

Hegemony, State Formation, and Cultural Revolution

My analysis also draws upon a number of recent developments within Marxism and historical materialist approaches.[57] Recent historical and sociological explorations of capitalist or bourgeois State formation have illuminated how crucial

to the formation of the contemporary State has been what can be called a 'bourgeois cultural revolution'.[58]

Building on earlier State forms, the capitalist class made itself the ruling class and forged contemporary State relations by attempting to remake society in its own image. Crucial to this process was the creation of approved or respectable social identities, which necessarily meant the denial of alternatives. State formation is therefore always an active process, always contested and resisted, and riveted with contradictions. Heterosexual hegemony, as a part of this process, was constructed at the expense of other social and sexual possibilities, such as emerging homosexual and lesbian cultures. Heterosexuality was established as 'normal'. Homosexuality and lesbianism were disadvantaged as perverted, sick, and criminal.[59]

This approach stresses the importance to capitalist and patriarchal rule of the cultural and moral regulation of social identities and practices. The oppressive regulation of social life establishes some forms of activity as acceptable, respectable, responsible, normal, and natural; some ways of life are empowered, others are devalued. This approach refuses to reduce capitalism to its economic dimensions alone. State formation is seen as central to capitalist development. Class relations include struggles over cultural norms, social identities, and sexualities. Non-economic relations are thereby crucial to class relations.[60] Within historical materialism using these insights, the relationship of class, State formation, and sexual rule can be explored.

A crucial aspect of this State formation and cultural revolution has been the establishment of social, cultural, and political forms of hegemony. 'Hegemony', as I use the term, derives from the writings of the Italian Marxist Antonio Gramsci in the 1920s and 1930s.[61] Hegemony unites the process of coercion and consent, viewing the two as often taking place through the same social practices. Hegemony occurs through the normalization or naturalization of existing relations and is achieved when one class can exert social authority and leadership over others. This includes the power to

> frame alternatives and contain communities, to win and shape consent so that the granting of legitimacy to the dominant classes appears not only 'spontaneous' but natural and 'normal'.[62]

Hegemony is, however, not simply imposed by State agencies and the ruling class. It must be continually re-established. It is therefore never total or exclusive.

> [Hegemony] is not self-securing, it is constructed, sustained, reconstructed, by particular agents and agencies, in part by violence.[63]

When successfully established, hegemony shapes, redefines, and incorporates the needs and concerns of the subordinated groups, so that they conform to the interests of ruling groups.[64]

The development, transformation, and struggle over cultural and social definitions, boundaries, acceptable knowledge, identities, and norms is a key terrain for the continuous organization and reorganization of hegemonic relations:

> The dominant culture represents itself as the culture. It tries to define and contain all other cultures within its most inclusive range. Its views of the world, unless challenged, will stand as the most natural, all-embracing culture.[65]

[. . .]

Hegemonic approaches can be used to explore lesbian and gay oppression and resistance.

Heterosexual hegemony came about with the emergence of distinct heterosexual and homosexual/lesbian identities and cultures over the last two centuries. Its bases are the relations of ruling class normality, sex and gender, the gender division of labour, family and kinship relations, State policies, and sexual policing, and it relies not only on consent, legitimation, and 'common sense', but also on moments of denial, silencing, and coercion. Heterosexuality is 'freely compelled' for many in this society. Coercive laws, police practices, 'queer-bashing', and limited social options all attempt to make heterosexuality compulsory (or compulsive).[66] At the same time, there is an active social construction of 'consent' to heterosexual desire through strategies of the naturalization and normalization of heterosexuality and the construction of heterosexual cultures.

Heterosexual hegemony is produced on many fronts—from family relations that often marginalize and sometimes exclude gays and lesbians,[67] to the violence we face on city streets, to State policies, to the medical profession, to sociology, sexology, and psychiatry, to the church, the school system, and the media. These forms of sexual regulation (which do not develop in a linear fashion)[68] interact with the social relations we live to produce heterosexist 'common sense'. There exist also conflicts between and within various agencies over definitions of homosexuality and jurisdictional disputes over who can best deal with the sexual deviant.

[. . .]

How these various forms of heterosexism interact, and how they are based in social practices and relations, is a question for social and historical investigation. It is sufficient to note here that all these ideas can be found in contemporary discourse. There is a continuing resiliency for anti-gay/anti-lesbian discourses formed in previous historical periods that can still be remobilized against us. In certain periods, some regulatory strategies and discourses achieve a degree of cogency for maintaining and reconstructing heterosexual hegemony.[69] Given the various social processes at play, heterosexual common sense clearly suffers from many internal contradictions.

My historical investigation involves an analysis of the social relations that have organized heterosexual hegemony. Heterosexual hegemony and contemporary lesbian and gay cultures are two sides of the same relational social process. Heterosexual hegemony necessarily involves lesbian and gay subordination. As Rachel Harrison and Frank Mort note:

> The 'deviant' subject is not absent from discourse but she/he is only permitted to speak from a subordinate position: as 'patient', as 'pervert', etc.[70]

Heterosexual hegemony, and oppressive sexual regulation more generally, are an integral aspect of the organization of class, State, gender, and race relations. [. . .]

Notes

1. This can be a danger in 'queer' and much discourse-driven theory.
2. See Dorothy E. Smith, *The Everyday World as Problematic* (Toronto: University of Toronto Press, 1987), pp. 128–135; 223–224.
3. See Michel Foucault, *The History of Sexuality. V. 1, An Introduction* (New York: Vintage, 1980), pp. 116–127.
4. See my unpublished paper '"Queer Theory" versus Heterosexual Hegemony: Towards a Historical Materialism for Gay Men and Lesbians' presented at the 'Queer Sites' lesbian and gay conference, Toronto, 14 May 1993.
5. Dorothy E. Smith, 'Feminist Reflections on Political Economy' in *Studies in Political Economy*, No. 30, Autumn 1989, pp. 37–59, and Lorna Weir, 'Socialist Feminism and the Politics of Sexuality' in Heather Jon Maroney and Meg Luxton, eds, *Feminism and Political Economy* (Toronto: Methuen, 1987), pp. 69–83.
6. See Andrew Parker, 'Unthinking Sex: Marx, Engels and the Scene of Writing' in Michael Warner, ed., *Fear of a Queer Planet: Queer Politics and Social Theory* (Minneapolis: University of Minnesota Press, 1993), pp. 19–41. Unfortunately, Parker does not focus on how lesbians and gay men can use the method of historical materialism, and also seems unable to view sex and sexuality as forms of human practice/production.
7. Fetishism 'is a definite social relation between men (sic) that assumes, in their eyes, the fantastic form of a relationship between things.' Karl Marx, *Capital: A Critique of Political Economy*, V. 1 (New York: International Publishers, 1967), p. 72.
8. See Sayer, *Marx's Method* (Sussex and New Jersey: Harvester/Humanities, 1983), pp. 8–9.
9. Dorothy E. Smith, 'Women, Class and Family' in *Socialist Register* 1983 (London: The Merlin Press, 1983), p. 7.
10. Robert A. Padgug, 'Sexual Matters: On Conceptualizing Sexuality in History' in *Radical History Review*, No. 20, Spring/Summer, 1979, p. 9. Also in other collections including *Passion and Power* and *Hidden from History*.
11. It is also to be remembered that all biological knowledge, like all other forms of knowledge, is socially constructed. See Suzanne J. Kessler and Wendy McKenna, *Gender: An Ethnomethodological Approach* (Chicago and London: The University of Chicago Press, 1978), especially pp. 42–80, and Donna Haraway, *Simians, Cyborgs, and Women* (New York: Routledge, 1991), especially pp. 7–68, among others.
12. This perspective draws some of its insights from Gayle Rubin's 'The Traffic in Women' in Rayna R. Reiter, ed., *Toward an Anthropology of Women* (New York: Monthly Review Press, 1975), and her notion of a 'sex/gender' system. I do not use sex/gender system because it tends to conflate questions of sexuality and gender and also because it suggests that sex/gender relations are some sort of system separate from other social relations rather than an integral aspect of them. It also suggests that this system has been static throughout history rather than historically transformed. In my view, sex and gender relations vary historically and always exist in articulation with class, race, and other social relations. They are therefore part of class relations in a broad sense. Rubin herself has now rejected her earlier approach. In 'Thinking Sex: Notes for a Radical Theory of the Politics of Sexuality' in Vance, ed., *Pleasure and Danger: Exploring Female Sexuality* (Boston and London: Routledge and Kegan Paul, 1984), pp. 307–309, she rejects this category, but in a pre-feminist regression asserts that sex and gender are two completely autonomous and separate systems. This later position of Rubin's continues to shape recent 'queer theory', including the influential work of Eve Kosofsky Sedgwick, who, in her *The Epistemology of*

the Closet (Berkeley and Los Angeles: University of California Press, 1990), uses Rubin's later work to argue for the need to separate gender and sexual analysis.

13. On 'sexual scripts', see the work of symbolic interactionists, such as J.H. Gagnon and William Simon, *Sexual Conduct* (Chicago: Aldine, 1973) and Kenneth Plummer, *Sexual Stigma* (London: Routledge and Kegan Paul, 1975).

14. As Marx states: 'all epochs of production have certain common traits, common characteristics. Production in general is an abstraction, but a rational abstraction insofar as it really brings out and fixes the common element . . . Still this general category, this common element sifted out by comparison, is itself segmented many times over and splits into different determinations. Some determinations belong to all epochs, some only to a few.' Karl Marx, *Grundrisse* (Hammondsworth: Penguin, 1973), p. 85.

15. See Derek Sayer, op. cit., for this type of view in relation to production. Also see Roslyn Wallach Bologh, *Dialectical Phenomenology: Marx's Method* (Boston, London, and Henley: Routledge and Kegan Paul, 1979).

16. See K.J. Dower, *Greek Homosexuality* (New York: Vintage, 1980); Michel Foucault, *The Use of Pleasure*. V. 2, *History of Sexuality* (New York: Pantheon, 1985); David Halperin, *One Hundred Years of Homosexuality* (New York and London: Routledge, 1990); Clellan Ford and Frank Beach, *Patterns of Sexual Behavior* (New York: Harper Colophon, 1972), p. 132; Vern Bullough, *Sexual Variance in Society and History* (Chicago and London: The University of Chicago Press, 1976), pp. 32–34.

17. On the Sambia see sources cited in Joseph Harry, *Gay Children Grown Up: Gender Culture and Gender Deviance* (New York: Praeger, 1982), p. 3.

18. See S.J. Kessler and W. McKenna, *Gender: An Ethnomethodological Approach*, op. cit. Despite its date of publication, this is still one of the best books on the social making of gender. In many ways, it provides a much better socially grounded account of gender than that which is common in post-structuralist or postmodemist theory, including within queer theory. Judith Butler's *Gender Trouble, Feminism and the Subversion of Identity* (New York and London: Routledge, 1990) is often cited within queer theory regarding gender. Despite Butler's use of the term 'performativity', she does not focus on gender as actual social performance or accomplishment, but instead on the performative effects of discourse. I would argue quite strongly that gender is not simply a discursive effect.

19. For a critique of these biological reductionist approaches, see Nelly Oudshoorn, *Beyond the Natural Body: An Archeology of Sex Hormones* (London and New York: Routledge, 1994), and Gail Vines, *Raging Hormones: Do They Rule Our Lives?* (Berkeley and Los Angeles: University of California Press, 1994).

20. On the 'natural attitude' toward gender, see Harold Garfinkel, *Studies in Ethnomethodology* (Englewood Cliffs, NJ: Prentice-Hall, 1967), and Kessler and McKenna, *Gender: An Ethnomethodological Approach*, op. cit.

21. On collecting categories and devices that bring together a range of different activities, practices, or groups under common administrative classifications so they can be dealt with by ruling agencies, see Philip Corrigan, 'On Moral Regulation' in *Sociological Review*, V. 29, 1981, pp. 313–316.

22. See the very interesting account developed by the Red Collective, who describe the 'givenness' of our sexuality and feelings that prevents analysis and change. *The Politics of Sexuality in Capitalism* (London: Red Collective and Publications Distributors Cooperative, 1978).

23. Ellen Ross and Rayna Rapp, 'Sex and Society: A Research Note from Social History and Anthropology' in *Comparative Studies in Society and History*, V. 23, 1981, p. 71; also in Snitow, et al., *Powers of Desire* (New York: Monthly Review, 1983).

24. J.H. Gagnon and William Simon, *Sexual Conduct* (Chicago: Aldine, 1973).

25. Ibid., p. 26.

26. Ibid., p. 5.

27. Unfortunately, valuable insights in Foucault's work, such as 'power/knowledge', are limited by his lack of attention to social standpoint and the deletion of active subjects from his discourse analysis. Foucaultian-derived notions of 'power/knowledge' often tend to be relatively ungrounded from the social practices that produce them. Sometimes 'power/knowledge' almost seems to be self-generating and not produced through social practices. For some useful critical analysis of this, see Dorothy E. Smith, 'The Social Organization of Textual Reality' in *The Conceptual Practices of Power* (Toronto: University of Toronto Press, 1990), pp. 70, 79–80.

28. On normalization as a strategy of power, see Michel Foucault, *Discipline and Punish* (New York: Vintage, 1995).

29. George L. Masse, *Toward the Final Solution: A History of European Racism* (New York: Harper Colophen, 1978), pp. 16–17, and his *Nationalism and Sexuality* (New York: Howard Fertig, 1985).

30. On Eurocentrism see Samir Amin, *Eurocentrism* (New York: Monthly Review Press, 1989), and Edward W. Said, *Orientalism* (New York: Vintage, 1979).

31. Jeffrey Weeks, 'Discourse, Desire and Sexual Deviance' in Plummer, ed., *The Making of the Modern Homosexual* (London: Hutchinson, 1981), p. 77.

32. This point comes from a lecture by Dorothy E. Smith in the Social Organization of Knowledge course, Sociology Dept., Ontario Institute for Studies in Education, Fall 1980.

33. Bronislaw Malinowski, *The Sexual Life of Savages in North-Western Melanesia: An Ethnographic Account of Courtship, Marriage, and Family Life Among the Natives of the Trobiand Islands, British New Guinea* (London: Routledge and Kegan Paul, 1968), pp. 395–402.

34. See Randolph Trumbach, 'London's Sodomites: Homosexual Behaviour and Western Culture in the Eighteenth Century' in *Journal of Social History*, V. 2, No. 1, Fall 1977, note 11, p. 26.

35. Isabel J. Hull, 'The Bourgeoisie and Its Discontents: Reflections on Nationalism and Respectability' in *Journal of Contemporary History,* V. 17, No. 2, April 1982, p. 258. Also see Krafft-Ebing, *Psychopathia Sexualis* (New York: C.P. Putnam's Sons, 1965), and Lorna Weir, 'Studies in the Medicalization of Sexual Danger', Ph.D. thesis, Dept. of Social and Political Thought, York University, Toronto, 1986, chapter on sex psychology.

36. Freud's psychoanalytical work was simultaneously a recognition of how sexual desire was organized in a particular class, patriarchal, racial, and historical setting, and a universalization of this experience, which made it ahistorical, thereby articulating new oppressive regulations of erotic life. Freud's work has been transformed and integrated into the strategies of heterosexual hegemony and sexual rule. While there is much to be learned from Freud's work, Freudian psychoanalysis has been incorporated into the present practices that define sex and normalize only a particular form of male-dominated heterosexuality. Also see Jennifer Terry's 'Theorizing Deviant Historiography' in *Differences,* V. 3, No. 2, Summer 1991, pp. 55–74. For one lesbian's struggle with the psychiatric system, see Persimmon Blackbridge and Sheila Gilhooly, *Still Sane* (Vancouver: Press Gang, 1985). Also see 'Mad, Angry, Gay and Proud: A Lesbian and Gay Supplement' in *Phoenix Rising,* V. 8, No. 3/4, July 1990.

37. On 'cutting out' operations, see Dorothy E. Smith's 'K Is Mentally Ill' in her *Texts, Facts, and Femininity: Exploring the Relations of Ruling* (London and New York: Routledge, 1990), pp. 12–51.

38. Lon G. Nungessar, *Homosexual Acts, Actors and Identities* (New York: Praegar, 1983), p. 55.

39. Arno Karlen, *Sexuality and Homosexuality* (New York: W.W. Norton, 1971), p. 185.

40. Diane Richardson, 'Theoretical Perspectives on Homosexuality' in John Hart and Diane Richardson, eds, *The Theory and Practice of Homosexuality* (London: Routledge and Kegan Paul, 1981), p. 34. The major exceptions were the Kinsey Studies and the psychological work of Evelyn Hooker, which was directed at uprooting the construct that gay men were mentally ill.

41. See George Smith's 'Overturning State's Evidence: From Social Constructionism to Historical Materialism', unpublished paper given at the 'Sex and the State Lesbian/Gay History Conference' in Toronto, July 1985; 'Policing the Gay Community: An Inquiry into Textually-Mediated Social Relations' in *International Journal of the Sociology of Law,* 1988, 16, pp. 163–183; and his 'Political Activist as Ethnographer' in *Social Problems,* V. 37, No. 4, Nov. 1990, pp. 629–648.

42. 'Moral Panics' are defined by Stan Cohen: A condition, episode, person or group of persons emerges to become defined as a threat to societal values and interests; its nature is presented in a stylized and stereotyped fashion by the mass media; the moral barricades are manned by editors, bishops, and politicians and other right-thinking people; socially accredited experts pronounce their diagnoses and solutions; ways of coping are evolved, or (more often) resorted to; the condition then disappears, submerges or deteriorates . . . Sometimes the panic is passed over and forgotten, but at other times it has more serious and long-term repercussions and it might produce changes in legal and social policy or even in the way in which societies conceive themselves.
Stan Cohen, *Folk Devils and Moral Panics* (London: MacGibbon and Kee, 1972), p. 9. Unfortunately, 'moral panic' tends to get so overused in the literature that it almost seems to be self-generating. I try to specifically locate and ground the notion of moral panic in social and institutional relations and practices actively constructed between the media, the police, the courts, 'citizen's groups', professional experts, and State agencies. These relations combine in different ways in different 'panics'. They are an active process of social organization. I do not see 'moral panics' as an explanation of a social process, rather as pointing toward an investigation of social relations.

43. See Richard J. Herrnstein and Charles Murray, *The Bell Curve: Intelligence and Class Structure in American Life* (New York: Free Press, 1994) and the controversies surrounding it. See Steven Fraser, *The Bell Curve Wars* (New York: Basic Books, 1995).

44. See 'Brain Sex', *Witness,* CTV TV, 1992.

45. See Dorothy E. Smith, 'No One Commits Suicide: Textual Analysis of Ideological Practices' (particularly the diagram on p. 14), unpublished paper, Feb. 1980. Also see Smith's 'The Social Construction of Documentary Reality' in *Sociological Inquiry,* 44:4, 1974, pp. 257–268. Revised versions of these articles appear in *The Conceptual Practices of Power,* op. cit.

46. This is not the same as what is referred to as feminist-standpoint theory, which implies that women have a common standpoint and perspective. Instead, Dorothy E. Smith's work argues for a shift in where we begin our inquiry to take up a particular social standpoint in exploring social relations. Standpoint is then a place from which to explore social relations and practice. The standpoints of oppressed groups allow us to see aspects of ruling relations not visible from within ruling institutions.

47. Dorothy E. Smith, 'Women, Class and Family', op. cit., p. 12.

48. Dorothy E. Smith, 'A Sociology for Women' in Sherman and Back, eds, *The Prism of Sex: Essays in the Sociology of Knowledge* (Madison: University of Wisconsin Press, 1979), pp. 135–187. A revised version of this article appears in *The Everyday World as Problematic,* op. cit.

49. Ibid., p. 137 in *The Everyday World as Problematic,* p. 51.

50. Also see Dorothy E. Smith, 'Femininity As Discourse' in her *Texts, Facts and Femininity: Exploring the Relations of Ruling* (London and New York: Routledge, 1990), pp. 159–208,

and her 'Women, Class and Family' in *The Socialist Register* (London: Merlin Press, 1983), pp. 1–44.

51. Dorothy E. Smith, 'The Experienced World as Problematic: A Feminist Method', the Twelfth Annual Soroken Lecture, University of Saskatchewan, Saskatoon, 28 January 1981, p. 17, also in *The Everyday World as Problematic.*

52. For important contributions, see George Smith's 'Policing the Gay Community: An Inquiry Into Textually-Mediated Social Relations' in *International Journal of the Sociology of Law,* op. cit.; his 'Political Activist as Ethnographer' in *Social Problems,* op. cit.; and his 'The Ideology of "Fag": The School Experience of Gay Students', unpublished paper, Ontario Institute for Studies in Education; and Madiha Didi Khayatt, *Lesbian Teachers, an Invisible Presence* (Albany: State University of New York Press, 1992); and her 'Compulsory Heterosexuality: Schools and Lesbian Students', in Marie Campbell and Ann Manicom, eds, *Knowledge, Experience and Ruling Relations: Studies in the Social Organization of Knowledge* (Toronto: University of Toronto Press, 1995).

53. See Mary McIntosh, 'The Homosexual Role', originally in *Social Problems,* V. 16, No. 2, Fall 1968, reprinted with a postscript in Plummer, ed., *The Making of the Modern Homosexual* (London: Hutchinson, 1981), pp. 38–43; and Kinsey, Gebhard, Pomeroy, and Martin, *Sexual Behavior in the Human Male* (Philadelphia: W.B. Saunders, 1953).

54. John Rechy, *City of Night* (New York: Grove Press, 1963), p. 40. This expression is also used by the character played by Keanu Reeves in the film *My Own Private Idaho.*

55. See Dorothy E. Smith, 'A Sociology for Women', op. cit.

56. Some inkling of this shifting in vantage point from 'outsider' to 'insider' can be seen in Joseph Styles, 'Outside/Insider Researching Gay Baths' in *Urban Life,* V. 8, No. 2, July 1979, pp. 135–152. Styles describes how an insider vantage point let him see things in a way that the outsider perspective obscured. On an insider's sociology, also see the work of Dorothy E. Smith, especially *The Everyday World as Problematic.*

57. Also offering important insights is recent work on governmentality influenced by the work of Michel Foucault. Among others, see Graham Burchell, Colin Gordon, and Peter Miller, eds, *The Foucault Effect: Studies in Governmentality* (Chicago: The University of Chicago Press, 1991), and Mike Gane and Terry Johnson, eds, *Foucault's New Domains* (London and New York: Routledge, 1993).

58. In particular, see Philip Corrigan and Derek Sayer, *The Great Arch: English State Formation as Cultural Revolution* (Oxford: Basil Blackwell, 1985).

59. See Philip Corrigan, 'Towards a Celebration of Difference(s): Notes for a Sociology of a Possible Everyday Future' in D. Robbins, ed., *Rethinking Social Inequality* (London: Gower, 1982).

60. See the work of the late E.P. Thompson, particularly *The Making of the English Working Class* (Hamondsworth: Penguin, 1968), and Dorothy E. Smith, 'Women, Class and Family', op. cit., for an account of women's activity in the organization of this broader notion of class relations.

61. See Antonio Gramsci, *Selections from the Prison Notebooks* (New York: International Publishers, 1971); Carl Boggs, *Gramsci's Marxism* (London: Pluto Press, 1976); Perry Anderson, 'The Antimonies of Antonio Gramsci' in *New Left Review,* No. 100, Nov. 1976–Jan. 1977, pp. 5–78; Chantal Mouffe, ed., *Gramsci and Marxist Theory* (London: Routledge and Kegan Paul, 1979); and Ernesto Laclau and Chantal Mouffe, *Hegemony and Socialist Strategy: Towards a Radical Democratic Politics* (London: Verso, 1985). Unfortunately, while Laclau and Mouffe trace some of the genealogy of the concept of hegemony, they treat hegemony as only a discursive concept, separating it from social practices and severing it from its historical, social, and organizational contexts. They completely sever hegemony from class relations and class struggles in their latest work. There are difficulties with notions of 'hegemony', especially if hegemony is construed as an explanatory category in and of itself. But it points us toward the relational and social character of social regulation in a clearer fashion than do terms like dominant culture or notions of domination. Unlike social or ideological reproduction, it suggests that social regulation is actively accomplished by individuals in diverse institutional sites and is always 'problematic'. It points us toward the social organization of ruling relations while including within it the activities and resistances of the subordinated. It is never total, never exclusive, and there is always the possibility of subversion and transformation. It is these opportunities we have to seize.

62. John Clarke, Stuart Hall, Tony Jefferson, and Brian Roberts, 'Subcultures, Cultures and Class: A Theoretical Overview' in Hall and Jefferson, eds, *Resistance Through Rituals* (London: Hutchinson, 1976), p. 38.

63. Corrigan and Sayer, *The Great Arch,* op. cit., p. 142.

64. See Gary Kinsman, 'Managing AIDS Organizing: "Consultation", "Partnership", and the National AIDS Strategy', in William K. Carrol, ed., *Organizing Dissent: Contemporary Social Movements in Theory and Practice* (Toronto: Garamond, 1992), pp. 215–231.

65. Clarke, et al., op .cit., p. 12.

66. See Adrienne Rich, 'Compulsory Heterosexuality and Lesbian Existence' in *Signs,* V. 5, No. 4, Summer 1980, pp. 631–660. Despite the many insights of this article, her suggestion that heterosexuality is simply 'compulsory' for women is rather one-sided. It does not adequately take into account that 'consent' to heterosexuality is also actively constructed through practices of normalization and naturalization. This is why I prefer heterosexual hegemony to compulsory heterosexuality since it includes these moments of coercion *and* consent.

67. See Carol-Anne O'Brien and Lorna Weir, 'Lesbians and Gay Men Inside and Outside Families' in Nancy Mandell and

Anne Duffy, eds, *Canadian Families: Diversity, Conflict and Change* (Toronto: Harcourt Brace Canada, 1995).

68. See Frank Mort, 'Sexuality: Regulation and Contestation' in Gay Left, ed., *Homosexuality: Power and Politics* (London: Allison & Busby, 1980), pp. 41–42.

69. See Gary Kinsman, 'The Textual Practices of Sexual Rule: Sexual Policing and Gay Men' in Marie Campbell and Ann Manicom, eds, *Knowledge, Experience and Ruling Relations:*

Studies in the Social Organization of Knowledge (Toronto: University of Toronto Press, 1995), pp. 80–95.

70. Rachel Harrison and Frank Mort, 'Patriarchal Aspects of Nineteenth-Century State Formation: Property Relations, Marriage and Divorce and Sexuality' in Philip Corrigan, ed., *Capitalism, State Formation and Marxist Theory* (London: Quartet, 1980), p. 106.

Destiny: The Data of Biology

Simone de Beauvoir

Woman? Very simple, say the fanciers of simple formulas: she is a womb, an ovary; she is a female—this word is sufficient to define her. In the mouth of a man the epithet *female* has the sound of an insult, yet he is not ashamed of his animal nature; on the contrary, he is proud if someone says of him: 'He is a male!' The term 'female' is derogatory not because it emphasizes woman's animality, but because it imprisons her in her sex; and if this sex seems to man to be contemptible and inimical even in harmless dumb animals, it is evidently because of the uneasy hostility stirred up in him by woman. Nevertheless he wishes to find in biology a justification for this sentiment. The word *female* brings up in his mind a saraband of imagery—a vast, round ovum engulfs and castrates the agile spermatozoon; the monstrous and swollen termite queen rules over the enslaved males; the female praying mantis and the spider, satiated with love, crush and devour their partners; the bitch in heat runs through the alleys, trailing behind her a wake of depraved odours; the she-monkey presents her posterior immodestly and then steals away with hypocritical coquetry; and the most superb wild beasts—the tigress, the lioness, the panther—bed down slavishly under the imperial embrace of the male. Females sluggish, eager, artful, stupid, callous, lustful, ferocious, abased—man projects them all at once upon woman. And the fact is that she is a female. But if we are willing to stop thinking in platitudes, two questions are immediately posed: what does the female denote in the animal kingdom? And what particular kind of female is manifest in woman?

Males and females are two types of individuals which are differentiated within a species for the function of reproduction; they can be defined only correlatively. But first it must be noted that even the *division* of a species into two sexes is not always clear-cut.

In nature it is not universally manifested. To speak only of animals, it is well known that among the microscopic one-celled forms—infusoria, amoebas, sporozoans, and the like—multiplication is fundamentally distinct from sexuality. Each cell divides and subdivides by itself. In many-celled animals or metazoans reproduction may take place asexually, either by schizogenesis—that is, by fission or cutting into two or more parts which become new individuals—or by blastogenesis—that is, by buds that separate and form new individuals. [. . .] In cases of parthenogenesis the egg of the virgin female develops into an embryo without fertilization by the male, which thus may play no role at all. In the honeybee copulation takes place, but the eggs may or may not be fertilized at the time of laying. The unfertilized eggs undergo development and produce the drones (males); in the aphids males are absent during a series of generations in which the eggs are unfertilized and produce females. Parthenogenesis has been induced artificially in the sea urchin, the starfish, the frog, and other species. [. . .]

Certain biologists in the past concluded from these facts that even in species capable of asexual propagation occasional fertilization is necessary to renew the vigour of the race—to accomplish 'rejuvenation'—through the mixing of hereditary material from two individuals. On this hypothesis sexuality might well appear to be an indispensable function in the most complex forms of life; only the lower organisms could multiply without sexuality, and even here vitality would after a time become exhausted. But today this hypothesis is largely abandoned; research has proved that under suitable conditions asexual multiplication can go on indefinitely without noticeable degeneration, a fact that is especially striking in the bacteria and Protozoa. [. . .]

The production of two types of gametes, the sperm and the egg, does not necessarily imply the existence of two distinct sexes; as a matter of fact, egg and sperm—two highly differentiated types of reproductive cells—may both be produced by the same individual. This occurs in normally hermaphroditic species, which are common among plants and are also to be found among the lower animals, such as annelid worms and mollusks. In them reproduction may be accomplished through self-fertilization or, more commonly, cross-fertilization. Here again certain biologists have attempted to account for the existing state of affairs. Some hold that the separation of the gonads (ovaries and testes) in two distinct individuals represents an evolutionary advance over hermaphroditism; others on the contrary regard the separate condition as primitive, and believe that hermaphroditism represents a degenerate state. These notions regarding the superiority of one system or the other imply the most debatable evolutionary theorizing. All that we can say for sure is that these two modes of reproduction coexist in nature, that they both succeed in accomplishing the survival of the species concerned. [. . .]

Thus we can regard the phenomenon of reproduction as founded in the very nature of being. But we must stop there. The perpetuation of the species does not necessitate sexual differentiation. True enough, this differentiation is characteristic of existents to such an extent that it belongs in any realistic definition of existence. But it nevertheless remains true that both a mind without a body and an immortal man are strictly inconceivable, whereas we can imagine a parthenogenetic or hermaphroditic society.

On the respective functions of the two sexes man has entertained a great variety of beliefs. At first they had no scientific basis, simply reflecting social myths. It was long thought—and it still is believed in certain primitive matriarchal societies—that the father plays no part in conception. Ancestral spirits in the form of living germs are supposed to find their way into the maternal body. With the advent of patriarchal institutions, the male laid eager claim to his posterity. It was still necessary to grant the mother a part in procreation, but it was conceded only that she carried and nourished the living seed, created by the father alone. Aristotle fancied that the fetus arose from the union of sperm and menstrual blood, woman furnishing only passive matter while the male principle contributed force, activity, movement, life. Hippocrates held to a similar doctrine, recognizing two kinds of seed, the weak or female and the strong or male. The theory of Aristotle survived through the Middle Ages and into modern times.

At the end of the seventeenth century Harvey killed female dogs shortly after copulation and found in the horns of the uterus small sacs that he thought were eggs but that were really embryos. The Danish anatomist Steno gave the name of ovaries to the female genital glands, previously called 'feminine testicles', and noted on their surface the small swellings that von Graaf in 1677 erroneously identified with the eggs and that are now called Graafian follicles. The ovary was still regarded as homologous to the male gland. In the same year, however, the 'spermatic animalcules' were discovered and it was proved that they penetrated into the uterus of the female; but it was supposed that they were simply nourished therein and that the coming individual was preformed in them. In 1694 a Dutchman, Hartsaker, drew a picture of the 'homunculus' hidden in the spermatozoon, and in 1699 another scientist said that he had seen the spermatozoon cast off a kind of molt under which appeared a little man, which he also drew. Under these imaginative hypotheses, woman was restricted to the nourishment of an active, living principle already preformed in perfection. These notions were not universally accepted, and they were argued into the nineteenth century. The use of the microscope enabled von Baer in 1827 to discover the mammalian egg, contained inside the Graafian follicle. Before long it was possible to study the cleavage of the egg—that is, the early stage of development through cell division—and in 1835 sarcode, later called protoplasm, was discovered and the true nature of the cell began to be realized. In 1879 the penetration of the spermatozoon into the starfish egg was observed, and thereupon the equivalence of the nuclei of the two gametes, egg and sperm, was established. The details of their union within the fertilized egg were first worked out in 1883 by a Belgian zoologist, van Beneden.

Aristotle's ideas were not wholly discredited, however. Hegel held that the two sexes were of necessity different, the one active and the other passive, and of course the female would be the passive one. 'Thus man, in consequence of that differentiation, is the active principle while woman is the passive principle because she remains underdeveloped in her unity.'[1] And even after the egg had been recognized as an active principle, men still tried to make a point of its quiescence as contrasted with the lively movements of the sperm. Today one notes an opposite tendency on the part of some scientists. The discoveries made in the course of experiments on parthenogenesis have led them to reduce the function of the sperm to that of a simple physico-chemical reagent. It has been shown that in certain species the stimulus of an acid or even of a needle-prick is enough to initiate the cleavage of the egg and the development of the embryo. On this basis it has been boldly suggested that the male gamete (sperm) is not necessary for reproduction, that it acts at most as a ferment; further, that perhaps in time the co-operation of the male will become unnecessary in procreation— the answer, it would seem, to many a woman's prayer. But there is no warrant for so bold an expectation, for nothing warrants us in universalizing specific life processes. The phenomena of asexual propagation and of parthenogenesis appear to be neither more nor less fundamental than those of sexual reproduction. I have said that the latter has no claim *a priori* to be considered basic; but neither does any fact indicate that it is reducible to any more fundamental mechanism.

Thus, admitting no *a priori* doctrine, no dubious theory, we are confronted by a fact for which we can offer no basis in the nature of things, nor any explanation through observed data, and the significance of which we cannot comprehend *a priori.* We can hope to grasp the significance of sexuality only by studying it in its concrete manifestations; and then perhaps the meaning of the word *female* will stand revealed.

I do not intend to offer here a philosophy of life; and I do not care to take sides prematurely in the dispute between the mechanistic and the purposive or teleological philosophies. It is to be noted, however, that all physiologists and biologists use more or less finalistic language, if only because they ascribe meaning to vital phenomena. I shall adopt their terminology. Without taking any stand on the relation between life and consciousness, we can assert that every biological fact implies transcendence, that every function involves a project, something to be done. Let my words be taken to imply no more than that.

In the vast majority of species male and female individuals co-operate in reproduction. They are defined primarily as male and female by the gametes which they produce—sperms and eggs respectively. [. . .] Sperms and eggs develop from similar primordial germ cells in the two sexes. The development of oocytes from the primordial cells in the female differs from that of spermatocytes in the male chiefly in regard to the protoplasm, but the nuclear phenomena are clearly the same. The biologist Ancel suggested in 1903 that the primordial germ cell is indifferent and undergoes development into sperm or egg depending upon which type of gonad, testis or ovary, contains it. However this may be, the primordial germ cells of each sex contain the same number of chromosomes (that characteristic of the species concerned), which number is reduced to one half by closely analogous processes in male and female. At the end of these developmental processes (called spermatogenesis in the male and oogenesis in the female) the gametes appear fully matured as sperms and eggs, differing enormously in some respects, as noted below, but being alike in that each contains a single set of equivalent chromosomes.

Today it is well known that the sex of offspring is determined by the chromosome constitution established at the time of fertilization. According to the species concerned, it is either the male gamete or the female gamete that accomplishes this result. In the mammals it is the sperm, of which two kinds are produced in equal numbers, one kind containing an X-chromosome (as do all the eggs), the other kind containing a Y-chromosome (not found in the eggs). Aside from the X- and Y-chromosomes, egg and sperm contain an equivalent set of these bodies. It is obvious that when sperm and egg unite in fertilization, the fertilized egg will contain two full sets of chromosomes, making up the number characteristic of the species—48 in man, for example. If fertilization is accomplished by an X-bearing sperm, the fertilized *egg* will contain two X-chromosomes and will develop into a female (XX). If the Y-bearing sperm fertilizes the egg, only one X-chromosome will be present and the sex will be male (XY). [. . .]

What we should note in particular at this point is that neither gamete can be regarded as superior to the other; when they unite, both lose their individuality in the fertilized egg. There are two common suppositions which—at least on this basic biological level—are clearly false. The first—that of the passivity of the female—is disproved by the fact that new life springs from the union of the two gametes; the living spark is not the exclusive property of either. The nucleus of the egg is a centre of vital activity exactly symmetrical with the nucleus of the sperm. The second false supposition contradicts the first—which does not seem to prevent their coexistence. It is to the effect that the permanence of the species is assured by the female, the male principle being of an explosive and transitory nature. As a matter of fact, the embryo carries on the germ plasm of the father as well as that of the mother and transmits them together to its descendants under now male, now female form.

It is, so to speak, an androgynous germ plasm, which outlives the male or female individuals that are its incarnations, whenever they produce offspring.

This said, we can turn our attention to secondary differences between egg and sperm, which are of the greatest interest. The essential peculiarity of the egg is that it is provided with means for nourishing and protecting the embryo; it stores up reserve material from which the fetus will build its tissues, material that is not living substance but inert yolk. In consequence the egg is of massive, commonly spherical form and relatively large. The size of birds' eggs is well known; in woman the egg is almost microscopic, about equal in size to a printed period (diameter .132–.135 mm), but the human sperm is far smaller (.04–.06 mm in length), so small that a cubic millimetre would hold 60 000. The sperm has a threadlike tail and a small, flattened oval head, which contains the chromosomes. No inert substance weighs it down; it is wholly alive. In its whole structure it is adapted for mobility. Whereas the egg, big with the future of the embryo, is stationary; enclosed within the female body or floating externally in water, it passively awaits fertilization. It is the male gamete that seeks it out. The sperm is always a naked cell; the egg may or may not be protected with shell and membranes according to the species; but in any case, when the sperm makes contact with the egg, it presses against it, sometimes shakes it, and bores into it. The tail is dropped and the head enlarges, forming the male nucleus, which now moves toward the egg nucleus. Meanwhile the egg quickly forms a membrane, which prevents the entrance of other sperms. In the starfish and other echinoderms, where fertilization takes place externally, it is easy to observe the onslaught of the sperms, which surround the egg like an aureole. The competition involved is an important phenomenon, and it occurs in most species. Being much smaller than the egg, the sperm is generally produced in far greater numbers (more than 200 000 000 to 1 in the human species), and so each egg has numerous suitors.

Thus the egg—active in its essential feature, the nucleus—is superficially passive; its compact mass, sealed up within itself, evokes nocturnal darkness and inward repose. It was the form of the sphere that to the ancients represented the circumscribed world, the impenetrable atom. Motionless, the egg waits; in contrast the sperm—free, slender, agile—typifies the impatience and the restlessness of existence. But allegory should not be pushed too far. The ovule has sometimes been likened to immanence, the sperm to transcendence, and it has been said that the sperm penetrates the female element only in losing its transcendence, its motility; it is seized and castrated by the inert mass that engulfs it after depriving it of its tail. This is magical action—disquieting, as is all passive action—whereas the activity of the male gamete is rational; it is movement measurable in terms of time and space. The truth is that these notions are hardly more than vagaries of the mind. Male and female gametes fuse in the fertilized egg; they are both suppressed in becoming a new whole. It is false to say that the egg greedily swallows the sperm, and equally so to say that the sperm victoriously commandeers the female cell's reserves, since in the act of fusion the individuality of both is lost. No doubt movement seems to the mechanistic mind to be an eminently rational phenomenon, but it is an idea no clearer for modern physics than action at a distance. [. . .]

It would be foolhardy indeed to deduce from such evidence that woman's place is in the home—and there are foolhardy men. In his book *Le Tempérament et le charactètere*, Alfred Fouillée undertakes to found his definition of woman *in toto* upon the egg and that of man upon the spermatozoon; and a number of supposedly

profound theories rest upon this play of doubtful analogies. It is a question to what philosophy of nature these dubious ideas pertain; not
to the laws of heredity, certainly, for, according
to these laws, men and women alike develop
from an egg and a sperm. I can only suppose
that in such misty minds there still float shreds
of the old philosophy of the Middle Ages which
taught that the cosmos is an exact reflection of
a microcosm—the egg is imagined to be a little
female, the woman a giant egg. These musings,
generally abandoned since the days of alchemy,
make a bizarre contrast with the scientific precision of the data upon which they are now based,
for modern biology conforms with difficulty to
medieval symbolism. But our theorizers do not
look too closely into the matter. In all honesty
it must be admitted that in any case it is a long
way from the egg to woman. In the unfertilized
egg not even the concept of femaleness is as yet
established. As Hegel justly remarks, the sexual
relation cannot be referred back to the relation
of the gametes. It is our duty, then, to study the
female organism as a whole.

[. . .]

The fact is that the individual, though its
genotypic sex is fixed at fertilization, can be profoundly affected by the environment in which it
develops. In the ants, bees, and termites the lar-
val nutrition determines whether the genotypic
female individual will become a fully developed
female ('queen') or a sexually retarded worker.
In these cases the whole organism is affected;
but the gonads do not play a part in establishing
the sexual differences of the body, or *soma*. In
the vertebrates, however, the hormones secreted
by the gonads are the essential regulators.
Numerous experiments show that by varying
the hormonal (endocrine) situation, sex can be
profoundly affected.

Grafting and castration experiments on
adult animals and man have contributed to the
modern theory of sexuality, according to which
the soma is in a way identical in male and female
vertebrates. It may be regarded as a kind of neutral element upon which the influence of the
gonad imposes the sexual characteristics.[2] Some
of the hormones secreted by the gonads act as
stimulators, others as inhibitors. Even the genital
tract itself is somatic, and embryological investigations show that it develops in the male or
female direction from an indifferent and in some
respects hermaphroditic condition under the
hormonal influence. Intersexuality may result
when the hormones are abnormal and hence neither one of the two sexual potentialities is exclusively realized.

Numerically equal in the species and developed similarly from like beginnings, the fully
formed male and female are basically equivalent. Both have reproductive glands—ovaries
or testes—in which the gametes are produced
by strictly corresponding processes, as we have
seen. These glands discharge their products
through ducts that are more or less complex
according to sex; in the female the egg may pass
directly to the outside through the oviduct, or it
may be retained for a time in the cloaca or the
uterus before expulsion; in the male the semen
may be deposited outside, or there may be a
copulatory organ through which it is introduced
into the body of the female. In these respects,
then, male and female appear to stand in a symmetrical relation to each other. To reveal their
peculiar, specific qualities it will be necessary to
study them from the functional point of view.

[. . .]

In nature nothing is ever perfectly clear.
The two types, male and female, are not always
sharply distinguished; while they sometimes
exhibit a dimorphism—in coat colour or in
arrangement of spotting or mottling—that
seems absolutely distinctive, yet it may happen,
on the contrary, that they are indistinguishable

and that even their functions are hardly differentiated, as in many fishes. All in all, however, and especially at the top of the animal scale, the two sexes represent two diverse aspects of the life of the species. The difference between them is not, as has been claimed, that between activity and passivity; for the nucleus of the egg is active and moreover the development of the embryo is an active, living process, not a mechanical unfolding. It would be too simple to define the difference as that between change and permanence: for the sperm can create only because its vitality is maintained in the fertilized egg, and the egg can persist only through developmental change, without which it deteriorates and disappears.

It is true, however, that in these two processes, *maintaining* and *creating* (both of which are active), the synthesis of becoming is not accomplished in the same manner. To *maintain* is to deny the scattering of instants, it is to establish continuity in their flow; to *create* is to strike out from temporal unity in general an irreducible, separate present. And it is true also that in the female it is the continuity of life that seeks accomplishment in spite of separation; while separation into new and individualized forces is incited by male initiative. The male is thus permitted to express himself freely; the energy of the species is well integrated into his own living activity. On the contrary, the individuality of the female is opposed by the interest of the species; it is as if she were possessed by foreign forces—alienated. And this explains why the contrast between the sexes is not reduced when—as in higher forms—the individuality of the organisms concerned is more pronounced. On the contrary, the contrast is increased. The male finds more and more varied ways in which to employ the forces he is master of; the female feels her enslavement more and more keenly, the conflict between her own interests and the reproductive forces is heightened. Parturition in cows

and mares is much more painful and dangerous than it is in mice and rabbits. Woman—the most individualized of females—seems to be the most fragile, most subject to this pain and danger: she who most dramatically fulfills the call of destiny and most profoundly differs from her male. [. . .]

The development of the male is comparatively simple. From birth to puberty his growth is almost regular; at the age of 15 or 16 spermatogenesis begins, and it continues into old age; with its appearance hormones are produced that establish the masculine bodily traits. From this point on, the male sex life is normally integrated with his individual existence: in desire and in coition his transcendence toward the species is, at one with his subjectivity—he *is* his body.

Woman's story is much more complex. In embryonic life the supply of oocytes is already built up, the ovary containing about 40 000 immature eggs, each in a follicle, of which perhaps 400 will ultimately reach maturation. From birth, the species has taken possession of woman and tends to tighten its grasp. In coming into the world woman experiences a kind of first puberty, as the oocytes enlarge suddenly; then the ovary is reduced to about a fifth of its former size—one might say that the child is granted a respite. While her body develops, her genital system remains almost stationary; some of the follicles enlarge, but they fail to mature. The growth of the little girl is similar to that of the boy; at the same age she is sometimes even taller and heavier than he is. But at puberty the species reasserts its claim. Under the influence of the ovarian secretions the number of developing follicles increases, the ovary receives more blood and grows larger, one of the follicles matures, ovulation occurs, and the menstrual cycle is initiated; the genital system assumes its definitive size and form, the body takes on feminine contours, and the endocrine balance is established. [. . .]

From puberty to menopause woman is the theatre of a play that unfolds within her and in which she is not personally concerned. Anglo-Saxons call menstruation 'the curse'; in truth the menstrual cycle is a burden, and a useless one from the point of view of the individual. In Aristotle's time it was believed that each month blood flowed away that was intended, if fertilization had occurred, to build up the blood and flesh of the infant, and the truth of that old notion lies in the fact that over and over again woman does sketch in outline the groundwork of gestation. In lower mammals this oestrus cycle is confined to a particular season, and it is not accompanied by a flow of blood; only in the primates (monkeys, apes, and the human species) is it marked each month by blood and more or less pain.[3] During about 14 days one of the Graafian follicles that enclose the eggs enlarges and matures, secreting the hormone folliculin (estrin). Ovulation occurs on about the fourteenth day: the follicle protrudes through the surface of the ovary and breaks open (sometimes with slight bleeding), the egg passes into the oviduct, and the wound develops into the corpus luteum. The latter secretes the hormone progesterone, which acts on the uterus during the second phase of the cycle. The lining of the uterus becomes thickened and glandular and full of blood vessels, forming in the womb a cradle to receive the fertilized egg. These cellular proliferations being irreversible, the edifice is not resorbed if fertilization has not occurred. In the lower mammals the debris may escape gradually or may be carried away by the lymphatic vessels; but in woman and the other primates, the thickened lining membrane (endometrium) breaks down suddenly, the blood vessels and blood spaces are opened, and the bloody mass trickles out as the menstrual flow. Then, while the corpus luteum regresses, the membrane that lines the uterus is reconstituted and a new follicular phase of the cycle begins.

This complex process, still mysterious in many of its details, involves the whole female organism, since there are hormonal reactions between the ovaries and other endocrine organs, such as the pituitary, the thyroid, and the adrenals, which affect the central nervous system, the sympathetic nervous system, and in consequence all the viscera. Almost all women—more than 85 per cent—show more or less distressing symptoms during the menstrual period. Blood pressure rises before the beginning of the flow and falls afterward; the pulse rate and often the temperature are increased, so that fever is frequent; pains in the abdomen are felt; often a tendency to constipation followed by diarrhea is observed; frequently there are also swelling of the liver, retention of urea, and albuminuria; many subjects have sore throat and difficulties with hearing and sight; perspiration is increased and accompanied at the beginning of the menses by an odour *sui generis,* which may be very strong and may persist throughout the period. The rate of basal metabolism is raised. The red blood count drops. The blood carries substances usually put on reserve in the tissues, especially calcium salts; the presence of these substances reacts on the ovaries, on the thyroid—which enlarges—and on the pituitary (regulator of the changes in the uterine lining described above)—which becomes more active. This glandular instability brings on a pronounced nervous instability. The central nervous system is affected, with frequent headache, and the sympathetic system is overactive; unconscious control through the central system is reduced, freeing convulsive reflexes and complexes and leading to a marked capriciousness of disposition. The woman is more emotional, more nervous, more irritable than usual, and may manifest serious psychic disturbance. It is during her periods that she feels her body most painfully as an obscure, alien thing; it is, indeed, the prey of a stubborn and foreign life that each month constructs and then tears down a cradle within it; each month all things are made ready for a child and then aborted in the crimson flow. Woman, like man, *is* her body;[4] but her body is something other than herself.

Woman experiences a more profound alienation when fertilization has occurred and the dividing egg passes down into the uterus and proceeds to develop there. True enough, pregnancy is a normal process, which, if it takes place under normal conditions of health and nutrition, is not harmful to the mother; certain interactions between her and the fetus become established which are even beneficial to her. In spite of an optimistic view having all too obvious social utility, however, gestation is a fatiguing task of no individual benefit to the woman[5] but on the contrary demanding heavy sacrifices. It is often associated in the first months with loss of appetite and vomiting, which are not observed in any female domesticated animal and which signalize the revolt of the organism against the invading species.[6] There is a loss of phosphorus, calcium, and iron—the last difficult to make good later; metabolic overactivity excites the endocrine system; the sympathetic nervous system is in a state of increased excitement; and the blood shows a lowered specific gravity, it is lacking in iron, and in general, it is similar 'to that of persons fasting, of victims of famine, of those who have been bled frequently, of convalescents'.[7] All that a healthy and well-nourished woman can hope for is to recoup these losses without too much difficulty after childbirth; but frequently serious accidents or at least dangerous disorders mark the course of pregnancy; and if the woman is not strong, if hygienic precautions are not taken, repeated childbearing will make her prematurely old and misshapen, as often among the rural poor. Childbirth itself is painful and dangerous. In this crisis it is most clearly evident that the body does not always work to the advantage of both species and individual at once; the infant may die, and, again, in being born it may kill its mother or leave her with a chronic ailment. Nursing is also a tiring service. A number of factors—especially the hormone prolactin—bring about the secretion of milk in the mammary glands; some soreness and often fever may accompany the process and in any case the nursing mother feeds the newborn from the resources of her own vitality. The conflict between species and individual, which sometimes assumes dramatic force at childbirth, endows the feminine body with a disturbing frailty. It has been well said that women 'have infirmity in the abdomen'; and it is true that they have within them a hostile element—it is the species gnawing at their vitals. Their maladies are often caused not by some infection from without but by some internal maladjustment; for example, a false inflammation of the endometrium is set up, through the reaction of the uterine lining to an abnormal excitation of the ovaries; if the corpus luteum persists instead of declining after menstruation, it causes inflammation of the oviducts and uterine lining, and so on.

In the end woman escapes the iron grasp of the species by way of still another serious crisis; the phenomena of the menopause, the inverse of puberty, appear between the ages of 45 and 50. Ovarian activity diminishes and disappears, with resulting impoverishment of the individual's vital forces. It may be supposed that the metabolic glands, the thyroid and pituitary, are compelled to make up in some fashion for the functioning of the ovaries; and thus, along with the depression natural to the change of life, are to be noted signs of excitation, such as high blood pressure, hot flashes, nervousness, and sometimes increased sexuality. Some women develop fat deposits at this time; others become masculinized. In many, a new endocrine balance becomes established. Woman is now delivered from the servitude imposed by her female nature, but she is not to be likened to a eunuch, for her vitality is unimpaired. And what is more, she is no longer the prey of overwhelming forces; she is herself, she and her body are one. It is sometimes said that women of a certain age constitute 'a third sex'; and, in truth, while they are not males, they are no longer females. Often, indeed, this release from female physiology is expressed in a health, a balance, a vigour that they lacked before.

In addition to the primary sexual characteristics, woman has various secondary sexual peculiarities that are more or less directly produced in consequence of the first, through hormonal action. On the average she is shorter than the male and lighter, her skeleton is more delicate, and the pelvis is larger in adaptation to the functions of pregnancy and childbirth; her connective tissues accumulate fat and her contours are thus more rounded than those of the male. Appearance in general—structure, skin, hair—is distinctly different in the two sexes. Muscular strength is much less in woman, about two thirds that of man; she has less respiratory capacity, the lungs and trachea being smaller. The larynx is relatively smaller, and in consequence the female voice is higher. The specific gravity of the blood is lower in woman and there is less hemoglobin; women are therefore less robust and more disposed to anemia than are males. Their pulse is more rapid, the vascular system less stable, with ready blushing. Instability is strikingly characteristic of woman's organization in general; among other things, man shows greater stability in the metabolism of calcium, woman fixing much less of this material and losing a good deal during menstruation and pregnancy. It would seem that in regard to calcium the ovaries exert a catabolic action, with resulting instability that brings on difficulties in the ovaries and in the thyroid, which is more developed in woman than in man. Irregularities

in the endocrine secretions react on the sympathetic nervous system, and nervous and muscular control is uncertain. This lack in stability and control underlies woman's emotionalism, which is bound up with circulatory fluctuations—palpitation of the heart, blushing, and so forth—and on this account women are subject to such displays of agitation as tears, hysterical laughter, and nervous crises.

It is obvious once more that many of these traits originate in woman's subordination to the species, and here we find the most striking conclusion of this survey: namely, that woman is of all mammalian females at once the one who is most profoundly alienated (her individuality the prey of outside forces), and the one who most violently resists this alienation; in no other is enslavement of the organism to reproduction more imperious or more unwillingly accepted. Crises of puberty and the menopause, monthly 'curse', long and often difficult pregnancy, painful and sometimes dangerous childbirth, illnesses, unexpected symptoms and complications—these are characteristic of the human female. It would seem that her lot is heavier than that of other females in just about the same degree that she goes beyond other females in the assertion of her individuality. In comparison with her the male seems infinitely favoured: his sexual life is not in opposition to his existence as a person, and biologically it runs an even course, without crises and generally without mishap. On the average, women live as long as men, or longer; but they are much more often ailing, and there are many times when they are not in command of themselves.

These biological considerations are extremely important. In the history of woman they play a part of the first rank and constitute an essential element in her situation. Throughout our further discussion we shall always bear them in mind. For, the body being the instrument of our grasp upon the world, the world is bound to seem a very different thing when apprehended in one manner or another. This accounts for our lengthy study of the biological facts; they are one of the keys to the understanding of woman. But I deny that they establish for her a fixed and inevitable destiny. They are insufficient for setting up a hierarchy of the sexes; they fail to explain why woman is the Other; they do not condemn her to remain in this subordinate role forever.

It has been frequently maintained that in physiology alone must be sought the answers to these questions: Are the chances for individual success the same in the two sexes? Which plays the more important role in the species? But it must be noted that the first of these problems is quite different in the case of woman, as compared with other females; for animal species are fixed and it is possible to define them in static terms—by merely collecting observations it can be decided whether the mare is as fast as the stallion, or whether male chimpanzees excel their mates in intelligence tests—whereas the human species is forever in a state of change, forever becoming.

[. . .]

Certainly these facts cannot be denied—but in themselves they have no significance. Once we adopt the human perspective, interpreting the body on a basis of existence, biology becomes an abstract science; whenever the physiological fact (for instance, muscular inferiority) takes on meaning, this meaning is at once seen as dependent on a whole context; the 'weakness' is revealed as such only in the light of the ends man proposes, the instruments he has available, and the laws he establishes. If he does not wish to seize the world, then the idea of a *grasp* on things has no sense; when in this seizure the full employment of bodily power is not required, above the available minimum, then differences in strength are annulled; wherever violence is contrary to custom, muscular force cannot be a basis for domination. [. . .]

But in any case it does not always happen that the male's individual privileges give him a position of superiority within the species, for in maternity the female acquires a kind of autonomy of her own. Sometimes, as in the baboons studied by Zuckermann[8] the male does dominate; but in many species the two members of the pair lead a separate life, and in the lion the two sexes share equally in the duties of the den. Here again the human situation cannot be reduced to any other; it is not as single individuals that human beings are to be defined in the first place; men and women have never stood opposed to each other in single combat; the couple is an original *Mitsein,* a basic combination; and as such it always appears as a permanent or temporary element in a larger collectivity.

Within such a society, which is more necessary to the species, male or female? At the level of the gametes, at the level of the biological functions of coition and pregnancy, the male principle creates to maintain, the female principle maintains to create, as we have seen; but what are the various aspects of this division of labour in different forms of social life? In sessile species, attached to other organisms or to substrata, in those furnished by nature with abundant sustenance obtainable without effort, the role of the male is limited to fecundation; where it is necessary to seek, to hunt, to fight in order to provide the food needed by the young, the male in many cases co-operates in their support. This co-operation becomes absolutely indispensable in a species where the offspring remain unable to take care of themselves for a long time after weaning; here the male's assistance becomes extremely important, for the lives he has begotten cannot be maintained without him. A single male can fecundate a number of females each year; but it requires a male for every female to assure the survival of the offspring after they are born, to defend them against enemies, to wrest from nature the wherewithal to satisfy their needs. In human history the equilibrium between the forces of production and of reproduction is brought about by different means under different economic conditions, and these conditions govern the relations of male and female to offspring and in consequence to each other. But here we are leaving the realm of biology; by its light alone we could never decide the primacy of one sex or the other in regard to the perpetuation of the species.

But in truth a society is not a species, for it is in a society that the species attains the status of existence—transcending itself toward the world and toward the future. Its ways and customs cannot be deduced from biology, for the individuals that compose the society are never abandoned to the dictates of their nature; they are subject rather to that second nature which is custom and in which are reflected the desires and the fears that express their essential nature. It is not merely as a body, but rather as a body subject to taboos, to laws, that the subject is conscious of himself and attains fulfillment—it is with reference to certain values that he evaluates himself. And, once again, it is not upon physiology that values can be based; rather, the facts of biology take on the values that the existent bestows upon them. If the respect or the fear inspired by woman prevents the use of violence toward her, then the muscular superiority of the male is no source of power. If custom decrees—as in certain Indian tribes—that the young girls are to choose their husbands, or if the father dictates the marriage choice, then the sexual aggressiveness of the male gives him no power of initiative, no advantage. The close bond between mother and child will be for her a source of dignity or indignity according to the value placed upon the child—which is highly variable—and this very bond, as we have seen, will be recognized or not according to the presumptions of the society concerned.

Thus we must view the facts of biology in the light of an ontological, economic, social, and psychological context. The enslavement of the female to the species and the limitations of her various powers are extremely important facts; the body of woman is one of the essential elements in her situation in the world. But that body is not enough to define her as woman; there is no true living reality except as manifested by the conscious individual through activities and in the bosom of a society. Biology is not enough to give an answer to the question that is before us: why is woman the *Other?* Our task is to discover how the nature of woman has been affected throughout the course of history; we are concerned to find out what humanity has made of the human female.

Notes

1. Hegel: *Philosophy of Nature*.
2. In connection with this view, it must be remembered that in man and many animals the soma is not strictly neutral, since all its cells are genotypically either male (XY) or female (XX). This is why the young individual normally produces either the male or the female hormonal environment, leading normally to the development of either male or female characteristics.—TR.
3. 'Analysis of these phenomena in recent years has shown that they are similar in woman and the higher monkeys and apes, especially in the genus Rhesus. *It is evidently easier to experiment with these animals*', writes Louis Gallien (*La Sexualité*).
   [In the United States extensive research has been done on the sex physiology of the larger apes by Yerkes and oth-ers, especially at the Laboratories of Primate Biology at Yale University and in Florida (Robert M. Yerkes: *Chimpanzees*; Yale University Press, 1943).—TR.]
4. 'So I am my body, in so far, at least, as my experience goes, and conversely my body is like a life model, or like a preliminary sketch, for my total being.' (Merleau-Ponty: *Phénoménologie de la perception*.)
5. I am taking here an exclusively physiological point of view. It is evident that maternity can be very advantageous psychologically for a woman, just as it can also be a disaster.
6. It may be said that these symptoms also signalize a faulty diet, according to some modern gynecologists.—TR.
7. Cf. H. Vignes in the *Traité de physiologie*, Vol. XI, edited by Roger and Binet.
8. *The Social Life of Monkeys and Apes* (1932).

Thinking Sex: Notes for a Radical Theory of the Politics of Sexuality

Gayle Rubin

I. The Sex Wars

> Asked his advice, Dr. J. Guerin affirmed that, after all other treatments had failed, he had succeeded in curing young girls affected by the vice of onanism by burning the clitoris with a hot iron. . . . I apply the hot point three times to each of the large labia and another on the clitoris . . . . After the first operation, from forty to fifty times a day, the number of voluptuous spasms was reduced to three or four. . . . We believe, then, that in cases similar to those submitted to your consideration, one should not hesitate to resort to the hot iron, and at an early hour, in order to combat clitoral and vaginal onanism in little girls.
>
> Demetrius Zambaco[1]

The time has come to think about sex. To some, sexuality may seem to be an unimportant topic, a frivolous diversion from the more critical problems of poverty, war, disease, racism, famine, or nuclear annihilation. But it is precisely at times such as these, when we live with the possibility of unthinkable destruction, that people are likely to become dangerously crazy about sexuality. Contemporary conflicts over sexual values and erotic conduct have much in common with the religious disputes of earlier centuries. They acquire immense symbolic weight. Disputes over sexual behaviour often become the vehicles for displacing social anxieties, and discharging their attendant emotional intensity. Consequently, sexuality should be treated with special respect in times of great social stress.

The realm of sexuality also has its own internal politics, inequities, and modes of oppression. As with other aspects of human behaviour, the concrete institutional forms of sexuality at any given time and place are products of human activity. They are imbued with conflicts of interest and political manoeuvring, both deliberate and incidental. In that sense, sex is always political. But there are also historical periods in which sexuality is more sharply contested and more overtly politicized. In such periods, the domain of erotic life is, in effect, renegotiated.

In England and the United States, the late nineteenth century was one such era. During that time, powerful social movements focused on 'vices' of all sorts. There were educational and political campaigns to encourage chastity, to eliminate prostitution, and to discourage masturbation, especially among the young. Morality crusaders attacked obscene literature, nude paintings, music halls, abortion, birth control information, and public dancing.[2] The consolidation of Victorian morality, and its apparatus of social, medical, and legal enforcement, was the outcome of a long period of struggle whose results have been bitterly contested ever since.

The consequences of these great nineteenth-century moral paroxysms are still with us. They have left a deep imprint on attitudes about sex, medical practice, child-rearing, parental anxieties, police conduct, and sex law.

The idea that masturbation is an unhealthy practice is part of that heritage. During the nineteenth century, it was commonly thought that 'premature' interest in sex, sexual excitement, and, above all, sexual release, would impair the health and maturation of a child. Theorists differed on the actual consequences of sexual precocity. Some thought it led to insanity, while others merely predicted stunted growth. To protect the young from premature arousal, parents tied children down at night so they would not touch themselves; doctors excised the clitorises of onanistic little girls.[3] Although the more gruesome techniques have been abandoned, the attitudes that produced them persist. The notion that sex *per se* is harmful to the young has been chiselled into extensive social and legal structures designed to insulate minors from sexual knowledge and experience.

[. . .]

Although sodomy statutes date from older strata of the law, when elements of canon law were adopted into civil codes, most of the laws used to arrest homosexuals and prostitutes come out of the Victorian campaigns against 'white slavery'. These campaigns produced the myriad prohibitions against solicitation, lewd behaviour, loitering for immoral purposes, age offences, and brothels and bawdy houses.

[. . .]

In the 1950s, in the United States, major shifts in the organization of sexuality took place. Instead of focusing on prostitution or masturbation, the anxieties of the 1950s condensed most specifically around the image of the 'homosexual menace' and the dubious spectre of the 'sex offender'. Just before and after World War II, the 'sex offender' became an object of public fear and scrutiny. Many states and cities, including Massachusetts, New Hampshire, New Jersey, New York State, New York City, and Michigan, launched investigations to gather information about this menace to public safety.[4] The term 'sex offender' sometimes applied to rapists, sometimes to 'child molesters', and eventually functioned as a code for homosexuals. In its

bureaucratic, medical, and popular versions, the sex offender discourse tended to blur distinctions between violent sexual assault and illegal but consensual acts such as sodomy. The criminal justice system incorporated these concepts when an epidemic of sexual psychopath laws swept through state legislatures.[5] These laws gave the psychological professions increased police powers over homosexuals and other sexual 'deviants'.

[. . .]

The current period bears some uncomfortable similarities to the 1880s and the 1950s. The 1977 campaign to repeal the Dade County, Florida, gay rights ordinance inaugurated a new wave of violence, state persecution, and legal initiatives directed against minority sexual populations and the commercial sex industry. For the last six years, the United States and Canada have undergone an extensive sexual repression in the political, not the psychological, sense. In the spring of 1977, a few weeks before the Dade County vote, the news media were suddenly full of reports of raids on gay cruising areas, arrests for prostitution, and investigations into the manufacture and distribution of pornographic materials. Since then, police activity against the gay community has increased exponentially. The gay press has documented hundreds of arrests, from the libraries of Boston to the streets of Houston and the beaches of San Francisco. Even the large, organized, and relatively powerful urban gay communities have been unable to stop these depredations. Gay bars and bath houses have been busted with alarming frequency, and police have gotten bolder. In one especially dramatic incident, police in Toronto raided all four of the city's gay baths. They broke into cubicles with crowbars and hauled almost 300 men out into the winter streets, clad in their bath towels. Even 'liberated' San Francisco has not been immune. There have been proceedings against several bars, countless arrests in the parks, and, in the fall of 1981, police arrested over 400 people in a series of sweeps of Polk Street, one of the thoroughfares of local gay nightlife. Queerbashing has become a significant recreational activity for young urban males. They come into gay neighbourhoods armed with baseball bats and looking for trouble, knowing that the adults in their lives either secretly approve or will look the other way.

The police crackdown has not been limited to homosexuals. Since 1977, enforcement of existing laws against prostitution and obscenity has been stepped up. Moreover, states and municipalities have been passing new and tighter regulations on commercial sex. Restrictive ordinances have been passed, zoning laws altered, licensing and safety codes amended, sentences increased, and evidentiary requirements relaxed. This subtle legal codification of more stringent controls over adult sexual behaviour has gone largely unnoticed outside of the gay press.

[. . .]

The experiences of art photographer Jacqueline Livingston exemplify the climate created by the child porn panic. An assistant professor of photography at Cornell University, Livingston was fired in 1978 after exhibiting pictures of male nudes which included photographs of her seven-year-old son masturbating. *Ms. Magazine, Chrysalis,* and *Art News* all refused to run ads for Livingston's posters of male nudes. At one point, Kodak confiscated some of her film, and for several months, Livingston lived with the threat of prosecution under the child pornography laws. The Tompkins County Department of Social Services investigated her fitness as a parent. Livingston's posters have been collected by the Museum of Modern Art, the Metropolitan, and other major museums. But she has paid a high cost in harassment and anxiety for her efforts to capture on film the uncensored male body at different ages.[6]

It is easy to see someone like Livingston as a victim of the child porn wars. It is harder for most people to sympathize with actual boy-lovers. Like communists and homosexuals in the 1950s, boy-lovers are so stigmatized that it is difficult to find defenders for their civil liberties, let alone for their erotic orientation. Consequently, the police have feasted on them. Local police, the FBI, and watchdog postal inspectors have joined to build a huge apparatus whose sole aim is to wipe out the community of men who love under-aged youth. In 20 years or so, when some of the smoke has cleared, it will be much easier to show that these men have been the victims of a savage and undeserved witch-hunt. A lot of people will be embarrassed by their collaboration with this persecution, but it will be too late to do much good for those men who have spent their lives in prison. While the misery of the boy-lovers affects very few, the other long-term legacy of the Dade County repeal affects almost everyone. The success of the anti-gay campaign ignited long-simmering passions of the American right, and sparked an extensive movement to compress the boundaries of acceptable sexual behaviour.

Right-wing ideology linking non-familial sex with communism and political weakness is nothing new. During the McCarthy period, Alfred Kinsey and his Institute for Sex Research were attacked for weakening the moral fibre of Americans and rendering them more vulnerable to communist influence. After congressional investigations and bad publicity, Kinsey's Rockefeller grant was terminated in 1954.[7]

[. . .]

Periods such as the 1880s in England, and the 1950s in the United States, recodify the relations of sexuality. The struggles that were fought leave a residue in the form of laws, social practices, and ideologies which then affect the way in which sexuality is experienced long after the immediate conflicts have faded. All the signs indicate that the present era is another of those watersheds in the politics of sex. The settlements that emerge from the 1980s will have an impact far into the future. It is therefore imperative to understand what is going on and what is at stake in order to make informed decisions about what policies to support and oppose.

It is difficult to make such decisions in the absence of a coherent and intelligent body of radical thought about sex. Unfortunately, progressive political analysis of sexuality is relatively underdeveloped. Much of what is available from the feminist movement has simply added to the mystification that shrouds the subject. There is an urgent need to develop radical perspectives on sexuality.

Paradoxically, an explosion of exciting scholarship and political writing about sex has been generated in these bleak years. In the 1950s, the early gay rights movement began and prospered while the bars were being raided and anti-gay laws were being passed. In the last six years, new erotic communities, political alliances, and analyses have been developed in the midst of the repression. In this essay, I will propose elements of a descriptive and conceptual framework for thinking about sex and its politics. I hope to contribute to the pressing task of creating an accurate, humane, and genuinely liberatory body of thought about sexuality.

II. Sexual thoughts

'You see, Tim', Phillip said suddenly, 'your argument isn't reasonable. Suppose I granted your first point that homosexuality is justifiable in certain instances and under certain controls. Then there is the catch: where does justification end and degeneracy begin? Society must condemn to protect. Permit even the intellectual homosexual a place of respect and the first bar is down. Then comes the next and the next until the sadist, the flagellist, the criminally insane demand their places, and society ceases to exist. So I ask again: where is the line drawn? Where does degeneracy begin if not at the beginning of individual freedom in such matters?'

(Fragment from a discussion between two gay men trying to decide if they may love each other, from a novel published in 1950.)[8]

A radical theory of sex must identify, describe, explain, and denounce erotic injustice and sexual oppression. Such a theory needs refined conceptual tools which can grasp the subject and hold it in view. It must build rich descriptions of sexuality as it exists in society and history. It requires a convincing critical language that can convey the barbarity of sexual persecution.

Several persistent features of thought about sex inhibit the development of such a theory. These assumptions are so pervasive in Western culture that they are rarely questioned. Thus, they tend to reappear in different political contexts, acquiring new rhetorical expressions but reproducing fundamental axioms.

One such axiom is sexual essentialism—the idea that sex is a natural force that exists prior to social life and shapes institutions. Sexual essentialism is embedded in the folk wisdoms of Western societies, which consider sex to be eternally unchanging, asocial, and transhistorical. Dominated for over a century by medicine, psychiatry, and psychology, the academic study of sex has reproduced essentialism. These fields classify sex as a property of individuals. It may reside in their hormones or their psyches. It may be construed as physiological or psychological. But within these ethnoscientific categories, sexuality has no history and no significant social determinants.

During the last five years, a sophisticated historical and theoretical scholarship has challenged sexual essentialism both explicitly and implicitly. [. . .]

Michel Foucault's *The History of Sexuality* has been the most influential and emblematic text of the new scholarship on sex. Foucault criticizes the traditional understanding of sexuality as a natural libido yearning to break free of social constraint. He argues that desires are not pre-existing biological entities, but rather, that they are constituted in the course of historically specific social practices. He emphasizes the generative aspects of the social organization of sex rather than its repressive elements by pointing out that new sexualities are constantly produced. And he points to a major discontinuity between kinship-based systems of sexuality and more modern forms.[9]

The new scholarship on sexual behaviour has given sex a history and created a constructivist alternative to sexual essentialism. Underlying this body of work is an assumption that sexuality is constituted in society and history, not biologically ordained.[10] This does not mean the biological capacities are not prerequisites for human sexuality. It does mean that human sexuality is not comprehensible in purely biological terms. Human organisms with human brains are necessary for human cultures, but no examination of the body or its parts can explain the nature and variety of human social systems. The belly's hunger gives no clues as to the complexities of cuisine. The body, the brain, the genitalia, and the capacity for language are all necessary for human sexuality. But they do not determine its content, its experiences, or its institutional forms. Moreover, we never encounter the body unmediated by the meanings that cultures give to it. [. . .]

Because of his emphasis on the ways that sexuality is produced, Foucault has been vulnerable to interpretations that deny or minimize the reality of sexual repression in the more political sense. Foucault makes it abundantly clear that he is not denying the existence of sexual repression so much as inscribing it within a large dynamic.[11] Sexuality in Western societies has been structured within an extremely punitive social framework, and has been subjected to very real formal and informal controls.

It is necessary to recognize repressive phenomena without resorting to the essentialist assumptions of the language of libido. It is important to hold repressive sexual practices in focus, even while situating them within a different totality and a more refined terminology.[12]

Most radical thought about sex has been embedded within a model of the instincts and their restraints. Concepts of sexual oppression have been lodged within that more biological understanding of sexuality. It is often easier to fall back on the notion of a natural libido subjected to inhumane repression than to reformulate concepts of sexual injustice within a more constructivist framework. But it is essential that we do so. We need a radical critique of sexual arrangements that has the conceptual elegance of Foucault and the evocative passion of Reich.

The new scholarship on sex has brought a welcome insistence that sexual terms be restricted to their proper historical and social contexts, and a cautionary skepticism toward sweeping generalizations. But it is important to be able to indicate groupings of erotic behaviour and general trends within erotic discourse. In addition to sexual essentialism, there are at least five other ideological formations whose grip on sexual thought is so strong that to fail to discuss them is to remain enmeshed within them. These are sex negativity, the fallacy of misplaced scale, the hierarchical valuation of sex acts, the domino theory of sexual peril, and the lack of a concept of benign sexual variation.

Of these five, the most important is sex negativity. Western cultures generally consider sex to be a dangerous, destructive negative force.[13] Most Christian tradition, following Paul, holds that sex is inherently sinful. It may be redeemed if performed within marriage for procreative purposes and if the pleasurable aspects are not enjoyed too much. In turn, this idea rests on the assumption that the genitalia are an intrinsically inferior part of the body, much lower and less holy than the mind, the 'soul', the 'heart', or even the upper part of the digestive system (the status of the excretory organs is close to that of the genitalia).[14] Such notions have by now acquired a life of their own and no longer depend solely on religion for their perseverance.

This culture always treats sex with suspicion. It construes and judges almost any sexual practice in terms of its worst possible expression. Sex is presumed guilty until proven innocent. Virtually all erotic behaviour is considered bad unless a specific reason to exempt it has been established. The most acceptable excuses are marriage, reproduction, and love. Sometimes scientific curiosity, aesthetic experience, or a long-term intimate relationship may serve. But the exercise of erotic capacity, intelligence, curiosity, or creativity all require pretexts that are unnecessary for other pleasures, such as the enjoyment of food, fiction, or astronomy.

What I call the fallacy of misplaced scale is a corollary of sex negativity. Susan Sontag once commented that since Christianity focused 'on sexual behaviour as the root of virtue, everything pertaining to sex has been a "special case" in our culture'.[15] Sex law has incorporated the religious attitude that heretical sex is an especially heinous sin that deserves the harshest punishments. Throughout much of European and American history, a single act of consensual anal penetration was grounds for execution. In some states, sodomy still carries 20-year prison sentences. Outside the law, sex is also a marked category. Small differences in value or behaviour are often experienced as cosmic threats.

Although people can be intolerant, silly, or pushy about what constitutes proper diet, differences in menu rarely provoke the kinds of rage, anxiety, and sheer terror that routinely accompany differences in erotic taste. Sexual acts are burdened with an excess of significance.

Modern Western societies appraise sex acts according to a hierarchical system of sexual value. Marital, reproductive heterosexuals are alone at the top of the erotic pyramid. Clamouring below are unmarried monogamous heterosexuals in couples, followed by most other heterosexuals. Solitary sex floats ambiguously. The powerful nineteenth-century stigma on masturbation lingers in less potent, modified forms, such as the idea that masturbation is an inferior substitute for partnered encounters. Stable, long-term lesbian and gay male couples are verging on respectability, but bar dykes and promiscuous gay men are hovering just above the groups at the very bottom of the pyramid. The most despised sexual castes currently include transsexuals, transvestites, fetishists, sadomasochists, sex workers such as prostitutes and porn models, and the lowliest of all, those whose eroticism transgresses generational boundaries.

Individuals whose behaviour stands high in this hierarchy are rewarded with certified mental health, respectability, legality, social and physical mobility, institutional support, and material benefits. As sexual behaviours or occupations fall lower on the scale, the individuals who practise them are subjected to a presumption of mental illness, disreputability, criminality, restricted social and physical mobility, loss of institutional support, and economic sanctions.

Extreme and punitive stigma maintains some sexual behaviours as low status and is an effective sanction against those who engage in them.

The intensity of this stigma is rooted in Western religious traditions. But most of its contemporary content derives from medical and psychiatric opprobrium.

[. . .]

Figure 1 diagrams a general version of the sexual value system. According to this system, sexuality that is 'good', 'normal', and 'natural' should ideally be heterosexual, marital, monogamous, reproductive, and non-commercial. It should be coupled, relational, within the same generation, and occur at home. It should not involve pornography, fetish objects, sex toys of any sort, or roles other than male and female. Any sex that violates these rules is 'bad', 'abnormal', or 'unnatural'. Bad sex may be homosexual, unmarried, promiscuous, non-procreative, or commercial. It may be masturbatory or take place at orgies, may be casual, may cross generational lines, and may take place in 'public', or at least in the bushes or the baths. It may involve the use of pornography, fetish objects, sex toys, or unusual roles (see Figure 1).

Figure 2 diagrams another aspect of the sexual hierarchy: the need to draw and maintain an imaginary line between good and bad sex. Most of the discourses on sex, be they religious, psychiatric, popular, or political, delimit a very small portion of human sexual capacity as sanctifiable, safe, healthy, mature, legal, or politically correct. The 'line' distinguishes these from all other erotic behaviours, which are understood to be the work of the devil, dangerous, psychopathological, infantile, or politically reprehensible. Arguments are then conducted over 'where to draw the line', and to determine what other activities, if any, may be permitted to cross over into acceptability.

All these models assume a domino theory of sexual peril. The line appears to stand between sexual order and chaos. It expresses the fear that if anything is permitted to cross this erotic DMZ,

the barrier against scary sex will crumble and something unspeakable will skitter across.

Most systems of sexual judgment—religious, psychological, feminist, or socialist—attempt to determine on which side of the line a particular act falls. Only sex acts on the good side of the line are accorded moral complexity. For instance, heterosexual encounters may be sublime or disgusting, free or forced, healing or destructive, romantic or mercenary. As long as it does not violate other rules, heterosexuality is acknowledged to exhibit the full range of human experience. In contrast, all sex acts on the bad side of the line are considered utterly repulsive and devoid of all emotional nuance. The further from the line a sex act is, the more it is depicted as a uniformly bad experience.

As a result of the sex conflicts of the last decade, some behaviour near the border is inching across it. Unmarried couples living together, masturbation, and some forms of homosexuality are moving in the direction of respectability (see Figure 2). Most homosexuality is still on the bad side of the line. But if it is coupled and monogamous, the society is beginning to recognize that it includes the full range of human interaction. Promiscuous homosexuality, sadomasochism, fetishism, transsexuality, and cross-generational encounters are still viewed as unmodulated horrors incapable of involving affection, love, free choice, kindness, or transcendence.

[. . .]

It is difficult to develop a pluralistic sexual ethics without a concept of benign sexual variation. Variation is a fundamental property of all life, from the simplest biological organisms to the most complex human social formations. Yet sexuality is supposed to conform to a single standard. One of the most tenacious ideas about sex is that there is one best way to do it, and that everyone should do it that way.

The charmed circle:
Good, Normal, Natural,
Blessed Sexuality

Heterosexual
Married
Monogamous
Procreative
Non-commercial
In pairs
In a relationship
Same generation
In private
No pornography
Bodies only
Vanilla

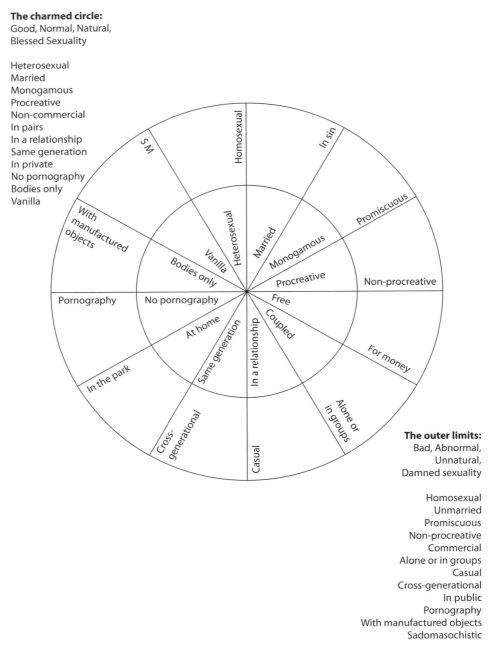

The outer limits:
Bad, Abnormal,
Unnatural,
Damned sexuality

Homosexual
Unmarried
Promiscuous
Non-procreative
Commercial
Alone or in groups
Casual
Cross-generational
In public
Pornography
With manufactured objects
Sadomasochistic

Figure 1 The Sex Hierarchy: the Charmed Circle versus Outer Limits

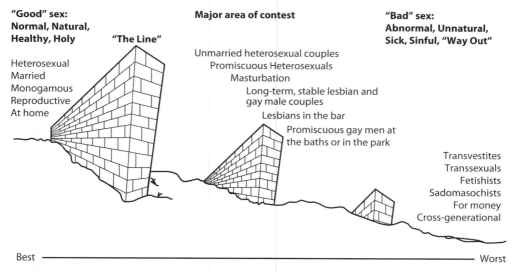

Figure 2 Sex Hierarchy: the Struggle over Where To Draw the Line

Most people find it difficult to grasp that whatever they like to do sexually will be thoroughly repulsive to someone else, and that whatever repels them sexually will be the most treasured delight of someone, somewhere. One need not like or perform a particular sex act in order to recognize that someone else will, and that this difference does not indicate a lack of good taste, mental health, or intelligence in either party. Most people mistake their sexual preferences for a universal system that will or should work for everyone.

This notion of a single ideal sexuality characterizes most systems of thought about sex. For religion, the ideal is procreative marriage. For psychology, it is mature heterosexuality. Although its content varies, the format of a single sexual standard is continually reconstituted within other rhetorical frameworks, including feminism and socialism. It is just as objectionable to insist that everyone should be lesbian, non-monogamous, or kinky, as to believe that everyone should be heterosexual, married, or vanilla—though the latter set of opinions are backed by considerably more coercive power than the former.

[. . .]

III. Sexual Transformation

As defined by the ancient civil or canonical codes, sodomy was a category of forbidden acts; their perpetrator was nothing more than the juridical subject of them. The nineteenth-century homosexual became a personage, a past, a case history, and a childhood, in addition to being a type of life, a life form, and a morphology, with an indiscreet anatomy and possibly a mysterious physiology. The sodomite had been a temporary aberration; the homosexual was now a species.

Michel Foucault[16]

In spite of many continuities with ancestral forms, modern sexual arrangements have a distinctive character which sets them apart from pre-existing systems. In Western Europe and the United States, industrialization and urbanization reshaped the traditional rural and peasant populations into a new urban industrial and service workforce. It generated new forms of state apparatus, reorganized family relations, altered gender roles, made possible new forms of identity, produced new varieties of social inequality, and created new formats for political and ideological conflict. It also gave rise to a new sexual system characterized by distinct types of sexual persons, populations, stratification, and political conflict.

[. . .]

Homosexuality is the best example of this process of erotic speciation. Homosexual behaviour is always present among humans. But in different societies and epochs it may be rewarded or punished, required or forbidden, a temporary experience or a life-long vocation. In some New Guinea societies, for example, homosexual activities are obligatory for all males. Homosexual acts are considered utterly masculine, roles are based on age, and partners are determined by kinship status.[17] Although these men engage in extensive homosexual and pedophile behaviour, they are neither homosexuals nor pederasts.

Nor was the sixteenth-century sodomite a homosexual. In 1631, Mervyn Touchet, Earl of Castlehaven, was tried and executed for sodomy. It is clear from the proceedings that the earl was not understood by himself or anyone else to be a particular kind of sexual individual. 'While from the twentieth-century viewpoint Lord Castlehaven obviously suffered from psychosexual problems requiring the services of an analyst, from the seventeenth-century viewpoint he had deliberately broken the Law of God and the Laws of England, and required the simpler services of an executioner'.[18] The earl did not slip into his tightest doublet and waltz down to the nearest gay tavern to mingle with his fellow sodomists. He stayed in his manor house and buggered his servants. Gay self-awareness, gay pubs, the sense of group commonality, and even the term 'homosexual' were not part of the earl's universe.

The New Guinea bachelor and the sodomite nobleman are only tangentially related to a modern gay man, who may migrate from rural Colorado to San Francisco in order to live in a gay neighbourhood, work in a gay business, and participate in an elaborate experience that includes a self-conscious identity, group solidarity, a literature, a press, and a high level of political activity. In modern, Western, industrial societies, homosexuality has acquired much of the institutional structure of an ethnic group.[19]

The relocation of homoeroticism into these quasi-ethnic, nucleated, sexually constituted communities is to some extent a consequence of the transfers of population brought about by industrialization. As labourers migrated to work in cities, there were increased opportunities for voluntary communities to form. Homosexually inclined women and men, who would have been vulnerable and isolated in most pre-industrial villages, began to congregate in small corners of the big cities. Most large nineteenth-century cities in Western Europe and North America had areas where men could cruise for other men. Lesbian communities seem to have coalesced more slowly and on a smaller scale. Nevertheless, by the 1890s, there were several cafes in Paris near the Place Pigalle which catered to a lesbian clientele, and it is likely that there were similar places in the other major capitals of Western Europe.

Areas like these acquired bad reputations, which alerted other interested individuals of their existence and location. In the United States, lesbian and gay male territories were well established in New York, Chicago, San Francisco, and Los Angeles in the 1950s. Sexually motivated migration to places such as Greenwich Village had become a sizable sociological phenomenon. By the late 1970s, sexual migration was occurring on a scale so significant that it began to have a recognizable impact on urban politics in the United States, with San Francisco being the most notable and notorious example.[20]

Prostitution has undergone a similar metamorphosis. Prostitution began to change from a temporary job to a more permanent occupation as a result of nineteenth-century agitation, legal reform, and police persecution. Prostitutes, who had been part of the general working-class population, became increasingly isolated as members of an outcast group.[21] Prostitutes and other sex workers differ from homosexuals and other sexual minorities. Sex work is an occupation, while sexual deviation is an erotic preference. Nevertheless, they share some common features of social organization. Like homosexuals, prostitutes are a criminal sexual population stigmatized on the basis of sexual activity. Prostitutes and male homosexuals are the primary prey of vice police everywhere.[22] Like gay men, prostitutes occupy well-demarcated urban territories and battle with police to defend and maintain those territories. The legal persecution of both populations is justified by an elaborate ideology which classifies them as dangerous and inferior undesirables who are not entitled to be left in peace.

Besides organizing homosexuals and prostitutes into localized populations, the 'modernization of sex' has generated a system of continual sexual ethnogenesis. Other populations of erotic dissidents—commonly known as the 'perversions' or the 'paraphilias'—also began to coalesce. Sexualities keep marching out of the *Diagnostic and Statistical Manual* and on to the pages of social history. At present, several other groups are trying to emulate the successes of homosexuals. Bisexuals, sadomasochists, individuals who prefer cross-generational encounters, transsexuals, and transvestites are all in various states of community formation and identity acquisition. The perversions are not proliferating as much as they are attempting to acquire social space, small businesses, political resources, and a measure of relief from the penalties for sexual heresy.

IV. Sexual Stratification

An entire sub-race was born, different— despite certain kinship ties—from the libertines of the past. From the end of the eighteenth century to our own, they circulated through the pores of society; they were always hounded, but not always by laws; were often locked up, but not always in prisons; were sick perhaps, but scandalous, dangerous victims, prey to a strange evil that also bore the name of vice and sometimes crime.

They were children wise beyond their years, precocious little girls, ambiguous schoolboys, dubious servants and educators, cruel or maniacal husbands, solitary collectors, ramblers with bizarre impulses; they haunted the houses of correction, the penal colonies, the tribunals, and the asylums; they carried their infamy to the doctors and their sickness to the judges. This was the numberless family of perverts who were on friendly terms with delinquents and akin to madmen.

Michel Foucault[23]

The industrial transformation of Western Europe and North America brought about new forms of social stratification. The resultant inequalities of class are well known and have been explored in detail by a century of scholarship. The construction of modern systems of racism and ethnic injustice has been well documented and critically assessed. Feminist thought has analyzed the prevailing organization of gender oppression. But although specific erotic groups, such as militant homosexuals and sex workers, have agitated against their own mistreatment, there has been no equivalent attempt to locate particular varieties of sexual persecution within a more general system of sexual stratification. Nevertheless, such a system exists, and in its contemporary form it is a consequence of Western industrialization.

Sex law is the most adamantine instrument of sexual stratification and erotic persecution. The state routinely intervenes in sexual behaviour at a level that would not be tolerated in other areas of social life. Most people are unaware of the extent of sex law, the quantity and qualities of illegal sexual behaviour, and the punitive character of legal sanctions. Although federal agencies may be involved in obscenity and prostitution cases, most sex laws are enacted at the state and municipal level, and enforcement is largely in the hands of local police. Thus, there is a tremendous amount of variation in the laws applicable to any given locale. Moreover, enforcement of sex laws varies dramatically with the local political climate. In spite of this legal thicket, one can make some tentative and qualified generalizations. My discussion of sex law does not apply to laws against sexual coercion, sexual assault, or rape. It does pertain to the myriad prohibitions on consensual sex and the 'status' offences such as statutory rape.

[. . .]

Sex law is not a perfect reflection of the prevailing moral evaluations of sexual conduct. Sexual variation *per se* is more specifically policed by the mental-health professions, popular ideology, and extra-legal social practice. Some of the most detested erotic behaviours, such as fetishism and sadomasochism, are not as closely or completely regulated by the criminal justice system

as somewhat less stigmatized practices, such as homosexuality. Areas of sexual behaviour come under the purview of the law when they become objects of social concern and political uproar. Each sex scare or morality campaign deposits new regulations as a kind of fossil record of its passage. The legal sediment is thickest—and sex law has its greatest potency—in areas involving obscenity, money, minors, and homosexuality.

Obscenity laws enforce a powerful taboo against direct representation of erotic activities. Current emphasis on the ways in which sexuality has become a focus of social attention should not be misused to undermine a critique of this prohibition. It is one thing to create sexual discourse in the form of psychoanalysis, or in the course of a morality crusade. It is quite another to graphically depict sex acts or genitalia. The first is socially permissible in a way the second is not. Sexual speech is forced into reticence, euphemism, and indirection. Freedom of speech about sex is a glaring exception to the protections of the First Amendment, which is not even considered applicable to purely sexual statements.

The anti-obscenity laws also form part of a group of statutes that make almost all sexual commerce illegal. Sex law incorporates a very strong prohibition against mixing sex and money, except via marriage. In addition to the obscenity statutes, other laws impinging on sexual commerce include anti-prostitution laws, alcoholic beverage regulations, and ordinances governing the location and operation of 'adult' businesses. The sex industry and the gay economy have both managed to circumvent some of this legislation, but that process has not been easy or simple. The underlying criminality of sex-oriented business keeps it marginal, underdeveloped, and distorted. Sex businesses can only operate in legal loopholes. This tends to keep investment down and to divert commercial activity toward the goal of staying out of jail rather than the delivery of goods and services. It also renders sex workers more vulnerable to exploitation and bad working conditions. If sex commerce were legal, sex workers would be more able to organize and agitate for higher pay, better conditions, greater control, and less stigma.

Whatever one thinks of the limitations of capitalist commerce, such an extreme exclusion from the market process would hardly be socially acceptable in other areas of activity. Imagine, for example, that the exchange of money for medical care, pharmacological advice, or psychological counselling were illegal. Medical practice would take place in a much less satisfactory fashion if doctors, nurses, druggists, and therapists could be hauled off to jail at the whim of the local 'health squad'. But that is essentially the situation of prostitutes, sex workers, and sex entrepreneurs.

Marx himself considered the capitalist market a revolutionary, if limited, force. He argued that capitalism was progressive in its dissolution of pre-capitalist superstition, prejudice, and the bonds of traditional modes of life. 'Hence the great civilizing influence of capital, its production of a state of society compared with which all earlier stages appear to be merely local progress and idolatry of nature.'[24] Keeping sex from realizing the positive effects of the market economy hardly makes it socialist.

The law is especially ferocious in maintaining the boundary between childhood 'innocence' and 'adult' sexuality. Rather than recognizing the sexuality of the young, and attempting to provide for it in a caring and responsible manner, our culture denies and punishes erotic interest and activity by anyone under the local age of consent. The amount of law devoted to protecting young people from premature exposure to sexuality is breathtaking.

The primary mechanism for insuring the separation of sexual generations is age of consent laws. These laws make no distinction between the most brutal rape and the most gentle romance. A 20-year-old convicted of sexual contact with a 17-year-old will face a severe sentence in virtually every state, regardless of the nature of the relationship.[25] Nor are minors permitted access to 'adult' sexuality in other forms. They are forbidden to see books, movies, or television in which sexuality is 'too' graphically portrayed. It is legal for young people to see hideous depictions of violence, but not to see explicit pictures of genitalia. Sexually active young people are frequently incarcerated in juvenile homes, or otherwise punished for their 'precocity'.

[. . .]

The only adult sexual behaviour that is legal in every state is the placement of the penis in the vagina in wedlock. Consenting adults statutes ameliorate this situation in fewer than half the states. Most states impose severe criminal penalties on consensual sodomy, homosexual contact short of sodomy, adultery, seduction, and adult incest. Sodomy laws vary a great deal. In some states, they apply equally to homosexual and heterosexual partners and regardless of marital status. Some state courts have ruled that married couples have the right to commit sodomy in private. Only homosexual sodomy is illegal in some states. Some sodomy statutes prohibit both anal sex and oral-genital contact. In other states, sodomy applies only to anal penetration, and oral sex is covered under separate statutes.[26]

Laws like these criminalize sexual behaviour that is freely chosen and avidly sought. The ideology embodied in them reflects the value hierarchies discussed above. That is, some sex acts are considered to be so intrinsically vile that no one should be allowed under any circumstance to perform them. The fact that individuals consent to or even prefer them is taken to be additional evidence of depravity. This system of sex law is similar to legalized racism. State prohibition of same-sex contact, anal penetration, and oral sex make homosexuals a criminal group denied the privileges of full citizenship. With such laws, prosecution is persecution. Even when they are not strictly enforced, as is usually the case, the members of criminalized sexual communities remain vulnerable to the possibility of arbitrary arrest, or to periods in which they become the objects of social panic. When those occur, the laws are in place and police action is swift. Even sporadic enforcement serves to remind individuals that they are members of a subject population. The occasional arrest for sodomy, lewd behaviour, solicitation, or oral sex keeps everyone else afraid, nervous, and circumspect.

The state also upholds the sexual hierarchy through bureaucratic regulation. Immigration policy still prohibits the admission of homosexuals (and other sexual 'deviates') into the United States. Military regulations bar homosexuals from serving in the armed forces. The fact that gay people cannot legally marry means that they cannot enjoy the same legal rights as heterosexuals in many matters, including inheritance, taxation, protection from testimony in court, and the acquisition of citizenship for foreign partners. These are but a few of the ways that the state reflects and maintains the social relations of sexuality. The law buttresses structures of power, codes of behaviour, and forms of prejudice. At their worst, sex law and sex regulation are simply sexual apartheid.

Although the legal apparatus of sex is staggering, most everyday social control is extra-legal. Less formal, but very effective social sanctions are imposed on members of 'inferior' sexual populations.

[. . .]

Families play a crucial role in enforcing sexual conformity. Much social pressure is brought to bear to deny erotic dissidents the comforts and resources that families provide. Popular ideology holds that families are not supposed to produce or harbour erotic nonconformity. Many families respond by trying to reform, punish, or exile sexually offending members. Many sexual migrants have been thrown out by their families, and many others are fleeing from the threat of institutionalization. Any random collection of homosexuals, sex workers, or miscellaneous perverts can provide heart-stopping stories of rejection and mistreatment by horrified families. Christmas is the great family holiday in the United States and consequently it is a time of considerable tension in the gay community. Half the inhabitants go off to their families of origin; many of those who remain in the gay ghettoes cannot do so, and relive their anger and grief.

In addition to economic penalties and strain on family relations, the stigma of erotic dissidence creates friction at all other levels of everyday life. The general public helps to penalize erotic nonconformity when, according to the values they have been taught, landlords refuse housing, neighbours call in the police, and hoodlums commit sanctioned battery. The ideologies of erotic inferiority and sexual danger decrease the power of sex perverts and sex workers in social encounters of all kinds. They have less protection from unscrupulous or criminal behaviour, less access to police protection, and less recourse to the courts. Dealings with institutions and bureaucracies—hospitals, police, coroners, banks, public officials—are more difficult.

Sex is a vector of oppression. The system of sexual oppression cuts across other modes of social inequality, sorting out individuals and groups according to its own intrinsic dynamics. It is not reducible to, or understandable in terms of, class, race, ethnicity, or gender. Wealth, white skin, male gender, and ethnic privileges can mitigate the effects of sexual stratification. A rich, white male pervert will generally be less affected than a poor, black, female pervert. But even the most privileged are not immune to sexual oppression. Some of the consequences of the system of sexual hierarchy are mere nuisances. Others are quite grave. In its most serious manifestations, the sexual system is a Kafkaesque nightmare in which unlucky victims become herds of human cattle whose identification, surveillance, apprehension, treatment, incarceration, and punishment produce jobs and self-satisfaction for thousands of vice police, prison officials, psychiatrists, and social workers.[27]

V. Sexual Conflicts

> The moral panic crystallizes widespread fears and anxieties, and often deals with them not by seeking the real causes of the problems and conditions which they demonstrate but by displacing them on to 'Folk Devils' in an identified social group (often the 'immoral' or 'degenerate'). Sexuality has had a peculiar centrality in such panics, and sexual 'deviants' have been omnipresent scapegoats.
>
> Jeffrey Weeks[28]

The sexual system is not a monolithic, omnipotent structure. There are continuous battles over the definitions, evaluations, arrangements, privileges, and costs of sexual behaviour. Political struggle over sex assumes characteristic forms.

Sexual ideology plays a crucial role in sexual experience. Consequently, definitions and evaluations of sexual conduct are objects of bitter contest. The confrontations between early gay liberation and the psychiatric establishment are the best example of this kind of fight, but there are constant skirmishes. Recurrent battles take place between the primary producers of sexual ideology—the churches, the family, the shrinks,

and the media—and the groups whose experience they name, distort, and endanger.

[. . .]

According to the mainstream media and popular prejudice, the marginal sexual worlds are bleak and dangerous. They are portrayed as impoverished, ugly, and inhabited by psychopaths and criminals. New migrants must be sufficiently motivated to resist the impact of such discouraging images. Attempts to counter negative propaganda with more realistic information generally meet with censorship, and there are continuous ideological struggles over which representations of sexual communities make it into the popular media.

Information on how to find, occupy, and live in the marginal sexual worlds is also suppressed. Navigational guides are scarce and inaccurate. In the past, fragments of rumour, distorted gossip, and bad publicity were the most available clues to the location of underground erotic communities. During the late 1960s and early 1970s, better information became available. Now groups like the Moral Majority want to rebuild the ideological walls around the sexual undergrounds and make transit in and out of them as difficult as possible.

Migration is expensive. Transportation costs, moving expenses, and the necessity of finding new jobs and housing are economic difficulties that sexual migrants must overcome. These are especially imposing barriers to the young, who are often the most desperate to move. There are, however, routes into the erotic communities which mark trails through the propaganda thicket and provide some economic shelter along the way. Higher education can be a route for young people from affluent backgrounds. In spite of serious limitations, the information on sexual behaviour at most colleges and universities is better than elsewhere, and most colleges and universities shelter small erotic networks of all sorts.

For poorer kids, the military is often the easiest way to get the hell out of wherever they are. Military prohibitions against homosexuality make this a perilous route. Although young queers continually attempt to use the armed forces to get out of intolerable hometown situations and closer to functional gay communities, they face the hazards of exposure, court martial, and dishonourable discharge.

Once in the cities, erotic populations tend to nucleate and to occupy some regular, visible territory. Churches and other anti-vice forces constantly put pressure on local authorities to contain such areas, reduce their visibility, or to drive their inhabitants out of town. There are periodic crackdowns in which local vice squads are unleashed on the populations they control. Gay men, prostitutes, and sometimes transvestites are sufficiently territorial and numerous to engage in intense battles with the cops over particular streets, parks, and alleys. Such border wars are usually inconclusive, but they result in many casualties.

[. . .]

Because sexuality in Western societies is so mystified, the wars over it are often fought at oblique angles, aimed at phony targets, conducted with misplaced passions, and are highly, intensely symbolic. Sexual activities often function as signifiers for personal and social apprehensions to which they have no intrinsic connection. During a moral panic, such fears attach to some unfortunate sexual activity or population. The media become ablaze with indignation, the public behaves like a rabid mob, the police are activated, and the state enacts new laws and regulations. When the furor has passed, some innocent erotic group has been decimated, and the state has extended its power into new areas of erotic behaviour.

The system of sexual stratification provides easy victims who lack the power to defend themselves, and a pre-existing apparatus for controlling their movements and curtailing their freedoms. The stigma against sexual dissidents renders them morally defenceless. Every moral panic has consequences on two levels. The target population suffers most, but everyone is affected by the social and legal changes.

Moral panics rarely alleviate any real problem, because they are aimed at chimeras and signifiers. They draw on the pre-existing discursive structure which invents victims in order to justify treating 'vices' as crimes. The criminalization of innocuous behaviours such as homosexuality, prostitution, obscenity, or recreational drug use, is rationalized by portraying them as menaces to health and safety, women and children, national security, the family, or civilization itself. Even when activity is acknowledged to be harmless, it may be banned because it is alleged to 'lead' to something ostensibly worse (another manifestation of the domino theory).[29] Great and mighty edifices have been built on the basis of such phantasms. Generally, the outbreak of a moral panic is preceded by an intensification of such scapegoating.

[. . .]

It is bad enough that the gay community must deal with the medical misfortune of having been the population in which a deadly disease first became widespread and visible. It is worse to have to deal with the social consequences as well. Even before the AIDS scare, Greece passed a law that enabled police to arrest suspected homosexuals and force them to submit to an examination for venereal disease. It is likely that until AIDS and its methods of transmission are understood, there will be all sorts of proposals to control it by punishing the gay community and by attacking its institutions. When the cause of Legionnaires' Disease was unknown, there were no calls to quarantine members of the American Legion or to shut down their meeting halls. The

Contagious Diseases Acts in England did little to control syphilis, but they caused a great deal of suffering for the women who came under their purview. The history of panic that has accompanied new epidemics, and of the casualties incurred by their scapegoats, should make everyone pause and consider with extreme skepticism any attempts to justify anti-gay policy initiatives on the basis of AIDS.

VI. The Limits of Feminism

> We know that in an overwhelmingly large number of cases, sex crime is associated with pornography. We know that sex criminals read it, are clearly influenced by it. I believe that, if we can eliminate the distribution of such items among impressionable children, we shall greatly reduce our frightening sex-crime rate.
>
> J. Edgar Hoover[30]

In the absence of a more articulated radical theory of sex, most progressives have turned to feminism for guidance. And the relationship between feminism and sex is complex. Because sexuality is a nexus of the relationships between genders, much of the oppression of women is borne by, mediated through, and constituted within, sexuality. Feminism has always been vitally interested in sex. But there have been two strains of feminist thought on the subject. One tendency has criticized the restrictions on women's sexual behaviour and denounced the high costs imposed on women for being sexually active. This tradition of feminist sexual thought has called for a sexual liberation that would work for women as well as for men. The second tendency has considered sexual liberalization to be inherently a mere extension of male privilege. This tradition resonates with conservative, anti-sexual discourse. With the advent of the anti-pornography movement, it achieved temporary hegemony over feminist analysis.

The anti-pornography movement and its texts have been the most extensive expression of this discourse.[31] In addition, proponents of this viewpoint have condemned virtually every variant of sexual expression as anti-feminist. Within this framework, monogamous lesbianism that occurs within long-term, intimate relationships and which does not involve playing with polarized roles, has replaced married, procreative heterosexuality at the top of the value hierarchy. Heterosexuality has been demoted to somewhere in the middle. Apart from this change, everything else looks more or less familiar. The lower depths are occupied by the usual groups and behaviours: prostitution, transsexuality, sadomasochism, and cross-generational activities.[32] Most gay male conduct, all casual sex, promiscuity, and lesbian behaviour that does involve roles or kink or non-monogamy are also censured.[33] Even sexual fantasy during masturbation is denounced as a phallocentric holdover.[34]

This discourse on sexuality is less a sexology than a demonology. It presents most sexual behaviour in the worst possible light. Its descriptions of erotic conduct always use the worst available example as if it were representative. It presents the most disgusting pornography, the most exploited forms of prostitution, and the least palatable or most shocking manifestations of sexual variation. This rhetorical tactic consistently misrepresents human sexuality in all its forms. The picture of human sexuality that emerges from this literature is unremittingly ugly.

In addition, this anti-porn rhetoric is a massive exercise in scapegoating. It criticizes nonroutine acts of love rather than routine acts of oppression, exploitation, or violence. This demon sexology directs legitimate anger at women's lack of personal safety against innocent individuals, practices, and communities. Anti-porn propaganda often implies that sexism originates within the commercial sex industry and subsequently infects the rest of society. This is sociologically nonsensical. The sex industry is hardly a feminist utopia. It reflects the sexism that exists in the society as a whole. We need to analyze and oppose the manifestations of gender inequality specific to the sex industry. But this is not the same as attempting to wipe out commercial sex.

Similarly, erotic minorities such as sadomasochists and transsexuals are as likely to exhibit sexist attitudes or behaviour as any other politically random social grouping. But to claim that they are inherently anti-feminist is sheer fantasy. A good deal of current feminist literature attributes the oppression of women to graphic representations of sex, prostitution, sex education, sadomasochism, male homosexuality, and transsexualism. Whatever happened to the family, religion, education, child-rearing practices, the media, the state, psychiatry, job discrimination, and unequal pay?

[. . .]

The development of this sexual system has taken place in the context of gender relations. Part of the modern ideology of sex is that lust is the province of men, purity that of women. It is no accident that pornography and the perversions have been considered part of the male domain. In the sex industry, women have been excluded from most production and consumption, and allowed to participate primarily as workers. In order to participate in the 'perversions', women have had to overcome serious limitations on their social mobility, their economic resources, and their sexual freedoms. Gender affects the operation of the sexual system, and the sexual system has had gender-specific manifestations. But although sex and gender are related, they are not the same thing, and they form the basis of two distinct arenas of social practice.

[. . .]

In the long run, feminism's critique of gender hierarchy must be incorporated into a radical theory of sex, and the critique of sexual oppression should enrich feminism. But an autonomous theory and politics specific to sexuality must be developed.

It is a mistake to substitute feminism for Marxism as the last word in social theory. Feminism is no more capable than Marxism of being the ultimate and complete account of all social inequality. Nor is feminism the residual theory which can take care of everything to which Marx did not attend. These critical tools were fashioned to handle very specific areas of social activity. Other areas of social life, their forms of power, and their characteristic modes of oppression, need their own conceptual implements. In this essay, I have argued for theoretical as well as sexual pluralism.

VII. Conclusion

> . . . these pleasures which we lightly call physical . . .
>
> Colette[35]

Like gender, sexuality is political. It is organized into systems of power, which reward and encourage some individuals and activities, while punishing and suppressing others. Like the capitalist organization of labour and its distribution of rewards and powers, the modern sexual system has been the object of political struggle since it emerged and as it has evolved. But if the disputes between labour and capital are mystified, sexual conflicts are completely camouflaged.

The legislative restructuring that took place at the end of the nineteenth century and in the early decades of the twentieth was a refracted response to the emergence of the modern erotic system. During that period, new erotic communities formed. It became possible to be a male homosexual or a lesbian in a way it had not been previously. Mass-produced erotica became available, and the possibilities for sexual commerce expanded. The first homosexual rights organizations were formed, and the first analyses of sexual oppression were articulated.[36]

The repression of the 1950s was in part a backlash to the expansion of sexual communities and possibilities which took place during World War II.[37] During the 1950s, gay rights organizations were established, the Kinsey reports were published, and lesbian literature flourished. The 1950s were a formative as well as a repressive era.

The current right-wing sexual counter-offensive is in part a reaction to the sexual liberalization of the 1960s and early 1970s. Moreover, it has brought about a unified and self-conscious coalition of sexual radicals. In one sense, what is now occurring is the emergence of a new sexual movement, aware of new issues and seeking a new theoretical basis. The sex wars out on the streets have been partly responsible for provoking a new intellectual focus on sexuality. The sexual system is shifting once again, and we are seeing many symptoms of its change.

In Western culture, sex is taken all too seriously. A person is not considered immoral, is not sent to prison, and is not expelled from her or his family, for enjoying spicy cuisine. But an individual may go through all this and more for enjoying shoe leather. Ultimately, of what possible social significance is it if a person likes to masturbate over a shoe? It may even be non-consensual, but since we do not ask permission of our shoes to wear them, it hardly seems necessary to obtain dispensation to come on them.

If sex is taken too seriously, sexual persecution is not taken seriously enough. There is systematic mistreatment of individuals and communities on the basis of erotic taste or behaviour. There are serious penalties for belonging to the various sexual occupational castes. The sexuality of the young is denied, adult sexuality is often treated like a variety of nuclear waste, and the graphic representation of sex takes place in a mire of legal and social circumlocution. Specific populations bear the brunt of the current system of erotic power, but their persecution upholds a system that affects everyone.

The 1980s have already been a time of great sexual suffering. They have also been a time of ferment and new possibility. It is up to all of us to try to prevent more barbarism and to encourage erotic creativity. Those who consider themselves progressive need to examine their preconceptions, update their sexual educations, and acquaint themselves with the existence and operation of sexual hierarchy. It is time to recognize the political dimensions of erotic life.

A Note on Definitions

Throughout this essay, I use terms such as 'homosexual', 'sex worker', and 'pervert'. I use 'homosexual' to refer to both women and men. If I want to be more specific, I use terms such 'lesbian' or 'gay male'. 'Sex worker' is intended to be more inclusive than 'prostitute', in order to encompass the many jobs of the sex industry. Sex worker includes erotic dancers, strippers, porn models, nude women who will talk to a customer via telephone hook-up and can be seen but not touched, phone partners, and the various other employees of sex businesses such as receptionists, janitors, and bankers. Obviously, it also includes prostitutes, hustlers, and 'male models'. I use the term 'pervert' as a shorthand for all the stigmatized sexual orientations. It used to cover male and female homosexuality as well but as these become less disreputable, the term has increasingly referred to the other 'deviations'. Terms such as 'pervert' and 'deviant' have, in general use, a connotation of disapproval, disgust, and dislike. I am using these terms in a denotative fashion, and do not intend them to convey any disapproval on my part.

Notes

1. Demetrius Zambaco, 'Onanism and Nervous Disorders in Two Little Girls', in François Peraldi (ed.), *Polysexuality, Semiotext(e)*, vol. IV, no. 1, 1981, pp. 31, 36.

2. Linda Gordon and Ellen Dubois, 'Seeking Ecstasy on the Battlefield: Danger and Pleasure in Nineteenth Century Feminist Sexual Thought', *Feminist Studies*, vol. 9, no. 1, Spring 1983; Steven Marcus, *The Other Victorians*, New York, New American Library, 1974; Mary Ryan, 'The Power of Women's Networks: A Case Study of Female Moral Reform in America', *Feminist Studies*, vol. 6, no. 1, 1979; Judith R. Walkowitz, *Prostitution and Victorian Society*, Cambridge, Cambridge University Press, 1980; Judith R. Walkowitz, 'Male Vice and Feminist Virtue: Feminism and the Politics of Prostitution in Nineteenth-Century Britain', *History Workshop Journal*, no. 13, Spring 1982; Jeffrey Weeks, *Sex, Politics* and *Society: The Regulation of Sexuality Since 1800*, New York, Longman, 1981.

3. G.J. Barker-Benfield, *The Horrors of the Half-Known Life*, New York, Harper Colophon, 1976; Marcus, op. cit.; Weeks, op. cit., especially pages 48–52; Zambaco, op. cit.

4. Commonwealth of Massachusetts, *Preliminary Report of the Special Commission Investigating the Prevalence of Sex Crimes*, 1947; State of New Hampshire, *Report of the Interim Commission of the State of New Hampshire to Study the Cause and Prevention of Serious Sex Crimes*, 1949; City of New York, *Report of the Mayor's Committee for the Study of Sex Offences*, 1939; State of New York, *Report to the Governor on a Study of 102 Sex Offenders at Sing Sing Prison*, 1950; Samuel Hartwell, *A Citizen's Handbook of Sexual Abnormalities and the Mental Hygiene Approach to Their Prevention*, State of Michigan, 1950; State of Michigan, *Report of the Governor's Study Commission on the Deviated Criminal Sex Offender*, 1951. This is merely a sampler.

5. Estelle B. Freedman, '"Uncontrolled Desire"; The Threat of the Sexual Psychopath in America, 1935–1960', paper presented at the Annual Meeting of the American Historical Association, San Francisco, December 1983.

6. George Stambolian, 'Creating the New Man: A Conversation with Jacqueline Livingston', *Christopher Street*, May 1980; 'Jacqueline Livingston', *Clothed with the Sun*, vol. 3, no. 1, May 1983.

7. Paul H. Gebhard, 'The Institute', in Martin S. Weinberg (ed.), *Sex Research: Studies from the Kinsey Institute*, New York, Oxford University Press, 1976.

8. James Barr, *Quartrefoil*, New York, Greenberg, 1950, p. 310.

9. Michel Foucault, *The History of Sexuality*, New York, Patheon, 1978.

10. A very useful discussion of these issues can be found in Robert Padgug, 'Sexual Matters: On Conceptualizing Sexuality in History', *Radical History Review*, no. 20, spring/summer 1979.

11. Foucault, op. cit., p. 11.

12. See the discussion in Weeks, *Sex, Politics and Society*, op, cit., p. 9.

13. See Weeks, *Sex, Politics and Society*, op. cit., p. 22.

14. See, for example, 'Pope Praises Couples for Self-Control', *San Francisco Chronicle*, October 13, 1980, p. 5; 'Pope Says Sexual Arousal Isn't a Sin If It's Ethical', *San Francisco Chronicle*, November 6, 1980, p. 33; 'Pope Condemns "Carnal Lust" As Abuse of Human Freedom', *San Francisco Chronicle*, January 15, 1981, p. 2; 'Pope Again Hits Abortion, Birth Control', *San Francisco Chronicle*, January 16, 1981, p. 13; and 'Sexuality, Not Sex in Heaven', *San Francisco Chronicle*, December 3, 1981, p. 50.

15. Susan Sontag, *Styles of Radical Will*, New York, Farrar, Strauss, & Giroux, 1969, p. 46.

16. Foucault, op. cit, p. 43.

17. Gilbert Herdt, *Guardians of the Flutes*, New York, McGraw-Hill, 1981; Raymond Kelly, 'Witchcraft and Sexual Relations', in Paula Brown and Georgeda Buchbinder (eds), *Man and Woman in the New Guinea Highlands*, Washington, DC, American Anthropological Association, 1976; Gayle Rubin, 'Coconuts: Aspects of Male/Female Relationships in New Guinea', unpublished ms., 1974; Gayle Rubin, review of *Guardians of the Flutes*, *Advocate*, 23 December 1982; J. Van Baal, *Dema*, The Hague, Nijhoff, 1966; F.E. Williams, *Papuans of the Trans-Fly*, Oxford, Clarendon, 1936.

18. Caroline Bingham, 'Seventeenth-Century Attitudes Toward Deviant Sex', *Journal of Interdisciplinary History*, spring 1971, p. 465.

19. Stephen O. Murray, 'The Institutional Elaboration of a Quasi-Ethnic Community', *International Review of Modern Sociology*, July–December 1979.

20. For further elaboration of these processes, see: Allan Bérubé, 'Behind the Spectre of San Francisco', *Body Politic*, April 1981; Allan Bérubé, 'Marching to a Different Drummer', *Advocate*, 15 October 1981; John D'Emilio, 'Gay Politics, Gay Community: San Francisco's Experience', *Socialist Review*, no. 55, January–February 1981; John D'Emilio, *Sexual Politics, Sexual Communities: The Making of the Homosexual Minority in the United States, 1940–1970*, Chicago, University of Chicago Press, 1983; Foucault, op. cit.; Bert Hansen, 'The Historical Construction of Homosexuality', *Radical History Review*, no. 20, spring/summer 1979; Jonathan Katz, *Gay American History*, New York, Thomas Y. Crowell, 1976; Jeffrey Weeks, *Coming Out: Homosexual Politics in Britain from the Nineteenth Century to the Present*, New York, Quartet, 1977; and Weeks, *Sex, Politics and Society*, op. cit.

21. Walkowitz, *Prostitution and Victorian Society*, op. cit.

22. Vice cops also harass all sex businesses, be these gay bars, gay baths, adult book stores, the producers and distributors of commercial erotica, or swing clubs.

23. Foucault, op. cit., p. 40.
24. Karl Marx, in David McLellan (ed.), *The Grundrisse,* New York, Harper & Row, 1971, p. 94.
25. Clark Norton, 'Sex in America', *Inquiry,* October 5, 1981. This article is a superb summary of much current sex law and should be required reading for anyone interested in sex.
26. Sarah Senefeld Beserra, Nancy M. Jewel, Melody West Matthews, and Elizabeth R. Gatov (eds), *Sex Code of California,* Public Education and Research Committee of California, 1973, pp. 163–8. This earlier edition of the *Sex Code of California* preceded the 1976 consenting adults statute and consequently gives a better overview of sodomy laws.
27. D'Emilio, *Sexual Politics, Sexual Communities,* op. cit., pp. 40–53, has an excellent discussion of gay oppression in the 1950s which covers many of the areas I have mentioned. The dynamics he describes, however, are operative in modified forms for other erotic populations, and in other periods. The specific model of gay oppression needs to be generalized to apply, with appropriate modifications, to other sexual groups.
28. Weeks, *Sex, Politics and Society,* op. cit., p. 14.
29. See Lysander Spooner, *Vices Are Not Crimes: A Vindication of Moral Liberty,* Cupertino, CA, Tanstaafl Press, 1977, pp. 25–9. Feminist anti-porn discourse fits right into the tradition of justifying attempts at moral control by claiming that such action will protect women and children from violence.
30. Cited in H. Montgomery Hyde, *A History of Pornography,* New York, Dell, 1965, p. 31.
31. See for example Laura Lederer (ed.), *Take Back the Night,* New York, William Morrow, 1980; Andrea Dworkin, *Pornography,* New York, Perigee, 1981. The *Newspage* of San Francisco's Women against Violence in Pornography and Media and the *Newsreport* of New York Women against Pornography are excellent sources.
32. Kathleen Barry, *Female Sexual Slavery,* Englewood Cliffs, NJ, Prentice-Hall, 1979; Janice Raymond, *The Transsexual Empire,* Boston, Beacon, 1979; Kathleen Barry, 'Sadomasochism: The New Backlash to Feminism', *Trivia,* no. 1, fall 1982; Robin Ruth Linden, Darlene R. Pagano, Diana E.H. Russell, and Susan Leigh Starr (eds), *Against Sadomasochism,* East Palo Alto, CA, Frog in the Well, 1982; and Florence Rush, *The Best Kept Secret,* New York, McGraw-Hill, 1980.
33. Sally Gearhart, 'An Open Letter to the Voters in District 5 and San Francisco's Gay Community', 1979; Adrienne Rich, *On Lies, Secrets, and Silence,* New York, W.W. Norton, 1979, p. 225. ('On the other hand, there is homosexual patriarchal culture, a culture created by homosexual men, reflecting such male stereotypes as dominance and submission as modes of relationship, and the separation of sex from emotional involvement—a culture tainted by profound hatred for women. The male "gay" culture has offered lesbians the imitation role stereotypes of "butch" and "femme", "active" and "passive", cruising, sadomasochism, and the violent, self-destructive world of "gay" bars.'); Judith Pasternak, 'The Strangest Bedfellows: Lesbian Feminism and the Sexual Revolution', *WomanNews,* October 1983; Adrienne Rich, 'Compulsory Heterosexuality and Lesbian Existence', in Ann Snitow, Christine Stansell, and Sharon Thompson (eds), *Powers of Desire: The Politics of Sexuality,* New York, Monthly Review Press, 1983.
34. Julia Penelope, 'And Now for the Really Hard Questions', *Sinister Wisdom,* no. 15, fall 1980, p. 103.
35. Colette, *The Ripening Seed,* translated and cited in Hannah Alderfer, Beth Jaker, and Marybeth Nelson, *Diary of a Conference on Sexuality,* New York, Faculty Press, 1982, p. 72.
36. John Lauritsen and David Thorstad, *The Early Homosexual Rights Movement in Germany,* New York, Times Change Press, 1974.
37. D'Emilio, *Sexual Politics, Sexual Communities,* op. cit.; Bérubé 'Behind the Spectre of San Francisco', op. cit.; Bérubé, 'Marching to a Different Drummer', op. cit.

The Incitement to Discourse

Michel Foucault

The seventeenth century, then, was the beginning of an age of repression emblematic of what we call the bourgeois societies, an age which perhaps we still have not completely left behind. Calling sex by its name thereafter became more difficult and more costly. As if in order to gain mastery over it in reality, it had first been necessary to subjugate it at the level of language, control its free circulation in speech, expunge it from the things that were said, and extinguish the words that rendered it too visibly present. And even these prohibitions, it seems, were afraid to name it. Without even having to pronounce the word, modern prudishness was able to ensure that one did not speak of sex, merely through the interplay of prohibitions that referred back to one another: instances of muteness which, by dint of saying nothing, imposed silence. Censorship.

Yet when one looks back over these last three centuries with their continual transformations, things appear in a very different light: around and apropos of sex, one sees a veritable discursive explosion. We must be clear on this point, however. It is quite possible that there was an expurgation—and a very rigorous one—of the authorized vocabulary. It may indeed be true that a whole rhetoric of allusion and metaphor was codified. Without question, new rules of propriety screened out some words: there was a policing of statements. A control over enunciations as well: where and when it was not possible to talk about such things became much more strictly defined; in which circumstances, among which speakers, and within which social relationships. Areas were thus established, if not of utter silence, at least of tact and discretion: between parents and children, for instance, or teachers and pupils, or masters and domestic servants. This almost certainly constituted a whole restrictive economy, one that was incorporated into that politics of language and speech—spontaneous on the one hand, concerted on the other—which accompanied the social redistributions of the classical period.

At the level of discourses and their domains, however, practically the opposite phenomenon occurred. There was a steady proliferation of discourses concerned with sex—specific discourses, different from one another both by their form and by their object: a discursive ferment that gathered momentum from the eighteenth century onward. Here I am thinking not so much of the probable increase in 'illicit' discourses, that is, discourses of infraction that crudely named sex by way of insult or mockery of the new code of decency; the tightening up

of the rules of decorum likely did produce, as a counter-effect, a valorization and intensification of indecent speech. But more important was the multiplication of discourses concerning sex in the field of exercise of power itself: an institutional incitement to speak about it, and to do so more and more; a determination on the part of the agencies of power to hear it spoken about, and to cause *it* to speak through explicit articulation and endlessly accumulated detail.

Consider the evolution of the Catholic pastoral and the sacrament of penance after the Council of Trent. Little by little, the nakedness of the questions formulated by the confession manuals of the Middle Ages, and a good number of those still in use in the seventeenth century, was veiled. One avoided entering into that degree of detail which some authors, such as Sanchez or Tamburini, had for a long time believed indispensable for the confession to be complete: description of the respective positions of the partners, the postures assumed, gestures, places touched, caresses, the precise moment of pleasure—an entire painstaking review of the sexual act in its very unfolding. Discretion was advised, with increasing emphasis. The greatest reserve was counselled when dealing with sins against purity: 'This matter is similar to pitch, for, however one might handle it, even to cast it far from oneself, it sticks nonetheless, and always soils.'[1] And later, Alfonso de' Liguori prescribed starting—and possibly going no further, especially when dealing with children—with questions that were 'roundabout and vague'.[2]

But while the language may have been refined, the scope of the confession—the confession of the flesh—continually increased. [. . .] According to the new pastoral, sex must not be named imprudently, but its aspects, its correlations, and its effects must be pursued down to their slenderest ramifications: a shadow in a daydream, an image too slowly dispelled, a badly exorcised complicity between the body's mechanics and the mind's complacency: everything had to be told. A twofold evolution tended to make the flesh into the root of all evil, shifting the most important moment of transgression from the act itself to the stirrings—so difficult to perceive and formulate—of desire. For this was an evil that afflicted the whole man, and in the most secret of forms: 'Examine diligently, therefore, all the faculties of your soul: memory, understanding, and will. Examine with precision all your senses as well. . . . Examine, moreover, all your thoughts, every word you speak, and all your actions. Examine even unto your dreams, to know if, once awakened, you did not give them your consent. And finally, do not think that in so sensitive and perilous a matter as this, there is anything trivial or insignificant.'[3] Discourse, therefore, had to trace the meeting line of the body and the soul, following all its meanderings: beneath the surface of the sins, it would lay bare the unbroken nervure of the flesh. Under the authority of a language that had been carefully expurgated so that it was no longer directly named, sex was taken charge of, tracked down as it were, by a discourse that aimed to allow it no obscurity, no respite.

It was here, perhaps, that the injunction, so peculiar to the West, was laid down for the first time, in the form of a general constraint. I am not talking about the obligation to admit to violations of the laws of sex, as required by traditional penance; but of the nearly infinite task of telling—telling oneself and another, as often as possible, everything that might concern the interplay of innumerable pleasures, sensations, and thoughts which, through the body and the soul, had some affinity with sex. This scheme for transforming sex into discourse had been devised long before in an ascetic and monastic setting. The seventeenth century made it into a rule for everyone. It would seem in actual fact that it could scarcely have applied to any but a

tiny elite; the great majority of the faithful who only went to confession on rare occasions in the course of the year escaped such complex prescriptions. But the important point no doubt is that this obligation was decreed, as an ideal at least, for every good Christian. An imperative was established: Not only will you confess to acts contravening the law, but you will seek to transform your desire, your every desire, into discourse. Insofar as possible, nothing was meant to elude this dictum, even if the words it employed had to be carefully neutralized. The Christian pastoral prescribed as a fundamental duty the task of passing everything having to do with sex through the endless mill of speech.[4] The forbidding of certain words, the decency of expressions, all the censorings of vocabulary, might well have been only secondary devices compared to that great subjugation: ways of rendering it morally acceptable and technically useful.

One could plot a line going straight from the seventeenth-century pastoral to what became its projection in literature, 'scandalous' literature at that. 'Tell everything', the directors would say time and again: 'not only consummated acts, but sensual touchings, all impure gazes, all obscene remarks . . . all consenting thoughts.'[5] Sade takes up the injunction in words that seem to have been retranscribed from the treatises of spiritual direction: 'Your narrations must be decorated with the most numerous and searching details; the precise way and extent to which we may judge how the passion you describe relates to human manners and man's character is determined by your willingness to disguise no circumstance; and what is more, the least circumstance is apt to have an immense influence upon the procuring of that kind of sensory irritation we expect from your stories.'[6] And again at the end of the nineteenth century, the anonymous author of *My Secret Life* submitted to the same prescription; outwardly, at least, this man was doubtless a kind of traditional libertine; but he conceived the idea of complementing his life—which he had almost totally dedicated to sexual activity—with a scrupulous account of every one of its episodes. He sometimes excuses himself by stressing his concern to educate young people, this man who had 11 volumes published, in a printing of only a few copies, which were devoted to the least adventures, pleasures, and sensations of his sex.[7] [. . .] But the guiding principle for the strangest of these practices, which was the fact of recounting them all, and in detail, from day to day, had been lodged in the heart of modern man for over two centuries. Rather than seeing in this singular man a courageous fugitive from a 'Victorianism' that would have compelled him to silence, I am inclined to think that, in an epoch dominated by (highly prolix) directives enjoining discretion and modesty, he was the most direct and in a way the most naive representative of a plurisecular injunction to talk about sex. The historical accident would consist rather of the reticences of 'Victorian puritanism'; at any rate, they were a digression, a refinement, a tactical diversion in the great process of transforming sex into discourse.

This nameless Englishman will serve better than his queen as the central figure for a sexuality whose main features were already taking shape with the Christian pastoral. [. . .] After all, the Christian pastoral also sought to produce specific effects on desire, by the mere fact of transforming it—fully and deliberately—into discourse: effects of mastery and detachment, to be sure, but also an effect of spiritual reconversion, of turning back to God, a physical effect of blissful suffering from feeling in one's body the pangs of temptation and the love that resists it. This is the essential thing: that Western man has been drawn for three centuries to the task of telling everything concerning his sex; that since the classical age there has been a constant optimi-

zation and an increasing valorization of the discourse on sex; and that this carefully analytical discourse was meant to yield multiple effects of displacement, intensification, reorientation, and modification of desire itself. Not only were the boundaries of what one could say about sex enlarged, and men compelled to hear it said; but more important, discourse was connected to sex by a complex organization with varying effects, by a deployment that cannot be adequately explained merely by referring it to a law of prohibition. A censorship of sex? There was installed rather an apparatus for producing an ever greater quantity of discourse about sex, capable of functioning and taking effect in its very economy.

This technique might have remained tied to the destiny of Christian spirituality if it had not been supported and relayed by other mechanisms. In the first place, by a 'public interest'. Not a collective curiosity or sensibility; not a new mentality; but power mechanisms that functioned in such a way that discourse on sex—for reasons that will have to be examined—became essential. Toward the beginning of the eighteenth century, there emerged a political, economic, and technical incitement to talk about sex. And not so much in the form of a general theory of sexuality as in the form of analysis, stocktaking, classification, and specification, of quantitative or causal studies. This need to take sex 'into account', to pronounce a discourse on sex that would not derive from morality alone but from rationality as well, was sufficiently new that at first it wondered at itself and sought apologies for its own existence. How could a discourse based on reason speak of *that?* 'Rarely have philosophers directed a steady gaze to these objects situated between disgust and ridicule, where one must avoid both hypocrisy and scandal.'[8] And nearly a century later, the medical establishment, which one might have expected to be less surprised by what it was about to formulate, still stumbled at the moment of speaking: 'The darkness that envelops these facts, the shame and disgust they inspire, have always repelled the observer's gaze. . . . For a long time I hesitated to introduce the loathsome picture into this study.'[9] What is essential is not in all these scruples, in the 'moralism' they betray, or in the hypocrisy one can suspect them of, but in the recognized necessity of overcoming this hesitation. One had to speak of sex; one had to speak publicly and in a manner that was not determined by the division between licit and illicit, even if the speaker maintained the distinction for himself (which is what these solemn and preliminary declarations were intended to show): one had to speak of it as of a thing to be not simply condemned or tolerated but managed, inserted into systems of utility, regulated for the greater good of all, made to function according to an optimum. Sex was not something one simply judged; it was a thing one administered. It was in the nature of a public potential; it called for management procedures; it had to be taken charge of by analytical discourses. In the eighteenth century, sex became a 'police' matter—in the full and strict sense given the term at the time: not the repression of disorder, but an ordered maximization of collective and individual forces: 'We must consolidate and augment, through the wisdom of its regulations, the internal power of the state; and since this power consists not only in the Republic in general, and in each of the members who constitute it, but also in the faculties and talents of those belonging to it, it follows that the police must concern themselves with these means and make them serve the public welfare. And they can only obtain this result through the knowledge they have of those different assets.'[10] A policing of sex: that is, not the rigour of a taboo, but the necessity of regulating sex through useful and public discourses.

A few examples will suffice. One of the great innovations in the techniques of power in the eighteenth century was the emergence of 'population' as an economic and political problem: population as wealth, population as manpower or labour capacity, population balanced between its own growth and the resources it commanded. Governments perceived that they were not dealing simply with subjects, or even with a 'people', but with a 'population', with its specific phenomena and its peculiar variables: birth and death rates, life expectancy, fertility, state of health, frequency of illnesses, patterns of diet and habitation. All these variables were situated at the point where the characteristic movements of life and the specific effects of institutions intersected: 'States are not populated in accordance with the natural progression of propagation, but by virtue of their industry, their products, and their different institutions. . . . Men multiply like the yields from the ground and in proportion to the advantages and resources they find in their labours.'[11] At the heart of this economic and political problem of population was sex: it was necessary to analyze the birthrate, the age of marriage, the legitimate and illegitimate births, the precocity and frequency of sexual relations, the ways of making them fertile or sterile, the effects of unmarried life or of the prohibitions, the impact of contraceptive practices—of those notorious 'deadly secrets' which demographers on the eve of the Revolution knew were already familiar to the inhabitants of the countryside.

Of course, it had long been asserted that a country had to be populated if it hoped to be rich and powerful; but this was the first time that a society had affirmed, in a constant way, that its future and its fortune were tied not only to the number and the uprightness of its citizens, to their marriage rules and family organization, but to the manner in which each individual made use of his sex. Things went from ritual lamenting over the unfruitful debauchery of the rich, bachelors, and libertines to a discourse in which the sexual conduct of the population was taken both as an object of analysis and as a target of intervention; there was a progression from the crudely populationist arguments of the mercantilist epoch to the much more subtle and calculated attempts at regulation that tended to favour or discourage—according to the objectives and exigencies of the moment—an increasing birthrate. Through the political economy of population there was formed a whole grid of observations regarding sex. There emerged the analysis of the modes of sexual conduct, their determinations and their effects, at the boundary line of the biological and the economic domains. There also appeared those systematic campaigns which, going beyond the traditional means—moral and religious exhortations, fiscal measures—tried to transform the sexual conduct of couples into a concerted economic and political behaviour. In time these new measures would become anchorage points for the different varieties of racism of the nineteenth and twentieth centuries. It was essential that the state know what was happening with its citizens' sex, and the use they made of it, but also that each individual be capable of controlling the use he made of it. Between the state and the individual, sex became an issue, and a public issue no less; a whole web of discourses, special knowledges, analyses, and injunctions settled upon it.

The situation was similar in the case of children's sex. [. . .] It is true that a longstanding 'freedom' of language between children and adults, or pupils and teachers, may have disappeared. No seventeenth-century pedagogue would have publicly advised his disciple, as did Erasmus in his *Dialogues,* on the choice of a good prostitute. And the boisterous laughter that had accompanied the precocious sexuality

of children for so long—and in all social classes, it seems—was gradually stilled. But this was not a plain and simple imposition of silence. Rather, it was a new regime of discourses. Not any less was said about it; on the contrary. But things were said in a different way; it was different people who said them, from different points of view, and in order to obtain different results. Silence itself—the things one declines to say, or is forbidden to name, the discretion that is required between different speakers—is less the absolute limit of discourse, the other side from which it is separated by a strict boundary, than an element that functions alongside the things said, with them and in relation to them within overall strategies. There is no binary division to be made between what one says and what one does not say; we must try to determine the different ways of not saying such things, how those who can and those who cannot speak of them are distributed, which type of discourse is authorized, or which form of discretion is required in either case. There is not one but many silences, and they are an integral part of the strategies that underlie and permeate discourses.

Take the secondary schools of the eighteenth century, for example. On the whole, one can have the impression that sex was hardly spoken of at all in these institutions. But one only has to glance over the architectural layout, the rules of discipline, and their whole internal organization: the question of sex was a constant preoccupation. The builders considered it explicitly. The organizers took it permanently into account. All who held a measure of authority were placed in a state of perpetual alert, which the fixtures, the precautions taken, the interplay of punishments and responsibilities, never ceased to reiterate. The space for classes, the shape of the tables, the planning of the recreation lessons, the distribution of the dormitories (with or without partitions, with or without curtains), the rules for monitoring bedtime and sleep periods—all this referred, in the most prolix manner, to the sexuality of children.[12] What one might call the internal discourse of the institution—the one it employed to address itself, and which circulated among those who made it function—was largely based on the assumption that this sexuality existed, that it was precocious, active, and ever present. But this was not all: the sex of the schoolboy became in the course of the eighteenth century—and quite apart from that of adolescents in general—a public problem. Doctors counselled the directors and professors of educational establishments, but they also gave their opinions to families; educators designed projects which they submitted to the authorities; schoolmasters turned to students, made recommendations to them, and drafted for their benefit books of exhortation, full of moral and medical examples. Around the schoolboy and his sex there proliferated a whole literature of precepts, opinions, observations, medical advice, clinical cases, outlines for reform, and plans for ideal institutions. With Basedow and the German 'philanthropic' movement, this transformation of adolescent sex into discourse grew to considerable dimensions. Salzmann even organized an experimental school which owed its exceptional character to a supervision and education of sex so well thought out that youth's universal sin would never need to be practised there. And with all these measures taken, the child was not to be simply the mute and unconscious object of attentions pre-arranged between adults only; a certain reasonable, limited, canonical, and truthful discourse on sex was prescribed for him—a kind of discursive orthopedics. The great festival organized at the Philanthropinum in May of 1776 can serve as a vignette in this regard. Taking the form of an examination, mixed with floral games, the awarding of prizes, and a board of review, this was the first solemn

communion of adolescent sex and reasonable discourse. In order to show the success of the sex education given the students, Basedow had invited all the dignitaries that Germany could muster (Goethe was one of the few to decline the invitation). Before the assembled public, one of the professors, a certain Wolke, asked the students selected questions concerning the mysteries of sex, birth, and procreation. He had them comment on engravings that depicted a pregnant woman, a couple, and a cradle. The replies were enlightened, offered without shame or embarrassment. No unseemly laughter intervened to disturb them—except from the very ranks of an adult audience more childish than the children themselves, and whom Wolke severely reprimanded. At the end, they all applauded these cherub-faced boys who, in front of adults, had skillfully woven the garlands of discourse and sex.[13]

It would be less than exact to say that the pedagogical institution has imposed a ponderous silence on the sex of children and adolescents. On the contrary, since the eighteenth century it has multiplied the forms of discourse on the subject; it has established various points of implantation for sex; it has coded contents and qualified speakers. Speaking about children's sex, inducing educators, physicians, administrators, and parents to speak of it, or speaking to them about it, causing children themselves to talk about it, and enclosing them in a web of discourses which sometimes address them, sometimes speak about them, or impose canonical bits of knowledge on them, or use them as a basis for constructing a science that is beyond their grasp—all this together enables us to link an intensification of the interventions of power to a multiplication of discourse. The sex of children and adolescents has become, since the eighteenth century, an important area of contention around which innumerable institutional devices and discursive strategies have been deployed. [. . .]

One could mention many other centres which in the eighteenth or nineteenth century began to produce discourses on sex. First there was medicine, via the 'nervous disorders'; next psychiatry, when it set out to discover the etiology of mental illnesses, focusing its gaze first on 'excess', then onanism, then frustration, then 'frauds against procreation', but especially when it annexed the whole of the sexual perversions as its own province; criminal justice, too, which had long been concerned with sexuality, particularly in the form of 'heinous' crimes and crimes against nature, but which, toward the middle of the nineteenth century, broadened its jurisdiction to include petty offenses, minor indecencies, insignificant perversions; and lastly, all those social controls, cropping up at the end of the last century, which screened the sexuality of couples, parents, and children. Dangerous and endangered adolescents—undertaking to protect, separate, and forewarn, signalling perils everywhere, awakening people's attention, calling for diagnoses, piling up reports, organizing therapies. These sites radiated discourses aimed at sex, intensifying people's awareness of it as a constant danger, and this in turn created a further incentive to talk about it.

One day in 1867, a farm hand from the village of Lapcourt, who was somewhat simple-minded, employed here then there, depending on the season, living hand-to-mouth from a little charity or in exchange for the worst sort of labour, sleeping in barns and stables, was turned in to the authorities. At the border of a field, he had obtained a few caresses from a little girl, just as he had done before and seen done by the village urchins round about him; for, at the edge of the wood, or in the ditch by the road leading to Saint-Nicolas, they would play the familiar game called 'curdled milk'. So he was pointed out by

the girl's parents to the mayor of the village, reported by the mayor to the gendarmes, led by the gendarmes to the judge, who indicted him and turned him over first to a doctor, then to two other experts who not only wrote their report but also had it published.[14] What is the significant thing about this story? The pettiness of it all; the fact that this everyday occurrence in the life of village sexuality, these inconsequential bucolic pleasures, could become, from a certain time, the object not only of a collective intolerance but of a judicial action, a medical intervention, a careful clinical examination, and an entire theoretical elaboration. The thing to note is that they went so far as to measure the brainpan, study the facial bone structure, and inspect for possible signs of degenerescence the anatomy of this personage who up to that moment had been an integral part of village life; that they made him talk; that they questioned him concerning his thoughts, inclinations, habits, sensations, and opinions. And then, acquitting him of any crime, they decided finally to make him into a pure object of medicine and knowledge—an object to be shut away till the end of his life in the hospital at Maréville, but also one to be made known to the world of learning through a detailed analysis. One can be fairly certain that during this same period the Lapcourt schoolmaster was instructing the little villagers to mind their language and not talk about all these things aloud. [. . .]

Between the licentious Englishman, who earnestly recorded for his own purposes the singular episodes of his secret life, and his contemporary, this village halfwit who would give a few pennies to the little girls for favours the older ones refused him, there was without doubt a profound connection: in any case, from one extreme to the other, sex became something to say, and to say exhaustively in accordance with deployments that were varied, but all, in their own way, compelling. Whether in the form of a subtle confession in confidence or an authoritarian interrogation, sex—be it refined or rustic—had to be put into words. A great polymorphous injunction bound the Englishman and the poor Lorrainese peasant alike. As history would have it, the latter was named Jouy.*

[. . .] These discourses on sex did not multiply apart from or against power, but in the very space and as the means of its exercise. Incitements to speak were orchestrated from all quarters, apparatuses everywhere for listening and recording, procedures for observing, questioning, and formulating. Sex was driven out of hiding and constrained to lead a discursive existence. From the singular imperialism that compels everyone to transform their sexuality into a perpetual discourse, to the manifold mechanisms which, in the areas of economy, pedagogy, medicine, and justice, incite, extract, distribute, and institutionalize the sexual discourse, an immense verbosity is what our civilization has required and organized. Surely no other type of society has ever accumulated—and in such a relatively short span of time—a similar quantity of discourses concerned with sex. It may well be that we talk about sex more than anything else; we set our minds to the task; we convince ourselves that we have never said enough on the subject, that, through inertia or submissiveness, we conceal from ourselves the blinding evidence, and that what is essential always eludes us, so that we must always start out once again in search of it. It is possible that where sex is concerned, the most long-winded, the most impatient of societies is our own.

But as this first overview shows, we are dealing less with *a* discourse on sex than with a multiplicity of discourses produced by a whole series of mechanisms operating in different institutions. [. . .] Rather than the uniform concern to hide sex, rather than a general prudishness of language, what distinguishes these last three centuries is the variety, the wide dispersion of devices that were invented for speaking about it, for having it be spoken about, for inducing it to speak of itself, for listening, recording, transcribing, and redistributing what is said about it: around sex, a whole network of varying, specific, and coercive transpositions into discourse. Rather than a massive censorship, beginning with the verbal proprieties imposed by the Age of Reason, what was involved was a regulated and polymorphous incitement to discourse.

The objection will doubtless be raised that if so many stimulations and constraining mechanisms were necessary in order to speak of sex, this was because there reigned over everyone a certain fundamental prohibition; only definite necessities—economic pressures, political requirements—were able to lift this prohibition and open a few approaches to the discourse on sex, but these were limited and carefully coded; so much talk about sex, so many insistent devices contrived for causing it to be talked about—but under strict conditions: does this not prove that it was an object of secrecy, and more important, that there is still an attempt to keep it that way? But this often-stated theme, that sex is outside of discourse and that only the removing of an obstacle, the breaking of a secret, can clear the way leading to it, is precisely what needs to be examined. Does it not partake of the injunction by which discourse is provoked? Is it not with the aim of inciting people to speak of sex that it is made to mirror, at the outer limit of every actual discourse, something akin to a secret whose discovery is imperative, a thing abusively reduced to silence, and at the same time difficult and necessary, dangerous and precious to divulge? We must not forget that by making sex

---

* Jouy sounds like the past participle of *jouir,* the French verb meaning to enjoy, to delight in (something), but also to have an organism, to come. (Translator's note)

into that which, above all else, had to be confessed, the Christian pastoral always presented it as the disquieting enigma: not a thing which stubbornly shows itself, but one which always hides, the insidious presence that speaks in a voice so muted and often disguised that one risks remaining deaf to it. Doubtless the secret does not reside in that basic reality in relation to which all the incitements to speak of sex are situated—whether they try to force the secret, or whether in some obscure way they reinforce it by the manner in which they speak of it. It is a question rather of a theme that forms part of the very mechanics of these incitements: a way of giving shape to the requirement to speak about the matter, a fable that is indispensable to the endlessly proliferating economy of the discourse on sex. What is peculiar to modern societies, in fact, is not that they consigned sex to a shadow existence, but that they dedicated themselves to speaking of it *ad infinitum,* while exploiting it as *the* secret.

Notes

1. Paolo Segneri, *L'Instruction du pénitent* (French trans. 1695), p. 301.
2. Alfonso de' Liguori, *Practique des confesseurs* (French trans. 1854), p. 40.
3. Segneri, *L'Instruction du pénitent*, pp. 301–2.
4. The reformed pastoral also laid down rules, albeit in a more discreet way, for putting sex into discourse.
5. Alfonso de' Liguori, *Préceptes sur le sixième commandement* (French trans. 1835), p. 5.
6. Donatien-Alphonse de Sade, *The 120 Days of Sodom,* trans. Austryn Wainhouse and Richard Seaver (New York: Grove Press, 1966), p. 271.
7. Anonymous, *My Secret Life* (New York: Grove Press, 1966).
8. Condorcet, cited by Jean-Louis Flandrin, *Familles: parenté, maison, sexualité dans l'ancienne société* (Paris: Hacette, 1976).
9. Auguste Tardieu, *Étude médico-légale sur les attentats aux moeurs* (1857), p. 114.
10. Johann von Justi, *Éléments généraux de police* (French trans. 1769), p. 20.
11. Claude-Jacques Herbert, *Essai sur la police générale des grains* (1753), pp. 320–1.

12. *Règalement de police pour les lycées* (1809), art. 67: 'There shall always be, during class and study hours, an instructor watching the exterior, so as to prevent students who have gone out to relieve themselves from stopping and congregating.'
    art. 68: 'After the evening prayer, the students will be conducted back to the dormitory, where the schoolmasters will put them to bed at once.'
    art. 69: 'The masters will not retire except after having made certain that every student is in bed.'
    art. 70: 'The beds shall be separated by partitions two metres in height. The dormitories shall be illuminated during the night.'
13. Johann Gottleib Schummel, *Fritzens Reïse nach Dessau* (1776), cited by Auguste Pinloche, *La Réforme de l'éducation en Allemagne au XVIIIe siècle* (1889), pp. 125–9.
14. H. Bonnet and J. Bulard, *Rapport médico-légal sur l'état mental de Ch.-J. Jouy*, January 4, 1968.

2 Contemporary Approaches and Applications

Gender and Sexual Harassment

Sandy Welsh

Even social scientists didn't study it, and they study everything that moves.

Catherine MacKinnon (1987:106; commenting on the lack of information about sexual harassment)

Twenty years ago, the study of sexual harassment focused on whether or not sexual harassment was a social problem worthy of study and on descriptive analyses of its prevalence. In recent years, research has shifted to more sophisticated empirical and theoretical analyses of the causes and consequences of this phenomenon. Research now exists that attempts to answer many of the fundamental questions surrounding sexual harassment: What is sexual harassment? How prevalent is sexual harassment? What are the predictors of sexual harassment? And what are the responses to and consequences of sexual harassment? This review outlines the major accomplishments in this field, some of its pitfalls, and research directions for the future.

What Is Sexual Harassment?

From a legal standpoint, sexual harassment is a form of sex discrimination composed of two forms of behaviour: quid pro quo harassment and hostile environment harassment. Quid pro quo harassment involves sexual threats or bribery that are made a condition of employment or used as the basis for employment decisions. Hostile environment harassment captures those behaviours, such as sexual jokes, comments, and touching, that interfere with an individual's ability to do her/his job or that create an 'intimidating, hostile or offensive working environment' (US EEOC 1980). This includes forms of gender harassment such as gender-based hazing and put-downs. After examining US legal decisions in sexual harassment cases, Schultz (1998b) comes to the following conclusion:

> Of course making a woman the object of sexual attention can also work to

undermine her image and self-confidence as a capable worker. Yet, much of the time, harassment assumes a form that has little or nothing to do with sexuality but everything to do with gender. (p. 1687)

At its core, sexual harassment is often about letting women know they are not welcome in certain workplaces and that they are not respected members of the work group (Reskin & Padavic 1994). Sexual harassment continues to hamper employment opportunities for many women and men.

The Prevalence and Measurement of Sexual Harassment

How Prevalent Is Sexual Harassment?

Considerable variation exists in the estimated proportions of women reporting experiences with sexual harassment.[1] Depending on the sample used, 16 per cent to 90 per cent of working women experience sexual harassment in their lifetime (e.g., Brooks & Perot 1991, Gutek 1985, Terpstra & Baker 1989, US MSPB 1981). [. . .] In Canada, studies using random samples of the general population, estimate that lifetime sexual harassment rates for women vary from 23 per cent (Welsh & Nierobisz 1997) to 51 per cent (Gruber 1997). [. . .] The brief overview of prevalence rates highlights one of the major problems confronting the empirical study of sexual harassment, as these differences are attributed, in part, to survey measurement issues.

Measuring Sexual Harassment

Some measurement issues identified as problematic in research on sexual harassment include differences in sampled populations, response rates, number of sexual harassment items, and context and timeframe of questions (see Gruber 1990, 1992, Fitzgerald & Shullman 1993, Arvey & Cavanaugh 1995, Welsh & Nierobisz 1997). For example, studies with higher survey response rates that use random samples tend to report lower prevalence rates than do other studies. As well, in early sexual harassment surveys there was little consensus as to how sexual harassment was defined. Most surveys provided a list of sexual behaviours derived in part from the EEOC definition. [. . .] Survey items also tended to be nonspecific such as asking about pressure for relationships or experiencing 'sexual remarks and teasing'. [. . .] As well, items should ask respondents about 'unwanted' sexual experiences and should not use the term 'sexual harassment' (Fitzgerald & Shullman 1993). In response to these early measurement problems, two comprehensive and fairly consistent schemes for measuring sexual harassment have emerged in the literature: the Sexual Experiences Questionnaire (Fitzgerald et al. 1988) and the Inventory of Sexual Harassment (Gruber 1992).

More work on measurement is needed. First, separate indicators or sub-scales of frequency, duration, directness, and offensiveness for specific types of harassment should be developed further. Because both the causes and impact of harassment are not consistent across all types of harassment, these more refined measures are necessary (Fitzgerald & Shullman 1993, Gruber et al. 1996, Gruber 1998). Second, cumulative or multidimensional measures of sexual harassment should be developed, as most harassment behaviours do not occur in isolation (Gruber et al. 1996, Fitzgerald et al. 1995a; for examples, see Schneider et al. 1997, Macmillan et al. 1996). Third, researchers other than the creators of the SEQ and the ISH need to perform reliability and validity tests on these measures (e.g., Stockdale & Hope 1997). These two measurement schemes represent the first step in developing standard harassment measures. [. . .] And finally, as is discussed in the next section, more attention is needed to the range of harassing behaviours included in sexual harassment measures. [. . .] What constitutes sexual harassment may be subjective, based on an individual's perceptions or the organizational context in which she works. In the following section, I discuss some of the implications of the subjective nature of sexual harassment for using survey data.

Is It Sexual Harassment? Labelling Sexual Behaviours

Although survey respondents often report being the targets of unwanted sexual behaviours, many respondents do not define these behaviours as sexual harassment (e.g., Fitzgerald et al. 1997b). Yet, when using survey responses, it is common for researchers to define all unwanted sexual behaviours as sexual harassment, whether the respondent defines them as such (see Gruber 1998 for notable exception). This phenomenon has led some to focus on the gap between objective and subjective perceptions of harassment or the likelihood respondents will label their experiences as sexual harassment (e.g., Vaux 1993, Folgero & Fjeldstad 1995, Williams 1997).

Some explanations are offered as to why respondents may be unwilling to label, or be more sensitive to, certain types of unwanted sexual behaviour. First, social psychologists find women and men both with more traditional sex role attitudes label fewer behaviours as sexual harassment (e.g., Johnson et al. 1991, Tangri & Hayes 1997). In terms of experiencing harassment though, this finding is not consistent across all work contexts (Rosenberg et al., 1993). Second, individual differences such as sexual orientation, race, and the organizational position of the harasser influence the self-labelling of harassment experiences (Giuffre & Williams 1994). Heterosexual norms in workplaces make sexual interaction between coworkers of the same race and sexual orientation seem less problematic. It is when sexual interaction crosses racial, sexual orientation, or organizational power lines that targets of the behaviour are more likely to label their experiences as sexual harassment. Third, the characteristics of the harassment matter as targets of harassment are more likely to label severe, pervasive, or frequent sexual behaviours as sexual harassment (Stockdale et al. 1995).[2]

Recent qualitative studies highlight how organizational culture contributes to employees' willingness and ability to label sexual behaviours as sexual harassment (e.g., Folgero & Fjeldstad 1995). In some masculine work cultures, women, in order to be seen as competent and as team players, may not define their experiences as sexual harassment (Collinson & Collinson 1996). As well, in other workplaces, sexual behaviours commonly understood as sexual harassment may in fact be requirements of the job (Williams 1997:4). That is, organizations may sanction or mandate the sexualized treatment of workers. For example, management may require waitresses to wear tight skirts (Loe 1996), customers in bars may be encouraged to 'talk dirty' to waitresses by ordering drinks with sexually loaded names like 'Screaming Orgasm' (Williams 1997:22; Giuffre & Williams 1994:387), or for new female coal miners sexualized hazing rituals may be considered part of their initiation into workgroups (e.g., Yount 1991).

In these sexually charged or permissive work cultures, degrading and sexual behaviours become an 'institutionalized' component of work and, thus, may not be considered sexual harassment (Williams 1997). This process of institutionalization involves the normalization of sexual harassment, whereby 'individual workers may not define their experiences as sexual harassment, even if they feel sexually degraded by them' (Williams 1997:26, Loe 1996).

[. . .]

This highlights an underlying tension between survey research and qualitative methods when studying sexual harassment. Williams (1997) criticizes survey research for emphasizing the harassment of women by men and for overlooking how heterosexual norms in organizations exploit workers' sexuality and may lead to same-sex harassment. Yet, it is not survey methods *per se* that are the problem. Just as the courts are slow to take up forms of harassment that do not fit 'our top-down, male-female sexual come-on image of harassment' (Schultz 1998a, 1998b), so are social science researchers. We know that workers tolerated hostile work environments long before these environments were recognized as such legally (Fitzgerald et al. 1997b:7). And, as qualitative research illustrates, workers continue to tolerate same-sex harassment and organizationally sanctioned harassment not captured in current measurement schemes. As we gain a better understanding of the range and context of unwanted sexual behaviours, sexual harassment's effective empirical measurement becomes not only more critical but more complicated.

Theories and Explanations of Sexual Harassment

If there is a weakness in studies of sexual harassment, it is the lack of systematic theoretical explanations for why sexual harassment occurs. Grounded in feminist, social psychological, and psychological frameworks, several models exist that break explanations of harassment into the primary correlates of sexual harassment (e.g., target characteristics, occupational/organizational characteristics, and offender characteristics) and theoretical explanations of sexual harassment (e.g.,

sex role spillover and power-dominance models, e.g., Stockdale 1996, Fitzgerald & Shullman 1993, Hulin et al. 1996). In the following section, I outline the most prominent explanations and theories of sexual harassment found in sociological analyses of sexual harassment.

Societal-Level Explanations and the Socio-cultural Model

The socio-cultural model posits that sexual harassment is a product of culturally legitimated power and status differences between men and women (Farley 1978, MacKinnon 1979). Socio-cultural explanations fit with the 'feminist' or 'dominance' model that emphasizes sexual harassment's origins in patriarchal society (e.g., MacKinnon 1979, Cockburn 1991, Stanko 1985, Rospenda et al. 1998, Padavic & Orcutt 1997). Sexual harassment is perceived to be an outgrowth of the gender socialization process and is a mechanism by which men assert power and dominance over women both at work and in society (Tangri et al. 1982). Proponents of this approach emphasize gender as a key predictor of who is at risk of harassment, in light of empirical evidence that women experience more harassment than men (Tangri et al. 1982, Gutek 1985, US MPSB 1981).

The socio-cultural model also emphasizes how individual-level correlates, such as age and marital status, mediate women's low status and lack of socio-cultural power (e.g., Kauppinen-Toropainen & Gruber 1993, Padavic & Orcutt 1997). For example, single women and young women may be viewed as more available for sexual interaction than do other women, and hence, they may experience higher levels of sexual harassment than other women (e.g., Gruber & Bjorn 1982, Lafontaine & Tredeau 1986, US MSPB 1981). Some argue that age not only captures the 'impact of youth per se' but is also a proxy for low seniority or poor job status (Gruber 1998:312). Individual-level correlates of age and marital status are mediated by occupational context (Kauppinen-Toropainen & Gruber 1993). For example, among older women in the United States, those who are professionals experience less harassment than do non-professional women (Kauppinen-Toropainen & Gruber 1993).

Organizational-Level Explanations

A diverse set of explanations for sexual harassment focus on the role of organizations, ranging from theoretical explanations of power to descriptions of organizational characteristics that are correlated with the likelihood of sexual harassment. Underlying many of these explanations are the ways power differences in organizations promote sexual harassment and perpetuate inequality (Rospenda et al. 1998:42).

Formal and Informal Organizational Power

Some organizational models emphasize how inequities in structural or formal power in organizations lead to harassment. Individuals with formal organizational power, such as managers, may use their position to harass subordinates (e.g., Benson & Thomson 1982, MacKinnon 1979). An underlying assumption is that it is men holding managerial positions who are harassing women subordinates. However, research showing that harassers are more likely to be coworkers (e.g., Gutek 1985) and that harassers may sometimes be subordinates (Grauerholz 1989, McKinney 1994, Rospenda et al. 1998) highlights the limitations of such explanations.

Most researchers agree that conceptualizations of organizational power must be broadened to include interpersonal modes of power (see Cleveland & Kerst 1993 for extensive review; Grauerholz 1996). For example, coworkers with individual or informal sources of power, such as personality, expertise, and access to critical information, may be more likely to engage in harassment than others (Cleveland & Kerst 1993). In terms of contrapower harassment, whereby a subordinate harasses someone with formal organizational power, socio-cultural power may compensate for the lack of organizational power (e.g., McKinney 1990, 1992). Rospenda and associates illustrate how socio-cultural and interpersonal forms of power are used by perpetrators to subordinate the victim's organizational power, as seen in the case of a white female senior faculty member harassed by a black administrator (1998:55). While formal organizational power still has contextualized effects in terms of who is harassed and how targets react to their harassment, it is clear that harassment studies need to incorporate the multiple hierarchies of power which 'can make people simultaneously powerful and powerless in relation to others' (Miller 1997:50). By doing so, we move away from always conceptualizing the harasser as male and powerful and the target as female and powerless.

Numerical and Normative Dominance

Numerically skewed sex ratios in work situations, such as female-dominated and male-dominated work groups, play a prominent role in explanations of sexual harassment. Some approaches focus on the gender roles associated with female- and male-dominated work situations (e.g., sex role spillover), while others discuss the issue in terms of numerical dominance of males over females in certain workplaces (contact hypothesis). In this review, I focus on the process by which numerically skewed work situations are linked to sexual harassment. In the following two sections, I discuss the primary ways normative dominance (gender roles) and numerical dominance (workgroup gender ratios) in work situations are used to explain the occurrence of sexual harassment (e.g., Gruber 1998).

Sex Role Spillover

Sex role spillover theory is considered one of the primary theories of sexual harassment (Tangri & Hayes 1997, Stockdale 1996). According to Gutek, when women's gender roles take precedence over their work roles, sex role 'spillover' occurs (Gutek & Morasch 1982, Gutek 1985). This happens most often when the gender ratio is heavily skewed toward either men or women because skewed situations render 'femaleness' more salient and visible (Kanter 1977, Stockdale 1996a:10). Under these circumstances, sexual harassment is more likely. For example, in female-dominated work situations, feminine roles become equated with the job, such as expectations that nurses are 'nurturing' or waitresses are 'sexy' (Gutek 1985, Nieva & Gutek 1981). In male-dominated workplaces, where women are competing with men for jobs, men attempt to emphasize women coworkers' status as women over their status as workers (DiTomaso 1989:88). Doing this allows men to put women in their 'proper' subordinate position. Overall, sex role spillover theory highlights how gender-based normative expectations prevail in numerically skewed work situations.

The Contact Hypothesis and Numerical Dominance

The contact hypothesis (Gutek et al. 1990, Gruber 1998) views harassment as a function of the contact between men and women in the workplace, rather than emphasizing the gender role expectations associated with certain jobs. Here, numerical dominance is seen as distinct from, though interrelated to, normative dominance (Gruber 1998). For example, a female secretary who works in an environment numerically dominated by males and who has more contact with men, will experience more severe harassment than her counterparts in integrated workplaces or those numerically dominated by females

(e.g., Gutek et al. 1990, Gruber 1997). Direct support for the contact hypothesis is found when measures of contact are based on respondents' reports of daily contact with men as opposed to occupational sex ratios (e.g., Kauppinen-Toropainen & Gruber 1993, Gutek et al. 1990, Gruber 1998).

Complicating numerical dominance are male-dominated or 'doubly-male' workgroups where both numerical and normative dominance are present. In these 'male preserves' (see Gruber 1997 for overview; Gruber 1998, Martin 1980, DiTomaso 1989) or 'masculine job gender contexts' (Hulin et al. 1996), 'the traditionality of an *occupation* creates a work culture that is an extension of male culture, and numerical dominance of the *workplace* by men heightens the visibility of, and hostility toward, women workers who are perceived as violating men's territory' (Gruber 1998:303). Ultimately this leads to extensive and aggressive forms of sexual harassment not usually found in other workgroups (e.g., Stanko 1985, Martin & Jurik 1996).

[. . .]

Organizational Culture

Because organizational culture represents the norms of appropriate behaviour and values held by organizational members (Hall 1994), it is not surprising researchers are turning to culture to explain why sexual harassment occurs in some organizations and not in others (e.g., Kauppinen-Toropainen & Gruber 1993, Hulin et al. 1996, Pryor et al. 1993). Early on, Gutek (1985) proposed that 'unprofessional' or disorganized ambiances, such as antagonistic relationships between coworkers or drinking on the job, would increase the likelihood of sexual harassment of women. More recently, Ragins & Scandura (1995) discuss how the physical nature of blue-collar work promotes a 'physical culture' resulting in more aggressive forms of sexual harassment (p. 449).

Organizational cultures that tolerate sexual harassment are linked to increased incidents of sexual harassment (e.g., Hulin et al. 1996, Pryor et al. 1993). Pryor and associates' (1993) person/situation framework illustrates how men who are highly likely to sexually harass are encouraged to do so by 'local' norms of sexual and aggressive behaviours supported by supervisors and peers. In contrast, proactive sexual harassment policies, or attempts to modify the workplace culture through training sessions and official complaint procedures, are particularly effective for reducing hostile environment harassment (Gruber 1998).

The Organization of Work

Relatively few studies incorporate how the technical organization of work, such as task characteristics, interacts with the social organization of work (e.g., DiTomaso 1989, Kauppinen-Toropainen & Gruber 1993, Lach & Gwartney-Gibbs 1993). In part, this gap is due to the influence of psychologists on the area and their predominant interest in individuals and their interactions (e.g., Stockdale 1996, Hulin et al. 1996). Looking at the organization of work, alienating work conditions, such as physically demanding or repetitive jobs, may be partly responsible for women's experiences of sexual harassment in male-typed jobs. Some researchers see men's harassment of women and sexual horseplay in the workplace as an attempt to forge human contact and to overcome boring work (e.g., Hearn & Parkin 1987:85; Hearn 1985). On the other hand, engaging in sexually aggressive behaviour and harassment may be an act of resistance that demonstrates opposition to women's presence in traditionally male jobs (e.g., Miller 1997, Hearn & Parkin 1987). As Cockburn reminds us, 'men's morale and solidarity in their struggle against the boss is sometimes achieved directly at the expense of women' (1991:148).

Gendered Organizations and Doing Gender

Recent attention by sexual harassment researchers to the gendered processes of organizations (e.g., Acker 1990) and to 'doing gender' (e.g., West & Zimmerman 1987, West & Fenstermaker 1995) has begun to clarify how the organization of work is connected to sexual harassment. As stated by Rogers & Henson (1997:234), 'sexual harassment is about particular constructions of gender, especially organizational imperatives to "do gender" in a particular manner' (Lorber 1994, West & Zimmerman 1987). For example, the deferential behaviour of temporary workers, stemming from the feminized and powerless status of their job, increases workers' vulnerability and potential for experiencing sexual harassment (Rogers & Henson 1997:224; see also Folgero & Fjeldstad 1995). Not surprising, studies that focus on the socially constructed nature of sexual harassment are qualitative. This research represents an important advance in the field by moving beyond variables of sex-ratios and organizational culture to explain sexual harassment, drawing our attention to how organizational norms of heterosexuality and power construct gender and facilitate sexual harassment (e.g., Schneider 1982, Collinson & Collinson 1989, Williams 1997, Rospenda et al. 1998).

[. . .]

Reactions to Sexual Harassment

Research suggests that women's responses to sexual harassment fall along a continuum of avoidance, diffusion, negotiation, and confrontation (Gruber 1989). Most women do not report their experiences of sexual harassment. Instead they are more likely to ignore the harassment (Benson & Thomson 1982, Cochran et al. 1997, Gruber & Bjorn 1982, Loy & Stewart 1984), to deflect the harassment by joking or going along with it (Gutek 1985, US MSPB 1981, 1987), or to avoid the harasser (Cochran et al. 1997, Culbertson et al. 1992, Gutek 1985, Schneider 1991; see Yoder & Aniakudo 1995 for exception). Women do not report harassment for a variety of reasons, ranging from a fear of retaliation or disbelief to a fear of losing ones' job or making the situation worse (Loy & Stewart 1984, Cochran et al. 1997, Schneider 1991, Fitzgerald et al. 1995b). Assertive or direct responses tend to occur in a variety of contexts, such as when the harassment is severe (Brooks & Perot 1991, Cochran et al. 1997, Gutek & Koss 1993, Livingston 1982, US MSPB 1981); when the harasser is not a supervisor (Gruber & Smith 1995); when policies and procedures are in place to combat sexual harassment (Gruber & Smith 1995); when the percentage of women in an occupation is either at parity with men or a threatening minority (Gruber & Bjorn 1986, Gruber & Smith 1995); and, finally, when the harassment target holds feminist attitudes (Gruber & Smith 1995, Brooks & Perot 1991). Respondents who are more tolerant of sexual harassment are less likely to see their experiences as severe and hence respond less assertively (Cochran et al. 1997. [. . .]

Qualitative studies suggest that responses to sexual harassment are grounded in the organization of power relations at work. Women and men temporary workers, with little control over employment assignments, have little recourse but to tolerate or ignore the harassment if they wish to continue receiving work assignments (Rogers & Henson 1997:230). On the other hand, African-American women firefighters, already considered outsiders and marginalized due to their race and gender, believe they have nothing to lose from fighting back against sexual harassment and confronting their harassers (Yoder & Aniakudo 1995). These studies support Williams' (1997) argument for contextualizing our understanding of sexual harassment. Although both temporary workers and African-American women firefighters are marginalized or vulnerable workers, they respond to sexual harassment in dramatically different ways.

Consequences of Sexual Harassment

Numerous studies outline the job-related, psychological, and somatic health consequences of sexual harassment. In terms of job consequences, sexual harassment is found to result in lowered morale, absenteeism (US MSPB 1981, 1987), decreased job satisfaction (Gruber 1992), decreased perception of equal opportunity (Newell et al. 1995), and damaged interpersonal work-relationships (Culbertson et al. 1992, DiTomaso 1989, Gutek 1985). Some victims are forced to quit or they lose their jobs (Coles 1986, Crull 1982, Gutek 1985, US MSPB 1981, 1987). Organizations also pay a price for harassment in terms of lost productivity, job turnover, and medical claims (US MSPB 1987). The psychological and physical health consequences of sexual harassment are also well-documented. Sexual harassment is linked to anxiety, depression, sleep disturbances, nausea, stress, and headaches (Crull 1982, Fitzgerald 1993, Gutek & Koss 1993).

[. . .]

Studying Sexual Harassment: An Agenda for the Future
Longitudinal Research and Multiplicity Sampling

Sexual harassment research in the past 10 years has moved away from a focus on prevalence rates to more sophisticated multivariate analyses of the antecedents and consequences of sexual harassment (e.g., Padavid & Orcutt 1997). Restricting many of the empirical analyses of harassment is a reliance on cross-sectional survey data. One positive trend away from this is the movement toward longitudinal data collection (e.g., Richman et al. 1997) because an understanding of the organizational context of harassment requires longitudinal data. For example, current analyses of the effect of organizational culture generally rely on respondents' perceptions of culture *after* they were sexually harassed. Without longitudinal data, the meaning behind the correlation between organizational tolerance and incidences of sexual harassment is unclear (Pryor et al. 1993).

Organizational researchers are also turning to multiplicity or 'bottom-up' sampling techniques to create samples linked across macro and micro levels (e.g., Parcel et al. 1991:74, Kalleberg et al. 1996). Future surveys of sexual harassment should incorporate this kind of sampling. By linking interviews with individuals, supervisors, and human resource managers, multiplicity sampling could provide data on the relationship between sexual harassment, organizational policies and context, and job-related outcomes. It is time for the use of more sophisticated data collection techniques if we are to continue to build our theoretical and empirical understandings.

Uncovering Gendered Processes: The Need for Qualitative Research

To counter the reliance on survey methods, a growing number of researchers are calling for the use of qualitative methods to study sexual harassment (Arvey & Cavanaugh 1995, Williams 1997). This is partly due to a belief that important concepts and processes are not adequately captured by survey items. For example, much is written about the connection between sexual harassment

and the gendered nature of organizations in terms of how 'organizational forms structure and are themselves structured by gender' (Savage & Witz 1992:8, Acker 1990, Adkins 1992). Yet, as discussed earlier, these gendered processes are difficult to capture using discrete survey items. As a result, researchers often use measures of gender roles and management's tolerance for sexual harassment as proxies for gendered processes existing in organizations. These measures do not tap the depth or identify the subtle ways in which organizational processes may 'institutionalize' sexual harassment as part of the job. As well, qualitative research is capable of uncovering the ambiguity that surrounds sexuality and sexual harassment in organizations (Williams 1997).

Race and Sexual Harassment

Several overviews comment on the paucity of research concerning sexual harassment, race, and ethnicity (e.g., Murrell 1996, Fitzgerald & Shullman 1993, Barak 1997). Much of this discussion is conceptual with an emphasis on the distinction between sexism and 'sexual racism' (e.g., Murrell 1996:56, Collins 1990) and on how racialized norms of sexual attractiveness limit job opportunities for women of colour (e.g., Williams 1997:29). A few early empirical studies found no overall difference in harassment rates for women of colour and white women (e.g., Gutek 1985, US MSPB 1981). On the other hand, some evidence exists that women of colour experience more severe forms of sexual harassment (e.g., Gruber & Bjorn 1982). Rospenda et al.'s (1998) analysis moves beyond the issue of prevalence to show how race intersects with class and gender in instances of contrapower harassment. For example, they theorize how norms of black masculinity may be a factor in the reluctance of a black male faculty member to report the harassment by a white male secretary (Rospenda et al. 1998:50). In many ways, MacKinnon's quotation cited at the beginning of the article still characterizes the state of research on race and sexual harassment.

Sexual Harassment of Men and Same-Sex Harassment

The sexual harassment of men, as well as same-sex harassment, are understudied phenomena (Vaux 1993, Williams 1997, Fitzgerald et al. 1997). In terms of the sexual harassment of men, Gutek's (1985) study found that men were more likely to interpret 'social-sexual' behaviour as non-threatening, whereas women interpreted the same behaviour as threatening. Men also identify some behaviours as harassing that are not identified by women (Berdahl et al. 1996). These behaviours include those perpetrated by women, such as verbal comments that negatively stereotype men (e.g., 'Men are pigs'). Men also report being labelled as unmasculine (e.g., being called 'fag' or 'pussy') when they do not participate with their male colleagues in jokes about women (Fitzgerald et al. 1997b:24). In order to understand the harassment of men, research on masculinity provides a useful starting point (e.g., Connell 1995).

Related to the sexual harassment of men are issues of same-sex harassment. Not only does the harassment of gays and lesbians need to be considered (e.g., Woods & Lucas 1993, Hall 1989), but the harassment of heterosexual men by heterosexual men should be examined. As discussed elsewhere in this review, studies illustrate how sexuality and 'hyper-masculinity' are part of many organizational cultures (e.g., Williams 1997). Heterosexual norms exclude or sexualize women, but they also constrain the behaviour of men. As others have mentioned, researchers need to incorporate the complexity of sexual exploitation and harassment found in organizations (e.g.,

Vaux 1993). As Williams points out, focusing on the harassment of women by men ignores 'other sexualized power dynamics in the workplace' (1997:33).

Conclusion

This review only touches the surface of many issues with which researchers are currently struggling. Beyond the specific scope of this review, but in need of further study, is the relationship of complaints of sexual harassment to legal and institutional environments. And, similar to research on the 'legalization of the workplace' (e.g., Sutton et al. 1994, Edelman 1992), the organizational adoption of sexual harassment policies and the potential increased regulation of workers' sexual interaction could be examined using insights from institutional approaches. Issues in the study of sexual harassment at work can draw from and inform a variety of sociological perspectives not previously considered.

What we know about sexual harassment is that its definition and occurrence is contextualized by organizational and individual factors. Gender will continue to remain central to the study of harassment, whether conceptualized as quantitative measures of gender ratios or more qualitative understandings of gender roles and gendered organizational processes. At this point, though, no unified theoretical framework has developed for explaining the occurrence of sexual harassment. Recent insights from social constructionists and other analyses of gendered organizations are among the most promising. As researchers move beyond cross-sectional surveys to more advanced survey techniques and more encompassing ethnographic studies, the task of sorting out the effects of gender, individual perceptions, and organizational context on sexual harassment will be assisted. As well, criminological theories are underutilized in the study of sexual harassment. One possible avenue is to incorporate routine activity theory that can provide insight into the interaction between organizational context and the presence of guardians and motivated offenders. The study of sexual harassment is in beginning stages, which means researchers are still struggling with issues related to measurement, data collection, and theoretical development. Yet it is these challenges that make this area one worth pursuing.

Notes

1. Most studies focus on the sexual harassment of women. Men's experiences are an understudied aspect of sexual harassment and are discussed later in this review. This discussion focuses on workplace sexual harassment. Researchers interested in the phenomenon of public harassment are referred to research by Gardner (1995).

2. Much debate exists over whether or not men and women hold different perceptions of sexual harassment. Gender differences in perceptions of harassment tend to disappear when the context of harassment (frequency, severity, and pervasiveness) are considered (Gutek & O'Connor 1995). Gutek (1995) provides a good overview of this issue and concludes that what women and men perceive as harassment, or as more or less severe harassment, is similar.

References

Acker, J. 1990. Hierarchies, jobs, bodies: A theory of gendered organizations. *Gender & Society* 4(2): 139–58.

Adkins, L. 1992. Sexual work and the employment of women in the service industries. In *Gender and Bureaucracy*, eds M. Savage, A. Witz, pp. 207–28. Oxford: Blackwell.

Arvey, R.D., Cavanaugh, M.A. 1995. Using surveys to assess the prevalence of sexual harassment: Some methodological problems. *J. Soc. Issues* 51(1): 39–52.

Barak, A. 1997. Cross-cultural perspectives on sexual harassment. See O'Donohue 1997, pp. 263–300.

Benson, D.J., Thomson, G.E. 1982. Sexual harassment on a university campus: The confluence of authority relations, sexual interest and gender stratification. *Soc. Probl.* 29: 236–51.

Berdahl, J.L., Magley, V.J., Waldo, C.R. 1996. The sexual harassment of men? Exploring the concept with theory and data. *Psychol. Women Q.* 20(4): 527–47.

Brooks, L., Perot, A.R. 1991. Reporting sexual harassment: Exploring a predictive model. *Psychol. Women Q.* 15(1): 31–47.

Cleveland, J.N., Kerst, M.E. 1993. Sexual harassment and perceptions of power: An under-articulated relationship. *J. Voc. Behav.* 42: 49–67.

Cochran, C.C., Frazier, P.A., Olson, A.M. 1997. Predictors of responses to unwanted sexual harassment. *Psychol. Women Q.* 21(2): 207–26.

Cockburn, C. 1991. *In the Way of Women: Men's Resistance to Sex Equality in Organizations.* Ithaca, NY: ILR.

Coles, F.S. 1986. Forced to quit: Sexual harassment complaints and agency response. *Sex Roles* 14: 81–95.

Collins, P.H. 1990. *Black Feminist Thought: Knowledge, Consciousness, and the Politics of Empowerment.* Boston: Irwin Hyman.

Collinson, D., Collinson, M. 1989. Sexuality in the workplace: The domination of men's sexuality. See Hearn et al. 1989, pp. 91–109.

Collinson, M., Collinson, D. 1996. 'It's only Dick': The sexual harassment of women managers in insurance sales. *Work, Employment & Society* 10(1): 29–56.

Connell, R.W. 1995. *Masculinities.* Berkeley: Univ. Calif. Press.

Crull, P. 1982. Stress effects of sexual harassment on the job: Implications for counseling. *Am. J. Orthopsychiatry* 52: 539–44.

Culbertson, A.L., Rosenfeld, P., Booth-Kewley, S., Magnusson, P. 1992. *Assessment of Sexual Harassment in the Navy: Results of the 1989 Navy-wide Survey.* San Diego, CA: Navy Personnel Res. Dev. Ctr.

DiTomaso, N. 1989. Sexuality in the workplace: Discrimination and harassment. See Hearn et al. 1989, pp. 71–90.

Edelman, L.B. 1992. Legal ambiguity and symbolic structures: Organizational mediation of civil rights law. *Am. J. Sociol.* 97(6): 1531–76.

Farley, L. 1978. *Sexual Shakedown: The Sexual Harassment of Women on the Job.* New York: McGraw-Hill.

Fitzgerald, L.F. 1993. Sexual harassment: Violence against women in the workplace. *Am. Psychol.* 48:1070–76.

Fitzgerald, L.F., Drasgow, F., Hulin, C., Gelfand, M., Magley, V. 1997a. The antecedents and consequences of sexual harassment in organizations. *J. Appl. Psychol.* 82(2): 578–89.

Fitzgerald, L.F., Gefland, M., Drasgow, R. 1995a. Measuring sexual harassment: Theoretical and psychometric advances. *Basic and Appl. Soc. Psychol.* 17(4): 425–45.

Fitzgerald, L.F., Shullman, S., 1993. Sexual harassment: A research agenda for the 1990s. *J. Voc. Behav.* 42: 5–27.

Fitzgerald, L.F., Shullman, S., Bailey, N., Richards, M., Sweeker, J., et al. 1988. The incidence and dimensions of sexual harassment in academia and the workplace. *J. Voc. Behav.* 32: 152–75.

Fitzgerald, L.F., Swan, S., Fischer, K. 1995b. Why didn't she just report him? The psychological and legal implications of women's responses to sexual harassment. *J. Soc. Issues* 51(l): 117–38.

Fitzgerald, L.F., Swan, S., Magley, V. 1997b. But was it really sexual harassment? Legal behavioral and psychological definitions of the workplace victimization of women. See O'Donohue 1997, pp. 5–28.

Folgero, I.S., Fjeldstad, I.H. 1995. On duty-off guard: Cultural norms and sexual harassment in service organizations. *Org. Stud.* 16(2): 299–313.

Gardner, C.B. 1995. *Passing By: Gender and Public Harassment.* Berkeley: Univ. Calif. Press.

Giuffre, P.A., Williams, C.L. 1994. Boundary lines: Labeling sexual harassment in restaurants. *Gender & Soc.* 8: 378–401.

Grauerholz, E. 1989. Sexual harassment of women professors by students: Exploring the dynamics of power, authority and gender in a university setting. *Sex Roles* 21(11/12): 789–801.

———. 1996. Sexual harassment in the academy: The case of women professors. See Stockdale 1996, 5: 29–50.

Gruber, J.E. 1989. How women handle sexual harassment: A literature review. *Sociol. Soc. Res.* 74: 3–9.

———. 1990. Methodological problems and policy implications in sexual harassment research. *Pop. Res. Policy Rev.* 9: 235–54.

———. 1992. A typology of personal and environmental sexual harassment: Research and policy implications from the 1990s. *Sex Roles* 22: 447–64.

———. 1997. An epidemiology of sexual harassment: Evidence from North America and Europe. See O'Donohue 1997, pp. 84–98.

———. 1998. The impact of male work environments and organizational policies on women's experiences of sexual harassment. *Gender & Soc.* 12(3): 301–20.

Gruber, J.E., Bjorn, L. 1982. Blue-collar blues: The sexual harassment of women autoworkers. *Work Occup.* 9(Aug.): 271–98.

———. 1986. Women's responses to sexual harassment: An analysis of socio-cultural, organizational, and personal resource models. *Soc. Sci. Q.* 67: 814–26.

Gruber, J.E., Kauppinen-Toropainen, K., Smith, M. 1996. Sexual harassment types and severity: Linking research and policy. See Stockdale l996, pp. 151–73.

Gruber, J.E., Smith, M. 1995. Women's responses to sexual harassment: A multivariate analysis. *Basic Appl. Soc. Psychol.* 17: 543–62.

Gutek, B.A. 1985. *Sex and the Workplace: The Impact of Sexual Behavior and Harassment on Women, Men, and Organizations.* San Francisco: Jossey-Bass.

———. 1995. How subjective is sexual harassment? An examination of rater effects. *Basic Appl. Soc. Psychol.* 17(4): 447–67.

Gutek, B.A., Cohen, A.G. 1987. Sex ratios, sex role spillover and sex at work: A comparison of men's and women's experiences. *Hum. Relat.* 40(2): 97–115.

Gutek, B.A., Cohen, A.G., Konrad, A.M. 1990. Predicting social–sexual behavior at work: A contact hypothesis. *Acad. Mgmt. J.* 33: 560–77.

Gutek, B.A., Koss, M. 1993. Changed women and changed organizations: Consequences and coping with sexual harassment. *J. Voc. Behav.* 42: 28–48.

Gutek, B.A., Morasch, B. 1982. Sex ratios, sex-role spillover, and sexual harassment of women at work. *J. Soc. Issues* 38: 55–74.

Gutek, B.A., O'Connor, M. 1995. The empirical basis for the reasonable woman standard. *J. Soc. Issues* 51: 151–66.

Hall, M. 1989. Private experiences in the public domain: Lesbians in organizations. See Hearn et al. 1989, pp. 125–38.

Hall, R.H. 1994. *Sociology of Work: Perspectives, Analyses, and Issues.* Thousand Oaks: Pine Forge.

Hearn, J. 1985. Men's sexuality at work. In *The Sexuality of Men,* eds A. Metcalf, M. Humphries, pp. 110–28. London: Pluto.

Hearn, J., Parkin, W. 1987. *'Sex' at 'Work': The Power and Paradox of Organisation Sexuality.* Brighton: Wheatsheaf.

Hearn, J., Sheppard, D.L., Tancred-Sheriff, P., Burrell, G. 1989. *The Sexuality of Organization.* London: Sage.

Holloway, W., Jefferson, T. 1996. PC or not PC: Sexual harassment and the question of ambivalence. *Hum. Relat.* 49(3): 373–93.

Hulin, C., Fitzgerald, L.F., Drasgow, F. 1996. Organizational influences on sexual harassment. See Stockdale 1996, pp. 127–51.

Johnson, C.B., Stockdale, M.S., Saal, F.E. 1991. Persistence of men's misperceptions of friendly cues across a variety of interpersonal encounters. *Psychol. Women Q.* 15: 463–75.

Kalleberg, A.D., Knocke, P.V., Marsden, P.V., Spaeth, J.L. 1996. *Organizations in America: Analyzing Their Structures and Human Resource Practices.* Thousand Oaks, CA: Sage.

Kanter, R.M. 1977. *Men and Women of the Corporation.* New York: Basic Books.

Kauppinen-Toropainen, K., Gruber, J.E. 1993. Antecedents and outcomes of woman-unfriendly experiences. *Psychol. Women Q.* 17: 421–56.

Lach, D.H., Gwartney-Gibbs, P.A. 1993. Sociological perspectives on sexual harassment and workplace dispute resolution. *J. Voc. Behav.* 42: 102–15.

Lafontaine, E., Tredeau, L. 1986. The frequency, sources and correlates of sexual harassment among women in traditional male occupations. *Sex Roles* 15(Oct.): 433–42.

Livingston, J. 1982. Responses to sexual harassment on the job: Legal, organizational, and individual actions. *J. Soc. Issues* 38: 5–22.

Loe, M. 1996. Working for men—at the intersection of power, gender, and sexuality. *Sociol. Inquiry* 66(4): 399–421.

Lorber, J. 1994. *Paradoxes of Gender*. New Haven, CT: Yale Univ. Press.

Loy, P., Stewart, L. 1984. The extent and effects of the sexual harassment of working women. *Sociol. Focus* 17: 31–43.

MacKinnon, C. 1979. *Sexual Harassment of Working Women*. New Haven, CT: Yale Univ. Press.

———. 1987. *Feminism Unmodified: Discourses on Life and Law*. Cambridge, MA: Harvard Univ. Press.

Macmillan, R., Nierobisz, A., Welsh, S. 1996. *Gender in Public: Harassment and Fear of Crime among Women*. Pres. Am. Sociol. Assoc. Meet., New York.

Martin, S. 1980. *Breaking and Entering: Policewomen on Patrol*. Berkeley: Univ. Calif. Press.

Martin, S., Jurik, N. 1996. *Doing Justice, Doing Gender*. Thousand Oaks, CA: Sage.

McKinney, K. 1990. Sexual harassment of university faculty by colleagues and students. *Sex Roles* 23: 421–38.

———. 1992. Contrapower sexual harassment: The effects of student sex and type of behavior on faculty perceptions. *Sex Roles* 27(11–12): 627–43.

———. 1994. Sexual harassment and college faculty members. *Deviant Behav.* 15(2): 171–91.

Miller, L.L. 1997. Not just weapons of the weak: Gender harassment as a form of protest for Army men. *Soc. Psychol. Q.* 60(1): 32–51.

Murrell, A.J. 1996. Sexual harassment and women of color: Issues, challenges, and future directions. See Stockdale 1996, pp. 51–66.

Newell, C.E., Rosenfeld, P., Culbertson, A.L. 1995. Sexual harassment experiences and equal opportunity perceptions of Navy women. *Sex Roles* 32(3–4): 159–68.

Nieva, V.F., Gutek, B.A. 1981. *Women and Work: A Psychological Perspective*. New York: Praeger.

O'Donohue, W. 1997. *Sexual Harassment: Theory, Research and Treatment*. New York: Allyn & Bacon.

Padavid, I., Orcutt, J.D. 1997. Perceptions of sexual harassment in the Florida legal system: A comparison of dominance and spillover explanations. *Gender Soc.* 11(5): 682–98.

Parcel, T.L., Kaufman, R.L., Jolly, L. 1991. Going up the ladder: Multiplicity sampling to create linked macro-to-micro organizational samples. *Social. Methodol.* 21: 43–79.

Pryor, J. 1987. Sexual harassment proclivities in men. *Sex Roles* 17: 269–90.

Pryor, J., Lavite, C., Stoller, L. 1993. A social psychological analysis of sexual harassment: The person/situation interaction. *J. Voc. Behav.* 42: 68–83.

Ragins, B.R., Scandura, T.A. 1995. Antecedents and work-related correlates of reported sexual harassment: An empirical investigation of competing hypotheses. *Sex Roles* 32(7–8): 429–55.

Reskin, B., Padavic, I. 1994. *Women and Men at Work*. Thousand Oaks, CA: Pine Forge.

Richman, J.A., Rospenda, K.M., Nawyn, S.J., Flaherty, J.A. 1997. Workplace harassment and the self-medicalization of distress: A conceptual model and case illustrations. *Cont. Drug Probl.* 24: 179–200.

Rogers, J., Henson, K. 1997. 'Hey, why don't you wear a shorter skirt?' Structural vulnerability and the organization of sexual harassment in temporary clerical employment. *Gender & Soc.* 11(2): 215–37.

Rosenberg, J., Perlstadt, H., Phillips, W.R.F. 1993. Now that we are here: Discrimination, disparagement, and harassment at work and the experience of women lawyers. *Gender & Soc.* 7: 415–33.

Rospenda, K.M., Richman, J.A., Nawyn, S.J. 1998. Doing power: The confluence of gender, race, and class in contrapower sexual harassment. *Gender & Soc.* 12(1): 40–60.

Savage, M., Witz A. 1992. *Gender and Bureaucracy*. Oxford: Blackwell.

Schneider, B.E. 1982. Consciousness about sexual harassment among heterosexual and lesbian women workers. *J. Soc. Issues* 38(4): 75–98.

———. 1991. Put up or shut up: Workplace sexual assaults. *Gender & Soc.* 5: 533–48.

Schneider, K., Swan, S., Fitzgerald, L.F. 1997. Job-related and psychological effects of sexual harassment in the workplace: Empirical evidence from two organizations. *J. Appl. Psychol.* 82: 401–15.

Schultz, V. 1998a. Sex is the least of it: Let's focus harassment law on work, not sex. *The Nation*, May 25.

———. 1998b. Reconceptualizing sexual harassment. *Yale Law Rev.* 107: 1683–805.

Stanko, E.A. 1985. *Intimate Intrusions: Women's Experience of Male Violence*. Boston: Routledge & Kegan Paul.

Stockdale, M.S. 1996. *Sexual Harassment in the Workplace: Perspectives, Frontiers and Response Strategies*, Vol. 5, Women and Work Series. Thousand Oaks, CA: Sage.

———. 1996a. What we know and what we need to learn about sexual harassment. See Stockdale 1996, pp. 3–25.

Stockdale, M.S., Hope, K.G. 1997. Confirmatory factor analysis of the U.S. Merit System's Protection Board's survey of sexual harassment: The fit of a three-factor model. *J. Voc. Behav.* 51: 338–57.

Stockdale, M.S., Vaux, A., Cashin, J. 1995. Acknowledging sexual harassment: A test of alternative models. *Basic Appl. Soc. Psychol.* 17: 469–96.

Sutton, J.R., Dobbin, F., Meyer, J.W., Scott, W.R. 1994. The legalization of the workplace. *Am. J. Sociol.* 99: 944–71.

Tangri, S., Burt, M., Johnson, L. 1982. Sexual harassment at work: Three explanatory models. *J. Soc. Issues* 38(Winter): 33–54.

Tangri, S., Hayes, S.M. 1997. Theories of sexual harassment. See O'Donohue, pp. 99–111.

Terpstra, D.E., Baker, D.D. 1989. The identification and classification of reactions to sexual harassment. *J. Org. Behav.* 10: 1–14.

US Equal Employment Opportunity Commission (US EEOC). 1980. Guidelines on discrimination because of sex. *Fed Reg.* 43: 74676–7.

US Merit System Protection Board (US MSPB). 1981. *Sexual Harassment in the Workplace: Is It a Problem?* Washington, DC: US Gen. Post Off.

———. 1987. *Sexual Harassment of Federal Workers: An Update.* Washington, DC: US GPO.

Vaux A. 1993. Paradigmatic assumptions in sexual harassment research: Being guided without being misled. *J. Voc. Behav.* 42: 116–35.

Welsh, S., Nierobisz, A. 1997. How prevalent is sexual harassment? A research note on measuring sexual harassment in Canada. *Can. J. Sociol.* 22(4): 505–22.

West, C., Fenstermaker, S. 1995. Doing difference. *Gender & Soc.* 9: 8–37.

West, C., Zimmerman, D.H. 1987. Doing gender. *Gender & Soc.* 1: 125–51.

Williams, C. 1997. Sexual harassment in organizations: A critique of current research and policy. *Sexuality Culture* 1: 19–43.

Woods, J.D., Lucas, J.H. 1993. *The Corporate Closet: The Professional Lives of Gay Men in America.* New York: Free Press.

Yoder, J, Aniakudo P. 1995. The response of African-American women firefighters to gender harassment at work. *Sex Roles* 32(3–4): 125–37.

Yount, K. 1991. Ladies, flirts, and tomboys: Strategies for managing sexual harassment in an underground coal mine. *J. Cant. Ethnogr.* 19: 396–422.

Bisexuality: Coping with Sexual Boundaries

Mariana Valverde

Ruth is 26, single, and a strong feminist. While she was attending university on the West Coast, she discovered feminism and almost simultaneously got drawn into a campus feminist group which turned out to be 100 per cent lesbian. At first she was a bit shocked. But soon she began to see the world through lesbian eyes, and it did not take long before she was flirting quite openly with Kate, a lesbian whom she thought might be interested in 'initiating' her. At first Kate was not receptive, not wanting to get involved with such a greenhorn, but Ruth's persistence paid off. The two women had a passionate affair that lasted eight months—until Kate's ex-lover returned from a year of study in Montreal and wooed Kate back. Ruth was very hurt but she played it cool. A year and two meaningless flings later, she left to go back East. There, living in a small Ontario town, she more or less forgot about her lesbianism, and a few months after moving back she got involved with a male musician. She told him something of her relationship with Kate, but he did not take it seriously, and simply said,

'Oh don't worry, it doesn't bother me.' So she did not bring it up again. She still subscribed to a couple of lesbian publications, and when they came in the mail she made a point of putting them where her male lover would not see them, without thinking about why.

Lynn is a lesbian, and her friend Laurie, who is a member of the same women's group, is bisexual. When they found that their friendship was quickly acquiring a sexual tinge, they both got a little frightened, and without talking to each other, both pondered a series of questions: How would this affect their work in the group? What about Lynn's ex-lover, who was also in the same group? What about Laurie's male lover? Would Laurie know how to manage two completely different relationships in two different worlds? And would Lynn not be too vulnerable?

Laurie talked only to her male lover before entering into the relationship. He accepted it as part of life with a feminist woman. Lynn talked to a few of her friends, who all said, 'Maybe a fling would be all right, but if you get in too deep it could be terrible; she'll ditch you for a man when the going gets rough.' But Lynn didn't think Laurie was like that. And she had too much of a crush on her to be able to stop herself.

Against all predictions, the relationship not only began but it prospered. If there was a women's event on Friday night Lynn and Laurie would go together, and then Laurie would be with her male lover on Saturday while Lynn went out with her other friends. Lynn found herself being closely questioned by all her lesbian friends, who thought it was too good to last.

But it wasn't. It lasted . . . until Lynn herself, whose views on men had undergone quite a drastic change for the better since getting to know (indirectly) Laurie's male lover, began to feel herself getting a crush on a heterosexual male friend. She blocked it for several months, thinking that it was just a phase and that she would get over it; after all, she was quite happy in her relationship with Laurie. By the crush refused to go away. She still spoke as a lesbian, wore lesbian buttons, socialized with her lesbian friends . . . but she had a secret crush on a man. Finally, she decided to tell Laurie about it.

Laurie said, 'Well, I'm certainly in no position to prevent you from having other relationships, especially with men. But it's funny you should get a crush on a man now; I have been thinking that I am probably a lesbian, or mostly a lesbian, anyway. . . .'

Ana comes from a working-class Italian family. She is 31 and divorced, and has a six-year-old boy. She doesn't want to get seriously involved with anyone, partly because her son had a hard time with the divorce and she thinks it would not be good if he got attached to somebody else, only to see that connection vanish. She has had two affairs with women in the last few years, one during a holiday in which she had left her son with his father, and one in a semi-surreptitious manner. She didn't want her son to find out and tell

his father about the strange woman in mommy's bedroom. At present Ana is attracted both to men and to women, and knows she could easily get into a relationship with either. But the lesbians she knows are wary of bisexuals; and the men she knows would probably freak out at the thought of her lesbian side, even if they pretended to be cool about it. She feels caught in a net. She hates having to be deceptive; even more, she hates having to *feel* devious and deceptive just because she is bisexual.

The women described above are all in some sense bisexual, but only Ana and Laurie think of themselves in those terms. Ruth might be perceived by some lesbians as a traitor, a 'true' lesbian who went straight because it was more convenient. Others might describe her as bisexual or as 'really' straight. And as for Lynn and Laurie, who knows? Underlying these opinions and judgments is the myth that everyone is 'really', 'deep down', *either* gay *or* straight—except for a very few people who might be allowed to be 'really' bisexual. This is the myth that we all have some inner core of sexual truth which exists and persists even while our surface behaviour patterns change. Some people think that this inner core is determined biologically by hormones and genes; others think it is determined by early psychological experiences. Those with a heterosexual bias might tend to believe that a particular person is 'really' heterosexual, unless that person protests strongly, while those with gay bias might tend to think that anyone who is in a grey area is 'really' gay. The debate about whether person X is 'really' gay or straight, however, fails to question the underlying assumption about the inner sexual core.

The way people use this myth is as follows. If a man who has been having sex with men since age 13 falls in love with a woman at age 32, this would be 'explained' by saying that the man was heterosexual all along but was afraid of women.

To go back to our fictional characters, Ruth's experiences could be neatly categorized by saying that she went through a 'lesbian phase' under the influence of feminism, and only later realized her 'true' heterosexual potential. An alternative but equally mythical explanation would be to say that she found her true nature in lesbianism but then entered a period of 'false consciousness' as a result of the failure of her relationship with Kate. The explanations could multiply.

Why are we so intent on assuming an inner core of sexual truth? Why do we have to rewrite our histories and dismiss experiences that were at the time extremely powerful as 'just a phase'? Would it not be better to work from the hypothesis that sexual orientation is not a given, like blue eyes or a tendency to gain weight, but is rather subject to profound changes—and is in fact constantly created and recreated—as our sexual and social experiences unfold?

Nobody knows how sexual orientation is in fact determined. One reason for this failure is that almost all research to date has concentrated on finding the 'causes' of homosexuality, as if heterosexuality had no cause. Thus, it might be better to work from a hypothesis that allows for both change and positive choices, rather than one which sees people as mere pawns of some hard, fixed core of sexual identity. It is true that there are some people who are exclusively attracted to either one gender or the other, and who from a very tender age felt 'pushed' by their exclusive desire. But many other people, and women in particular, experience their own sexual orientation as more fluid. This has to be recognized in any theory of sexual orientation, and clearly the category of bisexuality is an important conceptual tool in this type of analysis.

And yet, the rejection of hetero- and homosexuality as two different species with fixed boundaries does not mean that we should go to the other extreme and dismiss all differences in sexual orientation by blandly saying, 'but everyone is bisexual anyway'. This statement is often legitimized by reference to the Freudian model of sexual development, which sees early childhood sexuality as the child's pleasure in his/her own body. According to Freud, heterosexuality develops only by means of the resolution of the Oedipus complex. Prior to this, the child does not make gender distinctions in his/her desire, and is primarily focused either on autoerotic activities or on the mother (because she is the primary parent, not because she is female).

This theory can be used to suggest that bisexuals are closer to the innocence of pre-Oedipal childhood than those who have singled out one gender as the sole object of desire. One sometimes hears that bisexuality is superior to both the conformity of exclusive heterosexuality and the narrowness of exclusive homosexuality. In other words, this approach legitimizes bisexuality in the same way that conservative thought legitimizes exclusive heterosexuality, i.e., by reference to a myth of what is 'natural'. The only difference is that the bisexual myth emphasizes the innocence of early childhood, while the heterosexual myth emphasizes concepts such as 'maturity'.

The bisexual-as-innocent myth, however, is based on an incorrect reading of Freudian theory. One cannot assume that because babies and young children do not differentiate very much between genders—the significant distinctions are pleasure versus non-pleasure, mother versus absence of mother—therefore adults are in some essential way bisexual. The baby's generalized erotic drives, or 'polymorphous perversity' (as Freud called it), is not the same as or even the foundation for adult bisexual behaviour. The baby's erotic drives are not directed toward 'men' and 'women' as distinct genders, but rather toward autoerotic pleasures such as sucking one's thumb or touching one's genitals, or to the mother as object of desire and source of nurture and pleasure. The infant's sexuality is both pre-genital and pre-gendered.

The bisexual behaviour of adults who choose to eroticize both men and women is the furthest thing from this primeval innocence. Adult bisexuality is both genitally focused (unlike the child's oral, anal, and phallic eroticisms) and gender conscious. It is not an innocent, pre-genital eroticization of all bodily experience, but rather involves the selection of properly gendered men and women as objects of desire within the context of fairly rigid rules about what constitutes real sex.

The false analogy between the baby's polymorphous eroticism and the adult's bisexuality has been used to suggest that, far from being indecisive or fickle sexual beings (which is the view of mainstream society), bisexuals are 'closer to nature' and are even superior because of their non-exclusivity.

If the myth of a sexual state of nature (in which bisexuals get to play the noble savage) is a useful one in terms of the psychological self-justification of bisexuals, the myth also has certain political uses and consequences. By stressing the alleged 'essential' bisexuality of all human beings, heterosexuality and homosexuality tend to appear simply as alternative ways of narrowing down the original sexual drive. They tend to be presented as comparable choices, as 'sexual preferences'.

The model of 'sexual preference', as Adrienne Rich points out in her classic essay 'Compulsory Heterosexuality and Lesbian Existence'[1] is problematic mainly because it is based on the liberal myth that one makes one's sexual choices through individual preference. Rich points out that, given the enormous social weight of heterosexism, one cannot accurately describe heterosexuality as merely a personal preference, as though there were not countless social forces pushing one to be heterosexual. People do not generally choose heterosexuality out of a number of equally valid, equally respected lifestyles. Rather, people tend to

'naturally' become heterosexual as they become adult sexual beings. By speaking of homosexuality and heterosexuality (and for that matter bisexuality) as 'preferences', one is disguising and mystifying the institution that Rich calls 'compulsory heterosexuality'. As long as certain choices are punished while others are presented as natural, as the norm, it is naive to describe the complicated process of the construction of conformity and/or deviance by reference to a consumer-type notion of personal preference.

To point out that heterosexuality is not accurately described as a 'preference' is not to imply that homosexuality or bisexuality, as non-conformist lifestyles, are necessarily 'free' choices. As we said earlier, by stepping out of respectability one does not necessarily escape the grasp of the sexual experts; one does not step out of the realm of necessity and into the realm of pure freedom. Many people who are attracted to the 'wrong' gender feel *driven* by their own desires, feel compelled to seek homosexual partners, and do not experience their homosexuality as the exercise of freedom. However, even those people who have experienced their homosexual desires as dark forces governing them, rather than as freely chosen paths to self-fulfillment, are forced at some point to define themselves and ask how and why they have come to have such desire. One may choose to say, 'I was born gay', or 'I am bisexual because . . .'; but regardless of the answers that we give ourselves, we all have to spend some time thinking about the reasons why we took this particular path, and what the social consequences are. Heterosexuals do not have a comparable experience. Since we all 'naturally' grow up to be heterosexual, it is only the deviations that call out for an explanation; the norm appears as natural, and few heterosexual people ever wonder whatever caused them to be heterosexual.

Society does everything in its power to construct a certain pattern of heterosexual behaviour out of each child's autoerotic and polysexual drives. Sometimes the social forces are for one reason or another ineffectual, and the adolescent or adult 'discovers' certain deviant desires in her/himself. Society then does what it can to mould the deviant desires into one of the patterns provided by the experts. If it failed to give you a normal heterosexual identity, it will give you a deviant identity as a homosexual.

It is interesting that although bisexuality, like homosexuality, is just another deviant identity, it also functions as a rejection of the norm/deviance model. People who are bisexual, and not just in a transition between heterosexuality and homosexuality, are people who have resisted both society's first line of attack and its second offensive, i.e., they have resisted both the institution of heterosexuality and of homosexuality. This means that every day they have to make specific choices about how they will appear, with whom they will flirt, what style they will express in clothes and mannerisms.

However, the flexibility and ambiguity inherent in bisexuality do not suffice to allow bisexuals to hover comfortably somewhere 'above' the gay/straight split. Nobody can escape the social structures and ideologies that govern both gender formation and sexual-orientation formation, which have created hetero- and homosexuality as the main, institutionalized sexual identities. What bisexuals do is not so much escape the gay/straight split, but rather *manage* it. They are not above the fray, but participate in it by locating themselves at different points in the split according to the circumstances. Bisexuality is best seen not as a completely separate Third Option that removes itself from all the problems of both hetero- and homosexuality, but rather as a choice to combine the two lifestyles, the two erotic preferences, in one way or another.

This view of bisexuality as a combination of the two main sexual identities rather than a separate identity explains how there can be such huge differences among bisexuals. Homosexuals may be very different from each other—the closeted male politician who has secret affairs with boys does not have much in common with the lesbian feminist—but at the very least they all face a common social oppression and a marginalization into gay ghettoes. Bisexuals, on the other hand, do not have a common social experience upon which to build a specific *social* identity, although they do all share the problem of how to manage the gay/straight split and avoid feeling schizophrenic in the process.

Bisexuals who are unaware of the effects of heterosexism, and who see their situation as a purely individual choice with no significant social repercussions, often unwittingly reinforce, or at least go along with, heterosexist practices. If I have two lovers, one male and one female, it will not be easy to keep in mind that the heaps of social approval piled upon my 'straight' relationship should be taken with a grain of salt. I will 'naturally' tend to keep my lesbian relationship more private, without mentioning it to family and coworkers. [. . .]

On the other hand, bisexuals who are aware of how gay oppression and heterosexism shape the contours of their own lives are in a good position to challenge these oppressive social forces, even as they make it clear that they are fighting as bisexuals, not as honorary gays or pseudo-gays. Those bisexuals who see themselves as sometimes benefiting from the heterosexual privilege and at other times suffering gay oppression, and can see the different consequences of different ways of managing the gay/straight split, are also those who tend to take up gay rights as a cause that affects them personally.

However, up until now the gay community has not been at all encouraging or even tolerant of bisexuals who have a commitment to resisting heterosexism and gay oppression. Gay people have traditionally dismissed bisexuals as deceitful, unreliable, and cowardly. This negative view has unfortunately been confirmed by the existence of many bisexuals who maintain a public heterosexual image while indulging in gay relationships in private, thus escaping gay oppression in a way that gay people can never do. Gay people do have a right to demand that bisexuals do not fall into the easy trap of being publicly straight and privately gay. However, there are now bisexuals, especially feminist women, who are resisting that traditional easy approach and who are increasingly willing to be public about their gay side. They have to be welcomed and treated with respect for their sexual choice. Gay people have to stop assuming that everyone who is bisexual is simply either afraid of coming out or is in transition to being fully gay. The transition theory assumes that those who call themselves bisexual are 'really' gay, and this is as much an error as the belief that everyone is 'really' bisexual. Both rely on the assumption that sexual orientation is an inner essence, an assumption known as 'essentialism'.

Because of our society's firmly entrenched belief in sexual essentialism, we are all more or less uncomfortable with people who are sexually ambiguous. We insist that everyone have a fixed gender identity and a fixed sexual orientation. When we see someone in the street and we cannot tell if it is a man or a woman, we get uneasy and go out of our way to get a second look. We do not rest until we have determined the correct gender of this person (who is otherwise completely unimportant to us). Now, sexual orientation is not as visible on a person as gender, but we all derive a certain satisfaction from investigating people's sexual identities and proceeding to label them as X or Y. Bisexuality is threatening partly because it seems to challenge our classification system, thus putting into question fundamental notions about sexuality and gender. Thus, even if some traditional bisexual behaviour patterns

are questionable, and even though there is no such thing as an institutionalized bisexuality comparable to hetero- and homosexuality, I still think it is important to give sexual ambiguity a place in the sun of radical sexual thought. In other words, even though I share some of the gay skepticism about bisexuality, and am concerned to see bisexuals take a more active role in challenging heterosexism, I am also critical of the dogmatic view—found as much among gay people as among straight people—that bisexuals are inherently indecisive and immature. If the goals of feminism and gay liberation include the abolition of the gay/straight split, and its replacement by a social system which does not label and categorize people according to whom they are attracted, then bisexuality is an important part of the challenge to the status quo. Its role could involve vindicating and affirming sexual ambiguity, in a world which is presently extremely uncomfortable with any ambiguity. Bisexuality defies the experts' attempts to classify everything as either male or female, normal or deviant, good or bad.

[. . .]

Bisexuality does not exist as either a social institution or a psychological 'truth'. It only exists as a catch-all term for different erotic and social patterns whose common ground is an attempt to combine homo- and heterosexuality in a variety of ways. The term 'bisexual', then, merely tells us that someone can or does eroticize both men and women. It does not tell us anything about the morality or politics of that person. The decisions that inevitably have to be made about how to manage one's sexual life and one's social image will be based on extraneous factors (such as commitment to feminism).

However, there is one important way in which bisexuality plays a role in the struggle for a society free from sharp gender and sexual orientation boundaries. This lies in the implicit challenge to notions of essential and static sexual identities. Even those people who define themselves as 'definitely gay' or 'definitely straight' are often in the position of having to admit to desires that do not fit their current social identity. And in this sense it would be a great boon to all of us if there were more social space for self-defined bisexuals. This would mean that we would all be a little freer from exclusivist and essentialist definitions. Of course, because our society is rigidly gendered and is heterosexist in structure, it would be utopian to imagine that bisexuality could exist in a haven beyond gender and beyond gay oppression. But even a bisexuality with all the contradictions imposed on it by our society can help to challenge the sexual status quo. Contradictions, after all, are the moving force of history.

Note

1. Adrienne Rich, 'Compulsory Heterosexuality and Lesbian Existence', *Signs: A Journal of Women in Society* vol. 5, no. 4 (Summer 1980).

Making the Lives of Transsexual People Visible: Addressing the Politics of Social Erasure

Viviane Namaste

The following interview with Viviane Namaste was conducted by Clarice Kuhling and Gary Kinsman, and was published in New Socialist 39 *(January/ February 2003): 31–4. The format here is slightly different from that of the published interview.*

Q: Can you briefly describe for our readers what 'transsexual' and 'transgender' mean?
A: The term *transsexual* refers to individuals who are born in one sex—male or female—but who identify as members of the 'opposite' sex. They take hormones and undergo surgical intervention, usually including the genitals, to live as members of their chosen sex. Transsexuals are both male-to-female and female-to-male.

The term *transgender* is really popular in Anglo-American communities, and is used as an umbrella term to include all kinds of people who do not fit into normative relations between sex and gender. This would include, for instance, transsexuals, drag queens (men who perform as women on stage only, usually in a gay male club or social environment), intersexed individuals (people who are born with genitals that cannot be easily classified as 'male' or 'female'), drag kings (females who perform as men on the stage in lesbian cultural spaces), transvestites (heterosexual males who cross-dress in 'women's' clothes and who receive sexual gratification from this act), as well as people who do not identify with either of the categories 'male' or 'female'.

While the term *transgender* is currently one of the most popular, it needs to be pointed out at this stage in history that increasingly, transsexuals object to being included under a catch-all phrase of *transgender*. They argue that the health care and social service needs of transsexuals are quite specific, and that this specificity is lost when people use a vague term like *transgender*. Furthermore, the popularity of the term *transgender* emerges from the Anglo-American lesbian and gay community. While this discourse may have meaning for some transsexuals who understand their lives in these terms, it does not speak to the transsexuals who do not make sense of their lives, and their political struggles, within the confines of a lesbian/gay framework. It is important to point this out, because most of the Anglo-American writers and self-designated activists on 'transgender' issues come out of the lesbian/gay community and express themselves in those terms. My empirical research contradicts this underlying assumption, since most of the transsexuals I have interviewed do not articulate their needs according to a lesbian/gay framework.

All of this to say that questions of language are deeply political!

Q: Why did you title your book *Invisible Lives: The Erasure of Transsexual and Transgendered People*[1]?

A: Most of the academic approaches to transsexuality argue that transsexuals are produced by the medical and the psychiatric establishment. Alternatively, they use the case of transsexuality to illustrate the social construction of gender. There are all kinds of examples of this type of scholarship, and unfortunately, it does not appear that things are about to change in the near future.

There are a couple of things that need to be unpacked in this type of work. First, this work is always, and only, about identity. It limits itself to how and why transsexuals decide to live as members of the opposite sex. Or it uses transsexuals to speak about the relations between social norms and gender identity. What is left out of these accounts is any real understanding of what everyday life is like for transsexuals. So while critics are churning out books, articles, and essays on transsexuals and the transgendered, they have nothing to say about the very real circumstances in which transsexuals live. They cannot offer us even a tiny piece of information about transsexuals and the law, or access to health care, or the struggles

that transsexuals have with employment, or the situation of transsexuals in prison.

So my book begins with a critique of this kind of intellectual work. And I argue that, if we actually do some empirical research on some of the matters most pressing for transsexuals—civil status, access to health care, the decriminalization of prostitution, abusive police practices— we discover that transsexuals are quite literally shut out and excluded from the institutional world. They do not have access to many kinds of services, such as shelters for battered women. And so then I begin with this empirical data and I raise two questions with respect to theory. In the first instance, I argue that the theories concerned with the production of transsexuality have got it wrong: transsexuals are not, in point of fact, produced by the medical and psychiatric institution. Rather, they are continually *erased* from the institutional world—shut out from its programs, excluded from its terms of reference. And the second question I raise comes out of this reflection: I inquire about the relevance of writing theory that cannot make sense of the everyday world, and that actually contributes to the very invisibility of transsexuality that a critical theory needs to expose. This is part of a much broader debate in the university, especially within the social sciences, about the role and function of an intellectual. And I argue that if theory and university scholarship erase transsexuals in much the same way as do different institutional practices, then they are really part of the problem that needs to be understood, and not at all critical inquiry.

Q: What are some of the institutional forms of discrimination and oppression that transsexual and transgendered people face in patriarchal capitalist societies?

A: There are a variety of forms of discrimination. Access to services is one of the major barriers: detoxification programs especially, state funding for surgery, access to hormones in prison, access to emergency shelter. Much of this access is dependent on the individual attitudes of service providers. So when someone is uneducated about transsexuals and transvestites, they may refuse access to services based on misinformation or prejudice. Another type of discrimination comes out of a total lack of institutional policies for transsexuals. This is especially true for female-to-male transsexuals. In these instances, some people cannot get services because bureaucrats do not have a clear written directive.

Access to the media is a whole other form of institutional discrimination. Transsexuals are often required to give their autobiography on demand: How long have you known? Are you operated? How did your family take the news? These kinds of personal questions can provide some insight into the lives of transsexuals, but they are also, in a sense, quite invasive and rude. It is astounding to me that within 15 seconds of knowing an individual is transsexual, some [interviewers] feel comfortable enough to ask transsexual individuals to describe the physical appearance and sexual function of their genitals. How is it that cultural taboos regarding speaking openly about sexuality and genitalia with people you do not know well, go out the window when it comes to transsexuals? One of the effects of this demand is that it is difficult for transsexuals to address the real issues: cops who harass street prostitutes and escorts, access to health care and social services, changing one's name and sex.

The other issue with respect to access to the media is the whole affiliation with lesbian/gay and feminist communities. As I mentioned earlier, most of the self-designated activists emerge from lesbian/gay and/or feminist communities, and they frame the issues in these terms. This means that transsexuals who do not make sense of their lives according to lesbian/gay discourse have no voice. And I reiterate here that based on

my empirical research and observations within the milieu for more than 10 years, the majority of transsexuals do not make sense of their lives in lesbian/gay terms. Yet we never hear these voices. And even though we have some empirical research that challenges an equation amongst transsexuals and lesbians/gays—I refer here to my research as well as that of Henry Rubin, whose book on female-to-male transsexuals, *Self-Made Men*, has just been published by Vanderbilt University Press in 2003—our research and observations are ignored both by critics in queer theory as well as by transgender activists who align themselves with queer politics. So to return to the notion of institutions, transsexuals experience discrimination to the extent that they cannot express themselves in their own terms.

The last institutional barrier I want to cite is that of consultation. So often, the government develops policies without consulting transsexuals at all. Or in certain cases, consultation happens with middle-class non-prostitute transsexuals, who represent their unique interests without ensuring that the broader needs of transsexuals are addressed.

Q: Could you tell us a bit about the struggles of transsexuals in Quebec and the institutional relations they are up against when trying to get their 'sex' changed on official documents?
A: Legally, Quebec is a civil code jurisdiction, and within civil code jurisdictions, the body is legally inscribed as a matter of public order. This is quite different than the legal situation within a common law jurisdiction. What this means practically, in terms of name and sex change, is that transsexuals can only change their name after surgical intervention on the genitals. This legal framework is quite specific to civil code countries, and goes back to a long legacy of the Napoleonic Code. In terms of everyday life, this creates all kinds of problems: a female individual begins to take hormones, lives as

a man without detection, but their identity documents remain in the female name. Employment, access to health care, and everyday situations like picking up a registered letter from the post office become very problematic.

The situation is especially complicated for female-to-male transsexuals. The *Direction de l'état civil* (Office of Civil Status) clearly states that a male-to-female transsexual must undergo a vaginoplasty—the construction of the vagina—in order to change name and sex. Yet in the case of female-to-male transsexuals, in at least 1997 and 1998, the Office invoked a rather vague criterion of structurally changing the genital organs. It did not say if this meant a phalloplasty (the construction of a penis), or if it referred to removing the uterus and the ovaries alongside undergoing a double mastectomy and taking male hormones. So things are not always clear, and my research indicates that at certain times there is no standardized policy in this area. However, on a more positive note, it appears that since the late 1990s, the *Direction de l'état civil* is more clear with respect to the surgeries and procedures required for change of name and sex in the case of female-to-male transsexuals (hysterectomy, double mastectomy, hormone therapy).

In recent times, a court ruled that a male-to-female transgendered person in Quebec can add a female name to their birth certificate.[2] It will be interesting to see what kind of impact this has for transsexuals in Quebec, and if the access will be universal. The ruling specifies, for instance, that this modification can be made if the individual can demonstrate that they have lived as a woman for five years. Certainly, for transsexuals who 'transition' and are able to keep their jobs, providing such evidence is not difficult. But for individuals who do not work in any kind of legal economy, and who do not go to school, the proof of such an identity, established through official documents—pay stubs, school transcripts,

credit cards—is less certain. In this regard, while the ability to change one's name after five years is a definite improvement over not being able to do so at all before genital surgery, it is important to reflect on whether the administrative procedures favour middle-class transsexuals.

Q: What is the significance of the challenge to the two-gender dichotomous (male/female) system that transgendered and transsexual people raise? How can radical activists who are not transsexual or transgendered take up this critique of gender relations in the daily work that they do?

A: This question comes up again and again on the left. I am happy to have the opportunity to answer it, in a sense to undo this question, because it helps to illustrate some of the issues that I have raised in my previous answers.

Let me begin by briefly summarizing some of the underlying assumptions of this question. The question follows a line advanced by some self-designated transgender activists and repeated over and over again by queer theorists in universities. It argues that the binary sex/gender system, the exclusive division of the world into 'men' and 'women', is oppressive. And this argument further contends that this is oppressive not only to transsexuals, but indeed to men and women who consider themselves 'properly' sexed and gendered. And having made this critique of the binary sex/gender system, this position then goes on to state that social change can happen through some kind of disruption or displacement of the sex/gender system. That's where transgendered people come in, located within this framework as those who successfully challenge the status quo and point out a new way of going forward.

Now, having given a brief overview of what I see as some of the underlying assumptions of the question, let me return to the division I made earlier between 'transsexual' and 'transgendered'.

I said that more and more, a lot of transsexuals take a critical distance from the term *transgendered*. And this question allows us an opportunity to think through why. The question assumes that 'transgendered' people will see their bodies, identities, and lives as part of a broader process of social change, of disrupting the sex/gender binary. Now many transgendered people make such an argument: you can read it in the works of Leslie Feinberg, Riki Ann Wilchins, or Kate Bornstein.[3] But many transsexuals do not see themselves in these terms. They would situate themselves as 'men' and as 'women', not as 'gender radicals' or 'gender revolutionaries' or 'boyzzz' or 'grrrrrrls'.

Most transsexuals I know, and most I have interviewed, describe themselves as men or women. And there is a sense in which this position cannot be understood in relation to the question posed, 'What is the significance of the challenge to the two-gendered dichotomous system that transsexual and transgendered people raise?' Because transsexuals seek to have a different embodied position within that system, I hope it is clear here what I am trying to do—I hope to show how asking the question in this way forces transsexuals to speak a language that is foreign to us. And while it may have meaning and relevance for *transgendered* people, it has very little to do with the everyday lives of *transsexuals*.

Now it is usually assumed, in universities and even in progressive movements for social change, that people who adopt 'essentialist' positions are not politically progressive. But you know, I think that the interest in social constructionism in the Anglo-American university is in danger of blinding people to the very good political work that one can do from an essentialist position. And I will go out on a limb here—because to be a good thinker and activist and teacher means taking some risks—and I will say that in the case of transsexuals, essentialism has such a bad name!

Let me cite an example to help illustrate my case. It is so often assumed, as the question posed to me does, that in disrupting a binary sex/gender system, transgendered people are in the forefront of social change. I cited the works of Leslie Feinberg and Riki Ann Wilchins earlier. Both of these writers are located within this framework: they advocate a 'transgender' revolution. Now, this is supposed to be a position that is so much more sophisticated than those 'terrible' essentialist transsexuals. And the position advocated by Feinberg and Wilchins is the one cited by critics in queer theory. These are the authors who make it onto the course outlines of university studies. And it is all done by well-intentioned, well-meaning teachers who would situate themselves as allies of transsexuals.

But let us examine in more depth some of the political work of Feinberg and Wilchins. Wilchins has been not only active, but instrumental, in lobbying for the delisting of gender identity disorder from the manual of psychiatrists, the *Diagnostic and Statistical Manual of Mental Disorders IV*. And Feinberg also supports such a position, notably in publishing the 'International Bill of Gender Rights' in her book.[4] This Bill also contends that gender identity disorder has no place in the psychiatric diagnostic manual. If such a lobby is successful, it will mean that it will be impossible to pay for sex-reassignment surgery either through a private insurance company or through state/provincial health insurance. In this light, the activism of Wilchins and Feinberg supports the privatization of health care. (Feinberg represents herself as a Marxist activist, which is the biggest irony of all!) So here we have a case of some transgender activists, influenced by social constructionist theory, who argue that they are the cutting edge of social change. Yet they are involved in political work that is deeply conservative.

Now let us contrast this with the work of some transsexuals like Margaret O'Hartigan, who has been instrumental in ensuring that sex-reassignment surgery is paid for through state health insurance in Minnesota, and who has offered a trenchant critique of the funding of health care services in Oregon, including services for transsexuals. Now, O'Hartigan is an essentialist: she is not making any claims to disrupting the sex/gender binary, she is not hailing herself as the new vanguard of third-wave feminism. What she is doing, is the highly unglamorous work of research, lobbying, and activism to ensure that all transsexuals can have access to health care, regardless of their economic or financial resources. So here we have an example of an essentialist (gasp!) who is, in my opinion, doing some excellent political work.

Yet I want to go even further. In certain discussions in a university context, there is an acknowledgment that essentialism can be useful politically. Judith Butler, for example, recognizes that while her theoretical work interrogates the sign of 'woman', it is at times necessary to invoke the category 'woman' in order to make political gains.[5] This argument, of course, could easily be extended to the case of transsexuality: that one needs an identity of 'transsexual' in order to advance things politically. I can accept the terms of this argument. However, what I am saying today also goes far beyond this idea. I think that academics and activists set a very dangerous precedent if we maintain that people's identities are acceptable only if and when they can prove that they are politically useful. Who gets to decide what constitutes 'politically useful' anyway? To my mind, this still reinforces a dynamic in which transsexuals have to prove themselves: you see, we're really all right because we use our transsexual identity for some good law reform. I refuse to accept these terms.

I cited the case of Margaret Deidre O'Hartigan earlier, arguing that she was involved in some critical health care activism. Now, in very specific and practical terms, she and other activists in Portland, Oregon, engaged in a very detailed reading of the kinds of state coverage offered to its citizens.[6] And they found significant gender differences with respect to the ranking of different procedures for reimbursement. So for instance, state coverage paid for testicular implants in the case of a male who has lost his testicles, but did not allow for breast implants in the case of a woman who loses her breasts. This kind of activism, then, shows a clear gender bias in social policy. And in point of fact, the activism is not particularly premised on any kind of transsexual identity. So my earlier statement that this was good work being done by an essentialist is a bit unfair. The work is good, period. And whether or not O'Hartigan is an essentialist is irrelevant. So that is one of the points I am happy to make here today. In many university and activist contexts, essentialist identities can only be accepted to the extent that they clearly satisfy some unspecified political agenda. And I am saying something quite different, albeit perhaps unpopular in social constructionist circles. Accepting transsexuality means accepting that people live and identify as men and women, although they were not born in male or female bodies. And that this needs to be kept separate from political work. Some transsexuals situate themselves on the left, and do their political work from this perspective. Others are moderate, or deeply conservative politically. I want to say that if we accept transsexuality in and of itself, then we don't need to make it conditional on a particular political agenda.

So I hope it is clear, then, how the question posed to me contains kinds of assumptions that I do not accept. And so one of the things I hope to do is to encourage people to be deeply critical of the kinds of information and knowledge available on transsexuals, perhaps especially the knowledge advocated by 'transgendered' people.

In practical terms, this means reading more than Leslie Feinberg, Riki Ann Wilchins, Kate Bornstein, or Judith Butler.

That being said, and in a critical spirit of solidarity, I would encourage people in the labour movement and in progressive circles to openly critique the 'party line' when it comes to transsexuals and transgendered people. Feinberg and Wilchins and many others like them are invested and implicated in precisely the forms of economic and global capitalism that progressive people seek to understand and transform. You know, I think in the past five years, transgendered people have become so trendy. And sometimes I have a feeling that in part because of this trendiness, people are afraid to criticize what transgendered people say because they don't want to be called 'trans-phobic'. Don't get stuck there: some transgendered people are involved in regressive political work and it needs to be denounced.

I want to say two more things before concluding. Firstly, I want to encourage people to learn about what is going on here in Canada. Transsexuals have such a rich history in Canada, and prostitutes have been the first ones to organize to get services for transsexuals—in Montreal, in Vancouver, and in Toronto. Yet so much of the writing in English on transgendered people is produced by Americans. By studying how transsexuals have organized here in Canada, we can reframe some of the questions that people ask. Of course, since I live in Quebec, I would also encourage English Canadians to learn French, since it would allow them a whole other way to see and understand the world. But that's another interview!

I think it is most useful to think about these questions not in terms of the individual rights of transsexuals, but in terms of how these issues link with those of other marginalized populations, or with the functioning of the state in general. And I think that leftists can play a very important role in this regard. I am thinking, for instance, of a panel that Trish Salah organized around labour and prostitution at the Sexin' Change conference in October 2001 in Toronto. Prostitute activist Kara Gillis actually noted that this was one of the first times she had been invited to a specifically union/labour context, despite the fact that her activism frames prostitution as work. So organizing these kinds of events allows people to make broader connections and shifts the focus from a narrow one of 'transsexual rights'. Prostitute activist Mirha-Soleil Ross argued that day, for instance, that the decriminalization of prostitution would have a more positive impact on the lives of most transsexuals than any kind of human rights legislation. So that is something progressive people can do: integrate transsexual activists into your work not to speak about gender and transsexuality, but to make broader links concerning the regulation of marginalized people.

Notes

1. Chicago: University of Chicago Press, 2000.
2. The background and ruling of this case are available online at www.micheline.ca/page034-1-etat-civil.htm.
3. Leslie Feinberg, *Transgender Warriors: Making History from Joan of Arc to Dennis Rodman* (Boston: Beacon, 1996); Riki Ann Wilchins, *Read My Lips: Sexual Subversion and the End of Gender* (Ithaca: Firebrand Books, 1997); Kate Bornstein, *Gender Outlaw: On Men, Women, and the Rest of Us* (New York: Vintage Books, 1994).
4. Feinberg, *Transgender Warriors*.
5. Butler, 'Gender Insubordination', in Diana Fuss, ed. *Inside/Out: Lesbian Theories, Gay Theories* (New York: Routledge, 1991): 13–31.
6. Filisa Vistima Foundation, 'Re-prioritization of Coverage for Transexualism through the Oregon Medical Assistance Program', (28 February 1998). Available from Filisa Vistima Foundation, PO Box 82447, Portland, Oregon, 97282, USA.

The Regulation of First Nations Sexuality

Martin Cannon

Introduction

Several aspects of Canadian political reality have led historical sociologists to maintain that race, gender, and sexuality are not separate categories of experience and analysis but dynamic sets of social constructions which, as they interconnect, impact upon individuals and their (re)productive activities in distinctive, historically specific ways (Ng, 1993:50; Parr, 1995:356–360; McClintock, 1995). Informed by this understanding, any comprehensive analysis of Canada's Indian Act and early Indian policy should examine how configurations of racist, sexist, and heterosexist knowledges were manifested in the process(es) of colonization. Such an analysis would seek to document the endeavours toward making (European) heterosexuality compulsory within status Indian communities (Rich, 1993). Such an analysis, in its most ambitious sense, would illuminate the convergent discrimination(s) directed toward those preferring same-sex intimacies, and make a contribution toward an integrated theory of race, gender, and sexuality. Such an endeavour, though far from exhaustive, is the primary focus of this paper.

The first part of the paper will provide a critical review of the literature which suggests that a broad range of gender and erotic relationships existed among Aboriginal populations at early contact. Part of this exercise will be to specify homosexuality as an analytic category describing in turn the difficulty with using terms such as 'gay' and 'lesbian' to describe historic First Nations sexual categories (Midnight Sun, 1988:35; Whitehead, 1993). The second part of the paper will then document how racist sexism and heterosexism worked together to legislate and define First Nations political reality. Upon illustrating the interactive relationship among these systems of domination, I will conclude that none of the development of class relations, the regulation of sexuality, racism, or patriarchy can be explained as mutually exclusive.

Sexuality and Gender in Native North America

Even prior to Confederation and the emergence of the first statute entitled the Indian Act in 1876, the colonial enterprise in Canada had virtually enforced a system of Eurocentric policies, beliefs, and value systems upon First Nations. The earliest missionaries, for example, were determined to 'civilize' the Indian populations by attempting to indoctrinate a Christian ethos and patriarchal familial structure (Brodribb, 1984). It was within the context of such a conversion mission that same-sex erotic and sexual diversity was negatively evaluated and often condemned (Kinsman, 1987:71; Katz, 1983:28). This mission was a project fuelled by heterosexism.[1]

One of the often-quoted passages related to the views of the early missionaries is that of the Jesuit Joseph Francois Lafitau. Speaking of the erotic and gender relations which he observed among Native North Americans from 1711–1717, he noted:

> If there were women with manly courage who prided themselves upon the profession of warrior, which seems to become men alone, there were also men cowardly enough to live as women . . . they believe

they are honoured by debasing themselves to all of women's occupations; they never marry . . .

(Joseph Francois Lafitau, quoted in Katz, 1976:288)

The later diaries of the Jesuit Pedro Font resonated with the observations made by Lafitau. Making an assessment based on his observations taken from the expedition of Juan Bautista de Anza from 1775–76, he noted:

Among the women I saw men dressed like women, with whom they go about regularly, never joining the men . . . From this I inferred they must be hermaphrodites, but from what I learned later I understood that they were sodomites, dedicated to nefarious practices. From all the foregoing I conclude that in this matter of incontinence there will be much to do when the Holy Faith and the Christian religion are established among them. (Pedro Font, quoted in Katz, 1976:291)

[. . .]

The spectrum of erotic and gender diversity recorded in times of early contact suggests that same-sex relations were considered to be of some moral and political consequence.[2] Labelled as 'nefarious', the relations that did exist were seen as illegitimate. Clearly, there is no superior foundation for such 'common sense' forms of paternalistic judgment, but we can explain the claims to Euro-Christian pre-eminence as grounded in the ethos of the historical period.[3] Informed by notions of supremacy, ideologies of racial inferiority and of 'civilized' (hetero)sexual behaviour, the early Europeans saw First Nations (indeed all non-Europeans) as subordinate and underdeveloped entities (Miles, 1989; Said, 1978). Of pertinent interest in the aforementioned passages

is also the way they reveal the interrelated nature of all systems of oppression.

Configurations of racist, patriarchal, and heterosexist knowledges worked together to influence the views of the missionaries. Being a 'nefarious sodomite', for example, not only meant 'debasing' oneself by 'cowardly' appropriating the gender and assumed sexual roles of a devalued (in this case) female class, it was an 'unproductive' realm that, as I will describe in further detail, required complete refashioning. Salvation (sexual and otherwise) was to rest under the auspices of a religiously superior race of Europeans: a motive that was clearly racist. Salvation was something that required the regulation of a 'savage' sexuality thought antithetical to Christian decorum, gendered domestic relations, and moral rationality. There may be reason to suggest, however, that the view toward individuals referred to as 'nefarious' by the missionaries was an unshared sentiment among some of the original inhabitants of North America. It has been suggested that the *berdache* enjoyed an esteemed role within certain communities prior to contact.[4]

Among the Bella Coola Nation located in what is now called British Columbia, Franz Boas noted the special status accorded to the *berdache*, a status that was central to an origin myth on food (Boas, reprinted in Roscoe, 1988:81–84). Toleration of the *berdache* and even 'institutionalized homosexuality' is suggested in more contemporary anthropological literature and Native testimonials (Benedict, quoted in Roscoe, 1988:16–17; Mead, quoted in Roscoe, 1988:19; Owlfeather, 1988:100; Kenny, 1988:153). Sharing a similar perspective, Kenny (1988:26) has noted that:

Some tribes, such as the Minois, actually trained young men to become homosexuals and concubines of men. The

Cheyenne and Sioux of the plains may not have purposely trained young men to become *berdaches* but certainly accepted homosexuals more readily than perhaps other tribes.

In short, some have been inclined toward emphasizing the *berdache* as a recognized and legitimate social institution. Nonetheless, it is necessary to look upon this claim with some skepticism.

[. . .]

The evidence to substantiate the claim that the Native North American *berdache* was an equivalent to the modern day 'homosexual' is limited. As Harriet Whitehead explains, such cross-cultural investigations tend to posit a *shared sexual identity* between the gender-crossing *berdache* and modern 'homosexual': the very place where contradictions start to emerge (1993:498). Alluding to the importance of sex/gender systems, Whitehead explains:

> Western society foregrounds erotic orientation as the basis for dividing people into socially significant categories, but for Native North Americans, occupational pursuits and dress/demeanour were the important determinants of an individual's social classification, and sexual object choice was its trailing rather than leading edge (1993:498).

Whitehead does not suggest that the role of the *berdache* excluded same-sex sexual behaviour (1993:514). She illuminates instead a sex/gender system that renders one's chosen occupational behaviour of much greater importance than sexual object choice when it comes to social (re)classification (Whitehead, 1993:511; 513). The role of *berdache*, according to Whitehead, was more about gender-crossing than it was about sexual relations. In making this point, she alerts the

anthropologist and social historian alike to the weaknesses of 'homosexual' as an analytic category. This is a position that is broadened by constructionist theorists who are interested in the history of sexuality. Foucault is exemplary.

For Foucault, sexuality is not a natural given, but the name that is granted to a historical construct (1990:105; 127). Sexuality, in other words, is never more than a set of ever-varying developments tied to the mode of production and prevailing social/political realities (Foucault, 1990: 5–6; Padgug, 1989:58). In short, sexuality and subsequently related behaviour is socially constructed. Failing to recognize this category as such presents the social historian with conceptual and interpretive difficulties. [. . .]

It is necessary to distinguish between behaviour and identity when we apply an analytic category such as 'homosexual' to the historic past. We cannot take the sexual acts reported to have been witnessed by the missionaries and convert them to a history of personality or contemporary 'gay' identity. For on this question of identity, Robert Padgug insists:

> These identities are not inherent in the individual. In order to be gay . . . more than individual inclinations (however we might conceive of those) or homosexual activity is required; entire ranges of social attitudes and the construction of particular cultures, subcultures, and social relations are first necessary. (1989:60)

In sum, while it may be true that *homosexual behaviour* existed in history, we cannot call those whose behaviour was so inclined either 'gay', 'lesbian', or homosexual as these are known in the historic present.

[A different] problem with postulating on and about 'Native homosexuality' is in alluding to its prevalence as 'institutionalized'. The characterization of homosexuality threatens to foreground the homosexual sex act over and above the gender-crossing, occupational choice, and the distribution of (cross-gendered) tasks. The effect of this characterization is to suggest that sexual object choice was more important than gender-crossed behaviour in Native social classification systems. A mistaken consequence is thereby afforded to the homosexual or even heterosexual sex act since some *berdaches* 'lapsed into anatomic heterosexuality and on occasion even marriage without any loss of their cross-sex status' (Whitehead, 1993, 512; also see Schnarch, 1992:115). In sum, it is important to recognize when we speak of 'institutionalized homosexuality' that:

> [H]omosexual acts were not in any way immediately suggestive of an enduring disposition such as that which characterized the gender-crosser (or the 'homosexual' in our culture), and such acts were not confused with gender-crossing in the Native mind. (Whitehead, 1993:511)

This brief investigation on sexuality and cross-gendered behaviour in Native North America provides some insight into the diversity of erotic and gender relations that existed among a selection of Aboriginal populations at early contact. Through the use of secondary documents provided by Katz (1976), this investigation also illustrates the missionary response to such interactions. [. . .]

In short, the dynamic interplay between 'racial', sexual, and gendered types of knowledge both produced and organized missionary recordings. A similar set of ethnocentric understanding would later translate into a set of policy objectives. These colonial knowledges would influence the contemporary circumstances of Native 'gays' and 'lesbians', some of whom continue to identify as 'two-spirited' people. In the following section I explore the interactive relationship between racism, patriarchy, and heterosexism in early 'Indian' policy and the Indian Act.

Racism, Patriarchy, and Heterosexism in the Indian Act

In this section I will highlight the way in which the Indian Act, in the assumptions that it made about the kinship and social organization of First Nations, assumed homosexual behaviour out of existence. Further research is needed to illustrate more precisely the actual impact, or causal effect that government initiatives and legislation had on the suppression of homosexual behaviour and same-sex intimacies. For an initial analysis of how the *berdache* tradition is no longer as recognized an institution as it once was in Native communities, see Williams (1986:183–192), Roscoe (1988, Part II), and Brown (1997).

For well over 100 years, the Indian Act has been the central legislation governing the affairs of First Nations in Canada. Since its inception in 1876, the *Act* consolidated earlier policy and appointed the federal government in control of all aspects of 'Indian' life including education, social services, health care, and lands administration. For the purposes of this paper I will concentrate largely upon those sections of the Indian Act that deal with 'Indian' status and citizenship. These were the sections that fundamentally reorganized kinship relations and delineated who was, and who was not, eligible to be registered as an 'Indian' under the jurisdiction of the Indian Act.[5] While the historical development of these sections are most blatantly patriarchal, I will also illustrate how they combine to reveal an interactive relationship between racism, patriarchy, and heterosexism. It is necessary, in other words, to understand patriarchal discrimination *in relation to* racism and heterosexism. Moreover, these systems of domination cannot be understood outside of the formation of capitalist relations.

The implementation of the Reserve system in 1830s Upper Canada was among the earliest of statutory policies to affect First Nations prior to Confederation. This was a policy intended to resocialize First Nations into recognized 'British-agricultural-Christian patterns of behaviour' (Frideres, 1983:22). To that extent, the agricultural policy of the reserve system revealed underlying ideologies of racism and ethnocentrism. The Reserve system was intended to 'civilize' the 'Indian' who, in the eyes of the European, would be otherwise susceptible to nomadism and societal decline.

The agricultural component of the reserve system was also among the earliest of policies to commence with the social construction of gendered tasks. Commenting on the sexual division of labour associated with this policy, Ng has observed that 'men were taught farming skills such as how to clear land and hold a plow, [and] women, under the tutelage of the missionaries' wives and daughters were taught "civilized" domestic skills' (1993:54). The reserve system policy thus represented a further endeavour toward the reconstruction of gender relations among Aboriginal populations. [. . .] At the same time, these assumptions likely influenced the position of the *berdache* discussed earlier in the paper. Had systems that recognized and affirmed an engagement in cross-gendered occupations existed prior to European contact, they would not have been possible during the 1830s.

A continued emphasis toward gender hierarchicalization continued well into the late 1800s. Most notably, it emerged in the status and citizenship sections of 'Indian' policy. These were the sections that defined who was, and who was not, entitled to 'Indian' status. In the tradition of earlier statutes, these initiatives made invidious distinctions between male and female 'Indians'.

The status and citizenship sections of the Indian Act have historically excluded Aboriginal women from recognition as status 'Indians'. As early as 1869, for example, Native women marrying non-Native men lost status, along with their children, as defined under section 6 of *An Act for the Gradual Enfranchisement of Indians* ([S.C. 1869, c. 6 (32-33 Vict.)], reprinted in Venne, 1981:11–15).[6] This same loss of status did not apply to Native men or their children. In law, Native men retained their entitlement to status along with an ability to bestow it regardless of whom they married.

[. . .]

The status and citizenship sections of the 1869 policy carried connotations that were simultaneously racist, patriarchal, and heterosexist. As Jamieson (1986:118) has asserted 'the statute of 1869, especially section 6 . . . embodied the principle that, like other women, Indian women should be subject to their husbands'. At the level of 'common sense', in other words, it went unstated that all Native women (and children) take on the 'racial' status of their husbands at marriage. It also went unstated that Native women and men ought to be inclined toward the Euro-Christian institution of heterosexual marriage. By making marriage the only possible avenue through which to convey 'Indian' status and rights, the 1869 Act simply legislated European forms of heterosexuality compulsory in First Nations communities. Later legislation would only perpetuate such institutionalized domination.

In 1876, for example, the federal government passed the first legislation entitled the Indian Act. Like preceding legislation, this Act imposed patriarchal definitions of 'Indian' by again emphasizing patrilineal descent. Section 6 of the 1869 statute became section 3(c) of the Indian Act, only later to become section 12(1)(b) in the revised 1951 Indian Act.[7] Similar to previous legislation, the 1876 legislation did not require a loss of status for Native men. Native men retained their legal 'Indian' status and, under section 3, were able to bestow it onto the non-Native women they married. Section 3 of the Indian Act would later become section 11(1)(f) in the revised 1951 Act.[8] Historically, these legislated changes institutionalized descent through the male line and simply 'naturalized' the heterosexual nuclear family within First Nations communities.

Major changes to the Indian Act were common following 1876 and several systems of domination were upheld. In 1956, for example, an amendment to section 12(2) of the 1952 Act strengthened patriarchal definitions of 'Indian' by enabling individual Band members to contest the status and band membership of Native children thought to be 'illegitimate'. If an individual band member could prove that the father of a child was not an 'Indian', then the child would not be entitled to statutory registration or Band membership.[9] 'Indian' women's status, henceforth from 1956, ceased to be of any official legal significance in and of itself since only men could bestow legitimacy. It was by entrenching this system of relations that a discourse of patrilineage was offered to First Nations. At the same time, notions of 'illegitimacy' in the 1952 Act privileged heterosexual unions by emphasizing the importance of paternity to the exclusion of non-male partners. In this way, the existence—even possibility—of same-sex relationships in First Nations communities went unacknowledged.

[. . .]

The historical development of the Indian Act and other 'Indian' policy was a process coincident with the building of Canada as a nation. Between 1830 and 1950, for example, most of the Act's central prescriptions were being created. These were the years when Canada was moving toward an urbanized industrial economy. On that account, it is reasonable to speculate that the Indian Act and other 'Indian' policies were informed by ideologies congruent with the impending processes of social and economic change. The Indian Act may be (re)interpreted as a mechanism fashioning the human infrastructure necessary for the growth of capitalism. Informed by that understanding, the Reserve system of the 1830s may be revisited.

The agricultural policy of the 1830s not only placed emphasis on the state's motivation toward socializing 'Indians' into economically viable entities, it also made some fundamental distinctions between the male and female genders. Policy-makers of this new legislation, as mentioned, simply presupposed that 'Indian' men would learn agricultural skills; and women, domestic chores. In this way, policy-makers made 'common sense' assumptions about the gendered distribution of tasks. These assumptions were informed by ideologies of the sexual division of labour and the private and public spheres. It was within the broader context of these knowledges that the state mandated the regulation of gendered behaviour among First Nations. The imperative to divide tasks on the basis of gender must certainly have impacted upon women and also those inclined toward cross-gendered activity.

For women, capitalist and patriarchal knowledges combined to require that their labour be restricted to the private sphere. The implication of capitalist and patriarchal knowledges was to relegate women to the lower strata of the institutionalized gender hierarchy.[10] For those inclined to cross-gendered behaviour, capitalist and patriarchal knowledges relating to the sexual division of labour combined to mandate, even if unintentionally, the loss of gender flexibility. The effect of these knowledges was likely to have intensified gender classification systems making cross-gendered behaviour of considerable consequence. [. . .]

The status and citizenship sections of the Indian Act were as much about extending a project of invidious gender distinctions into First Nations communities as they were about the regulation of sexuality. The formulation of these sections were shaped through a historical context that ideologically prescribed the types of sexual behaviour thought most compatible with the mode of production. Capitalist and patriarchal knowledge relating to the (re)productive modes of sexuality combined in the 1800s to require the disavowal of same-sex relationships. Since only heterosexual marriage ensured a form of reproductive sexuality, these would become the only recognized unions through which to convey status in the Indian Act. Later Indian Act prescriptions on 'illegitimacy' would reveal a similar influence from the historical period.

The 'legitimacy' sections of the Indian Act were just as much inspired by the patriarchal emphasis on paternity as they were by the emerging productive relations of the late nineteenth century. The imperative of 'legitimacy', for example, was tied intimately to capitalist notions of private property. Those status provisions that upheld notions of 'illegitimacy' simply reflected a legal and social system which tried to ensure that only men could bequeath wealth onto their own children (Engels, 1942:76; O'Brien, 1981:54). The way that wealth was bequeathed was to declare that wives were the sole and exclusive property of their husbands and that subsequently, a man's children were those that his wife bore. It was in the broader context of wealth and the transference of property that the state endeavoured toward the regulation of women's sexuality. The imperative of paternity was largely to bring all First Nations into further congruence with a patriarchal system of private property.

[. . .]

Conclusion

A central conclusion of this paper is that the regulation of First Nations sexuality cannot be explained apart from, or without reference to, racist and patriarchal configurations as those emerged in the Euro-Christian and subsequent colonial contexts.

For the early missionaries, descriptions of sexuality were informed by both 'racial' and 'gendered' knowledges. 'Sodomy', for example, was a practice engaged in by a 'coarse natured' 'race' of people. The cross-gendered behaviour of the *berdache* was further constructed as effeminate. Informed by knowledges that linked sexuality with 'racial' difference, along with ideas that linked gender with masculinity and femininity, the Euro-Christian missions made the first attempt toward a 'civilizing' agenda. In any attempt to reconsider that agenda, the dynamic interrelationship among all systems of domination needs to be recounted.

Racist and patriarchal configurations also influenced the later agenda of nation building. Capitalist and patriarchal knowledges relating to the (re)productive modes of sexuality, for example, combined to require the disavowal of same-sex relationships in the status and citizenship sections of the Indian Act. By extension, the sexual division of labour intensified gender classification systems, in turn requiring the regulation of cross-gendered behaviour. All of these systems combined to deeply affect First Nations.

In short, the dynamic interplay between racist, patriarchal, and capitalist knowledges all influenced the regulation of First Nations sexuality. Any account of the history of this regulation, or theory of state formation, needs to illuminate that interrelationship.

Notes

1. By the term 'heterosexism', I mean the system of knowledges or 'political institution' through which heterosexuality is either implicitly or explicitly assumed to be the only acceptable or viable life option and/or sexual aim (Rich, 1993:232; Blumenfeld and Raymond, 1988:244–5).

2. The actual depth of missionary observation, comment and sentiment about 'sodomic practices' cannot be thoroughly discussed in a paper of this size. Testimonies can be analyzed more closely, however, in Katz (1983) and Williams (1986). Goldberg (1992) provides further analysis of the evidence in both Katz and Williams, along with an overview of the sexual practices of Indians from the vantage point of Spanish explorers.

3. I borrow the term 'common sense' from Himani Bannerji (1987) who draws attention to the way that systems of discrimination 'disappear from the social surface' and become ordinary ways of doing things of which we rarely have consciousness.

4. As Burns has noted (1988:1), *berdache* is the word used by early French explorers to describe male Indians who 'specialized in the work of women and formed emotional and sexual relationships with other men' (also see Kinsman, 1987:71).

5. The very first attempt to define the term 'Indian' and thereby racialize a heterogeneous and diverse group of people was made in 1850 under legislation entitled *An Act for the protection of the Indians in Upper Canada from imposition, and the property occupied and enjoyed by them from trespass and injury* (Library and Archives Canada, 2009).

6. As section 6 read: 'Provided always that any Indian woman marrying any other than an Indian, shall cease to be an Indian within the meaning of this Act, nor shall the children issue of such marriage be considered as Indians within the meaning of this Act . . .' (*An Act for the Gradual Enfranchisement of Indians* . . . [S.C. 1869, c.6. (32–33 Vict.)] reprinted in Venne, 1981:11).

7. As section 3(c) of the 1876 Act read: 'Provided that any Indian woman marrying any other than an Indian or a non-treaty Indian shall cease to be an Indian in any respect within the meaning of this Act . . .' (Indian Act [S.C. 1876, c. 18], reprinted in Venne, 1981:25). In 1951, this section was amended to read: 'The following persons are not entitled to be registered, namely . . . (b) a woman who is married to a person who is not an Indian' (Indian Act [S.C. 1951, c. 29], reprinted in Venne, 1981:319).

8. As section 3 of the 1876 Act read: 'The term "Indian" means, First. Any male person of Indian blood reputed to belong to a particular band; Secondly. Any child of such person; Thirdly. Any woman who is or was lawfully married to such person' (Indian Act [S.C. 1876, c. 18], reprinted in Venne, 1981:24). In 1951, this section was amended to read: 'Subject to section twelve, a person is entitled to be registered if that person . . . (f) is the wife or widow of a person who is entitled to be registered by virtue of paragraph (a), (b), (c), (d) or (e)' (Indian Act [S.C. 1951, c.29], reprinted in Venne, 1981:318–319).

9. As section 12(2) of the 1952 Act read: 'The addition to a Band List of the name of an illegitimate child described in paragraph (e) of section 11 may be protested at any time within twelve months after the addition, and if upon the protest it is decided that the father of the child was not an Indian, the child is not entitled to be registered under paragraph (e) of section 11' (Indian Act [R.S.C. 1952, c. 149], reprinted in Venne, 1981:360).

10. For many settlements, this meant a fundamental reconstruction of gender relations as some communities are said to have been egalitarian and matriarchal prior to contact. For a discussion of the matriarchal kinship organization and egalitarian relations among the Iroquoian Nations see Druke (1986:esp. 305). Also see Native Women's Association of Canada (1992) and Kirkness (1987/88:410–413).

References

Bannerji, Himani. 1987. Introducing Racism: Notes Toward an Anti-Racist Feminism. Resources for Feminist Research 16(1): 10–12.

Blumenfeld, Warren J., and Diane Raymond. 1988. Looking at Gay and Lesbian Life. Boston: Beacon Press.

Boswell, John. 1989. Revolutions, Universals, and Sexual Categories, pp. 17–36 in Martin Duberman, Martha Vicinus, and George Chauncey Jr. (eds): Hidden from History: Reclaiming the Gay and Lesbian Past. New York: Meridian.

Brodribb, Somer. 1984. The Traditional Roles of Native Women in Canada and the Impact of Colonization. The Canadian Journal of Native Studies 4(1): 85–103.

Brown, L.B. (ed.) 1997. Two Spirit People: American Indian Lesbian Women and Gay Men. New York: Haworth Press.

Burns, Randy. 1988. Preface, pp. 1–5 in Will Roscoe (ed.): Living the Spirit: A Gay American Indian Anthology. New York: St. Martin's Press.

Druke, Mary. 1986. Iroquois and Iroquoian in Canada, pp. 303–24 in R. Bruce Morrison and C. Roderick Wilson (eds): Native Peoples: The Canadian Experience. Toronto: McClelland & Stewart.

Engels, Frederic. 1942. The Origin of the Family, Private Property and the State. New York: International Publishers.

Foucault, Michel. 1990. The History of Sexuality: An Introduction, Volume 1. Trans. Robert Hurley. New York: Vintage Books [1978].

Frideres, James S. 1991. Indian and Northern Affairs Canada. The Indian Act Past and Present: A Manual on Registration and Entitlement Legislation. Ottawa: Indian Registration and Band Lists Directorate.

———. 1983. Native People in Canada: Contemporary Conflicts. Scarborough: Prentice-Hall.

Jamieson, Kathleen. 1986. Sex Discrimination and the Indian Act, pp. 112–36 in J. Rick Ponting (ed.): Arduous Journey: Canadian Indians and Decolonization. Toronto: McClelland & Stewart.

Katz, Jonathan. 1983. Gay/Lesbian Almanac. New York: Harper and Row.

———. 1976. Gay American History. New York: Thomas Y. Crowall.

Kenny, Maurice. 1988. Pima; United; and Winkte (poems) in Will Roscoe (ed.): Living the Spirit: A Gay American Indian Anthology. New York: St. Martin's Press.

Kinsman, Gary. 1987 Sexual Colonization of the Native Peoples, pp. 71–74 in Gary Kinsman (ed.): The Regulation of Desire: Sexuality in Canada. Montreal: Black Rose Books.

Kirkness, Verna. 1987/88. Emerging Native Women. Canadian Journal of Women and the Law 2: 408–415.

Library and Archives Canada. 2009. Aboriginal Resources and Services, http://www.collectionscanada.gc.ca/autochtone/020008-3000.3-e.html.

McClintock, Anne. 1995. Imperial Leather: Race, Gender and Sexuality in the Colonial Contest. New York: Routledge.

Midnight Sun, 1988. Sex/gender systems in native North America, pp. 32–47 in Will Roscoe (ed.): Living the Spirit: A Gay American Indian Anthology. New York: St. Martin's Press.

Miles, Robert. 1989. Racism. London: Routledge.

Native Women's Association of Canada. 1992. Matriarchy and the Canadian Charter: A Discussion Paper. Ottawa: Native Women's Association of Canada.

Ng, Roxana. 1993. Racism, Sexism, and Nation Building in Canada, pp. 50–59 in Cameron McCarthy and Warren Crichlow (eds): Race, Identity and Representation in Education. New York: Routledge.

O'Brien, Mary. 1981. The Politics of Reproduction. London: Routledge.

Owlfeather, M. 1988. Children of Grandmother Moon, pp. 97–105 in Will Roscoe (ed.): Living the Spirit: A Gay American Indian Anthology. New York: St. Martin's Press.

Padgug, Robert. 1989. Sexual Matters: Rethinking Sexuality in History, pp. 54–64 in Martin Duberman, Martha Vicinus, and George Chauncey Jr. (eds): Hidden From History: Reclaiming the Gay and Lesbian Past. New York: Meridian.

Parr, Joy. 1995. Gender, History and Historical Practice. Canadian Historical Review 76(3): 354–76.

Rich, Adrienne. 1993. Compulsory Heterosexuality and Lesbian Existence, in Henry Abelove, Michele Aina Barale, and David Halperin (eds): The Lesbian and Gay Studies Reader. New York: Routledge.

Roscoe, Will. 1988. Living the Spirit: A Gay American Indian Anthology. New York: St. Martin's Press.

Rubin, Gayle. 1975. The Traffic in Women: Notes on the Political Economy of Sex, pp. 157–210 in Reyna R. Reiter (ed.): Toward an Anthropology of Women. New York: Monthly Review.

Said, Edward. 1978. Orientalism. New York: Vintage Books.

Sanders, Douglas. 1972. The Bill of Rights and Indian Status. University of British Columbia Law Review 7(1): 81–105.

Schnarch, Brian. 1992. Neither Man nor Woman: Berdache— A Case for Non-Dichotomous Gender Construction. Anthropologica 34(1): 105–21.

Sharpe, Jim. 1992. History from Below, pp. 24–41 in Peter Burke (ed.): New Perspectives on Historical Writing. University Park, PA: Pennsylvania State University Press.

Goldberg, Jonathan. 1992. Sodometries: Renaissance Texts, Modern Sexualities. Stanford: Stanford University Press.

Venne, Sharon Helen. 1981. Indian Acts and Amendments 1868–1975: An Indexed Collection. Saskatoon: University of Saskatchewan Native Law Centre.

Whitehead, Harriet. 1993. The Bow and the Burden Strap: A New Look at Institutionalized Homosexuality in Native North America, pp. 498–527 in Henry Abelove, Michele Aina Barale, and David Halperin (eds): The Lesbian and Gay Studies Reader. New York: Routledge.

Williams, W. 1986. The Spirit and the Flesh: Sexual Diversity in American Indian Cultures. Boston: Beacon Press.

PART 1
Dialogue Box 1
When Did You Decide You Were 'Straight'?

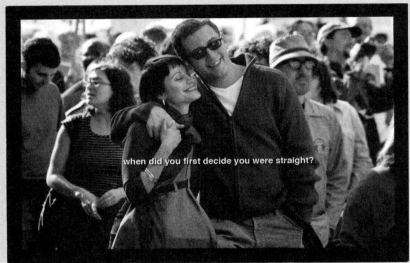

when did you first decide you were straight?

GlobalAware.org

Critical Conversations: Discussion Questions

1. The readings in chapter 1 were selected to show how older scholarship has influenced the work of more contemporary thinkers. What are some of the ways that you notice the ideas of Engels, de Beauvoir, or Foucault have influenced the thinking of Kinsman or Rubin?

2. Gayle Rubin writes, 'Most people find it difficult to grasp that whatever they like to do sexually will be thoroughly repulsive to someone else, and that whatever repels them sexually will be the most treasured delight of someone, somewhere' (p. 283). What is an aspect (something you do/like or don't do/ like) that is considered deviant? Where does this label come from? What is the rationale for the label?

3. Why is a biological explanation insufficient to explain human sexuality?

4. Are understandings of heterosexuality and homosexuality common across all cultures?

5. What does the structure of the economy have to do with the meanings that a society holds about sexuality and sexual activity?

6. Following the work of scholars such as Simone de Beauvoir, there has been a relative consensus in the social sciences that 'sex' refers to the biological distinctions between males and females and that 'gender' refers to the social or cultural distinctions between masculinity and femininity. However, this understanding is now being questioned by scholars. Based on these readings, why do you think these distinctions are now being questioned? [Editor's Note: This is an excellent question to return to periodically as you move through the readings in this collection. Does your answer change? What authors and ideas influence your changing response to this question?]

Glossary

Bisexuality Attraction to and sexual activity with members of either sex; the sexual identity premised on the desire for partners of both sexes.

Discourse Michel Foucault conceived of discourse as practices that form the objects of which they speak. Discourse might be more simply described as the particular organization and articulation of the practices, ideas, and speech through which our world is made known to us.

Feminism A diverse and international movement whose goal is the achievement of meaningful equality between men and women in all aspects of social, political and economic life. Feminism is both a social theory and a political practice.

Gender The socially constructed distinctions between men and women commonly taken to constitute masculinity and femininity. As these distinctions are socially constructed, they are also changeable across time, place, culture, and social groups.

Heteronormativity Beliefs and practices that produce heterosexuality as the normative (dominant, essential, and natural) sexuality.

Heterosexuality Opposite-sex sexual activities, desires, and to the sexual identity premised on the desire for these expressions of sexuality. The term came into common usage along with the term *homosexuality* in the late 1800s.

Homosexuality Originally referred to sexual activity and social networks among men who desired other men and was expanded to include same-sex sexual activity and relationships among women (lesbians). The term first appeared in print in Germany in 1869 (in a political pamphlet produced by Karl Maria Kertbeny [1824–1882]) and, by the turn of the century, was widely used in legal and medical discourses. In contemporary usage, homosexuality refers to same-sex sexual activities and to the sexual identities premised on the desire for these expressions of sexuality.

Marxism A diverse body of theories, political practices, and policies that are related to, or make reference to, the writings of Karl Marx and Friedrich Engels. Various forms of Marxism have been influential in the social sciences of academia and the political organization of many societies around the globe.

Post-structuralism A broad and interdisciplinary field of thought and social movement that has its origins in France during the 1960s and has since spread rapidly to other countries. Post-structural theories explore language as a system of signification rather than as simply a neutral representation of reality. Thus, post-structuralism is fundamentally concerned with the production and maintenance of 'politics of reality'.

Sexualities studies An interdisciplinary, international field of academic study. Sexualities studies in the social sciences explores the identities, cultures, acts, and desires we have come to understand as sexual, and how these understandings have been influenced by our larger social structures and cultures. The field of sexualities studies encourages us to appreciate the changeability of our cultural standards for sexual conduct.

Transgender An umbrella term, popular in Anglo-American communities, to include all kinds of people whose gendered self-presentation (expressed through mannerisms, dress, and even physiology) does not correspond to the behaviours associated with the members of their biological sex. This would include, for instance, transsexuals, drag queens (men who perform as women on stage only, usually in a gay male club or social environment), intersexed individuals (people who are born with genitals that cannot be easily classified as 'male' or 'female'), drag kings (females who perform as men on the stage in lesbian cultural spaces), transvestites (heterosexual males who cross-dress in 'women's' clothes and who receive sexual gratification from this act), as well as people who do not identify with either the category 'male' or 'female'.

Transsexual   Individuals born in one sex—male or female—but who identify as members of the 'opposite' sex. They take hormones and undergo surgical intervention, usually including the genitals, to live as members of their chosen sex. Transsexuals are both male-to-female and female-to-male.

Sexual Identities in Changing Social Contexts

Starting Points

1. How would you describe the sexual norms of your peers (what behaviours and desires are expected and acceptable)? How do you think these norms might change over the course of your life?
2. In 2005, same-sex marriage was legalized in Canada. What have you heard in the media and among friends and family about this change? What do you think about it?
3. Are there differences in what was or is considered appropriate sexual behaviour for people at your current age in your grandparents' generation, your parents' generation, and your generation?
4. How do everyday social rituals like a high school prom demonstrate and reinforce society's expectations of teenaged sexuality and sexual identity?

Introduction

> When experience is taken as the origin of knowledge, the vision of the individual subject (the person who had the experience or the historian who recounts it) becomes the bedrock of evidence on which explanation is built. Questions about the constructed nature of experience, about how subjects are constituted as different in the first place, about how one's vision is structured—about language (or discourse) and history—are left aside. The evidence of experience then becomes evidence for the fact of difference, rather than a way of exploring how difference is established, how it operates, how and in what ways it constitutes subjects who see and act in the world. (Scott 1993: 399–400)

When sexuality is discussed in undergraduate sociology classes, students often express the opinion that sex (identity, activities, and social arrangements) is 'just natural'. That is, we have sex the way we do because it is our nature or our biological destiny. While biology does certainly have something to do with it, as we saw in Part I there are many reasons to conclude that social, political, economic, and religious structures and traditions also have a great deal of influence on our sexuality. In the epigraph above, American historian Joan Wallach Scott argues that when we ignore the larger influences on our experiences, we lose the potential to understand ourselves as situated within a social, historical, and ideological context. It is this context that sets the possibilities or conditions of our experiences, including those through which we come to understand our sexualities. This section continues the analysis of the 'situatedness' of sexuality through the consideration of three related topics: the changing meanings about sexuality in Canadian society, the sexuality of young adults, and the changing patterns of long-term relationships. The first topic helps us appreciate that notions and experiences of sexualities within a society change over time. This understanding, in turn, is the foundation for further discussions about how considerations such as age, gender, and our political and legal systems are implicated in our experiences of sex and sexuality.

In Chapter 3, 'Change: The Shifting Meanings of Self and Sexuality', we explore the changes in public discourses about sex and sexuality through a historical focus. Discourse is popularly understood as what gets said about a particular topic, or the activity of communication. Scholars, however, have used the term *discourse* to describe the construction of the truth about some aspect of human activity. The most influential use of discourse as truth-making was offered by Michel Foucault, who conceived discourse as 'practices that systematically form the objects of which they speak' (Foucault, 2001: 49). An interesting example of the truth-making capacity of discourse is presented by Alan Hunt and Bruce Curtis, who consider the contemporary moral panic surrounding teenage oral sex. Their article offers an historical consideration of shifting expert and popular discourses on this sex act as it relates to age and marital status. Exactly who can 'properly' do what with whom is also the focus of the remaining articles in this chapter. Historian Steven Maynard uses case files of criminal prosecutions to analyze the gender and class expectations that shaped understandings of sexual relations between boys and men from 1890 to 1935. Court proceedings are also at issue in the excerpt from Velma Demerson's life history, *Incorrigible*. In 1939, at age 18, Demerson, a working-class white woman, was imprisoned in Ontario under the *Female Refuges Act* (1919–1958) for cohabiting out of wedlock with a Chinese man. Demerson's memoir, like Maynard's use of court records, encourages us to consider how experiences of race, class, and gender are embedded within discourses about 'dangerous' and 'immoral' sexualities. In the final article in this chapter, Canadian sociologist Mary Louise Adams uses Michel Foucault's conception of discourse and his understanding of how societies produce 'normal' sexualities to explore the underlying assumptions and politics of sex advice for Canadian teens in the 1950s. Adams demonstrates that these educational efforts were founded on a relatively new understanding in Canadian society—an understanding that held that 'normal' sexual activities and identities were a product of one's social and psychological environment, and thus an important societal resource that needed to be managed by public 'experts' such as teachers, police, and physicians.

The historical focus of chapter 3 provides a sense of the changeability of discourses about sexuality. In chapters 4 and 5, this sense helps us understand the various ways established knowledge about sex is institutionalized in contemporary society. Chapter 4, 'Young People Having Sex: Sexualities, Sexual Identities, and Sexual Behaviours', explores the role of social context in the production of sexual behaviours and identities. In the first article of this chapter, the sexual norms and mores of university students are the subject of a study of the influences of gendered discourses on attitudes toward and experiences of sexuality. This influence is not always recognized by social actors themselves, as demonstrated by sociologist Melanie Beres. Beres' interview-based study explores the production of choice and consent in short-term heterosexual encounters among young seasonal workers in the resort area of Jasper, Alberta. As a contrast to the supposed freedom of choice reported by Beres' interviewees, educators André P. Grace and Kris Wells examine the discourses surrounding the curtailment of personal choice. In 2002, Marc Hall, a student at a Toronto-area Catholic school, was denied permission to take his boyfriend to the senior prom. The authors examine how this event was politicized and critique the Catholic Church's attempt to 'privatize' queer sexuality. Similarly, the influence of authority on sexuality is also the focus of psychologists Cailey Hartwick, Serge Desmarais, and Karl Hennig's work. In this study, Hartwick and her colleagues survey male and female university students about the dynamics of sexual victimization. These authors pay particular attention to the experiences and characteristics of males who report being sexually coerced. Taken together, the selections in chapter 4 demonstrate the various ways established knowledge about sex is institutionalized.

Chapter 5, 'Sex for Life? Changing Patterns within Long-term Relationships', profiles three significant recent changes and trends within the established patterns of sexual relationships in Canada. These changes are the legalization of same-sex marriages, the increase of long-term cohabiting couples, and the increasing prominence of ethnically mixed marriages. Each of these phenomena will influence the patterns of socialization among Canadians for generations to come. In 'Until Death Do Us Part?' sociologist Adam Isaiah Green compares the 'sexual careers' of a sample of heterosexual and homosexual men in their twenties and thirties living in New York City. Green argues that differential access to marriage across these identities/communities encourages different patterns of sexual activities, relationships, and relational goals. This questioning of the role of marriage in our society is continued in Céline Le Bourdais and Évelyne Lapierre-Adamcyk's 'Changes in Conjugal Life in Canada'. In this study, the authors examine the trends in marriage and cohabitation across Canada and assess whether cohabitation has emerged as alternative to marriage or represents prelude to traditional marriage. The discursive dynamics of the legalization of same sex-marriage are probed by Mariana Valverde. Valverde uses a Foucauldian analysis to explore the phenomenon of the socially legitimate, or normal, same-sex relationship. In 'Ethnically Heterogamous Marriages: The Case of Asian Canadians', Jessie M. Tzeng examines the factors that predict the likelihood of marriage outside of one's own ethnic group. Tzeng's analysis highlights the importance of factors such as language, educational attainment, and socio-economic status when we are making our decisions as to whom and whether we should marry. Taken together, these articles demonstrate that even something that is as 'taken for granted' as the institution of marriage has effects upon and implications for our sexual identity that are not immediately obvious if we simply use our own experience as the basis of our social understanding. The authors whose work appears in chapter 5 encourage us to see beyond our own experiences and the either/or, for-or-against positions that structure these experiences and to become mindful of the complexities of the social construction of sexual and relational norms.

References

Foucault, Michel. 2001. *The Archeology of Knowledge*. London: Routledge.
Scott, Joan W. 1993. 'The Evidence of Experience', in Henry Abelove, Michèle Aina Barale, and David M. Halperin (eds), *The Lesbian and Gay Studies Reader*. New York: Routledge, pp. 397–415.

3 Change: The Shifting Meaning of Self and Sexuality

A Genealogy of the Genital Kiss: Oral Sex in the Twentieth Century

Alan Hunt and Bruce Curtis

Introduction

In this article we provide a genealogy of oral sex. It is a genealogy, in contrast to a chronological history, in that we explore the different contexts and discourses concerning oral sex that have occurred over time. It should be noted that the place of oral sex in homosexual communities and practices has been quite different than in the heterosexual population. Our analysis is confined to the role of oral sex within heterosexual practice.

At the beginning of the twenty-first century oral sex has become controversial; in short it has again become a problem, but a different sort of problem than it had been earlier. Oral sex has been problematized because it has left the marital bedroom and now figures in the tumultuous discourses about teenage sex. There is a scarcely veiled prurient interest indulged in by the media in the supposed proliferation of 'rainbow parties' at which teenage girls compete in oral sex by trying to leave the lowest lipstick ring on a boy's penis. Investigative journalists are easily

persuaded to make much of 'colour-coded sex'; practices in which girls wear coloured bracelets, where the colours indicate their preferred sexual practice, white signifying oral sex, red, vaginal sex, etc. Courts have imposed penalties on young men receiving oral sex from underage girls. School principals speak of a crisis of oral sex in the schoolyard. We explore the specific anxiety concerning teen oral sex in more detail below and elsewhere (Curtis and Hunt, 2007). Suffice it to say, that these and many other instances exemplify what Michel Foucault (1978) had described as an 'incitement to discourse' (p. 17). We may well be on the cusp of a 'policing of sex; that is, not the rigor of a taboo, but the necessity of regulating sex through useful and public discourses' (p. 25).

We develop a genealogy of oral sex here in a double sense in that we do not assume any linear continuity in oral sex as a stable and unchanging phenomenon, and we focus attention on the shifting ways in which oral sex has come to be treated as a problem. Our focus is on English-speaking countries, and draws on the marriage and sexual advice manuals of the twentieth century, texts and debates that crossed back and forth across the Atlantic with surprising alacrity. We do not claim that the advice given by manual writers provides direct access to the sexual practices of their readers. We do, however, claim that these texts generated what might fruitfully be called a sexual habitus that takes the form of sets of attitudes and dispositions shared by many in the social groups who were the intended audience of these texts. Thus, for example, at the beginning of our period many would have had a certain repugnance toward oral sex, but by the middle of the century, even though they may not personally have engaged in oral sex, most would probably have come to view it is a recognized feature of the sexual realm. We will show that through quite distinct phases oral sex became normalized, first cunnilingus and then fellatio, first as a physiological aid and then as a sexual pleasure in its own right. By the last decades of the century oral sex had taken its place in the sexual repertoire of most moderately adventurous heterosexuals having the distinct quality as an embodiment of both mutuality and intimacy. Then, rather suddenly, at the very end of the century oral sex becomes reproblematized in the context of controversies over teenage sexual practices where oral sex seemed to lose both mutuality and intimacy.

Foucault's (1996) work offers a valuable starting point for this inquiry in suggesting that for some social practice to enter the 'domain of thought' social, economic, or other processes must have made it uncertain, caused it to lose its familiarity, or to have provoked a certain number of difficulties around it.

> It is problematization that responds to these difficulties . . . it develops the conditions in which possible responses can be given; it defines the elements that will constitute what the different solutions attempt to respond to. This development of a given into a question, this transformation of a group of obstacles and difficulties into problems to which the diverse solutions will attempt to produce a response, this is what constitutes the point of problematization and the specific work of thought (p. 421).

One important caution is necessary. There is a common assumption that pervades everyday life that such practices as 'sexual intercourse' and 'oral sex' are natural and unchanging and that 'we' all know what these terms mean. [. . .] What gets subsumed under the umbrella of 'oral sex' often involves a dispersed set of practices and meanings.

It follows from the refusal of any assumption about the naturalness of sexual practices that there can be no sequential history of sexual conduct or of sexuality. There is no linear process of liberation or a reverse process of repression, but rather what should be anticipated is a series of shifting contexts in which the meaning and significance of particular sexual practices can and do change sometimes abruptly. [. . .]

Marriage and Sexual Advice Manuals

[. . .] It is important to our argument to stress that advice books should not be read as providing accurate accounts of the sexual practices of their readers. However, we do want to insist that these advice manuals participate in the articulation and formation of sexual desires and practices. These books instruct men as to the kind of women they should desire and how they should express their desire. In the same way, they tell women how to enhance their desirability and how to respond to their husband's desire. Thus we contend that neither sexual desire nor its practices are a universal, natural, or instinctual fact, and thus both sexual practices and sexual discourses have an inescapably historical dimension. It follows that we should avoid making assumptions about what they might have meant to people in earlier periods and, in particular, we should not assume that they carried today's meanings (Cook, 2004). Foucault (1978) captures this essential caution.

> Sexuality must not be thought of as a kind of natural given which power tries to hold in check, or as an obscure domain which knowledge tries gradually to uncover. It is the name that can be given to a historical construct: not a furtive reality that is difficult to grasp, but a great surface network in which the stimulation of bodies, the intensification of pleasures, the incitement to discourses, the formation of special knowledges, the strengthening of controls and resistances, are linked to one another, in accordance with a few major strategies of knowledge and power (p. 105).

By the early Victorian period, books primarily focused on marital sex had begun to appear. There were considerable barriers to their publication and restrictions on the contents of those that were published. The history of sexuality has been beset by the many ways in which sexual knowledge has been regarded as a form of 'dangerous knowledge'. Thus, the very idea of sex advice and education confronted the challenge that to speak of sex would promote sexual behaviour. [. . .] The writers and publishers of marital texts in the late nineteenth and early twentieth centuries were to run the gauntlet of the law for the next century. For instance, Ida Craddock (1897, 1899, 1900) published a series of marriage advice texts in the late 1890s and despite her claim to the blessing of the Women's Christian Temperance Union, her books were condemned by Anthony Comstock, who for 40 years as US Postal Inspector carried out a militant suppression of obscene literature in the mail. He denounced her books as 'the science of seduction'. Craddock was prosecuted for obscenity, found guilty, and committed suicide prior to sentence. In England, the publishers of Edward Charles's (1935) *The Sexual Impulse* were convicted on an obscenity charge largely because of his idiosyncratic rejection of sex in the bedroom in favour of sex in 'wild country, the warm, golden sand of a broken coast line, or the deep bed of pine needles in a wood' (p. 150).

The text writers sought to overcome the risks and barriers to publication by two tactics. The first was to write within a medical genre, making sure to use correct Latin names for body parts and physiological functions. The second tactic required the careful avoidance of explicit terminology by presenting the texts in a referential, even theological, idiom. For example, Ida Craddock, who was herself a believer in free love, refers only to marital sex in the most embellished terms. She advises wives to

> keep self-controlled, serene, tranquil and aspire to the highest. Pray to God, if you believe in God and in prayer; if not, think steadily and quietly what a beautiful thing it is to be at that moment of harmony with Nature in her inmost workings and rejoice that you and your husband are part of Nature, pulsating with her according to her law (Craddock, 1899; quoted Petersen, 1999, p. 16).

The result of these self-imposed restraints was that the marriage manuals of the early twentieth century remained reticent about the physical practices of sexual relations. [. . .] The key characteristic of the great majority of the texts of the period is a euphemism of everything to do with sex and sexuality. Van de Velde (1926) explicitly addresses the danger.

> If we cannot avoid occasional reference to certain abnormal sexual practices, *we shall emphatically state that they are abnormal* . . . it is our intention to keep the Hell-gate of the Realm of Sexual Perversion firmly closed (p. 144).

It is not surprising that there is a profound silence not only about oral sex, but about specific sexual practices. The descriptions of sexual practices are limited to the generalities of 'embraces' and 'caresses'. These silences and euphemisms were reinforced by the deep and pervasive discursive formation which located sex within the field of biological reproduction. Within this genre there was no need for a specific conception of female sexuality because as Claire Rayner (1968), the British sex advice columnist, was still saying as late as 1968 that sex for women was about baby-making. And Walker and Strauss, as late as 1954, classified both masturbation and oral sex as deviations, specifically as 'deviations of aim' (Walker & Strauss, 1954; quoted in Petersen, 1999, p. 115).

This reproductive ideology took its most explicit form in the longstanding distinction between approved sexuality directed toward the goal of conception and the disapproval of all non-reproductive sexuality that resulted in the condemnation, not only of homosexuality and extramarital sex, but the specific pursuit of sexual pleasure. [. . .]

A Woman's Right to Sexual Pleasure and Its Ramifications

The decisive rupture that occurred in the discursive formations which encompassed the sexual field came about, as do so many significant turning points, almost surreptitiously, without a fanfare. The emergence of a concern with female sexual pleasure had far-reaching consequences. It not only decisively impacted on the relations between males and females, but, more significantly for present purposes, it was to transform, if not the actual lived experience of women and men, then the discursive construction of the sexual encounter by extending it from a one-act play into a multi-act encounter. Its most distinctive manifestation was the discovery of foreplay. The very term *foreplay* is itself significant because the prior discursive construction had been one of great seriousness. So to invoke the theme of play was to usher in a profound transformation. One of the most explicit markers of this shift was Havelock Ellis's (1921) text, *The Play-Function of Sex*; it is not claimed that this probably not widely read text played any causal role, but rather that it provides a convenient marker. It would be a project of considerable significance to explore the invention of foreplay. Theodore van de Velde (1926), whose *Ideal Marriage* was probably the most influential marriage text until the early 1960s, serves as a particularly clear marker of an equal rights doctrine. For him 'ideal marriage' had to be grounded in mutuality, '*equal rights and equal joy in sexual union*' (p. 145; emphasis in original) and this required that the couple prepare each other's bodies for this joyous union.

[. . .]

In the period on either side of World War I, the market for texts on marriage and sex expanded, and more importantly the restricted circulation of such texts which had been a feature of the pre-War period was gradually undermined. From this point on more voices are heard that challenged the anti-sexual stance of the various strands of the social purity movement.

The key contention, namely, that sexual ignorance does not secure purity, but rather causes unhappiness, gained ground and soon became the standard point of entry for the newer texts. This was exemplified by the mild eugenicist Maurice Bigelow (1916), who insisted that physiological and psychological ignorance leads to marital disharmony. As against those he styled the sexual pessimists, he defended dancing—admitting that his own view had changed—as a good thing because modern dancing could teach sexual self-control.

Confirmation of the close link between contraception and the new form of discourse around sexuality is found in the texts of Marie Stopes and Margaret Sanger. Stopes (1918), the British champion of accessible contraception, in her sexual advice text, *Married Love*, promoted a romanticized defence of marital sex. She held that sexual compatibility provided the essential bond that could not be secured unless the relationship provided sexual satisfaction to the wife. Similarly, the American contraception pioneer Margaret Sanger's (1926) *Happiness in Marriage* invoked reference to the relationship between Pygmalion and Galatea. The husband's role, was like that of Pygmalion, 'his task is to bring to life the real woman of flesh and blood concealed in the statue he adores. It is the duty of the lover to accomplish this miracle by using all the resources he has at his command' (p. 130).

The thematic of these texts, and of the many that followed, which dominated the field for the next 50 years, is best captured as the advocacy of companionate marriage within which mutually satisfying marital sex provided the ongoing stability of the heterosexual relation. The signifier of successful marital sex was the achievement of mutual orgasm (Gordon, 1978). These texts all depended on a very specific conception of the dichotomous sexual physiology of females and males. As Sanger (1926) expresses it, the male, once aroused, is immediately ready for action, but his first duty is to awake his wife's desire

because, while the female is as sexual as the male, she is slower to arouse. [. . .]

The Opening for the Legitimation of Oral Sex

[. . .] Oral sex makes its appearance cautiously within a specifically physiological context. [. . .] If lubrication is not produced naturally then digital or oral stimulation may be necessary. Cunnilingus thus enters, not as a form of sexual pleasure for either the female or the male, but rather as an obligation essential to secure the physiological conditions for successful coitus.

Oliver Butterfield (1937/1969), in one of America's more durable manuals, *Sex Life in Marriage*, describes the transition to coitus.

> The man must understand that his wife may require anywhere from a few moments to an hour of fondling, caressing, and love-making before she is as ready for active intercourse as he may be within a few moments. Her sex organs are larger than his, both in size and number and are distributed over a wider area of her body. The inner walls of the vaginal opening need to become sensitive and thoroughly stimulated. . . . Just as it is necessary for the male organ to become stiff . . . so the soft external folds and the vaginal passage need to become fully prepared before intercourse can be truly satisfying. Such preparation usually takes longer in a woman than a man (p. 94).

Eustace Chesser (1947) similarly treats oral sex, or the 'genital kiss', pragmatically; 'the advantage of this kiss is that it provides natural lubrication' (p. 43). However, by the 1964 edition, he is more enthusiastic, insisting that oral sex has 'much to commend it' and is 'widely practiced', but the man 'must guard against anything which will frighten or disgust a woman who has little or no erotic experience' (p. 54).

[. . .]

The next significant discursive shift was one that questioned the paradigm of male sexual activity and female passivity. Its vehicle was a further extension of the companionate marriage that now breaks with a rigid gendered division of sexual labour. Max Exner (1937) articulates this transition by criticizing

> some of the more recent publications dealing with marriage that have fallen into the error of implying that the activities of foreplay are a function and responsibility of the husband only, and of implying that it consists essentially of a sort of mechanical process of stimulating the woman by manipulating her erotic areas. This is a serious error (p. 79).

It is in this way that fellatio makes its entrance. But it emerges only with a recognition of its problematic status. As Edwin Hirsch (1934) concedes, oral sex has often been defined as perversion and is 'generally regarded as loathsome and indicative of a sad degree of sexual perversion' (p. 225). Earlier, however, Havelock Ellis had recognized oral sex as normal particularly where it helped male erection. He expressed the view that 'whatever gives satisfaction and relief is good and right' (quoted in Hirsch, 1934, p. 227). Hirsch legitimizes oral sex by invoking a doctrine from the Indian *ars erotica*: 'Whatever things may be done by one of the lovers to the other, the same should be returned by the other.'

[. . .]

The emergence of discourses of sexual mutuality marks the culmination of the doctrine of companionate marriage. Thus van de Velde (1926) endorses the view that the genital kiss 'may be enjoyed alternately or sometimes simultaneously' (p. 171). Fellatio may also provide a substitute for coitus during menstruation.

Yet it is palpable that a certain reticence continues to surround oral sex. One part of this reserve is that fellatio has not freed itself from a certain uneasiness. This apprehension revolves around a configuration of different concerns. Foremost is the persistence of an unspoken taboo that may reflect a lingering hostility to non-reproductive sex. If fellatio ends with male ejaculation the 'goal' of penile-vaginal intercourse may not be achieved. Westheimer and Kravetz (1985) suggest that heterosexuals might be anxious that an interest in oral sex might imply a latent homosexuality (p. 201). Chesser (1964) cautioned women that some men may be shocked by what he regards as the 'forwardness' of a woman who attempts genital stimulation or that men who practise cunnilingus may be perceived as engaged in an act of 'self-abasement' or as a sign of masochism. [. . .] Many women experienced a persistent lack of comfort with their genital hygiene; 'down there' was somewhere they felt to be sexually unattractive; but it should be noted that perceptions of bodily and other odours have been historically contingent (Cohen & Johnson, 2005). This hesitation about hygiene still persists. Winks and Semans (2002) suggest that although most people practise oral sex, many of them are embarrassed while others are repulsed by the idea. They recognize that many may be concerned about body odour in a culture that has built an entire industry to mask or erase the body's natural smell. Others have suggested that because of the frequency of oral sex in heterosexual prostitution, it may have a negative image for many women (Robinson & Kruamer, 1983). Yet it seems that while some men and some women may feel some hesitation about cunnilingus, most authors concur with Paget's (2000) assessment that today most have rejected 'old myths having to do with oral sex being dirty or unnatural' (p. 134).

More generally the texts on either side of World War II evince the feeling that oral sex is not securely established as a 'normal' form of sexual pleasure. Even into the 1970s, Gagnon and Simon (1973) contend that oral sex was still regarded as unpleasant by many men and even more women. Such reservations reflect a persistence of assumptions about the context in which marital sex occurs. What is significant is that authors assume that they and their readers have a shared intuitive sense of what it means to 'have sex'—and we will see this is precisely one of the issues that has recently been contested. The assumed scenario of marital sex is that of its location in the bedroom, at the end of the day, husband and wife under the bedclothes; after some time devoted to foreplay, penile-vaginal intercourse occurs most frequently in the 'missionary position'. In this context, oral sex could be little more than an occasional variant in the sexual routine. When oral sex does occur, it is still located within the central ideological motif of the companionate marriage encapsulated in the ideal of pursuit of the mutual orgasm. Oral sex figures significantly as a technique to aid mutual orgasm and has thus become a core component of the eroticization of marriage.

Undoubtedly the major source of anxiety about the integration of oral sex into the normal sexual repertoire concerns whether oral sex was simply part of the regime of foreplay, which had by now become established as an ever present feature of the sexual encounter, or whether it culminates in male ejaculation. Reuben (1969), author of the well-known, but perhaps best forgotten, *Everything You Always Wanted to Know About Sex, But Were Afraid to Ask*, was concerned to rebut the suggestion that, if oral sex is so gratifying, it might replace penile-vaginal intercourse. He is very insistent that 'regular copulation is

even more enjoyable than fellatio and cunnilingus. The most desirable use of both stimulations is to make the final stage of intercourse as exciting and rewarding as possible' (pp. 64–65).

In the advice manuals there is a trend to incorporate questions around oral sex within the discourse of women's sexual rights. The new problem that arises once oral sex has been fully integrated is about whether it should lead to ejaculation. The answer given time and time again is that it is only acceptable if the female consents (Greenberg, Bruess & Haffner, 2004). Comfort (1972) lays down as a primary rule of good sex 'don't do anything you don't enjoy' (p. 73). But there is hesitation about addressing the issue of ejaculation. Only slowly were questions posed about whether it should occur inside or outside the mouth, about how semen tastes, and about whether it was in any way unhealthy or could cause pregnancy. Masters and Johnson (1986) addressed 'difficulties' experienced by women with oral sex but assured them that 'many find that with a little effort (and practice) they can easily develop a personal comfort' (p. 113). Only later did the question arise, so characteristic of an age obsessed by weight and calories, about the calorific value of semen. That the texts asked some of these questions, but always in a hesitant manner, can be interpreted as implying that oral sex was still some distance from having been normalized within heterosexual routines. In the most recent texts, anxieties about fellatio continue to be addressed in the form of a debate about whether to swallow or not. The responses are typical of an individualist ethos insisting that if you don't like it, don't do it, some make suggestions about simulating swallowing. However, Westheimer (1986) urges women to keep open the possibility that 'sometime' they might try it!

For oral sex to come into its own and to become thoroughly modernized sex had to become focused upon interpersonal intimacy and mutual bodily pleasure (Robinson, 1989). This required that the sexual encounter itself be reconfigured and relocated. First, it is no longer so squarely located within matrimony, although this did not mean that marriage was no longer important. Rather, sex was represented as occurring within any loving and lasting relationship. Next, the separation of sex from reproduction was completed and this involved an unambiguous commitment to pleasure as the primary motivation. In this context, it is reproductive sex that is different. It is timed and calculated outside the regular sex life of the partners. Modern sexual partners take affirmative decisions about when to seek conception and this calculation revolves around their whole life circumstances.

[. . .]

Oral Sex Comes of Age as Sexual Technique

The wave of texts that date from the mid-1960s became increasingly focused on providing instruction about sexual techniques. They shared much in common with the increasingly popular 'do-it-yourself' manuals that provide precise instructions on a wide range of self-help techniques. The most common focus of the texts of this period was on 'sexual positions', that is, the variety of configurations of bodies that made possible penile-vaginal intercourse. This focus may have been an unintended imitation of the Kama Sutra which was republished in paperback formats. The authors of such manuals conceived of their mission as being to spread variety in sexual practices in pursuit of sexual pleasure on the presumption that any couple sticking to one format would rapidly become bored. And 'variety' came to be presented (and indeed illustrated) as variation in sexual position. Such a preoccupation reflects an important link between sex and consumerist ethos in which variety is valorized.

If the manuals of the interwar period had detailed the techniques of foreplay and assumed that the readers knew about the basic mechanics of coitus, [. . .] the focus from the 1960s on was upon copulation as exemplified by Alex Comfort's (1972) *The Joy of Sex*. [. . .]

Toward the end of the twentieth century oral sex came to occupy an ever more prominent place in the discursive structure of what by now had ceased to be 'marriage manuals' but had become 'sex advice manuals'. There was no presumption that the implied readers who digest and practise the advice offered were married couples. Yet it should not be thought that oral sex had become 'the real thing'; that was still conceived as a precursor to penile-vaginal intercourse, but the variety of positions for coitus were presumed already to be familiar to the readers. In the quest for novelty the texts of the century's end devoted more attention to an ever more exhaustive compilation of sexual techniques. Characteristic of an unashamedly consumerist context more attention was given to 'sex aids' designed to supplement and vary the sexual experience.

Current sex manuals exist in an extremely competitive market; today's large bookstores contain a great profusion of such texts. Their most striking feature is that they have lost most of the medicalized trappings of earlier periods. Some authors do still make use of 'Dr', but even here the medical is made safely familiar, epitomized by 'Dr Ruth' who is a convivial friend rather than an expert. Their general style is enthusiastic, excited, and breathless, drawing on the journalistic style of *Cosmopolitan* with its injunction to experience 'great sex' by 'trying this, doing this'. Contemporary manuals celebrate this exuberance with titles such as Locker's (2003) *The Complete Idiot's Guide to Amazing Sex*, which promises 'techniques to add variety to your oral sex life' (p. 166) for which 'the following are lip-smacking ideas for things you can do while performing amazing oral sex on a woman' (p. 169). The quest for novelty and variety is exemplified by the suggestion that oral sex should be tried in 'exotic locations' such as at work, on trains, in planes, etc. *How to Give Her Absolute Pleasure* (Paget, 2000) makes it clear that the quest for enhanced pleasure requires practice and hard work. Men are informed that they need to learn what makes their partners 'hottest and come hardest'. This and other texts have a strong emphasis on acquiring correct techniques. Men are encouraged to practise drills such as holding a 'Life Saver' between the lips while licking from the inside out. Kate Taylor (2002) urges men to improve their skill by 'smothering her clitoris with your wet loose mouth and sucking on it gently' (p. 121). Chia, Chia, Abrams, and Abrams (2000) recommend that men even do exercises to strengthen their tongues. Yet this preoccupation with sexual technique turns sex into work; and as Lewis and Brisset (1967) had argued earlier, there is a tension, even a contradiction, between the pursuit of sexual pleasure and the acquisition of technique. This trend has reached a further peak with the publication of texts devoted exclusively to oral sex (Blue, 2002a; 2002b).

A strongly affirmative case for oral sex is made in the name of the sexual empowerment of women. In opposition to the strand of radical feminism which, during the pornography debates, had argued that oral sex degraded women, Lou Paget (1999) commends fellatio because it empowers women to take control. The empowerment suggested is one that valorizes female sexual initiative, 'this is something you do for him' (p. 135). She makes the interesting suggestion that men like fellatio because it allows them to surrender and to receive pleasure. This line of argument highlights the most general feature of this genre of sex advice that stresses the mutual responsibility of partners for the pleasure of the other.

The New Problematization of Oral Sex

It has become conventional, despite Foucault's strictures to the contrary, in chronological histories of twentieth-century sex to view the steady progress toward sexual modernization as having been disrupted by a sudden reversal that occurred in the 1980s (Dean, 1996; McLaren, 1999; Petersen, 1999). The emergence of the AIDS epidemic in the mid-1980s is the most frequently cited root of this reversal. [. . .] The impact of AIDS on the advice manuals of the period was evident, but it did not disrupt the now well-established commitment to the quest for mutual pleasure. Rather, the manuals' messages remained largely unchanged but with the addition of an explicit 'safe sex' content. Sari Locker's (2003) injunction captures the sexual ethos of the century's end; 'you should always be making your sexual choices based on what you think is best for your health and happiness' (p. 175). The return of sexual danger with the arrival of AIDS gave a specific direction to the longstanding tension between the presence of pleasure and danger in the field of sex (Dubois & Gordon, 1983; Vance, 1984). The problematic of sex, which had earlier in the century been fear of pregnancy, now became a fear of disease as reflected in another of Westheimer's offerings; her earlier *Dr. Ruth's Guide to Good Sex* (1983) becomes *Dr. Ruth's Guide to Safer Sex* (1992).

Paradoxically, this medicalization of sexual anxiety provided a quasi-medical normalization of oral sex. It is a characteristic trope that authors compare 'new' sexual practices favourably with other activities. Thus, Reuben (1969) claimed that oral sex was more hygienic than kissing. Oral sex was to be increasingly promoted as 'safer sex' employing the fashionable risk discourse to claim that AIDS, in particular, but other sexually transmitted diseases as well, were less likely to be transmitted by oral than penile-vaginal sex.

In Alex Comfort's (1991) revised edition of his bestseller, now called *The New Joy of Sex*, he retained the rather forced parallel between food and sex. Now oral sex is not only part of a great meal, but it is a safe and healthy course. He goes on to claim that there is no firm evidence of transmission of AIDS via oral sex. Other authors of the period are more cautious, claiming only that the risks are much lower than for other sexual practices. [. . .] But a new site of contestation emerged as part of a wider social problematization of the sexuality of children and young people.

Youth and Oral Sex

It is not our intention here to confront the complex phenomenon of the problematization of young people and sex (Curtis and Hunt, 2007). In order to explore the part played by oral sex in these controversies we note that once sexual practices become disconnected from both marriage and reproduction the field of sexuality and its associated practices (and, in addition, the earlier age of puberty and widening gap between puberty and marriage) opened to new configurations. We suggest that the place of oral sex in sexual repertoires has changed in significant ways.

It should be recalled that the sexuality of children has long been contested in many and varied forms. As Foucault (1978) observed

> all those social controls, cropping up at the end of the past century, which screened the sexuality of couples, parents and children, dangerous and endangered adolescents— undertaking to protect, separate and forewarn, signalling perils everywhere, awakening people's attention, calling for diagnoses, piling up reports, organizing therapies. These sites radiated discourses aimed at sex, intensifying people's awareness of

it as a constant danger, and this in turn created a further incentive to talk about it. (pp. 30–31)

The most obvious instance of this intensification of concern about children's sexuality has involved the various phases of preoccupation with masturbation from the eighteenth century to the end of the nineteenth century (Laqueur, 2003; Hunt, 1998). More recently, the focus shifted to premarital sex and teen pregnancies. The current phase, especially prominent in the United States, has been attempts to promote sexual abstinence. But as Zygmunt Bauman (1997, p. 151) notes, this search for a sexual purity confined within the family, results in the family itself being 'purified' of love and sexual suspicion coming to haunt all relations between adults and children; can we take photos of our kids who do not happen to have any clothes or can we sleep naked, take the kids into bed for a cuddle on Sunday morning? (Cover, 2003).

The major shift regarding the place of oral sex in contemporary sexual behaviour is a striking change of its place in sexual repertoires. With the normalization of oral sex within adult heterosexual relations after the 1960s, partners came to regard oral sex as a particularly intimate expression of heterosexual love. Typically, we suggest, adults started to engage in oral sex only after penile-vaginal intercourse had been established and regularized. [. . .]

Oral sex today has a rather different place for teenagers in that many engage in oral sex either before engaging in sexual intercourse or as a substitute for intercourse. One possible reason for this change stems from the heavy emphasis that has been placed in all forms of sex education and literature upon 'safer sex'. Another reason for this change may be linked to the return of concerns among girls and young women about maintaining their virginity. [. . .] These anxieties create a discourse within which the disciplining of bodies and sexuality thrives today. Discourses of 'safer sex' have come to play a significant role in the disciplining of pleasure. While not necessarily intended by sex educators, the message to practise 'safer sex' may have been interpreted by some young people in such a way that oral sex comes to be regarded as a safe alternative to intercourse. This view has gained endorsement from more liberal sex advice authors, most noticeably by Alex Comfort (1991). Others have been more cautious. Ruth Westheimer (1995) insists that oral sex is not entirely safe, 'you can get AIDS through oral sex' (p. 77).

It is evident that whatever its incidence the possibility or probability of oral sex among teens has fuelled adult anxieties. As Gelperin (2004) demonstrates, there has been increasing media coverage of stories about an 'epidemic' of teen oral sex. There have been numerous reports of teens attending 'oral sex parties'. Particularly prominent have been accounts of what the media have dubbed 'rainbow parties' at which girls wear different colour lipstick and the goal is for boys to get many different colours on their penises. These and similar events appear to have been inflated into urban legends. We know little about the accuracy of such stories, but the significance of their repetition and dissemination attests to the existence of anxieties which the media have been only too willing to amplify.

[. . .]

We have stressed that the sexual modernization of the twentieth century came to celebrate the quest for mutual pleasure within heterosexual relations in which oral sex came to figure prominently precisely because of its reciprocal potential. Today it is thought that among the young, oral sex is a sexual favour that girls perform for boys. [One educator] draws the positive inference that this puts the female in control and ends the situation in which most teen sex involved 'boys doing things to girls'. Many of the contemporary sex advice manuals confirm this view by valorizing female initiative and the positive value of an active role as the bringer of pleasure. Among the sex educators interviewed by Remez there were others who disputed the autonomy of girls in teen sexual relations and viewed oral sex as exploitative. Prinstein (2003), for example, suggests that girls providing fellatio may do so because of peer pressure in pursuit of an elusive social status and popularity. There is little to be gained from an abstract contest between empowerment and exploitation since normative assessment is only possible in the light of the contextual circumstances of specific sexual encounters.

Today oral sex leads a double life. It is firmly integrated within adult heterosexual relations as an important signifier of mutuality in the quest for pleasure. In contrast, among the young oral sex is a transitory contact that barely counts as 'having sex'. The closest we think it advisable to come to making a normative judgment is to express a certain regret that, after the long journey of oral sex within heterosexual relations toward establishing significant reciprocity and equality in gendered sexual roles, it is now criticized when practised by teens. It is especially significant that the quest for sexual autonomy of young people is now the target of a significant conservative reaction that has made oral sex a site of political contestation.

References

Bauman, Z. (1997). On the postmodern redeployment of sex: Foucault's *History of Sexuality* revisited. In *Postmodernity and Its Discontents* (pp. 141–51). New York, NY: New York University Press.

Bigelow, M. (1916). *Sex Education: A Series of Lectures Concerning Knowledge of Sex in its Relation to Human Life*. New York, NY: Macmillan.

Bland, L. (1995). *Banishing the Beast: English Feminism and Sexual Morality 1885–1918*. Harmondsworth: Penguin.

Blue, V. (2002a). *The Ultimate Guide to Cunnilingus: How to Go Down on a Woman and Give Her Exquisite Pleasure*. San Francisco, CA: Cleis Press.

———. (2002b). *The Ultimate Guide to Fellatio: How to Go Down on a Man and Give Him Mind-Blowing Pleasure*. San Francisco, CA: Cleis Press.

Butterfield, O.M. (1937/1969). *Sex Life in Marriage*. New York, NY: Emerson Books.

The Caraka Samhita (1949). Jamnagar, India: Jamnagar Shree.

Charles, E. (1935). *The Sexual Impulse: An Introduction to the Study of the Psychology, Physiology and Bio-Chemistry of the Sexual Impulse*. London, UK: Boriswood.

Chesser, E. (1947). *Love Without Fear. How to Achieve Sex Happiness in Marriage*. New York, NY: Roy Publishers.

———. (1964). *Love Without Fear: A Plain Guide to Sex Techniques for Every Married Adult*. London, UK: Jarrolds.

Chia, M., Chia, M., Abrams, D., & Abrams, R. (2000). *The Multi-Orgasmic Couple: Sexual Secrets Every Couple Should Know*. San Francisco, CA: HarperCollins.

Cohen, W.A. & Johnson, R. (Eds). (2005). *Filth, Dirt, Disgust, and Modern Life*. Minneapolis: University of Minnesota Press.

Comfort, A. (1972). *The Joy of Sex: A Gourmet Guide to Lovemaking*. New York, NY: Simon & Schuster.

———. (1991). *The New Joy of Sex*. New York, NY: Crown Publishers.

Cook, H. (2004). *The Long Sexual Revolution: English Women, Sex and Contraception, 1800–1975*. Oxford, UK: Oxford University Press.

Cover, R. (2003). The naked subject: Nudity, context and sexualization in contemporary culture. *Body & Society, 9*, 53–72.

Craddock, I.C. (1897). *Letter to a Prospective Bride*. Philadelphia, PA.

———. (1899). *Right Marital Living*. Chicago, IL.

———. (1900). *The Wedding Night*. Chicago, IL.

Curtis, B., & Hunt, A. (2007). The fellatio 'epidemic': Age relations and access to the erotic arts. *Sexualities, 10*, 5–28.

Dean, C.J. (1996). *Sexuality and Modern Western Culture*. New York, NY: Twayne.

Dodson, B. (1966). *Sex For One: The Joy of Selfloving*. New York, NY: Crown.

Dubois, E.C., & Gordon, L. (1983). Seeking ecstasy on the battlefield: Danger and pleasure in nineteenth-century feminist sexual thought. *Feminist Studies, 9*, 7–26.

Ellis, H.H. (1921). *The Play-Function of Sex*. London, UK: British Society for the Study of Sex Psychology.

Exner, M.J. (1937). *The Sexual Side of Marriage*. London, UK: G. Allen & Unwin, 1932, and New York, NY: Eugenics Publishing Co.

Foucault, M. (1978). *The History of Sexuality: Vol. I An Introduction* [1976]. New York, NY: Pantheon Books.

———. (1996). Problematics [1983]. In S. Lotringer (Ed.), *Foucault Live: Collected Interviews, 1961–1984* (2nd edn) (pp. 416–22). New York, NY: Semiotext(e).

Gagnon, J.H., & Simon, W. (1973). *Sexual Conduct: The Social Sources of Human Sexuality*. Chicago: Aldine Publishing Company.

———. (1987). The sexual scripting of oral genital contacts. *Archives of Sexual Behavior, 16*, 1–37.

Gay, P. (1984). *The Bourgeois Experience: Victoria to Freud (6 vols.) Vol. 1 The Education of the Senses*. Oxford, UK: Oxford University Press.

Gelperin, N. (2004). Oral sex and young adolescents: Insights from the 'oral sex lady'. *Sexuality Education, 9*, l–14.

Gordon, M. (1978). From unfortunate necessity to a cult of mutual orgasm: Sex in American marital education literature, 1830–1940. In J.M. Henslin & E. Sagarin (Eds), *The Sociology of Sex* (pp. 53–77). New York, NY: Schocken Books.

Greenberg, J.S., Bruess, C.E., & Haffner, D.W. (2004). *Exploring the Dimensions of Human Sexuality* (2nd edn). Sudbury, MA: Jones and Bartlett.

Hirsch, E.W. (1934). *The Power of Love: A Psychic and Physiologic Study of Regeneration*. Toronto, ON: McClelland and Stewart.

Hunt, A. (1998). The great masturbation panic and the discourses of moral regulation in nineteenth- and early twentieth-century Britain. *Journal of the History of Sexuality, 8*, 575–615.

———. (1999). *Governing Morals: A Social History of Moral Regulation*. Cambridge, UK: Cambridge University Press.

The Kama Sutra of Vatsyayana: The Classic Hindu Treatise on Love and Social Conduct (trans. Sir Richard E Burton). New York, NY: Arkana, 1991.

Laqueur, T.W. (2003). *Solitary Sex: A Cultural History of Masturbation*. New York, NY: Zone Books.

Lewis, L.S., & Brissett, D. (1967). Sex as work. *Social Problems, 15*, 8–18.

Locker, S. (2003). *The Complete Idiot's Guide to Amazing Sex* (2nd edn). Indianapolis, IN: Alpha Books.

Lyttelton, E. (1899). Instruction of the young in sexual knowledge. *International Journal of Ethics, 9*, 452–66.

McLaren, A. (1999). *Twentieth Century Sexuality: A History*. Oxford, UK: Blackwell.

Masters, W.H., & Johnson, V.E. (1986). *Masters and Johnson on Sex and Human Love*. Boston, MA: Little Brown.

Paget, L. (1999). *How To Be a Great Lover: Girlfriend-to-Girlfriend Totally Explicit Techniques that Will Blow His Mind*. New York, NY: Broadway Books.

———. (2000). *How to Give Her Absolute Pleasure: Totally Explicit Technique Every Woman Wants Her Man to Know*. New York, NY: Broadway Books.

Petersen, J.R. (1999). *The Century of Sex: Playboy's History of the Sexual Revolution, 1900–1999*. New York, NY: Grove Press.

Prinstein, M.J. (2003). Adolescent oral sex, peer, popularity, and perceptions of best friends' sexual behavior. *Journal of Pediatric Psychology, 28,* 243–49.

Rayner, C. (1968). *People in Love: A Modern Guide to Sex in Marriage*. London, UK: Collins.

Remez, L. (2000). Oral sex among adolescents: Is it sex or is it abstinence? *Family Planning Perspectives, 32,* 1–19.

Reuben, D. (1969). *Everything You Always Wanted to Know About Sex, But Were Afraid to Ask*. New York, NY: Bantam Books.

Robinson, P. (1989). *The Modernization of Sex: Havelock Ellis, Alfred Kinsey, William Masters, and Virgina Johnson* [1976]. Ithaca, NY: Cornell University Press.

Robinson, S.E., & Kruamer, H.W. (1983). Sex for money: Profile of a John. *Journal of Sexual Education and Therapy, 9,* 27–31.

Sanders, S.A., & Reinisch, J.M. (1999). Would you say you 'had sex' if . . .? *Journal of American Medical Association, 281,* 275–77.

Sanger, M. (1926). *Happiness in Marriage*. New York, NY: Brentano.

Singer, L. (1993). *Erotic Welfare: Sexual Theory and Politics in the Age of Epidemics*. New York, NY: Routledge.

Stopes, M.C. (1918). *Married Love: A New Contribution to the Solution of Sex Difficulties*. London, UK: A.C. Fifield.

Taylor, K. (2002). *The Good Orgasm Guide*. Georgetown: Georgetown Publications.

van de Velde, T.H. (1926). *Ideal Marriage: Its Physiology and Technique* (trans. Stella Browne). New York, NY: Random House.

Vance, C.S. (Ed.) (1984). *Pleasure and Danger: Exploring Female Sexuality*. London: Routledge.

Walker, K.M., & Strauss, B. (1954). *Sexual Disorders in the Male*. London, UK: Hamish Hamilton.

'Walter' (1966). *My Secret Life* [1880]. New York, NY: G. Legman.

Westheimer, R. (1983). *Dr. Ruth's Guide to Good Sex*. New York, NY: Warner Books.

———. (1986). *Dr. Ruth's Guide for Married Lovers*. New York, NY: Wing Books.

———. (1992). *Dr. Ruth's Guide to Safer Sex: Exciting, Sensible Directions for the 90s*. New York, NY: Warner Books.

———. (1995). *Sex for Dummies*. Foster City, CA: IDG Books.

Westheimer, R., & Kravetz, N. (1985). *First Love: A Young People's Guide to Sexual Information*. New York, NY: Warner Books.

Winks, C., & Semans, A. (2002). *The Good Vibrations Guide to Sex* (3rd edn). San Francisco, CA: Cleis Press.

'Horrible Temptations': Sex, Men, and Working-Class Male Youth in Urban Ontario, 1890–1935

Steven Maynard

As one man with a keen interest in boys observed about Toronto in 1898: 'You can scarcely walk a block without your attention being drawn to one or more of the class called street boys.' C.S. Clark went on to describe Toronto's street boys: 'Some of the boys live at home, but the majority are wanderers in the streets, selling papers generally, and sometimes forced to beg in the summer time they can live out all night, but in the winter they are obliged to patronize the cheap lodging houses . . . Their ages run from ten to sixteen years . . . They are generally sharp, shrewd lads with any number of bad habits and little or no principles . . . Some of the larger boys spend a considerable portion of their earnings for tobacco and drink, and they patronize all the theatres.'

Selling papers, begging, smoking, drinking, and theatre-going were only some of the vocations and vices of the street boy. 'When a newsboy gets to be seventeen years of age he finds that his avocation is at an end, it does not produce money enough and he has acquired lazy, listless habits . . . He becomes a vagrant and perhaps worse.' Clark had something quite specific in mind when he hinted at something worse than vagrancy. 'A boy of seventeen has visited nearly all the large cities of the United States, and the stories they tell of their experiences in Chicago in particular are absolutely revolting. The crime that banished Lord Somerset from London society is committed according to their reports, every night in some of the lodging houses in Chicago.' Clark also knew that Ontario boys did not have to roam as far away as Chicago. 'Consult some of the bell boys of the large hotels in Canada's leading cities, as I did, and find out what they can tell from their own experiences.'[1]

While they figured in the imaginations of muck-raking journalists, sexual relations between boys and men have generated little interest among historians. There are a few exceptions. Jeffrey Weeks noted some time ago that in late nineteenth-century England 'working-class youths featured prominently in all the major scandals, like the messenger boys in the Cleveland Street scandal'. The Cleveland Street affair of 1889–90 revolved around messenger boys who supplemented their post office incomes by working in a male brothel, servicing wealthy men, including Lord Arthur Somerset. As Weeks suggested, the Cleveland Street scandal, along with the stable lads and newsboys implicated in Oscar Wilde's trials, 'underscored the web of casual contacts and monetary exchanges that dominated the nineteenth-century homosexual world'.[2] On this side of the Atlantic, George Chauncey discovered that boys were involved in at least 40 per cent of all 'homosexual' offences prosecuted each year in early twentieth-century New York City, and he provides an intriguing discussion of 'wolves' and 'punks', an erotic system of intergenerational sex common among seamen, prisoners, and hoboes.[3]

Generally speaking, however, the history of sexual relations between boys and men remains unwritten. This is surprising given the prominent place the subject occupies on the contemporary political scene. One thinks immediately of the physical and sexual mistreatment of boys by men in state- and church-run orphanages, training schools, and residential schools. Beginning with the 1989 Newfoundland Royal Commission Mount Cashel (an orphanage for boys run by the Christian Brothers, a lay order of the Catholic Church), government inquiries and police investigations have documented the widespread abuse of boys in custodial institutions in nearly every province. Film and television dramatizations of particularly sensational cases such as *The Boys of St Vincent* (based on the Mount Cashel scandal) and *The Choirmaster* (based on the case of St George's Anglican Church, in Kingston, Ontario) have further focused public attention on the subject.[4] But as Lisa Duggan has pointed out, 'the intense contemporary discussions of children's sexuality and the sexual abuse of children have failed to generate much comparable historical exploration . . . [T]his rich and provocative area remains largely unexplored.'[5]

Intended as a contribution to the emerging field of Canadian lesbian and gay social history, this article is based on the case files of criminal prosecutions involving sexual relations between boys and men in urban Ontario from 1890 to 1935.[6] An analysis of the case files reveals that boys' sexual relations with men were marked by both sexual dangers and sexual possibilities.[7] This contradictory mix of danger and desire can be introduced through the stories of two boys.

Arnold and Garfield

In 1917, 15-year-old Arnold lived in Toronto. One day early in August, as Arnold explained to the police, 'I was coming out of the Star theatre. I met Thomas C. on Temperance Street.' According to his case file, Thomas was a single, 26-year-old 'sausage-casing expert'. 'I walked to the corner of Temperance and Yonge street. I said it is nice weather. He asked me if I would go to His Majesty's Theatre. I went with him. He got 2 seats at the wall. I was sitting next to him. He drew his hand up my leg. I then went with him to Bowles Lunch. After supper we went to the Hippodrome and after the show I went home.' On the day after Arnold first met Thomas, Arnold sought him out again. 'On Aug 5 I went to his room at 329 Jarvis and we went out and then I went home. Aug 6 I met him again . . . and we went to the Crown Theatre at Gerrard and Broadview and nothing happened. I went to his room on Aug 8. He opened my pants and handled my privates and I pulled his private person until there was a discharge and he did the same with me. He done this to me 8 times before Aug 31st.' In September, Arnold and Thomas left Toronto for western Canada, not returning until the end of the month. Asked by the court why he made the trip with Thomas, Arnold responded: 'He paid my way to the West and fed and clothed me all this time.' After their return to Toronto, Arnold and Thomas continued to see each other. As Arnold told the police, 'I slept with him on Dec. 17th . . . this was the last time.' It is unclear from the case file how their relationship was discovered, but Thomas was charged and arrested by an inspector of the Morality Department and shortly thereafter Arnold was picked up and compelled to testify against his friend.[8]

In 1904, Garfield was seven years old and lived with his family in London, Ontario. One Saturday, while passing by the hospital, Garfield encountered a stranger who, as he told the judge, 'asked me to go down the Hospital Hill and I wouldn't go'. The man, a teamster employed by the City of London, 'caught hold of me and dragged me down the hill and I caught hold of the hospital boulevard post and he said if I wouldn't let go he would cut my hands off. He took me down the hill then he undone the back of my pants which were fastened up with braces. He took my pants down. He undone the front of his pants . . . I was lying down and he was lying down too right on top of my back . . . He took out

a great big thing from the front of his trousers and he put in right behind me and I screamed it hurt. I could feel it. I screamed when he was taking me down the hill.'

As William E. explained to the London Police Court Magistrate, 'I am in the post office service. The boy Garfield is my son. I first heard of this trouble when I came home about a little after five o'clock . . . Garfield spoke to me about it. He told me what had occurred.' The next day, Garfield's father laid a charge against the man for indecently assaulting his son.[9]

Arnold and Garfield told very different stories about their sexual relations with a man; Arnold sought out his sexual encounter, boldly striking up a conversation with Thomas on the street. Their dates and gradual build-up to sex resembled something akin to a courtship, and Arnold used a matter-of-fact language to describe their reciprocal sexual relations. Arnold's relationship with Thomas appears to have been based on a mixture of economic need and an insatiable desire for the theatre. For Arnold, as for many other poor boys, sexual relations were rooted in a distinct moral economy in which working-class boys traded sex in exchange for food, shelter, amusement, money, and companionship. Garfield did not seek out his sexual encounter—he was forcibly taken by a man who used him for his own sexual purposes—and Garfield described his experience in the language of assault and harm. The locations of sexual danger for boys (along with more mutual relations) were embedded in the social relations of working-class boy life in household, neighbourhood, and a variety of institutional settings.[10] For the historian accustomed to dealing with power based on gender, race, and class, the case files of sexual relations between boys and men are a forceful reminder that age was also a significant axis of power. Always existing in complex relation to gender, class, and ethnicity, age shaped sexual relations in at least two distinct ways. First were the age differences between men and boys. Sexual danger for boys was grounded in men's greater age and physical strength, as well as in their positions of power over boys within a number of different organizational settings. Second, there were age differences between boys, older boys such as Arnold were able to turn men's interest to their own advantage, while younger boys like Garfield were more vulnerable to men's unsolicited and sometimes violent sexual advances.

The tales of Arnold and Garfield we read in the court records were not, of course, their own stories. Although boys and the men with whom they had sex supplied the plot lines, their stories were written by others. As the chief constable of St Catharines explained in police court with reference to a man arrested in 1931 on a charge of buggery with three young boys, 'after his arrest I had a conversation with him at the police office . . . [the] Deft, made a statement and Sergt Brown reduced it to writing and then it was read over to the Deft, twice and signed by the Deft.' Once in court, the testimony of boys and men was recorded by professional court stenographers who produced what they liked to call 'a true and faithful transcription of my shorthand notes taken' during the trial.[11] Having their stories transcribed and reduced to writing were only two of the ways boys' sexual relations were taken up and transformed by the legal process.[12]

[. . .]

Bowles Lunch and Burlesque

Some of the boys who appeared before Ontario courts involved in sexual relations with men were among those who lived on the street. As 16-year-old Henry explained to the Ottawa police court magistrate in 1922, 'I do not know where my father is and my mother is dead six years ago . . . I have no home.' Other boys moved back and forth between the street and various institutional homes. In Toronto and vicinity, boys moved in and out of the Newsboys' Lodging and Industrial Home, the Working Boys' Home, St Nicholas Home (the Roman Catholic newsboys' home), the Victoria Industrial School for Boys, and a number of training schools. The police statements of two boys involved in a case from 1911 indicated they were 'with the Salvation Army'. Key to survival was the distinctive culture boys developed in the streets. As Susan Houston has demonstrated, poor and working-class boys in late-Victorian urban Ontario forged their own 'street culture'. Boys 'who worked the streets', Houston has written, 'lived in an identifiable society of their own, frequenting the municipal baths and, more often, the pool halls and cheap theatricals'. Less well known is the fact that sites within boys' street culture often overlapped with those in urban homosexual subcultures. In devising their survival strategies, boys gave more than one meaning to 'working the street'.[13]

Boys drew on the resources of street and homosexual subcultures for food and shelter. In October 1929, 17-year-old John M. left the Bowmanville Training School for Boys just outside Toronto. He travelled to Ottawa 'to see what it was like'. John arrived in the city at two o'clock in the morning with no place to sleep. He headed for one of the few places open at such a late hour, the Bowles Lunch Counter. Cheap, all-night cafeterias and lunch counters were important social centres within homosexual subcultures. The Bowles chain of lunch counters turned up numerous times in the case files from Ottawa and Toronto. In Ottawa, the principal Bowles Lunch was located on Rideau Street near the railway station. In Toronto, Bowles Lunch counters were scattered throughout the downtown, but the spot most well known among homosexually active men was on the corner of Queen and Bay Streets. It was in this Bowles Lunch that

Arnold and Thomas had dinner before heading across the street to the Hippodrome. It is unclear whether John knew in advance that Bowles was a popular homosexual haunt, but it was not long before he met someone. As John explained, 'I went into Bowles Lunch near the Station on Rideau Street.' There he met Moise B., a single, 29-year-old labourer. Sitting next to each other in their booth at Bowles, they talked until six o'clock in the morning and then left for Moise's room 'above his father's shoemaking shop'. It was, according to John, 'an ordinary room' with 'a bed in one corner'. 'We got undressed and went to bed . . . we were laying there a while and after a while' they had sex. It was to be the beginning of a brief relationship. John moved in with Moise. According to John, they slept with each other every night and for the next month or so they had sex 'about four times a week'. John got a job at the Rideau Bowling Alley. Eventually, however, the police caught up with John, who apparently had left Bowmanville without permission and was sent back to the training school.[14]

Gossip about men circulated in the subaltern world of boys. As John said about Moise having sex with boys, 'all the lads in the bowling alley were telling me about it'. Or, as C.S. Clark noted about Toronto, 'men and their acts of indecency are the talk of boys all over the city'. For boys who were interested, such talk alerted them to the existence of men who had sex with boys and where those men could be found. When James M., a 17-year-old immigrant apprentice from England who resided in an Ottawa home for boys, went out for the evening, he set out for Bowles Lunch. There he met Moise, who had recently been separated from John following his abrupt return to Bowmanville. In exchange for sex, Moise took James 'for supper and after that took me to the Show'.[15]

As the stories of Arnold and John suggest, boys were crazy for 'the Show'. Rapidly expanding commercial amusement scenes in early twentieth-century Ontario cities were a magnet for boys. Carolyn Stange notes in her study of Toronto's working girls who sought out the pleasures of the city that, the number of 'places of amusement' soared from 9 in 1900 to 112 by 1915. Much like working girls who sometimes traded sexual favours with men to gain access to the city's amusements, boys with little or no money used sex as their ticket into the theatre. [. . .]

Not all encounters between boys and men were furtive sexual acts that took place in the public world of boys' street culture. Boys often went on to form elaborate, long-lasting relationships with the men they met. It was in 1924, at a friend's house, when 15-year-old Thomas H. first met Edward B., an Ottawa doctor. Details of their relationship—they were together for over a year—came out during the trial that followed charges laid against the doctor by police. As in other cases in which boys were forced to testify against the men with whom they had sex or shared a relationship, Thomas was reluctant to incriminate his friend. As the exasperated prosecuting lawyer said to Thomas, 'come on, please tell us, I have got your statement made before me—you know what had gone on between you and this man—please tell us how it started and what it was and get through with it—no use of boggling at it—come on or we will keep you all day if you don't.' During their time together, Thomas and Edward often used the doctor's motor car to go on excursions in the countryside. They went on fishing trips, one of their favourite destinations being just outside Woodlawn, where they stayed at a friend's cottage. Referring to one of their first fishing weekends, the lawyer asked Thomas: 'How did you come to get to bed with him?' As Thomas explained, 'There was the one bed and I went to bed with him [and] he brought me a discharge.' 'How often did this sort of thing occur?' the lawyer inquired. 'Every time we went on the trip there', was the response.

Thomas went on to testify that on some trips, 'we went out later in the car at night, and parked, and the same thing would happen.' Thomas also explained that they shared a bed and had sex on other trips they took together; for example, 'in the Hotel—in the Revere House at Brockville'. Questioned about their life in the city, Thomas divulged the details of the couple's various routines. Sometimes Thomas picked up the car at the garage and, recalling the doctor's instructions—'prime the pump six or eight times if any trouble in starting, don't run down battery [and] look out for skids'—he would 'take it to the Blue Bird Cafe and meet him [Edward] for supper'. Edward sometimes gave Thomas money. While the court suspected the money was payment for sexual services, Thomas countered that it was 'just a present like, to spend'. Even after an extensive interrogation, Thomas still resisted the court's attempt to make him understand his experience as wrong.

> Q. Did you know he was doing something he should not be doing?
> A. I did not know at the time.
> Q. You knew afterwards?
> A Well, I knew, but . . .
> Q. Did you ever try to stop him?
> A. No.

Thomas and Edward's relationship bears a close resemblance to a common pattern of homosexual relationship in the early twentieth century, in which working-class boys were kept by wealthier men in the context of often long-lasting, mutually rewarding partnerships.[16]

Prostitutes and Perverts

Boys traded sex with men for food, shelter, and admission to the theatre, but most often, in what is best described as a form of casual prostitution, boys exchanged sex for money. David K.'s experience was typical. In 1914, David met a man on Yonge Street outside Simpson's Hall who asked him to go to the theatre. David claimed that the man, Edward W., a single, 28-year-old driver, said 'it would be easy money for me to make 25 cents'. David and Edward went to the theatre where, according to David, 'I pulled his dickie up and down in the theatre . . . it was dark . . . he had his coat on and my hand worked under it.' Further detail about how such exchanges were negotiated is provided by a case from 1918 in which Francis D. and Henry M. arranged their encounter by writing notes back and forth on a small piece of paper. Entered as evidence during their trial, the scrap of paper was preserved in the case file. It is not clear where this note passing took place, but it appears to have begun with Henry asking, 'Do you want a dirty matter with me?' To which Francis replied, 'I will go with you on pleasure.' Before proceeding, however, there were evidently a number of details to consider, including age, penis size, and the price. Henry indicated that he was '15 years old,' to which Francis responded, 'I do like young boys.' Henry scribbled, 'My penis is about 5 in. long,' while Francis indicated his was '7 1/2 inches long' and asked whether 'you Will accept $1.00?' The price must have been right, as the note concluded, 'Where will we go?' 'Any place will do.'[17]

Given their importance as homosexual meeting places, theatres and their surrounding streets and lanes, especially those centred in the commercial amusement district around Queen and Bay, were a central site of prostitution in Toronto. Boys hung out in and around movie houses looking for men. About 8:30 PM on a summer evening in 1922, Morris approached a man 'outside the Reo Picture Show on Queen Street West near McCaul'. 'Let's go up the lane and do some dirty work', Morris suggested, 'I want to make some money to go to the show.' About the man with whom he had sex, Frank F. stated, 'I seen him at the Star Theatre. He asked me to go to his room . . . I went into his room. I took down my pants, he put his penis between my legs—he gave me 50 cents.' Some time later, when Frank needed another 50 cents, he knew where he might find the man: 'I met him at the Star the second time and I went to his room.'[18]

Boys who worked at hotels were particularly well placed to capitalize on their occupations. Sixteen-year-old William, a bell boy employed at the Vendome Hotel in Sarnia, supplemented his wages by having sex with men staying at the hotel. William described one such encounter for the court. 'He led me to the room and closed the door . . . [He] took his pants off and proceeded to open up his B.V.D.'S . . . He laid me on the bed and then laid on top of me.' Asked by the court why he had done so, William explained that the man 'asked me if I had any money and I told him no. He said I will give you some and also a job in the morning driving a truck . . . He handed me a dollar when he was finished and said to take it and keep quiet.' William, however, did not keep quiet; he reported the man to the police, who was then charged and found guilty of an indecent assault. It is not clear why William turned the man in; it may have been that although he was paid his one dollar—it was entered into the trial as an exhibit—he did not get a job driving a truck the morning after sex.[19]

Cases such as William's in which charges against men were laid by boys, not by the police, parents, or others, pose the question of why a boy would report to the police that he had been involved sexually with a man. Interestingly, almost all such cases involve scenarios in which boys were promised or expected something in return for sex, but the men failed to deliver. [. . .] Because such cases were relatively rare—most boys did not report their men to the police—it is difficult to get a firm grasp on the nature and extent of extortion. C.S. Clark believed it was a widespread practice among boys. Clark wrote that 'a youth of eighteen once informed me that he had blackmailed one of Canada's esteemed judiciary out of a modest sum of money, by catching him in the act of indecently assaulting one of the bell boys connected with a hotel . . . This is one case only, and they are countless . . . Some of Canada's leading citizens could be implicated just as Oscar Wilde was implicated, if some of these bell boys chose to make public what they knew.' [. . .]

How boys regarded their sexual relations with men—how, if at all, it shaped their self-perceptions—is an intriguing question. It would appear that for some boys, sex with men was an outgrowth of or gave rise to a sense of sexual difference or identity. Seventeen-year-old William C., for example, had sex with men for money. William's, however, was more than the occasional act of prostitution; he regularly provided sexual services to men in a male brothel on Toronto's Yonge Street. William presented himself in court as a 'self-confessed pervert'. Many other boys resisted the identity of prostitute and pervert. Sam B.'s straightforward exchange with William H., a 49-year-old clerical worker in Toronto in 1916, was typical. As Sam testified, William H. said 'he would give me a quarter to come up the lane. I did and he took out my cock and sucked it.' But as Sam insisted in court, 'it was not the way I supported myself'. Both prosecution and defence lawyers asked boys probing questions about prostitution, evidence that the court was aware of the existence or possibility of homosexual prostitution. Seventeen-year-old Wilfred T. insisted during cross-examination by the defence that 'I was not paid any money by the accused . . . It was not the way I supported myself.' While refusing to admit involvement in homosexual prostitution is not surprising in the context of a court examination, such a denial must have been at times simply an indication that many boys who occasionally traded sex for money did not regard themselves as perverts or prostitutes.[20]

Bootblacks and Boarders

In addition to street boys, occasional prostitutes, and confirmed perverts, many boys were the sons of working-class families and their sexual relations were embedded in the conditions of working-class life. As labour and social historians have demonstrated, working-class boys were expected to contribute to the family economy, including by going out to work. Many boys went to work in the street trades, where they found jobs as newsboys, messenger boys, and shoeshine boys. [. . .] Work in the street trades was unstable and poorly paid, so boys devised ways—from 'scrounging' to stealing—to supplement their modest wages. Some boys discovered that providing sexual favours to men was a way to earn pocket money. Alan, a 10-year-old newsboy from Sault Ste Marie, told the court that, in the summer of 1918, 'I was going to get my Sault Star to sell. This man was standing at the corner of Albert & Elgin Streets and asked me if I wanted to earn a nickel . . . He took me to Hiawatha Hotel where he took me to a room, and he took down his pants, then he took my hand and made me rub his [thing] and he gave me 7c. In about a couple of months I saw him again and he did the same thing again in a barn behind the St. Charles Hotel and he gave me 10c . . . I used to go to Hiawatha Hotel about every other day and I used to talk to this man and sold him papers.' The workplace could also be a site of sexual danger. Eleven-year-old Leo went to work as a shoeshine boy in June after school closed for the year. As Leo's father testified in court: 'The boy Leo asked me if he could work in shoe shine place of accused—I said "yes". At night when Leo came home I asked him how he was getting along at shoe shine place but he told me he would not work there for accused was a bad man and wanted him to do bad things.'[21]

Many working-class families supplemented the household economy by taking in boarders and, perhaps not surprisingly, sex between a boy and a male lodger was a common scenario. Consider the case of 13-year-old Sidney. In 1927, Sidney shared a bed with Joseph B., who had boarded in his family's household for about a year. During that time, as Sidney explained, 'he always fooled with my privates'. Displaying little knowledge of working-class life, the lawyer asked, 'Why did you go back to sleep with him on occasions after the first time this happened—you knew what he was doing to you—why didn't you go to sleep some place else?' 'I could not', replied Sidney, 'all the beds were occupied in the house—there was only that bed.' In often crowded households, people had to double up. Significantly, the charge against the lodger was laid not by Sidney's parents but by a truancy officer who had made it his business to investigate Sidney's sleeping arrangements. Whether Sidney's parents were aware of his sexual liaisons with the lodger is unclear. They did know that they slept in the same bed. As Sidney's father told the court, 'Yes, they both occupied the same room with the one bed.' When Sidney was asked whether he ever told anyone about having sex with the lodger, he replied, 'I did not say anything about it.' 'Why not?' asked the cross-examining lawyer. 'He used to give me things—cigarettes and things.'[22]

Ravines and Railway Yards

Boys, especially young boys, encountered men looking for sex in the spaces boys carved out of the city in which to play, including on the streets of their own neighbourhoods. Brothers Fred and Wilbert B., age 7 and 11, who lived at 28 Bain Avenue, Toronto, along with their 12-year-old friend Allan R., who lived just down the street at 22 Bain, all got caught up in a sexual scenario when a watchman pulled them into a shed not far from their street. Parks and ravines were another place boys could be found playing. Twelve-year-old Ben B. testified that 'I was coming from River-dale Park . . . [The accused] asked me to go with him. He asked me to take my pants down and . . . and he put his private in my backside. He was moving up and down. He gave me a one dollar bill after he had done it.' As a suspicious police constable testified, 'I saw [the accused] on Winchester Street near Riverdale Park I followed the prisoner and the boy up the Ravine. I saw the man getting off the boy who had his pants down.' Other sexual encounters took place in schoolyards, vacant lots, fields, and on the Don River Flats. Boys who ventured away from their neighbourhoods to go exploring might also encounter a man. Alleine W. met a man when he 'was down near the docks'. Henry B. encountered a labourer who 'works on the railway' when he was playing 'near the Gas Works'. According to Henry, 'he dragged me into a box car and did some things.'[23]

Because most of these boys did not seek out their sexual encounters but were discovered by men while at play, men had to devise ways to interest boys in sex. Ice cream and candy were two popular treats. As Sidney L. said about the man with whom he had sex, 'he treated me to Ice Cream'. With the 14 cents he received from a man, eight-year-old Albert M. 'bought two cones, I gave one cone to my brother and bought candy with the remaining four cents'. Napoleon R. was reluctant at first to go with a man down to the Grand Trunk railway yard; but agreed to go when the man promised, 'I shall give you a knife.' Once with a boy, some men turned conversation towards sex by asking the boy about girls. 'He asked me if I had ever gone or had to do with girls', 13-year-old Arthur N. told the court. 'He asked me dirty things about the body . . . He asked if I was old enough to do certain things . . . if I was old enough to have an emission.'[24]

When men's various methods to entice boys failed or once a boy began to resist, men could resort to physical coercion. As one young boy put it, 'he got me in the house. He hurt me down there, it is still sore.' The doctor who examined Tom backed up his story: 'I found the anus dilated and very red.' Twelve-year-old David T., on his way to meet his mother, encountered a man who 'asked me if I wanted a ride . . . I got in with him . . . then he grabbed me under the arms put me down on the ground, put his face against mine and laid on top of me making an up and down motion. He got off me I ran.' Norman C. met a man on Front Street who asked him to help carry a parcel. The man took him into the bushes 'and he took down my pants and opened his. He laid me on my stomach and put it into me. I tried to stop him and he forced me. He did it more than once.' As the doctor testified, 'I examined the boy and found marks of violence.'[25]

Boy Scouts and Big Brothers

In 1923, Charles F., 'an active worker in the Catholic Big Brother Movement' faced 'more than one charge of a disgusting nature' involving boys in his charge. Reform work, or 'boys' work' as it was often called, provided another social setting for sexual relations between boys and men. As historians have demonstrated, reform groups such as the Boys' Brigade, the YMCA, and the Boy Scouts, springing out of middle-class fears about the physical degeneration of the male working class and the effeminizing influence on boys of the domestic sphere, sought to restore boys to a proper state of manliness. In October 1923, Toronto boys gathered for a social at the Broadview YMCA, where they listened to speeches on 'the services a young man can render to his companions [which] emphasized the necessity of boys indulging in clean, wholesome recreation and companionship in order that they should be prepared for the duties of manhood.' Speeches were followed 'by activities in the gymnasium'. The objective of the east Toronto branch of the YMCA, known as the 'Railroad Branch—a home for Railwaymen away from home', was 'to make better men and boys . . . to create and develop a more wholesome atmosphere in which men and boys may spend their leisure time'. The Railroad Y pointed to its outdoor, physical program, which included 'all seasonable sports and has been of great assistance in developing better manhood' among boys.[26] Placing boys in the 'more wholesome atmosphere' of all-male groups nourished homosocial relations between boys and men. Those who worked with 'destitute boys' at the Toronto Boys' Home in 1915, for example, believed that boys needed to be 'taken in hand by a real friend—well dressed, loved, sent to school and watched over'.[27]

[. . .]

Rather than physical force, men who worked in reform groups relied on other forms of power to extract sexual compliance from boys. In 1932, Harvey B. was a single, 30-year-old curate and Sunday school teacher at a Toronto church. The local chapter of the Boy Scouts met at Harvey's church and, as one boy explained, 'Mr. [B.] was around with the scouts a great deal'. His usual routine involved offering boys rides in his automobile after Sunday School or a Scouts meeting. As Lloyd C. told police, 'He took me to his garage. He took off my clothes, loosened down my underwear and he started feeling my privates'. Another time, 'He asked me who my body belonged to. I said: "God, My Mother and Father". He said: "Is

it none of mine?" I said nothing, then he kissed me and asked me if I loved him, I said: "Yes sir".' Harvey managed to maintain the boys' silence for as long as he did by playing on his position of authority, both his position as assistant to the parish priest and as a scoutmaster. As 13-year-old Jack H. explained, after skipping Sunday school one week, Mr B. said, 'if I did not tell on him, he would not tell on me for not going to church'. Mr B. pursued a slightly different tack with Lloyd: he 'asked me to promise on my scout's honour not to say anything about it'.[28]

Sex rooted in men's institutional power over boys was highlighted in a scandal that rocked the city of Oshawa beginning in April 1927 and lasted for almost a year. It all began in early April when the assistant commissioner of the Ontario Provincial Police instructed one of his inspectors to investigate allegations that Mr Harley E., the superintendent of the Oshawa Children's Aid Society, had been involved sexually with boys who stayed at the CAS shelter. The Toronto-based OPP inspector travelled to Oshawa and he interviewed the chief constable of the Oshawa Police, who gave him the names of the boys said to have been involved. Some of the alleged incidents stretched back a number of years, so that by 1927 many of the boys were no longer at the shelter but scattered around the province. For the next several weeks, the inspector travelled around interviewing boys about their time at the Oshawa shelter. He found 17-year-old Edward P. working on a local farm. Edward told the inspector that in 1922 'on several occasions Mr. E. had him come up to his house when Mrs. E. was away and on those occasions had committed buggery on him'. Next the inspector went to the St John's Training School, where he interviewed three boys who had stayed at the shelter and 'all of whom stated that Mr. E. had on different occasions opened their pants and played with their privates'. The inspector's next stop was the Victoria Industrial School in Mimico, where he questioned 'about a dozen boys from Ontario County'. Here he heard similar stories, including from Reginald J., who claimed that not only had Mr E. meddled with him and his brother but that 'Harold W. had also been treated the same way by Mr E.; and that Harold got so bad that he had to be sent to the Ontario Hospital [for the insane] at Orillia'. Fifteen-year-old Nick S. told the inspector that when he 'was at the Shelter . . . Mr. E. came in and lifted up his night shirt and worked with his privates'. Following further investigations, charges were laid against Mr. E., he was arrested, brought before the Whitby Police Court magistrate, and remanded to jail to await trial. In court by the end of November, Mr E. elected trial by judge alone and pleaded not guilty. The case was prosecuted by the Ontario County crown attorney, and Mr E. was found guilty of one of the charges against him. He was sentenced to Kingston Penitentiary for three years. Mr. E appealed his sentence to the Ontario Supreme court. His lawyer [. . .] Nickle's defence strategy rested primarily on discrediting the boys' testimony, depicting them as untrustworthy and far from sexually innocent. Nickle grilled the boys about their sexual practices, getting them to admit that they masturbated. As the court reporter noted about Aubrey, Nickle 'drew from the boy in cross-examination that . . . he had been guilty himself of improper habits'. Nickle had Mr E. take the stand and deny all charges, and in his closing statement Nickle made what the court reporter described as 'a passionate appeal' on behalf of his client before the jury. The strategy paid off. The grand jurors returned a verdict of not guilty.

In none of Mr E.'s three trials did the structure of power within the CAS come under scrutiny. On one occasion between the appeal case and the final trial the county crown attorney wrote to the attorney general that '[Mr E.'s] position must be considered. He was the Ward in charge of these boys who were taken from their homes and placed under his care, and their whole lives were ruined by his actions'. But the superintendent's position was never seriously considered by the court. Instead, the judge and jury's focus was narrowed down to a set of legal issues through the defence lawyer's skillful rhetorical use of the concept of accomplice and technicalities such as the length of time permitted to elapse between an incident and when it was first reported. As Tina Loo suggests, 'the rules of legal rhetoric . . . result in removing actions from their social context'. What Loo writes about potlatch prosecutions might equally be said of many cases of sexual relations between boys and men: broader social 'meaning was lost in the course of the trials, pared away by a system of argument that resolved disputes by reducing them to a set of technical questions'. In Mr E.'s case, as in other cases involving state and voluntary boys' organizations, the issues of sexual coercion and the unequal relations of power between boys and men within institutional settings went unchallenged.[29]

Not all sexual relations between boys and men within organizational settings were of a coercive character. In 1922, Harold was 14 years old. He lived in Pickering with his foster parents. Harold had a long relationship with Edward, a 40-year-old scoutmaster. Edward lived in nearby Oshawa. They saw each other frequently, Edward making trips to Harold's home and becoming friends with Harold's foster family. Letters between Harold and Edward reveal an intense emotional and caring relationship. Rooted perhaps in their Boy Scouts connection, they shared an interest in nature. On 6 July 1922, Edward wrote to Harold on a small postcard-size piece of birch bark: 'I went to Newmarket & it rained all Saturday morning, but we went to Sutton & caught 82 fish . . . The ground hog is very tame. I saw one white rabbit, a nice large one. I may be down Sunday . . . This piece of bark came from Mr. Lewis's bush.' Letters from Harold to Edward focused on Harold's home life and the things the two planned to do together: 'I have just had my dinner . . . We are getting along fine on the farm . . . I need a blotter, the other is all used up so please send me one . . . Oh say, I forgot to tell you I got the Exhibition ticket so I think it will be alright . . . I will close for now, from yours very truly.' Edward often signed off his letters by encouraging Harold to help out around the house and to apply himself to religion and learning: 'Harold you must be good to Mr. & Mrs. Barlow, do all you can . . . behave & go to God in prayer before you go to bed, try & read good Book . . . Be good & learn all you can. Lots of love.'

[. . .]

Moral Reformers and Mothers

Much of the impetus to regulate sexual relations between boys and men was rooted in the more general middle-class apprehension about the working-class boy. This is what Toronto Chief of Police H.J. Grasett meant when he referred in 1891 to 'the boy question in Toronto' or, as he sometimes called it, the 'boy nuisance'. At the heart of the boy nuisance was the widely shared belief that working-class boys were responsible for a good deal of crime and vice in the city. Not surprisingly, much of the boy question was discussed with reference to the most visible boys—street boys—particularly the ever-present newsboy.[30] Testifying before the 1889 Royal Commission on the Relations of Labor and Capital, former Toronto mayor and moral reformer W.H. Howland related his conversations with 'respectable working people' who 'told me that their boys were all right until they began to sell newspapers on the street at eleven and twelve o'clock at night, but then they got demoralized . . .

I am satisfied that in every city a large portion of the petty crime is done by these boys.' For Howland, one of the chief sites of boys' demoralization was the street. In 1891, testifying this time before the Ontario Commission on Prisons and Reformatories investigating 'all matters appertaining to juvenile criminality and vice', he warned that 'the streets are full of temptation to children . . . There are hundreds of things in street life that attract children.' Howland was responsible for a number of solutions to the boy nuisance. He was the principal force behind the establishment in 1887 of the Victoria Industrial School for Boys. [. . .]

Working alongside the police, sometimes prodding them into action, were moral reformers active in the social purity movement. While most social purity activists focused their energies on women, prostitution, and the 'white slave trade', sex between men and boys did not go unnoticed. W.L. Clark, hired by the Methodist Church's Department of Temperance and Moral Reform in 1910 to give lectures to boys on sex hygiene and the 'secret vice', repeated the story of a boy who said he was taught to masturbate by 'a man in my home town'. Clark warned that boys were often 'taught that act by an older companion'. In his 'Private Talk to Young Men', B.G. Jeffries noted that 'in many cases the degrading habit ["the destructive sin of self-abuse"] has been taught by others, e.g., by elder boys at school . . . whilst in other cases fallen and depraved men have not hesitated to debauch the minds of mere children by teaching them this debasing Practice.' A committee of the Church of England considering the 'problems of marriage and sexual morality' in Canada in 1920 was 'compelled to notice the prevalence in some quarters of unnatural vice . . . to which they [boys] are often exposed from elders of their own sex'. The committee recommended that 'the aid of men of good and disciplined character is needed for the help of boys and young men . . . in combatting horrible temptations'.[31]

The Toronto Vigilance Committee, formed in 1911, included in its work efforts to aid in preventing boys being led astray by moral perverts. Reflecting the middle-class distrust of working-class children, the committee pinned responsibility for being led astray as much on boys as on 'moral perverts'. The Vigilance Committee encouraged its members to report all 'frivolous young girls and boys likely to be easily enticed into wrong doing'. [. . .]Theatres became one of the committee's favourite targets. The committee reminded the attorney general that while minors were prohibited from entering 'nickel-shows' and 'moving pictures' unless accompanied by an adult, 'these same minors can freely gain access to a theatre where a burlesque company is giving a risque performance and there, in a smoke-beclouded atmosphere, both hear and see things extremely detrimental'. During one visit to that 'training-school for immorality', the Star Burlesque Theatre, the Vigilance Committee noted that 'young boys of 8, 10, 12, and 15 years of age were in the gallery, unaccompanied by parents or guardians'. Whether or not they were card-carrying members of the Vigilance Committee or other moral reform organization, individual private citizens did report boys and men to the police. [. . .]

In addition to the Morality Department and moral reformers, working-class parents, especially mothers, played a key role in regulating sexual relations between their sons and men. Boys' sexual relations with men sometimes came to mothers' attention not because their sons told them about the encounter but because mothers discovered something amiss in the course of child care. In 1915, nine-year-old William had been doing 'dirty tricks' with a man in the neighbourhood. 'I have been there often', William testified,

'he gave me money to do dirty tricks . . . He told me not to tell my mother, that's why I did not.' Mrs H. explained to the court that while bathing William, she noticed 'his person was swollen . . . when I examined him it was sore.' Other times, boys told their mothers what happened and some mothers then went to the police. In 1915, Henry explained to the Ottawa court, 'The night before last I went to Matthews butcher shop' on Rideau Street. 'I waited at the door for my mother'. While Henry was waiting, a man came along and asked him if he wanted to go to the picture show and said 'that they would come back from the show and go to bed together'. As Bertha, Henry's mother, told the court, 'on the night of the 19th I was working over Matthew's butcher shop'. Bertha was a cleaning woman. 'My boy told me what the man said to him. I told a policeman.'[32]

Not all mothers went to the police. As feminist historians have demonstrated, while working-class women made use of the police and other social services when needed, at other times they resented the intrusion of police constables, truancy officers, rent collectors, and moral reformers into their neighbourhoods, preferring to supervise their own streets.[33] Rather than go to the police, some mothers confronted men themselves. When Josephine learned that her eight-year-old son Albert had a sexual encounter with one of her lodgers, she said, 'I sent for Adelard. I asked him what sort of evil thing do you show my children?' Other mothers simply urged their sons to stay away from such men. When in 1916 Oscar told his mother that a man once sucked his penis and gave him 25 cents, 'she told me not go near his place any more'. But as Oscar told the court, 'he has done this to me quite frequently for the past two years. He has always paid me 25 cents.'[34]

Mothers' different responses reflected the fact that working-class mothers had a range of understandings of sexual relations between boys and men. Certainly some mothers believed a wrong, an 'evil thing', had been done which required punishment. As Albert's mother said about Adelard. 'I told him I would have him punished for that.' [. . .]

Mothers too could take a rather pragmatic approach to their sons' sexual relations with men. For two months in 1921, Dominick lived with an Ottawa man in his house on Wilbrod Street. As Dominick told the court, 'I was to mind his house and take the dogs out . . . I took the dogs out in the morning 2 or 3 times.' Dominick's duties extended beyond domestic labour. 'I slept with him and three dogs in a bed in a room . . . The first night I slept with him he started to 'touch my private parts. On another night he put my privates in his mouth and wanted me to put his privates in my mouth.' Asked by the court how such an arrangement had been arrived at, Dominick said that he went to where I lived to hire me. He spoke to my mother.' Asked if he ever told his mother about the sex, he replied that 'I did not tell my mother about it. My mother told me I had to work.' In another case from Ottawa, one mother told the court the accused came to her house and 'told me he had done wrong [with my son] and asked me to allow him to settle with me by giving me money'. Lizzie settled for $50. Entered into the trial as a court exhibit was, as Lizzie explained, 'a receipt for $5 stating the balance of $45 was still due'.[35]

Although it is relatively easy to document that working-class parents had a range of responses toward boys' sexual relations with men, it is less easy to explain what accounts for the mix. We might speculate that working-class boys and their parents had their own sense of what posed real dangers and threats. In contrast to moral reformers who singled out sex and the streets, boys were more likely to point to their work and workplaces. Before the 1889 Royal Commission on the Relations of Labor and Capital, John Gale, an employee of the Dominion Telegraph Office,

told the commission that when he was between 11 and 12 he worked at an Ottawa mill where he lost his right arm taking blocks away from a circular saw. Joseph Lefebvre told a similar story—crushed against an axle, he lost both an arm and a leg working at a saw mill when he was 12. In view of the dangers and meagre remuneration of the workplace, it is perhaps not so hard to understand why some boys chose the streets and sex with men, in which a few minutes up a laneway or in a theatre might earn them as much as or more than a long day at a mill or factory. The actions of mothers who hired out their sons or who attempted to capitalize on the discovery of their sons' sexual relations were also rooted in the often harsh economic realities of working-class life. Certainly, some of the boys understood the situation in this way. Dominick's final response to the court's inability to understand his sexual relations with a man were the words, 'My mother is poor.'[36]

[. . .]

In our own time, marked by widespread cultural anxieties over shifting gender and sexual relations spurred on by the feminist and lesbian/gay liberation movements, the complex and multiple meanings of sexual relations between boys and men are invariably constructed as cases of 'child abuse' involving only boy victims and adult homosexual predators.[37] In the early twentieth century, the moral economy of many working-class boys and their families was more expansive, nuanced of both the dangers and the possibilities of sexual relations between boys and men. Whole communities might rise up when boys suffered at the hands of a man who used his position of trust and authority to wield sexual power over boys. At the same time, some working-class boys and their families recognized that, in a variety of ways, boys' sexual relations with men might provide a temporary escape from or way to alleviate their impoverishment. All of this suggests that early twentieth-century understandings of sexual relations between boys and men were markedly different from our own, highlighting the ways sexual meanings are subject to historical pressures and change.

Notes

1. C.S. Clark, *Of Toronto the Good* (Montreal 1898), 81–3, 90.
2. Jeffrey Weeks, *Coming Out: Homosexual Politics in Britain, from the Nineteenth Century to the Present* (London 1977), 39. Weeks went on to explore the world of working-class male youth and prostitution in an important article published in 1980, but his evidentiary base remained limited. As Weeks realized, 'the necessary detailed empirical research still has to be done'. Weeks, 'Inverts, Perverts, and Mary-Annes: Male Prostitution and the Regulation of Homosexuality in England in the Nineteenth and Early Twentieth Centuries,' *Journal of Homosexuality* 6 (fall/winter 1980–1), reprinted in M. Duberman, M. Vicinus, and G. Chauncey, eds, *Hidden from History: Reclaiming the Gay and Lesbian Past* (New York 1989), 197.
3. George Chauncey, *Gay New York: Gender, Urban Culture, and the Making of the Gay Male World, 1890–1940* (New York 1994), 140, 86–95.
4. The scandals have generated an uneven journalistic literature. See Michael Harris, *Unholy Orders: Tragedy at Mount Cashel* (Markham, ON 1990); Judy Steed, *Our Little Secret: Confronting Child Sexual Abuse in Canada* (Toronto 1994); Darcy Henton, *Boys Don't Cry: The True Story of Canada's Child Abuse Scandal* (Toronto 1995). For a more critical analysis that investigates how government inquiries reproduce homophobic equations of gay men as child molesters, see Gary Kinsman, 'The Hughes Commission: Making Homosexuality the Problem Once Again', *New Maritimes: A Regional Magazine of Culture and Politics II* (Jan./Feb. 1993), 17–19.
5. Lisa Duggan, 'From Instincts to Politics: Writing the History of Sexuality in the U.S.', *Journal of Sex Research* 27 (Feb. 1990): 108–9. An important exception, of course, is the work of feminist historians who, in writing the history of men's violence again women, also often examine the physical and sexual abuse of girls. See, for example, Linda Gordon, *Heroes of Their Own Lives: The Politics and History of Family Violence* (New York 1988), and Karen Dubinsky, *Improper Advances: Rape and Heterosexual Conflict in Ontario, 1880–1929* (Chicago 1993). See also Terry Chapman, '"Inquiring Minds Want to Know": The Handling of Children in Sex Assault Cases in the Canadian West, 1890–1920', in S. Smandych et al., eds, *Dimensions of Childhood: Essays on the History of Children and Youth in Canada* (Winnipeg 1990), 183–204.
6. This article is drawn from my Ph.D. dissertation, tentatively entitled 'Toronto the Gay: Sex, Men, and the Police in Urban Ontario, 1890–1940' (Queen's University, in progress). My search through court records housed at the Archives of Ontario turned up 313 cues involving 'homosexual' offences in Ontario for the period 1890–1935. It is not possible to pin down exactly how many or what percentage of these cases involved boys, as some cases did not specify the ages of (or provide other age-related information about) the parties involved. I have been able to identify 70 cases involving sexual relations between men and boys/male youth to examine for this article. These cases were processed under the criminal code categories of buggery, indecent assault upon a male, and gross indecency, the latter being by far the most frequent charge. On the legal history of these criminal code provisions, see Terry Chapman, '"An Oscar Wilde Type": "The Abominable Crime of Buggery" in Western Canada, 1890–1920', *Criminal Justice History 4* (1983): 97–118; and Chapman, 'Male Homosexuality: Legal Restraints and Social Attitudes in Western Canada, 1890–1920', in Louis Knafla, ed., *Law and Justice in a New Land: Essays in Western Canadian Legal History* (Toronto 1986), 277–92. The cases employed here come from two different sets of court records: Archives of Ontario, Criminal Court Records, RG 22, Criminal Assize Indictment Case Files, Series 392 (hereafter AO, Criminal Assize indictments, county/district, date, case number), and Archives of Ontario, Criminal Court Records, RG 2.2, Crown Attorney Prosecution Case Files, various series (hereafter AO, Crown Attorney Prosecution Case Files, country/district, date, case number). As the crown attorney prosecution case files remain largely unprocessed and stored in temporary boxes, I will not date box numbers. In order to be granted research access to the crown attorney's files I was required to enter into a research agreement with the archives. In accordance with that agreement, all names have been anonymized and all case numbers used here refer to my own numbering scheme and do not correspond to any numbers that may appear on the original case files.
7. There are some parallels here with the history of working-class girls and their sexual relations with men. As Christine Stansell has argued for nineteenth-century New York City, young girls learned 'early about their vulnerability to sexual harm from grown men . . . [but] also learned some ways to turn men's interest to their own purposes. Casual prostitution was one.' Stansell locates the way 'girls gambled with prostitution' firmly within the economic necessities dictated by life on the street as well as within girls'

desire for independence and amusement. By virtue of their gender, boys, especially older boys, stood a better chance than most girls in the luck of the sexual draw with men. But the dialectic between vulnerability to sexual harm and turning that vulnerability around to one's own purposes also characterizes much about boys' sexual relations with men in early twentieth-century urban Ontario. Stansell, *City of Women: Sex and Class in New York, 1789–1860* (New York 1986), 182.

8. AO, Crown Attorney Prosecution Case Files, York County, 1918, case 35.

9. AO, Criminal Assize Indictments, Middlesex County, 1904, case 191.

10. I want to underscore that in arguing that sexual danger and desire were rooted in boys' street culture and working-class life, I am not suggesting that sex between boys and men was somehow unique to working-class existence. My concentration on working-class male youth stems from my own interest in working-class history and from the nature of my sources (working-class and immigrant boys turn up in the court records more often than middle-class boys because the former were subject to greater police and legal surveillance). Middle-class boys also had sex with men, but the social organization of their sexual relations was different. For instance, rather than on the street, middle-class boys developed sexual relations with men in private boarding schools. On romantic friendships and sexual dangers in boys' boarding schools, see, for example, Jean Barman, *Growing Up British in British Columbia: Boys in Private School* (Vancouver 1984), and James Fitzgerald, *Old Boys: The Powerful Legacy of Upper Canada College* (Toronto 1994). See also E. Anthony Rotundo, 'Romantic Friendship: Male Intimacy and Middle-Class Youth in the Northern United States, 1800–1900', *Journal of Social History* 23 (fall 1989): 1–25.

11. AO, Crown Attorney Prosecution Case Files, Lincoln County, 1931, case 199, and Carleton County, 1925, case 155.

12. See, for example, James Chandler, Arnold I. Davidson, and Harry Harootunian, eds, *Questions of Evidence: Proof Practice, and Persuasion across the Disciplines* (Chicago 1994), and the special issue of PMLA on 'The Status of Evidence', *PMLA III* (Jan. 1996).

13. AO, Crown Attorney Prosecution Case Files, Carleton County, 1922, case 147; York County, 1911, case 8. Susan E. Houston, 'The "Waifs and Strays" of a Late Victorian City: Juvenile Delinquents in Toronto', in J. Parr, ed., *Childhood and Family in Canadian History* (Toronto 1982), 139.

14. AO, Crown Attorney Prosecution Case Files, Carleton County, 1929, case 171. I discuss Bowles Lunch and other late-night diners as homosexual sites in more detail elsewhere in my dissertation. The importance of these spaces was first drawn out by Chauncey in *Gay New York*, 163–77.

15. Clark, *Of Toronto the Good*. AO, Crown Attorney Prosecution Case Files, Carleton County, 1929, case 171. On immigrant apprentices, see Joy Parr, *Labouring Children: British Immigrant Apprentices to Canada, 1869–1924* (Montreal 1980).

16. AO, Crown Attorney Prosecution Case Files, Carleton County, 1925, case 155. On the pattern of homosexual relationships in the early twentieth century in which working-class male youths were kept by wealthier men, see Kevin Porter and Jeffrey Weeks, eds, *Between the Acts: Lives of Homosexual Men, 1885–1967* (London 1991). See also the wonderful photographic evidence of the long relationship between architect Montague Glover and Ralph Hall, his young, working-class chauffeur and lover, in James Gardiner, *A Class Apart: The Private Pictures of Montague Glover* (London 1992).

17. AO, Crown Attorney Prosecution Case Film York County, 1914, case 14; 1918, case 36.

18. Ibid., 1922, case 109; 1921, case 107.

19. AO, Criminal Assize Indictments, Lambton County, 1925, case 192.

20. AO, Crown Attorney Prosecution Case Files, York County, 1917, case 23; 1916, case 99; Carleton County, 1921, case 135.

21. AO, Crown Attorney Prosecution Case Files, Carleton County, 1917, case 128; Criminal Assize Indictments, Algoma District, 1919, case 207; Crown Attorney Prosecution Case Files, Algoma District, 1922, case 204. John Bullen, 'Hidden Workers: Child Labour and the Family Economy in Late Nineteenth-Century Urban Ontario', *Labour/Le Travail* 18 (fall 1986): 163–87; Neil Sutherland, '"We Always Had Things to Do": The Paid and Unpaid Work of Anglophone Children between the 1920s and the 1960s', *Labour/Le Travail* 25 (spring 1990): 105–41; Bettina Bradbury, *Working Families, Age, Gender and Daily Survival in Industrializing Montreal* (Toronto 1993).

22. AO, Crown Attorney Prosecution Case Files, Carleton County, 1927, case 164. On boarding as a working-class survival strategy, see Bettina Bradbury, 'Pigs, Cows, and Boarders: Non-wage Forms of Survival among Montreal Families, 1861–1891', *Labour/Le Travail* 14 (1984): 9–46.

23. AO, Crown Attorney Prosecution Case Files, York County, 1913, case 96; 1920, case 106; 1909, case 92; 1916, case 22.

24. Ibid., 1909, case 93; Carleton County, 1921, case 136; 1914, case 115; 1914, case 119.

25. Ibid., 1918, case 104; Algoma District, 1926, case 203; Carleton County, 1923, case 148; Algoma District, 1926, case 204; York County, 1907, case 90.

26. 'A Big Brother' and 'Soda', at Broadview "Y"', *Toronto Evening Telegram*, 24 Oct. 1923, 9 and 16. AO, Papers of the National Council of the YMCA, F814, Local Association Files, Series A, Toronto, box 37.

27. AO, Papers of the Toronto Boys' Home, mu 4932, Annual Report, Series C, I Oct. 1915 to 30 Sept. 1916, 12.

28. AO, Crown Attorney Prosecution Case Files, York County, 1932, case 113.

29. Ibid., Ontario County, 1928, and Criminal Assize Indictments, Ontario County, 1928, case 197. *Toronto Evening Telegram*, 13 April 1929, 28. Loo, 'Dan Cranmer's

Potlatch', 135, 158. Not all was lost in this case. During his time with the OPP and the county crown attorney, Aubrey explained that his brother Reginald had been in the Victoria Industrial School for more than four years and that he had been confined there by Mr E., without there ever having been a charge against him. The county crown attorney wrote to the government official responsible for the CAS, demanding an explanation: Reginald J. 'was sent to Victoria Industrial School by Mr. W.H.E. and apparently there is no charge against him . . . [we] cannot find any information concerning why this boy is confined to the Institution. My own opinion is that Mr. E. had him confined there to suit his own convenience . . . Let me hear from you why this boy is being confined as his is.' Indeed, there was no charge against Reginald and, perhaps to avoid any further bad publicity, the government official intervened personally in Reginald's case and promised his release. As J.J. Kelso wrote to the crown attorney. '[I] took this matter up with the Industrial School people and they have promised to give this boy special consideration next month. I believe they have an application for the boy from someone in the vicinity of Whitby.'

30. Report of the Commissioners Appointed to Enquire into the Prison and Reformatory System of Ontario, 1891 (Toronto 1891), 700. Toronto Police Department, 'Annual Report of the Chief Constable, 1890', Toronto City Council, Minutes, 1891, app. c, 27. For more on the turn-of-the-century 'boy problem', see Neil Sutherland, *Children in English Canadian Society Framing the Twentieth Century Consensus* (Toronto 1976), and Harry Hendrick, *Images of Youth: Age, Class, and the Male Youth Problem, 1880–1920* (London 1990).

31. W.L. Clark, *Our Sons* (Ontario 1914), 96–106, and B.G. Jeffries, *Search Lights on Health, Light on Dark Corners: A Complete Sexual Science and a Guide to Purity and Physical Manhood* (Toronto 1894), 437. Bulletin of the Council for Social Service of the Church of England in Canada, 51 (Oct.

1921): 12, found in National Archives of Canada, Papers of the Montreal Council of Women, MG 28, 1 164, vol. 12. Thanks to Robert Champagne for bringing this source to my attention.

32. AO, Crown Attorney Prosecution Case Files, Ontario County, 1915, case 195; Carleton County, 1915, case 121.

33. See Ellen Ross, *Love and Toil: Motherhood in Outcast London, 1870–1918* (New York 1993).

34. AO, Crown Attorney Prosecution Case Files, Carleton County, 19m, case 136; York County, 1916, case 101.

35. Ibid., Carleton County, 1921, case 135; 1924, case 115.

36. On boys' testimony before the Royal Commission on the Relations of Labor and Capital, see Greg Kealey, ed., *Canada Investigates Industrialism* (Toronto 1973), 195, 197,14, 199–200. On boys' labour in early twentieth-century Ontario, see Lorna F. Hurt, 'Overcoming the Inevitable: Restricting Child Factory Labour in Late Nineteenth Century Ontario', *Labour/Le Travail 2.1* (spring 1988): 87–121, and Jane Synge, 'The Transition from School to Work: Growing Up Working-Class in Early 20th Century Hamilton, Ontario', in K. Ishwaran, ed., *Childhood and Adolescence in Canada* (Toronto 1979), 249–69.

37. It scarcely needs pointing out that the historical shifts in the meaning of sexual relations between boys and men toward the currently hegemonic and homophobic understanding of such relations as the product of homosexual predation has done nothing to help those boys who have experienced sexual abuse at the hands of men. The identification of the sexual abuse of boys as a social problem is a very recent phenomenon. It has come about not through the efforts of those who obfuscate the issue of men's power by homosexualizing the abuse of boys but through the work of women and men, including lesbians and gay men, to confront child sexual abuse. See, for example, *Loving in Fear Lesbian and Gay Survivors of Childhood Sexual Abuse* (Toronto 1992).

Excerpt from *Incorrigible*

Velma Demerson

[Editor's Note: From 1919 to 1958 women judged to be 'idle' or 'dissolute' were arrested and jailed under the Ontario Female Refuges Act. This law was a striking example of the tendency in Canadian society to punish women for sexual behaviour that was not punishable for men. In this excerpt from her autobiography Incorrigible, *Velma Demerson, 18 at the*

time of her incarceration in 1939, recalls her experiences immediately after being removed by police from the Hamilton apartment she shared with her Chinese fiancé.]

I sit in the back seat of the police car with the two policemen in front as we drive through the downtown traffic. We stop at the side of a huge building where I'm escorted into the basement and put into a barred cell.

In a short time a woman comes and the door is unlocked. She directs me up the stairs and along a hallway, off which are numerous doors. We stop at one with an extended sign that reads *Barrister*. I think, *Thank God, a lawyer has come to help me.* The room is empty. The woman sits behind a desk and questions me.

'How old are you?' she asks.

'Eighteen.'

'What religion are you?' she enquires.

'Protestant.'

'No, I mean what church do you belong to?'

I pause to explain. 'I don't know. I was baptized Greek Orthodox. My mother belongs to the Church of England and I went to Sunday school there.'

It's becoming clear that this lady isn't a lawyer. 'Have you ever slept with anyone else besides the man you were living with?'

I hesitate. To save my boyfriend from blame I will have to damage my character.

'Two,' I say.

'What are their names?'

I give them to her. I suspect I'm pregnant, and I volunteer the information, hoping it will force a marriage. When she hears this she closes her book and returns me to the lockup.

*

A policeman unlocks the door of my cage and we again climb the stairs. We walk a considerable distance and stop at a heavy ornate door. We enter a large room with benches on the left side. I look for my father but don't see anyone, only a middle-aged man facing me from a distance. His seat is raised and he appears to be sitting on a podium. The walls are bare. I'm in a courtroom and the man facing me is Judge Browne. I'm standing with my back to the door.

I become aware of a policeman halfway down on the left-hand side. He's stating the address where he found me, saying my fiancé's name and that he was wearing a bathrobe and that I was wearing pyjamas.

I'm consumed with shame.

The judge asks, 'Are you pregnant?'

'Yes.'

'How far gone?'

'Three months. If you'll just let me out of here long enough, I'll get married.'

My words have no effect. Without hesitation, Judge Browne says, 'Remanded one week for sentence.'

'Remanded for sentence'—what does that mean?

The policeman who had escorted me to the courtroom must have been standing behind me. Immediately after the judge's remarks, he takes my arm and brings me back. I hear him say to another policeman, 'She loves him. Why won't they let her marry him?'

I walk back and forth in this barred cell in shock. How could it be that a judge, knowing I'm pregnant, would refuse to allow me to marry the father of my child?

*

Now I'm taken down the same concrete steps and put through the back door of a large van I hear them call the 'Black Maria'. I'm locked in, the sole passenger. Inside this dim enclosure is a long board seat at either side.

My head and throat ache. I'm alone, trapped, and voiceless. I throw myself on the floor and scream hysterically. I toss about and start screaming, 'Let me out!' I thrash about and bang on the sides of the van.

'Let me out!' I cry, over and over again.

A policeman peers in at me through the small wire-meshed window on the door.

'It won't do you any good—you can't get out,' he says.

Nothing I can do will help. I feel the car moving out into traffic and gaining momentum.

We stop at the jailhouse and climb the high steps to the reception office where I'm turned over to a guard and placed in one of a line of barred cells. I feel too distraught to take notice of anyone else who might be here.

I hold a dim hope that my fiancé might rescue me though I know it's impossible. A Chinese man can hardly come looking for a white woman without endangering himself.

I declared my immorality during the interview to protect my boyfriend. Otherwise he might have been charged with a morals offence. But nothing, it seems, would have saved me.

*

The wooden bench on which I sit serves as my bed for a week and there's no change of clothes. No pillow or blanket is supplied. A male guard unlocks the door when I request access to the washroom. When walking through the corridor, my heel slips and I fall backward; I hope it will cause a miscarriage.

The jail doctor gives me an internal examination in a cramped examining room.

It appears that I'm the only woman. At mealtimes I'm directed down some narrow steps to the basement where I sit at a long splintered wooden table with men and eat greasy stew.

Silence pervades except for the occasional guard who walks through, looking in. There's nothing to read. I sit and think. Only my father or mother can free me from this place. When will my father come? Where's my mother? I don't understand. She's in control of all situations. Doesn't she even want to talk to me? Does she know I'm pregnant? Would she be able to tolerate her daughter being pregnant outside of marriage? I have heard her say of a friend who had an illegitimate child, 'Esperance is weak-minded.' According to my mother, any woman who can't deal with an unwanted pregnancy is a country bumpkin.

*

[. . .]

My mother must have contacted my father, knowing full well his weakness.

'He's a coward,' she would say. He is a coward. In one great frenzy of fear for his social position, he came all the way to Toronto and had me arrested. He wasn't even in court for my sentencing. He has dispatched me and gone comfortably home. How can my father, so kind and affectionate when I was small, turn against me so viciously?

Had my English grandmother seen the picture of my fiancé hidden under the mattress when I visited Saint John? Had she snitched to my father? I remember she had once rented a room to a couple and then looked in their luggage when they went out. She found they weren't married and evicted them. She remained in the room and turned her back while they packed. There would be no immorality under her roof. She's such a snoop!

The separation from my fiancé consumes me. I imagine I see him at every turn. How must he feel? I told him I might be pregnant. Harry must surely know I'm in impossible circumstances. He probably thinks I went back to Saint John with my father, under duress, of course, but even if he went to the police station, who would provide him with information?

I keep going over my situation, looking for clues to account for my arrest. Why did my mother not have me arrested? Why my father? She couldn't have known it was possible. What law have I broken? Did my mother just choose to frighten my father? She knows the disgrace he fears within his own community, for he would be appalled to have his daughter running off with an Oriental.

My mother can't be terribly afraid of this. She has no particular social standing to protect. So why doesn't she come to see me, use her wiles to free me? She can hardly remain angry over the altercation with my boyfriend—such volatile scenes are customary to her. She has won the battle, I've been found. Why is she not visiting me and using her influence on me to return home? Of course, she played a role in my apprehension, but she couldn't have expected it to go so far. I've breached her authority but that's no longer important. She must know I'm pregnant—she would want me to have an abortion. She was never afraid I'd get pregnant perhaps because, before she was divorced, she had several self-induced abortions herself. She couldn't have known about the severe prejudice against the Chinese. Perhaps she can't get me out.

My mother has the feel of the downtown Church Street milieu. She doesn't for a moment believe I'm in danger of being influenced by sinister forces. She saw my boyfriend and knows he's working. My mother was never concerned with nationality.

However my father found out about my boyfriend, I can imagine that the police fuelled his feelings. Once a girl gets into Chinatown she's finished, according to them. They would fill my father with warnings about white slavery, vice, and drugs. All manner of evils would be laid at the feet of Chinese men.

These things could have been overcome. My father could have talked to me to ascertain if I was in danger. But he's not really concerned with my security. He's afraid that my association with a Chinese man will bring disgrace to his family. Only his own community is pure.

No doubt he learned the results of my court appearance. He hadn't apprehended me in time. I was pregnant. A Chinese grandchild! My God! I'd have to be put out of sight, at once.

My fiancé and I are in similar situations. Maybe that's what attracts us to each other. He's an outcast by virtue of his race. But I am also the object of discrimination. Because of my mother's divorce I am, like her, excluded from the world of stable, conforming families. The Chinese have been singled out by government legislation as undesirable and their families in China can't join them in Canada. Most of the Chinese here are men without mates and friendship with Canadian women is discouraged.

By statute the Chinese are singled out as the only people in Canada who cannot employ white women. My fiancé and I are lonely people who have found each other. We share the same enemies.

*

Days pass. I know my father won't tarry long in Toronto, but where's my mother? The possibility that my mother isn't going to rescue me occurs to me for the first time. I've been caught in a power struggle between two angry people—my parents. My father worked diligently to acquire a respectful place in the community. He's come a long way from the early days when my mother, a country girl, worked in his fledgling ice cream parlour. Her knowledge of the English language was an asset. There weren't many Greeks in the Maritimes then. When the business expanded and my mother's energies were no longer needed, she embarked on a vivid social life and became popular. My father wasn't interested and soon my mother became an obstacle to him. He started having affairs, which my mother learned about through the wife of his business partner.

My mother caught my father in our house with one of his waitresses. She had a witness, a male roomer. She had to 'keep him company' to ensure his testimony in her divorce action against my father and his employee. Already, she was selling her favours—it was the price for leaving one's husband. She must have been terrified. Failure would have meant returning to my father's house and his insults and humiliation. To leave would mean she'd risk losing her children; my father could also have used my mother's 'unwomanly' behaviour to have her committed to a mental institution.

There's a refuge called the Interprovincial Home for Young Women at Coverdale, near Moncton in New Brunswick. It's a Protestant home for women and girls from New Brunswick, Nova Scotia, and Prince Edward Island. A good number of those sentenced are older married women and girls who had committed an offence. But in Ontario, the *Female Refuges Act* allows an innocent woman to be confined, not for a crime but for being 'incorrigible' or 'idle and dissolute'.[1] Could a man put his wife in a refuge?

The loss of respect, the humiliation, still torments my mother. I know the extent of her despair and I cringe for my future. When the time was ripe she set the trap. He arrived and did her bidding. My incarceration at his hands is her victory. It's he who put his daughter in prison. Now she's holding the whip. As long as I'm here, she can plague him with my unhappiness, blackmail him to ensure secrecy, and guilt him mercilessly. 'He'll pay for his sins, he'll come crawling to me some day, and I'll have no mercy,' she always vowed. My father can no longer laugh at her. No one must know he has a daughter in prison or that she's pregnant by a Chinese.

I imagine going back to his community, screaming to the rooftops about what he's done to me, but then I would be mad just like my mother. He did the best he could, he'd say. I'm no longer his daughter. But he can't escape the blood ties of a Chinese grandchild.

It's unlikely my mother could have foreseen the escalation of my plight, the ruthlessness of the law. How does she feel about my pregnancy?

Is revenge against my father worth keeping me in jail?

Note

1. Section 15 states that any female between the ages of 15 and 35 may be brought before a judge by any person and charged with being idle and dissolute. A parent or guardian could charge a woman under 21 years with being incorrigible. This section was enacted in 1919. (*Female Refuges Act*, SOR 1937, c. 384.)

'Why Can't I Be Normal?': Sex Advice for Teens

Mary Louise Adams

In the years after the Second World War, 'normality' was a primary marker of difference between individuals and between groups of people. As defined by increasingly popular psychological and psychoanalytic theories, normality was the desired result of an individual's emotional and psychic evolution, a product of social and environmental factors.[1] Such had not been the case as recently as the 1920s when normality and abnormality were seen, primarily, as bodily and not psychic conditions.[2] While biological explanations have never been completely overturned, the relationship between biological and psychological theories has undergone substantial transformation over the course of this century.

[. . .]

What counted as normal and what did not were both discursively organized categories, articulated by and to a variety of institutions and practices. Science, the school, the family, medicine, and the field of mental health all contributed in significant ways to the production and circulation of the various discourses about normality that were available in mainstream, popular culture. While 'normal' was a term used to assess many aspects of post-war life, from cleaning habits to parenting styles, it was more often than not brought to bear on matters of sexuality and gender, perhaps because these, especially, were assumed to be fragile. They were understood to be the culmination of a delicate process of emotional development, one that might easily be corrupted—a perspective rooted in the increasing popularity of Freudian ideas. Sexuality, more than almost anything else, was understood as having the potential for abnormality in its expression.

Of course, concerns about sexuality were not unique to the post-war era. In Western cultures, the hierarchical opposition between appropriate and inappropriate sexualities has proven, historically, to be a common means of organizing the distribution of power. Those on the sanctioned side of the opposition—the normal, in the post-war case—benefit from the privileges of inclusion in the social order. Those on the undesirable side experience marginalization and exclusion. But as deconstructionists will tell us, the separation between the terms of any binary opposition is not complete. To some extent, the definition of each is located within the other. The one is what the other is not. The terms themselves are relative, making sense to us only as a dyad. If there was no abnormality, the concept of normality would not make sense. Nor would there be such a fuss about continually shoring it up.

With the widespread circulation of some aspects of Freudian theory, the line between normal and abnormal grew less distinct and so more threatening. Freudian suggestions that even the most 'natural' and 'normal' sexual instincts were open to perversion meant that sexual development came to be perceived as a process of potential peril. With the wrong influences, anyone's sexuality could veer hazardously

toward abnormality. Kinsey, claimed nervous commentators, had made that abundantly clear.

With the publication of his reports on male (1948) and female (1953) sexual behaviour, Alfred Kinsey and his team of researchers had shaken North Americans with carefully documented evidence of widespread variation in sexual practices.[3] As Eleanor Rumming wrote in *Saturday Night*, Kinsey's book called into question popularly accepted bounds of normality. 'Normality', she concluded, 'is what most people do. Dr Kinsey's book on the Human Male showed that what most people do is far more varied than public morality is prepared to admit.'[4] Rumming's definition of normality, based on statistical evidence and a liberal ethic, was not shared by everyone who wrote on Kinsey's work. And while Kinsey's own perspective was, in some sense, a liberal one, he didn't necessarily share Rumming's point of view.

Kinsey tried not to speak of either normality or abnormality, terms that he said had no place in a scientific vocabulary.[5] Instead Kinsey talked about biological possibilities and variations in human behaviour: 'Whatever the moral interpretation, there is no scientific reason for considering particular types of sexual activity as intrinsically, in their biological origins, normal or abnormal . . . Present-day legal determinations of sexual acts which are acceptable, or "natural", and those which are "contrary to nature" are not based on data obtained from biologists, nor from nature herself.'[6]

It was 'nature' that provided the single most important yardstick in Kinsey's work. He evaluated human behaviour not in terms of normality, which he considered to be a subjective quality, but in terms of its correspondence to the behaviour of other mammals. 'Interpretations of human behaviour would benefit', he said, 'if there were a more general understanding of basic mammalian behaviour'.[7] In this particular case, Kinsey was talking about the amount of time it takes for human males to ejaculate, the point being the unfairness of labelling men who ejaculate quickly as somehow sexually deficient. Chimpanzees, he said, can effect ejaculation in less than 20 seconds: 'It would be difficult to find another situation in which an individual who was quick and intense in his responses was labelled anything but superior.' While the word 'normal' was not used, it seems Kinsey did have an 'ideal' in mind. From this ideal there may be deviations—a markedly different concept from abnormality—but the ideal itself is the way 'nature' intended things to be.

[. . .]

Not surprisingly, Kinsey's rejection of a moral line of argument provided plenty of fodder for reviewers of all persuasions. Some, like Eleanor Rumming, translated the reports' findings into a call for the realignment of moral standards to reflect people's actual experiences.[8] Others worked feverishly to insert Kinsey into the very discourses he'd tried to decentre, asking, for instance, what the sex studies meant in terms of working definitions of normality. A piece in *Saturday Night* cited Yale psychiatrist Robert P. Knight, who used Kinsey to argue his own position that normality was definitely not a question of biological possibility. It was, instead, a product of well-kept moral standards: 'The common cold, says Dr Knight, has about the same incidence as homosexuality (that 37 per cent of all US males have some homosexual experience) in the Kinsey figures. But the prevalence of colds, says Knight, does not make them normal.'[9] That Kinsey had distinguished between medical normality (lack of any type of harmful or injurious physical condition) and sexual normality (a non-scientific, moral standard) was a point lost on Knight.[10] In Knight's construction, there was a fine line between normal and moral, a semiotic turn that would become perhaps too familiar to

the teenagers who negotiated the sexual terrain of the post-Kinsey years.

Advice for Teens

In popular magazines and in prescriptive literature and films, young people were offered tools and strategies to use in the construction of themselves as normal sexual beings. They were offered the promise of normality—a position of the inside of the social body—in exchange for conformity to rules and standards of behaviour that, in many cases, had implications beyond the sexual realm. Normal was about being middle class, normal was about whiteness and not being 'ethnic', normal was about proper expressions of gender.

Attempts to shape teenagers into proper adults were certainly not unique to the post–Second World War era. What is significant, however, is the way post-war efforts focused on sexuality as a requirement for the production of marriageable adults. In the 1940s and 1950s, adolescents were assumed by many to need sexual guidance before assuming their 'inevitable' marital roles. Around the turn of the century, by contrast, one prepared for marriage by learning gender-specific domestic and economic skills. Certainly, as Karen Dubinsky has pointed out, adolescents in earlier decades were warned about the dangers of sexual transgression,[11] but these warnings were not necessarily part of broader 'positive' and productive attempts to regulate the development of 'normal' sexual individuals. The latter did not begin until the 1920s and 1930s, when sexuality was increasingly being portrayed, via medical and popular instructional discourses, as important to heterosexual marriages.[12] The 'new' companionate marriages of the post–First World War era were to be held together by friendship and the sexual satisfaction of both husband and wife. Promoters of this 'new' form of heterosexual partnership advocated education about sex for those on the verge of marriage, warning of the danger to marriage of sexual 'deviations'. By the post-war years, companionate marriage was no longer new or unusual. Still, it was assumed that young people, at ever-decreasing ages, needed to be prepared for it. The growing prominence of psychological notions about the fragility of the process of attaining sexual maturity meant that one could rarely be too careful or too concerned about the brides and grooms of the future.

Sex advice for teens appeared in inexpensive pocketbooks, in pamphlets, in magazine articles, and in educational films on love, dating, and sex.[13] There are limits to using this type of prescriptive material for research purposes. Certainly it was not used by all young people, and it is difficult to determine who, in fact, did engage with it. One might also raise questions about the extent to which different groups of young people supported the ideas contained in the books, articles, and films, about the distance between 'advice' and 'reality'. But the possibility that young people did not subscribe to the information about sexuality and sexual behaviour they received from adults does not negate the role of that 'advice' in constructing the normative standards by which teens were judged. [. . .] Discursive constructions of good teenagers and bad teenagers, of healthy sexuality and immoral sexuality, may not have been the immediate determinants of teen behaviour, but they did influence the context of that behaviour and the meanings that would eventually be ascribed to it.

There was no explicitly Canadian popular discourse of teen advice. Canadians, expert and lay person alike, borrowed heavily from American work in this area. Canadian magazines published American authors and suggested the titles of American books to their readers. There was very little difference between what appeared in *Chatelaine*, for instance, and what was published in US pocketbooks. Marion Hilliard, who

to my knowledge was the only Canadian to have published sex advice books in this period, used British and American publishers.

Magazine advice columns and features directed at teens—primarily girls—were generally related to the etiquette of dating. They discussed the ways a young woman might go about attracting a young man, or, if she had one, how to keep him. Books covered a broader range of material and tended to address a mixed audience. Most spent some time on the physical basics of sex education—the workings of genitals and reproductive organs, where babies come from, and personal hygiene. This information was generally contextualized by lengthy discussions on the 'joys' of both masculinity and femininity (so long as they were expressed by the proper sorts of people in the proper sorts of ways). Thus established, the heterosexual framework was pursued through the stages of pre-dating, dating, engagement, and marriage, with related discussions about good grooming, how to hostess a party, how to meet your date's parents, and other essential skills of the successful girl or boy. The tone in both books and magazines was enthusiastic and upbeat. Being a modern boy or girl was a swell thing.

[. . .]

As with the advice books, post-war teens were also the target audience of growing numbers of educational films. While educational films were not new in and of themselves, the style and content of these 'how-to-grow-up' teenage-guidance films were unique to the post-war period. The films were more serious than the advice books, their tone set by the ever-present voice of a male narrator. Produced in Canada by the National Film Board and by private production houses, such as Crawley films in Ottawa, for distribution by American textbook publishers, the films played before 'captive' audiences in school classrooms, at youth groups, and, sometimes, on television. Perhaps because of this, their approach to content was more cautious than that followed by the advice authors. Whereas advice books were consumed privately, perhaps even secretly, films were viewed in public, sometimes in mixed groups of boys and girls. To some, who thought sex education the responsibility of parents and not the state, such materials were both ill-advised and dangerous. Boards of education could face protest by offended parents and embarrassed teachers for using them. Hence, the restrained tone of the films was not surprising. It probably helped facilitate the securing of an audience.

It's in the films that one sees most easily the way teen advice was implicated in the construction of post-war middle classness. These films flagged class in any number of ways, from simple matters like the predominance of spotless and well-furnished two-storey houses, where mothers were full-time homemakers (even if widowed), to the homogeneity of students in a classroom, to assumptions about dating, marriage, and future careers. [. . .]

A typical example was an American film called *Are You Popular?*, first produced in 1947 and updated in 1958. In both versions of this film, post-war class differences are central to the story line. To make its point the film contrasts Ginny and Caroline. Ginny is the unpopular girl, packaged in multiple working-class signifiers. Her jewellery is big and gaudy, her clothes are fussy, her hair is too old for her age, she 'yoo-hoos' the other kids in the cafeteria. And, we find out from the solemn-toned male narrator, she goes parking with boys at night. Caroline, on the other hand, is very popular, in an easy kind of way (which is, of course, the right way). She is dressed simply. She greets her friends calmly and pleasantly. She is 'interested in girls rather than boys'. She offers to help with the school play. She does not 'park' with the boys in their

cars.[14] She will, however, go on a date with a boy if it is okay with her mother. She will be home before an agreed-upon curfew. And, when she and her date arrive home, mother will greet them with a tray of fresh brownies. For both Caroline and Ginny, class, moral character, and popularity are indivisible.

In all of the films, all of the characters are white. None speak with accents or have 'foreign'-sounding names. There is no mention of the way religious or cultural differences might affect one's popularity or one's ability to date or how one approaches marriage. Several films do suggest, however, the importance of marrying someone from a similar background. Overall, nothing disrupts the seamless representation of middle-class dominant culture. Certainly nothing suggests that the advice on growing up given in both the books and the films might not be useful to everyone.

The Straightness of Normality

There was a remarkable conformity among the different advice books and films about what constituted normality. While it was talked about as a unitary category, normality, in these texts, differed for boys and girls, teens and adults. And while it was presented as a self-evident descriptive, normality was constructed through a complex formation of professional and popular discourses, all of which were easily bent to serve moral ends. Biological and psychological discourses, which at times contradicted each other, were tucked comfortably alongside the most 'unscientific' common sense. The end result of this eclectic approach was a peculiar mix of essentialist theory, moral coercion, and behaviouralist strategy that was all meant to inspire teens to 'do the right thing'.

At its most basic level, normality was grounded in notions of the supposedly biologically rooted mutual attraction of males and females. Addressing young women, Ann Landers wrote in her 1963 book, 'Of course you would not be normal if you were able to keep your mind off the boys, completely. And no normal boy is able to keep his mind off girls *completely* either.'[15] While heterosexual desire, on its own, wasn't enough to guarantee one's status as normal, it was essential. In the limited world of the teen manual, homosexuality marked the extreme outer edge of the abnormal. Homosexuality existed as that place in the books where discussions of abnormality were up front and explicit. It was a subject the more reticent films rarely touched.

In her 1960 book, *Sex and the Adolescent*, journalist Maxine Davis wrote, 'Human beings have always been frightened by phenomena which seem to be unnatural. For example, before they learned something about astronomy they were terrified by the eclipse of the sun by the moon; they thought it was the end of the world. Today, the average healthy adult has a *comparable* aversion to homosexuality; he thinks it a dreadful incurable disease or an unnatural emotional deformity' (emphasis mine).[16] And while Davis claimed she wanted to allay these types of fears, homosexuality remained, in her text, something vastly remote from everyday life. Indeed homosexuality was constructed as so outside the range of normal teen experience that it was presented in all of the books as an external threat. Homosexuals were other people—not, certainly, teens themselves. Thus, most of the information about homosexuality that found its way into these books was intended to help boys and girls to protect themselves from deviants.

[. . .]

Different writers had different explanations for the cause of a sexual aberration like same-sex desire. Frances Bruce Strain said it might be due to the unavailability of the opposite sex at a crucial time of development—for instance, in the case of boarding schools. She also suggested other reasons related to poor family conditions or unpleasant early experiences.[17] Lester Kirkendall looked primarily to the home to find the cause of homosexuality: 'Some [people] . . . are so unfortunate as to be blocked in their normal development by conflicts with their parents, unhappy home conditions, lack of opportunity to build friendships, timidity, poor social adjustment, and possibility poor physical conditions. A combination of factors thus produces the homosexual, an individual who might with better fortune have followed the normal process of maturing and growing up.'[18]

The developmental focus on the causes of homosexuality made it possible for the broad range and occurrence of same-sex affections in teenagers' own lives to be corralled and put to good ideological use. In typical models of heterosexual development, there existed a secure place for same-sex attractions, or crushes. Homosexual feelings or intimacies experienced by young people themselves were recuperated by advice writers as essential steps on the road to heterosexual normality. Most people, the writers claimed, go through some sort of homosexual 'phase' at some point in their lives. Evelyn Duvall, who was recommended to Canadians in *Chatelaine* magazine, constructed a continuum of affectional and sexual ties that began with 'same sex, same age' interests, passing through 'same sex, older age' crushes on the way to 'other sex, older age', before finally reaching the real thing, the 'other sex, same age' stage of 'love development'.[19] In this model, homosexual ties are seen as preparation or practice for heterosexual relationships. In their book *On Becoming a Woman*, Mary McGee Williams and Irene Kane discussed same-sex crushes as good training not only in sexuality, but also in terms of gender roles, 'There's nothing wrong with idolizing a woman—if it's kept under control *and* if she's a person worthy of your respect. As a matter of fact, it helps to have a model on whom you can pattern your behaviours, and it's a step in learning to be a woman, to learn to admire a good and admirable one.'[20]

Homoerotic desire in this sense was not only normal but desirable. Nevertheless, it was important that this 'not unusual part of growing up' did not expand into an active desire for physical contact—it was important to keep clear the boundaries between normal and abnormal. Should such transgressive feelings arise, the young person was advised to seek counselling to find out why his or her 'emotional development [was] being delayed beyond what [was] considered normal'.[21] The assumption was always that any same-sex sexual behaviour indicated a developmental stage that had been taken too far. Moreover, it was nothing a few new friends and some vigorous sports activity wouldn't put back on track.

Little attention was paid by these authors to concerns young people might have had about their own sexual identities, worries that they themselves might have been 'a little queer'. Ann Landers was the only writer to approach homosexuality from this angle, and she only talked about boys, claiming that they accounted for 70 per cent of her mail on the subject. They are the ones, she wrote, who were 'tortured with guilt and self-hatred . . . terrified that someone may learn they aren't "like everyone else".'[22] They were the ones who 'yearn to be normal'.

Perhaps because of the letters she received, Landers was more willing than her colleagues to make a distinction (albeit an unhappy one) between homosexuality as a phase and homosexuality as a tragic future. While she believed sexual identities to be the result of a process of emotional development, she saw that process as relatively quick and finite. However, she also claimed that cures were possible, although their chances of success were greater if 'the homosexual seeks professional help in his early teens'. But one wonders whether the young homosexual would have pursued such a course of action while everyone around him (or her, invisible though she was) was saying that homosexual feelings were a normal part of growing up. How was one to know the difference between homosexual desires that were 'twisted and sick' and those that were preparing one for heterosexual matrimony? The negotiation of the normal/abnormal boundary could be very complicated.

Never one to cut off hope, Landers stressed that much could be done in terms of 'adjustment' to homosexuality. She claimed that, 'Psychiatric therapy can, in most cases, give the homosexual some understanding and insight into his problem. It can help him to adjust to his condition and accept himself as he is.'[23] What that acceptance might look like in a society where homosexuality was rarely acknowledged, let alone tolerated, Landers didn't say. [. . .]

Most of the advice writers claimed that they wanted to reduce people's fear of homosexuality although, clearly, they weren't interested in calming young people's personal fears about living homosexual lives. Instead they focused on widespread social fears of homosexuals in the culture at large. It was widely believed in the 1950s, as it is by many today, that young people could be inducted into homosexuality by older homosexuals. In developmental theories of homosexuality, contact with an adult homosexual was one event that might send normal development astray. A particularly vitriolic version of this theory appeared in the American digest magazine *Coronet*:

All too often, we lose sight of the fact that the homosexual is an inveterate seducer of the young of bother sexes [sic], and that he presents a social problem because he is

not content with being degenerate himself;
he must have degenerate companions, and is
even seeking younger victims . . .

. . . He demands a partner. And the partner,
more often than not, must come from the
ranks of the young and innocent. (Emphasis in the original.)[24]

Davis wrote that if a young boy is seduced
by an older man and 'has repeated relationships with adult homosexuals, there is a serious
risk that his originally normal instincts may
eventually become permanently perverted'.[25]
Homosexuality, in this instance, is not something you perform or do, or something you are,
it is something that might happen to you. This
meant that, despite the 'naturalness' of heterosexuality and the abnormality of homosexuality,
young people were vulnerable to derailment
from the straight path. As long as homosexuality
was understood to be an external threat, notions
of the 'naturalness' and inevitability of heterosexuality were left unchallenged.

Normal Gender Makes Normal Sexuality

In teen advice books and films, the relationship
between sexuality and gender was a fluctuating
one. While post-war theories of homosexuality
relied less on notions of gender inversion than
earlier theories had,[26] theories of heterosexuality, by contrast, were heavily steeped in ideas
about the proper fit between gender and sexuality. Whereas one could be a homosexual without
feeling the inversion of gender, one could not be
a successful heterosexual if one's gender was out
of line.

Girls and boys who did not match prevailing
images of masculinity and femininity—sissies
and tomboys—were a challenge to the firmness

of the boundary that split off abnormal from normal. But, surprisingly, not a single writer mentioned the possibility that these children might
turn into homosexuals. Doing so might have
given too much credence to theories that homosexuality was a biological condition, as Kinsey
had tried to show, and not a perversion of normal
instincts or evidence of relaxed moral standards.
To succumb to biological arguments about the
basis of 'abnormalities' would have necessitated
an admission of the futility of sex education
and other regulatory measures as a prophylaxis
against deviations from social norms. Such arguments would have put these writers out of business. [. . .] While homosexuality was thought to
be the result of (failed) adolescent development,
sissyness and tomboyness were presented as
conditions that (successful) adolescent development could cure.

In the late 1940s, Kellogg's cereal company
ran a regular ad in *Chatelaine* magazine that was
formatted to look like a column by 'psychologist
Janet Power'. A 1948 installment was entitled
'Barbara Is a Tomboy'.[27] Psychologist Power (!)
responded to a letter from Barbara's mother
describing her daughter's habits and asking 'How
can I make Barbara more feminine, yet not curb
her high spirits?' Powers suggested that Barbara's
mother ignore 'her tomboy antics' and instead
praise Barbara 'for everything feminine she happens to do'. Barbara's mother was to encourage a closer relationship between Barbara and
her sister, to take Barbara shopping, and to give
both daughters more responsibility in the home.
Eventually, Barbara would calm down when she
learned how proud it makes her mother: 'Remember, stress CONSIDERATION OF OTHERS and
GOOD MANNERS. At first Barbara will obey just
to please you, but quiet, normal gentleness will
soon become a habit with her. Show Barbara it's
fun to be a DAUGHTER to you and FATHER—
not a tomboy!' (emphasis in original).[28]

Femininity in this case is a matter of behaviour modification; it is not something one feels, but something one learns. Several versions of this approach were expressed in teen advice books and guidance films. The writers made clear that while young women have an inherent capacity for femininity—it is, after all a 'natural' product of their biological femaleness—they need instruction so their femininity will attain the proper shape. 'Most of what goes into making a woman act and behave and feel like a woman is learned as she grows up . . . Learning to enjoy boys as persons, to like men without being afraid of them on the one hand or being too overwhelmed by them on the other, learning to enjoy the fine arts and skills of being a real woman, with all the satisfactions and challenges that lie before women today—these are important, and they are for you to learn.'[29]

But with questions around gender identity, as with other topics, there is a continual tension in these texts between 'modern' psychological theories and 'old-fashioned' explanations that draw on biology. Either set of theories could be easily adapted to meet the exigencies of moral discourses. That these two positions could, at times, be contradictory was a theoretical and narrative puzzle the advice writers left unsolved. In a book directed at parents and teachers, Frances Strain suggested tomboys and sissies be referred to the family doctor to determine 'the underlying physical basis' of 'the problem'. She also said that when children enter adolescence and their hormones start up 'either naturally or through medication, the minuses may both become pluses, delicate boys become virile and strong, stalwart girls become graceful and more feminine, ready to be to each other not pals but "dates" and sweethearts'.[30] Here, her advice differs from the behaviour-training approach of the Kellogg's ad. [. . .]

In most of the books and films, biology was presented as the source of things good, while environmental and psychological/emotional factors were what turned good things into bad ones. This is very clear in Strain's later book where she based her discussion of ideal genders on 'nature':

> Boys are to be fathers and providers. They become broad of shoulder, long of limb, fleet of foot, stronger, tougher and more combative. The animal world gives plenty of evidence of male equipment for this task of winning a wife, protecting and caring for a family. The magnificent antlers of the bull moose and his roaring mating call up in the north woods has inspired many a dainty little doe and won her to him. The bull seal with his mighty tusks, the lion with his massive head and mane, the game cock and his spurs, all of these are Life's provisions for the male of the species.[31]

Unnatural gender types, like sissies and tomboys, were frequently said to be the fault of parents; a bad home life could turn one's 'natural', normal constitution inside out. Learning to maintain gender boundaries, to express the right kind of masculinity or the right kind of femininity, was partially a matter of giving shape to the kind of biological urges evident in the 'animal world'. As Evelyn Duvall wrote, 'most young people have a strong urge to be normal . . .'[32] To do so, adolescents were to become the opposite halves of a heterosexual whole. Learning to date, then, was a means of building on biology, trying on heterosexuality and fulfilling gender requirements. The reader of *On Becoming a Woman* learns that womanliness, for instance, is not something complete unto itself; it is something to be 'practised' on men. To be a 'truly feminine woman', according to Williams and Kane, a woman had to 'really *like* men'.[33] This didn't mean, however, that she joined them for games on the ball field. Girls needed to like boys in ways that would make them into dates, not into pals. Although there were many ways for boys and girls to be together, only one was evidence that nature was unfolding as it should.

Dating as Heterosexual Practice

If anything marks post-war ideologies abut gender and sexuality and the relationship between the two categories, it's dating. Much has been written about dating as a fairly recent, North American institution. Beth Bailey, Ellen Rothman, and others have discussed the various historical factors that shaped the adoption of the 'dating system' by young Americans.[34] In most of this writing, dating appears as a series of events or customs that change with the economic and social climate. But, as Karen Dubinsky has pointed out, these histories of courtship fail to look at dating as a key aspect of the institutionalization of heterosexuality.[35] Neither have they looked at the ways that dating contributed to the construction of the teenager as a particular kind of sexual being, or at the ways that dating was as important for those who did not participate in it as it was for those who did.

[. . .] Paula Fass suggests that dating came about with the increasing numbers of coed colleges in the 1920s, and with the increasing enrollment in mixed-sex high schools.[36] It was in these institutions that youth began to be perceived as a distinct sector of society, a cohesive group with its own tastes, traditions, and norms. High schools also brought adolescents together in a way that made them targets of adult/expert observation and intervention. For instance, post–Second World War high schools provided the audience for the how-to-grow-up-properly films I've mentioned in this [article]. Without the large numbers of young people collected in state school systems it is unlikely such films would have been profitable.

As Kathy Peiss makes clear, 'dates' outside the home were not an invention of the middle class nor of the twentieth century. What was different about middle-class dates as they evolved in the 1920s and the decades that followed was that middle-class dating became *the* socially approved system of boy-girl interaction, with its own rituals and peer-enforced norms. Other situations in which boys and girls found themselves together in the service of their sexuality came to be censured. This transformation had a lot to do with changing economic conditions after the First World War, the growing proliferation of cars, and the availability of commercial amusements.[37] In order to date, one had to have money, somewhere to go, and a means of getting there.

By the interwar period, claims American historian Beth Bailey, dating had come to be organized along competitive 'economic' lines. In the 1930s, young men and women were keen to have as many dates as possible. Popularity was both an outcome of and a contributor to dating success. Bailey cites American sociologist Willard Waller who described the 'dating and rating system' as he saw it in the late 1930s.[38] To be popular and successful, Waller said, men had to have material advantages—access to disposable income, cars, the proper clothes, and so on. Women, of course, didn't compete on this same level. For a woman to be popular she herself had to be seen as valuable and in great demand. Thus, she tried to be seen with men who rated, turning down those who didn't or those who insulted her worth in the marketplace by asking her out at the last minute. As Bailey understands it, the rating and dating system was based on the conformity that was central to middle-class youth culture as well as on the competition that was a product of a nascent consumer society.[39]

By the 1950s, this constant changing of partners was all but lost as teenagers began to invest themselves in serial monogamy via the institution of 'going steady'. Again historians locate the source of this shift in the economic and social conditions of the larger society. After the war, says Bailey, teens used the dating system as a means of escaping the intense competition of the burgeoning consumer culture.[40] Elaine May says that dating habits were part of a larger search for security and stability during the cold war.[41] But dating was not merely a reflection of the larger economic and political circumstances. Dating was also a means of organizing social relations among youth. Peer-enforced standards of behaviour, encouraged by adults, brought the regulation of what was normal down to the level of young people themselves. As a public display of one's ability to fit in or not, 'going steady' was a requirement of popularity that made those who were not participating in its rituals obvious. Serial monogamy, with its lack of spontaneity—its stability—made the unattached especially visible. The problem is summed up by a young woman in Sylvia Fraser's autobiographical book about Hamilton, Ontario, in the 1950s: '"It's better to stay home than to go with someone you don't like", I assure her, knowing that I'm lying. All social life Hamilton High is strictly two-by-two, as in Noah's Ark. Not to date is to be an object of scorn or pity.'[42] Once on the outside of the couple world, the chances of getting in were fewer than they might have been in the constantly changing social scene of the thirties.

For all its significance as a teenage institution, going steady was not, by any means, free of adult influence. Teachers, journalists, filmmakers, advice-book writers, and parents all did their best to keep this form of dating consistent with larger social norms. While boys and girls could mark the boundaries of their social worlds in terms of who was with whom and who was alone, adults attempted to keep limits on the entire dating system, especially in terms of sexual expression and how interactions between boys and girls reflected contemporary ideologies about gender.

[. . .]

To the extent that it became institutionalized, with numerous ritual and structural intricacies, dating offered advice writers no end of opportunity to intervene in young lives. Dating, though the 'natural' expression of heterosexuality, was not something that just anyone could do properly—it had to be taught, and adults were more than happy to take on the job of teaching. As in the learning of masculinity and feminity, advice writers claimed no contradictions between their assertions that heterosexuality was 'natural' and the assumption that it was an identity and a practice that had to be achieved: 'Both girls and boys must learn how to be smooth in their dating. None of us is born with the attributes of being a good date . . . Such learning can be fun, and it is important without question. On it hangs our feeling of being a successful member of one sex or another.'[43] In this passage, Evelyn Duvall is talking grooming and being punctual and wearing the right clothes. But success as a dater, and as a young man or a young woman, was based on more weighty issues than these. Once one was in the dating system, one had to be able to stay there without 'getting into trouble'. Fears around the extent of sexual activity between daters as one topic on which the anti–going steady adults agreed with those who were for it. But while the latter thought going steady was a way to control sex between teenagers, the former believed it encouraged dangerous intimacies. Sidney Katz cited the results from a poll published in *Canadian High News* in which 82 per cent of parents were opposed to their daughters going steady. They were afraid 'something might happen'.[44] No mention was made of their sons.

Ann Landers shared the parents' concerns: 'It is unrealistic to assume that healthy, red-blooded high school kids can be together day in and day out, month after month—sometimes year after year—and keep their physical urges under perfect control.'[45] Sex, she warned, was a 'dangerous by-product of going steady'. Marion Hilliard thought the same: 'As a doctor I don't believe there is such a thing as a platonic relationship between a man and woman who are alone together a great deal.'[46] A strong sex drive was seen to be normal (for boys and girls, according to Hilliard), but a teenager needed to and could learn how to control it, because 'Uncontrolled, this force can take over and direct you.'[47] For those who agreed with Hilliard, sex education, like that found in the advice books, would give teenagers the moral grounding to stem their physical inclinations.

Some sources downplayed discussion of sex, perhaps because of a fear that too much sexual knowledge was, itself, a dangerous thing. Reading *Chatelaine's* regular column 'Teen Tempo', one could assume that the extent of teenage girls' concerns with sex stopped at whether or not to permit a goodnight kiss on the doorstep. Most dating how-to films, which were ostensibly presenting real teenage couples, managed to skip quickly over sex as an issue that might be of concern. In an American film called *Going Steady*, shown on a 1954 CBC talk show, *Youth Takes a Stand*, sex is introduced and dismissed in three short lines:

Marie: Going steady? Yes, I guess I have been going steady.
Mother: I hope Jeff doesn't feel he has the right to take liberties.
Marie: Oh mother.[48]

The film was shown as part of a special episode on going steady. The conversation between Marie and her mother contains the only reference to sex in the entire program. A 1957 film, *How Much Affection?*, produced by Crawley Films of Ottawa for McGraw-Hill Books in New York, is unusual in that it dances around sex without actually having to say the word:

Mary: Tonight the feeling between us kept getting stronger and stronger. And on the way home we stopped and parked. And then things seemed to happen, till we nearly—[Mary glances down at her dressing table, Mother stands by looking concerned, there is a long pause]—It was so close. Suddenly I realized what we were about to do. I asked Jeff to take me home. I guess he felt ashamed too. He said he was sorry, that it was his fault.
Mother: Do you think it was his fault?
Mary: Oh mother, I don't know what to think, I'm so mixed up. I don't even know if I want to go out with Jeff again.[49]

Mary and her mother have a talk about feeling 'warm and affectionate' and about times when 'your physical urges fight against your reason'. When Mary next runs into Jeff at school they apologize to each other. Later they see 'poor Eileen' and her baby on the street. Her baby was born five months after a hasty marriage to Fred. Her face looks haggard. We are to assume Mary and Jeff learn from her 'mistake'.

[. . .]

These reticent portrayals of teenage sexuality were at odds with advice-book discussions of sex as powerful and 'awe-inspiring'. Teenagers were supposed to learn about sex as a wonderful natural urge, and then they were to ignore or control that urge until they were legally sanctioned to express it. People like Marion Hilliard assumed it was impossible; she frankly told girls not to trust themselves and to keep out of any situation where sex might occur.[50] Other writers thought the right information presented in the 'right way' would prepare girls 'to deal with the power [their] "femaleness" places in [their] hands'.[51] While we all have urges, we are quite capable of keeping them under control. Heterosexual desires might have been normal, but only if expressed under certain conditions.

[. . .]

In the face of widespread sexual behaviour among adolescents, and despite timid discussions about goodnight kisses and popular articles by learned women and men on the dangers of petting, teenagers did continue to engage in a range of heterosexual activity, although as Breines says, it wasn't always pleasant or fun:

> I mention only in passing, despite its importance, the terror of pregnancy, shared by girls who considered or engaged in sexual intercourse. It mediated girls' appropriation of the pleasure-seeking ethos of sexualized consumerism and diminished their pleasure of heterosexual sex. The point . . . is not that this fear was unique to white, middle-class adolescents in the post-war years, but that this juxtaposition of sexual opportunities and encouragement with ignorance, condemnation, humiliation, and the unavailability or birth control is unusual.[52]

When the social norm meant waiting until marriage, teenagers who engaged in sexual activity—girls especially, though boys as well—played dangerously with their own social value and categorization. To meet their own needs and desires for sex as well as social requirements for at least the image of chastity, teenagers engaged in complicated negotiations around the categories of sexual activity. Can you kiss on the first date? the second? the third? What about after that? What is the correct relationship between the cost of a date and the percentage of her body a girl must share with a boy? What stretch of a hand or mouth turns necking into petting? Sexual activity took place on a graduated scale that culminated in 'going all the way'. So long as a couple went up in the scale in the proper order, at the proper stage of their dating relationship, the dating system could contain and sanction their intimacies. As an institution, going steady allowed both girls and boys to maintain their reputations while permitting them access to sex, in some cases, even intercourse, so long as they didn't get caught. Pregnancy was an incontestable marker of having crossed the line between normal/moral/good and abnormal/immoral/bad. Even homosexuality was easier to hide.

Early marriage was the ultimate solution to teenage sexual behaviour. In the 1950s the average age of marriage dropped to 22 years of age for Canadian women,[53] and not just because of 'shotgun weddings'. Marriage was a legitimate avenue of sexual expression for those young men and women who felt caught between the incitement to sex in the culture at large and the proscriptions against their own engagement in it. Early marriage was one way to bring changes in sexual behaviour into line with the established moral order; it could realign the boundary between abnormal and normal behaviour. As Williams and Kane put it, 'After going steady comes marriage, if life is to progress in an orderly fashion and it generally does.'[54] And while they, like other advice writers, hadn't intended that final step to come as early as it sometimes did, the vision of the sexual world that they promoted and helped to instill in popular culture made marriage the most obvious way to a positive resolution of the contradictions of young heterosexuality. As a *Chatelaine* editorial writer put it, 'Fortunately there continues to be something within all normal young people that makes them feel that marriage is good and meant for them.'[55]

The space between normality and its abnormal opposite was a powerful organizer and regulator of post-war life. As a category that could mark one's acceptability and cast one's future, normality had to be constantly fought for, despite ideological constructions of it as 'natural'. But while the classificatory power of normality had tremendous influence, it did not entirely determine the way people lived their lives, as Kinsey's figures suggested. As a discursive construction, normality was perhaps less responsible for shaping teenagers' daily activities than it was for curtailing the possible range of meanings that could be ascribed to them. Whether one felt normal or aspired to normality or not, it was always there for you and others to check yourself against.[56] At times, the consequences of not measuring up

were considerable. So-called abnormality was expressed at a terrible price, be it ostracism, incarceration, or psychiatrization. Homosexuality, unusual expressions of gender identity, promiscuity, and pregnancy were all evidence of an unsuccessful struggle to keep firm boundaries between outside threats to one's own psychosexual development and internal, 'natural' possibilities. As sexual beings in process, teenagers were assumed to be especially vulnerable. Hence, they were particularly singled out as targets for intervention by adults—if they were normal, the future would be normal too.

Notes

1. See Rose, Nikolas. *Governing the Soul: The Shaping of the Private Self*. London: Routledge 1990.
2. D'Emilio, John. *Sexual Politics, Sexual Communities: The Making of a Homosexual Minority in the United States, 1940–1970*. Chicago: University of Chicago Press 1983, 16.
3. Kinsey, Alfred, Wardell B. Pomeroy, and Clyde E. Martin. *Sexual Behavior in the Human Male*. Philadelphia: W.B. Saunders 1948; Kinsey, Alfred, Wardell B. Pomeroy, Clyde E. Martin, and Paul H. Gebhard. *Sexual Behavior in the Human Female*. New York: Pocket Books 1965 (originally published 1953).
4. Rumming, Eleanor. 'Dr. Kinsey and the Human Female'. *Saturday Night* (15 Aug. 1953): 7.
5. Kinsey et al., *Sexual Behavior in the Human Male*, 199.
6. Ibid., 202–3.
7. Ibid., 580.
8. See also Seeley, John R., and J.D. Griffin. 'The Kinsey Report'. *Canadian Welfare* (15 Oct. 1948): 42.
9. Hughes, Perry. 'Kinsey Again: Leers or Cheers?' *Saturday Night* (20 June 1950): 10.
10. Kinsey et al., *Sexual Behavior in the Human Male*, 201.
11. Dubinsky, Karen. *Improper Advances: Rape and Heterosexual Conflict in Ontario, 1880–1929*. Chicago: University of Chicago Press 1993. See also Odem, Mary. *Delinquent Daughters: Protecting and Policing Adolescent Female Sexuality in the United States, 1885–1920*. Chapel Hill: University of North Carolina Press 1995.
12. Simmons, Christina. 'Companionate Marriage and the Lesbian Threat'. *Frontiers* 4, no. 3 (1979): 54–9.
13. For the most part I gleaned the titles of books and pamphlets from bibliographies prepared by (1) teachers at the Toronto Board of Education, (2) the Canadian Youth Commission, and (3) contributors to the newsletter for

Ontario public health nurses. Other titles were mentioned as worthy of attention in Canadian magazine articles. In the end I've chosen six titles that span the mid-1940s to the early 1960s. The decision to include a particular book was based on three things: first, and most practically, on its current availability; second, on the number of references made to it or its author in other sources; and third, on its representativeness in terms of the genre as a whole. It's important to note that all six were published originally in the United States.
14. *Are You Popular?* Produced by Coronet Films, first in 1947 and re-made in 1958 with a new cast and updated dialogue. Both copies are available for viewing at Prelinger and Associates, New York.
15. Landers, Ann. *Ann Landers Talks to Teenagers about Sex*. Englewood Cliffs, NJ: Prentice-Hall 1963, 47.
16. Davis, Maxine. *Sex and the Adolescent*. New York: Permabooks 1960, 59.
17. Strain, Frances Bruce. *Teen Days: A Book for Boys and Girls*. New York: Appleton-Century-Crofts 1946, 160.
18. Kirkendall, Lester A. *Understanding Sex*. Life Adjustment Booklet. Rev. edn. Chicago: Science Research Associates 1957 (originally published 1947), 34.
19. Duvall, Evelyn Millis. *Facts of Life and Love for Teenagers*. New York: Association Press 1950, 202–6.
20. Williams, Mary McGee, and Irene Kane. *On Becoming a Woman*. New York: Dell 1958, 51.
21. Duvall, *Facts of Life and Love for Teenagers*, 274.
22. Landers, *Ann Landers Talks to Teenagers about Sex*, 81.
23. Ibid., 92.
24. Major, Ralph, H. 'New to Our Youth'. *Coronet* (Sept. 1950): 102.
25. Davis, *Sex and the Adolescent*, 228.

26. I am thinking particularly of sexological writings like Havelock Ellis's *Studies in the Psychology of Sex* (New York: Random House 1936), vol. I, part four, and Richard von Krafft-Ebing, *Psychopathia Sexualis* (New York: Paperback Library 1965 [originally published 1892]). Radclyffe Hall's *The Well of Loneliness* (New York: Permabooks 1951) also fits this model. An invert was, according to these writers, someone born with a bad match between their body and their *felt* gender. So Stephen, in *The Well of Loneliness*, felt she was very much a masculine soul living inside a feminine body.

27. *Chatelaine* (Sept. 1948), 106.

28. Ibid.

29. Duvall, *Facts of Life and Love for Teenagers*, 22.

30. Strain, Francis Bruce. *Sex Guidance in Family Life Education: A Handbook for the Schools*. New York: Macmillan 1942, 144.

31. Ibid., 75.

32. Duvall, *Facts of Life and Love for Teenagers*, 77.

33. Williams and Kane, *On Becoming a Woman*, 46 (emphasis in original).

34. See Bailey, Beth. *From Front Porch to Back Seat*. Baltimore: Johns Hopkins University Press 1988; Rothman, *Hands and Hearts: A History of Courtship in America*. New York: Basic Books 1984; D'Emilio, John, and Estelle Freedman, *Intimate Matters: A History of Sexuality in America*. New York: Harper and Row 1988.

35. Dubinsky, *Improper Advances*, 114.

36. Fass, Paula. *The Damned and the Beautiful: America Youth in the 1920s*. New York: Oxford 1997, 26l.

37. D'Emilio and Freedman, *Intimate Matters*, 258.

38. Bailey, *From Front Porch to Back Seat*, 26.

39. Ibid., 27.

40. Ibid., 53.

41. May, Elaine Tyler. *Homeward Bound: American Families in the Cold War Era*. New York: Basic Books 1988, 101.

42. Fraser, Sylvia. *My Father's House. A Memoir of Incest and Healing*. Toronto: Doubleday 1987, 71.

43. Duvall, *Facts of Life and Love for Teenagers*, 120.

44. Katz, Sidney. 'Going Steady: Is It Ruining Our Teen-Agers?' *Maclean's* (Jan. 1959): 10.

45. Landers, *Ann Landers Talks to Teenagers about Sex*, 19.

46. Hilliard, Marion. 'Dr. Marion Hilliard Talks to Single Women'. *Chatelaine* (Feb. 1956): 48.

47. Williams and Kane, *On Becoming a Woman*, 29.

48. *Going Steady*, produced by Coronet Films, 1951.

49. *How Much Affection?*, produced by Crawley Films for McGraw-Hill Books, 1957.

50. Hilliard, Marion. 'Dr. Marion Hilliard Helps Teen-age Girls Meet Their Biggest Problem'. *Chatelaine* (Oct. 1956): 100.

51. Williams and Kane, *On Becoming a Woman*, 28.

52. Breines, Wini. *Young, White and Miserable: Growing Up Female in the Fifties*. Boston: Beacon 1992, 115.

53. Prentice, Alison, Paula Bourne, Gail Cuthbert Brandt, Beth Light, Wendy Mitchinson, and Naomi Black. *Canadian Women: A History*. Toronto: Harcourt, Brace Jovanovich 1988, 311.

54. Williams and Kane, *On Becoming a Woman*, 149.

55. 'It's a Tough Time to Be in Love', (editorial). *Chatelaine* (May 1954): 1.

56. Rose, *Governing the Soul*, 11.

4 Young People Having Sex: Sexualities, Sexual Identities, and Sexual Behaviours

Canadian University Students' Perceptions of the Practices that Constitute 'Normal' Sexuality for Men and Women

Todd G. Morrison, Travis A. Ryan, Lisa Fox, Daragh T. McDermott, and Melanie A. Morrison

Introduction

Sexuality and sexual practices play a crucial role in defining the self as moral versus sinful and/or normal versus abnormal (Weeks, 1990). Knowledge of how people conceptualize their own sexual behaviours and attitudes and those of others is thus pertinent to a better understanding of human functioning. To this end, Rubin (1993, also this volume, pages 39–59), a feminist anthropologist, developed a categorization of various sexual practices as 'good/normal' or 'bad/abnormal' based on Western cultural standards. In the sexual hierarchy she constructed, certain practices defied categorization due to divided opinions. Some of these hard-to-categorize practices included activities such as masturbation and being in stable long-term gay or lesbian relationships. The latter was ambiguous because it combined homosexuality (which was 'bad') with monogamy (which was 'good'). At the top of Rubin's conceptualized hierarchy were married heterosexuals and at the bottom were fetishists and transsexuals, among others.

Rubin also discussed the socially constructed nature of human sexuality (i.e., the idea that religious, political, and medical institutions have embedded sexual scripts and norms into their public pedagogy). She asserted that these sexual scripts essentially shape human attitudes toward sexuality and the meanings that people attach to sexual practices. Rubin also referred to particular ideologies such as sexual essentialism and sex negativity that mould human sexuality and how it is perceived. When applied to sexuality, essentialism has been defined as the belief that 'sexual phenomena such as sexual orientation or gender reside within the individual in the form of hormones, personality traits, and so on' (DeLamater & Hyde, 1998, p. 13). Sex negativity refers to Western culture's branding of sex as a dangerous and inherently negative force. In particular, Christian doctrine has been viewed as erotophobic (i.e., some denominations denounce all sexual activity which is not amenable to procreation and/or does not occur within the confines of heterosexual marriage). Available evidence corroborates this point, as religiosity (measured in terms of self-identity and/or religious behaviours such as regular church attendance) correlates positively with more conservative attitudes toward sexuality (Duyan & Duyan, 2005; Cochran, Chamlin, Beeghley & Fenwick, 2004; de Visser, Smith, Richters & Rissel, 2007).

[. . .]

Rubin's (1993) model was sufficiently provocative that Stryker and Whittle (2006) described her article, which detailed the model and the related concepts outlined above, as 'a foundational text of queer theory' (p. 471). However, in its current form, the model has limitations. It is non-empirical and thus we do not actually know whether individuals categorize, for example, the use of sex toys as abnormal or a practice such as masturbation as indeterminate (i.e., neither normal nor abnormal). In addition, the model is grounded in an American understanding of human sexuality. Available research suggests that variations in sexual attitudes are evident among different cultural groups (Widmer, Treas & Newcomb, 1998). [. . .] Given these sorts of differences, the usefulness of Rubin's classification system in cultural contexts outside of America is unclear.

Since Rubin's model was formulated in the mid-1980s, it is possible that the assumptions she used in categorizing various practices as normal, abnormal, or indeterminate are now outdated. Indeed, Caron and Moskey (2002) found that attitudes toward sexuality have become more liberal over time. Reviewing General Social Survey data gathered between 1972 and 1998, Treas (2002) similarly reported that cohort turnover (i.e., the death of older generations and their replacement by younger generations) was responsible for a 'liberalizing effect on sexual attitudes' (p. 278).

Purposes of the Present Study

The primary purpose of the current study was to empirically investigate Rubin's sexual hierarchy using a self-report questionnaire in which Canadian university students indicated their perceptions of diverse sexual behaviours by rating them on a continuum of 'normality-abnormality'. Independent ratings were obtained for the behaviour performed by a man or a woman. Of particular interest was whether a sexual double standard would emerge. Previous research suggests that individuals evaluate women more negatively than men for engaging in some sexual behaviours (Fugère, Escoto, Cousins, Riggs & Haerich, 2008). For example, Marks and Fraley (2006) conducted two experimental studies in which American participants from a mid-western university read diary entries purportedly written by either a sexually active male or female. Five positive and five negative reactions that the actor indicated had been made by other people about his or her sexual exploits also were provided. Results indicated that participants both estimated and recalled more negative than positive comments about the female actor. According to the authors, such findings suggest that 'people's belief in the sexual double standard may lead them to be vigilant to information consistent with [that standard]' (p. 23). [. . .]

Another variation on the double standard comes from Aubrey's (2004) content analysis of American primetime television dramas targeting adolescent and young adult viewers. The author found that male characters were more likely than female characters to initiate sexual behaviour. In this analysis, initiations by either sex were defined as 'dialogue or behaviour that involved sexuality, sexual suggestiveness, sexual activities or sexual relationships' (p. 508) other than love or romance. Negative outcomes associated with such initiation (e.g., negative emotional, physical, and punitive consequences such as guilt, unwanted pregnancy, and punishment by parents) were more likely to occur when female characters initiated sexual behaviour.

The final purpose of the current study was to examine whether individuals' erotophilia-erotophobia, sexual experience, and religiosity would be correlated with their perceptions of sexual normalcy. A brief rationale for the choice of these variables is provided below.

Erotophobia-Erotophilia

Fisher, Byrne, White, and Kelley (1988) described erotophilia-erotophobia as a dimension of personality based on 'the disposition to respond to sexual cues along a negative-positive dimension of affect and evaluation' (p. 123). Humphreys and Newby (2007) viewed this as a trait disposition learned through socialization experiences in which erotophobia represents a 'generalized [negative] affective reaction' to sexual stimuli (p. 80) in contrast to erotophilia, which is characterized by a favourable affective reaction. Their research on university students suggests that individuals who are more erotophilic are more likely to incorporate new sexual behaviours into their relationships and to report having more lifetime intercourse partners. Erotophilic individuals also are more willing to be exposed to unsolicited sexually explicit material on the Internet (Shim, Lee & Paul, 2007) and to evidence greater levels of sociosexuality, i.e., a greater likelihood of engaging in 'any sexually intimate experience with another person including, at a minimum, deep passionate kissing' (Wright & Reise, 1997, p. 172).

Sexual Experience

Research suggests that whether individuals have engaged in sexual activity (typically defined as vaginal intercourse) is associated with a range of sexual attitudes (e.g., Duyan & Duyan, 2005). For example, McDonagh, Morrison, and McGuire (2008) found that male participants who had engaged in vaginal intercourse or performed/received oral sex evidenced lower levels of body-image self-consciousness during physical intimacy. Similarly, Morrison, Bearden, Ellis, and Harriman (2005) found that male and female participants categorized as non-virgins reported higher levels of sexual esteem. Their findings also revealed that non-virgins evidenced greater genital esteem, lower sexual anxiety, and more exposure to sexual material presented on television or on DVDs.

Religiosity

Studies suggest that the frequency with which individuals attend religious services, their self-identification as religious, and the degree to which religion guides their lives are correlated with various indicators of sexual attitudes and behaviour (e.g., Beckwith & Morrow, 2005). For example, Barkan (2006) reported that individuals who obtained higher scores on a multi-item measure of religiosity reported fewer sexual partners. Moreover, the magnitude of this association did not differ between male and female participants. Fischtein, Herold, and Desmarais (2007) similarly found that survey respondents who reported no religious attendance thought about sex more frequently, had first vaginal intercourse at a younger age, and had a greater number of lifetime sexual partners.

Hypotheses

Using a questionnaire methodology, this study assessed university students' perceptions of sexual normalcy. Possible correlates of those perceptions (specifically, erotophilia-erotophobia, sexual experience, and religiosity) also were examined. Based on the research summarized above, we proposed the following hypotheses:

Hypothesis 1: In comparison to female participants, males would be more likely to perceive a greater number of sexual practices to be 'normal'.

Hypothesis 2: A sexual double standard would be shown in that all participants (male and female) would perceive a greater number of the sexual practices to be 'normal' when performed by a male actor than when the same practices were performed by a female actor.

Hypothesis 3: Participants who were more erotophilic would perceive a greater number of sexual practices to be 'normal'.

Hypothesis 4: Participants who were more experienced sexually would perceive a greater number of sexual practices to be 'normal'.

Hypothesis 5: Participants reporting greater levels of religiosity would perceive a smaller number of sexual practices to be 'normal'.

Methods

Participants

A sample of 104 undergraduate students (68 females and 36 males) attending a post-secondary institution in Western Canada completed the research instruments described below. The respective mean ages of male and female participants were 19.53 years (SD = 2.78) and 19.15 years (SD = 2.10).

Measures

Normal Sexual Behaviours Inventory (NSBI; Kite, 1990)

This pedagogical tool contains 30 items that assess the extent to which various sexual practices are perceived as 'normal/abnormal'. Items were scored on a five-point Likert-type scale (1 = very normal,

2 = normal, 3 = don't know, 4 = abnormal, 5 = very abnormal). To minimize participant confusion, the inventory also provided definitions of key terms (e.g., enema and voyeurism). The content of the instrument was modified slightly for the present study. Specifically, three items concerning bestiality, necrophilia, and scat were removed because, in the last eight years, they have been unanimously categorized as non-normal by students of human sexuality and occupational therapy modules taught by the senior author. In addition, some new items were added to examine potentially non-normative sexual practices (e.g., a disabled person engaging in sexual relations with someone who is not disabled; a 'normal' weight person engaging in sexual relations with someone who is extremely overweight). Overall, the instrument used contained 33 items, with 25 from the original inventory.

Another important adaptation to the NSBI was the creation of separate male and female versions (e.g., an item targeting a female actor would read, 'A woman watching pornographic movies several times a week' and the item targeting a male actor would read, 'A man watching pornographic movies several times a week'). Male and female participants received either the male or female actor version. Another adaptation, to control for bias, was to vary direction of the response options. About half of the items on this measure used the response format '1 = very normal' to '5 = very abnormal', the others offered '1 = very abnormal' to '5 = very normal'. Barnette (2000) cites this variation in stem type as being highly effective in guarding against participant acquiescence. Possible scores ranged from 33 to 165 (higher scores represent narrower latitudes of sexual normalcy). For male respondents, alpha coefficients for the male actor and female actor versions of the inventory were .86 (95% CI = .76–.93) and .92 (95% CI = .85–.97), respectively. For female respondents, alphas were .86 (95% CI = .77–.92) and .88 (95% CI = .81–.93), respectively.

Religiosity

To measure religiosity, participants indicated whether they attended religious services (1 = never; 2 = on special occasions; 3 = now and then; 4 = usually) and whether they considered themselves to be religious (1 = very religious; 2 = fairly religious; 3 = slightly religious; 4 = not at all religious [reverse scored]).

Sexual Experience (Rothman, Kelly, Weinstein & O'Leary, 1999)

Participants were asked to respond *yes* or *no* to the following: 'Have you engaged in vaginal intercourse?', 'Have you engaged in anal intercourse?', 'Have you engaged in vaginal intercourse in the last 4 weeks?' and 'Have you engaged in anal intercourse in the last 4 weeks?' Rothman et al. (1999) used these items to determine a respondent's sexual status and experience (i.e., virgin or non-virgin; currently sexually active or not currently sexually active). Morrison, Harriman, Morrison, Bearden, and Ellis (2004) provide evidence suggesting that these items are valid.

Sexual Opinion Survey (SOS; Fisher, Byrne, White & Kelley, 1988)

The 21-item SOS is designed to assess people's tendency to respond to sexual cues along a negative-positive dimension of affect and evaluation (i.e., erotophobia-erotophilia). Half of the items describe a positive evaluative response to a sexual activity or situation whereas the other items describe a negative evaluative response to a sexual activity or situation. Seven items were negatively keyed in order to avoid response bias. In the current study, a five-point Likert scale (1 = strongly agree; 5 = strongly disagree) was used. As well, the item 'If I found that a close friend of mine was a homosexual, it would annoy me' was converted into two items to facilitate consideration of a gay or lesbian target (i.e., 'If I found that a close friend of mine was gay (lesbian), it would

annoy me'). This modification resulted in a 22-item version, with possible scores ranging from 22 to 110 (higher scores represent greater erotophilia). Fisher et al. (1988) provide evidence attesting to the psychometric soundness of the 21-item version of the SOS. In the current study, Cronbach's alphas were .78 for men (95% CI = .66–.87) and .90 for women (95% CI = .86–.93).

Procedures

The research instruments were administered to introductory psychology students during a regularly scheduled class mass testing session. Random distribution ensured that half of the participants received inventories featuring female actors, and half received the male actor version. With respect to completion of the inventory, participants read the following: 'Please rate whether each of the following activities represents "normal" or "abnormal" sexual behaviour by circling the appropriate number. Remember there are no right or wrong answers and you may classify the behaviour as abnormal or normal using whatever criteria you deem appropriate. Please read each item carefully.' It took participants approximately 25 minutes to complete all instruments.

Ethics approval was obtained from the Ethics Review Board (ERB) associated with the institution where the research was conducted. Prior to starting the study, all respondents were given consent forms. The content of these forms stated clearly that (a) participation was strictly voluntary; (b) the information gathered was anonymous and would be held in strictest confidence; and (c) respondents had the right to omit any items they wished or to withdraw from the study at any time without penalty or consequence. Participants received course credit for their involvement in the study. For the purposes of obtaining credit, students' names and identification numbers were recorded on separate forms.

Results

Sexual Experience of Participants

Among the 104 participants (68 female, 36 male), 62 per cent of the female respondents and 47 per cent of the male respondents reported that they had engaged in vaginal intercourse. Considering only those who had intercourse, 62 per cent of females and 29.4 per cent of males had intercourse in the preceding four weeks. Also among those with intercourse experience, 10 per cent of females and 19 per cent of males reported that they had engaged in anal sex, with one female and one male participant having engaged in this activity within the four weeks prior to completing the survey. With respect to sexual orientation, 96.2 per cent ($n = 100$) of participants saw themselves as 'exclusively heterosexual', 'primarily heterosexual', or 'more heterosexual than homosexual'. One participant identified as 'bisexual', one as 'primarily homosexual', one as 'exclusively homosexual', and one participant stated that she 'did not know' what her sexual orientation was, at present.

Overall Ratings of Behaviours

Table 1 reports the percentage of participants who rated the various behaviours of male or female actors as 'abnormal'. The percentage combines 'abnormal' and 'very abnormal' responses: Results show that participants' perceptions of normality varied greatly according to the types of sexual practices presented. For example, at one end of the spectrum only a small percentage of participants identified having sex somewhere other than a bed (e.g., on the floor, in the kitchen, etc.) as abnormal, while at the other end almost all considered it abnormal to become sexually aroused while watching children play. Despite this variability, the overall findings were not congruent with the expectation that university students would evidence liberal attitudes toward most of the sexual practices assessed by the NSBI. While some items may not assess 'liberality', it is noteworthy that, among those who assessed a male actor, 26 of the 33 items were perceived to be abnormal by at least 25 per cent of participants (15 items were perceived as abnormal by at least 50%). Similarly, among those who completed the inventory with a female actor, 24 of 33 items were classified as abnormal by at least 25 per cent of respondents, and 13 were perceived as abnormal by at least 50 per cent.

Effects of Sex of Participant and Sex of Actor on Perceptions of Normality

To determine whether perceptions of normality differed as a function of sex of participant and/or sex of actor, a multivariate analysis of variance (MANOVA) was conducted. The two sex variables were the fixed factors and each item on the inventory served as a dependent variable. To ensure compliance with the assumption of homogeneous covariance matrices (as assessed by Box's M test), two items from the inventory were removed ('A man [woman] becoming aroused by watching children play in a playground' and 'A man [woman] refusing to let his [her] partner seem him [her] masturbate'). For the remaining 31 items, Box's M was not statistically significant, $F = 1.09$, $p = $ ns.

Contrary to our prediction that men and women would differ on the NSBI, the multivariate effect for sex of the participant was not statistically significant, Wilks' lambda $= .60$, $F (31, 67) = 1.46$, $p = $ ns. Thus, overall, the men and women participating in this study evidenced statistically similar assessments of the normality of the various sexual activities measured. In accordance with our expectations, the multivariate effect for sex of the actor was statistically significant, Wilks' lambda $= .47$, $F (31, 67) = 2.46$, $p < .001$, suggesting that assessments of normality

Table 1 Percentages of Participants Who Identified Various Sexual Practices Engaged in by a Male or Female Actor as 'Very Abnormal or Abnormal'

ITEM	MALE TARGET	FEMALE TARGET
1. A man (woman) watching pornographic movies several times a week.	46.4	60.4
2. A man (woman) having sex with more than one man (woman) at the same time.	76.8	70.8
3. A man (woman) preferring oral sex over intercourse.	23.2	22.9
4. A man (woman) having sex somewhere other than a bed (e.g., floor, outdoors, etc.).	0.0	6.3
5. A man (woman) being sexually aroused by exposing himself (herself) in public.	62.5	62.5
6. A man (woman) fantasizing about being intimate with another man (woman).	44.6	25.0
7. A man (woman) fantasizing about being with a person other than his (her) partner during sexual intercourse.	35.7	27.1
8. A man (woman) being unable to achieve orgasm.	41.1	16.7
9. A man (woman) never engaging in masturbation.	87.5	45.8
10. A man (woman) being celibate.	39.3	16.7
11. A man (woman) in a wheelchair performing oral sex on someone who is able-bodied.	46.4	31.3
12. A normal weight man (woman) having sexual intercourse with a woman (man) who weighs 322 lbs.	32.1	25.0
13. A man (woman) enjoying being physically restrained during sex (e.g., bondage).	30.4	34.0
14. A man (woman) becoming aroused by voyeurism.	35.7	56.3
15. A man (woman) playing with food (e.g., chocolate sauce, whipped cream, etc) during sex.	19.6	12.5
16. A man (woman) preferring that his (her) partner initiates sex.	5.4	4.2
17. A man (woman) forcing a woman (man) to perform oral sex on him (her).	75.0	68.8
18. A man (woman) inflicting pain during sex.	78.6	64.6
19. A man (woman) receiving pain during sex.	75.0	56.3
20. A man (woman) using sex toys during sex.	23.2	14.6
21. A man (woman) having rape fantasies.	65.5	72.9
22. A man (woman) masturbating after marriage.	10.9	22.9
23. A man (woman) NOT being sexually aroused by a nude member of the opposite sex.	50.0	27.1
24. A man (woman) being sexually aroused by receiving an obscene phone call.	41.1	47.9
25. A man (woman) becoming sexually aroused by being urinated on.	94.6	83.3
26. A man (woman) being sexually aroused by soiling the clothing of the other sex.	87.5	83.3
27. A man (woman) becoming sexually aroused by watching children play in a playground.	100.0	91.7
28. A man (woman) placing nude photographs of himself (herself) on the Internet.	78.6	60.4
29. A man (woman) masturbating in front of a mirror.	37.5	39.6
30. A man (woman) driving sexual gratification from receiving an enema.	67.9	68.3
31. A man (woman) refusing to let his (her) partner see him masturbate.	17.9	19.5
32. A man (woman) being sexually aroused by making an obscene phone call.	55.4	39.0
33. A man (woman) dressing in women's (men's) clothing.	78.6	47.9

differed depending on whether participants completed the male or female version of the inventory. Inspection of the univariate F output revealed that participants saw it as more abnormal for a male actor to: (1) fantasize about being intimate with a member of the same sex, $F (1, 97) = 4.28$, $p < .05$, $d = .38$; (2) be unable to achieve orgasm, $F (1, 97) = 12.16$, $p < .001$, $d = .70$; (3) never engage in masturbation, Welch's $F (1, 72.92) = 22.20$, $p < .001$, $d = .94$; (4) be celibate, Welch's F (1, 101.75) = 6.02, $p < .001$, $d = .47$; 5); (5) dress in clothing of the opposite sex, Welch's F (1, 82.08) = 26.54, $p < .001$, $d = 1.02$; (6) receive pain during sex, Welch's F (1, 86.10) = 5.38, $p < .05$, $d = .47$; (7) become aroused by being urinated on, Welch's F (1, 63.19) = 3.86, $p = .05$, $d = .41$. Participants also saw it as more abnormal for a female to become aroused by voyeurism, Welch's F (1,102) = 10.85, $p < .001$, $d = -.63$. Finally, the multivariate effect for the sex of the participant X sex of the target interaction was not statistically significant, Wilks' lambda = .74, F (31,67) = .74, p = ns. Thus, male and female participants' evaluations did not become more or less similar as a function of the sex of the actor they were evaluating.

Associations between Erotophilia-Erotophobia and Perceptions of Normality

As hypothesized, participants who were more erotophobic (indicated by lower scores on the SOS) were more likely to evaluate the behaviours listed on the inventory as abnormal (male participants: r [n = 35] = $-.61$, $p < .001$; female participants: r [n = 66] = $-.58$, $p < .001$). In addition, male participants (M = 75.89, SD = 9.77) were more erotophilic than were female participants (M = 70.18, SD = 14.41), t (93.36) = 2.38, $p < .05$, d = 46. However, as indicated previously by the non-significant multivariate effect for participant's sex and contrary to our prediction, male participants (M = 108.19, SD = 15.94) and female participants (M= 106.76, SD = 14.34) did not differ in their scores on the NSBI, t (100) = .47, p = ns.

Intercourse Experience and Perceptions of Normality

No statistically significant differences on NSBI scores were noted between male participants who had (M = 105.24, SD = 13.09) or had not (M = 110.84, SD = 18.05) engaged in vaginal intercourse, t (34) = -1.06, p = ns, d = $-.35$. However, the predicted difference was obtained for female participants, with those who had not engaged in vaginal intercourse deeming the sexual behaviours on the inventory to be more abnormal (M = 113.76, SD = 12.56) in comparison to those who had engaged in vaginal intercourse (M = 102.49, SD = 13.78), t (64) -3.30, $p < .001$, d = $-.85$. Due to unequal ns, mean differences on the NSBI for the other measures of sexual experience (e.g., anal intercourse) could not be compared statistically.

Religiosity and Perceptions of Normality

As hypothesized, those who self-identified as more religious had lower scores on the SOS, signifying more negative affect related to sexual topics than those who self-identified as less religious: male participants, r (n = 35) = $-.54$, $p < .001$; female participants, r (n = 68) = $-.24$, $p < .05$. There was a statistically significant correlation between religious attendance and erotophilia-erotophobia scores for male participants, r (n = 35) = $-.37$, $p < .05$, suggesting that more frequent attendance was associated with more negative affect on sexual topics. This association was not found for female participants, r (n = 68) = $-.21$, p = ns. The correlations between the two indicators of religiosity (attendance and identity) and scores on the NSBI were not statistically significant (Male participants: religious attendance/inventory scores, r [n = 36] = .24, p = ns, and religious identity/inventory scores, r [n = 36] = .27, p = ns; Female participants: religious attendance/inventory scores, r [n = 66] = .19, p = ns, and religious identity/inventory scores, r [n = 66] = .24, p = ns).

Discussion

The central goal of this study was to empirically test Rubin's (1993) sexual hierarchy in which she divided sexual behaviours into two categories: the 'charmed circle' and the 'outer limits'. Falling into the 'charmed circle' were sexual practices that emphasized heterosexuality and monogamy; were procreative, dyadic, intra-generational; and did not involve pornography or sex toys. Those practices converse to the ones contained in the charmed circle were characteristic of the outer limits (e.g., practices that did not stress monogamy, procreation, etc.). Although participants were not particularly liberal in their sexual attitudes, results from the current study suggest that Rubin's division between the charmed circle and the outer limits requires some modification. For example, the individuals in our study did not regard the use of sex toys or engaging in sexual activity in a location other than a bed as particularly non-normative. Similarly, while Rubin asserts that masturbation is a 'major area of contest' in Western society (i.e., it is a sexual practice that is perceived as neither normal nor abnormal), such ambiguity was not apparent in our study. Indeed, only a small proportion of individuals thought it abnormal for a male actor or a female actor to masturbate after getting married and a substantial proportion of respondents believed it was abnormal for an individual, particularly a male actor, to never engage in masturbation. Such findings suggest that, for this sample at least, masturbation is deemed to be a normative practice; an observation that is congruent with other studies on this topic (e.g., Gerressu, Mercer, Graham, Wellings & Johnson, 2008).

Another purpose of the study was to document the existence of a sexual double standard across a wide range of sexual behaviours. Our results indicated that a sexual double standard was apparent for some of the items on the NSBI. However, contrary to what we expected, when differences did emerge, typically the male actor was accorded less sexual latitude than his female counterpart. Homosexual fantasy, disinterest in sexuality (as indicated by items assessing celibacy and not engaging in masturbation) as well as non-normative sexual practices such as achieving gratification from 'golden showers' (i.e., being urinated on) or the receipt of pain were deemed to be more abnormal for the male actor. Thus, our results underscore the conflictive nature of the sexual double standard when applied to men; it demands that they evidence greater interest in sexual matters yet also requires that this interest be channelled into modes of expression that are 'socially appropriate'—for example, in ways that do not involve submission or the 'wrong' object choice. Indeed, greater research attention should be given to the burden that some men may experience as a function of exposure to a sexual double standard that demands they evidence an interest in sexuality and 'should lead and control sexual interactions' (Kelly & Bazzini, 2002, p. 795).

Although our findings provide some evidence that suggests existence of a sexual double standard, for a majority of the items on the NSBI (i.e., 23 of 31 items after two were deleted), no differences were noted based on perceptions of male versus female actors. Thus, a 'single sexual standard' (Haavio-Mannila & Kontula, 2003) appeared to be the dominant pattern; one in which many of the practices listed were perceived to be abnormal, irrespective of whether they were performed by a male actor or a female actor.

[. . .]

Limitations and Future Directions

This study has several limitations that warrant discussion. First, the absence of sex of participant effects may be an artefact of our reliance on psychology undergraduates. In a recent study examining American college students' sexual attitudes, Dantzker and Eisenman (2007) found that those enrolled in a criminal justice program, traditionally regarded as attracting more conservative students, differed from those enrolled in other programs (specifically, psychology or philosophy). [. . .] To address this limitation, future research should target undergraduate students enrolled in disciplines characterized by greater levels of traditionalism. Sample homogeneity also may account for the low correlations observed between scores on the inventory and scores on the measures of religiosity.

Second, some of the items on the NSBI are potentially ambiguous. For example, 'receiving pain during sex' may refer to participation in masochism or dyspareunia (i.e., painful intercourse). Given what we envision to be the iterative nature of the inventory, this sort of ambiguity can be rectified. A related issue concerns the omission of items measuring: (1) perceptions of sexuality and the aging process; (2) sex work (e.g., engaging in sexual activity with an escort, street prostitute, etc.); and (3) double marginalization (i.e., individuals who occupy more than one space in Rubin's 'outer limits'—e.g., a gay man who is physically disabled). Again, future iterations of the inventory can address these gaps.

Third, the number of participants in this study is modest (approximately 100) particularly when each half assessed only male or female actors. As well, common to all sexological research, the issue of volunteer bias is a potential concern. There is evidence to suggest that those who volunteer to take part in sex research are qualitatively different from those who do not, with volunteers being more sexually liberal and more sexually experienced (e.g., Bogaert, 1996). Additional research with heterogeneous and larger samples is warranted.

A final limitation concerns the instructions provided on the NSBI. Given the exploratory nature of this research, we wanted participants to use whatever standards of normality they deemed appropriate. However, we did not determine the factors that were influential in shaping or reinforcing their perceptions of normal behaviour. [. . .] It is unclear whether participants relied on a specific model of normality when evaluating the NSBI or, alternatively, whether they employed different models of normality on a per-item basis. Future research should explore this question and also whether certain models are more likely to be used by certain groups of individuals. [. . .]

References

Aubrey, J.S. (2004). Sex and punishment: An examination of sexual consequences and the sexual double standard in teen programming. *Sex Roles, 50*, 505–14.

Barkan, S.E. (2006). Religiosity and premarital sex in adulthood. *Journal for the Scientific Study of Religion, 45*, 407–17.

Barnette, J.J. (2000). Effects of stem and Likert response option reversals on scale score consistency. If you feel the need, there is a better alternative to using those negatively worded stems. *Educational and Psychological Measurement, 60*, 361–70.

Beckwith, H.D., & Morrow, J.A. (2005). Sexual attitudes of college students: The impact of religiosity and spirituality. *College Student Journal, 39*, 357–66.

Bogaert, A.E. (1996). Volunteer bias in human sexuality research: Evidence for both sexuality and personality differences in males. *Archives of Sexual Behaviour, 25*, 125–40.

Caron, S.L., & Moskey, E.G. (2002). Changes over time in teenage sexual relationships: Comparing the high school class of 1950, 1975 and 2000. *Adolescence, 35*, 515–26.

Cochran, J.K., Chamlin, M.B., Beeghley, L., & Fenwick, M. (2004). Religion, religiosity, and non-marital sexual conduct: An application of reference group theory. *Sociological Inquiry, 30*, 45–62.

Dantzker, M.L., & Eisenman, R. (2007). Sexual attitudes of criminal justice college students: Attitudes toward homosexuality, pornography, and other sexual matter. *American Journal of Psychological Research, 3*, 43–48.

DeLamater, J.D., & Hyde, J.S. (1998). Essentialism vs. social constructionism in the study of human sexuality. *Journal of Sex Research, 35*, 10–18.

de Visser, R.O., Smith, A.M.A., Richters, J., & Rissel, C.E. (2007). Associations between religiosity and sexuality in a representative sample of Australian adults. *Archives of Sexual Behaviour, 36*, 33–46.

Duyan, V., & Duyan, G. (2005). Turkish social work students' attitudes toward sexuality. *Sex Roles, 52*, 697–706.

Fischtein, D.S., Herold, E.D., & Desmarais, S. (2007). How much does gender explain in sexual attitudes and behaviours? A survey of Canadian adults. *Archives of Sexual Behaviour, 36*, 451–61.

Fisher, W.A., Byrne, D., White, L.A., & Kelley, K. (1988). Erotophobia-erotophilia as a dimension of personality. *Journal of Sex Research, 25*, 123–51.

Fugère, M.A., Escoto, C., Cousins, A.J., Riggs, M.L., & Haerich, P. (2008). Sexual attitudes and double standards: A literature review focusing on participant gender and ethnic background. *Sexuality & Culture, 12*, 169–82.

Gerressu, M., Mercer, C.H., Graham, C.A., Wellings, K., & Johnson, A.M. (2008). Prevalence of masturbation and associated factors in a British national probability survey. *Archives of Sexual Behaviour, 37*, 266–78.

Haavio-Mannila, E., & Kontula, O. (2003). Single and double sexual standards in Finland, Estonia, and St. Petersburg. *Journal of Sex Research, 40*, 36–49.

Humphreys, T., & Newby, J. (2007). Initiating new sexual behaviours in heterosexual relationships. *The Canadian Journal of Human Sexuality, 16*, 77–88.

Kelly, J., & Bazzini, D.G. (2002). Gender, sexual experience, and the sexual double standard: Evaluations of female contraceptive behaviour. *Sex Roles, 45*, 785–99.

Kite, M.E. (1990). Defining normal sexual behaviour: A classroom exercise. *Teaching of Psychology, 17*, 18–19.

McDonagh, L., Morrison, T.G, & McGuire, B. (2008). The naked truth: Development of a scale designed to measure male body image self-consciousness during physical intimacy. *Journal of Men's Studies, 16*, 253–65.

Marks, M.J., & Fraley, R.C. (2006). Confirmation bias and the sexual double standard. *Sex Roles, 54*, 19–26.

Morrison, T.G., Bearden, A., Ellis, S.R., & Harriman, R. (2005). Correlates of genital perceptions among Canadian post-secondary students. *Electronic Journal of Human Sexuality, 8*. Retrieved 12 November 2007, from http://www.ejhs.org/volume8/GenitalPerceptions.htm

Morrison, T.G., Harriman, R., Morrison, M.A., Bearden, A., & Ellis, S. (2004). Correlates of exposure to sexually explicit material among Canadian postsecondary students. *The Canadian Journal of Human Sexuality, 13*, 143–56.

Rothman, A.J., Kelly, K.M., Weinstein, N.D., & O'Leary, A. (1999). Increasing the salience of risky sexual behaviour: Promoting interest in HIV antibody testing among heterosexually active young adults. *Journal of Applied Social Psychology, 29*, 531–51.

Rubin, G.S. (1993). Thinking sex: Notes for a radical theory of the politics of sexuality. In H. Abelove, M.A. Barale & D.M. Halperin (Eds), *The lesbian and gay studies reader* (pp. 3–44). New York, NY: Routledge.

Shim, J.W., Lee, S., & Paul, B. (2007). Who responds to unsolicited sexually explicit materials on the Internet?: The role of individual differences. *Cyber Psychology & Behaviour, 10*, 71–79.

Stryker, S., & Whittle, S. (2006). *The transgender studies reader*. New York, NY: Routledge.

Treas, J. (2002). How cohorts, education, and ideology shaped a new sexual revolution on American attitudes toward non-marital sex, 1972–1998. *Sociological Perspectives, 45*, 267–83.

Weeks, J. (1990). Sexuality and history revisited. In K.M. Phillips & B. Reay (Eds), *Sexualities in history* (pp. 27–41). London, UK: Mac Press.

Widmer, E.D., Treas, J., & Newcomb, R. (1998). Attitudes towards non-marital sex in 24 countries. *Journal of Sex Research, 35*, 349–58.

Wright, T.M., & Reise, S.P. (1997). Personality and unrestricted sexual behaviour: Correlations of sociosexuality in Caucasian and Asian college students. *Journal of Research in Personality, 31*, 166–92.

'It Just Happens': Negotiating Casual Heterosexual Sex

Melanie Beres

I begin this [reading] by highlighting ways that the negotiation of casual sex in Jasper is dominated by discourses that privilege male sexual desire. I discuss the three discourses of heterosexuality as outlined by Holloway (1984) and I argue for a fourth discourse within casual sex; I label it the 'it

just happens' discourse. Through this discourse casual sex is constructed as something that 'just happens' and is beyond control of the partners. I end with an analysis of the ways that women find spaces of power and agency within these discourses. Women do this by placing limits on casual sex, disrupting the 'coital imperative', and taking the typically 'male' position within the discourse and actively seeking casual sex.

The (Male) Models of Heterosexual Casual Sex in Jasper

'It Just Happens' Discourse

When I approached young adults in Jasper (YAJs) and told them about my study, I explained that I was interested in learning about how casual sex happens in Jasper, and how partners communicate their willingness to participate in casual sex. I began interviews by asking them about their lives in Jasper and about their past dating and sexual experiences. At some point during the interview I inevitably asked some version of the question 'How does casual sex happen?' or 'How do two people come to the understanding that they are going to have sex?' At this point many of the participants stopped and stared at me with perplexed looks on their faces. I interpreted their reactions as saying, 'Have you never had sex?' The presumption seemed to be that if I had sex at some point, then I would have known how it happened. The answer would have been obvious. The answer (of course) is that 'it just happens'. Almost all of the women and a few of the men responded with some version of this statement.

> *Samantha:* So you're like kind of like making eye contact, smiling at each other, and then all of a sudden we're like standing by each other talking. And just like . . . I don't know how it happened but we like, all of a sudden we were . . . (laughs) . . . we were just like talking and we were talking about that and like he started kissing me and we went back to my house. And it wasn't even a question of 'would you like to come

to my house?' You know what I mean? It was just like that. That's what happened. (laughs) And then in the middle of it, it was just like, oh my God!

> *Anne:* He, he just kissed me. Like he just, we were holding hands and dancing then he kissed me and I kissed him back and then it just . . . Yeah, we were hugging and kissing. I was, it was not . . . I don't know, it just happened.

> *James:* That's a really interesting question, because you don't really, I don't really analyze how it happens really, it just kind of happens.

This discourse of 'it just happens' reflects a sense that there is a force greater than and external to the two people involved in casual sex that is ultimately responsible for instigating sex. By using this discourse it seems more acceptable for women (and men) to engage in casual sex. By saying that it 'just happens' women are relinquishing responsibility for engaging in casual sex. Anne expresses this sense by saying that she 'felt a little less of a slut if it wasn't something I really intended on doing, it just happened'. Anne's comment also highlights her negotiation of the good girl/bad girl dichotomy. In order to maintain her 'good girl' image of herself, it is only acceptable to engage in casual sex that is 'accidental'. By adopting this discourse, women are relinquishing themselves and their male partners of responsibility. It suggests that men are just as susceptible to this force as women. There is no recognition that their male partner may have orchestrated the casual sex in any way.

Gwen provides a particularly poignant example.

> Yeah. And then so, yeah, and then he just kept talking. Like we didn't dance or anything. We just sat by the bar and talked for like two hours and he just kept feeding me

drinks. (laughs) But he was just drinking just as much as I was so it wasn't that big of a deal. So every time I'd get a drink, he would get a drink. And um . . . yeah, and then . . . And then I went to the washroom and then when I came out, he wasn't there. It was like okay, I'm just going to go home. And then I was walking outside and he like got a cab and stuff. And he was like, do you need a ride? Like I'll give you a cab and I'll give you a ride home. And then like sure, whatever. It was raining. It was ugly out. And then um . . . his friend was with him too and he said well why don't you just come over for a couple of beer? And I was like okay, I don't have to work until 3:30 the next day. I can do that. And um . . . so I went over. We had some beer. And then I was like okay, I'm going to go home. And he was like well no, let's just talk for a bit. And I was like okay, and then one thing led to another . . .

The way that Gwen tells the story, she sees it as a series of events that took place, finishing with 'and one thing led to another'. She does not see the man's behaviour as orchestrating her going home with him for casual sex. She dismisses his buying her lots of drinks, because he too is drinking. She does not think anything of him arranging a cab for her, or asking her home. She does not say anything to imply that his actions may have been planned—that he may be buying her alcohol to get her drunk so she would be more likely to go home with him. She ends the story with 'and one thing led to another', implying that neither one of them was in control of what was happening.

Most participants, especially women, expressed a sense that one thing led to another, rather than expressing an intent, or interest in engaging casual sex. James is one of the few men who also express this sense of 'it just happens'.

It's just something that happens, and you don't really know how it happened, but it happened. And ah, I've never had an experience where it happened and then she's been like 'I really didn't want that to happen' which I'm very thankful for. But you know, you go to an after party or something, right like you're already just hardcore making out on the dance floor let's say, right and you're doing dry humping and bumping and grinding and hanging off each other as you leave the bar. You get to the guy's party house or wherever you're at right, you're sitting around. The next thing you know, nobody's in the room and you're lying on each other and one thing leads to another. Right like, that's really the only way to put it, you start making out that leads to nakedness that leads to sex.

James was thankful that no woman has ever told him afterwards that she did not want to have sex. He said this as though he cannot control the situation or outcome—as though he has no access to the woman's comfort levels, interests, or desires. If sex can just happen, and he has no control over what happens, he then has no control over any potential consequences of the interaction. This use of the 'it just happens' discourse assumes that they are not responsible for negotiating casual sex. This results in a failure for men to take responsibility for their actions and the potential for these actions to create harm.

Agnes, among others, connected the 'it just happens' discourse with alcohol. 'Alcohol is a huge key, like huge, and it really makes you, it really limits you, your ability to make good, clear, conscious decisions.' I spoke with only one person who said that most often his casual sex hook-ups occur in the absence of alcohol, often with people he meets in coffee shops or on the street. All other participants mentioned that alcohol plays an important part in their casual sex experiences. When I asked Susan how casual sex happens, alcohol was the first thing she mentioned.

> Go to the bar. Start buying other people drinks and start drinking yourself. It's really really . . . it's all related to alcohol, I think. And for a lot or other people drugs, but I don't see that side of it because I've never been a part of that side of it. Um, but yeah, well it depends, well as a girl if that's what you're looking for when you come to Jasper. You dress really skanky and you get out on the dance floor and you drink lots. And there's gonna be a guy there. Guaranteed.

Many others mentioned being drunk as a necessary component of casual sex.

> *Teresa:* Yeah, we were, we were both pretty drunk. We were outside having a cigarette and I leaned over and kissed him. I was like, come on, you can sleep at my place tonight. So we walked home. I lived like not even a block away from the bar that we both worked at. And, and um . . . got inside . . . I put on a tee shirt and a pair of boxers. He was in his shorts. He was in there and apparently I had my own shirt off and both of our own shorts off within about half an hour and it was completely not an issue and it doesn't surprise me whatsoever cause he was very, very attractive.

While a few men commented that moderating the amount of alcohol was important when they are interested in casual sex, no women expressed similar sentiments. Women did not limit alcohol when they engaged in casual sex, and were much less likely to be able to maintain a level of control during the interaction. The alcohol can then be used as an excuse for how or why sex 'just happened'. The discourse of 'it just happens' creates a version of casual sex where the illusion is that neither partner is responsible. By positioning themselves within this discourse women can then feel like 'good girls' who do not actively seek sex, they are 'not slutty'. Women are also taking responsibility off their male partner. Men are not viewed as controlling sex, or as orchestrating the interaction. The sex just happened; the men were not in control over what took place any more than the women.

Male Sexual Drive Discourse

While most women and a few men began talking about casual sex through the 'it just happens' discourse, this was not the only way that hook-ups were conceptualized. Many men said they went out to parties or bars with an intention of hooking up, and they pay particular attention to what types of things women may want in men, or particular things to do to get women interested in them. For these men, casual sex does not just happen; it is something that they have to work for, and something they practise. Robert, a bouncer in one of the local bars said that he often sees men going from one group of women to another until they find someone willing to talk with them. Don said that he approaches a lot of women when he's looking for sex and that he knows he will get turned down frequently.

This fits in what Holloway (1984) describes as the male sexual drive discourse in which the men's sex drive is insatiable and that women's role in sexual activity is to be passive and go along with men's desires. Within this discourse, men are sexual subjects acting in ways to fulfill their desire for sex. Through this discourse men also secure their masculinity, by reinforcing their ever-present sex drive. Conversely, women are positioned as sexual objects, necessary for men to satiate their desire for sex without any desires of their own. Men reported many strategies that they used in order to find a sexual partner. For instance, some men said that they will often approach many women, with the idea that the more women they approach, the greater the likelihood that they will find one who will have sex with them.

Even once men were in conversation, or dancing with a particular woman, it was important for them to continue to monitor women's behaviours in ways that would increase the chance of 'getting laid'. For instance, it was important that women should feel as though that the situation was not threatening, and to feel comfortable and cared for.

> *Don:* You just give her a sense of security like, making them the focal point, and just looking out for them like, just simple sayings like, like obviously getting the door for them, like putting on their jacket but like actually pulling their hair back so it doesn't go under their jacket, like little things like that, and just looking out for them, even if it's just like creating some space for them, like in a crowded club or something like that just little things like that seemed to go a long way . . . you have to really play it by ear because it can be overdone . . . you have to give her her space and be relaxed then the same time just be conscientious and make her feel comfortable, you know offer them like something to drink, right. I'm not saying offering them a shot or something like that, but like can I get you a drink, would

you like my jacket, are you cold, and something like that.

Don is very deliberate in his approach with women; he sees himself in pursuit of sex and sees it as challenging to get women to have sex with him. He is quite aware of his actions and how they may help him reach his goal. While on the surface he seems concerned about women's comfort level, this is a means to an end, a way to get women to go to bed with him.

Don took up the male sexual drive discourse throughout his interview. When I first met him, he had just recently moved to Jasper, and had a girlfriend still living in their hometown. During the interview Don said that it was 'inevitable' that he would have casual sex during his time in Jasper. He seemed to believe that his sex drive was insatiable and it would be futile to resist his desire for casual sex. Don articulated his approach to women quite clearly and it was obvious that he thought carefully about how to approach women to get what he wants. He made references to the importance of 'knowing how to court a woman properly' and 'knowing your arts well'. By these he meant that it is important for men to know the right way, to approach women and talk to them, to make them feel comfortable, and to build a sense or trust.

[. . .]

He talked in detail about monitoring women's behaviour to gauge their comfort level and willingness to have sex. In particular, a woman's breathing was very important.

> It is all about the girl's breathing, and that's like, a lot of guys don't realize that, but that's like, that's your like light signal that's your red, yellow, green, right there it's her breathing and just playing that off and so you just gradually sort of progress things forward to taking off clothes.

For Don, it was important that he maintain control over the situation and over casual sex. He talked positively about situations where women initiated casual sex, as long as the woman was not too direct.

> The odd time that I get approached by a girl it works, like it's nice to see a girl of confidence and stuff like that but you can't be too direct because then it's just too easy, it kills it, like you know unless I was just slumming it you know, and going for raunchy sex.

Several other men talked in similar ways about women who are actively seeking sex.

> *Colin:* If they come on too strong, then you can kind of tell that they're kinda skanky. But if they come on sort of in a shy manner, then, then it's a good thing. Good cause it gives you room to open them up. You know what I mean? Like you've got to make them feel comfortable obviously or else it's just going to be stupid and suck . . . If they're really aggressive, it's just like no; I don't want to do this. Cause it's not really giving you a challenge. Cause if they're really aggressive, it's just like well okay, I'll just take my shorts off and let's go.

Thus, the chase becomes a 'natural' part of casual sex and courtship and seduction becomes the property of men.

A key component to the male sexual drive discourse is that men maintain control of the sexual experience. Overly sexually aggressive women threaten this control, men find this intimidating, and the women are then labelled 'slutty'.

Women were far less likely to articulate ways that casual sex happens. Even in cases where the women were interested in particular men, women waited for men to initiate contact.

> *Samantha:* It's usually the guy who makes the first move I guess, towards me if they can see I'm attracted to them or whatever.

Even when women initiate sex, they still take up the male sexual drive discourse by assuming that the men will be willing to engage in sex.

> *Agnes:* And I think it's more the girl to . . . be the one that decides whether or not it's going to happen because from my experience, there's not very many times when a guy won't have sex. In fact, more often than not, that's all they're in it for is and not like, looking for a relationship or just somebody to snuggle with.

Men also articulated this aspect of the male sexual drive discourse. When I asked men how they indicated their willingness for sex to their partners, many responded by saying that they do not have to demonstrate willingness.

> *Colin:* It's just like I'm a guy I'm ready, willing and able anywhere, anytime.

> *Gary:* I think it's probably pretty rare that the guy says Stop. I mean, I don't know with other guys for sure but . . . from, from what I know, then I say that the guy's not going to say Stop. Unless there's something else like he has a girlfriend or something like that.

This male sexual drive discourse was the discourse most frequently referred to by both women and men as they talked about casual sex. The male sexual drive discourse is different from 'it just happens' discourse in that both men and women who take up this discourse recognize that men actively pursue casual sex. This is viewed as the 'normal' and 'natural' way to engage in casual sex. It remained unquestioned by all but one female participant.

> *Stacy:* It's, it's so unfair that it's really assumed in our society that it's the guy's job to [initiate sex]. You know what I mean. It's the guy's job to invite the girl out on a date. It's the guy's job to initiate this. It's the guy's job to initiate that. Yeah, it's the guy's job to initiate sex. It's the guy's job to do everything. The girl's kind of the passive like you know? Passive partner who goes along with everything or doesn't. But is always like you know, things happen to her, she doesn't, you know what I mean? . . . Like don't treat me like some idiot! Like some damsel in fucking distress. So I think that that goes a long way in the bedroom too where like I don't expect him, you know what I mean? Like I'm willing to go out on a limb and face rejection, you know what I mean?

Have/Hold Discourse

While the male sexual drive discourse was the most frequently taken up, other discourses described by Holloway (1984) were alluded to by participants. Many women and a few men took up the have/hold discourse, which Holloway describes as the belief that sex comes with a committed and ongoing relationship. In this discourse women are positioned as the sexual subjects who were trying to establish a committed relationship with a man. Men are positioned as the objects of this discourse. Thus the have/hold discourse works with the male sexual drive discourse; men are attempting to satiate their sexual desires, and women participate in sex to build and maintain a committed relationship.

[. . .]

Agnes said that she learnt that if she wanted a relationship that she should not sleep with a man the first night they are together because she found that after she slept with a man on the first 'date', he would no longer speak to her.

> We ended up sleeping together and woke up the next morning, and we slept together again and then he like, never talked to me after that. And we were supposed to hang out on New Year's Eve together, cuz it was like two nights after that and umm, I phoned him on New Year's Eve, and asked him what he was doing, and he was like 'oh I think I'm just going to stay home'. He totally blew me off.

As a result, Agnes made a rule for herself and lets men know that she will not have sex with them right away. She will, though, have sex with them on the second date. By staying around for a second night, they demonstrated a certain level of interest or commitment. Unfortunately, she found that waiting until the second night they were together did not change the end result.

> I ended up hooking up with this friend of mine, but now I like have this thing where I won't sleep with guys on the first date, just because I don't like the feeling of being used the next day and for me that's a really big thing, and so, but this guy . . . we hooked up one night and then, I wouldn't sleep with him, so the next night, he ended up spending the night and I slept with him and then he never talked to me again. And so now, like even that little theory of mine, is totally like . . . blown out the window.

[. . .]

Agnes is not the only woman who spoke of similar ideas. Jane recounts a story where she met a man she was interested in. At first she thinks he is a real 'gentleman' because he does not try to sleep with her the first night they are together. They did, however, have sex the second night they were together. Afterwards she was angry because he is no longer speaking to her. She called him a 'really big slut' and a liar. She sees his actions as being dishonest because for her, having sex with someone is a sign that there is at least some interest and some commitment.

Even for some women who actively sought out one-night stands, their subject position was at least partially constructed through the have/hold discourse. After seeking out casual sex with a particular man Anne turned off her answering machine and purposely spent a lot of time out of the house for the following few days. She did not want to know if he had called or not.

> So it was not like I was expecting anything out of it, but still, I do have like, like, I had like little fantasies about him, like staying or something like that, or like us continuing the relationship, so there must be, and I went into it totally like chasing him. I just wanted to have, to basically have casual sex, but I still have the future flashes.

Anne has purposely tried to disregard and shed the have/hold discourse and went out looking for a one-night stand. Yet she still finds that she has what she calls 'future flashes' and that she fantasizes about a possible future with the man. She also mentioned a few times that she saw no reason why they could not be friends, or at least talk with one another after having casual sex.

> I had one one-night stand . . . and I just, I thought, like okay, well, you have sex with someone, and to me it doesn't matter, like sex . . . ok, I never felt like a slut when I do it, so I don't see other people . . . like I can never imagine other people thinking

of me as a slut, but like, so I thought that we could just hang out with these guys afterwards and be friends, but it's weird, like once you've done the act, it's, there's like very like a lack of interest . . . How are you supposed to meet anybody in this stupid town to hang out with, you know what I mean?

Here Anne takes up a different form of the have/hold discourse. She is not concerned with creating or maintaining a sexual or romantic relationship. However, she expects that she should be able to maintain a friendly relationship with men with whom she has had sex. She views the men as potential people to hang out with and party with, people who can be part of her larger social network. She resents that most often after she has sex with them, she is excluded from their social network.

Men do not take up this discourse as it relates to casual sex. Almost all the men expected not to engage in any sort of relationship with someone after they had sex, unless there was a relationship established before they had sex. A few men mentioned that they would delay having sex with a woman if they wanted to have a relationship with her:

> *Colin:* Well if you have a connection with this person and you're super attracted to them and you can see yourself being with them, then you won't fuck them the first date. Like if you really want a relationship with them, you're not going to spoil it by screwing them.

> *Don:* Like a really good one is going home to smoke pot or to do blow but like I've cut blow out of my life, that was like a high school thing. But like blow's really good because it shows that you really wanna talk to them because when you do a lot of blow

your dick is like a limp spaghetti, and it's just like useless for sex and so shows that you care about conversation and bullshit like that.

For men the have/hold discourse comes into play only when they want to develop a relationship with a woman, whereas to women, they often take it up whenever they are engaging in casual sex.

This discourse operates along with the male sexual drive discourse to enable casual sex among YAJs. Men engage in casual sex because of their 'natural' and insatiable drive for sexual gratification. Conversely, women participate in casual sex with the hope of developing a lasting and committed relationship.

Sexual Permissiveness Discourse

Both men and women deployed the sexual permissiveness discourse according to which casual sexual activity is considered normal and expected. Many of the men and women I spoke with were surprised at how many women in Jasper initiate and seek out casual sex. Robert said, 'When I lived in [another province], it was the guys. But like here, it's anybody who's, you know, guys or girls making the first move for sure.'

There was a sense that in Jasper it is a lot more acceptable for women to want casual sex, compared to other places.

Agnes: When I was in high school, somebody who like had casual sex and slept with a lot of people was called a slut. But I seldom ever hear that term. And I don't know if people have just grown up to realize that yeah, casual sex is something that you do when you get older. Like you know, just cause you sleep with a couple of people doesn't make you a bad person

or a slut for it. And I don't see that [in Jasper] at all.

Casual sex for women is accepted, rather than stigmatized, in Jasper (although if they are 'too' assertive or aggressive they risk being labelled a slut). Without this discourse, and the feeling that it is acceptable for women to have casual sex, it would be much more difficult for men to find willing partners. This discourse, while on the surface seems to support women's sexual desires, is necessary for men to engage in a lot of casual sex. This discourse can also obscure sexual double standards. It appears as though it is acceptable for both women and men to engage in casual sex. However, this is only acceptable if they are engaging in a 'masculine' version of casual sex and if women are adhering to normative constructions of femininity created through the male sexual drive discourse.

Women's Sexual Agency

The discourses discussed above create depictions of casual sex that benefit male sexual desires and needs and are subject to male initiation. However, within these discourses women carve out spaces to exercise agency over their own sexuality and engage in heterosexual casual sex. Women create different degrees of agency during their casual sex experiences. First, women take advantage of the perception that more men are interested in casual sex than women, and therefore women have more choice about with whom they have sex. Second, women exercise agency by interrupting sexual activity before they engage in casual sex. Third, they actively seek out and orchestrate casual sex to satisfy their own sexual desires.

Women exercise agency by taking advantage of the perception that there are a lot more men seeking casual sex than there are women, creating a situation where women have a lot of choice regarding with whom they go home.

Teresa: There's so many men looking for sex that, you know, women really have their pick and choose of the litter. If they're just looking a one-night stand [the men I've talked to] said that you really have to stick out like a sore thumb or like be right there.

Men and women sometimes argue that women have more power than men when it comes to casual sex, because they have the power of choice. Jane says that 'girls have a lot of power in whether they go home with a man or not. Guys just kind of take their chance and hope they get lucky.' If women are looking for casual sex it is much easier for them to find someone with whom to go home. In a sense they are taking advantage of the male sexual drive discourse and using it to their advantage to have casual sex when they desire it.

Additionally, women exercise agency within and around the male sexual drive discourse by placing limits on the sexual activity—getting what they want out of it and stopping the interaction when they are satisfied. Agnes says that 'I think too because the girl ultimately usually decides on . . . if there's going to be sex or not.' Thus, while casual sex operates on the presumption of a male model of sexuality women and men perceive that women act as the gatekeepers and determine whether or not casual sex will happen.

Men, as well as women, reported that women often act as limit-setters. Tim mentioned that sometimes women will be totally 'into making out', but they will not let him take off their pants. He reads this as an indication that they are menstruating; he suggests that many women get particularly 'horny' while they are menstruating. Regardless of whether or not these women are menstruating, taking up this strategy, or going along with

his suggestion that they are menstruating gives them a chance to engage in casual sexual activity that does not lead to penetration. James mentioned similar strategies used by a few women.

Like, you'll be with the girl and you'll be making out and she'll stop and be like, you know, 'I really like you but I don't wanna go all the way because of this reason.' Right, like, there are still virgins out there, believe it or not, who are like, saving themselves for marriage, it's a really romantic concept that I really still enjoy, but you . . . it's a rarity I'll say . . . but they'll still have tonnes and tonnes of fun, but they just won't go all the way.

By being up front and telling men their limits, these women are opening up possibilities for casual sexual activity that do not include penetration. James mentioned that often they would engage in oral sex or genital touching. When men mentioned these strategies, they did not mind that the women were placing limits on sexual activity. James mentioned later on that 'realistically again, you know, a lot of them are tourists they're not gonna be around the next day, so you have bad luck that night you always go out to couple nights later and maybe your luck's changed.' If one woman is not willing to participate fully in a male model of casual sex that includes sexual penetration, then another one will be later on.

Thus, these women are able to negotiate the 'coital imperative' (Jackson, 1984) of heterosexual sex by placing boundaries and limits around the sexual activity. This way, women are able to indirectly satisfy their own sexual desires while operating within normative heterosexual discourses. They do this without completely rejecting the coital imperative. By saying that they want to wait until marriage to have sex or that they are having their period, they imply that they would otherwise be willing to engage in intercourse and are recognizing the central role that intercourse plays in heterosexual relations.

While the women I interviewed did not talk about strategies that included claiming they were menstruating or that they wanted to remain virgins, many of them mentioned setting limits as a way to ensure control over their casual sex.

> *Agnes:* I just don't let it happen. I say no, like when they try to go that direction, I'm like 'no, I don't sleep with guys on the first date.'

Many women have a sense that they are in control of placing limits on sexual activity. Of course they do have to be careful how they approach setting these limits.

> *Laurie:* Well I guess, I would just, I don't know, I guess I would try to keep it kind of light and stuff, cause I don't want to piss them off right? Some guys could be weird and psycho (laughs) and so, I don't know I'd probably try to keep it light, put clothes on or whatever if I took my clothes off, and be like, 'oh, can you go?' or 'I'm gonna go home' or whatever.

While women exercised agency by setting limits and interrupting sexual activity prior to penetration, the reaction of the men they were with varied. In the examples discussed above the women's excuses were considered 'legitimate' by the men. However, if a man did not consider the excuses 'legitimate' he often becomes frustrated and women were labelled 'teases'. These consequences acted as constraints and attempted to limit women's access to these strategies to create their own agency.

[. . .]

The negotiation of heterosexual casual sex is a nuanced process laden with hegemonic and often contradictory discourses. Often, there is the sense that casual sex is not really negotiated at all, that it just happens when two people are together at the bar drinking. Running parallel to this discourse are the male sexual drive discourse and the sexual permissiveness discourse. The male sexual drive discourse is used to create a model of casual sex governed by notions of male sexual desire as being ever-present and never satisfied. This discourse simultaneously silences women's sexual desires and assumes that women play a passive role in sexual relations. For casual sex to take place, the sexual permissiveness discourse is deployed, allowing women to desire and participate in sex as long as it is the version of sex in the male sexual drive discourse—that is penetrative sex with 'no strings attached'. A few women, however, position themselves within the have/hold discourse and expect that after casual sex the possibility for a friendship or relationship still exists.

Within these discourses that privilege male desire, women have been able to carve out ways to negotiate casual sex that take into consideration their own desires. Women will place limits on the sexual activity or leave after their needs have been met. Sometimes women will take an even more active role in designing and orchestrating their own casual sex experiences that satisfy their desires. Women are adapting by recognizing that casual sex is often controlled by male sexual desire, then choosing when and how they participate in casual sex to get their own desires met.

Conclusion

When discussing issues of casual sex, YAJs first turn to a discourse of 'it just happens' and suggest that casual sex is a serendipitous event. However, through their stories the male sexual drive discourse is the dominant discourse operating in this environment. Casual sex is driven by the assumption that men are perpetually in search of sex. Perhaps surprisingly, the women deploy the have/hold discourse and report that one reason they engage in casual sex is for the possibility of developing a relationship with their casual partner. Finally, casual sex is dependent on the sexual permissiveness discourse that suggests that casual sex is permissible for both women and men (at least within the confines of the male sexual drive discourse). Finally, within these discourses women exert power through their choice in partners, by setting limits, and by taking what may be considered a typically masculine role and actively pursuing casual sex.

References

Hollway, W. 1984. 'Gender Difference and the Production of Subjectivity', in J. Henriques, W. Holloway, C. Urwin, C. Venn, and V. Walkerdine, eds, *Changing the Subject:* *Psychology, Social Regulation and Subjectivity*, pp. 227–63. New York: Routledge.

The Marc Hall Prom Predicament: Queer Individual Rights v. Institutional Church Rights in Canadian Public Education

André P. Grace and Kristopher Wells

Introduction: Marc Hall's Prom Request and the Privatization and Politicization of Queer

In writing our account of people and events surrounding Marc Hall's request to attend the prom in his Catholic high school with his boyfriend, we proceed not only inspired by Marc's courageous undertaking, but also motivated by our own histories of schooling as marginalized gay Canadian youth. We cannot escape the politics of our own locations, which are shaped by such influences as history, culture, and ideologies and communities of exclusion (Giroux, 1992). Thus we begin with narrative vignettes of our pasts that provide some explanation but never any apology for our collective passion.

André: I attended the same Catholic school from primary through junior high. That school was in a small community where everyone I knew was Catholic, and where life focused around the small church that had a granite grotto dedicated to Our Lady of Lourdes as its backdrop. As a young boy, the Catholic religion gave me some comfort, but it was always mixed with guilt and fear about being a bad boy, a sinner, and someone who might go to hell.

I spent high school in an all boys' Jesuit school that the principal-priest continuously referred to as a Roman Catholic public school. It was there that I had my first crushes on certain male teachers and other students. It was also there that I remember repeatedly experiencing or witnessing overt and subtle expressions (in word and in action) of heterosexism, sexism, and homophobia. Many students called me a faggot; some mentally and physically abused me. However, sometimes it was a teacher who became the problem.

For example, stamped indelibly in my memory is the response of that principal-priest—my grade-11 religion teacher—who, when one of my friends asked him about homosexuality during a religion class, abruptly responded, 'There's just no place to put it!' Apart from the inappropriateness of his response, I never forgot the homophobic sentiment in his retort. His words silenced me. I felt ashamed.

Silence and shame about my gayness are indelible parts of my history. While they have had enduring effects on my life, I have learned to live wholly as a gay person intellectually, emotionally, sexually, and so on. For me, the legacy of Catholic schooling is a wedge between sexuality and religion, which I see as two incompatible forces in my life. My peace now comes from people who respect my gayness and who do not reduce my physical expression of love for another man to an act of grave depravity.

Kris: My experience of schooling was not marred by religious ideology, practices, or interference. However, like André, both growing up queer and going to school were marked by invisibility and silences. In retrospect, I do not remember much about my public-school experience. In order to survive, I learned that it was best to simply turn off all my emotions and feelings. I dealt with my 'difference' by becoming an average student who always tried to blend in rather than stand out from the crowd.

As a queer youth, religion was always something outside my lifeworld. It was just another kind of oppression, an oppression that I avoided. I didn't need

religious people telling me that I was deviant, immoral, or disordered. I got enough of those messages in school hallways and in my classes every day.

Today I have tremendous respect and admiration for the many queer youth whose courage and convictions drive them to demand their human and civil rights. Instead of the invisibility and silences that marked my experiences of schooling, many making up today's queer student body are vocal, visible, and proud. They are making their schools key sites in their struggles for social justice and cultural recognition and respect.

The story regarding Marc Hall's request to have his principal give him permission to take his boyfriend Jean-Paul Dumond to his Catholic high-school prom is ultimately part of the larger narrative of what we perceive to be the Catholic Church's institutional efforts to privatize queer—to keep it hidden, invisible, silent, unannounced—in religion, education, and culture. In privatizing queer, the institutional Catholic Church aligns its actions to its particular exclusionary beliefs about queer without regard for broader public law and legislation that is in keeping with Section 15(1) of the Canadian Charter of Rights and Freedoms. This section has provided protection against discrimination on the ground of sexual orientation since 1995 when, in *Egan and Nesbit v. Canada*, the Supreme Court of Canada unanimously agreed that sexual orientation was a protected category under the Charter (MacDougall, 2000). Since then, sexual orientation has been *read in* to Section 15(1). In education, this decision has resulted in Canadian teachers' federations and associations amending their codes of professional conduct and statements of teachers' rights and responsibilities to include sexual orientation as a character of person to be protected against discrimination in keeping with the law of the land (CTF & ETFO, 2003).

Despite this remarkable change, we maintain that the Catholic Church continues to privatize queer by defining and setting parameters to it in institutional terms that segregate being religious from being sexual in ways that limit queer acceptability, access, and accommodation. For those who succumb to it, this privatization is about policing the queer body; that is, it is about 'silencing oneself, self-censorship, and self-consciousness in mind and body' (Frankham, 2001, p. 465). These self-guarded reactions represent complicity in maintaining the hegemony of heterosexism as a cultural technology, that systematically privileges heterosexuality, assumes that everyone is (or ought to be) heterosexual, and values heterosexuality while reducing homosexuality to deviance and intrinsic evil (Friend, 1998; Grace, Hill, Johnson & Lewis, 2004). [. . .] In this light, heterosexism is the precursor to homophobia, which is an ignorance-and-fear-based manifestation of symbolic and/or physical violence in relation to a homosexual positionality as an undesirable identity and expression. As Friend (1998) reminds us, 'Homophobia ensures that violating the rule of heterosexuality has consequences' (p. 142).

Institutional churches have been among the most invasive cultural forces in making certain that there are consequences for living queer. They 'historically have taught and often still teach children [and youth] that homosexuality is wrong and undesirable and that gays and lesbians are "bad"—unless perhaps they are ashamed of what they desire and repress their feelings' (MacDougall, 2000, p. 98). [. . .] As a gay Catholic youth, Marc Hall has resisted this privatization. Indeed in events leading up to the granting of an interlocutory injunction enabling him to take his boyfriend to the prom, Marc continuously made being, desiring, and acting queer personal and political. His resistance created a dilemma resulting in a lawsuit against his principal and Catholic School Board after they denied his request. The heart of the dilemma is captured in this question: Does the School Board's decision align with institutional church rights regarding the provision of denominational education as guaranteed in Section 93 of the Constitution Act, 1867, or does it violate Marc's individual human rights as protected under Section 15 of the Canadian Charter of Rights and Freedoms (Elliott & Paris, 2002; MacKinnon, 2002)? The Canadian judicial system still has to make a decision regarding this matter of institutional versus individual rights. The May 10, 2002, decision granting the interlocutory injunction did not address this more substantive issue.

[. . .]

Marc's story is also a story of the politicization of his prom predicament. To reflect the contextual, relational, and dispositional complexities of this story, we employed two research methods. First, we engaged extensively in document analysis. This included a chronological analysis of reports and commentaries, press releases, and newsletters from various news groups and organizations. We reviewed open letters written by those with vested interests in the prom predicament, including the Catholic bishop for the Durham region of Ontario, various politicians, and Egale Canada. We also examined legal records, including the legal factum prepared by the lawyers representing the Coalition in Support of Marc Hall and the court record prepared by Justice Robert MacKinnon in granting the interlocutory injunction. As well, we surveyed material from two key websites: the Marc Hall website called *Have Your Voice Heard* (Ryan, Hood & Hall, n.d.) and the Durham Catholic District School Board website (DCDSB, n.d.). Second, having built our knowledge and understanding of interest groups and events shaping the prom predicament, we conducted a two-hour, open-ended interview and held follow-up discussions with Marc who helped us build a deeper understanding of how he mediated the whole politicized process and how it affected him. The interview took place on October 3, 2002, nearly five months after his prom had taken place.

Drawing on these sources, we begin this paper with a chronology and analysis of events and interest groups shaping, and indeed politicizing, Marc's prom predicament. We incorporate a critique of Catholicized education and what we perceive as the Catholic Church's efforts to privatize queer by defining and setting parameters to queer in institutional terms that segregate being religious from being sexual. We discuss how we construe this privatization as a failure of the Catholic Church to treat queer Catholics, especially vulnerable queer Catholic youth, with dignity and integrity as they set untenable limits to queer acceptability, access, and accommodation. [. . .]

It's My Prom, too! The Unfolding of the Marc Hall Prom Predicament

Marc Takes a Stand: Choosing Resistance, Being Resilient

The stories of queer youth as at-risk individuals are well documented in narratives about confusion, depression, substance abuse, alienation, truancy, quitting school, gay bashing, running away, and suicide (Epstein, O'Flynn & Telford, 2001; Friend, 1998; Grace & Wells, 2001; Herdt, 1995; Human Rights Watch, 2001; Quinlivan & Town, 1999; Ryan & Futterman, 1998). Increasingly though, stories of at-risk youth are being transgressed by stories of queer youth as advocates, social activists, cultural workers, and survivors

(Friend, 1998; Grace & Wells, 2004; Weis & Fine, 2001). These stories of resilience locate queer youth as thrivers who mediate 'a paradoxical mix of empowerment and conflict' as they contest 'sanctioned silences and institutionalized invisibility' (Friend, 1998, pp. 138–39). Marc Hall is the epitome of these thrivers. He has been contesting the status quo and transgressing the limits to individual freedom put in his way, especially by the institutional Catholic Church as an exclusionary cultural formation. [. . .]

When the prom predicament erupted, Marc was 17 years old and a grade-12 student at Monsignor John Pereyma Catholic Secondary School in Oshawa, Ontario. He had recently declared his gay sexual orientation to his parents, friends, and his high school. Marc had attended Pereyma since grade 9, and he had also attended Catholic schools as an elementary and junior-high student. At the end of his grade-11 school year, Marc approached his English teacher with whom he had excellent rapport, asking her to speak to his principal Mike Powers about an issue he sensed might be problematic: Marc wanted to attend his Catholic high-school prom with his boyfriend Jean-Paul. With no response forthcoming from the principal after his English teacher spoke with him, Marc approached Mr Powers directly early in his grade-12 school year to request permission. With the principal seemingly avoiding him, Marc remained persistent. Finally, on February 25, 2002, Mr Powers refused Marc permission, maintaining that interacting with a same-sex partner at the prom would constitute a form of sexual activity that contravened the teachings of the Catholic Church (MacKinnon, 2002). Although the Catechism of the Catholic Church upholds that homosexuals should not be subjected to unjust discrimination, it nevertheless explicitly states, 'Basing itself on Sacred Scripture, which presents homosexual acts as acts of grave depravity, tradition has always declared that "homosexual acts are intrinsically disordered" . . . Under no circumstances can they be approved' (CCCB, 1994, at para. 2357, p. 480). During our interview with him, Marc provided this recollection of what he perceived as the Catholic Church's unjust discrimination toward him.

Marc: When I started school in grade 12 and more and more people were talking about the prom, I approached Mr Powers and asked to speak to him because he hadn't gotten back to me. I'd see him in the halls and tell him that I had to talk to him about something. I did this three or four times before he responded. One day I was sitting in my English class, and he buzzed me down to the office. After I walked into his office, he told me that he had been thinking about my request for several months. He said that he talked to our pastor about it as well as the school board. Basically, Mr Powers said that I couldn't bring JP [Jean-Paul] to the prom because it was against school policy and the Catholic teachings. I sat there in shock. While I had expected the worst, I still felt betrayed. I had learned in religion class to love thy neighbour and to treat everyone the way that you want to be treated. It felt like my pastor, the school board, and Mr Powers were all contradicting those teachings. That's when I got really upset. I started crying. He kept saying, 'I'm sorry! I'm sorry!' I got up and left the room.

In reality Marc was just another casualty of what has become known as the 1986 *Halloween Letter* in which the Catholic Church privatized queer in institutional terms by emphatically denying queer Catholics the individual right to live as whole persons in the fullness of their sexuality. These Catholic gatekeepers described 'the homosexual condition or tendency . . . as being "intrinsically disordered", and able in no case to be approved of' (DCD, n.d., p. 1). Having located the 'homosexual condition' (p. 1) as an 'objective disorder' (p. 2), they asserted, 'Although the particular inclination of the homosexual person is not a sin, it is a more or less strong tendency ordered toward an intrinsic moral evil' (p. 1). The CDF said that acting on the inclination was sinful, requiring a 'conversion from evil' (p. 5). Placing the institutional church above civil law and legislation, they emphatically stated, 'It is true that . . . [the Church's] position cannot be revised by pressure from civil legislation or the trend of the moment' (p. 4). [. . .]

The Halloween Letter, which we maintain represents symbolic excommunication of queer persons who choose to live full spiritual and sexual lives, continues to be the Catholic word on homosexuality and as such impacts the Catholic educational approach to it. [. . .]

The Prom Predicament Continues to Unfold

After his meeting with Mr Powers, Marc was very upset. When he got home, he told his parents about the devastating meeting with the principal. Deeply concerned, Audy and Emily Hall requested a meeting with Mr Powers with Marc present. During that meeting, which occurred the following week, Marc read a letter he had drafted to the principal. Marc told us about the origin of the letter.

Marc: When Mr Powers said no to me the first time, and I knew that he was going to have a meeting with my parents and me, that's when I wrote it. I read it to him in front of my parents.

In this excerpt from the letter, Marc demonstrated his determination and resilience in the face of what he perceived as unequal individual treatment due to his gay sexual orientation.

Marc: I just want to be treated like a normal human being, because guess what . . . that is what I am. I mean, look at me, I'm not here to cause trouble. I have an 82 per cent average, a lot of friends, and a great family . . . . Don't you see that I'm not fighting for this just because it's my prom? It's my whole life and the lives of other gay people. I'm fighting for what so many people don't understand. I'm trying to speed up the process of equality because I am sick of being treated like someone absent of feeling and emotion. I have been waiting for my prom since grade 9. Prom, to some people, is an important step in someone's life. It makes you realize that you're actually finishing high school and that this event is one of the last times you and your friends will all be together. So maybe I'll take things to the next level [to court], but it's better than not caring about anything . . . . Not only is what you are doing morally unjust, but you are also violating the laws of the Ontario Human Rights Act. Hopefully we can resolve this issue peacefully and before it escalates into a legal hearing. (Ryan, Hood & Hall, n.d., pp. 1–2)

Despite the letter and Marc's fervour, no progress was made at this meeting. In his conversation with us, Marc reflected, conveying his sense of sadness and loss.

Marc: After I read the speech I felt that what I wrote didn't mean anything to him. My mom thought that if she and my dad agreed that I could go with JP, then it would be okay. But Mr Powers still

said no, saying it was against the Catholic teachings. I just sat there and started crying again. He just said, 'I'm sorry.' Those were basically the two meetings—very, very emotional.

In refusing to change his mind, Mr Powers discriminated against Marc because he was gay. Moreover, he took *in loco parentis* to the extreme, overriding parental authority by ignoring Marc's parents' desire to have their son and Jean-Paul attend the prom together. The Halls have been loving and accepting parents. Their support for their gay son has grown through Marc's coming out and their coming to terms with his gayness. Marc recounts the emotional process that took its toll on all of them.

Marc: I actually remember the exact date that I came out to my parents—May 23rd, 2001. I actually remember the situation. My mom was downstairs watching *Wheel of Fortune* in the living room. I was upstairs in my room telling myself that I had to tell her. I went downstairs twice intending to do it, but each time I chickened out. Finally, the third time, I told her. I started off babbling about how people get older and have different sexual attractions, but when I came to the point of telling her I was gay I froze. My mom looked at me and said, 'I think I know what you are trying to say. Are you trying to tell me that you like boys?' I said, 'Yes.' She said, 'I kind of thought so.' And then the whole crying thing began.

A few days later she told my father. He continued to talk to me, asking little things like 'How was your day?' A few weeks later he and I went to the cemetery where my brother is buried. My dad started talking to my brother Marcel's grave, saying how

I was still the same person that I always was, and how he and my mom were going to take care of me. My dad said he would be behind me 100 per cent. Ever since then we've been really close. My mom and I have always been close.

My parents' point of view is that God created me the way I am, and they love all of me no matter what. The Catholic teachings say to love everybody basically. My parents' view never changed. My dad has said countless times that because the Catholic School Board made this decision doesn't mean that it is right. He also believes in a God who loves everyone. My dad says that he doesn't pray to the school board, he doesn't pray to the priest, he prays to God. My parents never rejected me, and supported me right from the beginning. If I never had their support I probably wouldn't have done anything.

Strong parental support like this is usually a key reason why queer youth like Marc thrive and are so resilient (Friend, 1998). Indeed many parents do not react so well when a child announces being queer (Grace & Wells, 2001; MacDougall, 2000). Some appear as traumatized by this announcement as they might be if they had been told that their child had a terminal illness. They experience a profound sense of loss and grief inextricably linked to cultural homophobia and interwoven in heteronormative thoughts like there will be no grandchildren. More compassionately, they may worry that their child might become a victim of violence. However, Marc's parents were able to put their love for their child first and move beyond any trauma to nurture their queer child. Throughout the prom predicament, Marc's parents remained supportive, despite the barrage of media attention and other difficulties emanating from the politicization of Marc's request.

All Marc wanted was to attend his prom with his boyfriend. However, in hegemonic terms, his wish amounted to a transgression of the prom as a heteronormalized rite of passage and a hyper-heterosexualized cultural technology.

> In secondary schools, the 'prom' . . . provides a space where, however uncomfortably, students are expected to interact, producing themselves as feminine and masculine in iconically heterosexual and exaggerated ways. The heterosexualization of this process is often unremarked, and young people are seen generally within a developmental discourse of 'normal' gender development. (Epstein, O'Flynn, & Telford 2001, p. 152)

As a hyper-heterosexualized cultural event, the school prom has functioned not only to replicate the masculine, the feminine, and the heterosexual pairing of male and female, but it has also operated to mark and police heterosexuality as the desired and assumed expression of sexuality. The heterosexual/homosexual binary assists this regulation as it 'function[s] to reinforce certain practices through signalling the disadvantages and dysfunctionality of other practices' (Frankham, 2001, p. 457). The Catholic prom, framed within the precepts and myths of Biblical patriarchy and religious tradition, which are cultural technologies of control, is perhaps the ultimate expression of hyper-heterosexual policing, even as it disdains any form of sexual expression by youth expected to be chaste and non-sexual. This is interesting if not hypocritical. [. . .] Indeed the Catholic Church as a regulative institution has policed gender and sexuality (Epstein & Johnson, 1998; Grace & Benson, 2000). Catholic schools are conduits for this policing. Thus across sex, sexual, and gender differences, 'everyone lives, daily, a relation to the heterosexual norm both within and outside the [Catholic] school' (Epstein & Johnson, 1994, p. 221).

The Politicization of Marc's Prom Predicament

In the aftermath of Marc's two distressing and unsuccessful meetings with his principal Mr Powers, a website *Have Your Voice Heard* was set up in response to his prom predicament. The home page featured a picture of Marc with Lance Ryan and Cassy Hood, two of his close friends who created the website where they set up a message board and posted the letter that Marc had written to his principal. On the home page Cassy, Lance, and Marc stated that the purpose of the website was to assist in the fight against the segregation of gay students in the schools of Durham region and elsewhere (Ryan, Hood & Hall, n.d.). In a website editorial entitled *Prejudice in Catholic Schools*, Cassy asserted that the principal's refusal to permit Marc to attend the prom with Jean-Paul was an act of discrimination and harassment. She categorically admonished educational leaders: 'Discrimination from peers is a large enough burden to homosexuals, but this kind of harassment coming from principals, teachers, and school boards is abominable. There is no excuse. It's illegal, immoral, and unfair' (Ryan, Hall & Hood, n.d., p. 1).

What followed next is a complex set of events. Through the involvement of diverse interest groups in the prom predicament, Marc experienced a politicization of his youth, his sexuality, and his individual right to participate in school activities. In a real sense his activism was not planned, but provoked. It was provoked not only by a Catholic Church and school that he felt had failed him, but also by supporters who saw this citizen student as a youth with a cause advanced

by Section 15(1) of the Canadian Charter of Rights and Freedoms. This section states:

> Every individual is equal before and under the law and has the right to the equal protection and equal benefit of the law without discrimination and, in particular, without discrimination based on race, national or ethnic origin, colour, religion, sex, age or mental or physical disability. (DJC, 2003, p. 4)

Although this equality provision protecting individual rights came into force in 1985, it took a decade before sexual orientation was *read into* Section 15(1) in *Egan and Nesbit v. Canada* (Lahey, 1999; MacDougall, 2000).

The politicization of the prom predicament was truly set in motion during the March break that came a few days after Marc and his parents met with Mr Powers. As Marc told us, news of his situation and the subsequent establishment of the website spread quickly.

Marc: During the March break more and more people got to see the website. In Windsor, Ontario, a guy named Chris Cecile who hosts a weekly radio show called *Queer Radio* saw the website. I think he's the one who got the whole thing rolling using email. That's when other radio stations and newspapers started to call me. After the March break, I got ambushed by TV cameras outside my school. That happened for a while. I did all my interviews during lunch break.

Another person that really stands out is George Smitherman. He's a gay MPP [Member of Provincial Parliament] from Toronto. He contacted me through the website email. We got together and started formulating plans to pressure the school board. He organized the press conferences at Queen's Park [home to the Ontario provincial legislature] and various rallies. He's been there from the beginning, and he's become a family friend.

The media coverage that escalated in the wake of this grassroots activism included national attention in a news story covering Marc's prom predicament that aired on the March 18, 2002 edition of CTV National News. Although the extent of the exposure was quite helpful in terms of the politicization process, it was much less helpful to Marc on a personal level because it left him even more visible and, consequently, more vulnerable to violence and retaliatory dangers (D'Augelli, 1998). Marc shared his experience of the threats and violence that came with openly taking a stand.

Marc: After the media interviews started at school, some students didn't like the idea of JP going to the prom with me. That's when a lot of name calling like 'faggot' and 'queer' started. The homophobia increased. For example, they shoved this piece of paper in my friend's locker. It was a really good drawing, but very morbid. It was an old cross and it had cobwebs and spiders and goblins and stuff on it. On the side of the cross someone wrote, 'Die Marc, Die!' On top of the drawing were the words, 'We're all out to kill Marc Hall!'

When the website first started, 95 per cent of the responses were supportive. As the whole thing continued though, more and more hate mail came. I also started getting letters and other mail at my school. Most of it was pretty supportive, but there was some negative stuff. One card had a

picture of a penis, and it said, 'Marc Hall sucks cock!' I just threw it out. I realized that if I took a stand like this, there would be some negative feedback.

The worst thing though was feeling unsafe. There was one point in which I was a little nervous. A police officer came to my house and told us that he received information that a group of guys had said they planned to ambush my family and me. My parents and I were all edgy after that. My dad put a piece of wood in the patio door for extra protection in case they broke the lock. That happened a few weeks after the whole media thing blew up.

The Prom Predicament Escalates

In a March 19, 2002 press release, Grant A. Andrews, Director of Education for the Durham Catholic District School Board, stated the school board's position regarding Mr Powers's decision.

This action is consistent with the views and values of the Durham Catholic District School Board. As a Catholic School Board, we are charged with upholding the values of the Church. The Church does not condemn an individual for his or her sexual orientation. However, the behaviours associated with a homosexual lifestyle are not consistent with Church teachings and our values as a Catholic School system. We are constitutionally entitled to administer our schools in a manner consistent with the teachings of the Church. (GALE-BC, 2002, p. 4)

This statement preceded the March 25, 2002 school-board meeting at which Marc, his parents, and numerous supporters were present.

Despite their presence, Mary Ann Martin, the board chair, said the prom issue was not on the agenda due to insufficient notice, so no one would be heard regarding the matter. Mike Shields, president of Local 222 of the Canadian Auto Workers, Canada's biggest union local and a strong advocate for gay rights, had attended this meeting as part of the Coalition in Support of Marc Hall. When Martin made her announcement, Shields angrily interjected, which resulted in police being called to escort him from board property (365Gay.com, 2002, p. 1).

Subsequently, school-board trustees acknowledged that even if proper protocol had been followed and supporters had been allowed to speak to the prom issue, they would not have changed their minds because they considered allowing Marc to attend his prom with his boyfriend tantamount to condoning homosexual behaviour (CBC News, 2002a). Thus the school board's decision was predetermined and fixed, bounded as it was by Catholic moral knowledge. [. . .]

In an April 4, 2002 open letter to Dalton McGuinty, a Catholic and then Leader of the Ontario Liberal Party and the Official Opposition, Anthony G. Meagher, Auxiliary Bishop of Toronto for the Northern and Durham regions, reiterated the school-board trustees' position. Appearing oblivious in the letter to his ultimate authority and responsibility as bishop of the Durham region, he maintained, 'The decision is obviously not mine to make in this issue' (Meagher, 2002, p. 1).

At a subsequent school-board hearing on April 8, 2002, the prom predicament was on the agenda and several individuals and groups made presentations. Prior to this hearing Marc, Cassy, and Lance had posted comments on their website. Rage and resilience permeated their words: 'We're trying to prove to them [the school board] how much more organized and sophisticated

we are! If they try to blow us off this time, let's watch the roof fall down on them!' (Ryan, Hood & Hall, n.d., notice board, p. 1). At the hearing George Smitherman suggested the prom issue touched on values undergirding our identity as a nation (Fisher, 2002). However, his comments and those of other supportive parties were made in vain. The Durham Catholic District School Board confirmed the principal's decision, denying Marc permission to attend his prom with Jean-Paul. Suggesting that taking a date to the prom is a form of romantic relationship, Mary Ann Martin, the school-board chair, read from an already prepared statement.

> The principal's decision and our decision to support the principal is [sic] consistent with the instruction of the Church to accept Marc with respect, compassion, and sensitivity. Just as the Church urges such an approach, it also draws a line. Like the Church, we accept and support Marc, but we also accept and respect the line that the Church has drawn. Marc wants us to help him cross this line at this Catholic school function. This we will not do. (Andrews, 2002, p. 1)

Hearing this decision, Marc cried. Still he maintained, 'I believe in justice and that God loves me for who I am' (CBC News, 2002b, p. 1). He exclaimed, 'They [the trustees] promote equality except in some cases. They take Jesus's rule [—do unto others as you would have them do unto you—] and bend it a little bit for their liking' (CBC Toronto, 2002, p. 1). The school board's decision served only to make Marc more resistant and resilient, intensifying his desire to attend his prom with his boyfriend. He left the hearing ready to have his lawyer take his case to court to ask a judge to reverse the school board's decision (CBC Toronto, 2002).

To the Courts: Marc's Prom Predicament and the Legal Hearing Seeking an Interlocutory Injunction

On May 6, 2002, a two-day legal hearing began in Whitby, Ontario (CBC News, 2002c). Justice Robert MacKinnon of the Ontario Court of Justice heard the case between plaintiff George Smitherman, in his capacity as litigation guardian of Marc Hall, and defendants Michael Powers and the Durham Catholic District School Board. David L. Corbett was the lead lawyer for the plaintiff; Peter D. Lauwers was the lawyer for the defendants. Through the hearing, Marc sought an interlocutory injunction restraining his high-school principal and the school board from preventing his attendance with his boyfriend at his Catholic high-school prom. However, this was Marc's immediate interest, as Justice MacKinnon (2002) noted.

> [T]he substantive thrust of his claims for trial, as pleaded, are for trial court declarations that his *Charter* rights have been violated. Included among the matters in issue for an eventual trial, if pursued, will be the question of whether the School Board's decision falls within its power to make decisions with respect to denominational matters and thus are protected under Section 93(1) of the Constitution Act, 1867 and whether the Board's decision violates individual human rights protected under the Canadian Charter of Rights and Freedoms, including the right to be free from discrimination on the basis of sexual orientation and age. (at para. 13)

In opening the case, David L. Corbett argued that, by accepting public funds, Catholic schools also accept a mandate to provide an education to every student in their care (Egale Canada, 2002). He also argued that the school board, in taking the position of respecting homosexuals while condemning homosexual conduct, made a distinction that had already been rejected by the Supreme Court of Canada in its ruling in the *British Columbia College of Teachers (BCCT) v. Trinity Western University (TWU)* in 2001. In that ruling, while the Supreme Court supported TWU's constitutional right to offer a 'full program [to] reflect . . . [its fundamentalist] Christian worldview' (*BCCT v. TWU*, 2001, at para. 2), it made the distinction between the broader right to hold discriminatory beliefs and the more limited right to act upon those beliefs.

In representing the principal and the Durham District Catholic School Board, Peter D. Lauwers argued that Catholic Schools are beyond Charter reach because of the constitutional protection guaranteed in Section 93 of the Constitution Act, 1867 (Egale Canada, 2002). He submitted that the plaintiff motion should be dismissed on that ground (MacKinnon, 2002).

[. . .]

In his judgment made just a few hours before Marc's prom on May 10, 2002, Justice Robert MacKinnon granted an interlocutory injunction. It provided an immediate order allowing Marc to attend his Catholic high-school prom with his boyfriend (Siu, 2002a). The principal and the school board had previously agreed not to cancel the prom if the injunction was granted (MacKinnon, 2002). In this poignant excerpt from the judgment, Justice MacKinnon speaks to protecting rights and promoting inclusion as fundamental Canadian values.

> In my view, the clear purpose of Section 15 is to value human dignity in a free society where difference is respected and equality is valued. The praiseworthy object of Section 15 of the Charter is to prevent discrimination and promote a society in

which all are secure in the knowledge that they are recognized as human beings equally deserving of concern, respect and consideration. . . . The record before me is rife with the effects of historic and continuing discrimination against gays. The evidence in this record clearly demonstrates the impact of stigmatization on gay men in terms of denial of self, personal rejection, discrimination and exposure to violence. . . . It is one of the distinguishing strengths of Canada as a nation that we value tolerance and respect for others. All of us have fundamental rights including expression, association, and religion . . . . We, as individuals and as institutions, must acknowledge the duties that accompany our rights. Mr Hall has a duty to accord to others who do not share his orientation the respect that they, with their religious values and beliefs, are due. Conversely, for the reasons I have given, the Principal and the Board have a duty to accord to Mr Hall the respect that he is due as he attends the prom with his date, his classmates and their dates. (MacKinnon, 2002)

Following the issuing of the interlocutory injunction enabling Marc to attend his prom with Jean-Paul, Marc's mom Emily Hall said, 'I am so very proud of him. He has opened the doors for other gay students' (Siu, 2002b, p. 2). During the interview Marc recounted the emotional events of that momentous decision day.

Marc: I remember every moment of that day. The judgment was to be made before five o'clock because that's when the prom started. I expected a phone call at any time. My tux was ready. We were all sitting in my kitchen. It was about two o'clock when we got the phone call. I got up and gripped the phone, and I thought, 'Please, please let me win!' I answered the phone, and David Corbett said, 'Marc, you're going to the prom!' I started jumping up and down and screaming. Everybody in the kitchen started cheering. Once I got off the phone, my mom phoned all my relatives in New Brunswick saying, 'We won! We won!' It was amazing. It was crazy, and it was quite a rush after the decision was made.

Shortly after the decision, dressed in tuxedos that had been laid out just in case the Justice's decision would be good news, Marc and Jean-Paul attended the prom. Marc recounted the unusual scenario and the politicization process that never stopped.

Marc: We had our champagne and then the limo came. When JP and I walked outside, people were clapping as we got into the limo. The first thing we did was go down to CAW [Canadian Auto Workers] Local 222 where we had this big, huge media event. We did the media event, but JP and I just wanted to go to the prom and be left alone.

As we were driving to the prom, there was a helicopter from Roger's Television following the limo. As we got to the gateway [where the prom was held], there were cameras and reporters everywhere. Thankfully they weren't allowed inside. Finally, we were at the prom. Students were shouting, 'You won!' The principal sat in his chair with his arms crossed, just slouching and staring at everybody. There were some teachers who congratulated me. Most of the students there said that they were really happy that I fought to take JP. They kept saying how happy they were that I was there.

The dinner was good, except we had rubber chicken and gross stuffing. JP and I danced together and slow danced, just like any other normal couple. We kissed just like any normal couple. The prom was worth fighting for, definitely!

Finally attending his prom with Jean-Paul is a testament to Marc's resilience. [. . .]

Canada has come a long way since December 22, 1967 when then Justice Minister Pierre Elliott Trudeau proposed amendments to the Criminal Code that resulted in the decriminalization of homosexuality. As Trudeau spearheaded this law reform and moved Canada away from state control of individual freedoms like those embodied and embedded in sexuality, he made the poignant and memorable assertion, 'The State has no business in the bedrooms of the nation' (Goldie, 2001, p.18). The amendments passed in 1969. During the Marc Hall legal hearing, Justice MacKinnon (2002) reminded us, 'The separation of church and state is a fundamental principle of our Canadian democracy and our constitutional law' (at para. 31). If we uphold this democratic principle in relation to schooling, then schools should carry out their public duties in accordance with strictly secular and non-sectarian democratic principles representative of the inclusive cultural democracy that the Canadian Charter of Rights and Freedoms protects. In this light, perhaps it is time to add a corollary to Pierre Elliott Trudeau's poignant statement and say, 'Institutional churches have no business in the classrooms of the nation.' Although Trudeau's statement was intended to protect the private sexual lives of individuals from public institutional (State) scrutiny, this corollary is different. It is intended to protect the sexual lives of individuals in public spaces like schools from the kind of Catholic institutionalized religious scrutiny embodied in the privatization of queer. Ultimately, the sexual lives of Canadians need to be protected in public *and* private spaces so queer and other persons can be, become, and belong fully and holistically as the Charter espouses. With the Marc Hall case dropped, this goal remains to be achieved.

References

Andrews, G.A. (2002, April 8). *Durham Catholic District School Board confirms principal's decision*. Retrieved 8 May 2002, from http://www.durhamrc.edu.on.ca/html/pr-04-08-02.html

British Columbia College of Teachers (BCCT) v. Trinity Western University (TWU), 2001 SCC 31. Retrieved 5 August 2005, from http://www.lexum.umontreal.ca/csc-scc/en/

Canadian Broadcasting Corporation News (CBC News). (2002a, March 26).

Catholic board meeting disrupted by gay student's supporters. Retrieved 5 August 2005, from http://www.cbc.ca/story/canada/national/2002/03/26/gay020326.html

———. (2002b, April 9). *Catholic school board rules against gay prom date*. Retrieved 5 August 2005, from http://cbc.ca/cgi-bin/templates/view.cgi?category=Canada&story=/news/2002/05/06/hall_020506

———. (2002c, May 6). *Gay teen takes Catholic school to court over prom date*. Retrieved 5 August 2005, from http://www.cbc.ca/stories/2002/05/06/hall_020506

CBC Toronto. (2002, April 9). *Board refuses bid for same-sex prom date*. Retrieved 5 August 2005, from http://toronto.cbc.ca/regional/servlet/View?filename=prom_090502

Canadian Conference of Catholic Bishops (CCCB). (1994). *Catechism of the Catholic Church*. Ottawa, ON: Publications Service, CCCB.

Canadian Teachers' Federation & The Elementary Teachers' Federation of Ontario (CTF & ETFO). (2003). *Seeing the rainbow: Teachers talk about bisexual, gay, lesbian, transgender and two-spirited realities*. Ottawa, ON: Authors.

D'Augelli, A.R. (1998). Developmental implications of victimization of lesbian, gay, and bisexual youths. In G.M. Herek (Ed.), *Stigma and sexual orientation: Understanding prejudice against lesbians, gay men, and bisexuals* (pp. 187–210). Thousand Oaks, CA: Sage Publications.

Department of Justice Canada (DJC). (2003). *Canadian Charter of Rights and Freedoms*. Retrieved 5 August 2005, from http://laws.justice.gc.ca/en/charter/index.html

Dignity Canada Dignité (DCD). (n.d.). *Vatican 'Halloween Letter' 1986: Letter to the bishops of the Catholic Church on the pastoral care of homosexual persons.* Retrieved 5 August 2005, from http://dignitycanada.org/halloweenletter.html

Durham Catholic District School Board (DCDSB). (n.d.). *Durham Catholic District School Board.* Retrieved 5 August 2005, from http://www.oshawa.ca/com_res/drrsccb.asp

Egale Canada. (2002, Summer). Court upholds gay student's bid to attend prom. *INFO-EGALE,* 1.

Elliott, D., & Paris, V. (2002, May 6). *Legal factum for the Coalition for Marc Hall.* Toronto: Authors.

Epstein, D., & Johnson, R. (1994). On the straight and the narrow: The heterosexual presumption, homophobias and schools. In D. Epstein (Ed.), *Challenging lesbian and gay inequalities in education* (pp. 197–230). Bristol, PA: Open University Press.

———. (1998). *Schooling sexualities.* Buckingham, UK: Open University Press.

Epstein, D., O'Flynn, S., & Telford, D. (2001). 'Othering' education: Sexualities, silences, and schooling. In W.G. Secada (Ed.), *Review of research in education 25, 2000–2001* (pp. 127–79). Washington, DC: American Educational Research Association.

Fisher, J. (2002, April 9). *Open letter to EGALE Educators' Network.* Ottawa, ON: Author.

Frankham, J. (2001). The 'open secret': Limitations on the expression of same-sex desire. *International Journal of Qualitative Studies in Education, 14*(4), 457–69.

Friend, R.A. (1998). Heterosexism, homophobia, and the culture of schooling. In S. Brooks (Ed.), *Invisible children in the society and its schools* (pp. 137–66). Mahwah, NJ: Lawrence Erlbaum Associates.

Gay & Lesbian Educators of British Columbia (GALE-BC). (2002, April). Student prevented from attending high school prom. *Gale Force, 12*(4), 4.

Giroux, H.A. (1992). *Border crossings.* New York: Routledge.

Goldie, T. (Ed.). (2001). *In a queer country: Gay & lesbian studies in the Canadian context.* Vancouver: Arsenal Pulp Press.

Grace, A.P., & Benson, F. J. (2000). Using autobiographical queer life narratives of teachers to connect personal, political, and pedagogical spaces. *International Journal of Inclusive Education, 4*(2), 89–109.

Grace, A.P., Hill, R.J., Johnson, C.W., & Lewis, J.B. (2004). In other words: Queer voices/dissident subjectivities impelling social change. *International Journal of Qualitative Studies in Education, 17*(3), 301–23.

Grace, A.P., & Wells, K. (2001). Getting an education in Edmonton, Alberta: The case of queer youth. *Torquere, Journal of the Canadian Lesbian and Gay Studies Association, 3,* 137–51.

———. (2004). Engaging sex-and-gender differences: Educational and cultural change initiatives in Alberta. In J. McNinch & M. Cronin (Eds), *I could not speak my heart: Education and social justice for gay and lesbian youth* (pp. 289–307). Regina, SK: Canadian Plains Research Centre, University of Regina.

Herdt, G. (1995). The protection of lesbian and gay youth. *Harvard Educational Review, 65*(2), 315–21.

Human Rights Watch. (2001). *Hatred in the hallways: Violence and discrimination against lesbian, gay, bisexual, and transgender students in U.S. schools.* Retrieved 5 August 2005, from http://www.hrw.org/reports/2001/uslgbt/

Lahey, K.A. (1999). *Are we persons yet? Law and sexuality in Canada.* Toronto: University of Toronto Press.

MacDougall, B. (2000). *Queer judgments: Homosexuality, expression, and the courts in Canada.* Toronto: University of Toronto Press.

MacKinnon, Justice R. (2002, May 10). *Smitherman v. Powers and the Durham Catholic District School Board.* (Court File No. 12-CV-227705CM3). Whitby, ON: Ontario Superior Court of Justice.

Meagher, Most Reverend A.G. (2002, April 4). *Open letter faxed to Mr. Dalton McGuinty, MPP.* Barrie, ON: Author.

Quinlivan, K., & Town, S. (1999). Queer pedagogy, educational practice and lesbian and gay youth. *International Journal of Qualitative Studies in Education, 12*(5), 509–24.

Ryan, C., & Futterman, D. (1998). *Lesbian and gay youth: Care & counseling.* New York: Columbia University Press.

Ryan, L., Hood, C., & Hall, M. (n.d.). *Have your voice heard.* Retrieved 4 April 2002, from http://geocities.com/rights_and_freedoms/

Siu, J. (2002a, May 10). *Off to the prom!* Retrieved 13 May 2002, from http://365gay.com

———. (2002b, May 11). *Prom fight not over.* Retrieved 11 May 2002, from http://365gay.com/newscontent/051102marcProm.htm

365Gay.com. (2002). *Prom date battle draws support from one of Canada's most powerful union bosses.* Retrieved 26 March 2002, from http://365gay.com

Weis, L., & Fine, M. (2001). Extraordinary conversations in public schools. *International Journal of Qualitative Studies in Education, 14*(4), 497–523.

Characteristics of Male and Female Victims of Sexual Coercion

Cailey Hartwick, Serge Desmarais, and Karl Henning

Introduction

Sexual coercion has been widely studied over the past several decades and is recognized as a prevalent social issue. However, past research has focused almost exclusively on coercion of females by males despite evidence that prevalence rates of sexual coercion of males by females may be as high as 58.5 per cent (Anderson & Sorenson, 1999). It has been argued that the lack of research on sexual coercion by females is due to the scientific community's adherence to the traditional script of sexual experiences (Anderson & Aymami, 1993; O'Sullivan & Byers, 1993). Sexual script theory (Simon & Gagnon, 1986) asserts that culturally constructed scripts structure sexual encounters and delineate what is expected of men and women by providing a model of masculinity and femininity. Men are expected to be avid initiators of sexual activity who are continuously seeking, or are at least amenable to any opportunity for a sexual encounter. In contrast, women are expected to be somewhat resistant to the sexual advances of men by controlling the amount of sexual access a pursuant man is permitted (Byers, 1996; Clements-Schreiber, Rempel & Desmarais, 1998; O'Sullivan & Byers, 1993).

[. . .]

Findings from past research on sexual coercion have been difficult to compare because the definition and measurement of sexual coercion have varied across studies. In the current study, we adopted the definition proposed by Struckman-Johnson and Struckman-Johnson (1994), who defined sexual coercion as 'an experience of being pressured or forced by another person to have contact which involved touching of sexual parts or sexual intercourse—oral, anal, or vaginal' (p. 96). Their definition incorporates 'psychological coercion, including verbal persuasion, threat of love withdrawal, bribery, and use of intoxication' (p. 96) without physical force or the intent to harm, and 'a higher level of coercion', physical coercion, which includes 'physical restraint, physical harm, physical intimidation, threat of harm, and use of weapons' (p. 96).

Since our chosen definition of sexual coercion covers a wide range of differing behaviours, it is difficult to find terms broad enough to satisfactorily characterize individuals' experiences across this spectrum. Terms such as 'perpetrator' and 'victim' are often used in the context of physical harm, intimidation, or forced intercourse (which is a crime) but they seem too strong or overstated to characterize some situations of psychological coercion, such as verbal pressuring (which is not a crime). We are aware of this limitation and have opted here for the terms 'initiator' and 'victim' on the understanding that 'initiator' may sometimes seem too benign or 'victim' too excessive for the circumstances involved.

The literature on women's sexual victimization provides strong indications for the variables that should be included in a predictive model of heterosexual coercion initiated by men. These include numerous contextual factors such as initiator strategies, characteristics of the initiator, characteristics of the victim, and the nature of the relationship between initiator and victim (for a review, see Adams-Curtis & Forbes, 2004). Research on men's experiences with female-initiated sexual coercion suggests consideration of factors such as initiator strategies and the relationship between initiators and victims; characteristics of male victims have yet to be examined. The present study expands upon existing findings regarding initiator strategies and the relationship between initiators and victims and breaks new ground by exploring the characteristics of male victims. The literature review that follows provides background for the hypotheses under investigation in this study.

Initiation of Sexual Coercion

Both men and women commonly report having experienced verbal or psychological coercion as well as being taken advantage of in an intoxicated state (Anderson & Aymami, 1993; Anderson & Sorenson, 1999; Krahe, Scheinberger-Olwig & Bieneck, 2003; Krahe, Waizenhofer & Moiler, 2003; Larimer, Lydum, Anderson & Turner, 1999; O'Sullivan, Byers & Finkelman, 1998; Struckman-Johnson & Struckman-Johnson, 1994). The few studies that have compared heterosexual coercion by both sexes suggest that men and women had experienced similar pressuring strategies in comparable proportions, with one exception. Women tend to report being physically forced into sexual activity more frequently than men, suggesting that male initiators are more likely to include physical force (Larimer et al., 1999).

The Relationship between Initiator and Victim

Research examining the nature of the relationship between male initiators and female victims indicates that sexual coercion is more likely to occur in more intimate relationships (for an early review see Craig, 1990; Gross, Winslett, Roberts & Gohm, 2006; Lannutti & Monahan, 2004; O'Sullivan & Byers, 1993; O'Sullivan et al., 1998). Though few studies have examined the relationship between female initiators and male victims, the available literature suggests a similar pattern in which men are more likely

to be coerced by friends or dating partners than strangers (Krahe et al., 2003; Struckman-Johnson & Struckman-Johnson, 1994). Given the limited number of studies examining the relationship between female initiators and male victims of sexual coercion, further research in this area is clearly warranted.

Characteristics of Victims

To date, the characteristics of males who have experienced heterosexual sexual coercion have not been investigated and, consequently, research on females with such experience must be used as a guide. Past research examining the characteristics of female victims has consistently demonstrated that having had a greater number of sexual partners is associated with having experienced sexual coercion (Lottes, 1991; Testa & Derman, 1999; Van Bruggen, Runtz & Kadlec, 2006). A history of sexual coercion in childhood has also been linked to experiencing adult sexual coercion and has been noted as a consistent predictor in a number of literature reviews (Messman & Long, 1996; Polusny & Follette, 1995) although contradictory results have also been published (Atkeson, Calhoun & Morris, 1989; Mandoki & Burkhart, 1989). Some researchers have found that women with lower self-esteem and lower levels of assertiveness are more likely to experience sexual coercion (Testa & Derman, 1999) while others have not found this association (Amik & Calhoun, 1987; Stets & Pirog-Good, 1987). In light of the mixed results, we believe there is a need for further research on the influence of self-esteem, assertiveness, and a history of sexual abuse.

[. . .]

Both male and female initiators differ significantly from individuals who do not report initiating sexual coercion in terms of their gender beliefs. Male initiators have been found to hold more traditional gender beliefs or to adhere more strongly to gender role stereotypes (Abbey, McAuslan, Zawacki, Clinton & Buck, 2001; for a review, Craig, 1990; Lackie & de Man, 1997; Loh, Gidycz, Lobo & Luthra, 2005; Muehlenhard & Linton, 1987; Senn et al., 2000). In contrast, while women who sexually coerce men are more likely to reject the traditional sexual roles for women, they are significantly more likely to endorse the traditional stereotype of men's sexual accessibility (Clements-Schreiber et al., 1998; Lottes, 1991; O'Sullivan & Byers, 1993). Consequently, it is apparent that endorsing traditional sex role beliefs is an important characteristic of initiators and that both initiators and victims share similar characteristics. In light of these findings the current study explored men and women's gender role beliefs and evaluated whether gender beliefs of victims have value in predicting the experience of sexual coercion.

Current Study and Hypotheses

The current study expanded upon and replicated past findings regarding the context of sexual coercion by men in comparison to women. Specifically, we replicated studies of the nature of the relationship between the initiator and victim, as well as typical pressuring strategies employed. We also examined characteristics of men and women who self-reported experiencing heterosexual coercion to determine whether victim characteristics are gender-specific and whether these characteristics have significant predictive value for members of both sexes.

We hypothesized:

(a) that sexual coercion would be more likely to take place in close relationships, such as friendships and dating relationships, than within relationships between strangers or acquaintances.

(b) that the number of romantic relationships and the length of romantic relationships would be significant predictors of victimization for both men and women.

(c) that both men and women would report the use of intoxication as the most common initiator strategy, followed by forms of verbal or relational coercion, and lastly, the threat or use of physical force.

(d) that men who had been sexually coerced would have similar characteristics to women who had experienced sexual coercion. Specifically that both male and female victims of sexual coercion would have a higher number of sexual partners, a history of childhood sexual victimization, lower self-esteem, and lower levels of assertiveness than participants who had not experienced sexual coercion.

(e) that both male and female victims would adhere to more traditional gender roles and stereotypes.

Methods
Participants

Initial participants were 251 male students and 267 female students enrolled at a mid-sized Canadian university. Errors or inconsistencies in questionnaire completion by participants resulted in the exclusion of 11 men and 8 women. The final sample was thus 240 male and 259 female participants. The mean age of participants was 19 ($SD = 2$). Most were white (90.8%), with Asian/Asian Canadian (7.2%), black/African Canadian (1%), and Latino/Hispanic or First Nations (less than 1%).

Procedures

Recruitment took place in a number of undergraduate classes including introductory psychology, biology, economics, and agriculture.

All participants were informed that the research involved completing an online questionnaire about their sexual experiences. The recruiter emphasized that participant responses were completely anonymous as identifying information, such as their name and student ID, was automatically saved in a separate electronic file that was not linked to questionnaire response data file. Participants were able to complete the 30-minute survey from any computer location; however, it was essential that participants completed the survey in one sitting. Submissions from IP addresses were not controlled, allowing students to make use of university campus computers. Participants could gain access to the website with a valid student ID; however, each student ID could only be used once. Measures were always presented in the same order as is the case in many online surveys due to the complexity of creating randomized questionnaire orders. Participants enrolled in an introductory psychology class received course credit whereas those who were recruited from other courses were entered into a draw for a monetary prize of $100.

Measures

Demographic Information

Participants were asked to select the ethnic description that best described them from a list that included 'Asian or Asian Canadian', 'black or African Canadian', 'Hispanic or Latino', 'First Nations', or 'white'. Participants were also asked to provide their age.

Childhood Sexual Experiences

The Unwanted Childhood Sexual Experiences Questionnaire (UCSEQ; Stevenson, 1998) is a 13-item scale derived from a larger questionnaire designed by Finkelhor (1979). Participants provided 'yes' or 'no' responses to statements regarding incidents of childhood sexual abuse (e.g., 'You touching an adult's sexual organs'). Participants were given a score of '1' if they responded 'yes' to an item indicating they had ever experienced an unwanted childhood sexual experience and a '0' if they responded 'no' to such an item which thus indicated they had not. [. . .]

History of Dating and Sexual Activity

To gain an understanding of participants' dating history they were asked to provide the number of past romantic relationships they had experienced, as well as the length of their longest romantic relationship. Participants were also asked to provide their total number of sexual partners and the age at which they first experienced sexual intercourse. The terms 'romantic relationship' and 'sexual intercourse' were not defined for participants and thus represent participant's interpretations.

Self-esteem

The Rosenberg Self-Esteem Inventory (Rosenberg, 1965) is a widely used and well-validated measure consisting of 10 items designed to assess self-esteem generally rather than within particular domains (e.g., 'I feel that I have a number of good qualities'). Each item was scored on a 4-point Likert scale ranging from 1 (*strongly disagree*) to 4 (*strongly agree*). Self-esteem items were summed to produce a total self-esteem score for each participant.

Assertiveness

The Rathus Assertiveness Schedule (Rathus, 1973) is a well-validated measure that assessed general assertiveness through 30 items (e.g., 'To be honest, people often take advantage of me'). Each item was scored on a 6-point Likert scale ranging from 1 (*very uncharacteristic of me*) to 6 (*very characteristic of me*). Assertiveness items were summed to produce a total assertiveness score for each participant.

Sexual Stereotypes

The Sexual Stereotypes Questionnaire (SSQ; Clements-Schreiber et al., 1998) was used to assess participants' beliefs about male and female sex drives (e.g., 'In general, men need sex more than women do'), as well as male sexual accessibility (e.g., 'It's easy for a woman to sexually arouse a man if she really wants to'). This is a 10-item measure with each item scored on a 5-point Likert scale ranging from 1 (*disagree strongly*) to 5 (*agree strongly*). SSQ items relating to gender specific sex drives were summed producing a total score for each participant. Reliability for the gender specific sex drives section of the SSQ was adequate (= .65). The SSQ items relating to male sexual accessibility were also summed to produce a total score for each participant.

Dependent Measure

Adult Experience with Sexual Coercion

The Sexual Experiences Questionnaire (SEQ) was developed for the current study to assess participants' adult experiences of sexual coercion by the opposite sex. The SEQ was based on the widely used and well-validated Sexual Experience Survey (SES) designed by Koss, Gidycz, and Wisniewski (1987). Previous research (Gylys & McNamara, 1996) has suggested that the SES inflates estimates of rape by using an overly broad definition and by collapsing the threat of physical force and the use of force together. Although there has also been research suggesting that the estimates are realistic (Alksnis, Desmarais, Senn & Hunter, 2000), as well as research demonstrating an underestimation of both the use and threat of physical sexual aggression (Testa, VanZile-Tamsen, Livingston & Koss, 2004), we refrained from collapsing threat and use of force, and also from labelling acts as 'rape'.

[…]

Results

History of Dating and Sexual Activity

A large majority of participants (86%) had been involved in at least one romantic relationship (range 0 to 10). There was a wide range of relationship lengths (one month to 12 years, $SD = 17.1$ months) with an average length of 17 months and a median length of 12 months. Most participants (79.7%) indicated that they had ever had sexual intercourse (mean age of first intercourse 17 years ($SD = 2.1$, range 13 to 23 years). Chi-square analysis revealed that a significantly greater percentage of males (84.2%) than females (74.9%) had ever had intercourse [$\chi^2 (1, N = 496) = 6.28$, $p = .001$]. Among those who had intercourse 40.4 per cent had one intercourse partner, 19.9 per cent had two, 12.1 per cent three, 7.6 per cent four, 4.5 per cent five, and the remaining 15.4 per cent had six or more sexual partners. An equivalent number of male (24.2%) and female (23.2%) participants reported some form of unwanted sexual contact prior to the age of 14 by someone who was at least 5 years older ($z = 0.13$, *ns*).

Prevalence of Coerced Sexual Experiences

Overall, a significantly greater percentage among all female participants (47.9%) than male participants (38.8%) reported being the victims of some form of coerced sexual activity, $\chi^2 (1, N = 499) = 4.2, p < .05$. While the coerced activities reported were not necessarily mutually exclusive (i.e., the same encounter could be reported more than once under different items), participants most frequently reported being coerced into kissing or fondling (women 34%, men 23.3%), followed by intercourse (women 21.2%, men 18.3%), and oral sex (women 4.2%, men 5.8%). Women were significantly more likely to have been coerced into kissing or fondling than men, $\chi^2 (1, N = 499) = 6.9, p < .01$; however, there was no significant gender difference in either coerced oral sex χ^2 (1, N = 499) = .66, *ns*, or coerced intercourse χ^2 (1, N = 499) = .66, *ns*. Consequently, the most prevalent experiences of sexual coercion for both sexes were associated with kissing and fondling and with sexual intercourse with a statistically significant gender difference found only with the former in that women were more likely than men to have experienced coerced kissing and fondling.

Initiator Strategies

Both men and women reported that initiators used guilt and intoxication to a greater extent than other strategies (see Figure 1). Women reported that guilt was the most commonly experienced coercive strategy (n_{women} = 73, 28.2%) whereas it was identified significantly less often by men (n_{men} = 31, 12.9%), χ^2 (1, N = 497) = 17.6, $p < .001$, for whom being taken advantage of when intoxicated was the most commonly experienced coercive strategy (n_{men} = 52.21.7%). Note that there was no significant gender difference in

the percentage of men and women who reported being coerced when intoxicated (n_{women} = 62, 23.9%), χ^2 (1, N = 497) = .42, *ns*. The remainder of the strategies were endorsed by too few respondents (less than 5%) to allow for meaningful statistical comparisons between men and women.

The Relationship between Initiator and Victim

Overall, the probability of experiencing sexual coercion, for both men and women, was relatively similar across types of relationships. However two noteworthy trends did emerge. First, strategies that manipulate the emotional connection between the victim and initiator, such as guilt or threatening to hurt oneself, were more commonly utilized by dating partners and friends than by strangers and acquaintances (89.6% of initiators who used guilt were dating partners or friends, in comparison to 10.4% of acquaintance and strangers, χ^2 (1, N = 113) = 60.84, $p < .001$. All 11 of the initiators who threatened to hurt themselves

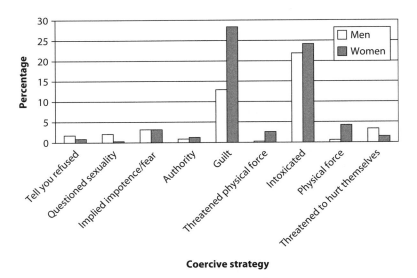

Figure 1 Prevalence Rates of Men and Women's Experiences With Sexual Coercion Strategies

Source: Cailey Hartwick, Serge Desmarais, and Karl Hennig, 'Characteristics of male and female victims of sexual coercion,' *The Canadian Journal of Human Sexuality*, 16, 1-2 (2007) p. 36.

Table 1 Results of Logistic Regression Analysis for Coerced Kissing and Fondling

PREDICTORS	B	S.E.	WALD	EXP (B)
Women				
Childhood sexual abuse	−.21	.32	.41	.81
Self-esteem	−.04	.03	1.72	.96
Assertiveness	.00	.01	.08	1.00
Number of partners	.01	.05	.03	.99
Number of relationships	.37	.14	6.60**	1.45
Length of relation-ships	−.03	.01	9.52**	.97
Male sexual accessibility	.03	.03	.80	1.03
Gender-dependent sex drives	−.07	.05	.02	.99
Men				
Childhood sexual abuse	−.41	.36	1.34	.66
Self-esteem	−.05	.03	2.00	.95
Assertiveness	−.00	.01	.06	.10
Number of partners	−.01	.04	.12	.99
Number of relationships	.06	.13	.26	1.07
Length of relationships	−.01	.01	.58	.99
Male sexual accessibility	.08	.04	3.48	1.08
Gender-dependent sex drives	.08	.06	1.74	1.09

Note: Nagelkerke $R2$ = .11 (women), .09 (men); ***p < .001; **p < .01; *p < .05

were dating partners or friends. Second, strangers or acquaintances more commonly employed strategies that do not rely on intimacy between the initiator and victim, such as intoxicating the victim (61.2% of such reports involved strangers or acquaintances, in comparison to 38.8% involving friends and dating partners, χ^2 (1, N = 122) = 5.24, p = .022).

Coerced Kissing and Fondling

A test of the full model regarding coerced kissing and fondling with all eight predictors against a constant only model was statistically reliable for women in the sample, χ^2 (5, N = 256) = 16.09, p < .01. This indicated that the predictors, as a set, reliably distinguish between those women who had experienced sexual coercion and those who had not. Table 1 provides the regression coefficients, standard errors, Wald statistics, and odds ratios for each predictor. According to the Wald criterion, the number of romantic relationships, Wald[1] = 6.60, p = .01, and the length of longest romantic relationship, Wald[1] = 9.52, p < .01, reliably predicted the experience of coerced kissing or fondling amongst women (Table 1). Women with a higher number of romantic relationships and relationships of a shorter duration were significantly more likely to be coerced into unwanted kissing or fondling than women with a smaller number of romantic relationships, or relationships of a longer duration.

A test of the full model regarding coerced kissing and fondling with all eight predictors against a constant only model was not statistically reliable for men, χ^2 (5, N = 239) = 6.89, *ns*. Thus, in contrast to women, the predictors, as a set, did not reliably distinguish between those men who had experienced sexual coercion and those who had not (Table 1).

Coerced Intercourse

For women, a test of the full model regarding coerced intercourse with all eight predictors against a constant only model was statistically reliable, χ^2 (5, N = 256) = 10.31, p < .05. As shown in Table 2, the number of sexual partners reported, Wald[1] = 17.31, p < .001, and a belief in males' sexual accessibility, Wald[1] = 4.55, p < .05, reliably predicted the experience of being coerced into sexual intercourse. Women who had a higher number of sexual partners were significantly more likely to report being coerced into sexual intercourse. Also, women who believed in the sexual accessibility of men were significantly more likely to report being coerced into sexual intercourse.

Table 2 Results of Logistic Regression Analysis for Intercourse

PREDICTORS	B	S.E.	WALD	EXP (B)
Women				
Childhood sexual abuse	−.55	.39	1.97	.58
Self-esteem	−.03	.04	.40	.97
Assertiveness	.02	.01	1.98	1.02
Number of partners	.28	.07	17.31***	1.32
Number of relationships	.22	.16	1.97	1.25
Length of relationships	.02	.01	2.90	1.02
Male sexual accessibility	.09	.04	4.55**	1.10
Gender-dependent sex drives	−.04	.06	.30	.97
Men				
Childhood sexual abuse	.11	.46	.05	1.11
Self-esteem	.02	.04	.15	1.02
Assertiveness	−.00	.01	.04	1.00
Number of partners	.21	.06	11.17**	1.23
Number of relationships	.35	.17	4.19*	1.42
Length of relationships	−.04	.02	4.83**	.96
Male sexual accessibility	.18	.06	9.85**	1.19
Gender-dependent sex drives	−.02	.07	.06	.98

Note: Nagelkerke $R2$ = .32 (women), .33 (men); ***p < .001; **p < .01; *p < .05

A test of the full model with coerced intercourse as the criterion was also statistically reliable for men in the sample, χ^2 (5, N = 239) = 20.69, p < .001. As was the case with females, the number of sexual partners, Wald[1] = 11.17, p = .001, and a belief in males' sexual accessibility, Wald[1] = 9.85, p < .01, reliably predicted men's experience of being coerced into sexual intercourse (Table 2). Men who had a higher number of sexual partners and those who believed in the sexual accessibility of men, were significantly more likely to have been coerced into sexual intercourse. At a lower level of significance, the number of relationships reported, Wald[1] = 4.19, p < .05, and the length of longest relationship, Wald[1] = 4.83, p < −.05, also predicted having been coerced into sexual intercourse for men. Men who had more romantic relationships, and those who had shorter romantic relationships, were significantly more likely to be coerced into sexual intercourse with women, than those who had fewer or longer romantic relationships.

Discussion

This study sought to compare men's and women's experience of heterosexual coercion and to assess whether a set of relevant attitudinal and personal characteristics could reliably predict the likelihood of various forms of coerced experiences. Accordingly, the current study attempted to replicate past findings on the prevalence and context of sexual coercion, specifically the pressuring strategies utilized, the sexual activities that ensued, and the relationship between the initiator and victim. In addition, we did gender comparisons to determine whether men and women who had experienced sexual coercion shared similar characteristics, and to explore the predictive value of such victim characteristics.

The consensual sexual behaviour reported in the current study is consistent with the Adams-Curtis and Forbes (2004) review of the normative sexual behaviour of university students. These authors suggested that approximately 70 per cent to 75 per cent of undergraduate students were sexually active; in our sample 79.7 per cent had ever had sexual intercourse and 86 per cent had been in a romantic relationship. Also consistent with our findings is the report of Adams-Curtis and Forbes (2004) that most university students had a relatively small number of sexual partners and that men had more partners than women. In these respects our sample appears to be fairly representative of university students in general.

Prevalence of Coerced Sexual Experiences

In line with previous research (Krahe et al., 2003; Larimer et al., 1999; Struckman-Johnson & Struckman-Johnson, 1994), roughly two out of every five men in the present study reported being coerced by a woman into unwanted sexual activity of some form. In comparison, almost half of female participants reported being coerced. Higher rates of sexual victimization among women are consistent with findings from past research (Hogben, Byrne & Hamburger, 1996; Stets & Pirog-Good, 1987. However, when sexual coercion experiences are categorized by type of sexual activity, our data revealed that women experienced significantly more coerced kissing or fondling (women 34%, men 23.3%), but not significantly more coerced oral sex (women 4.2%, men 5.8%), or coerced intercourse than men (women 21.2%, men 18.3%). This finding, which is also consistent with results from previous research (Larimer et al., 1999; Lottes, 1991), helps clarify the likelihood of different types of sexual coercion and the circumstances in which gender differences in experience of sexual coercion are most likely to occur.

Initiator Strategies

The current findings indicate that being purposefully intoxicated by the initiator is the most commonly experienced coercive strategy reported by men (21.7%), followed by the use of guilt (12.9%), whereas for women, guilt was the most commonly reported pressuring strategy (28.2%), followed by being intoxicated (23.9%). It is interesting to note that both of these commonly reported strategies require the participant to perceive the intention of the initiator. Consequently reports of these strategies are prone to subjectivity, as well as retrospective interpretation. Nevertheless, the results capture the victims' perceptions of their own experience. Women's greater likelihood of reporting being sexually coerced by the use of guilt can be explained in one of two ways. It is possible that male initiators use guilt as a pressuring strategy more frequently than female initiators or it may be that female victims are more susceptible to the use of guilt than male victims. Lewin (1985) asserts that women are socialized to believe that they should put men's needs ahead of their own. She suggests that women's self-images are more reliant on 'giving', which in turn makes it difficult for them to resist psychological pressure to engage in unwanted sexual activity. Note that we did not find the same gender difference in the reported use of intoxication as a coercive strategy. Both men and women indicated high rates of use of their intoxication by the initiator as a form of coercion, which [. . .] underscores the importance of including the use of intoxication as a coercive strategy when assessing incidents of sexual coercion.

The Relationship between Initiator and Victim

Prior research (for a review, Craig, 1990; Gross et al., 2006; Lannutti & Monahan, 2004; Lottes, 1991; O'Sullivan & Byers, 1993; O'Sullivan et al., 1998) has noted that the potential for coercion increases as does the level of closeness or intimacy in the relationship. Our findings provide only partial support for this argument since the probability of being coerced, for both men and women, was relatively similar across each type of relationship. However, two exceptions are worth noting and both are consistent with past research (Muehlenhard & Linton, 1987; Stets & Pirog-Good, 1987). First, strategies that manipulate the emotional connection between the victim and initiator, such as guilt or threatening to hurt oneself, were most commonly utilized by dating partners and friends. The second exception is essentially the reverse of the first whereby strangers or acquaintances were more likely to employ strategies, such as intoxication of the victim, that do not rely on intimacy between the initiator and victim. [. . .]

Characteristics of Victims

Two of our main objectives were to explore whether men and women who experience sexual coercion share similar personal characteristics and whether these characteristics have predictive value for women and men. Past research suggests that both male and female victims of sexual coercion would have a history of childhood sexual victimization, a higher number of sexual partners, lower self-esteem, and lower levels of assertiveness than participants who had not experienced sexual coercion. In addition, we hypothesized that both men and women who experienced coercion would adhere to more traditional gender roles and stereotypes.

Results regarding the predictive value of the relationship history variables were mixed. The number of romantic relationships that participants reported and the length of romantic relationships reported was predictive of coerced kissing and fondling for women and coerced intercourse for men. It is likely that the predictive value of these characteristics lies in the simple fact that

individuals who have more short-term partners have greater exposure to potential initiators of sexual coercion and thus more opportunity to be coerced (Lottes, 1991). However, it is prudent to point out that the two relationship variables did not significantly predict men's experience of coerced kissing and fondling or women's experience of coerced intercourse. This pattern of gender reversal is puzzling and certainly warrants further investigation.

In line with the notion of exposure and opportunity, the number of sexual partners reported was predictive of both men's and women's experience of coerced intercourse. However, this same variable did not predict coerced kissing and fondling for either men or women. This finding suggests that kissing and fondling are very distinct forms of sexual activity from sexual intercourse. Kissing and fondling often occur in the initial stages of a progression of sexual activity, and may mark a first attempt to initiate sexual activity in a previously platonic relationship. Accordingly, it is possible that coerced kissing and fondling is more context driven and less relationally driven than coerced intercourse.

Consistent with some past research (Clements-Schreiber et al., 1998), a belief in men's sexual accessibility predicted women's experience of sexual coercion such that a stronger belief in such accessibility was associated with higher rates of coercion. Interestingly, similar results were found for men. While both men and women can hold the same stereotype of men's sexual accessibility, i.e., that men are constantly desiring and always willing to engage in sexual activity, the endorsement of this stereotype likely has different ramifications for members of each sex. For men, endorsing the traditional sexual stereotype may lead to feelings of guilt when they are reluctant to engage in sexual activity, as they believe average men are always amenable to any sexual opportunity. Norris, Nurius, and

Dimeff (1996) suggest that feelings of guilt or responsibility make it more difficult for individuals to offer effective resistance. Accordingly, men who feel guilty about their own reluctance may have more difficulty offering effective resistance, and, as a consequence, are more vulnerable to being coerced into sexual activity. It is interesting that women who believe in men's sexual accessibility are also more likely to experience sexual coercion. It is possible that women who endorse the traditional male stereotype are more likely to believe that their own lack of desire does not warrant resistance relative to a man's higher sexual needs, or that resistance may be somewhat futile against a man's indomitable desire for sex. The link between belief in men's sexual accessibility and sexual coercion is compelling but an explanation of the full gender-based process that underlies our results will require further investigation as our explanations remain tentative.

Regardless of the sexual activity examined, neither self-esteem nor assertiveness reliably predicted sexual coercion for men or women. [. . .]

Similarly, a childhood history of sexual victimization was not predictive of sexual coercion regardless of gender or type of activity. [. . .]

Limitations

The current study joins many others in its use of undergraduate students as a convenient sample of participants. Although some research cited by Adams-Curtis and Forbes (2004) suggests that the sexual behaviour of university students corresponds to that of their peers in the general population, we would be cautious in broadly accepting that generalization in the context of the current study.

Conclusion

The current study reiterates the importance of studying both women's and men's experiences of sexual coercion and is part of a growing body of research (Anderson & Aymami, 1993; Byers & O'Sullivan, 1998; Davies, 2002; O'Sullivan, Lawrence, & Byers, 1994; O'Sullivan & Byers, 1993) that demonstrates the potential errors associated with a rigid adherence to the sexual script depicting men as constantly desiring sex and women as resistant gatekeepers. Normative assumptions about sexual standards for women and men have most likely evolved over the years and we believe it is imperative for sexuality researchers to keep pace with the reality of individuals' sexual attitudes and experiences as they require frequent contemporary re-examination.

Furthermore, our study draws attention to [. . .] the significance of victims' sex role beliefs as a promising potential predictor. Sexual script theory (Simon & Gagnon, 1986) suggests that strict adherence to scripted gender roles shape men's and women's attitudes and behaviours and influence the decisions they make when placed in situations that draw upon these scripts. As our findings indicate, the myth of men's sexual accessibility may predispose both men and women to experience sexual coercion, but we have argued that it may do so for entirely different reasons. Overall, our findings reinforce the value of including relational and sexual script variables when studying men's and women's sexual attitudes, cognitions, and behaviours and demonstrate the need to explore further how these scripts shape sexual experience in general and sexual coercion in particular.

References

Abbey, A., McAuslan, P., Zawacki, R., Clinton, A.M., Buck, P.O. (2001). Attitudinal, experimental, and situational predictors of sexual assault perpetration. *Journal of Interpersonal Violence, 16*, 784–807.

Adams-Curtis, L.E., & Forbes, G.B. (2004). College women's experiences of sexual coercion: A review of cultural, initiator, victim and situational variables. *Trauma, Violence, & Abuse, 5*, 91–122.

Alksnis, C., Desmarais, S., Senn, C., & Hunter, N. (2000). Methodologic concerns regarding estimates of physical violence in sexual coercion: Overstatement or understatement? *Archives of Sexual Behavior, 29*, 323–34.

Amik, C.E., & Calhoun, K.S. (1987). Resistance to sexual aggression: Personality, attitudinal and situational factors. *Archives of Sexual Behavior, 16*, 153–63.

Anderson, P.B., & Aymami, R. (1993). Reports of female initiation of sexual contact: Male and female differences. *Archives of Sexual Behavior, 22*, 335–43.

Anderson, P.B., & Sorensen, W. (1999). Male and female differences in reports of women's heterosexual initiation and aggression. *Archives of Sexual Behavior, 28*, 243–53.

Atkeson, B.M., Clahoun, K.S., & Morris, K.T. (1989). Victim resistance to rape: The relationships of previous victimization, demographics and situational factors. *Archives of Sexual Behavior, 18*, 497–507.

Byers, S. (1996). How well does the traditional sexual script explain sexual coercion? Review of a program of research. *Journal of Psychology and Human Sexuality, 8*, 7–25.

Byers, E.S., & O'Sullivan, L.F. (1998). Similar but different: Men's and women's experiences of sexual coercion. In P.B. Anderson & C. Struckman-Johnson (Eds), *Sexually Aggressive Women* (pp. 144–68). New York, NY: Guilford Press.

Clements-Schreiber, M.E., Rempel, J.K., & Desmarais, S. (1998). Women's sexual pressure tactics and adherence to related attitudes: A step towards prediction. *The Journal of Sex Research, 35*, 197–205.

Craig, M.E. (1990). Coercive sexuality in dating relationships. *Clinical Psychology Review, 10*, 395–423.

Davies, M. (2002). Male sexual assault victims: A selective review of the literature and implications for support services. *Aggression and Violent Behaviour, 7*, 203–14.

Finkelhor, D. (1979). *Sexually Victimized Children*. New York, NY: Free Press.

Gross, A.M., Winslett, A., Roberts, M., & Gohm, C.L. (2006). An examination of sexual violence against college women. *Violence Against Women, 12*, 288–300.

Gylys, J.A., & McNamara, J.R. (1996). A further examination of validity for the Sexual Experience Survey. *Behavioral Sciences and the Law, 14*, 245–60.

Hogben, M., Byrne, D., & Hamburger, M.E. (1996). Coercive heterosexual sexuality in dating relationships of college students: Implications of differential male-female experiences. *Journal of Psychology and Human Sexuality, 8*, 69–78.

Koss, M.P., Gidycz, C.A., & Wisniewski, N. (1987). The scope of rape: Incidence and prevalence of sexual aggression and victimization in a national sample of higher education students. *Journal of Consulting and Clinical Psychology, 55*, 162–70.

Krahe, B., Scheinberger-Olwig, R., & Bieneck, S. (2003). Men's reports of non-consensual sexual interactions with women: Prevalence and impact. *Archives of Sexual Behavior, 32*, 165–75.

Krahe, B., Waizenhofer, E., & Moiler, I. (2003). Women's sexual aggression against men: Prevalence and predictors. *Sex Roles, 49*, 219–32.

Lackie, L., & de Man, A.F. (1997). Correlates of sexual aggression among male university students. *Sex Roles, 37*, 451–57.

Lannutti, P.J., & Monahan, J.L. (2004). Resistance, persistence, and drinking: Examining goals of women's refusals of unwanted sexual advances. *Western Journal of Communication, 68*, 151–69.

Larimer, M.E., Lydum, A.R., Anderson, B.K., & Turner, A.P. (1999). Male and female victims of unwanted sexual contact in a college student sample: Prevalence rates, alcohol use, and depression symptoms. *Sex Roles, 40*, 295–308.

Lewin, M. (1985). Unwanted intercourse: The difficulty of saying no. *Psychology of Women Quarterly, 9*, 184–92.

Loh, C., Gidycz, C.A., Lobo, T.R., & Luthra, R. (2005). A prospective analysis of sexual assault perpetration: Risk factors related to perpetrator characteristics. *Journal of Interpersonal Violence, 20*, 1325–48.

Lottes, I.L. (1991). The relationship between nontraditional gender roles and sexual coercion. *Journal of Psychology and Human Sexuality, 4*, 89–109.

Mandoki, C.A., & Burkhart, B.R. (1989). Sexual victimization: Is there a vicious cycle? *Violence and Victims, 3*, 179–90.

Messman, T.L., & Long, P.J. (1996). Child sexual abuse and its relationship to revictimization in adult women: A review. *Clinical Psychology Review, 16*, 397–420.

Muehlenhard, C.L., & Linton, M.A. (1987). Date rape and sexual aggression in dating situations: Incidence and risk factors. *Journal of Canadian Psychology, 34*, 186–96.

Norris, J., Nurius, P.S., & Dimeff, L.A. (1996). Through her eyes: Factors affecting women's perception of and resistance to acquaintance sexual aggression threat. *Psychology of Women Quarterly, 20*, 123–45.

O'Sullivan, L.F., & Byers, E.S. (1993). Eroding stereotypes: College women's attempts to influence reluctant male sexual partners. *The Journal of Sex Research, 30*, 270–82.

O'Sullivan, L.F., Byers, E.S., & Finkelman, L. (1998). A comparison of male and female college students' experiences of sexual coercion. *Psychology of Women Quarterly, 22*, 177–95.

O'Sullivan, L.F., Lawrence, K., & Byers, E.S. (1994). Discrepancies in desired level of sexual intimacy in long-term relationships. *The Canadian Journal of Human Sexuality, 3*, 313–16.

Polusny, M.A., & Follette, V.M. (1995). Long term correlates of child sex abuse: Theory and review of empirical literature. *Applied and Preventative Psychology, 4*, 143–66.

Rathus, S.A. (1973). A 30-item schedule for assessing assertive behaviour. *Behaviour Therapy, 4*, 398–406.

Rosenberg, M. (1965). *Society and the adolescent self-image.* Princeton, NJ: Princeton University Press.

Senn, C.Y., Desmarais, S., Verberg, N., & Wood, E. (2000). Predicting coercive sexual behavior across the lifespan in a random sample of Canadian men. *Journal of Social and Personal Relationships, 17*, 95–113.

Simon, W., & Gagnon, J.H. (1986). Sexual scripts: Permanence and change. *Archives of Sexual Behavior, 15*, 97–120.

Stets, J.E., & Pirog-Good, M.A. (1987). Violence in dating relationships. *Social Psychology Quarterly, 50*, 237–46.

Stevenson, M.R. (1998). Unwanted childhood sexual experience questionnaire. In C.M. Davis, W.L. Yarber, R. Bauserman, G. Schreer & S.L. Davis (Eds). *Handbook of Sexuality-Related Measures* (pp. 28–29). Thousand Oaks, CA: Sage.

Struckman-Johnson, C., & Struckman-Johnson, D. (1994). Men pressured and forced into sexual experience. *Archives of Sexual Behavior, 23*, 93–114.

Testa, M., & Dermen, K.H. (1999). The differential correlates of sexual coercion and rape. *Journal of Interpersonal Violence, 14*, 548–61.

Testa, M., VanZile-Tamsen, C., Livingston, J.A., & Koss, M.P. (2004). Assessing women's experience of sexual aggression using the Sexual Experience Survey: Evidence for validity and implications for research. *Psychology of Women Quarterly, 28*, 256–65.

Van Bruggen, L.K., Runtz, M.G., & Kadlec, H. (2006). Sexual revictimization: The role of sexual self esteem and dysfunctional sexual behaviours. *Child Maltreatment, 11*, 131–45.

5 Sex for Life? Changing Patterns within Long-term Relationships

Until Death Do Us Part? The Impact of Differential Access to Marriage on a Sample of Urban Men

Adam Isaiah Green

Despite the changing nature of marriage and family over the last 50 years (Bianchi and Casper 2000; Coontz 2005), marriage continues to serve as an institution of paramount significance for heterosexuals—a 'master template' around which norms, practices, finances, and life decisions are organized (Swidler 2001). However, less clear is the impact of the *absence* of access to the institution of marriage for lesbians and gay men: How does the absence of marriage bear on processes of identity formation, the formulation of dyadic norms, and sexual decision making? To be sure, the hotly contested issue of same-sex marriage brings renewed significance to these questions.

This article presents a systematic comparison of the life histories of a sample of urban heterosexual and homosexual men[1] to examine the differential impact of marriage (and its absence) on sexual practices and dyadic formations and the meanings attached to them. These data demonstrate the profound impact of marriage—both its presence and absence—in shaping how urban heterosexual and homosexual men constructed

and selected sexual scripts, balanced erotic desires with dyadic commitment, and pursued sexually and emotionally fulfilling lives. Like the opposite poles of a compass, the possibility and impossibility of marriage provided contrasting navigational reference points, propelling heterosexual men into career trajectories characterized by a reduction of sexual partners and the gradual, if imperfect, adoption of monogamous norms and dyadic commitment and, conversely, driving homosexual men into sexual career trajectories characterized by increasing sexual exploration, dyadic innovation, and a re-evaluation of the meaning and value of monogamy. Yet, these contrasting structural positions aside, both sets of men articulate shared ambivalences around structured life paths that permit the satisfaction of some desires while frustrating or precluding altogether the realization of others. [. . .]

Herein is provided an overview of key themes in the literature related to marriage and the gay sexual career. Next is a diverse range of sexual careers to illustrate patterned processes whereby the institution of marriage (and its absence) impinges on and transforms the sexual behaviours, dyadic norms, and sensibilities of heterosexual and homosexual men. The treatment of marriage as an explicitly problematic feature of biography shows how its presence pushes heterosexual men (even heterosexual 'playboys') toward monogamy and, conversely, how its absence creates the conditions under which homosexual men (even homosexual 'monogamists') are pushed toward non-monogamy and dyadic innovation. The article concludes with a discussion of the implications of these life histories for the prospect of gay marriage and speculates on the potential impact of same-sex matrimony for gay men in US metropolitan areas.

Marriage and Sexuality: Key Themes in the Literature

> The relational and social worlds of homosexual men and women constitute major and intentional departures from the structures and expectations of heterosexual marriage. Homosexuals are marital nonconformists and are best understood in that framework (Fowlkes 1994:175).

The twentieth century was an era of dramatic change for marriage and the family in the United States and Western Europe (Coontz 2005). Women's increasing participation in the work force, the rise of the women's movement, and the sexual revolution have had a transformative impact on marriage and the family, producing demographic changes in the age at first marriage (Bianchi and Casper 2000), the delay of childbirth (Bachu and O'Connell 2000), the rising prominence of cohabitation (Bianchi and Casper 2000), and dramatically higher rates of divorce (Goldstein 1999; Goldstein and Kennedy 2001). Nonetheless, marriage and the family are 'here to stay'

(Bane 1976). More than 90 per cent of Americans marry and have children (Skolnick and Skolnick 1997) and, of those who divorce, most remarry (Bramlett and Mosher 2001), most within four years of divorce (Coleman et al. 2000). Moreover, despite increasingly permissive sexual practices after the sexual revolution of the 1960s, marital fidelity remains quite high (Laumann et al. 1994), and support for marital monogamy has actually *increased,* as indicated by General Social Survey respondents, 92 per cent of whom reported that extramarital sex was either 'always wrong' or 'almost always wrong' in 1998, up from 84 per cent in 1972 (Cherlin 2002). Indeed, even as the meaning of and participation in marriage vary across race and ethnicity (Ruggles 1994), class (Baca Zinn 1997), creed (Lamanna and Reidman 2003), and generation (Bumpass, Sweet, and Cherlin 1991), few social scientists would contest the paramount role of marriage in shaping heterosexual dyads, sexual practices, and sexual norms.

Over the last three decades, lesbian and gay careers have also been the subject of an expanding body of academic research. In this literature, the absence of marriage is regarded as an implicit structural backdrop against which lesbians and gay men build alternative, nonconformist, self-conscious, or liberated sexual lives (Bech 1997; Weeks, Heaphy, and Donovan 2001). [. . .] On the whole, this stream of research situates the non-marital status of homosexuals as an implicit point of departure from which other facets of lesbian and gay careers, such as sexual practice and coupling, are explored.

An alternative treatment of the matrimonial void is found in a body of literature that emphasizes self-conscious invention by lesbians and gay men who reject dominant heterosexual values and experience the absence of marriage as an 'opening up of choices' (Weeks et al. 2001:111). [. . .] A similar but more explicitly politicized treatment is seen in the works of DeCecco (1990), Rechy

(1977), and Weeks (1985), who suggest that gay men do not simply reinvent themselves outside of traditional parameters but, further, provide a vital counterpoint to heteronormativity—most notably through non-monogamous practices.

Yet another stream of lesbian- and gay-themed literature de-emphasizes politicized formulations of homosexual practices in favour of more explicit structural and social psychological processes. Herdt and Boxer (1992), for instance, suggest that 'becoming gay' is marked by a process of 'unlearning' heterosexual goals, including the idea of reproductive heterosexual marriage and monogamy.

Also, in a somewhat different vein, Laumann et al. (1994), Peplau (1993), and Kurdek and Schmitt (1987) suggest that lesbian and gay relationships may be less stable than heterosexual relationships because the absence of marriage diminishes barriers to dyadic dissolution. Thus, opportunity costs associated with divorce render the conjugal unit a more stable dyad than its homosexual counterpart.

In total, widely varied lesbian- and gay-themed literatures bring in the absence of marriage—more or less directly—in theorizing homosexual careers. However, this rich and suggestive body of research raises for lesbians and gay men important questions about the impact of the matrimonial void that are as yet unanswered. How does the inability to marry matter in homosexual life histories? How does the exclusion from marriage bear on self-concept, the development of sexual and dyadic norms, the acquisition and authorship of sexual scripts, and the processes of sexual decision making over the life course? Are lesbians and gay men 'marital nonconformists' as suggested by Fowlkes (1994), iconoclastic sexual actors who reject the constraints of matrimony and monogamy? Are they ideologically motivated actors who draw from and provide a vital critique of marriage and family institutions? Further, do

the sexual and dyadic forms and practices of lesbians and gay men arise as a function of social psychological adaptations to stigma and institutional constraint? [. . .] In an effort to address these questions, this article compares the sexual careers of urban heterosexual and homosexual men in an original piece of research.

Method

The research supporting this article was conducted between 2000 and 2003, a period during which sexual orientation served as a categorical axis of inclusion and exclusion in the United States (i.e., heterosexuals could marry; homosexuals could not). [. . .] This article focuses on male heterosexual and homosexual life histories for their potential as an instructive point of comparison. Sixty homosexual and 50 heterosexual men between the ages of 21 and 52 and residing in New York City engaged in interviews. A targeted, community-based sampling procedure for hidden populations recruited the respondents (Watters and Biernacki 1989), with starting points from a diverse range of local community sites in Manhattan's West Village and Chelsea. The audio-recorded interviews were semi-structured in a private space of the respondents' choosing and typically lasted between two and four hours. An interview schedule with matching chronological sections for gay and straight men created a comparable sexual career profile for each participant. As part of the analytic process, a code for each interview originated from principles of grounded theory (Strauss and Corbin 1998). Open coding established general salient categories, and axial coding revealed dimensions of variation within and across these concepts. Finally, a third analytic process mapped sequences of sexual conduct across cases, thus identifying patterned turning points (i.e., moments or experiences that trigger decisive shifts in life pathways; Elder 1985).

As a whole, respondents characterized themselves as middle-class (93%) and holders of college degrees (89%), and just over one-fourth (27.5%) held graduate degrees. To maximize the possibility for identifying racial patterns in the sexual career, recruitment restricted study participants to those identifying as either 'white' or 'black'. In total, one-half of the homosexual respondents identified as black; the other half identified as white-Caucasian. Heterosexual respondents identified as white-Caucasian (94%), with those remaining identifying as black.[2] At the time of interview, 43 per cent of the homosexual men and 52 per cent of the heterosexual men were in relationships, whereas 24 per cent of the total heterosexual sample were or had been married.

[. . .]

A series of cases in the following sections highlight the impact of marriage (and its absence) over a period of the life history, extending roughly from adolescence to early mid-life. These particular life histories tease out patterns in the ways in which very different heterosexual and homosexual men respond to and negotiate access to and exclusion from marriage, respectively. These histories aim neither to enumerate an exhaustive catalogue of sexual careers nor to present the most common careers. Rather, the central strategy for data presentation in this analysis is to distill processes associated with the sexual career that are specific to sexual orientation among men who otherwise have divergent motives and desires.

Data: Sex and Sexual Orientation over the Life History

Starting Points: The Institutionalization of Heterosexuality

[. . .] Well before reaching a normative age of marriageability, gay and straight men in this study perceived heterosexual, monogamous commitment and wedlock as universal rites of passage to adulthood. Paul, for instance, a white homosexual man in his mid-thirties, recalls vividly daydreaming about marriage and family both in childhood and early adolescence. His parents' divorce intensified these expectations and rendered formal kinship all the more important to him:

> Yes, I wanted to have a beautiful wife, and have six to eight children. It was very important to me because I never had a father. [I] wanted to create something which I did not have and was a big black-hole in my life.

On the issue of marriage, Derek—a black gay man in his mid-thirties—invokes a conception of the 'American dream' founded on matrimony and middle-class consumption:

> Yep . . . That was the thing to do. That was the social order. That's what I was expected to do. I wanted to be married, with sons, the house, cars, garage, dog. I wanted those . . .

Similarly, Steve, a white heterosexual in his mid-thirties, anticipated marriage as a way to replicate the 'social order' of his early family life:

> I thought about it. That's the right thing to do . . . Just from seeing it all my life . . . I wanted to find somebody to share my future with, and to build a future with together . . .

And Lane, a black, heterosexual in his mid-thirties, echoes these sentiments:

> I knew someday I'd be married. You know, you fall in love and you find that special one to spend your time with. I thought

about basically two kids, girls and a dog—raising them, living the right way, and having a happy life.

Beside marriage and family, another thing that was rarely questioned in childhood and early adolescence was sexual orientation. Like being a husband and a father, being heterosexual was often just an assumption, even in the face of contrary erotic feelings. Indeed, participants conceived of heterosexuality, marriage, and family as inextricably bound arenas in which expectations for future dyadic forms and adult identity were grounded. Jim—gay, white, and in his early twenties—demonstrates this:

> Given the town that I grew up in and my family, there weren't many other ways of life that I saw . . . It seemed very normal, and just what would happen. It only made sense that I would get married and have children . . . what else would I do?

The assumption of heterosexuality in childhood and adolescence is not surprising. Strong early attachments to heterosexual families and communities consolidate, or in some cases compel, heterosexual representations and practices (Rich 1990). Within Steve's and Jim's neighbourhoods, for instance, there were no homosexuals of whom they had knowledge. Though homosexual childhood exploration was not unheard of, it did not confer a sexual 'identity' on the boys involved. [. . .] In total, even before the first pubescent sexual impulse took form, heterosexual marriage and family served as master templates for most future-to-be straight and gay boys, despite differences in their own family structures. However, by the time adolescence set in, distinctions in their sexual desires initiated divergent life choices.

Heterosexual Men

Sexuality in Adolescence and Young Adulthood: Negotiating the Pull of Formal Kinship

Despite a growing proliferation of sexual scripts, adolescent heterosexuals encounter a socialization process that anticipates future heteronormative rites of passage, including future monogamous commitment, marriage, and family. As Gagnon and Simon (1973:69) note, even when young men falsely profess affection to young women in exchange for sex, these same men nonetheless learn to invest in the rhetoric of love and commitment, perhaps later to become what they thought they were only pretending to be. However, for some heterosexual men, dating in adolescence and early adulthood was not merely 'play' but the courtship phase of a long-term commitment and marriage. Collin, white and in his late twenties, took the marriage patterns of his family very seriously when he proposed to his college girlfriend at the age of 21:

> Based on what my parents told me, I thought that you . . . graduate from college, got your career, got married and had kids, the whole dream, and I bought it. I thought I would be married by . . . twenty-two without a doubt . . . I never questioned it.

Fred, a white man in his late forties, had no relationship as stable as Collin's during high school, though he recalls actively framing his short-term romantic encounters and sexual desires in the context of a marriage and family trajectory:

> There was the dating and mating process . . . acting out all sort of ritualistic notions of boy meets girl, we get married, have a family . . . You meet someone, and aside from the sexual attraction . . . I mean it's very easy to imagine what it would be like to be married to this person.

Not all heterosexual men experience their adolescent sexuality in direct reference to marriage. In fact, the attachment of sexual desire to institutionalized social forms and pathways is a process that may occur slowly and unevenly. Steve (mentioned earlier) had a steady and active sex life that started in his early teens, including frequent intercourse with young women whom he barely knew, and no thoughts of long-term commitment. Nonetheless, in high school, Steve dated Lori exclusively for eight months. Steve's parents took a liking to her, and their positive sentiments about the couple were clear. Yet, despite Lori's persistent efforts to establish formal terms for the dyad, Steve avoided discussions about their relationship and broke up with her in search of new sexual partners. Valuing sexual exploration over sexual fidelity, Steve would forgo monogamous relationships until his late twenties.

[. . .]

The intervention of marriage and family institutions in the lives of Collin, Fred, and Steve continued throughout their twenties, though each man navigated them in unique ways. For instance, in his early twenties, Collin grew unsure that he could remain faithful to his fiancée, Tracy. Because Collin believed that marriage and monogamy are inextricably linked, he could not reconcile his external sexual interests and eventually broke off the engagement. During his mid-twenties, Collin casually dated a series of women, finding his status as a bachelor highly pleasurable. Nonetheless, now in his late twenties, Collin regards bachelorhood negatively; that is, he speaks of wanting a relationship, 'something . . . to be a part of'. Recently, Collin reunited with his former fiancée and is now committed to marriage. In making this life transition, Collin draws on monogamous norms attendant to marriage, performing a cost-benefit analysis of his choice. His decision to marry is premised on years of preparation for reward and sacrifice:

There will be times that things outside the marriage will be pulling on me—work, other women; marriage is not all that glamorous . . . but something I want to be a part of.

Like Collin, Fred spent his early twenties in the 1970s indulging in the pleasures of the era, including 'free love', sexual experimentation, and heavy drug use:

There was always a level of romance . . . but they were mostly for sex. And they weren't permanent because . . . I wasn't ready to settle down. I was still a rabble rouser. I mean, they felt very deep and very real, but they also weren't very long.

By his mid- and late twenties, however, Fred's sexual career entered a new phase as his peers began to pair off into engaged and married dyads. This shift is described by Fred less as the result of waning desire for sexual variety than as the mounting weight of marriage bearing down on him:

In the mid-twenties now, everyone starts to say 'O.K., it's time to get married—it's time to get set up. Oh my God, I am an adult!' So at that point in time I say, 'Oh shit, what am I going to do?' I got to settle down . . . racing . . . I need to . . . have like a real relationship. So I met this girl, and after three months she moved into my apartment. It lasted probably a year and a half. Maybe I was in love for the first few months . . . I said to myself, 'Oh wow, this is what it's like to have a wife . . .'

By contrast, in college Steve and his fraternity brothers had no concern for 'settling down', enjoying instead the sexual pleasures of the moment. After graduation, Steve embarked on a series of occupational pursuits, including male dancer and personal trainer. Then, he lived the life of a travelling playboy:

> At this point it just got crazier . . . I was around a whole different lifestyle with the dancers . . . I didn't really have relationships at that point. We'd date, have a good time, enjoy each other's company. Usually two or three dates and then we had sex.

At 26, Steve met Dena—a swinger—and began the most active part of his sexual career that included partner swapping and ménages à trois. However, by the age of 28, Steve began to re-evaluate his lifestyle with Dena and the meaning of their relationship. At this point, too, Steve observed that some of his friends from college were reducing their numbers of sexual partners, replacing these with longer-term, committed relationships and articulating rising expectations of meeting the 'right' woman. Steve's self-concept entered the gravitational pull of marriage and family institutions. Then, Steve began to replace sexual scripts founded on erotic exploration and bachelorhood with scripts premised on monogamy and long-term, dyadic commitment: what he referred to as 'a future':

> . . . I could never see myself being with her for life . . . The lifestyle was too much . . . It lost its appeal . . . I felt like it was fun, but it wasn't going to help me get to the next step . . . a future.

The sexual careers of Collin, Fred, and Steve were negotiated in the shadow of marriage and family institutions during their adolescence and early adulthood. To the extent that more than 90 per cent of Americans marry and have children (Skolnick and Skolnick 1997), the patterned turning points in these men's sexual careers are consistent with the marriage trajectories of most heterosexual men. Though each man in this group actively sought out sexual and emotional satisfaction in unique ways, the structural conditions in which their (hetero) sexual careers were embedded established a template of possibilities and pressures that would ultimately pull them in the direction of long-term, monogamous commitment and circumscribe their selection of sexual scripts.

Maturing Phases of the Sexual Career: 'Getting to the Next Step'

At 29, when Steve grew restless with Dena and the swinger lifestyle, his friends set him up with Lindsey. Over a period of months, the relationship developed in a way that Steve had never experienced before. His interest in Lindsey extends considerably beyond sexual attraction:

> I was never really in love before, but I was in love with her and sure of it . . . Like I had a reason to want to make more money and y'know, focus, because now I had somebody else that I met and I was like . . . I think it's love—I definitely do.

At the time of his interview, Steve had been with Lindsey for nearly four years. Still, the last two years of the relationship had not been without tensions. In fact, Lindsey had made demands on Steve that he had not been fully prepared to meet, including monogamous commitment, financial responsibilities, and ultimately 'the ring':

> We broke up a couple of times, probably because I wasn't giving her what she wanted. She wanted to feel more secure with me and I didn't give her any reason to feel secure. I was all over the place, buying toys . . . but I mean emotionally secure—commitment. [Under his breath he laughs

and mutters] I guess I am just learning how to agree with it . . . I mean . . . She wants the ring, buddy! She wants to get married—always bringing it up.

Whereas Steve reports feeling pressured into marriage, other heterosexual men welcome the opportunity, even after their former marriages failed. Jack, white and in his late forties, expresses renewed interest in marriage after the divorce from his wife and the subsequent loneliness he feels without her. However, he believes that marriage imposes on men sexual restrictions that are 'at war with a lot of viscerally male feelings'. In the course of his 11-year marriage, Jack was not able to remain monogamous beyond the first year. Infidelity occurred not for lack of appreciation of the relationship; quite the contrary, Jack felt that marriage to Kate was good for him, providing stability and support amid the chaos of lost job opportunities, financial difficulties, and a strong propensity to drink. [. . .] Though his chief regret is that Kate found out about one of his affairs, his marriage leaves him pondering the value of monogamy and his own failed role as a husband:

> I'm probably divorced today more than anything because I screwed around and she found out about it . . . I have a lot of trouble being monogamous . . . But I think it could be important, I just don't know how people do it. I mean, I guess it's important from the standpoint of 'trust'; that word always comes up.

By contrast, Eric, white and in his mid-forties, had no problem remaining monogamous to his first wife. However, Eric was ambivalent about the prospects of marriage and, later, resentful of the burdens of married life. After 10 years of monogamous marriage, Eric and his spouse divorced because she felt that his occupational pursuits and musical interests were too great to accommodate the needs of the dyad. [. . .]

As a newly single man, Eric resents the pressure he feels from friends and family to remarry and become a parent. In certain respects, Eric wishes he could lead a life free from marriage and family institutions. Commenting on parenthood, Eric states:

> I can't see myself with that type of responsibility. I'd feel like I was in prison. But there's one frustrating aspect of this. Whenever I speak to people who have children, I consistently find that they're incapable of understanding a person who doesn't want to have children . . . They always . . . have this attitude—it's like condescending . . . that once you've crossed the line and become a parent, that it's so wonderful that they feel sorry for people who haven't done it.

Lane, a single black man in his mid-thirties, echoes Eric's sentiments:

> I want to be married . . . I think most of my friends feel similarly the way I do. But in talking with many of them, it has got its good and bad. They wish for what they don't have. They wish they were single again; but then again, they like their relationships. The married ones say that the single ones, 'oh they just have freedom . . . you can enjoy life as you want to without having to answer to someone.' I guess, less responsibility.

Though Jack finds the married dyad too sexually restrictive and Eric finds marriage and parenthood to be too demanding of his time, Rob, a white, 50-year-old high-school teacher, has managed to have a satisfying, monogamous marriage. [. . .] Twenty years into marriage, Rob reports sustained devotion to his wife and two children: 'I would be lost without them.'

And Lane (already mentioned) hopes to have the kind of marriage that Rob has obtained. Having spent the last 20 years of his life in short-term 'hook-ups' and with prostitutes and now in his mid-thirties, he is prepared to 'take the plunge'. He frames his current interest in monogamous marriage as the end product of a long phase of emotional growth and preparation:

> I'm emotionally ready . . . I don't have a desire to go after meaningless relationships. Now, the gratification is not that important. What's important, now, is meeting that quality lady. [In the future] I'll be with a family, possibly two children, a dog, a cat, living life fully. . . . Who knows, there might be one right around the corner who is the right one.

Steve, Collin, Jack, Eric, Rob, and Lane represent very different heterosexual men encountering the intervention of marriage and family institutions in their adulthood. Though these institutions did not determine sexual or dyadic outcomes, they did exercise substantial effects in shaping their sexual careers. For such men as Rob, Collin, and most married men (75%) in the study, marriage, parenthood, and the informal structural supports that buttress their relationships present the conditions through which they are overriding their non-monogamous sexual interests in favour of committed—if somewhat burdened—marriage and family lives. Jack and Eric, by contrast, like a minority (25%) of ever-married men in the study, reject particular constraints that come with marriage and yet, each has come to experience his sexuality in relation to the marital template, including the norm of monogamy and companionate partnership. [. . .]

Homosexual Men

Sexuality in Adolescence and Young Adulthood: Pushed to the Margins of Straight Communities

Though such heterosexual men as Steve and Collin were first experiencing heterosexual desires that connected them to the larger social structure, gay men such as Paul reached puberty in suburban communities wherein homosexuals were received with dismay and scorn. Try as he might to suppress his desires or rationalize them away, Paul's earliest sexual feelings were unwavering. Given the pervasive institutionalization of heterosexuality in the context of family, peers, church, and community, Paul's sexual feelings created a profound sense of discontinuity from his prior sense of self and worldview.

> I did not believe I could be gay. I just eliminated that option because of its stigma, socially to my peers and friends and what I thought of as society and my future. I did not believe this was a possible way to live . . . I could not accept that I was a young man attracted to other men. That threatened the very foundation of my being.

Chip, black and in his mid-twenties, identified a few potentially accepting friends, but felt this was not enough of a base of support to 'come out' as a teenager:

> My friends always said to me, 'Are you gay?' 'What's going on here?' And I always denied it. And they didn't really pass judgment— my friends-friends. [. . .] Nobody in my church would have been accepting of it . . . I couldn't live with that, y'know . . . People call you a 'fag' or a 'sissy' or a 'girl'. I was never physically assaulted but . . . I treaded on careful water.

Unlike Paul or Chip, Dan, a white man in his late twenties, accepted in early adolescence that he was homosexual but found the extreme homophobic attitudes of his parents and peers too oppressive to act on his sexual desires. Stigmatized at school and thrown out of his house, Dan developed acute anxiety in the process of 'coming out':

> I would say in general it was a frightfully homophobic environment. [At school] there were so many incidents—everything from public humiliation to my locker being defaced, to notes on the blackboard . . . Y'know, the usual high-school torture stories. It wasn't pretty.

In contrast, Tom, white and in his late forties, *did* act on his homosexual desires when he was a teenager. Still, these experiences occurred in public venues, were always anonymous, rarely involved verbal exchanges, and were never discussed with friends or family. Hence, the marginality of his eroticism constrained the substance and form of his sexual experiences. When asked about how he conceived of these interactions, Tom reports denying their significance: 'I rationalized it as just experiencing diversity in life. I compartmentalized it and forgot about it.'

The negative responses of these men to their homoeroticism represent a nearly universal feature in the lives of sexual minority youth (Savin-Williams 1995). Loath to report homosexual desires, gay youth often face fundamental conflicts between their emerging sexual feelings and their prior community attachments. Unlike minorities who may draw from vertical intergenerational bonds in ethnic communities, homosexuals are usually born into heterosexual families that cannot understand or provide support for their child's emerging sexual feelings and identity. Thus, gay youth are at increased risk for substance abuse and suicide (Ferguson, Horwood, and Beautrais 1999).

[. . .]

In total, most gay men in this study (78 per cent), including younger men in their twenties, experienced their homosexuality as a problematic, emerging life pathway without concrete precedent and with limited cultural support. As Chip remarked:

> I think there was a sense of anticipation— like, now, what do I do? Like, is there a ritual? Am I supposed to put something on? Like, I didn't really know what the protocol was.

For these men, being homosexual was more than just a 'road less travelled'; rather, it was a status that pushed them to the margins of their heterosexual communities and forced them to question the relevance of prior sexual scripts and life paths. In such 'unsettled lives' (Swidler 2001:89–107), life presents circumstances for which 'established strategies of action' are no longer relevant or effective. Thus, individuals must seek out new symbolic resources and new settings to anchor and reconstruct the self. As seen further, for gay study participants, the search for identity and community recalls just such a challenge.

Maturing Phases of the Sexual Career: In Search of the 'Citadel of Young Gaydom'

Though heterosexual men of this study reach their late twenties and begin to consider their sexuality seriously in relation to larger institutions and life paths, homosexual men simultaneously confront a divergent set of institutional possibilities and pressures. By the time Paul reached 30, a string of career successes in his public life stood in stark contrast to the profound guilt and depression that accompanied his homosexual trysts.

Consequently, at 31, he sought out psychotherapy and received anti-depressant medication. Within a year, Paul's depression lifted, and he first imagined the possibility of living his life as a gay man. But how could he do this in suburban Pennsylvania, in the setting of old community attachments, heterosexual friendship networks, and business ties? It was inconceivable. Thus, Paul made periodic trips to Manhattan in search of a safe space to explore his budding gay identification.

His travels to an urban gay community represent a journey that generations of homosexuals have undertaken in pursuit of sexual freedom and self-acceptance. Located in large urban centres, gay ghettos function like a 'gay Israel' (Fitzgerald 1986:48), supporting homoerotic sociality and protecting their inhabitants from the insults of heterosexism and homophobia. Perhaps the single most critical institutional formation that grew out of and facilitated the intensification of modern urban gay culture has been the gay bar and bathhouse (Murray 1996). Operating within a closely bound territory and with a shared clientele, gay bars, nightclubs, bathhouses, gyms, and the streets that connect them constitute the spatial nodes of an urban gay sexual field.

Paul's exodus to Manhattan's downtown gay sexual field—what he termed 'the citadel of young gaydom'—served as one of the most profound turning points of his life:

> So I started coming every weekend—and just embracing it! [Paul's voice becomes elevated and hurried with excitement.] And it was like wild! I was just like free! I mean the first weekend I was here [in Manhattan] I went to the Eagle, and I went to the Spike, and I went to the Lure! And I was like 'wow!'—I am walking up Eighth Avenue being exhilarated. I am in the deep West Village, seeing these huge, massive guys hugging and kissing while

roller-blading and I just couldn't stop smiling! Everywhere—at the bus, at the train station, at the ATM machines, in restaurants on the streets, in the park—I mean everywhere, there was this complete acceptance and normalization of everything that I had thought was deviant and wrong. It was wonderful! [Paul laughs with joy.]

Invigorated by his new experiences, Paul sought out gay bars, nightclubs, and bathhouses, using these as launch pads into gay life. Within two years, Paul relocated to Brooklyn, acquired gay friends, and estimates he had sex with 60 sexual partners per year, most of whom he met in Manhattan at the gym or at bars. At 35, Paul has 'come out' of the closet and 'come in' to the urban gay sexual field with a vengeance.

Gary, a white college professor in his late thirties, also came to Manhattan in his early thirties to escape the homophobic conditions of his home in Minnesota. Having fought his homosexual desires throughout his teens and twenties, Gary once believed that homosexuals were pathological deviants and their lifestyle abhorrent. However, when a career opportunity arose in Manhattan, Gary called off his engagement to Tina, his fiancée of four years. Once in Manhattan, Gary began to explore his previously taboo homosexual desires. Thus, Gary recalculated what life would be like as a gay man:

> I didn't think too much about politics. But I mean, I knew that, O.K., if I am going to be gay, I am not going to be married. The whole children thing—well there goes the kids! . . . There's no kids in the picture! . . . And I fully believed that a monogamous relationship was far less possible.

Immersing himself in the sexual institutions of the gay ghetto, Gary sought out an emotionally fulfilling gay lifestyle. Unlike Paul, however, Gary does not feel the same degree of identification or satisfaction with the downtown gay sexual field. Though he enjoys sexual exploration, he also reports frustration with what he perceives to be the non-monogamous sexual ethic of the gay 'scene'. [. . .]

In his mid-thirties, Gary had a three-year monogamous relationship but, after the break-up, he found himself in the same situation as before: lots of available sexual partners but few men willing to invest in a monogamous relationship. Though this may have been more acceptable to him at a younger age, Gary—now nearing 40—is both hopeful and discouraged about the viability of finding a monogamous partner:

> As I got more familiar with the gay community and the gay culture, just realizing, y'know, would I ever be able to have a monogamous relationship with anyone? That was elusive—that concept, with a man, in New York, with someone I was attracted to and really happy with. That seemed elusive to me. Hearing people breaking up, my own experiences—I'd meet somebody, have sex with them, call them to have a date, and nothing. [Gary's voice grows angry.] I mean, I don't know how many times I went through that, y'know? It was like a revolving door.

Even as many urban gay men seek out and are processed through the social institutions of the downtown sexual field, each man actively chooses the quality of his participation. However, individuals who make sexual and dyadic choices that are inconsistent with these institutions provide an instructive example of its influence on sexual practice and self-concept. Jim, for instance, a white man in his early twenties, illustrates the 'push' of Manhattan's gay

sexual field in his efforts to resist its influences. Jim often socializes with friends at bars and nightclubs. Yet, he reports feeling different from his friends, particularly with respect to sexual practices. He frames this difference as a problem that he struggles to resolve:

> I feel uptight. I feel like I need to relax. There are times that I wish I could just chill and mess around with people . . . I am sort of frustrated with myself and my inability to do that.

When asked to clarify these feelings, Jim wrestles between thinking that he is hung up about his homosexuality and that his sensibilities are simply different from those of his friends.

> I just wish I was more . . . I don't know . . . I don't know if I am hung up . . . I don't think it's an issue of being gay . . . I seem . . . I am reluctant to just 'go for it'. Partly because that's what I see around me, there's a part of it that I find exciting.

Jim's reluctance to engage in the casual sexual practices of his peers is reflected in the number of partners he reports in an average year—in the single digits. Asked whether he envisioned himself in the future either as a single man or in a relationship, Jim wavers, citing what he perceives to be the lack of dyadic 'know-how' in the gay community he has come to know:

> I think it would be nice to have someone eventually I could connect with . . . I think I would like to find that someday. It just feels that everyone is always looking for the next best thing . . . y'know . . . I think because there isn't a model in the gay community of steady relationships. No one knows how to do it . . . In the

gay community, there's always a way out. There aren't many people who are like, 'No, we need to stay together.' Usually, it's like, 'Oh, I'm attracted to somebody else.'

Derek (mentioned earlier) also expresses trepidations about Manhattan gay life, particularly with regard to pressures he perceives toward non-monogamy.

> I would have to see [about an open dyad]. I would be open to discussing it. I don't know how I would work in an open relationship . . . I still have problems with it. I only take this attitude because I look at what is going on in the community and I see very few monogamous relationships. That's the only reason I'd say I'm even open to considering it.

If such men as Gary, Jim, and Derek find in urban gay life obstacles to realizing monogamous relationships, others find that they can build the conditions under which a new relationship forms. In these instances, the possibilities of dyadic innovation inspire a shift in prior commitments to monogamous norms. Kevin, black and in his late twenties, describes how a relationship with a sexually adventurous boyfriend constituted a turning point that exposed him to alternative ways of thinking about the value of monogamy for the dyad:

> In the beginning, when we started this [open relationship], I was jealous. And then it wore off quickly when I started seeing the benefits for myself . . . Stan introduced me to the bathhouse. I think because of him I became more involved in the whole gay sexual experience. He told me that in every relationship he's ever been in he after a while just wants to have

sex with other people . . . So I would come to New York City to visit him, and if I was here for an extended period of time, he would have no problem letting me borrow his bathhouse club card . . . So there were perks on both ends.

Some gay men draw on their experiences with open dyads to re-imagine traditional dyadic arrangements, including the marital unit, with its implicit, if not fully realized, attachment to a monogamous norm. Thus, Andy, black and in his mid-twenties, views open dyads as the optimal arrangement, even in marriage—a perspective he credits to urban gay life:

> I would be interested in marriage [to a man] . . . It would not be a traditional monogamous one, though. It would possibly be more like the relationship I have. More and more, I don't understand how anyone could expect [that] the person they're marrying is never going to sleep with another person, or why that should have to be the case.

Jamie and Peter, both white and in their late twenties and early thirties, respectively, have enjoyed an open relationship for five years, after a first year of monogamy. Their relationship is not unlike the kind of marital unit that Andy imagines: Both partners articulate a commitment to being together; neither partner expects sexual fidelity from the other:

> In our first year together we were only with each other and we both felt that it was important to do that, plus we really didn't have any desire to go outside the relationship. But after a while you just feel strong enough in your relationship and in your bond together that sexual desire for other guys doesn't get in the way of that.

Asked to describe the open dyad, Peter enumerates the rules of exchange but, also, a process of negotiation wherein the partners discovered the limits of their comfort zone:

> Usually if we play it's with a guy that both of us have seen and like, maybe at a club or the gym, or even just out around town [Chelsea]. We'll play together, usually not more than once or twice, though there was recently one guy [Rick] that we would fool around with on a regular basis, but that got a little complicated after a while, and so we made the decision to stop seeing him. [. . .]

If Peter and Jamie have negotiated a successful open relationship, other men sit at the cusp of balancing commitment, sexual freedom, and dyadic innovation. Ed, a white man in his mid-thirties, is in a five-year monogamous relationship with Will, a former minister. When Ed was single, he felt unfulfilled with the erotic marketplace and spent his leisure time in alternative pursuits, including theatre, a cycling club, and church events, where he eventually met his current partner. Ed still prefers these latter outlets, as they are more hospitable to his relationship and in greater alignment with his interests. [. . .] Recently, his boyfriend, Will, expressed interest in finding a third sexual partner. Though Will has only 'joked' about this possibility, he is vocal about the men he finds attractive, and he receives validation for these desires when the couple socializes at a gay bar among friends who are single or in open relationships. Somewhat reluctantly, Ed concedes, one future evening may bring an opportunity to open up the dyad to new possibilities.

As for Paul, when asked about his current interest in establishing a relationship with a man, his response represents a marked departure from his years spent in the closet. In fact, Paul might very well pursue a long-term relationship with a male partner. Such an arrangement is now imaginable. However, in the same breath, he also reports a growing aversion to dating. He likens dates to 'a tiring performance' in which he has to be 'charming and affable'. As Paul joyfully observes, there is a nearly limitless supply of attractive guys on every street corner in Chelsea, many of whom are looking for or are receptive to a sexual encounter: 'What's there to stop them?' This has prompted Paul's most recent normative turning point, as he re-evaluates the value of monogamy. When once-monogamous dyadic commitment represented the staple of building a solid relationship, he is now less certain of this. As with Andy and Peter, plenty of Paul's gay friends have formalized open relationships and negotiated non-monogamy, and many of them find this to be an appealing dyadic innovation from the traditional, heteronormative construction.

Discussion

To the extent that prehomosexual and preheterosexual boys undergo the same ranges of socialization and community attachments in childhood, it is not surprising that both gay and straight men inherit the expectations of marriage and parenthood. Indeed, despite the diminution of the traditional nuclear family structure in the late twentieth century, most of the US population continues to marry, remarry if divorced, and procreate (Bramlett and Mosher 2001). In this study, regardless of the dyadic preferences or marital intentions of heterosexual men during adolescence and adulthood, marriage and family institutions served as a master template around which sexuality developed and was negotiated.

[. . .]

On the whole, heterosexual men in this study described sexual careers that were profoundly shaped by the institution of marriage, as it produced a pull out of sexual nightlife, a marked reduction in sexual partner change, a reining-in of the libido, and a transformation in script appropriation from those emphasizing bachelorhood and sexual exploration to scripts emphasizing paternity, monogamy, and conjugal status. However, rather than having a uniform effect on the men in this study, marriage more accurately provided a package of possibilities and constraints, a menu of options around which the sexual career was organized and navigated.

By contrast, homosexual men were categorically excluded from marriage; yet, this exclusion was no less significant than the paramount importance of marriage for heterosexuals. In fact, precisely because marriage and family represent fundamental milestones in American life, many gay men experienced their homosexuality as a fundamental problem, triggering developmental discontinuity and the dismantling of formerly held cultural and existential assumptions. For these men, irrespective of race, adolescence was a time during which the impact of homosexual status set in, including the realization that the marriage and family trajectories of their own families or those prescribed by religious institutions and the larger community were no longer applicable. Moreover, anti-gay sentiments in families, at school, in churches and synagogues, and in neighbourhoods more broadly only confirmed their outsider status. These were the conditions on which 'unsettled lives' took form (Swidler 2001). As with Weber's (1946) 'switchmen', homosexual identification directed these men toward an alternative set of train tracks into adulthood. However, where would these tracks lead and with what result?

For the men in this study, homosexual desires led them to Manhattan in search of a 'gay self'. There, these men sought out key entry points into gay sociality through the downtown gay sexual field, with its nightlife centre and overlapping, semi-coordinated social institutions, networks, and associated urban streets. [. . .] Thus, the search for a gay self brought with it newly structured sexual options and norms within the social institutions of the gay social world.

Heterosexual men, too, such as Steve and Lane, indicate the ways in which bars and nightclubs encourage a consumptive sexual ethos. However, as their cases aptly demonstrate, kinship institutions compete with these sites over time, producing opposing channels for anchoring the self and the intimate dyad. Indeed, marriage and family do not simply provide an alternative path; rather, they establish social conditions that pull heterosexual men toward a circumscribed future—and penalize deviation. [. . .]

Taken together, the life histories recorded in this study illustrate the profound impact of marriage, and its absence, on the sexual careers of heterosexual and homosexual men, respectively. By dint of nothing more than their sexual orientation, these individuals encountered divergent institutionalized life pathways that installed contrasting navigational reference points, pushing them into divergent sexual career trajectories. However, if differential access to marriage provides contrasting pressures—toward reduced sexual exploration and monogamy for the one and increased sexual exploration and non-monogamy in the other—the narratives of both sets of men reveal shared tensions around the problem of intimacy, commitment, and self-fulfillment. Indeed, if matrimony facilitates the pairing of emotional intimacy and sexual desire, it at the same time valorizes a mode of commitment that leaves some heterosexual men restless and unsatisfied, with the ironic effect of destabilizing the dyad. Yet, conversely, the sexual freedoms associated with urban gay life provide their own kind of constraint as some homosexual men struggle to find satisfying committed relationships. In short, neither access to nor exclusion from the institution of marriage produces sexual careers free of conflict; rather, both structural positions set into motion struggles for self-fulfillment in the context of life paths that facilitate the satisfaction of some desires while frustrating or precluding altogether the realization of others.

Conclusion

As the issue of gay marriage takes centre stage in the United States, questions regarding the impact of matrimony have renewed salience. This article examines the role of marriage in the life history and demonstrates how marriage continues to serve as an institution of paramount significance for the development of sexual and dyadic norms and practices among both heterosexual and homosexual men.

It should be cautioned that the findings of this study are suggestive and not intended as a definitive statement about the general impact of marriage—and its absence—on larger segments of the population. For instance, inferences regarding the impact of differential access to marriage on heterosexual and homosexual women is beyond the scope of this article. That differences between genders may exist would not be surprising, in part because men and women may differ in their physiological responses to sexual stimuli, psychosexual development, gender and sexual socialization, sexual stigma, and socio-economic status, all potentially critical factors in shaping the sexual career. Similarly, class and ethnoracial statuses may mediate the impact of kinship institutions in ways that the present middle-class, highly educated sample of black and white men cannot illuminate. Further, the fact that both black and white homosexual study participants show similarities in certain aspects of gay urban resocialization is not meant to collapse these two groups in terms of other dimensions of the sexual career, including the formation of social networks and sociosexual status within the downtown sexual field (Green 2005).

Following the lead of some Western countries, the United States may legalize same-sex marriage in the coming decade. Combined with more favourable adoption policies and the continued erosion of compulsory heterosexuality (Rich 1990), the sexual careers of homosexual and heterosexual men may bear fewer differences. Less certain, however, is the extent to which same-sex marriage will yield traditional marital forms. Indeed, even as a same-sex marriage movement is well underway in the United States, the historical exclusion from marriage may provide the structural foundation on which same-sex spouses will re-imagine matrimony. In this sense, same-sex marriage may constitute less a fossilized dyadic arrangement than a late modern point of departure.

Notes

1. All respondents self-identified as 'heterosexual' or 'homosexual'.
2. Recruitment of black homosexual men met the goals of the sampling frame, but recruitment of black heterosexual men did not. Consequently, the study does not permit a comparison of black men between sexual orientations.

References

Baca Zinn, Maxine. 1997. 'Families on the Fault Line'. pp. 297–315 in *Family in Transition,* edited by A. Skolnick and J. Skolnick. New York: Longman.

Bachu, Amaru, and Martin O'Connell. 2000. 'Fertility of American Women'. In *Current Population Reports.* Washington, DC: US Census Bureau.

Bane, M.J. 1976. *Here to Stay.* New York: Basic Books.

Bech, Henning. 1997. *When Men Meet.* Chicago: University of Chicago Press.

Bianchi, Suzanne M., and Casper M. Lynne. 2000. 'American Families'. In *Population Bulletin* 55:4. Washington, DC: Population Reference Bureau.

Bramlett, Matthew D., and William D. Mosher. 2001. 'First Marriage Dissolution, Divorce, and Remarriage: United States'. *Advance Data from Vital and Health Statistics, 323.* Hyattsville, MD: National Center for Health Statistics.

Bumpass, Larry, James A. Sweet, and Andrew Cherlin. 1991. 'The Role of Cohabitation in Declining Rates of Marriage'. *Journal of Marriage and Family* 53:913–27.

Cherlin, Andrew. 2002. *Public and Private Families: An Introduction,* 3rd edn. New York: McGraw Hill.

Coleman, M., L. Ganong, and M. Fine. 2000. 'Reinvestigating Remarriage: Another Decade of Progress'. *Journal of Marriage and Family* 62:1288–307.

Coontz, Stephanie. 2005. *Marriage, a History: From Obedience to Intimacy or How Love Conquered Marriage.* New York: Viking.

DeCecco, John. 1990. 'The Homosexual as Acts or Persons: A Conversation with John DeCecco'. pp. 132–69 in *Homosexuality as Behavior and Identity,* vol. 2, *Dialogues of Sexual Revolution,* edited by L.D. Mass. New York: Harrington Park.

Elder, Glen H., Jr. 1985. 'Perspectives on the Lifecourse'. pp. 23–49 in *Lifecourse Dynamics,* edited by G. Elder. Ithaca, NY: Cornell University Press.

Ferguson, D.M., J. Horwood, and AL. Beautrais. 1999. 'Is Sexual Orientation Related to Mental Health Problems and Suicidality in Young People?' *Archives of General Psychiatry* 56:876–80.

Fitzgerald, Frances. 1986. *Cities on a Hill.* New York: Simon and Shuster.

Fowlkes, Martha. 1994. 'Single Worlds and Homosexual Lifestyles: Patterns of Sexuality and Intimacy'. pp. 151–86 in *Sexuality across the Life Course,* edited by A. Rossi. Chicago: University of Chicago Press.

Gagnon, John, and William Simon. 1973. *Sexual Conduct.* Chicago: Aldine.

Goldstein, Joshua. 1999. 'The Leveling of Divorce in the United States'. *Demography* 36:409–14.

Goldstein, Joshua R., and Catherine T. Kennedy. 2001. 'Marriage Delayed or Marriage Forgone? New Cohort Forecasts of First Marriage for US Women'. Paper presented at the annual meeting of the Population Association of America, Los Angeles, California.

Green, Adam Isaiah. 2005. 'The Kind that All White Men Want: Race and the Role of Subtle Status Characteristics in a Sample of Urban Gay Men'. *Social Theory and Health* 3:206–27.

Herdt, Gilbert, and Andrew Boxer. 1992. 'Introduction: Culture, History, and the Course of Gay Men'. pp. 1–28 in *Gay Culture in America: Essays from the Field,* edited by G. Herdt. Boston: Beacon Press.

Kurdek, L., and J.D. Schmitt. 1987. 'Perceived Emotional Support from Families and Friends in Members of Homosexual, Married and Heterosexual Cohabitating Couples'. *Journal of Homosexuality* 14:57–68.

Lamanna, Marry Ann, and Agnes Riedmann. 2003. *Marriage and Families: Making Choices in a Diverse Society*, 8th edn. New York: Wadsworth.

Laumann, Edward, John Gagnon, Robert Michael, and Stuart Michael. 1994. *The Social Organization of Sexuality: Sexual Practices in the United States.* Chicago: University of Chicago Press.

Murray, Stephen. 1996. *American Gay.* Chicago: University of Chicago Press.

Peplau, Letitia A. 1993. 'Lesbian and Gay Relationship'. pp. 395–419 in *Psychological Perspectives on Lesbian and Gay Male Experience,* edited by L. Garnets and D.C. Kimmel. New York: Columbia University Press.

Rechy, John. 1977. *The Sexual Outlaw.* New York: Grove Press.

Rich, Adrienne. 1990. 'Compulsory Heterosexuality and Lesbian Existence'. *Signs* 5:631–60.

Ruggles, Steven. 1994. 'The Origins of African-American Family Structure'. *American Sociological Review* 59:136–51.

Savin-Williams, Ritch. 1995. 'Lesbian, Gay Male, and Bisexual Adolescents'. pp. 165–9 in *Lesbian, Gay, and Bisexual Identities over the Lifespan. Psychological Perspectives,* edited by A.R. D'Augelli and C.J. Patterson. New York: Oxford University Press.

Skolnick Arlene and Jerome Skolnick. 1997. 'Introduction: Family in Transition'. pp. 1–16 in *Family in Transition,* edited by A. Skolnick and J. Skolnick. New York: Longman.

Strauss, Anselm, and Juliet Corbin. 1998. *Basics of Qualitative Research. Techniques and Procedures for Developing Grounded Theory.* Thousand Oaks, CA: Sage.

Swidler, Ann. 2001. *Talk of Love: How Culture Matters.* Chicago: University of Chicago Press.

Watters, John K., and Peter Biernacki. 1989. 'Targeted Sampling: Options and Considerations for the Study of Hidden Populations'. *Social Problems* 36:416–30.

Weber, Max. 1946. 'Bureaucracy'. pp. 196–240 in *From Max Weber,* edited by H. Gerth and C. Wright Mills. New York: Oxford University Press.

Weeks, Jeffrey. 1985. *Sexuality and Its Discontents: Meanings, Myths and Modern Sexualities.* London: Routledge and Kegan Paul.

Weeks, Jeffrey, Brian Heaphy, and Catherine Donovan. 2001. *Same Sex Intimacies: Families of Choice and Other Life Experiments.* New York: Routledge.

Weinberg, Martin, and Collin Williams. 1975. *Male Homosexuality.* New York: Oxford University Press.

Changes in Conjugal Life in Canada: Is Cohabitation Progressively Replacing Marriage?

Céline Le Bourdais and Évelyne Lapierre-Adamcyk with the collaboration of Philippe Pacaut

In the last 30 years, most Western countries have witnessed formidable changes in the foundation of the family institution. Demographic indicators point to a postponement of marriage and to a decline in the proportion of individuals who are likely to marry during their lifetime. Marriage has also been characterized by growing levels of instability, with divorce rates showing that it is not that uncommon among these countries to find that one marriage out of two is likely to dissolve. The dramatic increase in cohabiting unions over the last 30 years—first as a way for young adults to start their conjugal life, and more recently, as an environment in which to start and raise a family—further led researchers to question the 'future of marriage' (title of Jessie Bernard's well-known book and the theme of the 2003 National Council on Family Relations [NCFR] annual conference). Currently, the recognition of same-sex marriage has prompted debates about the meaning of marriage. How has the institution of marriage changed in recent decades, and how do these changes vary across cultures and across countries? [. . .]

One of the ways to document the weakening of marriage and its change in meaning is to look more closely at the progression of cohabitation over time. [. . .] [In this article, we] describe the demographic trends of marriage and cohabitation in Canada, and . . . assess whether cohabitation constitutes a new stage in the progression to marriage or an alternative to marriage altogether. After addressing these issues, we close by discussing possible explanations underlying the observed changes. By contrasting the evolution of demographic behaviours adopted across the different regions in Canada, we show that cohabitation has reached different stages of development in Quebec as opposed to elsewhere in Canada, as formulated by Kiernan (2001). In the former, cohabitation seems now to be nearly indistinguishable from marriage, as it is in Sweden, whereas in the latter, cohabitation is still accepted predominantly as a childless phase of conjugal life, as is the case in the United States.

The Decline of Marriage

Profound changes have transformed the conjugal life of Canadians in recent decades. Figure 1 presents the evolution of total female marriage rates, calculated by combining marriage vital statistics and census population counts, and exemplifies the fall of marriage over the last 30 years. [. . .]

As can be seen in Figure 1, marriage was still very popular throughout the 1960s; more than nine women out of ten would marry over the course of their life. In the mid-1970s, marriage started to lose ground progressively, and by the turn of the century, just slightly over half of women were expected to marry in Canada. In Quebec, the fall was far more drastic: From nearly 90 per cent in the 1960s, the proportion of women who would marry at least once in their life fell to 50 per cent in 1984, and only one woman in three is now expected to marry according to most recent data. The gap separating Quebec's women from their counterparts living elsewhere in Canada widened throughout the period studied as Quebecers deserted marriage. By 2000, 60 per cent of women living

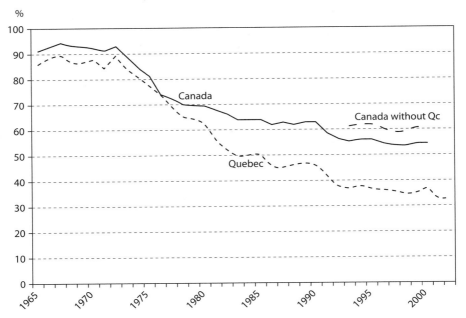

Figure 1 Total Female Marriage Rate, Canada and Quebec, 1965–2002

Sources: Duchesne (2003), Dumas and Péron (1992), Dumas and Bélanger (1994), Bélanger (2003).

outside Quebec were expected to marry at least once, compared with less than 40 per cent of those living in Quebec. When measured for men, total marriage rates are generally slightly lower but follow similar trends.

The decline of marriage has also been accompanied by a postponement of the age at first marriage. When marriage was widespread, it was relatively precocious, with an average age of 25.4 years among men and 22.5 years among women in Canada in 1960 (26.0 and 23.5 in Quebec, respectively; Duchesne, 2003; Dumas & Péron, 1992). Now that marriage has become less popular, individuals marry approximately five years later. In 2001, the age at first marriage was 30.2 and 28.2 years, respectively, for men and women in Canada (30.6 and 28.8 years in Quebec in 2002; Duchesne, 2003; Statistics Canada, 2003a).

Not only has marriage become less popular but it has also become more unstable since the adoption of the Divorce Law by the Canadian Parliament in 1968. In 1970, the total divorce rate was approximately 10 per cent, indicating that one marriage in ten would eventually end in divorce. Although fluctuating depending on the courts' availability and because of modifications to the Divorce Law introduced in 1985, the divorce rate increased steadily in the following years until it reached a plateau in the 1990s. Thirty years after divorce became more easily accessible, the rate has multiplied by four. In Canada as a whole, nearly 40 per cent of couples are expected to divorce. Interestingly, in Quebec, where marriage is least popular, it is most fragile, with nearly one couple out of two likely to divorce (Lapierre-Adamcyk & Le Bourdais, 2004).

Although marriage is on the decline and divorce is on the rise, one cannot conclude that conjugal life has receded to the same extent. From survey data, we know that the majority of Canadian men and women wish 'to have a lasting relationship as a couple' (Lapierre-Adamcyk, Le Bourdais & Marcil-Gratton, 1999). Hence, the decline of marriage has been mostly offset by the growth of cohabiting unions that began in Western Europe after May 1968. In this first phase, cohabitation emerged as an 'avant-garde phenomenon' that was adopted by a small fraction of the young, and often well-educated, population (Kiernan, 2001).

The Growth of Cohabiting Unions as a Form of Conjugal Life

Because of its informal and unstable nature, the importance of cohabitation is often difficult to measure and varies depending on point of view. In Canada, cohabiting unions were recognized as an alternative form of conjugal life from the beginning. As early as the 1971 census, long before cohabitation had become commonplace, cohabiting couples were instructed to consider themselves as 'married'; they were thus counted as *couples,* but they remained invisible among the larger number of married couples (Le Bourdais & Juby, 2001). In 1981, Statistics Canada maintained this instruction on marital status, but included *common-law partner* as a category to describe the relationship of individuals with the householder, permitting estimation of the number of cohabiting unions for heads of household. The 1986 census was the first to collect direct information on both marital and common-law status of all household members, and to allow a full count of cohabiting couples. [. . .]

Figure 2 presents the percentages of couples who were identified as cohabiting across Canada in three different censuses. In 1981, 6 per cent of couples were cohabiting in Canada. The proportion varied from 3.4 per cent in the Atlantic region to roughly 7 per cent in the provinces of Quebec and British Columbia. In the 1970s, cohabitation was still a relatively new phenomenon. [. . .]

From that point on, the evolution of cohabitation took a very different course in Quebec from the rest of Canada. During the 1980s, the percentage of couples who were cohabiting in Quebec more than doubled to 19 per cent in 1991. The increase continued unabatedly throughout the 1990s. In 20 years, the proportion of couples who were cohabiting was multiplied by more than 4 in Quebec, but only by 1.9 in British Columbia. [. . .] As of 2001, the popularity of cohabitation in Quebec is as widespread as it is in Sweden, where 30 per cent of couples are cohabiting, and clearly greater than in France (17.5%) or the United States (8.2%; Statistics Canada, 2002b). The percentage in Canada outside Quebec (12%) falls between these two countries.

Census data give an idea of the percentage of individuals who are cohabiting at a given point in time. In large part, these percentages are composed of young individuals who chose cohabitation to start their conjugal life, but they underestimate the extent to which this phenomenon occurs because cohabitating individuals can marry or separate before the census date. Moreover, as divorce rose, census data also increasingly included proportions of individuals who opted for a consensual union after a first marriage dissolved.

Figure 3 presents the cumulative probabilities (derived from life table estimates) that women experience a first union, through marriage or cohabitation, in five different cohorts. This figure first shows that the vast majority of individuals

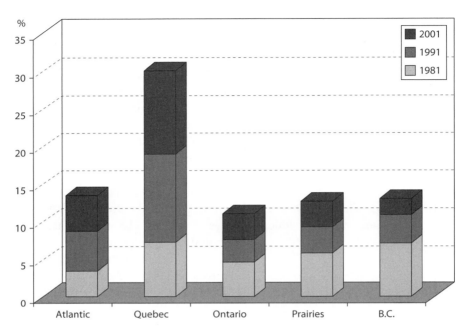

Figure 2 Percentages of Couples Cohabiting in Canada by Region of Residence, 1981, 1991, 2001

Source: Statistics Canada for 1981: *Canadian Families: diversity and change* (cat. 12F0061XPF). For 1991, *1996 Census* (table 93F0022XDB96008). For 2001, *2001 Census* (table 97F005XCB01006).

across all cohorts still form conjugal unions: Well above 90 per cent of women born in the 1960s or earlier had formed a union at least once in their life, and 84 per cent of those born in the 1970s had already done so by age 29.

How women started their conjugal life changed drastically across cohorts, however. In the oldest cohort born in the 1930s (ages 60–69 in 2001), 93 per cent of women married directly, and only 2 per cent began by living with a cohabiting partner. The percentage of women cohabiting in their first union throughout the 1970s rose to 27 per cent among those born in the 1950s, and to 42 per cent among those born in the 1960s. Among the youngest cohorts who entered their first union during the 1990s, cohabitation has become the favoured way to start conjugal life. By age 29, 53 per cent of women had formed a

consensual union, as compared with only 31 per cent who had married directly. The percentage of women who will eventually marry directly in the youngest cohorts should be slightly higher as they get older, however, because age at first marriage is increasing as individuals postpone marriage. The figures presented for Canada as a whole are similar to those observed in the United States, where 43 per cent of the first unions concluded by women in the early 1980s and 54 per cent of those formed in the early 1990s began with cohabitation (Bumpass & Lu, 2000).

[. . .]

Choosing marriage (or cohabitation) to begin conjugal life affects, but does not preclude, the likelihood that women experience cohabitation (or marriage) subsequently. On the one hand, although only 8 per cent of women born in the

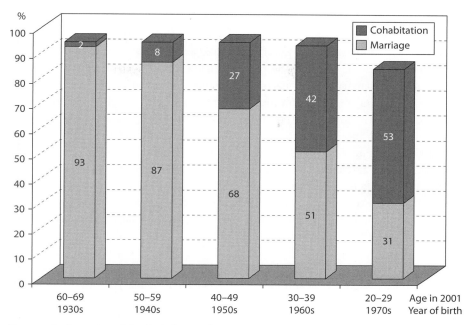

Figure 3 Cumulated Probabilities That Women in Canada Enter Their First Union through Marriage or Cohabitation, by Age Cohorts

Source: 2001 General Social Survey on Family; Statistics Canada (2002a), Figure 1.

1940s experienced cohabitation at the beginning of their conjugal life (see Figure 3), another 11 per cent did so after their first marriage dissolved (Statistics Canada, 2002a). On the other hand, 78 per cent of women born during the 1960s had married at least once, compared with 51 per cent who had married without first cohabiting. Put differently, older generations of women were more likely to experience cohabitation later in the course of their life, after marrying young, whereas more recent generations are more inclined to marry later—if they ever do—after having first cohabited. It is difficult to forecast the proportion of women who will eventually marry among the youngest cohorts. One thing is certain, though: It is likely to remain quite low in Quebec, where the total marriage rate has been well below 40 per cent for more than 10 years.

As we have seen, cohabitation has progressively replaced marriage, at least in Quebec, as a way to start conjugal life. We know from various studies, however, that cohabiting unions are more short-lived than marriages, and that they have become even less stable over time (Bumpass & Lu, 2000; Dumas & Bélanger, 1997; Statistics Canada, 2002a). A partial explanation for the rising instability of cohabiting unions can perhaps be found in the wide diversity of existing unions. For a significant proportion of couples, cohabitation has replaced 'going steady' relationships, which do not necessarily involve any long-term engagement. For another group, cohabiting unions constitute a 'prelude to marriage' or a 'trial marriage'—that is, a period in which to test the solidity of the relationship while completing schooling and attaining professional achievement (Villeneuve-Gokalp, 1991). As cohabitation has become more socially acceptable, it seems to have attracted larger numbers of less committed couples. As a result, the proportion of cohabitors who married their partners within three to five years of the beginning of the union has decreased, while the proportion of those who separated has increased (Bumpass & Lu, 2000; Turcotte & Bélanger, 1997; for a review, see Smock & Gupta, 2001). Concomitantly, the percentage of cohabiting unions that endured longer than three to five years has increased, both in Canada and in the United States, partly countervailing the trend toward rising instability. Again, the situation in Quebec differs from that observed elsewhere in Canada. Cohabitations are of longer duration in Quebec, and they are less likely to transform into marriage (Le Bourdais & Marcil-Gratton, 1996; Turcotte & Bélanger, 1997).

Transitions outside cohabiting unions tend to occur relatively early after the union starts. Hence, two years after the beginning of the union, the likelihood of experiencing separation or marriage falls quite abruptly (Brown, 2000). These results tend to suggest that cohabitation, in Canada as in the United States, has successfully completed its second phase; it is 'either a prelude to or a probationary period where the strength of the relationship may be tested prior to committing to marriage and is predominantly a childless phase' (Kiernan, 2001, p. 5). The passage to the next stage requires cohabitation to become an alternative to marriage, allowing individuals to fulfill both conjugal and parental roles.

The Growth of Cohabiting Unions as a Form of Family Life

The percentage of non-marital births has increased sharply over the last 20 years. In the early 1980s, approximately one birth in six

occurred outside marriage in Canada (Marcil-Gratton, 1998). By 2000, nearly one child in three was born to an unmarried mother (Statistics Canada, 2003b). These figures roughly compare to those observed in the United States (Cherlin, 2004), but increasingly differ from the situation experienced in Quebec, where nearly 60 per cent of all registered births in 2000 were to unmarried mothers (Duchesne, 2003). [. . .]

To be born outside marriage does not necessarily mean to be born to a single mother. In fact, the percentage of children born to an unknown or non-declared father was only 3.4 per cent in 2002 in Quebec, a slight decrease from previous years (Duchesne, 2003). This suggests that nonmarital births are more closely associated with the decline of marriage and the progression of cohabitation than with an increase of formerly 'illegitimate' births.

[. . .]

In Kiernan's (2001) third stage of the partnership transition, cohabitation is socially acceptable, and 'becoming a parent is no longer restricted to marriage' (p. 5). Now that cohabitation has become the modal way in which to give birth, the transition to this third stage seems to have been successfully achieved in Quebec. Elsewhere in Canada, however, if half of children born in the late 1990s were born to parents who had cohabited, only 30 per cent (15% out of 51%) were born within a cohabiting union. This suggests that cohabiting unions have not yet become an alternative setting in which to become a parent, and that women who become pregnant while living with a cohabiting partner will tend to legalize their union before the birth of the child. In a way, the evolution of family life in Canada outside Quebec parallels that observed in the United States, where only a small fraction of the increase in non-marital births was due to a decline in the likelihood that pregnant cohabiting mothers will marry before the birth of their child (Raley, 2001). The greatest portion of the increase seems to be attributable to rising percentages of women cohabiting, and to the greater likelihood that single pregnant women start cohabiting (rather than marry). These results led Raley to conclude, along with Manning (1993), that cohabitation was perhaps becoming a trial marriage among singles, but that it was still too early to conclude that it had become a substitute for marriage.

If cohabitation is to be considered a substitute for marriage, it needs to provide not only a family setting in which to give birth but also a lasting arrangement in which to raise children. Previous studies have shown that cohabiting couples giving birth to a child appear to be more stable than childless unions (Wu & Balakrishnan, 1995). But are these couples as solid as married couples with children? Can we expect the risk of family disruption to vary according to historical context—that is, in relation to the importance and acceptance of cohabitation as a way to start family life? Can we expect the gap in family disruptions between marriages and cohabitations to narrow as cohabitation has become the modal way in which to form a family in Quebec?

The distribution of children according to the family setting in which they live at a given moment provides an indirect indication of the duration of families across the country, depending upon the type of parental union. In 2001 in Canada, over 80 per cent of children aged 0–14 years were living with two parents who were either their biological parents, adoptive parents, or stepparents. Census data do not allow distinction among biological families, adoptive families, and stepfamilies because respondents are instructed to declare as 'son' or 'daughter' their biological children, adopted children, or stepchildren. Between 17 per cent and 20 per cent were living with a single parent, usually the mother (8 times out of 10). Outside Quebec,

the percentage of children living with cohabiting parents was relatively low, ranging between 7 per cent in Ontario and 11 per cent in the Atlantic provinces. It was clearly higher in Quebec, where it reached 30 per cent, reflecting the longer duration of cohabiting unions in this province (Statistics Canada, 2002c). [. . .]

The only way to directly compare the stability of marriages and cohabiting unions with children is to use longitudinal data and to begin at the moment a child is born. This is precisely the approach we took in two studies of family disruption in Canada (Desrosiers & Le Bourdais, 1996; Le Bourdais, Neill & Marcil-Gratton, 2000). The most recent study was based on retrospective information collected from respondents to the 1995 General Social Survey, who had become mothers for the first time in an intact family (i.e., within a union with their child's father) between 1970 and 1995. We examined the relative risks of family disruption faced by these women, according to their conjugal situation at the time of first birth and their region of residence (Quebec vs. elsewhere in Canada). We used a proportional hazards model to control for a series of variables that were shown to be associated with conjugal and family instability (age of the mother at the beginning of the union, period in which the child was born, mother's level of education and presence in the labour market), and we introduced an interaction variable that combined the effects of region of residence and type of union to allow the effect of conjugal status on the risk of separation to vary across the two regions of residence. We wanted to evaluate whether the higher risks of separation attached to cohabiting families were similar across the country, even though this family type is far more numerous in Quebec, and to check how they compared, within each region, in relation to married families.

Table 1 presents the results of this analysis. Compared with the families formed directly

Table 1 Relative Risks of Family Disruption Among 'Intact' Families, by Type of Union and Region of Residence at Birth of First Child

| | REGION OF RESIDENCE | |
	QUEBEC	CANADA WITHOUT QUEBEC
TYPE OF UNION		
Direct marriage	1.45	1.00
Marriage following cohabitation	1.46	1.66
Cohabitation	3.47	4.94

through marriage in Canada outside Quebec (the reference category), married couples who lived together before marriage appeared to have a 1.66 greater chance of separating following the birth of their first child. In other words, starting conjugal life through cohabitation rather than marriage increased by two-thirds the risk of separation among parents who had already married by the time their first child was born. Conjugal instability was much greater among cohabiting-couple families. For those who were still cohabiting at the birth of the child, the risk of disruption was nearly five times higher than that observed for those who had married directly, even after controlling for mothers' sociodemographic characteristics (i.e., highest level of education completed at the time of the survey; preconjugal conception; age and school enrollment status at the beginning of the union; period of family formation; employment status; cumulated duration of employment; and cumulated number of work interruptions through the family episode).

Compared with their counterparts living elsewhere in Canada, Quebec families formed within direct marriage appeared more unstable, with a risk of separation that is 45 per cent greater. In Quebec, however, married couples who lived together before marriage formed equally stable families as those who did not. Cohabiting families in Quebec appeared to be more fragile than

those whose parents had married by the time the first child was born, but the difference between the two groups was not nearly as large as that observed elsewhere in Canada. In Quebec, cohabiting-couple families were 2.5 times (relative risk of 3.47 compared with 1.45) more likely to separate than those married directly, whereas they were 5 times more likely to do so in the rest of Canada.

As the context in which families are formed changed—that is, as cohabitation became progressively more acceptable and widespread—the risk of separation associated with the different types of unions also changed. [. . .] [A]s direct marriage becomes increasingly unusual, it no longer provides a guarantee of stability, and as cohabitation becomes more widespread, it becomes more stable. For these reasons, the promotion of marriage as the only way to raise a family may have little value and, of greater importance, could well result in the opposite—that is, in a desertion of family life altogether, as seems to have occurred in countries such as Italy or Japan, where fertility has fallen to a very low level (Livi-Bacci & Salvini, 2000).

Cohabiting Unions in Canada: Rights and Benefits for Adults and Children

Canada adopted a very pragmatic approach in relation to the growth of cohabitation. Just as the statistical agency was prone to recognizing cohabiting couples as the equivalent of married couples from the beginning, cohabitors rapidly gained access to social programs and benefits. In the absence of a contract or ceremony to clearly mark the start of the union, a criterion of duration (usually 1–3 years) of living together is usually used before cohabiting couples can access benefits, but this criterion is often waived if the couple has a child. As long as they live together, cohabiting couples now seem to have the same benefits and advantages as married couples: They have a right to 'equality' of treatment, a right that was confirmed by the Supreme Court of Canada in 1995 (Goubau, 2004).

Many areas of family law, however, such as laws governing union dissolution and child support, remain under provincial jurisdiction. Some differences exist across provinces, mostly the way that cohabiting couples are treated at separation. Some provinces, such as Alberta and Quebec, have been reluctant to provide total equality for married and cohabiting couples in terms of sharing assets at separation, but for opposite reasons. On the one hand, in Alberta, where marriage was judged the ideal family context, it was felt that additional recognition of cohabitation would undermine marriage. In Quebec, on the other hand, the justification for not assimilating cohabitation to marriage was based on the respect of the freedom of choice of cohabiting partners, who deliberately preferred cohabitation to marriage in order to avoid the rights and obligations attached to the latter (Le Bourdais & Juby, 2001). [. . .]

Although respecting the conjugal choices of adults, the courts and governments have aimed to ensure the protection of children irrespective of their parents' situation. In Canada, children now have the same rights and privileges, no matter the family circumstances of their birth, and birth statistics no longer classify as 'illegitimate' births that occurred outside marriage. Parents, whether married or cohabiting, together or separated, have the same responsibilities and obligations toward their children. As much as possible, policies and laws have aimed to reduce the effect of parental separation on children's well-being. In December 2002, a new initiative, the Child-Centred Family Justice Strategy, was developed, aimed at the needs of children and at the reduction of the level of conflict between parents. [. . .]

Officially, children are entitled to the same rights and benefits, irrespective of the conjugal status of their parents. Interestingly, though, the reality appears to be slightly different. Because cohabiting parents are not required, at separation, to share the assets accumulated through the union, children are likely to suffer more difficult economic conditions following parental separation if they were living in a cohabiting rather than married family (Dubreuil, 1999). Moreover, cohabiting fathers are less likely to maintain frequent contact with their children or provide child support on a regular basis following separation (Marcil-Gratton & Le Bourdais, 1999). Sole custody to the mother, rather than joint custody, has also been shown to be more frequent after the dissolution of a cohabiting union. Consequently, children and adults are likely to experience different living conditions following family disruption, depending on whether the parents were married or cohabiting.

The Divergent Evolution of Cohabitation in Quebec and Elsewhere in Canada

The data presented here have revealed profound changes in the processes of union and family formation and dissolution in Canada, and show how institutions such as the law and the national statistical agency have adapted to these transformations. Our analysis has contrasted the evolution of the demographic behaviours adopted in Quebec with that elsewhere in Canada, and led us to conclude that cohabitation has reached different stages of development across the country.

Outside Quebec, cohabitation seems to have successfully achieved the second stage of Kiernan's (2001) model of partnership transition, but to have not yet attained the third: It has become widely accepted as a form of conjugal life—that is, as a prelude or probationary period in which to test the strength of the relationship before marrying—but not yet as an environment in which to become a parent. In that respect, Canada without Quebec closely resembles the United States, where cohabitation still predominantly remains a childless phase of conjugal life.

In Quebec, though, the progression of cohabitation is far more advanced. Now that cohabitation has become the modal way in which to give birth in Quebec (i.e., an alternative to marriage in order to have children), clearly the transition to the third stage of development appears to have been fully completed. Has Quebec also achieved the transition to the fourth stage of Kiernan's (2001) model in which 'cohabitation and marriage become indistinguishable with children being born and reared within both' (p. 5)? To help distinguish between these two stages, Heuveline and Timberlake (in press) have introduced a further criterion to those advanced by Kiernan: Unlike unmarried couples who, in the previous stage, opted for cohabitation as an *alternative* to marriage, those formed in the latter stage would be *indifferent* to marrying, because of the widespread acceptability of cohabitation and the provision of institutional supports that discriminate little between married and cohabiting families.

[. . .]

We cannot end this article without raising some hypotheses to explain the divergent evolution of cohabitation in Quebec as compared with elsewhere in Canada. Part of the answer probably lies in the different religious and cultural backgrounds of the two societies (for a similar argument, see Laplante, 2004; Pollard & Wu, 1998). Up to the 1960s, Quebec society was under the yoke of the Catholic Church, which controlled most aspects of Quebecers' lives. During the 1960s, a vast movement of secularization, known as the Quiet Revolution,

touched all aspects of society, including health, education, and social services, and led to the development of a modern state. Individuals rapidly embraced this revolution and progressively deserted the Church and abandoned its precepts. In the wake of this movement, Quebec women, who had maintained traditional behaviours in terms of contraception and family life, enthusiastically adopted the pill as a contraceptive method, and couples progressively did away not only with religious marriage but also with the 'institution' of marriage altogether. Consequently, the total fertility rate and the total marriage rate plunged rapidly in Quebec, as it did in other Catholic societies, such as Spain, Italy, and, to a lesser degree, France (Le Bourdais & Marcil-Gratton, 1996). Elsewhere in Canada, the Protestant Church exerted less control over civil society and adapted more easily to the changes observed in family behaviours. Non-Catholic Canadians thus did not feel that they had to break away from their church to fulfill their personal aspirations for conjugal and family life.

[. . .] We argue that much of the evolution observed in Quebec has to do with changes in men's and women's roles. As Théry (1993) argued, the principal motor of recent conjugal changes is to be found in the redefinition of men's and women's roles in society and in conjugal relationships. Families remain, to this day, the last places where equality between men and women does not seem to be fully recognized. As societies are promoting greater equality within families, deep changes are likely to occur and lead to ongoing family transformations. Interestingly, the few studies that aimed to document existing differences between marriage and cohabitation have found that the organization of daily life is more egalitarian within the latter than in the former. Cohabiting partners are more prone than married couples to sharing domestic work (Shelton & John, 1993). They are also more likely to share paid work, as cohabiting women are more involved in the labour market (Le Bourdais & Sauriol, 1998). By contrast, married couples are more inclined than cohabiting partners to pool their financial resources (for a review, see Seltzer, 2000). These studies suggest that cohabitation and marriage constitute two different forms of conjugal engagement, each characterized by different forms of relationships. Cohabitation is based on a greater equality and professional autonomy of partners, whereas marriage rests on greater specialization and complementarity between spouses (Villeneuve-Gokalp, 1991). This interpretation is further supported by Brines and Joyner's (1999) study that showed that similar levels of earnings were associated with greater stability among cohabiting couples, whereas marital stability was more closely linked to specialization of labour, and thus, to unequal earnings.

In Quebec, we argue that the tremendous progression of cohabitation has to do with profound changes in men's and women's roles and expectations brought about in large part by the feminist movement that is stronger and more deeply rooted than elsewhere in Canada. Quebec couples strive for greater equality between men and women, and cohabitation perhaps offers them the best opportunity in this regard. In that sense, cohabitation is probably here to stay, because both Quebec men and women express attitudes more favourable to a redefinition of conjugal unions than other Canadians (Lapierre et al., 1999). As long as cohabitation and marriage represent two different models of conjugal and family life, however, cohabitation remains an alternative to rather than a true substitute for marriage.

References

Bélanger, A. (2003). *Report on the demographic situation in Canada 2002* (cat. 91-209-XPE). Ottawa, Ontario: Statistics Canada.

Brines, J., & Joyner, K. (1999). The ties that bind: Principles of cohesion in cohabitation and marriage. *American Journal of Sociology, 64*, 333–55.

Brown, S.L. (2000). Union transitions among cohabitors: The significance of relationship assessments and expectations. *Journal of Marriage and the Family, 62*, 833–46.

Bumpass, L.L., & Lu, H.-H. (2000). Trends in cohabitation and implications for children's family contexts in the United States. *Population Studies, 54*, 29–41.

Cherlin, A.J. (2004). The deinstitutionalization of American marriage. *Journal of Marriage and Family, 66*, 848–61.

Desrosiers, H., & Le Bourdais, C. (1996). Progression des unions libres et avenir des familles biparentales [The rise of cohabitation and its impact on two-parent families]. *Recherches féministes, 9*, 65–83.

Dubreuil, C. (1999). L'union de fait au Québec: Inexistence dans le Code civil [Consensual union in Quebec: Non-existence in the Civil Code]. *Cahiers québécois de démographie, 28*, 229–36.

Duchesne, L. (2003). *La situation démographique au Québec, bilan 2003* [The demographic situation in Quebec, 2003]. Quebec: Institut de la statistique du Québec.

Dumas, J., & Bélanger, A. (1994). *Report on the demographic situation in Canada 1994* (cat. 91-209E). Ottawa, Ontario: Statistics Canada.

———. (1997). *Report on the demographic situation in Canada 1996* (cat. 91-209E). Ottawa, Ontario: Statistics Canada.

Dumas, J., & Péron, Y. (1992). *Marriage and conjugal life in Canada* (cat. 91-534F). Ottawa, Ontario: Statistics Canada.

Goubau, D. (2004). La notion de conjoint: La loi et la societe avancent-elles au même pas? [The notion of couples: Are law and society progressing at the same speed?]. In *Actes de la XVIᵉ Conférence des juristes de l'État* (pp. 39–60). Cowansville, Quebec: Éditions Yvon Blais.

Heuveline, P., & Timberlake, J.M. (in press). The role of cohabitation in family formation: The United States in comparative perspective. *Journal of Marriage and Family* [Special issue].

Juby, H., Marcil-Gratton, N., & Le Bourdais, C. (in press). *When parents separate: Further findings from the National Longitudinal Survey of Children and Youth*. Phase 2 research report of the project, 'The Impact of Parents' Family Transitions on Children's Family Environment and Economic Well-Being: A Longitudinal Assessment'. Ottawa, Ontario: Department of Justice Canada, Child Support Team.

Kiernan, K. (2001). Cohabitation in Western Europe: Trends, issues and implications. In A. Booth & A.C. Crouter (Eds), *Just living together: Implications of cohabitation on families, children, and social policy* (pp. 3–31). Mahwah, NJ: Erlbaum.

Lapierre-Adamcyk, É., & Le Bourdais, C. (2004). Couples et familles: Une réalité sociologique et démographique en constante évolution [Couples and families: Sociological and demographic arrangements in constant evolution]. In *Actes de la XVIᵉ Conference des juristes de l'État* (pp. 61–86). Cowansville, Quebec: Éditions Yvon Blais.

Lapierre-Adamcyk, É., Le Bourdais, C., & Marcil-Gratton, N. (1999). La signification du choix de l'union libre au Québec et en Ontario [The meaning of choosing cohabitation in Quebec and in Ontario]. *Cahiers québécois de démographie, 28*, 199–227.

Laplante, B. (2004). *The diffusion of cohabitation in Quebec and Ontario and the power of norms in religion.* Montreal, Quebec: Institut national de la recherche scientifique (INRS)— Urbanisation, Culture et Société.

Le Bourdais, C., & Juby, H. (2001). The impact of cohabitation on the family life course in contemporary North America: Insights from across the border. In A. Booth & A.C. Crouter (Eds), *Just living together: Implications of cohabitation on families, children, and social policy* (pp. 107–18). Mahwah, NJ: Erlbaum.

Le Bourdais, C., & Marcil-Gratton, N. (1996). Family transformations across the Canadian/American border: When the laggard becomes the leader. *Journal of Comparative Family Studies, XXVII*, 415–36.

Le Bourdais, C., Neill, G., & Marcil-Gratton, N. (2000). L'effet du type d'union sur la stabilité des familles dites 'intactes' [The effect of union type on the stability of 'intact' families]. *Recherches sociographiques, 41*, 53–74.

Le Bourdais, C., & Sauriol, A. (1998). *La part des pères dans la division du travail domestique au sein des familles canadiennes* [Father's share in the division of domestic labour among Canadian families] (Études et Documents No. 69). Montreal, Quebec: INRS-Urbanisation.

Livi-Bacci, M., & Salvini, S. (2000). Trop de famille et trop peu d'enfants: La fécondité en Italie depuis 1960 [Too much family and too few children: Fertility in Italy since 1960]. *Cahiers québécois de démographie, 29*, 231–54.

Manning, W.D. (1993). Marriage and cohabitation following premarital conception. *Journal of Marriage and the Family, 55*, 839–50.

Marcil-Gratton, N. (1998). *Growing up with mom and dad? The intricate family life courses of Canadian children* (cat. 89-566-XIE). Ottawa, Ontario: Statistics Canada.

Marcil-Gratton, N., & Le Bourdais, C. (1999). *Custody, access and child support. Findings from the National Longitudinal Survey of Children and Youth.* Retrieved 27 May 2004, from the Department of Justice Canada, Child Support Team website: http://canada.justice.gc.ca/en/ps/pad/reports/index.html#res

Pollard, M.S., & Wu, Z. (1998). Divergence of marriage patterns in Quebec and elsewhere in Canada. *Population Development Review, 24*, 329–56.

Raley, R.K. (2001). Increasing fertility in cohabiting unions: Evidence for the second demographic transition in the United States? *Demography, 38*, 59–66.

Seltzer, J.A. (2000). Families formed outside of marriage. *Journal of Marriage and the Family, 62*, 1247–68.

Shelton, B.A., & John, D. (1993). Does marital status make a difference? *Journal of Family Issues, 14*, 401–20.

Smock, P.J., & Gupta, S. (2001). Cohabitation in contemporary North America. In A. Booth & A.C. Crouter (Eds.), *Just living together: Implications of cohabitation on families, children, and social policy* (pp. 53–84). Mahwah, NJ: Erlbaum.

Statistics Canada. (2002a). *Changing conjugal life in Canada* (cat. 89-576-XIE). Ottawa, Ontario: Author.

———. (2002b). *Profile of Canadian families and households: Diversification continues* (cat. 96F0030XIE2001003). Ottawa, Ontario: Author.

———. (2002c). *2001 census* (Table 97F0005XCB0l002). Ottawa, Ontario: Author.

———. (2003a, November 20). Marriages. *The Daily* (pp. 11–12, cat. 11-001-XIE). Ottawa, Ontario: Author.

———. (2003b). *Annual demographic statistics 2002* (cat. 91-213-XIE). Ottawa, Ontario: Author.

Théry, I. (1993). *Le démariage* [Unmarrying]. Paris: Odile Jacob.

Turcotte, P., & Bélanger, A. (1997). *The dynamics of formation and dissolution of first common-law unions in Canada.* Ottawa, Ontario: Statistics Canada.

Villeneuve-Gokalp, C. (1991). From marriage to informal union: Recent changes in the behavior of French couples. *Population: An English selection, 3*, 81–111.

Wu, Z., & Balakrishnan, T. R. (1995). Dissolution of premarital cohabitation in Canada. *Demography, 32*, 521–32.

A New Entity in the History of Sexuality: The Respectable Same-Sex Couple

Mariana Valverde

In *The History of Sexuality: Volume 1,* Michel Foucault argued that 'homosexuality' is a relatively recent invention, distinct from earlier forms of same-sex love and lust. 'Homosexuality' could only emerge when European scientific knowledges began to peer into—and construct—an inner 'self', a personal identity that the nineteenth century saw as a matter of physiology and that the twentieth century regarded as fundamentally psychological. Sexuality—in the West but not in the East—came to be regarded as that which is most secret and therefore most authentic about 'the self', the key, in other words, to personal identity.

Before the rise of modern scientific knowledges, law governed sexuality as a set of acts, mainly distinguishing 'unnatural' from 'natural' acts. Many law codes still contain prohibitions against sodomy and other 'unnatural' acts. And, exceptionally among advanced industrial democracies, the United States criminalized sodomy in many states until the very late date of 2003, when such laws were declared unconstitutional by the Supreme Court. Nevertheless, the persistence of 'sodomy' in legal codes owes more to the difficulties involved in changing and modernizing law than to any real belief that 'sodomy' is a useful category: it is highly doubtful that any of the men charged under sodomy laws in the waning years of US sodomy statutes thought of themselves as 'sodomites'. Of course some people, especially men, have sex with people of the same sex without thinking of themselves as gay. But it is not inappropriate, when making a large-scale generalization, to say, in line with Foucault's famous thesis, that the regulation of the self has been increasingly dominated by the notion of 'identity'. What you did with various body parts came to be regarded, throughout the course of the twentieth century, mainly as a clue about what kind of person you were. And 'the homosexual' was probably the most successful of all deviant identities. It was invented at the same time as the hysteric, the nymphomaniac, and the kleptomaniac, but unlike these marginal entities/identities, it ended up occupying a very central place in the constitution of twentieth-century human beings and social groups. Although subsequent research has shown that Foucault's contrast is far too sharp, the point

about the shift from governing sexuality through acts to governing through identities has been generally accepted by historians and social scientists.

But what has happened since the 1970s, when Foucault was writing about sexuality? Let me suggest, half jokingly but half seriously, that we have been witnesses to a historic event. This is the emergence, in the space occupied by 'homosexuality', of a new sexual object/subject: the respectable same-sex couple. If the medieval soldier charged with sodomy was not 'a homosexual', as Foucault argued, so too, we can argue, the respectable same-sex couple (to which I am assigning the acronym 'RSSC') is not two homosexuals added together. Let me explain.

Almost 20 years ago, Jean Baudrillard wrote a little book, *Forget Foucault*, which, amidst much envy, contained a prescient passage:

> And what if Foucault spoke to us so well of sexuality . . . only because its form, this great production . . . of our culture was, like that of power, in the process of disappearing? Sex, like man, or the category of the social, may only last for a while. And what if sex's reality effect, which is at the horizon of the discourse on sexuality, also started to fade away radically . . .? Foucault's hypothesis itself suggests how mortal sex is, sooner or later.[1]

It certainly seems true that the particular form of the inner self that is 'sexuality'—the object of inquiries from 1890s sexology to sex-change clinics—may indeed be now fading.

Young people who would rather be 'queer' than 'gay' are leading the way. The term 'queer' blurs the boundaries of the homosexual self of tormented 1950s autobiographies and medico-legal inquiries. Queer is a purposefully vague name for a nonconformist lifestyle that is 'post-homosexual', historically if not biographically. And AIDS discourse has also given rise to a new, post-homosexual object: the man who has sex with men. Contrary to Foucault's discussion of the disciplinary gaze, AIDS experts don't care one bit whether this personage is gay.

But the queer youth and the 'man who has sex with men' are marginal by comparison with the legally and culturally prominent figure of the RSSC. This is likely more apparent in Canada, where gay/lesbian marriage began to be legalized as early as 2003, than south of the 49th parallel; but given the speed with which Americans rushed to San Francisco city hall during February of 2004, when gay/lesbian marriage was for a time provided in a more or less legal manner, perhaps the Canadian situation is relevant elsewhere, even in Bush's America.

The pictures that were used in the media are of particular importance for understanding how the RSSC is something new, rather than the addition of two homosexuals. As marriage for gays and lesbians approached legality, around 2003, Canadians were treated to an unprecedented visual display of respectable homosexuality: an extended series of photos displaying not the ashamed and effeminate homosexuals that used to be posed in dark corners in 1960s reportage of steamy gay life, but rather an array of perfect 'same-sex' couples, usually shown in the full glare of sunlight, a lighting convention at odds with representations of the classic homosexual. A look at the photographs that are still available, somewhat after the fact, proves enlightening. The first lesson in social semiotics is provided by an analysis focusing on that most important of all signs of marriage, notably, the wedding dress. A number of the lesbian couples who got married at the San Francisco city hall wore wedding dresses, as seen in one of the photos (Figure 1). And I can also attest to the presence of wedding dresses from personal experience. I happened to be in San Francisco in mid-February 2004 (where my partner and I were constantly asked

AP Photo/Erin Lubin

Figure 1

if we had come to get married by well-meaning Americans not aware of the fact we could have gotten married in Toronto quite easily, if that was our desire). My partner and I, used to the idea of gay/lesbian marriage but not to the flashier styles of US lesbians, were quite struck by seeing young lesbians in full wedding white waiting for the subway in the Berkeley mass transit station. It was very difficult to tell whether the wedding dresses were being worn in straight-up imitation of marriage or in playful parody. It is quite possible, given the mixed feelings gays and lesbians have about marriage, that the wearers were not themselves very clear about their intentions. By contrast, the available photos of Canadian lesbian couples (Figure 2) did not reveal a single wedding dress. All the couples depicted looked earnest and serious, sort of butch, and dressed in office attire: no wedding dresses; no playfulness; no parody—but also, no imitation of marriage. Perhaps Canada really is a more boring and earnest country; the lesbians do seem just to be wanting to get married, as opposed to wanting to dress up and have a really good time.

But what about the male couples? The first thing that one notices is that none of the men in US or Canadian pictures (Figure 3) of gay male weddings wear white dresses. Drag queens seem to have vanished from view. Nearly all of the men featured in the newspaper photographs

CP Photo/Kevin Frayer

Figure 2

CP Photo/Kevin Frayer

Figure 3

wore shirts and ties; nearly all were middle-class, middle-aged, and white. They looked either like soft-spoken librarians or like beefy stockbrokers—not like we expect homosexuals to look.

But perhaps pictures of actual weddings, or rather of that small sample of weddings that happened to be covered by the media, are not representative. I thus turned to another source, the *Toronto Star*'s Pride Day special section, published 19 June 2004. Toronto Pride Day is a significant event because it draws around three-quarters of a million people, many of them US gays and lesbians. The local press now covers this event in a booster-ish manner, just like any other event that contributes to the local economy and to the local myth that Toronto is the mecca of multiculturalism and

tolerance. This special section of Canada's largest circulation daily had two main articles. One featured the 73-year-old homosexual activist, George Hislop, wistfully reminiscing about the days of illegality. This story was obviously meant to represent the ghost of gay lives past. The community's future, by contrast, was embodied not in a young queer person or a transsexual activist, but, predictably, in images of a RSSC. Equally predictable, the couple in question was made up of two middle-class men. The couple is portrayed as totally immersed in the financial and logistical challenges of their upcoming wedding. In what can best be described as a feminist nightmare vision, both are obsessing about the colour scheme, the food, the entertainment, and the guest list.

I looked in vain for something that the RSSC might have had in common with Hislop. Sex, perhaps? Foucault would have said that in the end it is sex that holds the RSSC together and links it to both the homosexual of the 1960s and the eighteenth-century sodomite. But nothing about sex was said or even faintly implied in the article about this gay male couple. The two men who were about to tie the knot seemed to be far too engrossed in the details of their wedding to even think about sex. The travel of relatives from Brazil to Toronto was one key logistical challenge discussed at length. Other practices of consumerism were also discussed in fine-grained voyeuristic detail. The readers aren't given even a distant hint that these two men might sometimes have sex with one another. Instead, the readership is excitedly told how much the flower arrangements and the rental of a pleasure boat on Lake Ontario are going to cost. The frisson experienced by the reader clearly has nothing to do with any sex that might be going on (indeed, one suspects little time or energy will in fact be available for sex, at least, for the marrying couple). Other than the RSSC itself, the only people cited in the article are wedding professionals. These entrepreneurs offer up-to-date information about the new consumer niche and advise readers who operate small businesses not to neglect the gay marriage market (the gay male marriage market at any rate; lesbian weddings aren't mentioned). Readers (including business people) thus learn from authoritative sources that gay and lesbian couples always pay for their own wedding, with no parental involvement, which is apparently a key marketing point.

The *Star*'s coverage of Pride Day certainly supports Baudrillard's claim that if homosexuality did not die with Foucault in 1984, it is dying or dead now. Hislop, who despite his advanced age likes to shock people by saying he likes boys, probably knows many florists; but he is otherwise wholly unconcerned with weddings and, indeed, with consumption. In the days of homosexuality, activism meant poverty. Hislop, who is still fighting in the courts to get the Canadian government to retroactively include him in the same-sex pension arrangements that have been made available in recent years (his partner died a few years before the cut-off date for same-sex pensions), does not come across as a consumer at all.

But what about law? Putting away the newspaper, I turned to the relevant decisions of the Supreme Court of Canada, the decisions that were key in paving the way for gay/lesbian weddings, in pursuit of the vanishing homosexual. Instead of sexuality, homo or otherwise, I found two non-sexual themes. The two themes that run throughout the decisions are (1) family and (2) finance/consumption. Conjugality, family, and impoverishment were the sole themes of the Court's descriptions of the retirement struggles of James Egan and his partner in the 1995 case *Egan v. Canada*, a landmark decision that first declared that discrimination against gays and lesbians was in Canada just as illegal as discrimination on the basis of race or religion. Neither sex nor sexuality are mentioned in either the majority or the minority *Egan* decision. 'Sexual orientation' is the only sex-like term in

the Court's text—but this is not a *sexual* identity. As I have argued elsewhere with much more evidence than can be presented here, sexual orientation in Canadian law actually refers not so much to homosexuality as a sexual identity, but to an urban lifestyle, partly political and partly consumerist. Particularly in cases involving mayoral declarations about Pride Day, the 'gay community' is constructed as a quasi-ethnic group, a group that is entitled to rights because it has cultural and social solidity: it organizes bowling leagues, AIDS support groups, and all the other sort of community organizations that ethnic groups in Canada have long had. The Pride Day cases too are remarkably silent about sex; they are all about 'culture' and 'community', the sort of entities that official Canadian multiculturalism can easily accommodate. But perhaps the desexualization of gay rights in this decision is due to the fact that the *Egan* case was about pension benefits. A couple that has been together 40 years is unlikely to have a sexy aura. Perhaps the Egans are not sexual, and hence not homosexuals, by virtue of the fact that they were challenging pension regulations.

So what about the other famous RSSC of Canadian law, then? Another notable Canadian legal case involved a lesbian couple known as 'M and H' (to preserve their privacy). A 2001 Supreme Court decision, which stopped short of actually legalizing gay marriage, extended exactly the same recognition of heterosexual common-law couples to lesbian and gay couples, a recognition that involves compulsory support obligations after living together for two years. M and H are two women. They are not elderly. They weren't trying to get their pension. And they were undoubtedly presenting themselves as lesbians when they went to court. They could thus be sexual/homosexual. But their sexuality too is completely erased. Their issue was divorce, or rather, alimony. In a nutshell, M was unemployed or precariously employed, while H owned considerable property. When they split up, M claimed a right to alimony. The Supreme Court eventually ruled that H and others in similar positions did indeed have an obligation to support their expartners.

Not infrequently, people divorce for reasons related to sexuality; but this is not contemplated anywhere in the legal texts. The Court's recounting of their relationship is wholly devoted to financial matters. Of course, a claim for alimony is all about money; but nevertheless, some reference to the initial romance might have been found relevant, if only to explain the somewhat careless joining of finances that later caused discord. Let us turn to the Supreme Court text to see if there are any homosexuals.

> M and H are women who met while on vacation in 1980. It is agreed that in 1982 they started living together in a same-sex relationship that continued for at least five years. . . . During that time they occupied a home which H had owned since 1974. H paid for the upkeep of the home. . . . In 1983, M and H purchased a business property together. In 1986, they purchased as joint tenants a vacation property in the country. They later sold the business property and used the proceeds to finance the construction of a home on the country property.

> As a result of a dramatic downturn in the advertising business in the late 1980s, the parties' debt increased significantly. H took a job outside the firm and placed a mortgage on her home to pay for her expenses and those of M. M also tried to find employment but was unsuccessful. . . .

By September of 1992, M and H's relationship had deteriorated.[2]

The sheer ordinariness of the details given here is no doubt intended: writing up 'the facts' in this dreary-details-of-domestic-life manner furthers the justices' project to normalize same-sex marriage. Amidst the property relations, sex is nowhere to be found; neither is homosexuality. Nobody even inquires whether they sleep together, much less what they do in bed: the famous disciplinary gaze has vanished.

The RSSC of the *Toronto Star* pre-wedding photos and the RSSC of M and H occupy opposite ends of the marital happiness spectrum. But neither entity is made up of two homosexuals. Nobody cares about their sexuality—including, apparently, the parties involved. The non-sexual transactions that make up the everyday fabric of coupledom are what the texts find worth recounting. In the *Star*, one finds that the narrative of the happy Toronto couple is wholly made up of florists' bills and plane tickets for relatives. The narrative of the divorcing couple of the M and H Supreme Court decision, for its part, is made up of joint tenancy agreements and bank loan documents.

The RSSC is still a very new object in the legal (and economic) horizon. It would thus be premature to make any grand claims about its 'essence'. But it is clear that Hislop's reminiscences of homosexuality and its pleasures and dangers are precisely that—reminiscences. Bank loans, florists' bills, joint bank accounts, renovated gentrified downtown homes, and worries about the relatives are the pieces that make up the new, post-homosexual entity that Canadian jurisprudence has helped to fabricate: the respectable 'same-sex' couple. Like other proper homosexuals, Foucault is no doubt turning over in his grave.

Notes

1. Jean Baudrillard, *Forget Foucault* (New York: Semiotexte, 1987), 13.

2. Attorney General for *Ontario v. M and H*, par. 9–13.

Ethnically Heterogamous Marriages: The Case of Asian Canadians

Jessie M. Tzeng

Introduction

In an ethnically diverse society, such as Canada, the increases in intersection of group affiliations may promote intermarriage. A person often belongs to several social groups, for example, people live in a neighbourhood, have an occupation, belong to an ethnic group, are members of a religious group, and have a socio-economic status. Thus, the increasing social interactions among individuals of different backgrounds in modern society promote intergroup relations which in turn foster intermarriage (Blau, Beeker, and Fitzpatrick, 1984). In addition, the apparent growth of cultural pluralism which stresses the acceptance of various ethnicities within a society also shortens the social distances among persons of different ethnic backgrounds and may encourage intermarriage.

Many recent empirical studies suggest that various kinds of intermarriage have become more common over the course of this century (Kitano, Yeung, Chai, and Hatanaka, 1984; Lieberson and Waters, 1988; Kalmijn, 1993). However, the question of who marries whom remains a complicated mate selection process for intermarried couples. The traditional theory of homogamy (like attracts like) is insufficient to explain interracial assortative mating because individuals in interracial relationships face unconventional and unique challenges when compared to couples in interracial relationships. To better understand the mechanism behind interracial marriage selection, one needs to further explore the forces of pull and push in the decision to intermarry and the role which achieved socio-economic status plays in the process of interracial assortative mating.

Dynamics in Intermarriage: Forces of Pull and Push

In principle, there are two major forces, pull and push, operating simultaneously in the interracial assortative mating. Young people today may assume that their choice of mate is completely autonomous; however, many factors, in fact, do place limits on autonomy, whether we consciously recognize their impact or not. One of the major influences on marital autonomy is the principle of endogamy which requires a person to choose a partner from his or her own group (Larson, Goltz, and Hobart, 1994). This is one of the major pull sources constraining individuals from marrying someone outside their own group. Historically both family and society strongly opposed intermarriage. Almost all racial and ethnic groups have resisted intermarriage to protect and maintain their ethnic identities. Though there was no law prohibiting marriages between individuals from different racial and ethnic groups in Canada, intermarriage taboo exists not only in the importance of maintaining purity of one's own race or consistency of socialization for the younger generations, but also in the prevention of creating incompatible norms between members of diverse ethnic groups (Tinker, 1973; Merton, 1941). [. . .]

Looking back in history, despite the persistence of negative attitudes and reactions toward intermarriage, people continue to intermarry which may be a result of the following favourable push factors. First, recent social, economic, and political environment changes provide some evidence that the society has become more open and tolerant to racial and cultural heterogeneity (Spickard, 1989; Goldstein and Segall, 1991).

Namely, a higher rate of interracial marriage is possible because social proximity is common across many areas of social life, thereby providing evidence of shortening social distances between different racial and ethnic groups. Second, significant changes in the racial and ethnic distributions of the population will inevitably increase the probability of intermarriage. As the opportunities for individuals to come into contact with someone outside their own group increase, so does the likelihood of intermarriage. Third, research suggests that individuals from various racial and ethnic groups with higher socio-economic status are more likely to enter intermarriage (Glick, 1970; Tinker, 1973; Fitzpatrick and Gurak, 1979; Sung, 1990). [. . .] On the one hand, individuals with higher socio-economic status are more appealing to potential partners in the marriage market, both within and outside their own ethnic group. Since everyone is searching for a 'better half' as a marriage partner, individuals from racial and ethnic groups with favourable socio-economic positions increase their chance of outmarrying. On the other hand, this may also suggest that individuals from various racial and ethnic groups with higher socio-economic status have a more liberal attitude toward marriage and are less likely to be bounded by traditional family or cultural norms, and thus, are more likely to select mates outside their own group. Overall, it is argued that the number of interracial marriages will continue to rise as physical and social barriers between peoples diminish and the traditional approaches to mate selection will be replaced by the individual's choice (Sung, 1990).

Given the expansion of education and of women's participation in the labour force in the past few decades, young adults of all races are increasingly more likely to meet their potential spouses in school or at work. As a result of the current social forces, we are tempted to argue that the push force will play a more significant role than the pull force in an individual's marital choice.

The Significance of Achieved Status and Mate Selection

Some empirical evidence supports the theory of homogamy that persons marry others either with similar ascribed family background or, increasingly, with similar achieved socio-economic status. Couples who share similar cultural resources, either from ascribed or from achieved status, are more likely to enjoy similar views or agree with each other on certain issues and behaviours. On the one hand, the ascribed cultural characteristics from one's family of origin, including social class, religion, and race/ethnicity, are believed to have a major impact on an individual's choice of a future partner (Hollingshead, 1950). Among the many ascribed cultural characteristics used to describe the process of assortative mating, race and ethnicity is one of the most significant characteristics to represent one's cultural heritage. In particular, persons who were born and raised in Asian families have very distinctive cultural traits, such as unique physical appearance, languages, subcultures, values, norms, lifestyles, attitude, customs, and beliefs, all of which contribute to the uniqueness of their personalities, attitudes, social activities, and social circles and eventually affect their preference or choice of future mates.

On the other hand, the achieved cultural characteristics associated with individuals' socio-economic status, such as language capability of the host society, educational attainment, and labour market experience, are obtained by individuals through external institutions outside the home over time. The role of one's socio-economic resources is becoming more important than race and ethnicity in the process of mate selection due to the great expansion of education in the second half of the twentieth century, the greater flexibility in social mobility, and the changing role of women in the labour force.

For Asian immigrants, language ability is an important achieved characteristic clearly related to the assimilation process (White, Biddlecom, and Guo, 1993), because most Asian countries from which immigrants come do not use English or French as their official languages. Not only is the ability to speak English and/or French in Canada necessary for survival and assimilation in the host society, it helps to shorten the distance and to increase contact between individuals from different racial and ethnic groups. If immigrants lack knowledge of the official language, then there are cumulative as well as social and cultural barriers between immigrant groups and the host society (Stevens and Schoen, 1988). [. . .] [T]he most obvious channel for communication between spouses is language, and when there is no common language between the potential marital partners, the channels of communication are blocked; thus, the odds of intermarriage will be small (Sung, 1990). Accordingly, Asian immigrants' knowledge of English and/or French will facilitate their propensity to intermarry in Canada (Castonguay, 1982).

In addition, numerous studies show that an individual's educational attainment and labour market experience have become influential predictors in the process of marriage selection (Mare, 1991; Kalmijn, 1991, 1993; Qian and Preston, 1993; Schmitt, 1971; Hout, 1982). Educational attainment probably is one of the most significant social influences on the marriage process in many ways (Qian and Preston, 1993). Since education is often looked upon as being a key determinant of long-term socio-economic status, research shows that the level of schooling varies positively with the propensity to marry (South, 1991). Following the exchange theory of mate selection (Merton, 1941), the higher

the educational attainment of individuals, the more desirable they are in the marriage market, thus increasing their chances to marry. In addition, there has been a high level of marriage homogamy by education in the US as well as in Canada (Sweet and Bumpass, 1987; Schoen and Wooldredge, 1989; Mare, 1991; Ishwaran, 1992). Most people tend to marry those with a similar level of education due to their comparable values, goals, interests, and outlooks on life.

Among the most significant social changes in the recent decades has been the increasing participation of women in the labour force (Cherlin, 1992; Bianchi and Spain, 1986). The labour market experience of women may have two opposite effects on the overall propensity to marry. On the one hand, the new economic independence gained by employed women reduces the comparative gains from marriage, thereby reducing the propensity to marry (Becker, 1981). On the other hand, women's full-time labour force participation may be viewed as potential marital capital which will contribute to the total family income, thus increasing their desirability in the marriage market.

In view of people's general interest to marry up and/or marry homogamously, the high educational attainment and labour force participation of Asians may affect their odds of marrying someone outside their own group. However, for many individuals of Asian origin, the newly learned cultural traits may be in great conflict or competition with traditional cultural characteristics. Individuals with an Asian background have one of the strongest family traditions and kinship ties, and it is extremely important for the members in each group to preserve and pass their cultural heritage from one generation to the next. Marriage, for most Asian families, is important for its effect on family continuity and for maintaining the family line, not just for two individuals (Tinker, 1973). If, among Asian groups, the family tradition still plays an important role (even implicitly) in the individual's choice of spouse, then the increasing trend of interracial marriage expected for Asian groups due to their high socio-economic achievement would have been offset or lessened to a certain degree.

How one balances or weighs the two cultural forces when it comes to the individual's choice of a marital partner may vary with different groups and change over time. Thus, in this paper, I investigate the association between socio-economic achievement and intermarriage for Asians in Canada and examine the changes in the importance of an individual's achieved socio-economic status on his or her propensity to intermarry.

Intermarriage in Canada

This paper is aimed toward a better understanding of recent unique patterns in interracial marriage for Asians in Canada. Canada is widely regarded as an ethnoracially complex but remarkably ordered society of immigrants and refugees, aboriginal peoples, and colonizing groups (Fleras and Elliott, 1992). The immigrant population represented 16 per cent (4.3 million persons) of Canada's population in 1991, almost unchanged since 1951 when the immigration population was 15 per cent (Badets and Chui, 1994). Although the proportion of immigrants living in Canada has remained stable for the past 50 years, the distribution of immigrant population has become much more diverse now than it was a few decades ago. For example, in 1961, 90 per cent of immigrants in Canada were from Europe, partly because immigration policy had systematically excluded non-white people; however, the proportion of European immigrants dropped significantly to less than a quarter in 1991. Among the new immigrant population, people reporting Asian origins were the fastest growing group between 1981 and 1991. In 1991, more than 40 per cent of immigrants came from Asia and the Pacific, while only 21 per cent were from Europe (Statistics Canada, 1993). The shift in the source of immigrants from European to non-European countries has altered Canada's ethnic and linguistic composition and has created a greater diversity in the new 'Canadian mosaic'.[1]

[. . .] Migration . . . is a major factor leading to interracial unions (Sung, 1990). If Asians or other racial and ethnic groups had not migrated to Canada, intermarriage would be less likely to occur. In the late 1980s, about 14 per cent of the total married couples in Canada involved one foreign-born spouse and 9 per cent of the marriages were made up of two foreign-born persons (Dumas, 1990). [. . .]

As a result of increasing Asian immigration to Canada in the past two decades, those reporting single Asian origins represented about 5 per cent of the total population in 1991, and this trend is likely to persist with current immigration policies. Nevertheless, not only has systematic empirical research on intermarriage for individuals with Asian origins rarely been conducted in Canada, but also little attention has been paid to married couples' socio-economic status in the study of interracial marriages. [. . .] Recent studies in marriages have described the tendency for persons to choose partners of similar educational attainment (Mare, 1991), occupation (Hout, 1982), and other social standings. In addition, in his recent research, Kalmijn (1991, 1993) suggests that educational homogamy has increased its importance over social origin homogamy, such as class and race, in marriage selection in the US during recent decades. Thus, the focus of this paper is to examine the patterns and changes in intermarriage for Asians in Canada from 1981 to 1991, focusing on the effects of married couples' individual characteristics and socio-economic status on intermarriage.

Data and Method

Sample

To examine intermarriage for various Asian groups in Canada, it would have been more fruitful to use the individual file from recent Canadian censuses which would provide detailed information on the respondent's ethnic origin,[2] place of birth, and other individual characteristics. However, the individual identification codes in each census file were removed from public access and the data was randomly rearranged to ensure its total confidentiality. Thus, it is impossible to identify married couples from this data structure. As a result of this constraint in using individual census records, I have resorted to the family census file for this analysis.

[. . .]

I used the Family Public Use Microdata Sample file (PUMS-F) of the 1981 (1%) and 1991 (3%) Canadian censuses to extract the sample for this project. Although it is far from ideal to use an individual's place of birth to approximate one's race and ethnicity, it does provide some advantages. For example, instead of studying interracial marriages for various generations, I focus on changes and patterns of interracial marriage for foreign-born first-generation Asians only. Studies show later generation immigrants are much more likely to outmarry than the first-generation immigrants due to the acculturation or assimilation process and the decreasing pressure from the ethnic group (Tinker, 1973; Pagnini and Morgan, 1990). By examining the relevant correlates and interracial marriage for foreign-born, first-generation, Asian immigrants, I am able to delineate the effect of generation on intermarriage. In addition, an important advantage of using family census data is that it provides rich information on married couples' joint distributions of age, immigration status, educational attainment, labour market characteristics, and other important social demographic characteristics which are crucial in the study of interracial marriage.

The extract is in a sample of 1756 and 10 598 married couples[3] in which one of the partners or both spouses were born in Asia and were older than 15 years of age by the time of the survey in 1981 and 1991, respectively. The rationale for the selected time frame is that the Asian population was too small to become a category in the census data before 1980. Plus a significant population growth was evident for Asian-origin groups in Canada only during the recent years. The study of this particular time period allows us to obtain a closer inspection of the recent past and of potential future trends of intermarriage for various Asians in Canada.

Variables and Method

A logistic response model is used to explore the relative importance of couples' individual characteristics and socio-economic status for the race/ethnicity heterogamy over time. The dependent variable in the analysis is whether or not one of the spouses reports an ethnic origin other than Asian origins, that is, whether the couples intermarry or not. More specifically, the dependent variable in the model is the log odds of intermarriage for Asians. The independent variables include several major influences on intermarriage such as age, immigrant status, language capability, and socio-economic achievement of both spouses.

Findings

Changes and Temporal Patterns of In- and Outmarriages

Table 1 presents descriptive statistics on selective spouses' characteristics for Asian in- and outmarriages in Canada for 1981 and 1991. Contrary to the popular belief, inmarriage rates for Asians

Table 1 Descriptive Statics for Selective Variables

VARIABLES	1981			1991		
	IN-MAR.	OUT-MAR. HUSBAND	OUT-MAR. WIFE	IN-MAR.	OUT-MAR. HUSBAND	OUT-MAR. WIFE
Marriage rate	75.5	12.8	11.7	80.1	9.7	10.2
Husband's age	42.0	42.2	42.8	45.3	42.2	43.6
Wife's age	38.2	37.8	38.8	41.4	38.8	39.8
YEARS OF IMMIGRATION (HUSBAND)						
< = 10	64.1	42.7	18.9	45.7	24.9	10.6
>10	35.9	56.4	30.1	49.9	70.8	32.7
n/a		0.9	51.0	4.4	4.4	56.7
YEARS OF IMMIGRATION (WIFE)						
< = 10	71.6	30.8	45.1	48.7	12.1	30.4
>10	28.4	24.7	53.4	46.5	29.8	64.8
n/a		44.5	1.5	4.8	58.1	4.8
OFFICIAL LANGUAGE (HUSBAND)						
English and/or French	89.2	98.7	98.5	88.2	98.6	99.1
Neither	10.8	1.3	1.5	11.8	1.4	0.9
OFFICIAL LANGUAGE (WIFE)						
English and/or French	81.1	97.8	98.1	82.8	98.9	98.1
Neither	18.9	2.2	1.9	17.2	1.1	1.9
EDUCATION (HUSBAND)						
<12	25.7	14.5	12.6	28.1	15.1	16.4
12–13	29.9	36.1	46.1	22.3	19.9	24.3
14+	44.4	49.3	41.3	49.6	65.0	59.3
EDUCATION (WIFE)						
<12	36.1	23.3	12.1	35.8	16.0	15.1
12–13	33.4	48.0	52.4	27.1	30.8	26.3
14+	30.5	28.6	35.4	37.1	53.2	58.6
EMPLOYMENT STATUS (HUSBAND)						
Not employed	13.4	9.7	3.9	18.7	10.8	10.9
Part-time	3.3	2.2	3.9	4.3	5.8	5.6
Full-time	83.3	88.1	92.2	77.0	83.3	83.4
EMPLOYMENT STATUS (WIFE)						
Not employed	37.0	34.4	35.9	33.6	24.9	25.8
Part-time	13.2	15.4	21.4	11.1	20.0	17.5
Full-time	49.8	50.2	42.7	55.4	55.2	56.7

increase from 75.5 per cent in 1981 to 80.1 per cent in 1991. Accordingly, both male and female outmarriage rates were somewhat lower in 1991 than in 1981, with male outmarriage rates dropping twice as much as female outmarriage rate (3.1% vs. 1.5%) during the 10-year period. As a result, Asian women have a slightly higher outmarriage rate than Asian men in 1991; however, the gaps in outmarriage rates between Asian men and women are small in both time periods. Thus, a significant gender difference in intermarriage found in other studies (Tinker, 1973; Kitano et al., 1984) is not evident for Asian men and women in our data.

The average ages for husbands and wives in our sample are 42.3 and 38.27 in 1981; 43.7 and 40 in 1991. The respondents in our sample are in their middle-age because the age composition of the immigrant population differs markedly from that of non-immigrants in Canada (Fleras and Elliott, 1992). The immigrant population in Canada is older than the native-born population because most people who immigrate to Canada do so when they are adults. More specifically, the inmarried couples in 1981 were about three years younger than those couples in 1991. However, the changes in the age distributions are within one year for both male and female outmarriers from 1981 to 1991. The average differences between husbands and wives in all marriage types range from 3.3 to 4.4 years.

In both time periods, there are more outmarried couples than inmarried couples who have no children in their family, and the proportions are higher in 1991 than in 1981. In particular, female outmarriers have the highest proportion of being childless—32 per cent and 38.2 per cent in 1981 and 1991, respectively. In addition, male outmarriers in 1981 and female outmarriers in 1991 have the lowest proportions of having more than three children in their families. Nevertheless, the majority of couples have one or two children in their families regardless of marriage types. For all marriages, about one-third of the couples have

children under the age of six. This is consistent with the literature in that intermarried couples tend to have fewer children due to their concern about adjustment problems for their children or their lack of time to have children if both of them are highly devoted to the labour force (Eberhard and Waldron, 1977; Sung, 1990).

The majority of Asians who married within group had been in Canada less than 10 years by the time of survey in 1981. In 1981, more than 50 per cent of male (56.4%) and female (53.4%) outmarriers had been in the country for more than 10 years. However, for those who marry within group in 1991, about half of them had been in Canada for more than 10 years and the other half had been in the country for less than 10 years. In addition, among outmarriers, 70.8 per cent of men and 64.8 per cent of women had been living in Canada for more than 10 years by the time of survey in 1991.

As to language capability, those who were unable to speak either English or French were more likely to marry within the Asian group. About 10 per cent of men and 20 per cent of women who had no knowledge of English or French were in inmarriages. On the other hand, more than 98 per cent of the outmarriers were able to speak English, French, or both English and French in 1981 and 1991.

The lower half of Table 1 describes couples' labour force characteristics for both in- and outmarriages. The overall educational attainment increased for all Asians during the period of 1981–1991. For inmarriages, the proportion of husbands and wives with more than 14 years of schooling increased more than 5 per cent from 1981 to 1991. The upward shift in educational achievement was even more significant for Asian outmarriers. The proportions of male and female outmarriers who were in the highest educational category increased from 49.3 per cent to 65 per cent and from 35.4 per cent to 58.6 per cent in the 10-year period, respectively.

The changes in the labour force participation for husbands and wives show somewhat different patterns during this period. There was about a 5–6 per cent decrease in full-time employment for both in- and outmarried Asian males. On the contrary, the proportions of full-time employment increased from 49.8 per cent to 55.4 per cent for wives in inmarriages and from 42.7 per cent to 56.7 per cent for female outmarriers. In addition, the proportions of housewives for Asian females in both types of marriages declined, especially for female outmarriers.

The Effects of Individual Characteristics and Socio-economic Factors on Intermarriage

[...] The multivariate analyses presented in Table 2 examine the effects of both Asian husbands' and wives' social demographic and socio-economic characteristics on the log odds of interracial marriage in 1981 and 1991, respectively. For models in Table 2, I report the logit coefficients, beta, and their standard deviations, se (beta).

Age

The results show that the effect of husband's age on the odds of interracial marriage is much stronger in 1991 than in 1981 except for the oldest age group. Husbands who were 35–44 or 45–54 years old are about 66 per cent ($100[\exp(-1.079)-1]$) or 65 per cent ($100[\exp(-1.050)-1]$) less likely to be intermarried than those who were 15–24 years of age in 1991. Wife's age consistently shows a negative effect on the probability of intermarriage in both years. Namely, older wives are less likely than those who were 15–24 years old to marry out, especially for those who were older than 65 years of age in 1981 and those who were 55–64 years of age in 1991. I also examine the

Table 2 Logistic Models of Asian Interracial Marriages in Canada

	1981		1991	
	BETA	**SE(BETA)**	**BETA**	**SE(BETA)**
HUSBAND'S AGE (15–24)				
25–34	0.057	0.452	−0.761	0.208
35–44	−0.446	0.503	−1.079	0.227
45–54	0.006	0.558	−1.050	0.252
55–64	−0.019	0.640	−0.592	0.281
65+	1.386	0.760	0.027	0.331
WIFE'S AGE (15–24)				
25–34	−0.363	0.272	−0.042	0.138
35–44	−0.556	0.349	−0.375	0.167
45–54	−0.428	0.440	−0.495	0.202
55–64	−0.308	0.555	−0.737	0.248
65+	−1.625	0.768	−0.390	0.301
AGE HOMOGAMY (HUSBAND − WIFE = 0–3)				
Husband − Wife >3	0.167	0.158	0.138	0.068
Husband − Wife <0	0.212	0.199	0.481	0.081

(Continued)

Table 2 Logistic Models of Asian Interracial Marriages in Canada (*continued*)

	1981		1991	
	BETA	**SE(BETA)**	**BETA**	**SE(BETA)**
YEARS OF IMMIGRATION (>10 YRS) (NEITHER)				
Husband only	1.982	0.256	1.866	0.123
Wife only	1.234	0.196	1.854	0.110
Both	1.859	0.166	1.954	0.086
OFFICIAL LANGUAGE (BOTH)				
Husband only	−2.069	0.531	−1.795	0.260
Wife only	−1.311	1.134	−0.984	0.388
Neither	−1.715	0.492	−2.074	0.257
HUSBAND'S EDUCATION (< = 11)				
12–13	0.704	0.233	0.231	0.097
14+	0.467	0.280	0.336	0.117
WIFE'S EDUCATION (< = 11)				
12–13	0.448	0.193	0.475	0.090
14+	0.114	0.255	0.744	0.109
EDUCATIONAL HOMOGAMY (H = W)				
H > W	0.098	0.180	0.135	0.071
H < W	0.755	0.194	0.550	0.085
H'S EMPLOYMENT STATUS (NOT EMPLOYED)				
Part-time	−0.162	0.601	0.398	0.175
Full-time	−0.454	0.793	0.275	0.258
W'S EMPLOYMENT STATUS (NOT EMPLOYED)				
Part-time	0.093	0.194	0.325	0.092
Full-time	0.513	0.774	−0.045	0.243
EMPLOYMENT HOMOGAMY (H = W)				
H > W	0.751	0.756	0.155	0.228
H < W	−0.858	0.655	0.429	0.222
Selected Deviance	1586.200		8812.000	
Degrees of Freedom	1738.000		10567.000	

effect of age homogamy on intermarriage. The results indicate that age heterogamous Asian couples are more likely than age homogamous couples (i.e., wife's age is equal to or less than three years younger than her husband's) to intermarry in both years. Especially in 1991, older wife–younger husband couples are about 62 per cent

$(100[\exp(0.481)–1])$ more likely to intermarry than age homogamous couples.

Years of Immigration
The results also indicate the durations of immigration for both husband and wife significantly predict whether they enter intermarriage or not.

Couples in which either one of the spouses or both spouses had been in Canada for more than 10 years are much more likely to be intermarried than those couples who had been in the country for less than 10 years. For example, if both spouses had been in Canada for more than 10 years, they are at least five times (1981: 100[exp(1.859)–1]; 1991: 100[exp(1.954)–1) more likely to marry out than those had been in the country less than 10 years. The effects of durations of immigration on the log odds of entering intermarriage have remained quite stable during the 10-year period.

Official Language

Furthermore, the ability to speak either English and/or French increases one's probability to marry someone outside the Asian group. As shown from both years, when either one of the spouses or neither spouse speaks the official languages, the chance of outmarrying is reduced. Although the negative effects on the probability of intermarriage have lessened from 1981 to 1991 for couples with only one of the spouses speaking the official languages, they are still highly significant. In addition, when neither spouse speaks one of the official languages, couples are about 87 per cent less likely to intermarry than those couples who both have the ability to speak English or French in 1991. The ability to negotiate life in the host society using the official languages helps the immigrants to achieve social and economic assimilation, which in turn can facilitate intermarriage (White et al., 1993).

Education

The results from the lower panel of Table 2 show that the odds of interracial marriage varies positively with the educational attainment of husbands and wives for both years. In particular, the magnitude of the effects of wife's educational attainment is about twice that of husband's in

1991. The models also indicate that educational heterogamous couples are, in general, more likely than homogamous couples to experience interracial marriage, especially when the wife has more years of schooling. Apparently, the high level of marriage homogamy by education found in recent years for married couples in North America are not witnessed in the intermarried Asian couples in Canada.

Employment Status

The odds of interracial marriage are not affected by husband's and wife's employment status in 1981. However, the odds of outmarriage vary positively with husband's and wife's employment status in 1991, except for wife's full-time employment. And employment heterogamous couples are also more likely to be intermarried than employment homogamous couples in 1991, especially when wives work more than their husbands. The effects of employment heterogamy are consistent with that of educational heterogamy on intermarriage. That is, couples in which wives work more than their husbands are about 54 per cent more likely to be intermarried than employment homogamous couples in 1991.

Conclusions

Our results indicate the increasingly significant roles which the achieved socio-economic characteristics play in interracial assortative mating. [. . .] The results are, in large part, in agreement with prior research. I find older individuals and those without any knowledge of English or French are less likely to marry out. Whereas, the propensity to intermarry is higher for age heterogamous couples, and when either one or both spouses have been in Canada for more than 10 years.

I then examine the effects of couples' socio-economic characteristics on the odds of intermarriage. Our results indicate that educational attainment positively affects one's probability of interracial marriage. In addition, couples in which wives have higher educational achievement are also more likely to intermarry than educationally homogamous couples. As for the effect of labour force experience, I did not observe the same main effects of husband's and wife's employment status on intermarriage for both 1981 and 1991. In particular, the employment effect is not significant in 1981. On the contrary, in 1991, employment heterogamous couples are more likely to be intermarried than employment homogamous couples, especially when wives work more than their husbands.

Thus, the results suggest age, educational, and employment heterogamous Asian couples vary positively with the odds of intermarriage. In particular, the most unconventional couples, in which the wife is older, more educated, and with a higher level of labour force participation than the husband, are more likely to be intermarried. These results may suggest that Asian women do have more to gain by intermarriage (Tinker, 1973). In general, older ages of the wives in intermarriage are highly correlated with their higher educational attainment and labour market experience. Also, highly educated or full-time employed Asian women are more likely to intermarry due to their quest for a more egalitarian marriage and their desire to avoid traditional constraints set

upon an Asian wife if she were to marry within her cultural group.

However, to my surprise, the rates of Asian intermarriage did not increase from 1981 to 1991 as I originally thought. The reasons for these decreasing rates may be due to the following. First, there is a larger selection as well as a more balanced sex ratio within one's own ethnic group as more Asian-origin groups immigrate to Canada. Most prior research suggests that population size and a balanced sex ratio positively correlate with inmarriage (Besanceney, 1965; Alba and Golden, 1986; Sung, 1990). Second, with a growing consciousness of multiculturalism in the Canadian society, many racial and ethnic minorities including Asians, are increasingly aware of their cultural and linguistic heritage as a positive component of personal identity and are anxious to remain culturally distinct, which may pose cultural constraints on intermarriage (Fleras and Elliott, 1992). Though I observe a declining trend in intermarriage over this 10-year period, it is premature to predict a downward trend in Asian intermarriage in Canada, because I only include the first-generation, foreign-born Asians in this sample, which usually has much lower outmarriage rates than later generations of immigrants. In addition, there may exist a large variation in the patterns of intermarriage for various Asian ethnic groups, which was not captured in this study.

Notes

1. Although people of British (Anglophones) and French (Francophones) backgrounds are still the largest ethnic groups in Canada, neither of them account for a majority of the population (Statistics Canada, 1993).
2. Respondent's race/ethnicity was not included in Canadian censuses.
3. The reasons for such a big difference in our sample sizes of the two census years are the following. First, the population was much larger in 1991 than in 1981; thus, the gap is partly due to the sampling of a small percentage (1%) from a smaller population in 1981 and of a large percentage (3%) from a larger population in 1991. In addition, the Asian population was also much larger in 1991 than in 1981, which further affects the sample sizes in the two years under study.

References

Alba, R.D., & R.M. Golden. 1986. 'Patterns of Ethnic Marriage in the United States'. *Social Forces 65*: 202–23.

Badets, J., & T.W. Chui. 1994. 'Canada's Changing Immigrant Population'. Statistics Canada—Catalogue No. 96-311E. Scarborough, Ontario: Prentice Hall, Canada Inc.

Becker, G.S. 1981. *A Treatise on the Family*. Cambridge: Harvard University Press.

Besanceney, P.H. 1965. 'On Reporting Rates of Intermarriage'. *American Journal of Sociology 70*(6): 717–21.

Bianchi, S.M., & D. Spain. 1986. *American Women in Transition*. New York: Russell Sage Foundation.

Blau, P.M., C. Beeker & K.M. Fitzpatrick. 1984. 'Intersecting Social Affiliations and Intermarriage'. *Social Forces 62*(3): 585–605.

Castonguay, C. 1982. 'Intermarriage and Language Shift in Canada, 1971 and 1976'. *Canadian Journal of Sociology 7*(3): 263–77.

Cherlin, A.J. 1992. *Marriage. Divorce. Remarriage*. Cambridge: Harvard University Press.

Dumas, J. 1990. 'Report on the Demographic Situation in Canada, 1988'. Statistics Canada—Catalogue No. 91-209E. Ottawa: Statistics Canada.

Eberhard, M., & J. Waldron. 1977. 'Intercultural Marriage and Child Rearing'. In W.S. Tseng, et al. (eds.), *Adjustment in Intercultural Marriage*. Honolulu: University of Hawaii Press.

Fitzpatrick, J.T., & D.T. Gurak. 1979. *Hispanic intermarriage in New York City: 1975*. New York: Fordham University Hispanic Research Center.

Fleras, A., & J.L. Elliott. 1992. *Multiculturalism in Canada: The Challenge of Diversity*. Scarborough, Ontario: Nelson Canada.

Glick, P. 1970. 'Intermarriage among Ethnic Groups in the United States'. *Social Biology 17*(4): 293–98.

Goldstein, J., & A. Segall. 1991. 'Ethnic Intermarriage and Ethnic Identity'. In Jean E. Veevers (ed.), *Continuity & Change in Marriage and Family*. Toronto: Holt, Rinehart and Winston of Canada, Limited.

Hollingshead, A.B. 1950. 'Cultural Factors in the Selection of Marriage Mates'. *American Sociological Review 15*: 619–27.

Hout, M. 1982. 'The Association Between Husbands' and Wives' Occupations in Two-Earner Families'. *American Journal of Sociology 88*: 397–409.

Ishwaran, K. 1992. *Family and Marriage: Cross-Cultural Perspectives*. Toronto: Thompson Educational Publishing, Inc.

Kalmijn. M. 1991. 'Status Homogamy in the United States'. *American Journal of Sociology 97*(2): 496–523.

———. 1993. 'Trends in Black/White Intermarriage'. *Social Forces 72*(1): 119–46.

Kitano, H.H., W.-T. Yeung, L. Chai & H. Hatanaka. 1984. 'Asian-American Interracial Marriage'. *Journal of Marriage and the Family 46*(1): 179–90.

Larson, L.E., J.W. Goltz & C.W. Hobart. 1994. *Families in Canada*. Scarborough, Ontario: Prentice Hall Canada Inc.

Lieberson, S., & M.C. Waters. 1988. *From Many Strands: Ethnic and Racial Groups in Contemporary America*. New York: Russell Sage.

Mare, R.D. 1991. 'Five Decades of Educational Assortative Mating'. *American Sociological Review 56*: 15–32.

Merton, R.K. 1941. 'Intermarriage and Social Structure: Fact and Theory'. *Psychiatry 4*: 361–74.

Pagnini, D.L., & S.P. Morgan. 1990. 'Intermarriage and Social Distance among U.S. Immigrants at the Turn of the Century'. *American Journal of Sociology 96*(2): 405–32.

Qian, Z., & S.H. Preston. 1993. 'Changes in American Marriage, 1972 to 1987: Availability and Forces of Attraction by Age and Education'. *American Sociological Review 58*: 482–95.

Schoen, R., & J. Wooldredge. 1989. 'Marriage Choices in North Carolina and Virginia, 1969–71 and 1979–81'. *Journal of Marriage and the Family 51*: 465–81.

Schmitt, R.C. 1971. 'Recent Trends in Hawaiian interracial Marriage Rates by Occupation'. *Journal of Marriage and the Family 33*: 373–74.

South, S.J. 1991. 'Sociodemographic Differentials in Mate Selection Preferences'. *Journal of Marriage and the Family 53*: 928–40.

Spickard, P.R. 1989. *Mixed Blood: Intermarriage and Ethnic Identity in Twentieth-Century America*. Madison, WI: The University of Wisconsin Press.

Statistics Canada. 1988. 'Marriage and Conjugal Life in Canada'. Statistics Canada—Demography Division. Ottawa: Statistics Canada.

———. 1993. 'Ethnic Origin and Occupied Private Dwellings'. *The Daily*, Statistics Canada—Catalogue No. 96-304E. Ottawa: Statistics Canada.

Stevens, G., & R. Schoen. 1988. 'Linguistic Intermarriage in the United States'. *Journal of Marriage and the Family 50*: 267–79.

Sung, B.L. 1990. *Chinese American Intermarriage*. New York: Center for Migration Studies.

Sweet, J.A., & L.L. Bumpass. 1987. *American Families and Households*. New York: Russell Sage Foundation.

Tinker, J.N. 1973. 'Intermarriage and Ethnic Boundaries: The Japanese American Case'. *Journal of Social Issues 29*(2): 49–66.

White, M.J., A.E. Biddlecom & S. Guo. 1993. 'Immigration, Naturalization, and Residential Assimilation among Asian Americans in 1980'. *Social Forces 72*(1): 93–117.

PART II
Dialogue Box 2
Whistler Guys Study

Jennifer Matthews, a Masters student in Health Promotion Studies at the University of Alberta, was interested in exploring some of the gaps in sexual health promotion campaigns, specifically in relation to young men, drinking, and sex. She chose to do an interview-based study with men between 19–31 living in Whistler, British Columbia, about 'what they see as the risks and pleasures of sex under the influence' (Matthews, 2007). Her results are very similar to Beres' findings as discussed in chapter 4. More information about Matthews' study is available at http://www.whistlerguysstudy.com.

Critical Conversations: Discussion Questions

1. Based on your readings, how would you describe 'normal' sexuality? What are some of the social forces (i.e., trends, structures, and institutions) that have led to changes in popular understandings of 'normal' sexuality?

2. What do you think of the commentary in Melanie Beres' study that casual sexual encounters 'just happen'? Is this experience more typical of a particular age group, sexual orientation, or gender? Explain.

3. How do public attitudes about young adults' sexualities seem to have changed from those discussed in chapter 3 (particularly in Maynard and Demerson) and the contemporary discussions by the authors in chapter 4?

4. Adam Isaiah Green argues in 'Until Death Do Us Part?' that differential access to the institution of marriage influences the community and identity development of homosexuals and heterosexuals. How do you think the experience of bisexuality is influenced by the institution of marriage?

5. What was the most surprising or shocking thing you read about in this section? Why? How do your own place in society and your socialization influence your response?

6. What are some examples from the readings of how gender, race, and/or class influence expectations about sexuality?

Glossary

EGALE (Equal Rights for Gays and Lesbians Everywhere) – EGALE Canada is a national organization committed to advancing equality and justice to lesbian, gay, bisexual, and trans-identified people, and their families, across Canada. EGALE has intervened before the Supreme Court of Canada, appeared before many federal parliamentary committees, and been involved in public education at local, national, and global levels. (www.egale.ca)

Normativity/normalization The function of the privileged discourses in society through which we create our understandings of what is normal and natural in human social behaviour.

Norms Expectations for appearance and behaviour in particular social circumstances (e.g. work, family, school, and dating) that become guidelines for everyday living. Failure to adhere to norms has consequences that serve to encourage conformity.

Sex A term that commonly refers to aspects of our physiological configuration (male, female, intersex), our social identity (as the presumed foundation of our gender identity), and our erotic life (sexual activities and sexual relationships). The complexity and intermingling of these meanings and the social processes and practices through which they are produced and maintained demonstrates that 'sex', in all three of its articulations, is a socially constructed category.

Socialization The life-long processes and practices by which individuals learn to become members of a society.

Status and Stigma: Sex and Sexualities in Social Institutions

Starting Points

1. The topics of health and sexuality relate to each other in a variety of ways. Beyond the usual discussions around sexual health (e.g., sexually transmitted infections, contraception, consent), what are some other connections between health and sexuality?
2. What did you learn about sex in school (K–12)? Who taught you that information (e.g., teachers, classmates, etc.)?
3. What tends to be the first question that new parents are asked about their baby? What are some of the implications of this question (and the answer to it)?
4. How would you describe the relationship between media portrayals of sexuality and popular attitudes toward sexuality?

Introduction

In this section, we explore how our experience of sexuality is constructed through some of our more prominent social institutions: the health care system, the education system, and the mass media. In sociology, the term *social institution* refers to stable patterns of social relationships that develop over a long period of time, have achieved a high level of consensus within a society, and facilitate the accomplishment of recognized social goals (Tepperman and Curtis, 2009). These patterns of relationships, while stable, do also change over time. The family is the most widely acknowledged and, arguably, the oldest of our contemporary social institutions. As we saw in chapter 5, in Canada, the structure of the family is changing in part through the legitimation of same-sex relationships and changing attitudes about cohabitation and inter-racial marriage. As well as facilitating the accomplishment of social goals such as child-rearing, the family and other social institutions also communicate values and norms including those that shape our experiences of sexuality. We need to continue to examine these influences in order to better understand the role of sexuality in society.

Chapter 6, 'Health, Illness, and Sexualities', profiles some of the contemporary Canadian scholarship on sexualities from the related fields of sociology of health and illness and sociology of medicine. One of the things generally taken for granted about our bodies in society is that we are born either male or female and that this designation is based on our genitalia. Critical social theorist Morgan Holmes demonstrates the fallacy of this common-sense understanding through an examination of the routine and invasive treatment of infants born with ambiguous genitalia. As we see from Holmes' work, perceptions of our bodies, our health, and our sexualities are often entwined. Additionally, because we want to pay attention to the politics of who is allowed to do what with whom, we are also always interested in how these perceptions are embedded within broader social discourses such as race, class, and citizenship. Sociologist and activist OmiSoore Dryden analyzes the exclusions of sexuality and race embedded in the current blood donor–screening process in Canada. The delivery of and priorities within contemporary health care are also often influenced by trends and pressures in the broader society. An example of such influence is found in Richard Carpiano's 'Passive Medicalization: The Case of Viagra and Erectile Dysfunction'. Carpiano explores the social construction of illness through an analysis of the development and marketing of Viagra.

These first three articles by Holmes, Dryden, and Carpiano all speak to the experience of stigma as it relates to health, illness, and sexuality. The concept of stigma is used by sociologists to describe 'a relationship of devaluation' involving appearance, behaviour, or social group (Scott and Marshall, 2005). This concept is the central analytical framework utilized by health care researchers Elizabeth Saewyc, Colleen Poon, Yuko Homma, and Carol Skay as they explore the risks of being seen as queer and the connection between this stigma and incidences of teen pregnancy. These readings demonstrate the important influences that social factors have on both experiences of health and illness and on the expression of our sexuality.

As previously mentioned, our education system is an important social institution within Canadian society. As such, it exerts considerable influence on the development of our understandings of our sexuality and the sexualities of others. The selections in chapter 7, 'Sex Education and Sex in Education', resituate the discussions of youth sexuality in chapter 4 and health and identity from chapter 6 in the context of the Canadian public education system. In this chapter, the assembled authors explore concerns about teen sexuality, sexual health education (SHE), and community authority over school curricula. Collectively, their work helps us explore the politics of controversy, change, and consensus in relation to issues of sexuality in education.

Stephanie Mitelman and Jo Visser outline the construction of a contemporary moral panic around teen sexual activities. These authors suggest that educators can play an important role in promoting healthy and responsible decision–making by youth in sexual matters. Mitelman and Visser call for 'sex education and risk reduction education' (p. 301 in this volume) in our schools. The next two articles in this chapter explore prospects for such initiatives. The Sex Information and Education Council of Canada's information guide, 'Sexual Health Education in the Schools: Questions and Answers', addresses common concerns about SHE.

Psychologists E. Sandra Byers, Heather Sears, Susan Voyer, Jennifer Thurlow, Jacqueline Cohen, and Angela Weaver examine the attitudes of New Brunswick students from grades 9 to 12 toward SHE. Reading across these three articles, it becomes clear that while there is a strong general consensus in Canadian society in favour of SHE, this consensus breaks down in the details, such as which students should be educated and when such education should begin. The final selection in this chapter explores an incident related to the breakdown of this consensus. Social geographer Damian Collins examines the debates surrounding the Supreme Court of Canada's decision regarding the inclusion of books portraying same-sex parents on a grade 1 reading list. These articles demonstrate some of the debates, controversies, and tensions about sexuality within the Canadian education system.

The articles in chapter 8 display the varying approaches in Canadian sexualities studies to the influence of mass media on social norms of sexuality and gender. When the topic is sexuality, perhaps no social institution receives more attention than the media. Even before Elvis Presley first rocked his hips for an international television audience, social commentators and community leaders were worried about the influence of media representations on social morals (Adams, 1997). Within the landscape of our contemporary celebrity and consumer culture, the power of mass media to offer lessons about belonging in contemporary society (Fleras, 2003) has become of increasing interest to today's scholars. These lessons are not only about beauty, success, happiness, and desirability, but are also often about sex and sexuality.

Musicologist Charity Marsh profiles the response of Canadian broadcaster MuchMusic to Madonna's video 'What It Feels Like for a Girl' (2001). Marsh critiques the common dismissal of popular figures such as Madonna who, while complicit in the production of dominant norms and values, challenge the boundaries of gender and sexuality. Madonna is also a subject of analysis for Anita Shaw. Through an examination of Madonna's 'Papa Don't Preach' (1986) video and the feature film *Juno* (2007), Shaw explores the persistent, though changing, stigma of pregnant teenagers. Prostitution is another activity that is heavily stigmatized in Canadian society. In 'The Lone Streetwalker', Shawna Ferris analyzes print media portrayals of female prostitutes and finds that these representations undermine sex workers' voices while simultaneously highlighting their risk for victimization. The final article in this chapter continues the analysis of the sensationalization of sex crime through an examination of local televised news programming. Criminologist Kenneth Dowler finds that the reportage of sex crimes tends to focus on narratives of fear and victim credibility.

Throughout this collection, readers have been asked to pay attention to their knowledge about sexualities and how they came to this knowledge. Without a doubt, our principal social institutions, including health care, education, and the mass media, play a central role in the development of our knowledge of sexuality and our sense of our own sexuality.

References

Adams, Mary Louise. 1997. *The Trouble with Normal: Post-War Youth and the Making of Heterosexuality*. Toronto: University of Toronto Press.

Fleras, Augie. 2003. *Mass Media Communication in Canada*. Toronto: Thomson Nelson.

Scott, John, and Robert Marshall. 2005. *A Dictionary of Sociology*, 3rd edn. Oxford, UK: Oxford University Press, p. 639.

Tepperman, Lorne, and James Curtis. 2009. *Principles of Sociology: Canadian Perspectives*, 2nd edn. Toronto: Oxford University Press.

6 Health, Illness, and Sexualities

Mind the Gaps: Intersex and (Re-productive) Spaces in Disability Studies and Bioethics

M. Morgan Holmes

Introduction

With a few notable exceptions disability studies have not taken account of intersexuality.[1-2] Moreover, it is principally through the lenses of feminist and queer-theory oriented ethical discussions but not through 'straight' bioethics that modes valuing intersex *difference* have been proposed.[3-4] Meanwhile, the medical presupposition that intersex characteristics are inherently disabling to social viability remains the taken-for-granted truth from which clinical practice proceeds. On this point, the bioethicist and philosopher Carl Elliott has argued that to ask clinical practice to change its view of intersex is to fail to understand that:

> . . . we treat these children the way we do because this is how we see the world. And it isn't just the way doctors see the world; it is the way the parents see the world, and most importantly, it is the way that the children themselves are taught to see the world. It is the fact that they do not fit into this way of seeing the world that causes the problems (p. 39).[5]

Because Elliott is generally thought to be a 'radical' bioethicist, his comments on intersex are surprising; however, as I will argue in this paper, his assertion is congruent with his attitude toward other forms of difference in children, and with his belief in the fundamental correctness of the clinical perspective.

Elliott's assertion contradicts Suzanne Kessler's findings on the clinical encounter between the parents of an intersexed child and those in charge of its medical assessment and treatment.[6] Kessler showed that clinicians had *to teach* the parents how to understand intersexuality in clinical terms, and *to learn* its meaning according to medical priorities: that is, to see the children's appearance as problematic and to apprehend intersex as appropriately serious but absolutely repairable with medical intervention. If we can understand that this process of teaching and learning is rendered possible and enforced through the clinical encounter, then we can understand that the social crisis and inability to view the child as a person begins not with the child's appearance, but with the medical discourse that frames and shapes the viewing angle that parents are to take. Elliott is correct that this may be how 'we' do and see things, but it is important to understand that some cultures do not, and that without the clinical encounter we would likely still see intersex in terms of difference but not necessarily of monstrosity that forecloses on the child's species membership as a human, and subsequent status as a person.

Clinicians assume that unhappiness in the form of isolation *will result* if the intersexed child's body is not altered through techno-medical intervention. Arthur Frank reminds us, however, that any technology that promises to put an end to human unhappiness takes place in a larger social context of mutually sustaining market forces at play between the consumers, suppliers, and builders of medical technologies (p. 46).[7] In cases of intersex, it is the parents who demand or consume treatment; however, it is the children who have to live not only with medicine's technical shortcomings, but also with the awareness of the message conveyed through intervention, namely, that in their intersexed bodies they were unacceptable, perhaps unlovable, and certainly unrecognizable as persons. The literature demonstrating the harm done to self-perception is growing rapidly.[8–14] Crucially, Frank observes that when a medical technology is known to have a high failure rate it can nonetheless continue as the dominant mode of management because clinicians have successfully 'blamed failure on the patient'.[8–14] As we shall see, blaming the patient remains a powerful

means of saving face for those who have specialized in the diagnosis and treatment of intersex.

There is a need to wrest intersex management away from the medical domain. And there is good reason to address intersex principally through a critical disability studies apparatus that may hold in abeyance the common sense attitudes that not only fail to provide well-being, but which are moving in the face of that failure, to eradicate intersex altogether through the use of invasive prenatal technologies, including selective termination. However, I also maintain a critical stance toward tendencies in disability studies that make a 'straw woman' out of feminist concerns for women's reproductive autonomy, and argue that we need not pit women's reproductive autonomy against those whose lives are described as 'lives of difference'.[15] I address these concerns in the paper's final section.

Biopower and the Clinical Setting

In the world of the clinic into which they are born, intersexed infants and children face a prevailing perception that they are so seriously damaged it is impossible even to conceive of admitting them to the category of personhood without performing extensive and immediate medical and surgical intervention on them. The birth of an intersexed child has until very recently been described with near unanimity in the medical literature as a crisis, with these alarmist tones calming only very recently in favour of other, more subtle means of promoting immediate surgical intervention,[16] and continues to be unequivocally described as a 'medical and social emergency' (p. 388).[17] Most important here, however, is to point out that it is a function of power, rather than a statement of fact, to attribute the source of crisis to the birth of the intersexed child. The crisis in the clinic ought instead to be understood as a failure of the discourses of personhood in which expectant parents and their attendants invest.

Long before the birth of a child, those awaiting its arrival are encouraged to imagine its future as either male or female, and to map out the various, usually opposing, gendered divisions of aspirations, fantasies, labour, and so forth. Much of the internal structure of these expectations hinges on heteronormative assumptions about genital appearance as a 'natural' signifier of desires and sexual identity, and thus reifies and naturalizes gender as an effect of anatomy and biology. On the point of such expectation and the horror that parents must face when a newborn does not meet it, D.F.M. Thomas offers the following:

> Ambiguous genitalia and intersex states are serious disorders with profound and potentially lifelong implications for the affected individual. Gender assignment is often an imperfect exercise and where the long-term outcomes of genital reconstruction in infancy have been documented they have proved disappointing. There is widespread recognition of the need for long-term functional and psychosexual outcomes studies to formulate a more evidence-based approach. Aggressive and unnecessary early surgery is unjustifiable. However, the approach advocated by some patient groups, which envisages leaving some girls with an obviously uncorrected male genital phenotype, is likely to prove unacceptable to most parents (p. 50).[16]

Thomas' statement appears in an article that acts as an apologia for the still dominant clinical practice of rapid surgical intervention. While Thomas admits that surgical outcomes have been less than optimal, he charges that patient groups have been 'unjustified' and 'strident' in their 'misinformed' criticism of the motivations of doctors who treat intersexuality who, he asserts, 'have always been motivated by the wish to do what they genuinely believe to be in the best interests of their young patients and their families' (p. 47).[16] That is, in spite of his acknowledgment that early surgery is 'unjustifiable' when it is both aggressive and unnecessary, Thomas allows for any surgical intervention not deemed to be either. We should, then, pose the question to Thomas, 'Aggressive and unnecessary according to whose measure?' [. . .] Disability scholar Thomas Couser[18] explains that the difference between the medical and patient assessments is a struggle over who gets to tell the story that will make sense of one's ill self or body, of one's self or body in treatment, and of one's self or body after treatment:

> . . . even when medical treatment may be objectively successful, patients may feel they have been poorly treated. They often express anger at depersonalizing treatment and sometimes advocate alternative modalities. . . . just as patients wish to vanquish the illness that alters their lives, they may also wish to regain control of their life narratives which they have yielded up to 'objective' medical authority (p. 10).[18]

Couser's observations speak to the experiences of persons who at least agree with their practitioners that they were sick, and had experienced themselves as *ill* and for whom the struggle to re-personalize the meaning of that experience persists. With intersex, there is an extra layer of struggle as most of us who were treated as children did not experience ourselves as *ill*, and there is little agreement in the intersex population with the medical assessment of our bodies as diseased, rather than merely different. However, in common with those who have experienced illness, intersexed persons inhabit what Couser describes as 'colonized bodies' (p. 11),[18] granted little opportunity to speak authoritatively and granted little credence by medical audiences. [. . .] Thus, we are made by our colonizers not to matter, first as impossible intersexes, and after treatment as the no-longer intersexed.

Instead of addressing questions of epistemic and empirical power to label any intervention as appropriate or not, D.F.M. Thomas' essay directs attention away from concerns about power and toward an image of the clinician as benevolent caregiver. Moreover, the continued focus on the taken-as-obvious right course of using surgery to assign the child both a sex and gender ought to, and yet does not, signal to all concerned that sex and gender both arise as manifestations of cultural, not biological, imperative.

In focusing on an asserted benevolence grounded in the concern of the clinician for the 'best interests' of intersexed children and their families, Thomas denies any negative bias—such as sexism and heteronormative prejudice—in the motivation to treat quickly and aggressively. Summing up the enormous body of medical literature on intersex, Myra Hird concludes that '[t]here is consistent concern in the medical literature that an unstable gender identity will precipitate homosexual desire' (p. 1069).[19] The claim for medical benevolence 'works' only if one agrees with Thomas (and the practices he defends) that gender instability is the only possible outcome for a male with an 'inadequate phallus', or for a girl with 'an obviously uncorrected male genital phenotype' (p. 50).[16] Indeed, Thomas' language asserts that a child cannot have a 'clear' gender in the absence of a 'clear' anatomy that more-or-less meets the ideal for one sex or the other. However, Thomas' account fails to acknowledge that the anatomical model for sex *is* an ideal, and thus, by definition, something impossible for any individual body to possess or perform.

Disability, Intersex, and the Problem of the Ideal Body

From birth forward, recognition of the personhood of the child requires inclusion of all the narrative components that instantiate recognition, and which begin at the very least with the performative pronouncement of a sex upon which to hang a subject/identity. The pronouncement of a sex, Judith Butler explains, sets into play the recognition of a subject who is also recognizable to itself as such (pp. 231–32).[20] But more than requiring just the pronouncement of sex, the very concept of personhood requires an entire and productive discourse around its being in order for its existence to become articulate, and from which the status 'person' must articulate.* Butler explains:

> Where there is an 'I' who utters and speaks and thereby produces an effect in discourse, there is first a discourse which precedes and enables that 'I' and forms in language the constraining trajectory of its will. Thus there is no 'I' who stands *behind* discourse and executes its volitional will through discourse. On the contrary the 'I' comes into being *through* being called, named, interpellated . . . and this discursive constitution takes place prior to the 'I'; it is the transitive invocation of the 'I' (p. 225).[21] (Emphasis in the original.)

Butler's point does not apply uniquely to the manner in which intersexed children are apprehended and managed in the clinical setting, but to the manner that persons *in general* are instantiated as subjects. I draw attention to the point here only to help locate the imperative motivating clinical practice as the extra step required for all those already formed subjects to recognize and treat the intersexed child *as a person*. I reject the clinical characterization of intersex as a form of calamity, but must acknowledge that *something* about the child has interrupted the discursive trajectory that the expectant family and their attendants had been following.

Current clinical practice is instantiated and assumed as an obvious requirement to return the child to the discursive trajectory; moreover, it assumes that through fairly simple surgical practice clinicians will be able to effect the bodily type that would otherwise—if left alone in its confounding state—render impossible the conditions of/for the child's status as a person to be recognized. Critically, in the stance that Butler explains so well, personhood does not emanate from the individual/body, but from those around the individual/body who have the privilege and power to recognize or to deny the personhood of the individual/body they confront. [. . .] For my purposes here, the crucial point is not to settle what it means to be a person, but to question the taken-for-granted position that without a clear sex a child cannot become a person.

When an intersexed child is born, the level of concordance between parents and clinicians tends to be far higher than over questions of how to treat a child living what James Overboe, parsing Agamben, refers to as a 'bare life'.[23] [. . .] With intersex the problem is not a lack of will to provide treatment, but rather an excessive commitment to invasive treatment. The clinical standards of care for intersex assert that only through treatment to erase their ambiguous traits can the intersexed become fully human with the capacity for development as persons. With intersex the 'best interests' and 'quality of life' questions articulate at/from the point of acquiring human subjectivity: 'it' may obviously have a life, but 'it' will not become a person unless, as Iain Morland observes, some narratives can be held in abeyance while others are effected through surgical alteration of

the children's bodies.[24] At the very least, when intersexed children are identified, the unintelligibility of a subject position from which a clear sense of self (a requirement for self-reflection) may develop is presupposed and their potential to develop into persons is assumed to be thus threatened. It may even be that the intersexed infant is thought to lack the criteria for inclusion in species membership as a *human being,* insofar as the development of the intersexed body is thought to be arrested at some ambiguous embryological stage. Intersexed infants clearly have the capacity—if brought out of their embryonic status—to meet the criteria of species membership, and eventually to achieve full status as persons, but that achievement is structured as possible only if surgical technologies and prenatal interventions vault them past their ambiguous embryonic stage into human species membership. [. . .] Given this set of cultural assumptions there is little reason for clinicians and parents to be in conflict over how to proceed or what to withhold; it is obvious to the adult stakeholders that to withhold surgical 'correction' is to forestall unnecessarily the development of the child's identity.

It is worth pointing out that parents of non-responsive infants with severe neurological impairments have an easier time attributing the qualities of personhood to their children than do the parents of intersexed children. It may be, as Carl Elliott suggests, that 'anencephalics are, after all, living infants who often look very much like ordinary infants' (p. 95).[25] If the very sick infant *appears* very much like typical infants it is understandable that parents would have difficulty in perceiving the infant as a child who would be better off not to exist. While it disturbs Elliott to witness parents celebrating the birthdays of such children (p. 94),[25] I can only imagine how much worse it would disturb parents of such a child *not to celebrate* his or her birthday. Nonetheless, unable to see in the child what the parents see there, Elliott concludes his article in despair:

> We see that the lives of these children may have deep significance for their families. Yet on the other hand, we recognize that these lives fail to meet the criteria by which we count our own lives as meaningful. We try to convince ourselves that we should protect vulnerable lives, but we cannot imagine this as a life we would want to continue living. We say all lives deserve respect, but our measure of the good life does not include a life like this. We say that all lives are equal in the eyes of God, but we wonder why God has allowed such a life to come into being (p. 101).[25]

Elliott is unable to grant that there is a reasonable attachment of the parents to their anencephalic children, and finds no satisfactory answer for how the clinicians ought to decide to proceed. What remains stable in the face of his disquiet is the assumption that it is, in fact, the clinicians' place to decide how to proceed. Elliott has decided that a 'meaningful life is inaccessible to any child with severe neurological impairment' and his consternation, crucially, is over the inability of the parents to take the same view (p. 100).[25] Unable to do what they think 'right', clinicians and ethicists are frustrated by parents who continue to treat their anencephalic children as persons.

As Elliott's remarks cited above show us, clinicians have an easier time following their own sensibilities about the course of treatment because the parents of intersexed children are as unable as medical specialists to perceive the children as viable persons. It seems that where the typical appearance of anencephalic infants makes it easier for their parents to perceive the children as persons—though the parents' perception may have little effect on the treatment

decisions of clinicians—the atypical appearance of intersexed children makes it a simpler matter for parents to acquiesce to the clinical view and to accept surgical interference as the obviously right course. In either situation, the clinical view of the atypical child as a defective child prevails.

While the clinical decision to treat or not is very much at odds in the examples Elliott works with (anencephaly and intersex), there is no doubt in his view that in either scenario parents are reasonably acting in concordance with the larger culture when they cede to the expertise of the clinical assessment. While Elliott finds it 'hard to blame parents for seeking or consenting to surgery for their intersexed children' and hard to see the reason in parents' demands for continued life-support for their 'braindamaged' children, I disagree (p. 38).[5] Like Hilde Nelson, I find it difficult to condone willfully refusing to fulfill our duty to treat with care those children on whom we have conferred the capacity for personhood, and question the medical demand for parents to acquiesce to the view that their children cannot reasonably have a personhood in their anomalous 'state of exception'.[26]

Sexing the Intersexed

From a clinical perspective, the desire to 'manage' (i.e., to treat) the intersexed child's body through surgical and medical means is the volitional discourse that precedes the 'I' that the child will become. That is, where in typical births a simple pronouncement of sex is all that is required for the discursive constitution of the subject to be established, when an intersexed infant is born, technical intervention must occur prior to the pronouncement of sex. [. . .] Standard medical and surgical intervention to sex the intersexed has been described metaphorically by Anne Fausto-Sterling as a kind of 'shoehorning' in which surgeons alter the child's body to fit the constraints of a binary sex schema.[27] It is actually a little less like shoehorning, and rather more like the version of the Cinderella story in which the step-sisters attempt the removal of their toes and heels in order to fit into the ridiculous slippers that will verify their marriageability.

Indeed, the violent mutilation of heels and toes in the familiar Cinderella story illuminates the second major requirement of clinical intervention: the demand for silence. For just as the reader knows that the *ugly* step-sisters cannot make themselves suitable marriage partners for a prince, so too do the step-sisters know that they cannot really conceal the failure of their bodies to meet the ideal. The problem for the sisters is their *awareness* that they are imposters who know as much as we do that they do not 'belong' in the castle. To belong to the order of things, common wisdom says, one must remain ignorant of one's own divergence from the ideal. Cinderella herself is saved/kept ignorant of her own deviation from the ideal and consequent unsuitability for a prince by a narrative conceit that the body mirrors the interior and true quality of the soul; she may be a scullery maid but her beauty reflects an aristocratic soul. Indeed, in some versions of the Cinderella story, when the step-sisters repent for their cruelty, they are transformed into beauties who are married to noblemen in Cinderella and her prince's court. Intersexed children then must, like Cinderella, not be allowed awareness of their unsuitability for entry to the Gender Castle, and like fairy-godmothers who can supply the requirements for entry to the castle, surgeons supply the keys to the magic kingdom in the form of surgically fashioned genitals. David Hester sums up the situation thusly:

> Success of the adoption of the gender assignment is premised on the intersexed individual *not knowing they are intersexed*. Truth telling within this protocol is seen as

threatening the very success of the protocol, since it would mean informing the parent and the child/young adult that the gender of the child was in question (p. 27).[28]

Kathryn Pauly Morgan explains in her own parable, 'Gender Dimorph Utopia', that surgical and other medical technologies such as those employed in the management of intersexed infants and children are thought to stave off a form of 'gender-disability' that clinicians assume to be the obvious outcome of any nonconformity to the usual, oppositional dimorphism imposed on everything from appearance, gendered preferences, and individual behaviour to interpersonal relations and general societal membership:

> To maximize individual well-being and societal stability, diagnostic and interventionist technologies should be used—prenatally and postnatally—in order to eradicate genetically and/or hormonally gender-disabled fetuses. All gender ambiguous babies (i.e., babies with ambiguous genitalia) are to be labelled 'temporarily intersexed' and surgically corrected as soon after birth as possible so that they may fit into the proper gender location (p. 301).[2]

Regardless of how self-evident the current clinical approach to intersex seems, there are other, perhaps better, ways that we can treat intersexed children. That is, we have not to treat the child in the medical sense, but to revise how we think of 'treatment' itself, and not to define it solely as a set of clinically grounded options but as a set of behaviours and attitudes that we can take toward a child, or toward a fetus perceived to have a chromosomal, hormonal, or genetic profile likely to express itself in some form of intersexuality. If we understand treatment as an attitude or as a behaviour/stance that we take toward one another, then we can proceed from there to see that any 'need for treatment' arises not in the taken-as-obvious 'problem' of intersex characteristics in the child; instead, there is a need for a change in attitude emanating from the parents, the wider family, clinicians, social workers, and so forth. The reason that we need to turn away from the standard clinical treatment, and toward a new attitude of acceptance is that the standard treatments undermine the (formerly) intersexed adult's sense of authenticity as persons, and as gendered subjects.

We must take as obvious the *personhood* of the intersexed child rather than take as obvious that the personhood of the intersexed child is somehow obscured by the state of the genitals. After all, it is worth remembering that any passer-by who sees the child will apprehend a person, not an 'it'.

Typical Perspectives

Tom Koch argues that bioethics has become a practice and perspective in which 'debate is restricted to operational judgments based upon [unquestioned values]' (p. 252).[22] Bioethics has thus become a mode of thinking and of clinical practice in which only the same questions arise again and again, no longer really as questions but as the accepted ideology, purview, and practice of the field. [. . .] The crucial divide between bioethicists and disability studies scholars lies in the refusal of bioethicists to see lives with disability as lives with value.

Koch challenges and reframes such assessments of disability and quality of life by asserting a language of difference rather than of disability. As a person of difference himself, Koch refuses the term 'disability', and instead focuses attention on the manner in which the lives of persons of difference (the term he chooses over 'persons with disability' or 'disabled persons') are devalued. [. . .] Koch argues, medicine and the larger social world simply take for granted that lives lived with and through difference are to be avoided. [. . .]

The failure to value difference is a critical target of many rights-oriented movements aimed at the elimination of the social prejudices that prevent specific groups from accessing and exercising full rights as human subjects. The civil rights movement, the various women's movements, and the contemporary gay, lesbian, bisexual, and transgender/transsexual (GLBT) rights movement all appeal to the broader social world to extend full inclusion in the social contract to persons who have been marginalized on the basis of race, sex, gender, and sexuality (or a combination of these). As a part of the general civil rights tradition, disability rights advocacy also uses argument, education, and demonstration to demand recognition as full human subjects.

Queer theory, the GLBT movement, and critical disability activism/scholarship have an overlapping interest in 'resisting the marginalizing force of the private [and] insist, of course, that gender, sexuality and sex are issues of public concern', explain McRuer and Wilkerson (p. 10).[29] The point is that once identified as a person with a disability, or an inappropriate (i.e., queer) sexuality, we lose the personal privacy that others take for granted, while other aspects of our lives can be commanded to be private in oppressive ways, becoming simultaneously a matter of very public discourse and highly secretive management to facilitate our entry into the 'normal' world (p. 8).[29]

Successful entry into the 'normal world' generally requires as a condition of entry that we assimilate with it. The terrible consequence of contradictory imperatives to be at once on display as the *demonstrative* case for interested clinicians and medical students and to have to remain ignorant, or, at the very least, *silent* about our embodied difference is that both heteronormative and ableist perceptions of sexuality and embodied difference go unquestioned in the public domain that insists on our silence but cannot itself refrain from speaking about the problem we present to the usual narrative course of human being.

Thus, our entry may raise questions regarding which aspects of our differences we must sacrifice in order to access the rights and privileges of membership in the larger, hegemonic group. For example, claims for retaining the positive value of difference frequently face charges of essentialism. [. . .] Here, then, I return the focus of the paper to the particular manner in which the value of difference plays out for intersexuals, whose form of 'difference' is located in or on bodily terrain hidden from view by virtue of being located in areas deemed 'private', and generally rendered apparent only through invasive inspection. [. . .]

Arguments regarding the clinical treatment of intersex turn on its head the value of difference/refusal of care position that Koch advocates and that Overboe demands. The intersex rights movement has said not 'If you respect difference in life as you should then you will ensure my continued clinical care', but rather, 'If you value difference in life as you should then you must refuse clinical intervention as it is done for your sake and your interests, not mine'.

Thus, intersex activists use arguments grounded in a Difference Perspective, but it is simultaneously to normative ideologies of individual autonomy often rejected by disability scholars that intersex activists often appeal. My own work argues, for example, that we should take more seriously the manner in which surgery on intersexed infants and children interferes with their development as potentially autonomous subjects, and that we ought to take a more

'hands off' approach to allow intersexed children time to determine for themselves if and how they wish to 'deal with' their differences at some deferred date.[30] By and large, the contemporary intersex movement asks that guardians not bind their wishes for their children to be either male or female so closely to the bodies of their intersexed children as to impose clinical interventions that the child cannot be included in determining, and to recognize that if they are to have reciprocal relationships with their children as adults at a later date then *nothing,* rather than *something,* must be done now.

The argument is not purely a relational one about the value of difference, for it retains aspects of the individualist ideology that Koch describes as objectifying.[15] However, in the combination of both the difference perspective and the individual autonomy perspective a third mode of (e)valuation arises. Bioethicists and disability scholars alike may then be curious to know how we ought to apply this third way to the issue of prenatal selection—a classic beginning-of-life issue with which both groups are concerned. Before I introduce the terms through which I think a third approach could be built, it is necessary to examine the prenatal diagnostic tools being developed for intersex, and their relation to selective abortion.

Intersex, Prenatal Selection, Diagnosis and Valuing Difference

The final move of the paper is to discuss the manner in which prenatal technologies, through the use of particular narratives (disease, intervention, cure, inevitable death, future predictions of sex, of quality of life, etc.) confer or deny species membership and personhood on a child not-yet born to its expectant parents. The idea of the *expectant* warrants some further scrutiny, for it is specifically against the expected that Tanya Titchkosky explains the *unexpected* becomes problematic (pp. 96–128).[31] If the last half-century has seen the narrativization of personhood, sex, and subjectivity in the post-natal period of an intersexed child's life, prenatal interventions into pregnancies push back the timeframe in which the expected becomes the unexpected, the problematic, the not-quite-human.

Prenatal selection and diagnostic technologies and their eugenic potential are increasingly a concern for the intersexed. At least two forms of intersex—androgen insensitivity syndrome (AIS) and congenital adrenal hyperplasia (CAH)—are detectable in a developing fetus and some clinicians propose that we ought to use prenatal diagnostic tools to prevent intersex births from occurring.[32–34] [. . .]

In the majority of cases, there are no health considerations associated with intersexuality. In some cases, there are minor health or quality of life considerations; in a small percentage of cases (in CAH and Turner syndrome, especially), there can be serious considerations regarding metabolism (in CAH) and organ formation (in Turner syndrome).

Current *in utero* treatments can alter the outward manifestations of CAH, but cannot alter the underlying metabolic complications. *In utero* treatment, then, is effective only for pushing back the point at which parents make decisions about the appearance of their children. [. . .]

It is possible to identify Turner, Klinefelter, and Androgen Insensitivity Syndrome through prenatal testing, but [there are currently] no therapies available to reverse them. However, health considerations for these syndromes are far from clear and often overstated: many people with these conditions suffer no associated illnesses. The identification of any of these syndromes fails to provide a compelling reason for terminating a pregnancy.

Dorothy Wertz's research shows that 49 per cent of genetic professionals, and 48 per cent of primary care physicians would favour selective abortion of fetuses with Klinefelter Syndrome. Meanwhile, 42 per cent of genetics professionals and 37 per cent of primary care physicians favour selective abortion of fetuses with Turner Syndrome.[35] To give a sense of how these outcomes compare with the only even remotely close circumstance on the chart of potential identifications, I should point out that only 3 per cent of genetics professionals and 3 per cent of primary care physicians would favour selective abortion of a fetus who was not the sex desired by the parents.[35]

In addition, Wertz shows that the number of genetic professionals and primary care physicians who would terminate for Klinefelter or Turner syndrome is significantly higher than the numbers for schizophrenia, alcoholism, or Alzheimer's. In a separate test for other measures and with other health care providers, only about 12 per cent would focus on the positive aspects for Klinefelter syndrome and only about 16 per cent would do so with Turner syndrome. Furthermore, the number of genetics professionals and physicians who would emphasize the positive are only slighter higher than the numbers for Alzheimer's and schizophrenia (p. 279).[36]

The essays in *Prenatal Testing and Disability Rights* show that extremely negative attitudes of genetic counsellors, primary physicians, and families prevail in attitudes toward pregnancies and fetuses in which conditions such as AIS, CAH, Klinefelter, or Turner Syndrome are identified.[36] [. . .] As Sharpe and Earle argue, the problem is not rooted in women's right to abortion and, therefore, the solution to the problem is not to curtail that right, as doing so undermines both the status of the right as such, and the status of women as persons under the law.[37] Rather, the problem begins with clinical attitudes and with social demands and limitations that place exceptional demands specifically on mothers. [. . .]

In this paper, I have argued that claims such as those Elliott makes, according to which medical care providers have no special obligation to diverge from the values of our society in general when it comes to the perception of lives of difference, form an unconvincing apologia for the support of hegemonic, often oppressive attitudes and behaviours when those who wield biopower could instead urge us all to do better, to resist oppressive attitudes, and use technology to prepare for greater accommodations.

Approaches to concerns over prenatal technologies and disability rights that suggest the debate revolves exclusively around the question of abortion inevitably pit women's rights claims against disability rights claims. Such approaches assume that women who terminate pregnancies for reasons of disability or difference act in bad faith and '[challenge] the legitimacy of individual choices on the grounds that they emanate from wider beliefs and values. . . . On this argument, a case could be made for denying virtually any individual the right to exercise virtually any preference' (pp. 143–44).[38] In addition, such stances imply that there could never be disabled women who might use prenatal and other reproductive technologies, or at least that no self-respecting women with disabilities would do so.

I propose that we ought not extrapolate from the specifics of intersex to the more general questions of what it means to be human, how to value human life, and what it means to be a person, but ought instead to pursue the specifics of difference and autonomy on a case-by-case basis, being attentive to the positive value of lives lived with difference, and to the need of persons to exercise their own level of qualified autonomy within

the networks of social support that enable the qualified autonomy of all persons. I imagine the third mode as one in which we recognize that how we use reproductive technologies is not simply a question of whether we choose to continue a pregnancy or not. In my imagined third mode, neither an apologist stance from bioethicists favouring soft eugenic practices, nor a disability activist stance, which would deny women their own autonomy, would have priority. Rather than assume that women are merely vehicles through which to enact other social objectives, this third mode will be attentive to the value of difference, open to the encouragement of movement away from a quality assurance attitude toward reproduction. A third mode approach will recognize that women are autonomous persons with the right to exercise that autonomy to protect their own bodies, reproductive labour, and mothering. A third mode will also seek to protect the rights of children born with atypical physical, sensory, and/or cognitive traits, aiding them to develop the greatest level of autonomy possible at maturity. Autonomy may always be provisional, but to deny some their bodily integrity—as with intersexed children—on the grounds that autonomy is only provisional at best is to continue to divide the world into groups of people who are more and less deserving, with some more able to exercise their provisional autonomy than others. In practice this means adopting a policy of non-interference for any atypical features more troubling to parents than to infants, and while the appearance-based features of intersex are my primary concern here, there are clearly other types of corporeal anomaly to which such a stance could apply. Cochlear implantation for deaf infants is one example; surgery for various cranio-facial anomalies, such as cleft-lip, is another. My proposal also requires that we move away from assertions that typically make women out to be adversaries who will always choose to terminate any fetus in which an anomaly is diagnosed. As Chloë Atkins has argued in a paper that discusses with nuance and depth how women think about their pregnancies in relation to medical discourses they encounter, women are increasingly refusing prenatal diagnostics, and increasingly refusing the pathologization of bodily, sensory, and cognitive difference in their fetuses (p. 107).[39]

If we are to develop this third mode, we need to demand that bioethics discourses not aim to make us complacent about medical knowledge/power. We need to curtail eugenic tendencies in prenatal technologies so that we may value human variability more rather than less. We need to listen seriously to the narratives of adult intersexed persons when they discuss the ways in which medicine, however well intentioned its traditional approach, has failed to meet their

needs because it has treated the child as a problem to be fixed, instead of treating the child as an eventual adult who will decide for itself whether its body is problematic. And, even while we demand that medicine rethink its pathologization of intersex and other forms of difference, we need to be careful not to build a disability stance that vilifies all women whose exercise of their reproductive agency leads to termination. This last stance is important because logically, we cannot grant agency to exercise a right of autonomy if we insist that only one outcome is correct. Ultimately, the rights we recognize for one person inform the terrain on which we recognize rights for others. Because I insist that we must protect the development of autonomy in intersexed children, I also recognize their right to choose surgeries to alter appearance later in life. [. . .]

Note

* For a much longer discussion of how concepts of personhood and their implications for care provision and citizenship are structured, see Martha Nussbaum (2006)[40] especially Chapters 2 and 3, and Eva Feder Kittay (2005).

Notes

1. Tremain, S. (2001). On the government of disability. *Social Theory and Practice, 27*(4), 617–36.
2. Morgan, K.P. (2005). Gender police. In S. Tremain (Ed.), *Foucault and the government of disability* (pp. 298–328). Ann Arbor: University of Michigan Press.
3. Roen, K. (2005). Queer kids: Toward ethical clinical interactions with intersex people. In M. Shildrick & R. Mykitiuk (Eds), *Ethics of the body* (pp. 259–78). Cambridge (MA): MIT.
4. Dreger, A. (1999). *Intersex in the age of ethics*. Boston: Harvard University Press.
5. Elliott, C. (1998). Why can't we go on as three? *Hastings Center Report, 28*(3), 36–39.
6. Kessler, S. (1990). The medical construction of gender: Case management of intersexed infants. *Signs, 16*(1), 3–26.
7. Frank, A. (2005). The perfect storm of enhancement. *Hastings Center Report, 35*(1), 46–47.
8. Anonymous. Our 12 year old selves [monograph on the Internet]. AISSG; 2008 [cited 2008 Mar 12]. Available from: http://www.medhelp.org/ais/debates/12YEAROLD.HTM#Start.
9. Anonymous (1996). Sex, lies and ideology. *Alias, 1*(6), 7.
10. Anonymous (1994). Once a dark secret. BMJ, *308*, 542, Feb 19.
11. Chase, C. (1998). Affronting reason. In D. Atkins (Ed.), *Looking queer* (pp. 205–19). London and New York: Haworth.
12. Coventry, M. (1998). The tyranny of the esthetic. *On The Issues, VII*(3), 16–20+.
13. Groveman, S. (1998). The Hanukkah bush: Ethical implications in the clinical management of intersex. *Clinical Ethics, 9*(4), 356–59.
14. Harmon-Smith, H. (1998). Ten commandments. *Clinical Ethics, 9*(4), 371.
15. Koch, T. (2004). The difference that difference makes: Bioethics and the challenge of 'disability'. *Journal of Medicine and Philosophy, 29*(6), 697–716.
16. Thomas, D.F.M. (2004). Gender assignment: Background and current controversies. *British Journal of Urology International, 93*(Suppl 3), 47–50.
17. Özbey, H., Darendeliler, F., Kayserili, H., Korkmazlar, U., & Salman, T. (2004). Gender assignment in female

congenital adrenal hyperplasia: A difficult experience. *British Journal of Urology International, 94*, 388–91.

18. Couser, T. (1997). *Recovering bodies*. Madison: University of Wisconsin Press.

19. Hird, M. (2003). Considerations for a psychoanalytic theory of gender identity and sexual desire: The case of intersex. *Signs, 28*(4), 1068–91.

20. Butler, J. (1994). *Bodies that matter: On the discursive limits of sex*. London and New York: Routledge.

21. Butler, J. (2004). *Undoing gender*. New York: Routledge.

22. Koch, T. (2006). Bioethics as ideology. *Journal of Medicine and Philosophy, 31*(3), 251–67.

23. Overboe, J. (2007). Disability and genetics: Affirming the bare life (the state of exception). *Canadian Review of Sociology and Anthropology, 44*(2), 219–35.

24. Morland, I. (2005). *Narrating intersex: On the ethical critique of the medical management of intersexuality, 1985–2005* [dissertation] (p. 306). Royal Holloway, University of London.

25. Elliott, C. (2001). Attitudes, souls and persons: Children with severe neurological impairment. In C. Elliott (Ed.), *Slow cures and bad philosophers: Essays in Wittgenstein, medicine and bioethics* (pp. 89–102). Durham (NC): Duke University Press.

26. Nelson, H. (2002). What child is this? *Hastings Center Report, 36*(2), 29–38.

27. Fausto-Sterling, A. (1993). The five sexes: Why male and female are not enough. *The Sciences, 33*(2), 20–24 March/April.

28. Hester, J.D. (2004). Intersex(es) and informed consent: How physicians' rhetoric constrains choice. *Theoretical Medicine, 25*, 21–49.

29. McRuer, R., & Wilkerson, A. (2003). Cripping the (queer) nation. *GLQ, 9*(1–2), 1–23.

30. Holmes, M. (2006). Deciding fate or protecting a developing autonomy?: Intersex children and the Colombian Constitutional Court. In S. Minter, P. Currah & R. Juang (Eds.), *Transgender rights* (pp. 102–21). Minneapolis: University of Minnesota.

31. Titchkosky, T. (2003). *Disability, self and society*. Toronto: University of Toronto Press.

32. American Academy of Pediatrics (2000). Technical report: Congenital adrenal hyperplasia. *Pediatrics, 106*(6), 1511–18.

33. New, M. (2001). Prenatal treatment of CAH: US experience. *Endocrinology and Metabolism Clinics of North America, 20*(1), 1–14.

34. Donohoe, P.K., Powell, D.M., & Lee, M.M. (1991). Clinical management of intersex abnormalities. *Current Problems in Surgery, 28*(8), 513–79.

35. Wertz, D. (2000). Drawing lines: Notes for policymakers. In E. Parens & A. Asch (Eds), *Prenatal testing and disability rights* (pp. 261–87). Washington: Georgetown University Press.

36. Parens, E., & Asch, A. (2000). *Prenatal testing and disability rights*. Washington: Georgetown University Press.

37. Atkins, C. (2008). The choice of two mothers: Disability, gender, sexuality, and prenatal testing. *Cultural Studies <=>Critical Methodologies, 8*(1), 106–29.

38. Sharpe, K., & Earle, S. (2002). Feminism, abortion and disability: Irreconcilable differences? *Disability and Society, 17*(2), 137–45.

39. Lindemann, H. Shotgun weddings. *Bioethics Forum* [serial on the Internet]. 2007 Aug 30 [cited 2008 Mar 5]. Available from: http://www.bioethicsforum.org/abortion-Italy-Down-Syndrome.asp.

40. Nussbaum, M. (2006). *Frontiers of justice*. Cambridge (MA): Belknap.

Canadians Denied: A Queer Diasporic Analysis of the Canadian Blood Donor

OmiSoore Dryden

When you click on the 'Donor' section of the Canadian Blood Services' (CBS) website, you are met with a picture of a white man, with his right arm outstretched, as if he is about to roll up his sleeve, preparing himself to donate blood. The text begins with the statement, 'Donors are the heart of our blood supply system . . .' and closes with gratitude and a seemingly gentle command,

'If you are already a donor, thank you; if not, **"it's in you to give"**. Please book an appointment today' (CBS n.d., emphasis in the original).

However, while it may be 'in you to give', your blood may not be wanted.

In detailing the eligibility requirements for blood donations, Canadian Blood Services also dedicates two webpages to temporary and indefinite deferrals. On the page titled, 'Indefinite Deferrals', Canadian Blood Services catalogues and details six factors that lead to indefinite deferrals from the blood donation process. These factors are: '1) Geographic Deferrals; 2) Possible Exposure to CJD [Creutzfeldt Jakob Disease] or vCJD [Variant Creutzfeldt Jakob Disease]; 3) HIV High Risk Activities; 4) Disease; 5) Diabetes; and 6) False Reactive (False Positive) Test Results' (CBS n.d.). It is in the third factor that we find the following statement, 'All men who have had sex with another man, even once, since 1977 are indefinitely deferred' (CBS n.d.). Canadian Blood Services' use of the words 'defer' and 'deferral' may suggest that a person's opportunity to donate blood is just merely postponed, when in fact their body has been permanently banned from this process.

Canadian Blood Services' blood donor screening process is a significant part of a larger system that is intended to protect the blood supply from debilitating and deadly infection, in particular HIV/AIDS. The provisions for deferral target particular bodies for temporary or indefinite deferral. Bisexual men, gay men, and men who have sex with men are specific examples of bodies that are indefinitely deferred.

According to Canadian Blood Services' website and its television and radio commercials, the most precious gift one can give is to donate one's blood and give the gift of life. Canadian Blood Services positions the blood donor as heroic, generous, selfless, thoughtful, and moral, the traits of an ideal, proper, and authentic Canadian citizen. What does it mean then if bisexual and gay men are barred from donating blood? When bisexual and gay Canadian men attempt to donate their blood are they positioned as heroic, selfless, and moral? Or are they considered unethical, improper, and un-Canadian in their attempts?

Lesbian and gay political and legal groups, such as the professional organization Egale Canada (Equality for Gays and Lesbians Everywhere), along with other ad hoc organizations formed on college and university campuses and over the Internet, are actively engaged in having the ban against bisexual and gay men removed. While I find this an important intervention, I am concerned with how these initiatives position bisexual and gay men. Currently, in the challenges brought to the blood donor screening process, lesbian and gay political groups have only focused upon the conflation of HIV/AIDS infection with gay bodies and the resulting exclusion of gay blood,[1] without taking into consideration that HIV/AIDS infection is also intimately tied to other bodies and that gay bodies are rarely just gay. Other categories of people (sex workers, people addicted to drugs, people from continental Africa, and the people who have sex with people from these groups) are considered to be at greater risk for HIV/AIDS infection and are therefore also subject to indefinite deferral in Canadian Blood Services' attempts to safeguard the blood supply from these infections.

Not only am I intrigued by the refusal to acknowledge or incorporate the 'just gay' body as a proper and acceptable (non-tainted) blood-donating Canadian, but I also seek to explore the complex conceptual link between 'homosexuality' and 'race', particularly with how this link further disrupts the normative positioning of the blood donor body/subject. Blood has been used to tie an individual to the nation, and within the nation; HIV/AIDS and Hepatitis C has tied tainted blood to individuals who are gay, sex workers, addicted to drugs, from Haiti (in the beginning of the tainted blood crisis of the late 1970s and early 1980s), and from continental Africa (currently). In this paper, I examine how Canadian Blood Services operates as a technology of

Canadian nationalism as it posits the blood donor as an ideal, proper, and acceptable Canadian and the effect this has on the bodies of African gay-Canadians.

The blood business in Canada is intimately connected to Canadian nationalism. In January 1940, the Canadian Red Cross Society urged Canadians to 'make a date with a wounded solider', and thus the first blood donor clinic occurred (Picard 1995, 9). The creation of a voluntary blood donation system during the Second World War positioned blood donation as a patriotic act—the Canadian thing to do. Canadian Blood Services relied on this history when faced with the daunting task of having to rebuild the blood supply system in Canada after the tainted blood crisis. 'It's in you to give' effectively reminds Canadians that voluntary blood donation fulfills the international narratives of generosity, nice-ness, morality and tolerance and therefore becomes as archetypically Canadian as the national anthem, hockey games, multiculturalism, and the Charter of Rights and Freedoms.

In an effort to be considered an ideal and proper Canadian, and consequently included in all things Canadian, lesbian and gay political organizations have focused on specific questions included in the blood donor questionnaire that directly target bisexual men, gay men, and men who have sex with men. I'll come back to this discussion in a moment. Instead, I begin my analysis by focusing on the following sample of declarative statements and phrases made by Canadian Blood Services on their website and YouTube channel.

- 'Without *generous and committed* donors, there would be no blood system in Canada.' (CBS n.d., Donor section, my emphasis)
- 'Canada's blood system is founded on the principle of *gratuity*.' (CBS n.d., my emphasis)

- 'Canadian Blood Services . . . [is] dedicated to ensuring that Canadians have access to *safe and secure* supplies of blood and blood products . . .' (CBS n.d., Media Room, my emphasis)
- 'Canadian Blood Services is committed to maintaining the *Canadian tradition* of unpaid and volunteer donations for both whole blood and plasma. In fact, research shows that Canadians donate blood because *they want to help their fellow Canadians* in need.' (CBS n.d., FAQ, my emphasis)
- '. . . finding more and more communities coming to us and asking us how they can be a difference in their community. *How they can be Canadian*. And we are telling them, you know what, *to really be Canadian is about giving blood* [. . .] and that is *what being Canadian is about*.' (YouTube: CBS n.d., Official Channel, my emphasis)

The words and phrases I've highlighted provide valuable information regarding the discursive practices utilized by Canadian Blood Services in the construction of the ideal and proper blood donor body/subject. The use of seemingly explicit and definitive language in an effort to produce distinct types of knowledge relies on deliberate and specific erasures. In my exploration of how African gay-Canadians destabilize the blood donor body, I employ a theoretical framework which also makes use of destabilizing constructions—queer diasporic analysis.

Queer diasporic analysis is a post-structural critical theory that not only draws upon the critical practice of deconstruction but also draws upon discourse analysis as posited by Michel Foucault. I draw upon queer diasporic scholars Rinaldo Walcott and Gayatri Gopinath who describe this form of analysis as a suturing of queer theory with/to diasporic analysis in order to 'recuperate those desires, practices and subjectivities that are rendered impossible and unimaginable' (Gopinath 2005b, 11) within conventional nationalist imaginaries. Queer diasporic analysis utilizes the need to employ a genealogy of the present that takes into account how the body/subject is constructed differently and divergently through time, space, and place. Additionally, this analysis insists on the intersectional, interlocking use of multiple fields and disciplines, specifically the discursive practices of race, nation, diaspora, and sexuality. [. . .]

Gayatri Gopinath posits that queer diasporic analysis considers how specific racial, sexual, and gender configurations, when read simultaneously, 'exceed the nation's boundaries and contest its absolutist logic' (Gopinath 2005a, 160). The potential of an analysis framed through diasporic queerness suggests and makes prominent the destabilizing, disappeared 'other'. This analysis challenges the technologies of nationalism by insisting on foregrounding the excluded, and putting forth a contrapuntal reading of belonging, home, and the ideal, authentic and natural body politic. Queer diasporic analysis carries with it a hope of new meanings, new possibilities, and the space to think what was previously unthought and unthinkable.

With specific attention to African/Haitian bodies, I draw upon Rinaldo Walcott, who uses queer diaspora to read 'race', specifically blackness, back into the Canadian nation. In his article, 'Somewhere Out There: The New Black Queer Theory', Walcott maps how queer diasporic analysis can be applied when exploring black queer subjects within the nation. In this passage, he speaks to HIV/AIDS and the usefulness of queer diasporic analysis. He states, 'HIV/AIDS connects across the diaspora as much as it disconnects, raising the difficult issues of instability and indeterminacy as both diaspora and queer theory throw up those terms for

consideration and analysis in the making and unmaking of community; thus offering us more complex and complicated encounters with how we belong on the basis of race, gender and sexuality' (Walcott 2007, 34).

Walcott cautions that blackness can, should, and is being read outside of the imperial borders of the United States in spite of the dominant presence of American (and African American) productions of culture in Canada. By firmly placing blackness in Canada, the possibilities for analysis and critique are furthered, specifically in relation to black queers in the diaspora (Walcott 2001; 2003; 2007). [. . .]

To place Canada into useful dialogue, conversation, and even antagonism, I turn to Canada's violently instituted origins.

Canada, a colonial settler society, is fraught with the grandiose denials of its exceptionally violent history. The discourse of being founded by two nations, as opposed to being invaded by two nations, significantly structures the imagined political community that is the nation. Additionally, founding nations are relied on not only as the moral markers for the nation, but also as the marker by which bodies are measured for citizenship. Bodies from the founding nations are therefore positioned as ideal, exalted (Thobani 2007), and as Canadian-Canadian (Mackey 2002, 33).[2] Other bodies are raced and subsequently positioned as less than ideal, improper, and not truly Canadian. Instead, I suggest that these constructed positions are haunted by, or filled with, tensions, disquiet, and pestering caused from the unsuccessful repression of the colonial formation of Canada.

Current accounts of Canada being a civil nation—a generous, nice, moral, and tolerant nation—make it difficult for the nation to imagine, comprehend, and hold the violence with which and upon which it is founded. An othering of indigenous and not-white bodies is a significant tenet within European and American discursive schools of race, (Somerville 1995)[3] and Canada is a nation deeply dependent upon the discourses of race and the practices of racism. [. . .] The nation knows itself not simply by who is included, but specifically by who is othered in that inclusion.

Canada's multiculturalism policy and the perpetual estrangement of the raced body are interlocking tools in the technology of Canadian nationalism. After all, a nation that risks its safety and security to include these othered bodies must be a generous, tolerant, moral, and gracious nation. Racism and racial discrimination are effectively understood to happen elsewhere (or in the very distant past), and this narrative instructs the discursive practice of innocence. To maintain the discourse of innocence requires an aggressive adherence to Canadian discursive practice of multiculturalism and its disavowal that racism, historically and currently, occurs within the nation. We see the effects of this discursive practice when slavery in Canada is not only denied, but also aggressively disavowed.

Slavery in Canada[4] lasted for over 200 years; however, because Canada's slave institution was smaller in scope than the slave institutions in the geographical regions currently known as the United States, Caribbean, and Latin America, it is often considered 'too small to warrant intellectual or political consideration' (McKittrick 2006, 97). However, by not taking Canada's slave institutions into consideration, blackness and black bodies are effectively placed outside the boundaries of how we understand Canada and Canadian society. Even though 'black' people continue to make Canada home, Canadian 'black' bodies are often considered recent arrivals whilst simultaneously belonging elsewhere. The Caribbean region and the United States are considered more appropriate spaces/places for 'black' bodies and continental Africa is irrevocably positioned as the geographical, environmental, and historical producer of 'black' bodies. [. . .]

These are the narratives of Canada I read back into the nation when I come across the words and phrases declaratively used by Canadian Blood Service in their construction of the donor body. I take the realities of the violence of colonialism, racism, race discourse, and the absented presence of blackness into account when I am confronted with words and phrases such as 'safe and secure', 'Canadian tradition', 'fellow Canadians', and 'to really be Canadian'.

Even though the white European body is positioned as the ideal Canadian-Canadian, this body must also adhere to restrictive narratives regarding sex, sexuality, and gender. These restrictive narratives posit that ideal Canadians must control their sexual urges if they are to become proper Canadians; in this case, virtuous and moral. The Canadian-Canadian sexual subject is monogamous and only engages in sexual activities for the purposes of procreation. The Canadian-Canadian sexual subject is responsible for replenishing the nation's population with healthy and ideal bodies. Sexual activities should not be overly enjoyed, not engaged in excessively or outside of the monogamous coupling. [. . .] In other words, these sexual activities occur between a man and his wife. Sexual activities that occur outside of monogamous marriage are considered deviant practices which may threaten and undo the well-being of the family and therefore of the nation. Feminist political, social, and legal actions have effectively shifted many of these regulations; however many of these beliefs still exist in the discursive practices of misogyny, patriarchy, and homophobia.

Seeking recognition as Canadian-Canadians, lesbian and gay political and legal rights movements in Canada challenged the nation's narratives on the ideal, proper, and authentic sexual Canadian subject, which resulted in many successes. Same-sex sexual activities were decriminalized; homosexuality was no longer officially considered a mental illness; lesbians and gays retained access and their legal rights to their children; and were granted unrestricted access to the adoption process. Most recently, lesbians and gays gained the right to be legally married.

In order to achieve these legal rights within the state, lesbian and gay political and legal rights organizations not only took up an essentialist construction of a gay body, but also actively engaged in putting forward an ideal 'just gay' Canadian sexual subject. This 'just gay' sexual body was not only sex-gender-genital compliant but also embraced the narratives of monogamy and family. This 'just gay' Canadian sexual subject became a simple, cohesive, and innocent subject. In her article 'Marrying Citizens! Raced Subjects? Re-thinking the Terrain of Equal Marriage Discourse', Suzanne Lenon contends that 'The coherency of this "just gay" legal subject is produced and made legible in part through the occlusion of whiteness as a racial category—it is a norm to which no racial reference need be made' (Lenon 2005, 413).

With the coherency of the 'just gay' subject being produced through the occlusion of whiteness as a racial category, it is important to examine the challenges launched by Egale Canada and other ad hoc lesbian and gay political groups against Canadian Blood Services.

The following questions are identified by Egale Canada and other ad hoc lesbian and gay political groups as being discriminatory to bisexual men, gay men, and men who have sex with men.

- Question #12: Have you ever had an AIDS (HIV) test other than for donating blood?
- Question #19: Male donors: Have you had sex with a man, even one time since 1977?

- Question #22: Female donors: In the last 12 months, have you had sex with a man who had sex, even one time since 1977, with another man?
- Question #29: In the past 6 months, have you had sex with someone whose sexual background you don't know? (CBS, 'Record of Donation' April 2009, 2)

Egale Canada and other ad hoc organizations find that the focus on a particular group of people, as opposed to high-risk behaviours, is misleading in terms of HIV/AIDS information and blood safety. To assume that only bisexual men, gay men, and men who have sex with men engage in unprotected anal sex is deceptive and fictitious. It is important to explore why Canadian Blood Services does not believe that heterosexual couples would participate in unprotected anal sex with their partners and with people outside of their coupling. The 'just gay' body positioned in these challenges, as constructed by Egale and other organizations, is a gay man in a monogamous married couple where he and his husband have protected sex consistently and also test negative for HIV.

I am interested in what happens to this 'just gay' body when other questions from the questionnaire are introduced into the analysis. I suggest the following questions:

- Question #30 a): Were you born in or have you lived in Africa since 1977?
- Question #30 b): Since 1977, did you receive blood transfusions or blood products in Africa?
- Question #30 c): Have you had sexual contact with anyone who was born in or lived in Africa since 1977 (CBS, 'Record of Donation' April 2009, 2)

The bifurcation of 'sexuality' from 'race' effectively posits questions 12, 19, 22, and 29 as disconnected and independent from question 30, sections a, b, and c. However, as queer diasporic analysis illustrates, the African gay-Canadian body is a very real presence, which means that these questions must be read collectively and concurrently.

The desire of Egale Canada and other organizations to have 'just gay' bodies included within the current configuration of Canadian-Canadians requires a separation of sexuality from race. Additionally for the 'just gay' body to be considered a 'good' subject, he/she must be sex/gender compliant, married, monogamous, family oriented, and white, and take up the national narratives regarding the 'just black' body (recently arrived and belonging elsewhere). The reading of gay-Canadian with/through blackness disrupts not only the challenges launched by lesbian and gay political groups against Canadian Blood Services but also disrupts the discursive practices utilized by CBS in their construction of an ideal and proper blood donor body/subject.

Queer diasporic analysis understands that the donor is heavily regulated through the exaltation of Eurocentric heteronormativity, and because of this, the only *good* gay is the one who does his duty by not attempting to donate his blood. This is what it means to engage a blood donor system that is founded upon a racist, heteropatriarchal, and homophobic system. The complexity of bodies in and of the nation exceeds the binary structures of representation. [. . .]

As a tool of Canadian nationalism, Canadian Blood Services must ensure that the narratives of the nation are not only adhered to diligently, but also are protected, safe and secure. And as a technology of nationalism, Canadian Blood Services mimics the discursive practices of the nation. Consequently, like the nation, Canadian Blood Services may tolerate difference among potential blood donor bodies; however, it will not relinquish its construction of the ideal blood body and the othered body that remains positioned as inherently threatening the blood supply. Self-evident truths do not come from the body, they are in fact constructed and then written upon and through the body; therefore, what does this mean for the safety and security of the blood supply?

The opportunity to donate blood is clearly felt as a process of belonging, even though the Canadian Blood Services' blood donor is a haunted, violently instituted, and over-determined subject. Canadian Blood Services' inability to take into account the so-called 'impossible subjects' of queer diasporic populations within the nation is as much a danger to the blood system as are former, current, and future diseases.

Notes

1. I draw on two documents—Egale Canada's press release and Angela Lambert's article. Egale Canada's press release entitled, '"It's in You to Give" But Not If You Are a Gay or Bisexual Man' dated 12 June 2007, focuses upon CBS's continued intention to exclude gay and bisexual men from donating blood and also calls attention to CBS's focus on ' . . . sexual orientation rather than on unsafe sexual practices'. In Angela Lambert's article, 'The Impact of Heterosexism on Our Emergency Blood Supply', dated June 2000, Lambert cites an education campaign run by the Canadian Federation of Students where they challenge Canadian Blood Services to focus on high-risk behaviours and not gay men.

2. I borrow this term from the work of Eva Mackey. Mackey posits that in order to have 'normal personhood', it is imperative to understand one's self through a defined, differentiated, and enclosed identity. 'Canadian-Canadian' is such a term. The term is coined by an interview subject who is attempting to establish herself as a proper and ideal Canadian, someone who is white yet not 'raced' (Mackey 2002).

3. I am specifically referencing Somerville's work on monogeny and polygeny.

4. During the practice of slavery in Canada, the nation held the designations 'British North America' and 'New France'.

References

CBS (Canadian Blood Services). www.bloodservices.ca Web. Retrieved February 2007.

Egale Canada. "'It's in You to Give" But Not If You Are a Gay or Bisexual Man' 2007. www.egale.ca Web. Retrieved April 2008.

Gopinath, G. 'Bollywood Spectacles: Queer Diasporic Critique in the Aftermath of 9/11', *Social Text*, 23.3–4 (2005a): 157–69.

———. *Impossible Desires: Queer Diasporas and South Asian Public Cultures*. Durham and London: Duke University Press, 2005b.

Lambert, A. 'The Impact of Heterosexism on Our Emergency Blood Supply', 2000. www.mun.ca/the/news/emergency blood.html Web. Retrieved February 2007.

Lenon, S. 'Marrying Citizens! Raced Subjects? Re-thinking the Terrain of Equal Marriage Discourse', *Canadian Journal of Women and the Law* 17.2 (2005): 405–21.

Mackey, E. *The House of Difference: Cultural Politics and National Identity in Canada*. Toronto: University of Toronto Press, 2002.

McKittrick, K. *Demonic Grounds: Black Women and the Cartographies of Struggle*. Minneapolis: University of Minnesota Press, 2006.

Picard, A. *The Gift of Death: Confronting Canada's Tainted Blood Tragedy*. Toronto: HarperCollins Publishers Ltd., 1995.

Somerville, S. *Queering the Color Line: Race and the Invention of Homosexuality in American Culture*. Durham and London: Duke University Press, 1995.

Thobani, S. *Exalted Subjects: Studies in the Making of Race and Nation in Canada*. Toronto: University of Toronto Press, 2007.

Walcott, R. 'Caribbean Pop Culture in Canada: Or, The Impossibility of Belonging to the Nation', *Small Axe 9*, March 2001: pp. 231–39.

———. 'Beyond the "Nation Thing": Black Studies, Cultural Studies and Diaspora Discourse (Or the Post-Black Studies Moment)', *Decolonizing the Academy: African Diaspora Studies*, C. Davies, M. Gadsby, C. Peterson, and H. Williams, eds. Trenton, New Jersey: Africa World Press, Inc., 2003, pp. 107–24.

———. 'Somewhere Out There: The New Black Queer Theory', *Blackness and Sexualities*, M. Wright and A. Schuhmann, eds. Berlin: Lit Verlag, 2007, pp. 29–40.

YouTube: Canadian Blood Services Official Channel. www.youtube.com/user/18882DONATE Web. Retrieved January 2009.

Passive Medicalization: The Case of Viagra and Erectile Dysfunction

Richard M. Carpiano

Available for prescription use only since 27 March 1998, Viagra (sildenafil citrate) has changed the way Americans view erectile dysfunction (ED). With nearly 2.9 million prescriptions written during its first three months on the US market (Lamberg 1998), Viagra's popularity has many social and cultural consequences for both the US health care delivery system and the population as a whole. What implications does such a 'lifestyle' drug have for medicalization and social control?

With Viagra's introduction, a new model of medicalization—'passive medicalization'—has emerged that has pushed treatment of ED further into the realm of biomedicine while ignoring psychosocial correlates and etiologies. In this form of passive medicalization, the medical field did not necessarily make an initial attempt to further medicalize a problem that has larger social ties (in this case, ED). Instead, the general public has turned to the medical field for a way to combat this side effect of socially rooted problems. In the case of Viagra, the medical field did not establish an organized crusade against a social problem but has merely acted as a gatekeeper for those obtaining a temporary treatment for an illness that can be caused by social factors—in essence, becoming a passive control agent that profits from the demands of the public.

In exploring the emergence of this passive medicalization, it is important first to examine the ED etiology debate. Although ED affects 10–20 million US men (Fabbri, Aversa, and Isidori 1997), debate has long existed over whether it is a psychogenic or biogenic condition. As awareness of ED has increased, two themes have emerged in the literature: (a) It is viewed as a socially legitimate problem that can be treated medically and (b) despite the frequent involvement of emotional and interpersonal factors, medical treatments are viewed as more efficient and effective than psychological treatments (Levine 1992). [. . .] Theories on the medicalization of ED, however, need to be stretched further in order to examine the role that individual action plays in promoting medicalization. Prior work has proposed the idea that medicalization can result when physicians are generally uninvolved or their initial involvement is minimal (e.g., Conrad and Schneider 1980). Although studies have not addressed non-physician–promoted medicalization for ED, it proves to be an important perspective to consider in understanding the various factors surrounding the increasing prescription of Viagra and ED's passive medicalization.

The Passive Medicalization of Viagra

[. . .] In examining the Viagra demand, it is necessary to investigate social constructions of health and illness in clarifying how social forces contribute to human understanding of, and action toward, health and illness (Brown 1996). Analyzing how the individual man recognizes that he has some form of ED leads to an examination of numerous social forces that help influence one's judgment that a problem exists. Because medicine does not have a standard definition for what constitutes a normal erection (Tiefer 1994), a man's decision of whether he has some form of

ED is influenced by other societal factors. Media (particularly advertising) help create socially constructed notions of what defines a proper body. Individual ideals regarding sexuality are moulded from these images and reinforce notions that connect healthy living and sexual functioning (both being synonymous with 'normal'). 'Normal' or 'healthy' sexual function is reinforced socially and culturally as being phallocentric, whereby the penis becomes the focal point of sexual activity from which pleasure emanates (for both partners; Tiefer 1994). Therefore, when ED is experienced (to any degree), most men believe that they have a medical problem and are, ultimately, less than healthy, regardless of whether their ED is psychogenic or biogenic in nature.

Cultural norms of masculinity also contribute to negative feelings that emanate from ED. Within US culture, the notion of being a man is closely tied to ideals of sexual potency and the ability to achieve an erection. Consequently, having ED makes one feel like less of a man (Zilbergeld 1992). Many societal ideals about sexual fitness lay rooted in ideals of reproduction. The existing belief that a man with ED is unhealthy or disabled can also affect the individual's well-being. Men with ED may see themselves as less desirable, equating ideals of 'unhealthy' with 'unattractive'. Some feel that women will not want to enter into a relationship with them because they are unable to perform intravaginal sex. In addition, for some older men, ED may convey the message that the sufferer is getting older, a stigma within itself that many men try to hide (e.g., through exercise, hair dyes, or cosmetic surgery).

Social influences affect not only an individual's perception of an illness but also how the individual pursues treatment. For some men, seeking treatment represents an acceptance that they do have a problem. Accepting a problem, however, can mean accepting the stigma of the disease as well (i.e., that they are unhealthy or unable to perform for their partners). Individuals also construct appropriate treatment modalities not on medical criteria alone but on factors such as family responsibilities, perceived stigma, and interference with work (Brown 1996). In considering social factors that promote insecurity and stigma, it becomes evident why Viagra became so much in demand. By merely taking a pill, the sufferer may be able to resolve any insecurity problems that may result from social stereotypes of ED, 'health', and even aging. In addition, the ease of taking a pill eliminates the need for counselling, permitting the individual to avoid addressing any possible psychogenic causes of his ED, the embarrassment of talking to someone repeatedly about his problem, and the inconvenience of having to reschedule work, family, or other obligations in order to attend numerous therapy appointments.

The Role of the Medical Field

Most work on medicalization has focused on the medical professions or physician specialty associations placing themselves into the arena of a particular social problem. Although this may be true for many problems such as alcoholism and child hyperactivity, the answer is not as clear for ED. The medical field (specifically urologists) has medicalized ED in many respects through the development of various devices and drugs and by classifying impotency as ED (Tiefer 1994). These efforts have shifted the focus of ED treatment away from psychogenic causes and centred attention on biogenic causes, and on Viagra as a biogenic way to treat ED.

Initially tested as a heart medication, Viagra was not initially developed for ED. Therefore, if any group can be held responsible for the initial push to get Viagra on the market, it is the pharmaceutical industry. In the past, ED treatments

(i.e., penile pumps, implants, and injections) were developed only with the intention of curing or managing the condition. Urologists took a leading role in their development and solicited the assistance of manufacturers to produce and market the new products (Tiefer 1994). Although the profession has certainly profited from Viagra's popularity with the patient influx, the specialization itself (as well as the medical field as a whole) can take almost no credit for contributing to the Viagra phenomenon.

Furthermore, because no clinical definition exists for what comprises a normal erection (Tiefer 1994), any erection that is not fully erect can be viewed as a problem by the patient, even if he has no problems functioning sexually. The fact that urologists did not help develop Viagra, combined with the lack of a definition for a normal erection, tends to lend further credence to the argument that Viagra has been passively medicalized.

Nevertheless, by prescribing Viagra for any degree of ED (from long-term, full inability to achieve an erection to isolated incidents of ED attributable to work stress) without performing extensive medical diagnostic tests or recommending psychological counselling either as an alternative or accompaniment to the medication, the medical profession's passivity encourages medicalization. The readiness to prescribe Viagra also ignores many larger social issues that may be the root cause of the patient's ED. Examining a number of Viagra efficacy studies presented at the 1998 annual meeting (Padma-Nathan 1998) of the American Urological Association (most of which were funded by Pfizer Pharmaceuticals) or published in leading medical journals (e.g., Marks et al. 1999), one can easily argue that this practice of treating only symptoms and not curing the illness that is the source of the symptoms has been further perpetuated.

Because, as with most drugs, no regulations exist regarding which physicians can prescribe

Viagra, urologists are not the only ones prescribing it (Borzo 1998). Furthermore, Viagra was on the market before many doctors (especially urologists) were introduced to the drug and before Pfizer product representatives were trained about the drug and sent into the field (Borzo 1998). In fact, in the initial weeks, physicians had only the package insert to inform them about the drug's indications, counterindications, and interactions with other drugs (Borzo 1998).

Waitzkin (1989) argued that doctors, for many conditions, tend to prescribe medication or other treatments for a patient's problem but overlook aspects of the patient's lifestyle that may be creating the problem in the first place (i.e., work stress or marital problems). Essentially, prescribing medication for various conditions becomes little more than 'medical duct-tape' for the patient's problems—it corrects the problem but never completely fixes it. In failing to inform patients of the larger lifestyle nature and cause of their ED, the medical profession is exerting another form of social control by perpetuating the patient's ignorance of the full context of his condition.

Faced with the enormous popularity of the drug and the constant drive to maintain costs, health insurers have been too heavily immersed in a debate regarding paying for Viagra to be active in the drug's promotion. A central issue of this debate concerns whether sexual function is a 'medical necessity'. [. . .] If nothing else, the health insurance industry debate on covering Viagra has presented more ways to impede further medicalization of ED than to promote it (although it has demonstrated the ability of the insurers to regulate sexual activity). Finally, in considering the latest trends in pharmaceutical advertising, it is easy to also blame the pharmaceutical industry (Pfizer specifically) for Viagra's popularity and the further medicalization of ED. However, initial advertising for Viagra was minimal in comparison to other drugs (i.e., Claritin for allergies and Valtrex for genital herpes). Arguably, news programs, newspaper articles, and word of mouth were more responsible in helping to promote the new drug.

Overall, in assessing who may have been responsible for creating the Viagra craze, all evidence points to factors outside of the medical field itself. [. . .] Essentially, the field has merely served as a provider and a gatekeeper (at best, a loosely organized agent of social control) for a product that society can use in fighting a consequence of social problems—passively pushing ED further into the realm of medical treatment and ultimately overlooking the full psychological and socio-cultural context of the condition.

Conclusion

Although ED was already a medicalized condition before Viagra was introduced, Viagra presents a variation on an old theme. In this case, medicalization has been promoted through public demand influenced by socio-cultural constructions and norms of health and masculinity. The challenge to combat the problem was accepted by the health care field, yet has not been sufficiently controlled by the profession in terms of regulating ED diagnosis, Viagra prescriptions, and coverage of the patient's costs. Therefore, a passive, as opposed to an active, medicalization has emerged, whereby the health care field has the power to control the problem yet is still struggling with issues over how this control should be executed. Whether this passive medicalization will transform into a more active model of control remains to be seen, especially as the drug is still relatively new.

Although there is no denying that certain men require medical treatment for their ED (i.e., because of nerve damage, diabetes, or prostate surgery), the passive medicalization of Viagra poses several implications for the user, his intimate partner, and society at large. First, like other medical treatments, a Viagra prescription ignores the full context of the patient's ED. Second, Viagra maintains the sexual status quo by perpetuating the belief that sex can only be satisfying when it involves vaginal penetration. Third, health insurance coverage for Viagra establishes a gendered double standard for medications. While some insurers cover the cost of Viagra, many still refuse to cover birth control pills or other forms of female contraception (Mann 1998). Finally, as part of the latest trend in online medicine, Internet pharmacy sites have emerged, selling Viagra and other medications (i.e., Propecia for hair loss) at supposedly cheaper rates than local pharmacies. Although many men faking ED (or at least severe forms of it) may seek out a physician prescription for Viagra to enhance sex, these websites provide an easier way to obtain the drug illegally by merely filling out an online questionnaire and consent form. Even if the patient's condition is legitimate, these sites provide a way to bypass the doctor's office, removing some of the medical field's ability to regulate Viagra's distribution.

In designing policy, it is imperative that the health care field consider the social implications of Viagra consumption. Although Viagra has the potential to help men and their partners, it can also open a Pandora's box in the process, creating problems not only for users and their partners but also for how society views sexuality and medical care overall—that the cure for sexual and relationship difficulties is merely a 'magic bullet' away.

With the increase in marketing campaigns for drugs that essentially promote better living through medication (i.e., Paxil for social anxiety disorder), it is quite possible that passive medicalization of other conditions may take place as we head into the new millennium. In thinking about the Viagra phenomenon, passive medicalization, and the emergence and marketing of a number of new 'lifestyle drugs' in the past few years (e.g., Paxil, Valtrex, and Vioxx for arthritis), medical sociology needs to be mindful that pharmaceutical innovations are having an ever increasing impact on improving quality of life. Consequently, the emergence of this new age of pharmaceuticals warrants much-needed sociological inquiry into issues related to the development, marketing, popularity, prescription, use, and policy issues of medications—essentially, the development of a 'sociology of pharmaceuticals', a subfield within medical sociology itself. One can hope that an increase in the number of such studies will soon emerge in the literature.

References

Borzo, Greg. 1998. 'Viagra Raises Demand, Questions'. *American Medical News* 41(21): 25–6.

Brown, Phil. 1996. 'Naming and Framing: The Social Construction of Diagnosis and Illness'. pp. 92–122 in *Perspectives in Medical Sociology*, 2nd edn, edited by Phil Brown. Prospect Heights, IL: Waveland Press.

Conrad, Peter, and Joseph Schneider. 1980. *Deviance and Medicalization: From Badness to Sickness*. St. Louis: Mosby.

Fabbri, A., A. Aversa, and A. Isidori. 1997. 'Erectile Dysfunction: An Overview'. *Human Reproduction Update* 3(5): 455–66.

Lamberg, Lynne. 1998. 'New Drug for Erectile Dysfunction Boon for Many, "Viagravation" for some'. *JAMA* 280(10): 867–69.

Levine, S.B. 1992. 'Intrapsychic and Interpersonal Aspects of Impotence: Psychogenic Erectile Dysfunction'. pp. 198–225 in *Erectile Disorders: Assessment and Treatment*, edited by R.C. Rosen and S.R. Leiblum. New York: Guilford Press.

Mann, Judy. 1998. 'The Pharmaceutical Double Standard'. *The Washington Post*, May 22, p. E03.

Marks, L.S., C. Duda, F.J. Dorey, M.L. Macairan, and P.B. Santos. 1999. 'Treatment of Erectile Dysfunction with Sildenafil'. *Urology* 53(1): 19–24.

Padma-Nathan, Harin. 1998. 'A 24-Week, Fixed Dose Study to Assess the Efficacy and Safety of Sildenafil (Viagra) in Men with Erectile Dysfunction'. Paper presented at the 1998 Annual Meeting of the American Urological Association.

Tiefer, Leonore. 1994. 'The Medicalization of Impotence: Normalizing Phallocentrism'. *Gender & Society* 8: 363–77.

Waitzkin, Howard. 1989. 'A Critical Theory of Medical Discourse: Ideology, Social Control, and the Processing of

Social Context in Medical Encounters'. *Journal of Health and Social Behavior* 30: 220–39.

Zilbergeld, Bernie. 1992. *The New Male Sexuality*. New York: Bantam Books.

Stigma Management? The Links between Enacted Stigma and Teen Pregnancy Trends among Gay, Lesbian, and Bisexual Students in British Columbia

Elizabeth M. Saewyc, Colleen S. Poon, Yuko Homma, and Carol L. Skay

Introduction

Adolescence is a critical period in sexual development: from the physical changes of puberty (Patton & Viner, 2007), to the awakening of sexual attractions and awareness of sexual orientation (Rosario et al., 1996), to first romantic relationships, and decisions about initiating various sexual behaviours (Boyce, Doherty, Fortin & MacKinnon, 2003; Maticka-Tyndale, 2001; Wellings et al., 2007), these milestones most often occur during the teen years. However, for a significant minority of teens, this critical time period may also include other experiences that can affect their sexual development and long-term sexual health. Sexual debut may be coerced, for example, a result of sexual abuse or sexual assault, or sexual violence may occur after a youth is already sexually active. Either experience can lead to a variety of negative sexual health issues (Saewyc, Magee & Pettingell, 2004). Depending on the population, as many as one in three teens may experience sexual violence before reaching adulthood (Saewyc, Pettingell & Magee, 2003; Saewyc, Skay, et al., 2006; Tonkin, Murphy, Lee, Saewyc & the McCreary Centre Society, 2005). Unprotected sexual behaviours may result in sexually transmitted infections (Maticka-Tyndale, 2001), which can affect future fertility, or even life expectancy. Similarly, unprotected sexual

intercourse with opposite-sex partners can result in teen pregnancy, requiring subsequent decisions for abortion or birth (Statistics Canada, 2007), adoption or parenthood. Each year since 2000, around 1.5 per cent of Canadian females between the ages of 15 and 19 years have given birth (Statistics Canada), suggesting nearly 10 per cent of girls will give birth at some point during their teens; some provincial population-based surveys suggest a slightly smaller per cent of adolescent boys are also involved in pregnancy and parenthood (Tonkin et al., 2005).

A sexual orientation that does not match the expectations or norms in a young person's social and familial environments may be stigmatized, creating issues around disclosure, acceptance or rejection, and personal safety that other adolescents may not need to negotiate as part of their sexual development (D'Augelli, Hershberger & Pilkington, 1998). For lesbian, gay, bisexual, Two Spirit, and questioning (LGBTQ) youth, all of the listed issues affecting sexual development may be particularly salient. Despite improvements in status for LGBTQ populations in Canada over the past several years (such as legal recognition for same-gender marriages), non-heterosexual identities are still stigmatized in many social settings, especially for adolescents (Saewyc, Skay, et al., 2006; Saewyc, Poon, et al., 2007). Disclosure of LGBTQ identity—even suspicion of LGBTQ identity without disclosure—can evoke a variety of negative reactions, such as exclusion, harassment, discrimination, and even violence (Reis & Saewyc, 1999; Saewyc, Singh, Reis & Flynn, 2000; Saewyc, Skay, et al., 2006). These reactions, which can also be considered *enacted stigma,* are thought to contribute to a number of health disparities that have been observed for sexual minority youth, such as distress and suicide attempts, problem substance use, and other risks (Bagley & Tremblay, 2000; Hershberger, Pilkington & D'Augelli, 1997; Marshal et al., 2008; Robin et al., 2002; Russell & Joyner, 2001; Saewyc, 2007). [. . .]

Teen Pregnancy among Sexual Minority Youth

A number of population-based surveys of youth in Canada and the US in the past two decades have documented higher rates of teen pregnancy involvement among sexual minority youth compared to heterosexual peers, often 2 to 10 times higher (Blake et al., 2001; Saewyc, Bearinger, Blum & Resnick, 1999; Saewyc, Pettingell, & Skay, 2004). [. . .] Though the surveys used differing measures of orientation, bisexual and lesbian or gay teens were more likely to report pregnancy involvement than heterosexual peers their age. Only one study has reported any information related to teen parenting among LGB youth (Forrest & Saewyc, 2004); among Minnesota 9th and 12th graders in 1998 who were teen parents, one in three teen fathers reported same- or both-gender sexual partners in the past year, as did one in eight teen mothers.

Possible Explanations for Higher Teen Pregnancy Rates among Sexual Minority Youth

Why teen pregnancy—especially higher rates of teen pregnancy—for LGB youth? As with other health disparities, before identifying unique reasons related to sexual orientation, we should first consider factors linked to teen pregnancy in the general population, and explore whether LGB youth are more likely to have those risks in their lives (Saewyc, 2005). In order for teen pregnancy to occur, unprotected opposite-sex intercourse between sexually mature, fertile young people at or near ovulation is required, since assistive reproductive technologies such as in vitro fertilization are generally not offered to adolescents. The risk of pregnancy increases with earlier sexual debut, more frequent sexual intercourse, more sexual partners, and ineffective methods of contraception, including withdrawal, no method, and inaccurate or sporadic use of effective methods (Klein & the Committee on Adolescence, 2005). Sexually abused adolescents are more likely to report all of these risk behaviours (Saewyc, Magee & Pettingell 2004); similarly, runaway and homeless youth are at higher risk for teen pregnancy, in part because survival sex or sexual exploitation can increase the frequency of sex and make it difficult to negotiate contraception (Warf et al., in press). A number of studies have documented that LGB youth have equal or higher rates of these risk factors for teen pregnancy compared to their heterosexual peers (Saewyc, 2005). [. . .]

Beyond higher risk for these common factors of pregnancy involvement, LGB youth may also have factors specific to their experiences and stigmatized identity. Goffman's theory of stigma management (1968) asserts people may engage in a number of strategies to either avoid or to cope with stigma. For LGB youth this may include avoiding disclosure, and simultaneously engaging in heterosexual dating and sexual behaviours as a form of 'camouflage', to avoid being identified as LGB and targeted for enacted stigma (Saewyc et al., 1999). Those who experience harassment and discrimination may choose pregnancy involvement as a way to deny their orientation, to prevent further enacted stigma. Increased substance use and abuse as a way of coping with stigma (Marshal et al., 2008; Poon et al., 2006) can also lead to unintended, and often unprotected, sexual behaviour. Alternately, if sexual education programs ignore LGB youth sexual health issues, they may conclude that the information is irrelevant to their lives, and 'tune out' important information about contraception and safer sexual practices. As a result, they may be unprepared for healthy decision making when engaging in opposite-gender sexual behaviour.

Teen pregnancy rates have been falling among youth in both Canada and the US since the early 1990s (McKay, 2006). Birth rates have also declined, although more recent news reports suggest birth rates rose in 2006 among adolescents in the US for the first time in 14 years (Reinberg, 2007). Data for 2006 are not yet available in Canada, but birth rates in 2005 among Canadian girls age 15–19 continued their downward trend (Statistics Canada, 2007). The declines in teen pregnancy and birth rates in the US have been attributed to both delay in initiating sexual intercourse and improved contraception use among sexually active teens (Santelli et al., 2004). At the same time, national studies in the US have documented significant declines in substantiated sexual abuse cases and self-reported sexual victimization rates among youth, which may have further contributed to the drop in teen pregnancy rates (Finkelhor & Jones, 2004). Similar studies have not been undertaken in Canada. [. . .]

Have these declining pregnancy trends also occurred among LGB youth? Some preliminary evidence from the US and Canada from the 1990s has suggested LGB youth may actually have increasing trends (Saewyc, Pettingell & Skay, 2004), possibly linked to experiences of sexual violence and enacted stigma. [. . .]

Purposes of the Present Study

As part of an ongoing series of studies exploring risk exposures and health disparities among sexual minority youth across North America, the purposes of this particular study were to:

1. Identify the disparities in teen pregnancy involvement between heterosexual, bisexual, and gay or lesbian adolescents among three cohorts of BC youth in school;

2. Document any disparities in potential risk factors for teen pregnancy, such as exposure to sexual violence, or risky sexual behaviours, between heterosexual and sexual minority teens of the same gender and age; and

3. Explore trends in pregnancy involvement among each of the orientation and gender groups, and concurrent changing trends in risk exposures that may help explain the findings.

Based on preliminary work in other youth health surveys, we hypothesized that bisexual youth would be at higher risk for teen pregnancy involvement than their heterosexual peers, as would gay and lesbian teens, but there would not necessarily be significant differences between gay and bisexual males or lesbian and bisexual females. We also expected sexual minority adolescents would generally report higher levels of common risk factors for teen pregnancy involvement, and that trends in teen pregnancy would mirror trends in those risk factors, as well as trends in exposure to discrimination and other forms of enacted stigma.

Methods

Sample and Procedures

This secondary analysis explored the BC Adolescent Health Surveys (BC AHS) of 1992, 1998, and 2003. The BC AHS is a cluster-stratified random survey of classrooms of students in grades 7 through 12 in public schools across the province, with an overall participation rate of about 72–76 per cent. Detailed description of the survey sampling and administration methods are described elsewhere (Saewyc, Taylor, et al., 2008). In all, more than 70 000 youth have participated in the BC AHS since 1992.

The pencil-and-paper questionnaire of health and risk behaviours was administered by public health nurses and nursing students in each year. After survey completion, the data were weighted by Statistics Canada consultants to adjust for differential probability of sampling and differential response rates, then scaled to the provincial enrollment. For these analyses, the final weighted sample for each year included only those youth who indicated gender, age, and sexual orientation (less than 10 per cent of youth were excluded from each year's sample due to key missing data; see Table 1 for weighted sample size and demographic information for each year).

Measures

For this analysis, measures include demographic variables such as gender and age, as well as items assessing sexual orientation, specific sexual behaviours, exposures to other key correlates of teen pregnancy such as sexual victimization, and teen pregnancy involvement. Sexual orientation was a measure of self-labelling defined by attraction, with categories ranging from '100% heterosexual', 'mostly heterosexual', 'bisexual', 'mostly homosexual', '100% homosexual; gay/lesbian', and 'not sure'. Based on extensive measurement evaluation and power issues (Saewyc, Bauer, et al., 2004), the 'mostly homosexual' and '100% homosexual' youth were combined into a single group (i.e., gay/lesbian, Table 1). The 'not sure' were excluded from analyses because the wide variety of those selecting that option renders it unclear how they are answering, i.e., whether they are not sure of their sexual orientation, or not sure what the question was asking. The 'mostly heterosexual' were included in analyses, despite the heterogeneity of the group (a significant number were younger students or recent immigrants who spoke a language other than English most of the time at home), but their results were seldom significantly different from 100 per cent heterosexual youth, and so their data are not shown. Specific sexual behaviours from items on the survey were recoded to represent specific risks for pregnancy involvement; for example, age of first sexual intercourse was dichotomized to be <14 years, or 14 years and older. Pregnancy involvement was originally asked as number of times pregnant, but for this analysis, was dichotomized to ever/never pregnant. Eight different measures of victimization and discrimination in the 2003 BC AHS were incorporated into an *enacted stigma* composite measure that included, for the past year: discrimination on the basis of race, physical appearance, or sexual orientation; being excluded by others at school, being insulted or teased, being physically assaulted; or verbal or physical sexual harassment. Lifetime sexual abuse was not included in this measure. The enacted stigma composite score showed good reliability across various groups of students in 2003, and has been reported elsewhere (Meininger et al., 2007; Poon et al., 2006; Saewyc, Clark, et al., 2006; Saewyc, Poon, et al., 2007).

Table 1 Demographics for Those Indicating Sexual Orientation in the *BC AHS*, by Year

	FEMALE			MALE		
	1992	1998	2003	1992	1998	2003
WEIGHTED N	121,100	148,009	133,539	118,924	133,567	131,593
% female each year	50.5	52.6	50.4			
Sexual orientation, %						
100% heterosexual	91.4	89.8	86.6	93.6	93.7	95.0
mostly heterosexual*	6.7	8.0	9.8	4.3	4.3	3.4
bisexual	1.8	1.9	3.2	1.6	1.2	0.9
gay/lesbian	0.2	0.3	0.3	0.5	0.9	0.7

*Specific results for 'mostly heterosexual' youth not shown in subsequent tables

Analysis

All analyses were conducted separately by gender. Analyses included chi-square tests of the prevalence of pregnancy involvement and various risk factors within each orientation group, to test trends over time between 1992 and 2003, and 1998 and 2003 (Fleiss, 1981). Because the rates of sexual experience differ among the orientation groups, and can in part contribute to trends, we report trends for prevalence of pregnancy both as a rate among all youth by orientation group, then for sexually experienced youth only. Similarly, the prevalence of sexual behaviours is prone to maturational effects (Saewyc, Taylor, et al., 2008), and the sexual orientation groups were significantly different in age, with gay and lesbian youth older on average than heterosexual teens. Therefore, in testing disparities between heterosexual teens and their gay, lesbian, bisexual, or mostly heterosexual peers we controlled for age, using multivariable logistic regressions to calculate age-adjusted odds ratios of pregnancy and common risk factors for pregnancy.

The complex stratified sampling of classrooms in the BC AHS design would usually suggest the need for statistical procedures to compensate for potential clustering effects, using software such as SUDAAN or SPSS Complex Samples. However, an extensive analysis of the sample's distribution of the small percentages of lesbian, gay, and bisexual adolescents throughout the province indicated there were no design effects: clustering effects cannot occur with only one or two students in a classroom, and the LGB youth appeared to be randomly distributed across the province. Therefore, for these analyses, SPSS 15.0 was used without adjustment for the complex sampling method, save for incorporating the weights. Given the large sample size for each cohort, to reduce the risk of Type I error, we set alpha to <.01 for comparisons between orientation groups; however, for tests of trends within bisexual and lesbian or gay groups, we set alpha to <.05 for these smaller samples.

Results

Disparities in Pregnancy Involvement and Related Risk Behaviours for Gay and Bisexual Male Students

Table 2 shows the age-adjusted odds ratios and 95 per cent confidence intervals comparing pregnancy involvement and related risk behaviours for the gay and bisexual male students vs. their heterosexual peers in each survey year. In all years, gay and bisexual male youth were more likely than heterosexual youth their age to have ever had sexual intercourse. Among the male youth who ever had sexual intercourse, gay and bisexual youth had higher age-adjusted odds (3.53–7.49) of having participated in a pregnancy than heterosexual male teens. With respect to risk factors for pregnancy involvement, gay and bisexual youth were more likely than age-matched male heterosexual peers to have had first intercourse before age 14 and to have had two or more sexual partners. Similar differences also applied for lack of condom use at last intercourse (with the exception that gay males in 2003 did not differ from heterosexual peers in this respect) and in substance use before last intercourse (with the exception that bisexual males did not differ from heterosexual peers in this respect, $p = 0.89$).

Table 2 Age-adjusted Odds Ratios (AOR) Comparing Pregnancy Involvement and Related Risk Behaviours among Gay, Bisexual, and Heterosexual Male Students in *BC ACH* 1992, 1998, and 2003

	1992		1998		2003	
	AOR	(95% CI)	AOR	(95% CI)	AOR	(95% CI)
MALE						
Ever had sexual intercourse						
Bisexual	1.31	(1.19–1.45)	2.42	(2.17–2.70)	2.44	(2.16–2.76)
Gay	6.18	(5.05–7.57)	4.02	(3.55–4.55)	1.28	(1.10–1.48)
Pregnancy involvement[a]						
Bisexual	4.66	(3.94–5.52)	6.02	(5.02–7.22)	3.61	(2.86–4.56)
Gay	7.39	(5.96–9.16)	3.52	(2.81–4.42)	3.56	(2.58–4.92)
Early first intercourse (before age 14)[a]						
Bisexual	1.58	(1.34–1.87)	2.24	(1.86–2.70)	2.23	(1.84–2.69)
Gay	5.09	(3.88–6.68)	1.90	(1.57–2.30)	2.57	(1.95–3.37)
2 or more lifetime sexual partners[a]						
Bisexual	1.24	(1.07–1.45)	7.53	(5.68–9.97)	1.47	(1.23–1.76)
Gay	3.24	(2.49–4.21)	4.63	(3.68–5.82)	1.67	(1.30–2.15)
Substance use before last intercourse[a]						
Bisexual	1.80	(1.56–2.07)	1.42	(1.20–1.66)	NS	(0.84–1.22)
Gay	4.84	(3.93–5.97)	1.49	(1.27–1.75)	0.35	(0.25–0.49)
Lack of condom use at last intercourse[a]						
Bisexual	2.12	(1.83–2.44)	1.74	(1.48–2.05)	3.47	(2.92–4.12)
Gay	2.03	(1.66–2.48)	1.51	(1.29–1.77)	NS	(0.77–1.32)

Note: 100% heterosexual = reference group, all AOR p < .01 except where noted
[a] Among male youth who have ever had sexual intercourse

Disparities in Pregnancy Involvement and Related Risk Behaviours for Lesbian and Bisexual Female Students

Table 3 shows the age-adjusted odds ratios and 95 per cent confidence intervals comparing having been pregnant and related risk behaviours for the lesbian and bisexual female adolescents to their heterosexual peers in each survey year. In all years (except for bisexual females in 1992), lesbian and bisexual female students were more likely than heterosexual female students their age to have ever had sexual intercourse. Among female students who ever had sexual intercourse, lesbian and bisexual females had higher age-adjusted odds (1.8–3.4) of having been pregnant compared to heterosexual female teens. With respect to risk factors for ever having been pregnant, lesbian and bisexual female students were more likely than age-matched heterosexual peers to have had first intercourse before age 14 (with the exception of lesbian youth in 1992) and to have had two or more sexual partners (with the exception of lesbian youth in 1998, $p = 0.15$). In all years, lesbian

Table 3 Age-adjusted Odds Ratios (AOR) Comparing Pregnancy Experience and Related Risk Behaviours among Lesbian, Bisexual, and Heterosexual Female Students in *BC AHS* 1992, 1998, and 2003

	1992		1998		2003	
	AOR	(95% CI)	AOR	(95% CI)	AOR	(95% CI)
FEMALE						
Ever had sexual intercourse						
Bisexual	0.74	(0.67–0.83)	3.55	(3.26–3.87)	3.96	(3.70–4.24)
Lesbian	2.42	(1.76–3.32)	5.37	(4.34–6.64)	1.36	(1.09–1.70)
Pregnancy experience[a]						
Bisexual	3.40	(2.81–411)	2.96	(2.56–3.36)	1.81	(1.55–2.10)
Lesbian	2.38	(1.32–4.30)	2.37	(1.60–3.50)	2.63	(1.55–4.44)
Early first intercourse (before age 14)[a]						
Bisexual	2.81	(2.23–3.55)	3.22	(2.83–3.66)	2.25	(2.01–2.53)
Lesbian	NS	(0.82–2.80)	7.45	(5.23–10.60)	11.76	(7.67–18.03)
2 or more lifetime sexual partners[a]						
Bisexual	1.76	(1.45–2.14)	2.93	(2.59–3.31)	2.29	(2.10–2.49)
Lesbian	—[b]		NS	(0.61–1.08)	7.80	(4.94–12.32)
Substance use before last intercourse[a]						
Bisexual	NS	(0.94–1.37)	1.67	(1.49–1.86)	1.39	(1.27–1.52)
Lesbian	7.25	(4.52–11.64)	0.46	(0.32–0.66)	NS	(0.70–1.56)
Lack of condom use at last intercourse[a]						
Bisexual	3.86	(3.15–4.72)	1.75	(1.57–1.96)	1.28	(1.17–1.40)
Lesbian	2.69	(1.70–4.28)	1.49	(1.12–1.98)	2.94	(2.02–4.28)

Note: 100% heterosexual = reference group, all AOR p < .01 except where noted (NS)

[a] Among female teens who have ever had intercourse

[b] All lesbian students reported two or more lifetime sexual partners

and bisexual female students were more likely than heterosexual female peers to report lack of condom use at last intercourse and in substance use before last intercourse (with the exception that bisexual females in 2003 did not differ from heterosexual peers in this latter respect, $p = 0.82$).

Trends in Pregnancy Involvement and Related Risk Behaviours by Orientation

Table 4 reports trends for the total sample in each sexual orientation group for having had sexual intercourse and having experienced sexual abuse.

Table 4 Trends in Prevalence of Pregnancy Involvement and Related Risk Exposures by Orientation in *BC AHS* 1992, 1998, and 2003

	MALE %			FEMALE %		
	1992	**1998**	**2003**	**1992**	**1998**	**2003**
Heterosexual teens						
Ever had sexual intercourse	35.1	25.1	23.8	30.0	22.4	22.2
Sexual abuse history	3.2	2.6	2.0	21.0	14.3	10.8
Pregnancy[a]	6.2	6.4	5.3	10.2	8.0	5.3
Early sexual debut (<14 years)[a]	41.4	33.4	23.9	29.4	21.5	13.8
2+ sexual partners in lifetime[a]	62.8	57.5	58.8	55.0	49.8	47.8
Substance use before last sex[a]	27.4	37.2	32.3	22.8	28.7	26.2
No condom at last sex[a]	35.5	35.5	25.6	47.2	46.9	34.2
Bisexual teens						
Ever had sexual intercourse	41.0	40.6	44.7	27.4	53.3	55.7
Sexual abuse history	14.9	21.9	14.8	34.8	31.9	36.2
Pregnancy[a]	23.4	28.9	16.8	26.7	20.4	8.8
Early sexual debut (<14 years)[a]	56.4	59.7	42.7	44.1	39.6	26.0
2+ sexual partners in lifetime[a]	66.5	91.1	66.7	68.0	74.4	68.6
Substance use before last sex[a]	38.9	45.2	31.8	25.3	39.7	33.9
No condom at last sex[a]	52.5	47.1	53.5	75.5	60.6	38.1
Gay or lesbian teens						
Ever had sexual intercourse	75.6	56.3	37.5	40.4	51.3	27.4
Sexual abuse history	22.5	22.7	6.3	43.4	22.8	29.1
Pregnancy[a]	32.7	19.2	16.8	17.3	14.6	12.6
Early sexual debut (<14 years)[a]	76.0	54.8	41.7	64.6	67.9	48.4
2+ sexual partners in lifetime[a]	83.5	86.3	69.2	100.0	42.9	87.9
Substance use before last sex[a]	62.6	46.6	14.0	69.5	17.9	27.4
No condom at last sex[a]	51.3	43.8	25.3	61.7	52.5	60.5

[a] Among sexually-experienced youth
All *p*-values for chi-square tests of trends <0.05 to <0.01, except where noted in the text.

Data only for youth in these groups who have ever had sexual intercourse is also presented for pregnancy involvement, first intercourse before age 14, multiple lifetime partners, substance use before last intercourse, and lack of condom use at last intercourse.

Heterosexual Youth Trends

For both sexes, one of the most obvious changes between 1992 and 2003 is a decline in prevalence of sexual abuse, particularly among heterosexual females, for whom it was reduced by half. Among heterosexual teens who have ever had intercourse, this reduction in sexual victimization likely helps to explain the reduction in early age of first sexual intercourse as well. Another decline that may help explain lower heterosexual teen pregnancy is in sexual experience overall, as both sexes reported lower prevalence of ever having sexual intercourse in 2003 compared to previous years. This contribution to the declines is further suggested when we look only at youth who have ever had intercourse: among sexually experienced heterosexual males, teen pregnancy involvement did not actually decline significantly between 1992 and 1998, but only between 1998 and 2003. Another improvement was in condom use at last intercourse, where the percentage of heterosexual teens reporting they did not use condoms last time was lower overall, although almost all of that decrease occurred between 1998 and 2003.

In contrast to these overall declining trends, two risk behaviours among heterosexual youth who had ever had intercourse showed periods of increasing trends. For example, heterosexual male reports of two or more lifetime sexual partners declined overall from 1992 to 2003 but, in fact, rose between 1998 and 2003 (in contrast to a continued decrease among heterosexual females). Substance use before last intercourse increased for both sexes between 1992 and 2003 but did so in both cases with a rise between

1992 and 1998 and a slight decrease between 1998 and 2003 (Table 4).

Bisexual Youth Trends

The trends for the total sample of bisexual teens of both genders look quite different from those of their heterosexual peers. The percentage of bisexual males who had ever had sexual intercourse increased somewhat from 1992 to 2003, and doubled for bisexual females during that period. Similarly, the prevalence of sexual abuse among bisexual females increased between 1998 and 2003, rather than decreased, while prevalence of sexual abuse among bisexual males increased in 1998, then dropped in 2003 back to the 1992 prevalence. A number of risk factors showed a similar peak in 1998, for both males and females, which may help explain their increases in teen pregnancy rates during that year, before declining in 2003. For example, early sexual debut was not significantly different in 1998, but then significantly declined for both males and females in 2003. Multiple sexual partners and substance use before last sex both peaked in 1998, dropping in 2003. Unlike bisexual youth in general, or among sexually experienced bisexual males, among sexually experienced bisexual females, teen pregnancy rates actually declined, and condom use at last intercourse significantly improved: lack of condom use at last intercourse dropped by nearly half between 1992 and 2003. These counteracting trends may help explain the differences between pregnancy involvement overall for bisexual female students.

Lesbian and Gay Youth Trends

For lesbian teens, the trends in risk exposures are also quite different from heterosexual peers, and show different patterns even from bisexual female peers. For example, while rates of ever having sexual intercourse increased between 1992 and 1998, they declined sharply by 2003. In contrast, sexual abuse rates declined between 1992 and

1998, then began increasing again between 1998 and 2003. That same decline-then-increase pattern was also found for lesbian students' trends in number of lifetime partners, and substance use before last intercourse, although the opposite pattern was reported for initiation of sexual intercourse before age 14. Condom use at last sex was relatively unchanged across years, as was teen pregnancy among sexually experienced lesbian students; it appeared to decline, but differences were not significant. The extent to which these different trends contribute to teen pregnancy may be harder to assess for lesbian teens; for example, the increasing rates of multiple sexual partners, substance use with sex and lack of condom use may not be relevant if lesbians were reporting mostly same-gender sexual partners, but gender of sexual partners was only asked on the BC AHS in 2003.

Unlike the other sexual minority groups, gay male students overall showed a marked and consistent decline in teen pregnancy involvement, and this was supported by declines in every risk exposure measured. The rate of gay students reporting ever having intercourse dropped by half between 1992 and 2003, while sexual abuse history declined by nearly 75 per cent. These two declines clearly contributed to the decline in early sexual experience among gay males. Among sexually experienced gay students, teen pregnancy also declined between 1992 and 2003, fuelled perhaps in part by strong improvements in condom use with sexual intercourse, and declines in substance use before sex.

The Link between Enacted Stigma and Pregnancy Involvement

Although not available for all years of the BC AHS, the *enacted stigma* measure provides another measure of exclusion or marginalization that may be salient in explaining the disparities in teen pregnancy involvement for sexual minority youth, as does the individual item about sexual orientation discrimination. Table 5 compares the percentage of bisexual, lesbian, or gay teens who reported experiencing sexual orientation

Table 5 Relationships between Pregnancy Involvement and Enacted Stigma among Bisexual and Gay/Lesbian Youth (2003 *BC AHS*)

	PREGNANCY INVOLVEMENT	% DISCRIMINATED AGAINST IN PAST YEAR DUE TO SEXUAL ORIENTATION	P^a	MEAN ENACTED STIGMA SCORE, RANGE 0-8 (SD)	P^b
MALE					
Bisexual	No	32.4	<0.001	2.90 (2.09)	<0.001
	Yes	84.3		4.09 (1.60)	
Gay	No	60.4	<0.001	3.10 (1.92)	0.959
	Yes	18.4		3.08 (2.34)	
FEMALE					
Bisexual	No	2.67	<0.001	3.01 (1.95)	<0.001
	Yes	48.3		4.43 (2.26)	
Lesbian	No	42.7	<0.001	3.48 (2.25)	<0.001
	Yes	100.0		7.00 (0.00)	

[a] Chi-square tests
[b] Independent sample *t*-tests

discrimination for those who have been involved in pregnancy vs. those who have not. Similarly, the table displays the mean enacted stigma scores and *t*-test results between those who have been involved in pregnancy and those who have not.

For lesbian and bisexual female students, and for bisexual male students, those who had been involved in pregnancy were more than twice as likely to report experiencing discrimination in the past year due to their sexual orientation. Those involved in pregnancy also reported a significantly greater number of types of harassment and discrimination, as shown by higher enacted stigma scores. However, gay students reported opposite results: those who had ever been involved in pregnancy were nearly two-thirds less likely to report discrimination in the past year because of their sexual orientation, and those who had caused a pregnancy showed no difference in experiences of enacted stigma than those who had not.

Discussion

Within these three cohorts of BC high school students more than a decade apart, the evidence is clear: lesbian, gay, and bisexual teens in British Columbia are at significantly higher risk for pregnancy involvement during their teen years than their heterosexual peers, with odds of two to seven times the rate of heterosexual students' pregnancy involvement. [. . .] What explains this higher risk among BC students? It appears in great part due to disparities in risk factors for teen pregnancy compared to heterosexual teens, such as higher rates of ever having sexual intercourse, and higher odds of early sexual intercourse initiation (often in the context of sexual abuse), multiple lifetime partners, substance use before sex, and lack of condom use or other effective contraception. These disparities have also been noted in other school-based studies of sexual minority youth in the US and elsewhere. In addition to these common teen pregnancy risk factors, teen pregnancy involvement for lesbian

and bisexual teens was also significantly associated with discrimination due to sexual orientation and more experiences of exclusion, harassment, and violence (enacted stigma). Lesbian and bisexual teens who reported pregnancy involvement were significantly more likely to report discrimination and harassment than teens of their same orientation who have never been pregnant—which suggests that there may be some unique risk factors for sexual minority youth related to issues of societal stigma and social exclusion.

The good news is that teen pregnancy rates declined among all orientation groups between 1992 and 2003, although the strength of those declines among sexual minority youth varied by group, with most groups reporting an increase in 1998 before declining in 2003. For heterosexual students, trends in related risk factors appear to closely mirror the trends in pregnancy involvement, with declines in sexual abuse, youth waiting longer to begin having sex, and, among those who are sexually active, engaging in fewer risky behaviours, and improved contraception.

In contrast, trends in teen pregnancy and related risk behaviours are far less consistent for sexual minority teens over the course of the same decade. For bisexual female students, competing trends—increasing numbers who were sexually experienced, plus rising rates of sexual abuse, substance use with sex, and multiple partners, set against lower rates of early initiation of intercourse and increased rates of condom use with last intercourse—may help explain the increase then decline in teen pregnancy rates for bisexual females over that decade. Lesbian students show somewhat different competing trends, but they too help explain the increase, then decline, in teen pregnancy rates overall. Similarly, for bisexual male students, the trends in both sexual experience and sexual risk behaviours, with many rates peaking in 1998 before beginning to decline, strongly mirror their pattern of pregnancy involvement. Thus, for sexual minority youth in general, higher rates of teen pregnancy involvement may well be mostly due to higher rates of risks related to pregnancy in the general population, although enacted stigma and discrimination also appear to play a role in teen pregnancy involvement for these youth.

Documenting the higher risks and changing trends is important, but does not completely address the question of *why* LGB youth are facing these disparities—why are they engaging in riskier sexual behaviours, at earlier ages? While the surveys themselves do not ask why, so cannot provide definite answers, the results do suggest some potential reasons. The higher rates of sexual abuse among LGB youth may be one key. Sexual violence is a potent predictor of risky sexual behaviours and teen pregnancy involvement in general (Saewyc, Magee & Pettingell, 2004); a reason for this is that the trauma-inducing nature of sexual abuse also engenders shame and stigma, altered perceptions about sexual behaviours, and difficulty negotiating condom use or other self-care practices in sexual relationships (Finkelhor & Browne, 1985). Indeed, maltreatment of any sort during childhood and adolescence causes a cascade of physiological and psychological changes during development, and these stressors subsequently induce a variety of negative coping responses (DeBellis, 2001). The combined stigma of sexual orientation status, and sexual victimization, along with the stress of ongoing enacted stigma experiences, may both increase the distress among LGB youth and precipitate risky coping behaviours that can lead to pregnancy. It should be noted that the timing of the sexual abuse, the enacted stigma, and the pregnancy involvement are not clear from the questions asked, so we cannot be sure which came first, and whether the pregnancy involvement was unintended, or an attempt at stigma management. Pregnancy involvement may be intentional, as a way of changing status and reaching for a more positive identity of parenthood, as has been suggested in other studies. The BC AHS cannot help determine this, because it does not include such questions.

Among sexual minority teens, gay males stand out as an anomaly. Like heterosexual teens, their rates of teen pregnancy involvement decline steadily over the decade, as do their rates of sexual experience, exposure to sexual abuse and early sexual initiation, and all the other risk behaviours, which provides further support to the proposed reasons for the higher risk. Unlike the other sexual minority groups, gay males who have been involved in pregnancy were less likely to report anti-gay discrimination, or were no more likely to experience enacted stigma than their gay peers who had not been involved in pregnancy. There are no specific other studies that appear to help explain this difference for gay males, but it warrants further examination, both in future BC cohorts and in school-based surveys in other regions that include sexual orientation questions and teen pregnancy involvement.

Beyond overt stigma and hostility, another possible contributor to higher rates of teen pregnancy involvement is a disparity in the levels of supportive resources or protective factors in the lives of lesbian, gay, and bisexual youth. Protective factors such as connectedness to family or school have been linked to lower rates of pregnancy involvement among adolescents in the US and in British Columbia (Kirby, Lepore & Ryan, 2005; Saewyc, Taylor, et al., 2008), yet many sexual minority youth feel less connected to family or school than their heterosexual peers (Saewyc, et al., 2009). To the extent they have fewer supportive resources to draw upon, LGB youth may be more motivated to reach for those caring connections through parenthood.

[. . .]

Conclusions

The results of our study suggest that reducing rates of teen pregnancy among LGB youth will require a focus on reducing levels of stigma and sexual violence toward them. This may in part require interventions in the wider community, but efforts to create friendlier, more supportive atmospheres within schools, and interventions to reduce sexual harassment and sexual violence in adolescent relationships in general, may both have an effect on sexual violence and harassment directed toward LGB youth within the school setting. Sexual health education topics should include discussion of sexual abuse as well as healthy relationships, with the awareness that such content may elicit disclosure of abuse, so health educators should be prepared to address that disclosure as well as their duty to report. Sexual health curriculum should also include non-judgmental, factual information about sexual orientation development, and LGB-related sexual health issues, in order to engage the awareness of even closeted LGB youth about their risks for pregnancy involvement. Finally, interventions to foster positive family and school connectedness for LGB youth may be an additional approach to reducing the distress, improving sexual health behaviours, and reducing unintended teen pregnancy.

These findings also suggest directions for further research. First, it is important to document whether these disparities and trends continue in BC, and whether they exist among LGB youth in other regions of Canada. This can only be done by incorporating measures of sexual orientation, teen pregnancy involvement, sexual health behaviours, and sexual victimization into other regularly recurring population-focused surveys of youth health and risk behaviours, whether in other provinces in Canada, or in national surveys. To our knowledge, only the Atlantic provincial youth drug use surveys have recently included a measure of sexual orientation, and have some of the measures of sexual risk behaviour, but do not include questions about teen pregnancy involvement or experiences of sexual violence (Poulin & Elliott, 2007). The 2008 BC AHS is currently under way, and includes most of the same measures as previous surveys, allowing us to eventually document whether the trends continue or alter.

Second, beyond documenting the disparities and trends, it is important to learn *why,* and that requires in-depth qualitative exploration of the meanings of sexual behaviour, intentions, pregnancy experiences, and pregnancy decisions among lesbian, gay, and bisexual adolescents who have been involved in a pregnancy. This will help identify potential other factors associated with pregnancy involvement, test and refine theories around this particular health disparity for LGB youth, and the specific perspectives and reasons identified by young people themselves.

Third, we need to know more about the hidden phenomenon of LGB teen parenting. Not all teen pregnancies among LGB youth end in abortion; what are their experiences in deciding to give birth, involvement in maternity care, and involvement in subsequent parenting? What supports can they draw upon as young parents? Both qualitative studies with LGB teen parents, as well as including items about teen parenting on large-scale population-based surveys of youth, will help us better identify this elusive population.

Fourth, we need to conduct, with Canadian datasets, studies replicating the Massachusetts analyses around supportive sexual health education (Blake et al., 2001) and supportive school environments (Goodenow et al., 2006) and their influence on health disparities for LGB youth. This will help document such effects within the Canadian contexts, to guide policy and practice in schools. Finally, research should include intervention studies to assess the effectiveness of programs to address stigma reduction, sexual violence prevention, fostering healthy sexual decision making, and reducing unintended pregnancy involvement for LGB youth.

Lesbian, gay, and bisexual teens are at higher risk for teen pregnancy involvement than their heterosexual peers, and higher rates of sexual violence and enacted stigma help explain this disparity. The declining rates of pregnancy for heterosexual teens since the early 1990s are also found among gay males, but rates for lesbian and bisexual teens have only begun to decline in the later 1990s. Of even greater concern, some of the most potent risk factors for teen pregnancy—sexual abuse and early sexual experience—have increasing trends for lesbian and bisexual female students, which suggests the declines in teen pregnancy in 2003 may not continue in future cohorts. Reducing stigma for LGBTQ youth, and preventing the harassment and sexual violence they may be targeted for, could be important strategies for preventing unwanted teen pregnancies.

References

Bagley, C., & Tremblay, P. (2000). Elevated rates of suicidal behavior in gay, lesbian, and bisexual youth. *Crisis: The Journal of Crisis Intervention and Suicide Prevention, 21,* 111–17.

Blake, S.M., Ledsky, R., Lehman, T., Goodenow, C., Sawyer, R., & Hack, T. (2001). Preventing sexual risk behaviors among gay, lesbian, and bisexual adolescents: The benefits of gay-sensitive HIV instruction in schools. *American Journal of Public Health, 91,* 940–46.

Boyce, W., Doherty, M., Fortin, C., & MacKinnon, D. (2003). *Canadian Youth, Sexual Health, and HIV/AIDS Study: Factors Influencing Knowledge, Attitudes and Behaviors.* Toronto, ON: Council of Ministers of Education.

D'Augelli, A.R., Hershberger, S.L., & Pilkington, N.W. (1998). Lesbian, gay, and bisexual youth and their families: Disclosure of sexual orientation and its consequences. *American Journal of Orthopsychiatry, 68,* 361–71; discussion 372–75.

DeBellis, M.D. (2001). Developmental traumatology: The psychobiological development of maltreated children and its implications for research, treatment, and policy. *Developmental Psychopathology, 13,* 539–64.

Finkelhor, D., & Browne A. (1985). The traumatic impact of child sexual abuse: A conceptualization. *American Journal of Orthopsychiatry, 55,* 530–40.

Finkelhor, D., & Jones, L.M. (2004). Explanations for the decline in child sexual abuse cases. *OJJDP Juvenile Justice Bulletin,* #NCJ 199298: U.S. Department of Justice, Office of Juvenile Justice and Delinquency Prevention, January 2004.

Fleiss, J.L. (1981). *Statistical Methods for Rates and Proportions,* (2nd edn). New York, NY: Wiley.

Forrest, R., & Saewyc, E.M. (2004). Sexual minority teen parents: Demographics of an unexpected population. [Abstract]. *Journal of Adolescent Health, 34,* 122.

Goffman, E. (1968). Management of spoiled identity. In E. Rubington and M.S. Weinberg (Eds), *Deviance: The Interactionist Perspective. Text and Readings in the Sociology of Deviance* (pp. 344–48). New York, NY: The MacMillan Company.

Goodenow, C., Szalacha, L., & Westheimer, K. (2006). School support groups, other school factors, and the safety of sexual minority adolescents. *Psychology in the Schools, 43,* 573–89.

Hershberger, S.L., Pilkington, N.W., & D'Augelli, A.R. (1997). Predictors of suicide attempts among gay, lesbian and bisexual youth. *Journal of Adolescent Research, 12,* 477–97.

Kirby D., Lepore G., & Ryan J. (2005). *Sexual risk and protective factors. Factors affecting teen sexual behavior, teen pregnancy, childbearing, and sexually transmitted disease: Which are important? Which can you change?* National Campaign to Prevent Teen Pregnancy, USA. http://www.thenationalcampaign.org/resources/works/PWWTWabout.aspx.

Klein, J.M., & the Committee on Adolescence. (2005). Adolescent pregnancy: Current trends and issues. *Pediatrics, 116,* 281–86.

Marshal, M.P., Friedman, M.S., Stall, R., King, K.M., Miles, J., Gold, M.A., et al. (2008). Sexual orientation and adolescent substance use: A meta-analysis and methodological review. *Addiction, 103,* 546–56.

Maticka-Tyndale, E. (2001). Sexual health and Canadian youth: How do we measure up? *The Canadian Journal of Human Sexuality, 10,* 1–17.

McKay A. (2006). Trends in teen pregnancy in Canada with comparisons to U.S.A. and England/Wales. *The Canadian Journal of Human Sexuality, 15,* 157–61.

Meininger, E., Saewyc, E., Skay, C., Clark, T., Poon, C., Robinson, E., Pettingell, S., & Homma, Y. (2007). Enacted stigma and HIV risk behaviors in sexual minority youth of European heritage across three countries. [Abstract]. *Journal of Adolescent Health, 40,* S27.

Patton, G.C., & Viner, R. (2007). Pubertal transitions in health. *Lancet, 369,* 1130–39.

Poon, C., Saewyc, E., Skay, C., Homma, Y., & Barney, L. (2006). Stigma and substance use in Asian GLB youth. Paper presented at the 17th International Conference on the Reduction of Drug Related Harm, 1 May 2006, in Vancouver.

Poulin C., & Elliott D. (2007). *Student drug use surveys in the Atlantic provinces: Atlantic technical report.* Halifax, NS: Dalhousie University.

Reinberg, S. (2007). Teen birth rates up for first time in 14 years, U.S. reports. *U.S. News and World Report,* online, 5 December 2007. Accessed on 3 March 2008 at http://health.usnews.com/usnews/health/healthday/ 071205/teen-birth-rates-up-for-first-time-in-14-years-us-reports.htm.

Reis, B., and Saewyc, E. (1999). *Eighty-three Thousand Youth: Selected findings of eight population-based studies as they pertain to anti-gay harassment and the safety and well-being of sexual minority students.* Safe Schools Coalition of Washington, May 1999. Available from http://www.safe-schoolscoalition.org/83000youth.pdf.

Robin, L., Brener, N.D., Donahue, S.F., Hack, T., Hale, K., & Goodenow, C. (2002). Associations between health risk behaviors and opposite-, same-, and both sex sexual partners in representative samples of Vermont and Massachusetts high school students. *Archives of Pediatric and Adolescent Medicine, 156,* 349–55.

Rosario, M., Meyer-Bahlburg, H.F., Hunter, J., Exner, T.M., Gwadz, M., & Arden, K.M. (1996). The psychosexual development of urban lesbian, gay, and bisexual youths. *Journal of Sex Research, 33,* 113–26.

Russell, S.T., & Joyner, K. (2001). Adolescent sexual orientation and suicide risk: Evidence from a national study. *American Journal of Public Health, 91,* 1276–81.

Saewyc, E.M. (2005). Chapter 5: Teen pregnancy among gay, lesbian, and bisexual youths: Influences of stigma, sexual abuse, and sexual orientation. In A. Omoto & H. Kurtzman (Eds), *Sexual Orientation and Mental Health: Examining Identity and Development in Lesbian, Gay, and Bisexual People* (pp. 95–116). APA Press.

———. (2007). Contested conclusions: What claims can (and cannot) be made from the current research on gay, lesbian, and bisexual teen suicide attempts? *Journal of LGBT Health Research, 3,* 79–87.

Saewyc, E.M., Bauer, G.R., Skay, C.L., Bearinger, L.H., Resnick, M.D., Reis, E., & Murphy, A. (2004). Measuring sexual orientation in adolescent health surveys: Evaluation of eight school-based surveys. *Journal of Adolescent Health, 35,* 345e.l–e.16.

Saewyc, E., Bearinger, L., Blum, R., & Resnick, M. (1999). Sexual intercourse, abuse and pregnancy among adolescent women: Does sexual orientation make a difference? *Family Planning Perspectives, 31,* 27–131.

Saewyc, E., Clark, T., Barney, L., Poon, C., Skay, C., Pettingell, S., Meininger, E., Robinson, E., Murphy, A., and Watson, P. (2006). Enacted stigma and HIV risk behaviors among sexual minority Native youth in Canada, New Zealand, and U.S. schools. Paper presented at Embracing our Traditions, Values, and Teachings: Native Peoples of North America HIV/AIDS Conference, 2–6 May 2006, in Anchorage, Alaska, US.

Saewyc, E.M., Homma, Y., Skay, C.L., Bearinger, L., Resnick, M., & Reis E. (2009). Protective factors in the lives of bisexual adolescents in North America. *American Journal of Public Health, 99,* 110–17. PubMedCentral ID#: PMC2636603.

Saewyc, E.M., Magee, L., & Pettingell, S. (2004). Teenage pregnancy and associated risk behaviors among sexually-abused adolescents. *Perspectives in Sexual and Reproductive Health, 36,* 98–105.

Saewyc, E.M., Pettingell, S.L., & Magee, L.L. (2003). The prevalence of sexual abuse among adolescents in school. *Journal of School Nursing, 19,* 266–72.

Saewyc, E.M., Pettingell, S.L., & Skay, C.L. (2004). Teen pregnancy among sexual minority youth in population-based surveys of the 1990s: Countertrends in a population at risk. [Abstract]. *Journal of Adolescent Health, 34,* 125–26.

Saewyc, E., Poon, C., Wang, N., Homma, Y., Smith, A., & the McCreary Centre Society. (2007). *Not Yet Equal: The Health of Lesbian, Gay, & Bisexual Youth in BC.* Vancouver, BC: McCreary Centre Society. ISBN #: 978-1-895438-84-5. Available at http://www.mcs.bc.ca.

Saewyc, E., Richens, K., Skay, C.L., Reis, E., Poon, C., & Murphy, A. (2006). Sexual orientation, sexual abuse, and HIV-risk behaviors among adolescents in the Pacific Northwest. *American Journal of Public Health, 96,* 1104–1110.

Saewyc, E.M., Singh, N., Reis, E., & Flynn, T. (2000). The intersections of racial, gender, and orientation harassment in school and health risk behaviors among adolescents. [Abstract]. *Journal of Adolescent Health, 26,* 148.

Saewyc, E.M., Skay, C.L., Bearinger, L.H., & Resnick, M.D. (2005). The prevalence of protective factors in the lives of bisexual adolescents in the U.S. and Canada. [Abstract]. *Journal of Adolescent Health, 36,* 136–137.

Saewyc, E.M., Skay, C.L., Reis, E., Pettingell, S.E., Bearinger, L.H., Resnick, M.D., Murphy, A., Combs, L. (2006). Hazards of stigma: The sexual and physical abuse of gay, lesbian, and bisexual adolescents in the U.S. and Canada. *Child Welfare, 85*(2), 196–213.

Saewyc, E., Taylor, D., Homma, Y., & Ogilvie, G. (2008). Trends in sexual health and risk behaviours among adolescent students in British Columbia. *Canadian Journal of Human Sexuality, 17*(1–2), 1–13.

Santelli, J.S., Abma, J., Ventura, S., Lindberg, L., Morrow, B., Anderson, J.E., Lyss, S., & Hamilton, B.E. (2004). Can changes in sexual behaviors among high school students explain the decline in teen pregnancy rates in the 1990s? *Journal of Adolescent Health, 35,* 80–90.

Statistics Canada (2007). *Births 2005.* Catalogue #84F0210X-IE. Available from http://www.statcan.ca.

Statistics Canada. CANSIM Table 102-4505, Age-specific fertility rates for females age 15–19, from 2000 to 2005, Canada, provinces and territories. Accessed 01/03/08 from http://cansim2.statcan.ca.

Tonkin, R., Murphy, A., Lee, Z., Saewyc, E., & the McCreary Centre Society. (2005). British Columbia youth health trends: A retrospective, 1992–2003. Vancouver, BC: McCreary Centre Society. ISBN #: 1-895438-71-3. Available from http://www.mcs.bc.ca.

Warf, C., Rew, L., Neavel, C., Saewyc, E., Ensign, J., & Ammerman, S. (in press). Health and health needs of homeless and runaway youth: A position paper of the Society for Adolescent Medicine. *Journal of Adolescent Health.*

Wellings, K., Collumbien, M., Slaymaker, E., Singh, S., Hodges, Z., Patel, D., & Bajos, N. (2007). Sexual behaviour in context: A global perspective. *Lancet, 368,* 1706–28.

7 Sex Information and Educational Council of Canada

Trends in Adolescent Sexuality: A Look at Canadian Youth

Stephanie Mitelman and Jo Visser

Statistics Canada released data showing what other kinds of trouble teens and pre-teens are embracing. Some 13 per cent of youth have had sexual intercourse before they reach the age of 15, while condom use among this age group is erratic at best, leaving teens open to pregnancy and potentially deadly sexually transmitted infections.

('Vital to keep tabs on kids', *Daily Mercury*, Guelph Ontario, 9 May 2005)

With the media moral panic that is hitting news-stands lately, such articles like the one above that appeared in the Guelph *Daily Mercury* are not uncommon. Coloured bracelets, rainbow parties, oral sex in public places, does this reflect what our kids are experiencing? We are very quick to call all of this an epidemic. In the media frenzy about oral sex in school bathrooms and the back of the bus, there is a plethora of this kind of reporting—reporting that is not always accurate and constructs a skewed picture of adolescence and the troubled teen. For example, what the *Daily Mercury* article does not make clear is that in the Statistics Canada survey (of which it is quoting), it was 13 per cent of 14–15 year olds (not all youth) who reported some form of sexual behaviour (not just intercourse), which included masturbation. What comes with this kind of media phenomenon ('leaving teens open to . . . ') is an atmosphere of fear and inaccurate information, which can be more dangerous in itself. Therefore, not only are sex education programs vital for helping youth make healthy decisions about sex and life choices, but they are important for helping people deconstruct the media information that exists—from *Sex and the City*, to the Internet, to daily newspapers.

Are Teens Having Sex?

The answer is yes. What may be surprising is how teens define—or do not define—sex. Most teenagers do not consider petting or oral sex as 'sex'. While there has been lots of discussion about this, it is important to understand that this debate is equally split among adults as well. With that being said, 50 per cent of teenagers are having sex by the age of 17, and this increases with age. Ten per cent of Canadian teens between 12 and 14 years old have had sexual intercourse, and 35 per cent of sexually active Canadians, aged 15–17, have had two or more sexual partners (Maticka-Tyndale, 2001). In self-reported surveys, not surprisingly, males tend to over report, whereas females tend to under report about their sexual activity.

As educators, it is important for us to understand the reasons why teenagers engage in sex in order to start a dialogue and move toward education. The reasons teens have sex are much the same reasons that adults have sex: to alleviate sense of loneliness, to express emotion, to escape boredom, because they are aroused, and because they can. The different motivators for adults and for teens include such factors as the need to feel older, for attention, to be popular, and an increased need for self-esteem. It is important to note that the issue of self-esteem and earlier sexual behaviour work in opposite ways for boys and girls. In the case of boys, sexual behaviour is correlated to a higher self-esteem, while in girls it is correlated to a lowered self-esteem. An additional factor for teens is the well-understood concept of peer pressure and the influence of peer associations at this stage of life.

Factors Contributing to Earlier Sexual Involvement

Many researchers have tried to pinpoint the indicators of earlier sexual involvement. While 'early sexual involvement' is not always exactly well defined, we use it here to mean sexual involvement in early adolescence below the Canadian average of sexual debuts (17 years). The majority of these factors are connected to adolescent risk-taking behaviours, which is a fundamental characteristic of their life-stage development. Another important element of adolescence is the

notion of optimistic bias (i.e., 'It won't happen to me.'). This belief/attitude permeates most of adolescence and the adolescent decision-making processes.

The likelihood of using drugs and alcohol increases the likelihood of early sexual activity, but on its own does not preclude, prescribe, or predict sexual behaviours. There have been many correlations drawn between adolescent sexual behaviours and other factors, but it is important to understand that these are not direct causations. Some connecting factors include the use of drugs and/or alcohol, lower academic performance, peer pressure, and peer associations. Being involved in dating and romantic relationships also increases the opportunity for sexual exploration. As well, one of the strongest connections is the belief that friends have done it or are doing it. Socio-familial factors include fewer religious commitments, more distant relationships with parents, lack of parental supervision, and good old social rebellion. Another element to take note of is biology and the perception of physical maturity, especially in young girls. The concept of precocious puberty (beginning puberty at an early age) may bring up potentially distorted views of maturity, which for some girls can, in some cases, lead to either a perception of emotional maturity, or unwanted sexual advances on behalf of boys and men.

Trends and Sexual Behaviour

In a nutshell, there is good news and some not-so-good news. Statistically, adolescents are initiating sex at earlier ages; however, the rate of Canadian teen pregnancies is declining, and has been declining for the past 20 years. This decline has also led to a decline in teen abortion rates (although a third of all teen pregnancies continue to end in abortion). This shift is largely attributed to a widespread use and effectiveness of lower dose contraception. New methods of administering contraception have also made birth control more appealing than ever before. As a result, Canadian teens are more likely to seek out contraception.

Despite the decrease in adolescent pregnancies, there has been an increase in the transmission of sexually transmitted infections (STIs), including HIV/AIDS, among youth. Teens are still disproportionately at risk for STIs for a number of social reasons: teens are more likely to have multiple partners over a given period of time, have unprotected sex, and to choose higher risk partners.

Cause for great concern is the risky sexual behaviour of youth between the ages of 15 and 25. In a recent survey conducted by the Sex Information Education Council of Canada (SIECCAN, 2005), of sexually active people between the ages of 15 and 25, 40 per cent used a condom at last intercourse, but are less likely to use condoms if they are just with one partner. Eighty per cent of girls and 60 per cent of boys who have been infected with chlamydia do not know they are infected. Finally, as well as not defining oral sex as 'sex', most teens do not know that oral sex is not safe sex. Most teens, and adults alike, are not aware of the potential for transferring STIs to the mouth or back of the throat. Oral sex and teens is not a new thing, but it is certainly an issue we are talking more about. Eighteen per cent of 12 to 15 year olds have experienced oral sex. In the Canadian Youth, Sexual Health and HIV/AIDS Study (Boyce, et al. 2003) of 11 000 Grade 7, 9, 11 students, when asked the question *'Have you ever engaged in oral sex?',* 32 per cent of male grade 9 students and 53 per cent of male grade 11 students answered 'yes'. Twenty-eight per cent of female grade 9 students and 52 per cent of female grade 11 students said 'yes'.

There are two important points about understanding adolescent oral sex. The first is that in a post-AIDS society, even with the gaps in knowledge around HIV/AIDS transmission, teens have managed to construct a set of norms around a lower risk sexual behaviour. Secondly, we must be careful not to construct the oral sex phenomenon through an adult lens, because the adult lens, as well as the feminist perspective, would have us believe that engaging in and performing oral sex on boys is degrading to girls. While this certainly may be the case in some instances, a majority of teenage girls would construct their reality of this activity as power enhancing. This is not to deny that there still exist double standards regarding male and female sexual behaviours, which is another reason why sex education is vital to dispel myths and to cut through age-old double standards. While some teens may experience oral sex as a casual activity, anecdotally we know that most teens do it in the construction of a monogamous intimate relationship. It is important to keep in mind, however, the way in which long-term relationships and monogamy are defined by teens, and that they tend to be shorter in length than adult relationships. Thus, a changing in partners is more rapid than in adulthood.

Education is especially needed around HIV/AIDS, if only to dispel some dangerous myths that continue to prevail. Most commonly heard in the classroom is that there is a cure for AIDS, AIDS is a gay disease, and AIDS happens mostly in Africa. The rate of HIV/AIDS within the heterosexual community in Canada is increasing at a noticeable rate. In 1998, 11 per cent of new HIV infections were spread through heterosexual contact. In 2003, 33 per cent of new HIV infections were spread through heterosexual contact, a 20 per cent increase in five years. Among young heterosexual women, the numbers have increased: in 1994, females aged 15–29 years old represented 10 per cent of AIDS diagnosis. By 2003, females aged 15–29 years old represented

41 per cent of AIDS diagnosis. That is an increase of 30 per cent in nine years (Hawaleshka, 2005).

HIV statistics for Native populations are increasingly alarming, as well. From 1998 to 2001, an estimated 605 Aboriginal persons tested positive to HIV, making up 26 per cent of all reported cases in Canada. And, 30 per cent of Aboriginal people living with AIDS are under 30 years old (Information Centre on Aboriginal Health, 2001). As well, rates of bacterial STIs (such as chlamydia) in the James Bay region are 10 times the provincial rate. In 2000, there were 24 cases of gonorrhea per 100 000 within the Cree population, compared to 9 in 100 000 for the rest of Quebec. Teenage pregnancy rates within the Cree population are also high: 10–14 year old girls are six times more likely to give birth than their provincial average, 15–19 year olds are eight times more likely, and 20–24 year olds are twice as likely.

Given all this information, there is an urgent need for improving upon the sex education and risk reduction education in the schools where we have the largest access to our youth. The three largest target groups for increased risk reduction education are youth (under 25), heterosexual women, and Aboriginal groups.

[. . .]

References

Boyce, W., Doherty, M., Fortin, C., and MacKinnon, D. (2003). Canadian Youth, Sexual Health and HIV/AIDS Study. Council of Ministers of Education, Canada. Available at www.cmec.ca/Publications/Lists/Publications/Attachments/180/CYSHHAS_2002_EN.pdf

Hawaleshka, D. (2005). HIV striking straight young women. *Maclean's Magazine*, 30 May 2005.

Information Centre on Aboriginal Health (2001).

Maticka-Tyndale, E. (2001). Sexual health and Canadian youth: How do we measure up? *Canadian Journal of Human Sexuality, 10*(1–2): 1–17.

Sex Information Education Council of Canada (SIECCAN) (2005). Vital to keep tabs on kids. *Daily Mercury*, Guelph, Ontario, 9 May 2005.

Sexual Health Education in the Schools: Questions & Answers (3rd edition)

Sex Information and Education Council of Canada (SIECCAN)

Introduction

Access to effective, broadly based sexual health education is an important contributing factor to the health and well-being of Canadian youth (Public Health Agency of Canada, 2008). School-based programs are an essential avenue for providing sexual health education to young people. Educators, public health professionals, administrators, and others who are committed to providing high quality sexual health education in the schools are often asked to explain the rationale, philosophy, and content of proposed or existing sexual health education programs.

This document, prepared by SIECCAN, the Sex Information and Education Council of Canada (www.sieccan.org) is designed to support the provision of high quality sexual health education in Canadian schools. It provides answers to some of the most common questions that parents, communities, educators, program planners, school and health administrators, and governments may have about sexual health education in the schools.

Canada is a pluralistic society in which people with differing philosophical, cultural, and religious values live together in a society structured upon basic democratic principles. Canadians have diverse values and opinions related to human sexuality.

Philosophically, this document reflects the democratic, principled approach to sexual health education embodied in the Public Health Agency of Canada's (2008) Canadian Guidelines for Sexual Health Education. The Guidelines are based on the principle that sexual health education should be accessible to all people and that it should be provided in an age-appropriate, culturally sensitive manner that is respectful of an individual's right to make informed choices about sexual and reproductive health.

The answers to common questions about sexual health education provided in this document are based upon and informed by the findings of up-to-date and credible scientific research. An evidence-based approach combined with a respect for democratic principles and values offers a strong foundation for the development and implementation of high quality sexual health education programs in Canadian schools.

Sexual Health and Canadian Youth: How Are We Doing?

Sexual health is multidimensional and involves the achievement of positive outcomes such as mutually rewarding interpersonal relationships and desired parenthood as well as the avoidance of negative outcomes such as unwanted pregnancy and STI/HIV infection (Public Health Agency of Canada, 2008). Trends in teen pregnancy,

sexually transmitted infections, age of first intercourse, and condom use are often used to generally assess the status of the sexual health of Canadian youth.

With respect to teenage pregnancy, it can be assumed that a large proportion of teen pregnancies, particularly among younger teens, are unintended. Teen pregnancy rates are therefore a reasonably direct indicator of young women's opportunities and capacity to control this aspect of their sexual and reproductive health. In Canada, the pregnancy rate (live births/induced abortions/fetal loss) for both younger (age 15–17) and older (age 18–19) teenage women has fallen significantly over the last several decades (McKay, 2006). [. . .]

Sexually transmitted infections (STI) pose a significant threat to the health and well-being of Canadian youth and the prevalence of common STI such as Chlamydia and human papillomavirus (HPV) is highest among youth and young adults. Chlamydia is of particular concern because, if left untreated, it can have serious long-term consequences for the reproductive health of women (Public Health Agency of Canada, 2006). Reported rates (the number of positive test reports made to public health agencies) of Chlamydia have been increasing steadily in recent years (Public Health Agency of Canada, 2009). However, it is important to recognize that reported rates are not a measure of prevalence (the percentage of the population that is infected) and that much of the increase in the reported rate of Chlamydia is likely due to the increasing use of more sensitive testing technologies and a greater number of young people being tested (McKay & Barrett, 2008). Nevertheless, small scale prevalence studies in Canada have found rates of Chlamydia infection ranging from 3.4 per cent among young women tested at family physician's offices (Richardson, Sellors, Mackinnon, et al., 2003) to 10.9 per cent among female street youth

(Shields, Wong, Mann, et al., 2004). In sum, the prevalence of Chlamydia infection among youth and young adult Canadians is unacceptably high.

For a majority of Canadians, first sexual intercourse occurs during the teenage years (Maticka-Tyndale, 2008; Rotermann, 2008). Overall, the percentage of Canadian youth who report ever having had sexual intercourse has declined since the mid-1990s (Rotermann, 2008; Saewyc, Taylor, Homma & Ogilvie, 2008). For example, data from the Canadian Community Health Survey indicates that the percentage of 18/19-year-olds who had ever had intercourse declined from 70 per cent in 1996/1997 to 65 per cent in 2005 (Rotermann, 2008). Research from both Canada and the United States indicates that oral sex is about as common as intercourse and typically occurs at about the same time as intercourse, although up to a quarter of teens may begin having oral sex before starting to have intercourse (Maticka-Tyndale, 2008).

The percentage of sexually active Canadian youth who report using a condom at last intercourse has increased in recent years (Rotermann, 2008; Saewyc et al., 2008). For example, among the participants in the BC Adolescent Health Survey, condom use rose from 64.6 per cent in 1992 to 74.9 per cent in 2003 (Saewyc et al., 2008). Short-term trends are encouraging as well: For teens aged 15–19 participating in the Canadian Community Health Survey condom use at last intercourse rose from 72 per cent in 2003 to 75 per cent in 2005 (Rotermann, 2008).

While condom use among sexually active Canadian youth has clearly increased overall, there is also a persistent trend for the relatively high rates of condom use among younger sexually active teens to decline as teens get older (Rotermann, 2008; Saewyc et al., 2008). For example, among Canadian Community Health Survey participants aged 15–19, 81 per cent of sexually active 15–17-year-olds reported using a condom at last intercourse compared to 70 per cent of 18–19-year-olds (Rotermann, 2008). This pattern of condom use declining with age among sexually active young people has been clearly evident in other surveys of Canadian youth (Boyce, Doherty, Fortin & MacKinnon, 2003; Saewyc et al., 2008). The propensity for older sexually active teens and young adults in Canada to discontinue consistent condom use is a clear indication that many young people in Canada underestimate their risk for sexually transmitted infection (Chlamydia reported rates are highest among 20–24-year-olds).

On basic indicators of sexual health, Canadian young people have made progress in many respects. Rates of teenage pregnancy have declined steadily, the percentage of teens who have had intercourse has also declined in recent years, and rates of condom use among sexually active young people have increased. However, there are important challenges that remain to be adequately addressed. The prevalence of sexually transmitted infections among Canadian young people is unacceptably high and poses a significant threat to their current and long-term health and well-being. Many gay, lesbian, bisexual, and questioning youth receive insufficient sexual health education relevant to their needs (for full discussion of the range of sexual health challenges facing Canadian youth see Maticka-Tyndale, 2008). [. . .]

Why Do We Need Sexual Health Education in the Schools?

'Sexual health is a key aspect of personal health and social welfare that influences individuals across their life span' (Public Health Agency of Canada, 2008, p. 2). Because sexual health is a key component of overall health and well-being, 'Sexual health education should be available to all Canadians as an important component of health promotion and services' (Health Canada, 2003,

p. 1). In principle, all Canadians, including youth, have a right to the information, motivation/personal insight, and skills necessary to prevent negative sexual health outcomes (e.g., sexually transmitted infections including HIV, unplanned pregnancy) and to enhance sexual health (e.g., positive self-image and self-worth, integration of sexuality into mutually satisfying relationships).

Data from Statistics Canada show that 65 per cent of Canadian youth aged 18–19 have experienced sexual intercourse at least once (Rotermann, 2008), clearly indicating that most Canadians become sexually active during the teenage years. In order to ensure that youth are adequately equipped with the information, motivation/personal insight, and skills to protect their sexual and reproductive health, 'it is imperative that schools, in cooperation with parents, the community, and health care professionals, play a major role in sexual health education and promotion' (Society of Obstetricians and Gynecologists of Canada, 2004, p. 596).

As stated by the Public Health Agency of Canada (2008),

> Since schools are the only formal educational institution to have meaningful (and mandatory) contact with nearly every young person, they are in a unique position to provide children, adolescents, and young adults with the knowledge, understanding, skills, and attitudes they will need to make and act upon decisions that promote sexual health throughout their lives (p. 19).
>
> [. . .]

Do Parents Want Sexual Health Education Taught in the Schools?

Parents and guardians are an important and primary source of guidance for young people concerning sexual behaviour and values. Many youth look to their parents as a valuable source of sexuality information (Frappier, Kaufman, Baltzer, et al., 2008).

Parents also recognize that the schools should play a key role in the sexual health education of their children. Studies conducted in different parts of Canada have consistently found that over 85 per cent of parents agreed with the statement 'Sexual health education should be provided in the schools' and a majority of these parents approved of schools providing young people with information on a wide range of sexual health topics including puberty, reproduction, healthy relationships, STI/AIDS prevention, birth control, abstinence, sexual orientation, and sexual abuse/coercion (Langille, Langille, Beazley & Doncaster, 1996; McKay, Pietrusiak & Holowaty, 1998; Weaver, Byers, Sears, Cohen & Randall, 2002). A more recent survey from Saskatchewan (Advisory Committee on Family Planning, 2008) found that 92 per cent of parents strongly agreed or agreed that sexual health education should be provided in the schools and 91 per cent indicated that sexual health education that is appropriate for a child's age and developmental level should start before Grade 9.

Do Young People Want Sexual Health Education Taught in the Schools?

Surveys of youth have clearly shown that young people in Canada want sexual health education to be taught in school (Byers, Sears, Voyer, et al., 2003a; Byers, Sears, Voyer, et al., 2003b; McKay & Holowaty, 1997). For example, a survey of high school youth found that 92 per cent agreed that 'Sexual health education should be provided in the schools' and they rated the following topics as either 'very important' or 'extremely important': puberty, reproduction, personal safety, sexual coercion and sexual assault, sexual decision making in dating relationships, birth control and safer sex practices, and STIs (Byers et al., 2003a). National surveys of youth in Canada have found that schools are the most frequently cited main source of information on sexuality issues (human sexuality, puberty, birth control, HIV/AIDS) (Boyce, Doherty, Fortin & Mackinnon, 2003) and rank highest as the most useful/valuable source of sexual health information (Frappier et al., 2008).

What Values Are Taught in School-based Sexual Health Education?

Canada is a pluralistic society in which different people have different values and perspectives toward human sexuality. At the same time, Canadians are united by their respect for the basic and fundamental values and principles of a democratic society. An emphasis on democratic values provides the overall philosophical framework for many school-based sexual health education programs. [. . .] Thus, the Canadian Guidelines for Sexual Health Education are intended to inform sexual health programming that:

Focuses on the self-worth, respect and dignity of the individual;

Is provided in an age-appropriate, culturally sensitive manner that is respectful of individual sexual diversity, abilities, and choices;

Helps individuals to become more sensitive and aware of the impact their behaviours and actions may have on others and society;

Does not discriminate on the basis of age, race, ethnicity, gender identity, sexual orientation, socioeconomic background,

physical/cognitive abilities and religious background in terms of access to relevant, appropriate, accurate and comprehensive information (Public Health Agency of Canada, 2008, p. 11–12).

These statements acknowledge that sexual health education programs should not be 'value free', but rather that:

Effective sexual health education recognizes that responsible individuals may choose a variety of paths to achieve sexual health;

Effective sexual health education supports informed decision making by providing individuals with the knowledge, personal insight, motivation, and behavioural skills that are consistent with each individual's personal values and choices (Public Health Agency of Canada, 2008, p. 25).

Does Providing Youth with Sexual Health Education Lead to Earlier or More Frequent Sexual Activity?

The impact of sexual health education on the sexual behaviour of youth has been extensively examined in a large number of evaluation research studies. A meta-analysis of 174 studies examining the impact of different types of sexual health promotion interventions found that these programs do not inadvertently increase the frequency of sexual behaviour or number of sexual partners (Smoak, Scott-Sheldon, Johnson & Carey, 2006). More specifically, from a review of 83 studies measuring the impact of curriculum-based sexual health education programs, Kirby, Laris, and Rolleri (2007) concluded that 'The evidence is strong that programs do not hasten or increase sexual behaviour but, instead, some programs delay or decrease sexual behaviours or increase condom or contraceptive use' (p. 206).

Is There Clear Evidence that Sexual Health Education Can Effectively Help Youth Reduce Their Risk of Unintended Pregnancy and STI/HIV Infection?

There is a large body of rigorous evidence in the form of peer-reviewed published studies measuring the behavioural impact of well-designed adolescent sexual health interventions that leads to the definitive conclusion that such programs can have a significant positive impact on sexual health behaviours (e.g., delaying first intercourse, increasing use of condoms). [. . .] For comprehensive reviews of the evaluation research literature demonstrating the positive behavioural impact of sexual health education see Bennett and Assefi (2005) and Kirby, Laris, and Rolleri (2005; 2007).

Are 'Abstinence-only' Programs an Appropriate and Effective Form of School-based Sexual Health Education?

In general, the primary objectives of 'abstinence-only' programs are to encourage young people to not engage in sexual activity until they are married and to teach youth ' . . . that sexual activity outside the context of marriage is likely to have harmful psychological and physical effects' (Title V, Section 510 of the US Social Security Act cited in Trenholm, Devaney, Fortson, et al., 2007). 'Abstinence-only' programs purposefully do not teach young people the importance of consistent contraceptive use for unintended pregnancy

prevention or condom use for STI/HIV infection prevention.

[. . .]

For young people who have not become sexually active, delaying first intercourse can be an effective way to avoid unwanted pregnancy and STI/HIV infection. Therefore, it is important that school-based sexual health education for youth include, as one component of a broadly based program, the relevant information, motivation, and behavioural skills needed to act on and affirm the choice not to engage in sexual activity.

The Public Health Agency of Canada's (2008) Canadian Guidelines for Sexual Health Education state that 'Effective sexual health education recognizes that responsible individuals may choose a variety of paths to achieve sexual health' (p. 25). Educational programs that withhold information necessary for individuals to make voluntary, informed decisions about their sexual health are unethical (World Association for Sexual Health, 2008). 'Abstinence-only' policies may violate the human rights of young people because they withhold potentially life-saving information on HIV and other STI (Ott & Santelli, 2007). According to Statistics Canada the average age of first sexual intercourse among Canadian young people aged 15 to 24 who have had intercourse is 16.5 years for both males and females (Rotermann, 2005). It is therefore vitally important that school-based sexual health education provides youth with the information, motivation, and behavioural skills to consistently practise effective contraception and safer sex practices such as condom use when and if they become sexually active. [. . .]

A substantial body of research evidence clearly indicates that most 'abstinence-only' sex education programs are ineffective in reducing adolescent sexual behaviour. For example, a multiple site randomized trial evaluation of 'abstinence-only' programs authorized by the United States Congress and submitted to the US Department of Health and Human Services found that students who had participated in these programs were not more likely to be abstinent or to delay first intercourse or to have fewer sexual partners than students who did not receive 'abstinence-only' education (Trenholm, Devany, Fortson, et al., 2007). [. . .]

What Are the Key Ingredients of Behaviourally Effective Sexual Health Education Programs?

The first and most important ingredients of effective sexual health education programs in the schools are that sufficient classroom time is allocated to the teaching of this important topic and that the teachers/educators who provide it are adequately trained and motivated to do so (Society of Obstetricians and Gynecologists of Canada, 2004). As stated by the Public Health Agency of Canada (2008), 'Sexual health education should be presented by confident, well-trained, knowledgeable and non-judgmental individuals who receive strong administrative support' (p. 18). In addition, it is clear from the research on sexual health promotion that behaviourally effective programs are based and structured on theoretical models of behaviour change that enable educators to understand and influence sexual health behaviour (Albarracin, Gillette, Earl, et al., 2005; Kirby, Laris & Rolleri, 2007; Public Health Agency of Canada, 2008).

[. . .]

There is an extensive body of research that has indentified the key ingredients of effective sexual health promotion programming (for a summary and review of this literature see Albarracin, Gillette, Earl, et al., 2005; Fisher & Fisher, 1998; Kirby, Laris & Rolleri, 2007; Public Health Agency of Canada, 2008; World Association for Sexual Health, 2008). This research has clearly demonstrated that effective sexual health education programs will contain the following:

1. A realistic and sufficient allocation of classroom time to achieve program objectives.

2. Provide teachers/educators with the necessary training and administrative support to deliver the program effectively.

3. Employ sound teaching methods including the utilization of well-tested theoretical models to develop and implement programming (e.g., IMB Model, Social Cognitive Theory, Transtheoretical Model, Theory of Reasoned Action/Theory of Planned Behaviour).

4. Use elicitation research to identify student characteristics, needs, and optimal learning styles including tailoring instruction to student's ethnocultural background, sexual orientation, and developmental stage.

5. Specifically target the behaviours that lead to negative sexual health outcomes such as STI/HIV infection and unintended pregnancy.

6. Deliver and consistently reinforce prevention messages related to sexual limit-setting (e.g., delaying first intercourse; choosing not to have intercourse), consistent condom use and other forms of contraception.

7. Include program activities that address the individual's environment and social context including peer and partner pressures related to adolescent sexuality.

8. Incorporate the necessary information, motivation, and behavioural skills to effectively enact and maintain behaviours to promote sexual health.

9. Provide clear examples of and opportunities to practise (e.g., role plays) sexual limit setting, condom use negotiation, and other communication skills so that students are active participants in the program, not passive recipients.

10. Incorporate appropriate and effective evaluation tools to assess program strengths and weaknesses in order to improve subsequent programming.

What Is the Impact of Making Condoms Available to Teenagers?

Research has clearly and consistently shown that making condoms accessible to young people does not result in earlier or more frequent sexual activity. The same research studies also show that condom distribution programs can significantly increase condom use among teens who are sexually active (Blake, Ledsky, Goodnow et al., 2003; Guttmacher et al., 1997; Schuster, Bell, Berry & Kanouse, 1998). For example, Blake et al. (2003) in their study of high schools in Massachusetts found that students enrolled in schools with condom availability programs were not more likely to report ever having intercourse but sexually active students attending schools with condom availability programs were significantly more likely to have used a condom at last intercourse than sexually active students without condom availability programs (72% vs. 56%). This finding is consistent with other research studies on the impact of school-based condom availability programs. [. . .]

Are Condoms Effective in Preventing HIV and Other STIs?

According to the Public Health Agency (2002), 'Condoms used consistently and correctly provide protection against getting or spreading STIs including HIV' (p. 1) and the Canadian Guidelines on Sexually Transmitted Infections (Public Health Agency of Canada, 2006) indicate that clinical and public health professionals, including physicians and nurses, should strongly recommend consistent condom use to prevent STIs among at-risk persons (pp. 334–38). The importance of condom use for prevention of STIs is echoed by the World Health Organization (WHO, 2000): 'Condoms are the only contraceptive method proven to reduce the risk of all sexually transmitted infections (STIs), including HIV' (p. 1).

According to the US Centers for Disease Control and Prevention (CDC, 2008), 'Laboratory studies have demonstrated that latex condoms provide an essentially impermeable barrier to particles the size of HIV' (pp. 2–3) and that 'Latex condoms, when used consistently and correctly, are highly effective in preventing the sexual transmission of HIV' (p. 2). A laboratory study carried out by the US Food and Drug Administration found that under extreme and highly unlikely conditions of stress (i.e., 'worst-case condom barrier effectiveness') using a latex condom was estimated to reduce exposure to HIV by at least 10 000 times compared to not using a condom (Carey et al., 1992).

There is also strong evidence that consistent condom use significantly reduces the risk of transmission of Chlamydia and gonorrhea (Gallo, Steiner, Warner, et al., 2007; Paz-Bailey, Koumans, Sternberg et al., 2005; Warner, Stone, Macaluso et al., 2006), herpes (HSV-2) (Wald, Langenberg, Krantz et al., 2005), and human papilloma virus (HPV) (Winer, Hughes, Feng et al., 2006).

In sum there is strong and conclusive evidence that consistent condom use significantly reduces the risk of sexually transmitted infections. Sexual health educators have a duty to inform youth who are sexually active, or who will become sexually active, about the benefits of condom use and to stress that ' . . . like any other prevention tool, condoms work only when they are used. Consistent and correct use is essential for optimal risk reduction' (Steiner & Cates, 2006, p. 2642).

Should School-based Sexual Health Education Address the Issue of Sexual Diversity?

The available research data on sexual orientation among Canadian youth (Boyce et al., 2003; McCreary Centre Society, 2007) indicates that most school classrooms in Canada will likely have at least one or more students who are not heterosexual. The Public Health Agency of Canada's (2008) Canadian Guidelines for Sexual Health Education suggest that educational programs should address the sexual health needs of all students, including those who are gay, lesbian, bisexual, transgendered, or questioning. As well, the Guidelines note that an understanding of sexual diversity issues is an important component of sexual health education.

Surveys of Canadian parents indicate that a majority want sexual orientation addressed in school-based sexual health education programs (Advisory Committee on Family Planning, 2008; Langille, Langille, Beazley & Doncaster, 1996; McKay, Pietrusiak & Holowaty, 1998; Weaver, Byers, Sears, Cohen & Randall, 2002). For example, in a study of New Brunswick parents, Weaver et al. (2002) found that over 80 per cent supported the inclusion of the topic of 'homosexuality' in the sexual health curriculum. In a study of the effectiveness of sexual health education in British Columbia schools (Options for Sexual Health, 2004), parents, students, educators and public health workers acknowledged that the sexual health curriculum often failed to meet the needs of sexually diverse students, and that sexual diversity issues warranted more attention.

A supportive, non-threatening school environment has been recognized as being one protective factor that can potentially reduce the risk of negative health and social outcomes among youth (Saewyc, Homma & Skay, 2009).

However, preliminary results (Egale Canada, 2008) from a national survey on homophobia in Canadian schools indicates that over two-thirds of lesbian, gay, bisexual, transgendered, and questioning youth felt unsafe in their schools. Over half of these students reported being verbally harassed and over a quarter report being physically harassed because of their sexual orientation. The inclusion of sexual diversity issues in the sexual health curriculum can help encourage understanding and respect among students, and will contribute to a supportive and safe school environment that is the right of all students (for more information on sexual diversity and the educational needs of LGBTQ youth see Public Health Agency of Canada, 2008).

How Should School-based Sexual Health Education Address the Issue of Emergency Contraception?

The provision of accurate information about contraception allows youth to make informed sexual and reproductive health choices. With respect to emergency contraception (EC), it is important that clear information is provided about how the methods work, when they can be used for maximum effectiveness, and where they can be accessed. [. . .]

In Canada, ECP [emergency contraception protection] is available without a prescription from a licensed pharmacist. Minor youth do not need the permission of their parents or guardians to obtain ECP. Pharmacists are required to inform potential users about the drug, how it works and possible side effects. Pharmacists can refuse to supply ECP to minors only if there is reasonable doubt about the minor's ability to comprehend the information given. The insertion of a post-coital IUD [intrauterine device] must be done in a medical setting. In Canada, the age of consent for medical treatment can differ across provinces and territories. However, the concept of the mature minor will also apply on a case-by-case basis (Rozovsky, 2004). In provinces that haven't legislated an age of consent for medical treatment, the concept of the mature minor applies in every instance. This means that a youth can have an IUD inserted if the health practitioner believes that the information about the treatment, including possible risks and consequences, was fully understood by the patient (for more information on ECP, see Pancham & Dunn, 2007). Youth should be made aware of any relevant provincial or territorial legislation that could affect their access to sexual health services.

How Should School-based Sexual Health Education Address the Issue of New Laws on the Age of Sexual Consent?

Age of consent refers to the age at which people are able to make their own decisions about sexual activity. In Canada, the age of consent was raised from 14 to 16 in 2008 (for a summary of the contents of the legislation and discussion of its implications see Wong, 2006). Effective sexual health education should provide students with a clear understanding of how age of consent is interpreted under the law. Educators should make youth aware that the intent of the legislation is to target adult sexual predators, not youth themselves and that the new legislation does not affect the right of young people to access sexual health education or sexual and reproductive health services. A five-year peer group provision allows for youth aged 14 or 15 to have consensual sex with partners who are no more than five years older than themselves. As well, youth aged 12 and 13 can have consensual sex with other youth who are not more than two years older than themselves.

Certain sexual activities are prohibited for those under the age of 18. The Criminal Code of Canada states that persons under the age of 18 cannot engage in anal intercourse except if they are legally married. Someone under the age of 18 cannot legally consent to have sex with a person in a position of authority such as a teacher, health care provider, coach, lawyer or family member. Persons under the age of 18 cannot legally consent to engage in sexual activity involving prostitution or pornography.

What Are the Social and Economic Benefits to Society of Implementing Broadly Based Sexual Health Education in the Schools?

[. . .] There is a growing recognition that the attainment and maintenance of sexual health for individuals, couples, and families is an important component of the overall well-being of the community (World Association for Sexual Health, 2008). Broadly based sexual health education in the schools can make a significant positive contribution to the health and well-being of the community.

It is equally important to recognize that neglecting to provide broadly based sexual health education programs can have far reaching social and economic consequences. For example, untreated Chlamydia infection (a common STI among Canadian youth and young adults) can lead to severe medical conditions including pelvic inflammatory disease (PID) and infertility, chronic pelvic pain, and ectopic pregnancy (Public Health Agency of Canada, 2006). It has been estimated that in Canada the costs of these conditions are approximately $1942 for inpatient PID treatment, $6469 for ectopic pregnancy, $324 for chronic pelvic pain, and $12 169 for the lifetime cost of infertility treatment

(Goeree, Jang, Blackhouse et al., 2001). Goeree and Gully (1993) estimated that in 1990, the total cost of Chlamydia and associated sequelae was approximately $89 million and the total cost of gonorrhea and associated sequelae was approximately $54 million. Given that the number of cases of these infections that are diagnosed annually has increased significantly since 1990 (see Public Health Agency of Canada, 2009), the total costs associated with these infections have also likely increased. [. . .]

The socio-economic outcomes of teen pregnancy and parenthood are complex and do not lend themselves to simplistic conclusions on cause and effect (for a review of this literature see Best Start, 2007; 2008; Bissell, 2000). However it is fair to assume that, particularly for younger teens, unintended pregnancy and child-bearing can have social and economic consequences for the young woman, her family, and the community.

[. . .]

How Can the Canadian Guidelines for Sexual Health Education Contribute to the Initiation and Maintenance of High Quality Sexual Health Education Programming in the Schools?

The Canadian Guidelines for Sexual Health Education (Public Health Agency of Canada, 2008) are designed to guide and unify professionals working in fields that provide sexual health education. The Guidelines are grounded in evidence-based research placed in a Canadian context and offer curriculum and program planners, educators, and policy-makers clear direction for the initiation, development, implementation, and evaluation of effective sexual health education programs.

For example, at the initiation stage, the Guidelines can be used to facilitate discussion of the rationale and philosophy of school-based sexuality education with parents and other community stakeholders. The Guidelines include a checklist for assessing existing programs with respect to philosophy, accessibility, comprehensiveness, effectiveness of educational approaches and methods, training and administrative support, and planning/evaluation/updating/social development.

The Guidelines suggest a basic three-step process to sexual health education development:

Assessment

program planners assess the target population's sexual health education needs;

Intervention

program planners develop and implement relevant and appropriate sexual health education programs;

Evaluation

program planners measure the effectiveness of the program and identify areas requiring modification.

At the curriculum development and implementation stages, the Guidelines provide a framework for effective program content based on the information-motivation-behavioural skills (IMB) model (Fisher & Fisher, 1998) for sexual health enhancement and problem prevention. The Guidelines specify that effective sexual health education integrates four key components: acquisition of knowledge; development of motivation and critical insight; development of skills; and creation of an environment conducive to sexual health.

In summary, the Canadian Guidelines for Sexual Health Education provide a clear, easy-to-apply, evidence-based guide to the initiation, development, implementation, and evaluation of sexual health education in Canadian schools. The Guidelines are available online from the Public Health Agency of Canada (www.phac-aspc.gc.ca/publicat/cgshe-ldnemss/index-eng.php).

References

Advisory Committee on Family Planning. (2008). *Sexual health education survey: Urban and rural comparative.* Conducted by Fast Consulting, Saskatoon, SK, for the Advisory Committee on Family Planning, Saskatoon, Saskatchewan.

Albarracin, D., Gillette, J.C., Earl, A., et al. (2005). A test of the major assumptions about behavior change: A comprehensive look at the effects of passive and active HIV-prevention interventions since the beginning of the epidemic. *Psychological Bulletin, 31,* 856–897.

Bennett, S.E., and Assefi, N.P. (2005). School-based teenage pregnancy prevention programs: a systematic review of randomized controlled trials. *Journal of Adolescent Health, 36*(1), 72–81.

Best Start. (2007). *Update report on teen pregnancy prevention.* Toronto, ON: Best Start: Ontario's Maternal, Newborn and Early Child Development Resource Centre.

———. (2008). *Teen pregnancy prevention: Exploring out-of-school approaches.* Toronto, ON: Best Start: Ontario's Maternal, Newborn and Early Child Development Resource Centre.

Bissell, M. (2000). Socio-economic outcomes of teen pregnancy and parenthood: A review of the literature. *The Canadian Journal of Human Sexuality, 9,* 1919–204.

Blake, S.M., Ledsky, R., Goodenow, C., et al. (2003). Condom availability programs in Massachusetts high schools: Relationships with condom use and sexual behavior. *American Journal of Public Health, 93,* 955–962.

Boyce, W., Doherty, M., Fortin, C., & MacKinnon, D. (2003). Canadian youth, sexual health and HIV/AIDS study. Council of Ministers of Education, Canada.

Byers, E.S., Sears, H.A., Voyer, S.D., et al. (2003a). An adolescent perspective on sexual health education at school and at home: I. High school students. *The Canadian Journal of Human Sexuality, 12,* 1–17.

——— (2003b). An adolescent perspective on sexual health education at school and at home: II. Middle school students. *The Canadian Journal of Human Sexuality, 12,* 19–33.

Carey, R.F., Herman, W.A., Retta S.M., et al. (1992). Effectiveness of latex condoms as a barrier to human immunodeficiency virus-sized particles under conditions of simulated use. *Sexually Transmitted Diseases, 19,* 230–34.

CDC. (2008). *2008 Compendium of evidence-based prevention interventions.* Atlanta, GA: Centers for Disease Control and Prevention. http://www.cdc.gov/HIV/topics/research/prs/print/evidence-based-interventions.htm

Egale Canada. (2008). Backgrounder: Egale Canada first national survey on homophobia in Canadian schools: Phase one results. http://www.egale.ca/extra/1393-Homophobia-Backgrounder.pdf

Fisher, W.A., & Fisher, J.D. (1998). Understanding and promoting sexual and reproductive health behavior: Theory and method. *Annual Review of Sex Research, 9,* 39–76.

Frappier, J-Y., Kaufman, M., Baltzer, F., et al. (2008). Sex and sexual health: A survey of Canadian youth and mothers. *Pediatric and Child Health, 13,* 25–30.

Gallo, M.F., Steiner, M.J., Warner, L., et al. (2007). Self-reported condom use is associated with reduced risk of Chlamydia, gonorrhea and trichomoniasis. *Sexually Transmitted Diseases, 34,* 829–33.

Goeree, R., & Gully, P. (1993). *The burden of Chlamydial and Gonococcal infection in Canada. New reproductive technologies and the health care system: The case for evidence-based medicine,* Vol. 11. Research studies of the Royal Commission on New Reproductive Technologies. Ottawa, ON: Minister of Supply and Services.

Goeree, R., Jang, D., Blackhouse, G., et al. (2001). Cost-effectiveness of screening swab or urine specimens for Chlamydia trachomatis from young Canadian women in Ontario. *Sexually Transmitted Diseases, 28,* 701–9.

Guttmacher, S., et al. (1997). Condom availability in New York City public schools: Relationships to condom use and sexual behavior. *American Journal of Public Health, 87,* 1427–33.

Health Canada. (2003). *Canadian guidelines for sexual health education* (2nd edn). Ottawa, ON: Population and Public Health Branch, Health Canada.

Kirby, D., Laris, B.A., & Rolleri, L. (2005). *Impact of sex and HIV education programs on sexual behaviors of youth in developing and developed countries.* Research Triangle Park, NC: Family Health International.

———. (2007). Sex and HIV education programs: Their impact on sexual behaviors of young people throughout the world. *Journal of Adolescent Health, 40,* 206–17.

Langille, D.B., Langille, D.J., Beazley, R., & Doncaster, H. (1996). *Amherst parents' attitudes towards school-based sexual health education.* Halifax, NS: Dalhousie University.

McCreary Centre Society. (2007). *Not yet equal: The health of lesbian, gay, & bisexual youth in BC.* Vancouver, BC: McCreary Centre Society.

McKay, A. (2006). Trends in teen pregnancy in Canada with comparisons to U.S.A. and England/Wales. *The Canadian Journal of Human Sexuality, 15,* 157–62.

McKay, A., & Barrett, M. (2008). Rising reported rates of Chlamydia among young women in Canada: What do they tell us about trends in the actual prevalence of the infection? *The Canadian Journal of Human Sexuality, 17,* 61–69.

McKay, A., & Holowaty, P. (1997). Sexual health education: A study of adolescents' opinions, self-perceived needs, and current and preferred sources of information. *The Canadian Journal of Human Sexuality, 6,* 29–38.

McKay, A., Pietrusiak, M.A., & Holowaty, P. (1998). Parents' opinions and attitudes towards sexuality education in the schools. *The Canadian Journal of Human Sexuality, 6,* 29–38.

Maticka-Tyndale, E. (2008). Sexuality and sexual health of Canadian adolescents: Yesterday, today and tomorrow. *The Canadian Journal of Human Sexuality, 17,* 85–95.

Options for Sexual Health. (2004). *An assessment of the effectiveness of sexual health education in BC schools.* Vancouver, BC: Options for Sexual Health.

Ott, M.A., & Santelli, J.S. (2007). Abstinence and abstinence-only education. *Current Opinion in Obstetrics and Gynecology, 19,* 446–52.

Pancham, A., & Dunn, S. (2007). Emergency contraception in Canada: An overview and recent developments. *The Canadian Journal of Human Sexuality, 16,* 129–33.

Paz-Bailey, G., Koumans, E., & Sternberg, M., et al. (2005). The effect of correct and consistent condom use on chlamydial and gonococcal infection among urban adolescents. *Archives of Pediatric and Adolescent Medicine, 159,* 536–42.

Public Health Agency of Canada. (2002). *Condoms, Sexually transmitted infections, safer sex and you.* Ottawa, ON: Public Health Agency of Canada. http://www.phac-aspc.gc.ca/publicat/epiu-aepi/std-mts/condom-eng.php

———. (2006). *Canadian guidelines on sexually transmitted infections.* 2006 edn. Ottawa, ON: Public Health Agency of Canada.

———. (2008). *Canadian guidelines for sexual health education* (3rd edn). Ottawa, ON: Public Health Agency of Canada.

———. (2009). Brief report on sexually transmitted infections in Canada: 2006. Surveillance and Epidemiology Section, Public Health Agency of Canada.

Richardson, E., Sellors, J.W., Mackinnon, S., et al. (2003). Prevalence of Chlamydia trachomatis infections and specimen collection preference among women, using self-collected vaginal swabs in community settings. *Sexually Transmitted Diseases, 30,* 880–85.

Rotermann, M. (2005). Sex, condoms, and STDs among young people. *Health Reports, 16,* 39–45.

———. (2008). Trends in teen sexual behaviour and condom use. *Health Reports, 19,* 1–5.

Rozovsky, F. (2004). *Canadian law of consent to treatment.* (3rd edn). Toronto, ON: Butterworths of Canada.

Saewyc, E., Homma, Y., Skay, C., et al. (2009). Protective factors in the lives of bisexual adolescents in North America. *American Journal of Public Health, 99,* 110–17.

Saewyc, E., Taylor, D., Homma, Y., & Ogilvie, G. (2008). Trends in sexual health and risk behaviours among adolescent students in British Columbia. *The Canadian Journal of Human Sexuality, 17,* 1–14.

Schuster, M., Bell, R., Berry, S., & Kanouse, D. (1998). Impact of a high school condom availability program on sexual attitudes and behaviors. *Family Planning Perspectives, 30,* 67–72.

Shields, S., Wong, T., Mann, J. et al. (2004). Prevalence and correlates of Chlamydia infection in Canadian street youth. *Journal of Adolescent Health, 34,* 384–90.

Smoak, N.D., Scott-Sheldon, L.A., Johnson, B.T., & Carey, M.P. (2006). Sexual risk interventions do not inadvertently increase the overall frequency of sexual behavior: A meta-analysis of 174 studies with 116,735 participants. *Journal of Acquired Immunodeficiency Syndrome, 41,* 374–84.

Society of Obstetricians and Gynecologists of Canada. (2004). SOGC policy statement: school-based and school-linked sexual health education in Canada. *JOGC, 26,* 596–600.

Steiner, M.J., & Cates, W. (2006). Condoms and sexually transmitted infections. *The New England Journal of Medicine, 354,* 2642–43.

Trenholm, C., Devaney, B., Fortson, K., et al. (2007). Impacts of four Title V, Section 510 abstinence education programs, final report. Mathematica Policy Research, Inc. Submitted to: U.S. Department of Health and Human Services. http://aspe.hhs.gov/hsp/abstinence07/

Wald, A., Langenberg, A., Krantz, E. et al. (2005). The relationship between condom use and herpes simplex virus infection. *Annals of Internal Medicine, 143,* 707–13.

Warner, L., Stone, K.M., Macaluso, M. et al. (2006). Condom use and risk of gonorrhea and Chlamydia: a systematic review of design and measurement factors assessed in epidemiologic studies. *Sexually Transmitted Diseases, 33,* 36–51.

Weaver, A.D., Byers, E.S., Sears, H.A., Cohen, J.N., & Randall, H. (2002). Sexual health education at school and at home: Attitudes and experiences of New Brunswick parents. *The Canadian Journal of Human Sexuality, 11,* 19–31.

Winer, R.L., Hughes, J.P., Feng, Q., et al. (2006). Condom use and the risk of genital human papillomavirus infection in young women. *The New England Journal of Medicine, 354,* 2645–54.

Wong, J.P. (2006). Age of consent to sexual activity in Canada: Background to proposed new legislation on 'age of protection'. *The Canadian Journal of Human Sexuality, 15,* 163–169.

World Association for Sexual Health. (2008). *Sexual health for the millennium: A declaration and technical document.* Minneapolis, MN: World Association for Sexology.

World Health Organization (WHO). (2000). Effectiveness of male latex condoms in protecting against pregnancy and sexually transmitted infections. Fact Sheet No. 243. http://apps.who.int/inf-fs/en/fact243.html

An Adolescent Perspective on Sexual Health Education at School and at Home: 1. High School Students

E. Sandra Byers, Heather A. Sears, Susan D. Voyer, Jennifer L. Thurlow, Jacqueline N. Cohen, and Angela D. Weaver

Introduction

School is a primary source of sexual health information for Canadian youths (McKay & Holowaty, 1997). Well-planned and effectively delivered sexual health education (SHE) can help young people enhance their sexual health and avoid negative sexual outcomes, such as unwanted pregnancy (Baldwin, Whitely & Baldwin, 1990; Kirby, 2001; Mackie & Oickle, 1996; Munro, Doherty-Poirier, Mayan & Salmon, 1994), Although SHE is taught in all Canadian provinces and territories, the nature of these programs varies considerably and not all major topics are included (Barrett 1994; McCall et al., 1999).

Most SHE programs are based on adults' views, but likely would be more successful if the perspectives of adolescents were incorporated into their design (Campbell & Campbell, 1990; Fisher & Fisher, 1992; Maticka-Tyndale, 1995; McKay & Holowaty, 1997). Given that teenagers view sex education as one of their most important educational needs (Cairns, Collins & Hiebert, 1994), elicitation research that evaluates whether the curriculum addresses students' needs is vital (McKay, Fisher, Maticka-Tyndale & Barrett, 2001; McKay & Halowaty, 1997). It is also important to assess whether youths see their parents as meeting SHE needs, because parents and teachers believe strongly that schools *and* parents should share responsibility for providing SHE and that discussions at home are an important part of students' SHE (Cohen, Byers, Sears & Weaver, 2001; Weaver, Byers, Sears, Cohen & Randall, 2002). Therefore, the purpose of this study was to assess students' SHE needs and their perceptions of the quality of the SHE they have received at school and at home. The present survey of high school students was one of four studies assessing the attitudes and ideas of New Brunswick parents, teachers, middle school students, and high school students toward SHE (Byers et al., 2001; Cohen et al., 2001; Weaver et al., 2002).

Attitudes Toward Sexual Health Education

Surveys of Canadian parents and teachers have found strong support for school-based SHE (Cohen et al., 2001; McKay, Pietrusiak & Holowaty, 1998; Weaver et al., 2002). Studies with adolescents have also shown that youths feel positively about SHE. For example, McKay and Holowaty (1997) surveyed 406 adolescents in grades 7 to 12 in one rural Ontario school district and found that 89 per cent viewed SHE as an important part of the curriculum. [. . .] However, no large-scale survey of New Brunswick students' attitudes toward SHE has been conducted. Thus, the first goal of this study was to assess New Brunswick students' attitudes toward SHE at school. We evaluated students' general attitude toward school-based SHE and compared this opinion to their opinion about schools and parents sharing responsibility for SHE. We also assessed their attitudes toward the inclusion of specific researcher-defined sexual health topics. In addition, we evaluated whether students' gender and grade level were associated with their attitudes. In order to identify discrepancies between the current curriculum and students' learning priorities, we asked youths to identify two questions they had about sexual health.

Effectiveness of Sexual Health Education

Research has demonstrated that SHE is most effective when it goes beyond information and also includes motivational and skill-building opportunities (Fisher & Fisher, 1992; Kirby, 1992). Consistent with these results, students want a comprehensive SHE program that provides detailed information on specific sexual health topics (e.g., preventing and treating STDs, methods of birth control) as well as explicit instruction on skills (Eisenberg & Wagenaar, 1997; McKay & Holowaty, 1997). However, Canadian curricula primarily focus on enhancing knowledge about the biological aspects of sexuality (McCall et al., 1999). Students are aware of the deficiencies in school-based SHE and view the curriculum as one of the barriers to effective SHE (Langille et al., 2000). [. . .] Building on this work, we assessed students' opinions about the quality of the SHE they had received at school, and the extent to which it addressed their perceived needs. We also extended past elicitation research by asking students to indicate the grade level at which they believed SHE should start as well as the grade level at which they would have liked to learn about each of a number of specific sexual health topics. In addition, we asked students to rate the extent to which each of 10 sexual health topics was covered in the school-based SHE they had received.

Teaching Quality and Teaching Methods

Students report that SHE is more effective when they perceive their teachers as knowledgeable, comfortable with the subject matter, and non-judgmental; and when teachers use discussion, guest speakers, and experiential learning activities instead of, or in addition to, lecturing (Eisenberg & Wagenaar, 1997; Langille et al., 2000). [. . .] Thus, we assessed students' opinions about their sexual health teachers as well as the teaching methods used by these teachers. We also asked students to rate how helpful each method would be for teaching sexual health.

The composition of the class may also contribute to the effectiveness of SHE, from the teachers' and the students' perspectives. Cohen et al. (2001) found that most female teachers preferred teaching single-sex classes whereas most male teachers were equally comfortable with teaching either single-sex or coed classes. McKay and Holowaty (1997) reported that 60 per cent of girls and 35 per cent of boys thought that single-sex classes would be appropriate for some sexual health topics and would make them feel more comfortable. Some girls have indicated that they are embarrassed to ask questions in front of boys who make inappropriate jokes or act disrespectfully (Langille et al., 2000). It is not known, however, whether these preferences differ across grade level. Therefore, we examined students' preferences for single-sex or coed sexual health classes.

Sexual Health Education at Home

Parents and school are students' two preferred sources of sexual health information, although parents are not often a primary source of this information (Ansuini, Fiddler-Woite & Woite, 1996; King et al., 1988; McKay & Holowaty, 1997). Sexual health education at home is important because high quality parent-child communication about sexuality has been linked to a decrease in sexual risk behaviour and negative sexual health outcomes (Meschke, Bartholomae & Zentall, 2002). [. . .]

Some students want to talk more to their parents about sexuality than they currently do. However, many of them do not know how to raise the topic with their parents or fear that their parents will disapprove if they talk to them openly about sex (Eisenberg & Wagenaar, 1997; Hampton, Smith, Jeffery & McWatters, 2001), Many parents are aware that what they are offering for SHE could be improved. In a previous study, we found that only one-third of parents felt that they had done an excellent or very good job providing SHE at home, and parents, on average, indicated that they had rarely encouraged their children to ask questions about sexuality (Weaver et al., 2002). Therefore, we asked students about the SHE they received from their parents, including how often their parents encouraged them to ask questions. Because some parents delay more extensive, albeit still limited, discussions of sexual health topics with their children (Weaver et al., 2002), we also evaluated whether students at higher grade levels were more positive about the SHE they had received at home than students at lower grade levels. Finally, we assessed the extent to which girls and boys want to talk more to their parents about sexuality than they currently do.

Method

Participants

Surveys were completed by 1663 high school students who were attending grades 9 to 12 in eight schools in New Brunswick. Each grade was equally represented and about half (54%) of the participants were girls (21 students did not indicate their gender). About three-quarters of the teenagers (78%) lived in two-parent families, 16 per cent lived in one-parent families, and 3 per cent lived in a joint custody situation. According to the youths, most mothers had completed high school (36%),

community college or technical school (20%), or university (33%) and were employed outside the home (75%). Similarly, most fathers had completed high school (30%), community college or technical school (18%), or university (32%) and were employed outside the home (91%). In terms of their dating history, 89 per cent of the adolescents reported that they had had at least one boyfriend or girlfriend, and 69 per cent had dated someone for longer than two months.

Measure

The survey was divided into seven parts. Part A elicited students' general opinions, rated on 5-point Likert scales, about SHE in school, such as whether SHE should be provided in school, whether the school and parents should share responsibility for the provision of SHE, their perceptions of the quality of the SHE that they have received in school, and whether the SHE they have received covered the topics in which they were most interested. Youths also indicated the grade level at which they thought SHE should begin (K–3, 4–5, 6–8, 9–12, or 'There should be no sexual health education in schools'). Part B asked students to rate, on a 5-point scale ranging from 1 (not at all important) to 5 (extremely important), how important it is to include each of 10 topics in a sexual health curriculum (see Table 1 for a list of the topics). In Part C, students reported the grade that they were in the last time they received SHE. They then indicated how well each of the 10 topics listed in Part B had been covered in the SHE they had received in school, using a 5-point scale ranging from 'not covered at all' (1) to 'covered very well' (5). Using an open-ended format, they also were asked to list any two sexual health questions about which they would like to learn.

Part D assessed youths' opinions about their most recent sexual health teacher. Each question had an option for them to indicate that they had never had SHE. Using 5-point scales, they reported how comfortable they thought their instructor was ('not at all comfortable' to 'very comfortable'), how often their instructor encouraged them to ask questions ('not at all' to 'very often'), and how well their instructor answered questions ('poor' to 'excellent'). They were also asked about their preference for single-sex versus coed SHE classes. Next, students indicated which of eight teaching methods their teacher used as well as the extent to which they thought each method would help them learn about sexual health ('it wouldn't help at all' [1], 'it would help somewhat' [2], 'it would help a lot' [3]). The methods listed were lecturing, videotapes, readings, group discussion, guest speakers, individual projects, role play, drama and games, and a question box.

In Part E, students reported the grade level at which they would have liked to learn about each of 27 sexual health topics (K–5, 6–8, 9–12, or 'This topic should not be included'; see Table 2 for a list of the topics). In Part F, they rated the SHE they had received from their parent(s) or guardian on a 5-point scale ranging from 'excellent' to 'poor', and indicated how often their parents or guardian encouraged them to ask questions ('very often' to 'not at all'). They also reported on separate 5-point Likert scales ranging from 'strongly agree' to 'strongly disagree', whether they wished their parents had talked to them more about sexuality and whether they wished they knew more about sexuality. In Part G, youths provided demographic information, including their gender, grade level, with whom they were living, and each parent's level of education and employment status.

Procedure

This study was conducted in the spring of 2001 as part of a project that also assessed parent and teacher attitudes toward SHE. Six high schools and two combined middle and high schools (grades 6–12) were selected geographically from around the province so that, in keeping with New Brunswick demographics, an approximately equal number of students were attending schools in rural and urban communities.

Following ethics approval from the University of New Brunswick, the New Brunswick Department of Education sent a letter describing the project to the directors of the selected school districts and notified them about which schools had been chosen to participate. The researchers then contacted the principals of the selected schools by telephone in order to obtain their consent to participate in the study, to explain the procedure, and to verify the number of students in the school. Members of the research team administered the survey to youths at school during one class period. Before the surveys were distributed, students were informed about the nature and purpose of the study and were asked to read and sign a consent form if they wished to participate. They were informed that they could omit any questions they were uncomfortable answering and that they could withdraw from the study at any time. Only 15 students declined to complete the survey. In addition, three surveys were excluded because they had extensive missing data.

Data Analysis

Frequencies and means were used to describe students' responses to individual objective questions. The effects of gender and grade level on the variables assessed were analyzed using 2 (gender) X 4 (grade level) ANOVAs or MANOVAs, unless otherwise indicated. Due to the large sample size, we set alpha at a conservative level ($p < .001$), and only interpreted results as significant when they accounted for 4 per cent or more of the variance (η^2). An effect size of about 1 per cent is considered small, 9–10 per cent medium, and 25 per cent large (Cohen,

Cohen & West, 2003). Follow-up mean comparisons were performed using Tukey's HSD.

To evaluate students' responses to the open-ended item that asked them to list any two questions about sexual health that they would like to learn about, we used content analysis. This technique is commonly used in survey research (Weber, 1990). One of the authors reviewed all responses given by students in one of the large schools and then read and reread the responses until patterns emerged. Three themes were identified which focused on the nature of the question. The themes concerned seven sexual health topics. The themes and topics were confirmed using the responses from students at the other schools.

Results

Attitudes Toward Sexual Health Education

The vast majority of adolescents were in support of school-based SHE, with 92 per cent either agreeing or strongly agreeing that SHE should be provided in school. In addition, many of the students (77%) either agreed or strongly agreed that the school and parents should share this responsibility. We examined variation by gender and grade in students' attitudes toward school-based SHE using a 2 (gender) X 4 (grade) ANOVA. Neither of the main effects nor their interaction was significant. However, students' attitudes toward schools and parents sharing responsibility for SHE did vary by gender and grade, $F(1, 1630) = 85.64, p < .001, \eta^2 = .05$ and $F(3, 1630) = 25.22, p < .001, \eta^2 = .04$. Girls were more positive about schools and parents sharing responsibility for SHE than boys ($Ms = 4.19$ and 3.77, respectively); and grade 12 students were more positive ($M = 4.34$) than grade 9, 10, or 11 students ($Ms = 3.79, 3.93,$ and 3.97, respectively). The gender by grade interaction was not significant. Finally, we examined

mean-level differences between students' attitudes toward school-based SHE and toward schools and parents sharing this responsibility using a paired-samples t-test, $t(1659) = 20.06, p < .001, \eta^2 = .20$. Students agreed more strongly with the view that SHE should be provided in school ($M = 4.43$) than with the view that it should be a shared responsibility ($M = 3.99$).

Perceived Importance of Specific Sexual Health Topics

Youths were asked to rate the importance of including each of 10 sexual health topics in the SHE curriculum. Examination of their median responses showed that they viewed all 10 topics as important (see Table 1). They thought it was extremely important that the curriculum include information on sexually transmitted diseases and birth control methods. They rated the topics of sexual coercion and assault, personal safety, sexual decision making, reproduction, and puberty as very important. While they tended to place less importance on the topics of sexual pleasure and enjoyment, abstinence, and correct names for genitals than other topics, they still rated these topics as 'important' overall. However, as the middle option was labelled 'important' rather than 'neutral', it is possible that the topics of sexual pleasure and enjoyment, abstinence, and correct names for genitals were, in fact, viewed as neither 'important nor unimportant'. The results of a MANOVA, with the 10 topics as dependent variables, revealed a significant main effect for gender. $F_{mult}(10, 1529) = 39.03, p < .001, \eta^2 = .20$. The results of the follow-up univariate ANOVAs are presented in Table 7.3.1. The girls rated two topics as more important than the boys: sexual coercion and assault, and abstinence. Conversely, the girls rated sexual pleasure and enjoyment as less important than the boys did. The main effect for grade level and the interaction were not significant.

Table 1 Importance High School Students Assigned to Possible Topics in the Sexual Health Curriculum

TOPIC	MEAN RATINGS (SD)[a]					
	MEDIAN	TOTAL	GIRLS	BOYS	$F(1, 1538)$	η^2
Sexually transmitted diseases	5	4.5 (0.8)	4.6 (0.7)	4.4 (0.9)	18.73	.02
Birth control methods & safer sex practices	5	4.4 (0.9)	4.5 (0.8)	4.2 (1.0)	27.48	.02
Sexual coercion & sexual assault	4	4.1 (1.0)	4.3 (0.9)	3.9 (1.0)	59.27*	.04
Personal safety	4	4.0 (1.0)	4.2 (0.9)	3.9 (1.0)	24.74	.02
Sexual decision-making in dating relationships	4	3.8 (1.1)	3.9 (1.0)	3.6 (1.1)	37.54	.02
Reproduction	4	3.8 (1.0)	3.9 (0.9)	3.7 ((1.0)	17.29	.01
Puberty	4	3.7 (1.0)	3.9 (0.9)	3.6 (1.0)	32.79	.02
Sexual pleasure & enjoyment	3	3.2 (1.1)	2.8 (1.3)	3.7 (1.3)	327.27*	.12
Abstinence	3	3.1 (1.2)	3.3 (1.2)	2.8 (1.3)	121.92*	.05
Correct names for genitals	3	3.0 (1.1)	3.0 (1.0)	2.9 (1.2)	3.01	.00

Note: N = 707 boys and 839 girls.
1 = not at all important, 2 = somewhat important, 3 = important, 4 = very important, 5 = extremely important.
[a] Responses rank ordered for total sample.
*p < .001 and η^2 > .04.

Preferred Grade Level for Introducing Specific Sexual Health Topics

About one-quarter of the students (23%) thought that SHE should begin in elementary school. In contrast, about two-thirds (67%) of youths thought that SHE should begin in grades 6–8. The analysis showed that students' opinions about when SHE should start did not differ significantly by gender, grade level, or their interaction.

Students were also asked to indicate the grade level at which they would have liked to learn about each of 27 sexual health topics. The results are summarized in Table 2. There was strong support for the inclusion of all 27 topics in the curriculum: between 79 per cent and 99 per cent of youths wanted to learn about each topic at some grade level. Examination of the median responses showed that students wanted all topics taught by grades 6–8. However, there were several topics that a substantial minority

of teens (more than 25%) would like to have learned about in elementary school, including personal safety, correct names for genitals, being comfortable with the other sex, body image, and sexual coercion and assault. Further, students were divided in their opinions about the appropriate grade level for several topics. For example, the median response for the topic of personal safety suggests that students would have liked to learn about this issue in grades 6–8, but just under half of students would have liked to learn about it in elementary school. Similarly, the median response for teenage prostitution, sex as part of a loving relationship, building equal romantic relationships, and sexual pleasure and orgasm was grades 6–8, but a substantial percentage of students wanted to learn about these topics in high school. There were only four topics that more than 10 per cent of students thought should be excluded from the curriculum: masturbation, pornography, homosexuality, and teenage prostitution. However, even these potentially controversial topics had the support of the majority of students—86 per cent, 79 per cent, 82 per cent, 85 per cent respectively.

The relationship between students' preferred timing for each of the 27 sexual health topics and their gender and grade level was assessed using separate ANOVAS. Separate ANOVAS rather than a single MANOVA were used so that students who indicated that the topic should not be included in the curriculum could be excluded on an analysis-by-analysis basis. As summarized in Table 2, there was a significant gender difference on only 1 of the 27 topics: The girls would like to learn about menstruation in a younger grade than the boys. The main effects for grade level and the gender by grade level interactions were not significant.

Table 2 Grade Level at which High School Students Would Like to Learn about Specific Sexual Health Topics

TOPIC	PERCENT INDICATING EACH GRADE LEVEL[a]			SHOULD NOT BE INCLUDED	GRADE LEVEL SCORE[b] MEAN (SD)		F	η^2
	K–5 (1)	6–8 (2)	9–12 (3)		GIRLS	BOYS		
Personal safety	45.9	44.9	9.3	1.7	1.54 (0.63)	1.75 (0.65)	38.84	.02
Correct names for genitals	31.8	63.4	4.8	2.0	1.73 (0.54)	1.72 (0.54)	0.14	.00
Being comfortable with the other sex	27.6	60.0	12.4	1.7	1.80 (0.61)	1.91 (0.61)	11.34	.01
Body image	25.6	67.0	7.4	1.4	1.77 (0.54)	1.87 (0.55)	15.63	.01
Sexual coercion & sexual assault	25.6	60.3	14.2	1.3	1.82 (0.64)	1.96 (0.59)	19.76	.01
Puberty	19.5	77.7	2.9	0.3	1.79 (0.45)	1.89 (0.43)	22.44	.01
Menstruation	18.8	74.2	6.9	2.2	1.78 (0.50)	2.01 (0.46)	90.43*	.06
Wet dreams	13.6	79.0	7.4	5.0	1.93 (0.46)	1.95 (0.46)	0.54	.00
Abstinence	12.2	70.2	17.6	8.5	2.06 (0.51)	2.05 (0.51)	0.02	.00
Masturbation	11.3	75.7	13.0	14.0	2.08 (0.48)	1.95 (0.51)	22.72	.02
Reproduction and birth	10.6	66.2	23.2	0.9	2.15 (0.58)	2.10 (0.56)	3.01	.00
Pornography	10.6	52.7	36.6	21.3	2.33 (0.60)	2.19 (0.66)	14.28	01
Sexual behaviour (e.g., French kissing)	10.2	72.2	17.6	3.1	2.06 (0.51)	2.19 (0.55)	0.97	.00
Homosexuality	10.1	58.4	31.6	18.5	2.24 (0.61)	2.18 (0.61)	3.31	.00
Sexually transmitted diseases/AIDS	8.9	70.4	20.7	0.3	2.15 (0.52)	2.08 (0.54)	5.76	.00
Communicating about sex	7.7	59.1	33.2	1.4	2.28 (0.58)	2.23 (0.59)	2.67	.00
Dealing with peer pressure to be sexually active	7.4	73.2	19.4	2.1	2.11 (0.50)	2.13 (0.50)	0.47	.00
Sexuality in the media	7.4	63.6	28.9	8.1	2.34 (0.57)	2.18 (0.56)	3.34	.00
Attraction, love, intimacy	6.8	52.0	41.2	3.4	2.39 (0.60)	2.29 (0.60)	9.39	.01

Table 2 Grade Level at which High School Students Would Like to Learn about Specific Sexual Health Topics (*continued*)

TOPIC	PERCENT INDICATING EACH GRADE LEVEL[a]			SHOULD NOT BE INCLUDED	GRADE LEVEL SCORE[b] MEAN (SD)		F	η²
	K–5 (1)	6–8 (2)	9–12 (3)		GIRLS	BOYS		
Sex as part of a loving relationship	6.3	52.1	41.7	4.1	2.38 (0.60)	2.33 (0.59)	3.04	.00
Sexual problems & concerns	5.5	63.1	31.5	1.6	2.30 (0.56)	2.21 (0.53)	11.72	.01
Teenage prostitution	5.0	53.8	41.2	14.7	2.40 (0.56)	2.32 (0.59)	8.53	.01
Sexual decision-making in dating relationships	4.5	64.2	31.3	3.7	2.28 (0.52)	2.25 (0.56)	1.02	.00
Sexual pleasure & orgasm	4.3	50.4	45.3	9.2	2.49 (0.55)	2.32 (0.59)	35.93	.03
Building equal romantic relationships	4.2	52.2	43.6	4.2	2.48 (0.56)	2.35 (0.57)	7.80	.01
Teen pregnancy/parenting	3.7	62.1	34.3	0.5	2.31 (0.53)	2.30 (0.55)	0.47	.00
Birth control methods & safer sex practices	3.6	63.3	33.1	0.4	2.34 (0.53)	2.24 (0.53)	11.72	.01

Note: N = 707 boys and 839 girls.
[a] 'Percent indicating each grade level' and ANOVAs are based on those students who reported that they wanted the topic included. Responses rank ordered for grades K-5.
[b] Score determined by assigning a value of 1 to grades K–5, 2 to grades 6–8 and 3 to grades 9–12.
*$p < 0.001$ and η² > .04.

Perceptions of Sexual Health Education at School

Students were asked about the quality of the SHE they had received at school. Eight percent reported that they had not received any school-based SHE. The remainder of the students had last received SHE in elementary school (2%), middle school (53%), or high school (38%). Of the students who had received SHE, more than half (55%) rated it as fair or poor and only a few students (13%) rated it as excellent or very good. Thus, the majority or students were dissatisfied with the quality of the school-based SHE they had received. Similarly, only 28 per cent of youths agreed or strongly agreed that the SHE they had received at school covered the topics in which they were most interested. A MANOVA, with these two items as the dependent variables, revealed

that these ratings did not differ by gender, grade level, or their interaction.

Students who had received SHE were asked to indicate how well each of 10 sexual health topics had been covered. They reported that with the exception of sexual pleasure/enjoyment, all of the topics were covered to some degree (see Table 3). Examination of the median responses showed that none of the topics were rated on average, as having been 'covered very well' and only puberty was rated as having been 'covered well'. Correct names for genitals, reproduction, sexually transmitted diseases, birth control methods, and sexual coercion and assault were all rated as 'covered' whereas abstinence, sexual decision making, and personal safety were topics that were rated as 'covered poorly'. Results of a MANOVA with coverage of the 10 topics as the dependent variables, yielded a significant

Table 3 Extent to Which Sexual Health Topics Were Covered in Sexual Health Education Classes

| TOPIC | MEAN RATINGS (SD)[a] | | | | | |
	MEDIAN	TOTAL	GIRLS	BOYS	F(1, 1446)	η²
Puberty	4	3.6 (0.9)	3.7 (0.9)	3.6 (0.9)	2.04	.00
Correct names for genitals	3	3.4 (1.0)	3.4 (1.0)	3.4 (1.0)	0.30	.00
Reproduction	3	3.4 (1.1)	3.3 (1.1)	3.4 (1.0)	1.51	.00
Sexually transmitted diseases	3	3.2 (1.2)	3.1 (1.2)	3.3 (1.1)	22.67	.02
Birth control methods & safer sex practices	3	2.9 (1.2)	2.8 (1.3)	3.1 (1.2)	14.94	.01
Sexual coercion & sexual assault	3	2.6 (1.1)	2.5 (1.1)	2.7 (1.1)	14.16	.01
Abstinence	2	2.4 (1.2)	2.4 (1.2)	2.5 (1.2)	1.16	.00
Sexual decision-making in dating relationships	2	2.4 (1.1)	2.3 (1.1)	2.4 (1.1)	0.72	.00
Personal safety	2	2.3 (1.2)	2.1 (1.1)	2.4 (1.2)	14.01	.01
Sexual pleasure & enjoyment	1	1.8 (1.1)	1.6 (0.9)	2.0 (1.2)	41.83	.03

Note: N = 666 boys and 788 girls. 1 = not covered at all, 2 = covered poorly, 3 = covered, 4 = covered well, 5 = covered very well.
[a] Responses rank ordered for total sample.
*p < 0.001 and η² > .04.

main effect for gender, F_{mult} (10, 1437) = 8.25, $p < .001$, $\eta^2 = .05$. However, follow-up ANOVAs showed no significant differences (i.e., none of the differences accounted for more than 4% of the variance) (see Table 3). The main effect for grade level and the interaction were also not significant.

Student Interests

Students were asked to list any two questions about sexual health that they would like to learn about. Five hundred and seventeen students (31%) provided at least one response for a total of 897 questions. Three primary themes and seven sexual health topics emerged from a content analysis of their responses. The three themes were: Facts and information, practical skills, and values clarification. Each theme involved questions about a number of sexual health topics. Thus, one student wrote 'How to put on a condom' and another student asked 'How effective are condoms?' Both responses, were coded as concerning the same topic (birth

control/abstinence/safer sex), but different themes (skills versus information).

Theme #1: Facts and Information

Most responses were requests for facts and information, most frequently with respect to reproduction/biological functions, birth control/abstinence/safer sex, sexually transmitted infections, and sexual techniques/activities. The following are examples of requests for information: 'What % of teenagers have sex?'; 'How many types of STDs are there?'; and, 'What happens when you have sex?'

Theme #2: Practical Skills

Many students wanted to learn practical skills. The main areas in which they requested skills training were birth control/abstinence/safe sex, sexual techniques/activities, sexual decision making/dating relationships, and personal safety/sexual coercion/assault/abuse. For example, students asked: 'How do you tell someone how far you want to go?'; 'What different things can you say or do to feel less pressured into having sex?'; and 'How do you go about using birth control?'

Theme #3: Values Clarification

Some students asked questions related to values clarification. Many of these questions focused on either sexual techniques/activities or sexual decision making/dating relationships. For example, one student wrote 'Is it all right to have sexual practices in the teen years if careful?' and another wrote, 'How far should you go on a date?'

Students wrote questions about seven sexual health topics. The most frequent topics were birth control/abstinence/safe sex (22% of questions), reproduction/biological functions (19%), sexual techniques/activities (18%), and sexually transmitted diseases (16%). The per cent of responses corresponding to other topics were sexual decision making/dating relationships (8%); sexual violence (personal safety/sexual coercion/sexual assault/sexual abuse) (7%); and sexual pleasure and enjoyment (6%). In addition, 4 per cent of the questions were on other idiosyncratic topics, including comments about the school sexual health curriculum or resources.

Perceptions of Sexual Health Education Teachers and Teaching Methods

Students who had received SHE were also asked questions about their most recent SHE teacher.

In terms of teacher comfort, 59 per cent of youths reported that their teacher was 'pretty comfortable' or 'very comfortable' with the topics discussed. Similarly, 60 per cent of students reported that their teacher encouraged them to ask questions very often or quite often. Forty per cent of students felt that their teacher answered their questions very well or excellently; an additional 34 per cent felt that their questions were answered well. Results of a MANOVA, with the comfort of the instructor, the extent to which they encouraged questions, and their skill at answering questions as dependent variables, yielded no significant effects for gender, grade level, or the gender by grade level interaction.

The high school students reported that the most frequently used teaching method for covering SHE information was videos (80%) followed closely by lectures (76%). A question box (69%), readings (63%), and group discussions (62%) were also commonly used. Guest speakers (25%), role play and games (17%), and individual projects (15%) were used much less frequently. Students indicated that they thought a question box, videos, and group discussion would be the three most helpful teaching methods for sexual health topics (see Table 4). Nonetheless, they felt that all the techniques would be at least somewhat helpful. [. . .]

Table 4 High School Students' Ratings of the Helpfulness of Teaching Methods for Sexual Health

METHOD	MEAN RATINGS (SD)[a]					
	MEDIAN	TOTAL	GIRLS	BOYS	F(8, 1398)	η^2
Question box	3	2.5 (0.6)	2.6 (0.6)	2.4 (0.7)	13.95	.02
Videos	3	2.5 (0.6)	2.5 (0.6)	2.5 (0.6)	1.97	.00
Group discussion	3	2.4 (0.6)	2.5 (0.6)	2.3 (0.7)	12.19	.02
Guest speakers	2	2.3 (0.7)	2.4 (0.7)	2.2 (0.7)	16.61	.03
Lecturing	2	2.0 (0.6)	2.0 (0.6)	2.0 (0.7)	2.47	.01
Readings	2	2.0 (0.6)	2.0 (0.6)	1.9 (0.6)	0.59	.00
Role play, drama, games	2	1.9 (0.8)	1.9 (0.8)	1.9 (0.8)	0.13	.00
Individual projects	2	1.7 (0.7)	1.8 (0.7)	1.6 (0.7)	7.44	.01

Note: $N = 707$ boys and 839 girls. 1 = no help at all, 2 = help somewhat, 3 = help a lot.
[a] Responses rank ordered for total sample.
$p > 0.001$ and $\eta^2 > .04$.

Most of the students who had received SHE at school were taught in coed classes (93%). When asked about their preference for single-sex or coed classes, 11 per cent of students indicated that they preferred to be taught separately, 57 per cent preferred to be taught together, and 32 per cent did not have a preference. The girls (16%) were more likely than the boys (6%) to indicate a preference for single-sex classes, χ^2 (1, $N = 1631$) = 46.27, $p < .001$, $\eta^2 = .17$. However, grade level was not significantly related to students' preference for single-sex classes.

Perceptions of Sexual Health Education at Home

When asked to rate how well their parents or guardian had done in providing the SHE they needed, about two-thirds of the students gave ratings of excellent, very good, or good; the other one-third of youths indicated that their parents had done only a fair or poor job. Most students (80%) also reported that they were rarely or never encouraged to ask questions about sexuality at home. Further, almost half of the students (46%) disagreed or strongly disagreed that they wanted their parents to talk to them more about sexuality; 40 per cent were neutral. Results of three ANOVAs indicated that neither gender nor grade level was significantly related to students' evaluation of the information provided to them by their parents, how frequently they were encouraged to ask questions, or the extent to which they wished that their parents had talked to them more about sex. When students were asked whether they wished they knew more about sexuality and sexual health, about one-third of them agreed or strongly agreed; 45 per cent neither agreed nor disagreed with this statement. These ratings were not related to students' gender, grade level, or the gender by grade interaction.

Discussion

This study provides information on SHE at school and at home from the adolescent's perspective. Most high school students have received SHE at school. Therefore, they are in an excellent position to provide information about the nature and content of SHE as well as aspects of SHE that they did not receive but feel that they needed. This information is important for the design of SHE curricula (Campbell & Campbell, 1990; McKay & Holowaty, 1997). As there were very few gender and grade level differences, overall, the conclusions from this study are the same for girls and boys, and for students across the high school years. However, the sample did consist of predominately white youths (consistent with the demographics of New Brunswick) who were attending English schools. As a result the extent to which our findings apply to Francophone adolescents, adolescents from other ethnic and cultural groups, or to teenagers who are not in school is not known.

Attitudes Toward Sexual Health Education

One of the clearest conclusions of this study is that New Brunswick high school students overwhelmingly support having SHE in school. This is consistent with the results of McKay and Holowaty's (1997) survey of Ontario students, and with surveys of New Brunswick parents and teachers (Cohen et al., 2001; Weaver, et al., 2002). It is also clear that these students want a comprehensive SHE curriculum that includes a broad range of sexuality topics. Further, only a minority of students indicated that any of 27 specific topics including those that are often considered controversial (e.g., masturbation, homosexuality), should be excluded from the SHE curriculum. It appears, then, that the vast majority students want even these more controversial topics included in the SHE they receive.

What are high school students' views about the best grade level for SHE? The majority indicated that SHE should begin in middle school, and that each of 27 specific topics should be introduced by middle school. However, approximately one-quarter of students preferred to have some SHE in elementary school, particularly topics such as personal safety, body image, sexual coercion, and being comfortable with the other sex. Given that we did not provide details about the meaning of each of the listed topics and that few students had received SHE in elementary school, it is possible that some additional students would support SHE in the lower grades if they knew more about what would be covered.

Conversely, more than 40 per cent of students indicated that some sexual health topics should not be covered until high school, specifically, sex as part of a loving relationship, attraction/love/intimacy, teenage prostitution, building equal romantic relationships, and sexual pleasure and orgasm. It is likely that many high school students' opinions about the preferred timing of these topics have been influenced by their own developmental experiences, especially issues related to sexuality and sexual health that they and their peers are currently facing in their dating relationships. Since older adolescents are more likely to focus on reciprocity and interdependence in dating relationships (Adams, Laursen & Wilder, 2001; Brown, 1999), it makes sense that these students would see the high school grades as the appropriate time to learn about these issues. However, they may not have considered that SHE for specific topics is more effective if it precedes experience (McKay, 2000). They also may not have taken into account that their peers who are on an earlier developmental timetable (e.g., as a result of going through puberty early, experiencing sexual violence in the home, or becoming sexually active at a very young age) would benefit from discussions of these (and other) topics at an earlier grade level.

Quality of School-Based Sexual Health Education

Our findings suggest that for many New Brunswick high school students their needs are not being sufficiently met by the SHE curriculum. Only 13 per cent of students rated the quality of the SHE they received at school as very good or excellent and 55 per cent rated it fair or poor. In addition, about one-third of the students reported that the topics of most interest to them were not covered in the SHE that they had received; of the topics that were covered, only puberty was 'covered well'; and 8 per cent of students had not received any SHE at all. Langille et al. (2000) also identified problems with the curriculum as a barrier to effective SHE.

Students specifically [. . .] indicated that they want SHE to teach practical skills. Research has found that in order to achieve desired outcomes, SHE must provide motivation, enhance behavioural skills, and be timed to be both age- and experience-appropriate in addition to providing information (Fisher & Fisher, 1998; 2000; Haffner, 1996; Kirby, 1992; Melchert & Burnett, 1990). In New Brunswick, as elsewhere in Canada, the SHE curriculum has focused on knowledge and attitudes with less attention to developing skills and increasing motivation (Boyce, Warren & King, 2000). The students in this study were clearly expressing their dissatisfaction with this approach.

Sexual Health Education Teachers and Teaching Methods

About 60 per cent of high school students indicated that their most recent SHE teacher was comfortable with the topics discussed, and that she or he often encouraged them to ask sexual health questions. Many students (40%) felt that teachers answered questions well; another one-third felt that they did so acceptably. These data suggest that more than half of SHE teachers are doing a reasonable job implementing this curriculum. However, they also identify a significant proportion of teachers who do not appear comfortable in this role, and thus may be less successful at delivering effective SHE (Eisenberg & Wagenaar, 1997; Hamilton & Levenson Gingiss, 1993; Langille et al., 2000). Further, teachers' comfort varies across topics (Cohen et al., 2001). As we did not ask the students about their teacher's comfort with each topic covered in the SHE curriculum, it may be that teachers are not covering topics that make them uncomfortable. [. . .]

Turning to the delivery of SHE at school, the students reported that videos and lectures were the teaching methods used most frequently. In contrast, they indicated that a range of teaching methods, especially a question box, videos, and group discussions, would be helpful. Similarly, Eisenberg and Wagenaar (1997) found that students preferred non-lecture teaching methods. The vast majority of students were taught SHE in coed classes, and the majority of students preferred to be taught in coed classes. However, a small minority of youths (more girls than boys) preferred single-sex SHE classes. Others (e.g., McKay & Holowaty, 1997) have reported that many students view single-sex classes as being more appropriate for some sexual health topics. Thus, as these authors pointed out, at least some single-sex classes may be beneficial to allow students, particularly girls, an opportunity to discuss feelings and issues that they may feel uncomfortable talking about in coed settings.

Sexual Health Education at Home

A majority of the high school students (77%) thought that parents and schools should share responsibility for SHE. This proportion is significantly lower than the proportion of youths who supported SHE at school, perhaps because many students have not had positive experiences with SHE at home. In this sample, only 36 per cent of students rated their parents as doing an excellent or very good job of providing them with SHE; an approximately equal number rated the SHE they received from their parents as fair or poor. In addition, 80 per cent of students reported that their parents rarely encouraged them to ask questions about sexuality. Thus, when students were asked if they wished their parents talked to them more about sexuality, almost half of them preferred that their parents *not* talk to them more about sex. [. . .]

It is also noteworthy that adolescents appear to prefer learning about sexual health at school rather than at home, even though more of them were dissatisfied with the quality of the SHE they received at school (55%) than with the SHE they received at home (37%). It may be that youths have higher expectations regarding the depth or nature of sexuality information they expect to receive from teachers as opposed to parents, and their ratings reflect their disappointment with the school-based information that they did receive. This pattern may also illustrate the extent to which adolescents are reluctant to engage in conversations about sexual health topics with their parents, which emerges from specific reservations as well as the quality of the parent-adolescent relationship (Jaccard, Dittus & Gordon, 2000). Since many high school students in this study indicated that they wished they knew more about sexuality, it is critical that researchers and practitioners find ways to facilitate discussions about sexual health between youths and their parents and teachers.

Gender and Grade Level Differences

Although some results indicated that gender was linked to high school students' attitudes toward and experiences with SHE, in general, these differences were very small and accounted for only small proportions of variance in the variables. There were two exceptions. Girls were more likely than boys to support parents' role in SHE, perhaps because parents, particularly mothers, discuss sex more often with their daughters than their sons (Moore, Peterson & Furstenberg, 1986; Raffaelli, Bogenschneider & Flood, 1998). However, it appears that although more girls are in favour of parental involvement in SHE in theory, parents are not doing a better job of providing sexual health information to their high-school-aged daughters than they are to their high-school-aged sons from either their children's or their own perspective (Weaver et al., 2001).

Boys and girls also differed in their ratings of the importance of three out of ten sexual health topics. The girls clearly rated sexual coercion and assault and abstinence as more important in the school curriculum than did boys. Boys rated the topic of sexual pleasure and enjoyment as more important than did girls. Since girls are more likely than boys to experience sexual coercion and sexual violence in their homes and dating relationships, and are at risk for experiencing specific negative outcomes associated with sexual activity (i.e., STIs and unwanted pregnancy) (Health Canada, 1998; Price et al., 2000: Putnam, 2003), it is not surprising that they perceived these topics as being more important than did boys.

It should be noted, however, that boys gave the topic of sexual coercion and assault their third highest rating (as did girls), placing it in importance above the topic of sexual pleasure and enjoyment. Sex differences in experiences of girls and boys may explain why girls were more likely than boys to prefer single-sex SHE classes and why some girls wanted menstruation taught in a younger grade (i.e., they view some topics as more personally relevant to them). In contrast, in keeping with the traditional sexual script that prescribes that boys' status is enhanced and girs status is diminished by high interest in sexual activity (Byers, 1996), the boys rated sexual pleasure and enjoyment as more important than did girls.

There were also few links between grade level and high school students' attitudes toward and experiences with SHE, although Grade 12 students were more supportive of SHE as a shared responsibility between schools and parents than youths in earlier grades. It may be that students' awareness of the discrepancy between the SHE they have received at home and their need for SHE may emerge over the high school years as they mature cognitively and emotionally, become more involved in dating relationships, attempt to negotiate intimacy and autonomy in these relationships, and encounter specific difficulties in this regard (e.g., try to resolve conflicts or discuss sex with their partner) (Brooks-Gunn & Paikoff, 1997; Grover & Nangle, 2003).

References

Adams, R.W., Laursen, B., & Wilder, D. (2001). Characteristics of closeness in adolescent romantic relationships. *Journal of Adolescence, 24,* 353–63.

Ansuini, C.G., Fiddler-Woite, J., & Woite, R.S. (1996). The source, accuracy, and impact of initial sexuality information on lifetime wellness. *Adolescence, 31,* 283–89.

Baldwin, J.L., Whitely, S., & Baldwin, J.D. (1990). Changing AIDS and fertility-related behaviour: The effectiveness of sexual education. *Journal of Sex Research, 27,* 245–63.

Barrett, M. (1994). Sexuality education in Canadian schools: An overview in 1994. *Canadian Journal of Human Sexuality, 3,* 199–208.

Boyce, W.F., Warren, W.K., & King, A.J.C. (2000). The effectiveness of a school-based HIV education program: A longitudinal comparative evaluation. *Canadian Journal of Program Evaluation, 15,* 93–116.

Brooks-Gunn, J., Paikoff, R. (1997). Sexuality and developmental transitions during adolescence. In J. Schulenberg,

J.L. Maggs & K. Hurrelmann (Eds), *Health Risks and Developmental Transitions During Adolescence* (pp. 190–219). New York: Cambridge University Press.

Brown, B. (1999). 'You're going out with who?': Peer group influences on adolescent romantic relationships. In W. Furman, B. Brown & C. Feiring (Eds), *The Development of Romantic Relationships in Adolescence* (pp. 291–329). New York: Cambridge University Press.

Byers, E.S. (1996). How well does the traditional sexual script explain sexual coercion?: Review of a program of research. *Journal of Psychology and Human Sexuality, 8,* 7–25.

Byers, E.S., Sears, H.A., Boyer, S.D., Thurlow, J.L., Cohen, J.N., & Weaver, A.D. (2001, November). *New Brunswick Students' Ideas About Sexual Health Education.* Report prepared for the New Brunswick Department of Education. www.gnb.ca/0000/publications/ss/studentsexeducation.pdf.

Cairns, K.V., Collins, S.D., & Hiebert, B. (1994). Adolescents? Self-perceived needs for sexuality education. *Canadian Journal of Human Sexuality, 3,* 245–51.

Campbell, T.A., & Campbell, D.E. (1990). Considering the adolescent's point of view: A marketing model for sex education. *Journal of Sex Education & Therapy, 16,* 185–93.

Cohen, J., Cohen, P., & West, S.G. (2003). *Applied Multiple Regression/Correlation for the Behavioural Sciences* (3rd edn). Mahwah, NJ: Lawrence Erlbaum.

Cohen, J.N., Byers, E.S., Sears, H.A., & Weaver, A.D. (2001). *New Brunswick Teachers' Ideas About Sexual Health Education.* Fredericton, NB: University of New Brunswick, Psychology Department. www.gnb.ca/0000/publications/ss/nbparentidea.pdf.

Eisenberg, M.E., & Wagenaar, A. (1997). Viewpoints of Minnesota students on school-based sexuality education. *Journal of School Health, 67,* 322–27.

Fisher, J.D., & Fisher, W.A. (1992). Changing AIDS-risk behavior. *Psychological Bulletin, 111,* 453–74.

———. (2000). Theoretical approaches to individual level change in HIV-risk behavior. In J. Peterson & R. DiClemente (Eds), *Handbook of HIV Prevention* (pp. 3–55). New York: Plenum.

Fisher, W.A., & Fisher, J.D. (1998). Understanding and promoting sexual and reproductive health behavior: Theory and method. *Annual Review of Sex Research, 9,* 39–76.

Grover, R.L., & Nangle, D.W. (2003). Adolescent perceptions of problematic heterosocial situations: A focus group study. *Journal of Youth and Adolescence, 32,* 129–39.

Haffner, D. (1996). Sexual health for America's adolescents. *Journal of School Health, 55,* 151–52.

Hamilton, R., & Levenson Gingiss, P. (1993). The relationship of teacher attitudes to course implementation and student responses. *Teaching & Teacher Education, 9,* 193–204.

Hampton, M.R., Smith, P., Jeffery, B., & McWatters, B. (2001). Sexual experience, contraception, and STI prevention among high school students: Results form a Canadian urban centre. *Canadian Journal of Human Sexuality, 10,* 111–26.

Health Canada. (1998). *Sexually transmitted disease surveillance in Canada: 1995 annual report, 24S1.* http://www.hc-sc.gc.ca/pphb-dgspsp/publicat/ccdr-rmtc/98vol24/24s1/stdp_e.html.

Jaccard, J., Dittus, P.J., & Gordon, V.V. (2000). Parent-teen communication about premarital sex: Factors associated with the extent of communication. *Journal of Adolescent Research, 15,* 187–208.

King, A.J.C., Beazley, R.P., Warren, W.K., Hankins, C.A., Robertson, A.S., & Radford, J.L. (1998). *Canada Youth and AIDS Study.* Kingston, ON: Queen's University.

Kirby, D. (1992). School-based programs to reduce sexual risk-taking behaviors. *Journal of School Health, 62,* 280–287.

———. (2001). *Emerging answers: Research findings on programs to reduce teen pregnancy.* Washington: National Campaign to Prevent Teen Pregnancy.

Langille, D., Graham, J., Marshall, E., Blake, M., Chitty, C., & Doncaster-Scott, H. (2000). *Developing Understanding from Young Women's Experiences in Obtaining Sexual Health Services and Education in a Nova Scotia Community: Lessons for educators, physicians, and pharmacies.* Halifax, NS: Dalhousie University, Department of Community Health and Epidemiology.

Mackie, W., & Oickle, P. (1996). Comprehensive school health: The physician as advocate. *Canadian Medical Association Journal, 156,* 1301–5.

Maticka-Tyndale, E., (1995). Can we? Have we? Prevention of sexual transmission of HIV. *Canadian Journal of Human Sexuality, 4,* 79–102.

McCall, D., Beazley, R., Doherty-Poirier, M., Lovato, C., MacKinnon, D., Otis, J., & Shannon, M. (1999). *Schools, Public Health, Sexuality, and HIV: A status report.* Toronto, ON: Council of Ministers of Education.

McKay, A. (2000). Common questions about sexual health education. *Canadian Journal of Human Sexuality, 9,* 129–37.

McKay, A., & Holowaty, P. (1997). Sexual health education: A study of adolescents' opinions, self-perceived needs, and current and preferred sources of information. *Canadian Journal of Human Sexuality, 6,* 29–38.

McKay, A., Fisher, W.A., Maticka-Tyndale, E., & Barrett, M. (2001). Adolescent sexual health education. Does it work? Can it work better? An analysis of recent research and media reports. *The Canadian Journal of Human Sexuality, 10,* 127–35.

McKay, A., Pietrusiak, M., & Holowaty, P. (1998). Parents' opinions and attitudes toward sexuality education in the schools. *Canadian Journal of Human Sexuality, 7,* 139–145.

Melchert, J., & Burnett, K.F. (1990). Attitudes, knowledge, and sexual behavior of high-risk adolescents: Implications for counseling and sexuality education. *Journal of Counseling & Development, 68,* 293–98.

Meschke, L.L., Bartholomae, S., & Zentall, S.R. (2002). Adolescent sexuality and parent-adolescent processes: Promoting healthy teen choices. *Journal of Adolescent Health, 31,* 264–79.

Moore, K.A., Peterson, J.L., & Furstenberg, F.F. (1986). Parental attitudes and the occurrence of early sexual activity. *Journal of Marriage and the Family, 48,* 777–82.

Munro, B., Doherty-Poirier, M., Mayan, M.L., & Salmon, T. (1994). Instructional strategies used in HIV/AIDS education: Correlations with students' knowledge, attitudes, and intended behavior. *Canadian Journal of Human Sexuality, 3,* 237–43.

Price, E.L., Byers, E.S., Sears, H.A., Whelan, J., Saint-Pierre, M., & The Dating Violence Research Team (2000). *Dating Violence Amongst Students in Grades 7, 9 and 11 in New Brunswick: A Summary of Two Studies.* Fredericton: The Muriel McQueen Fergusson Centre for Family Violence Research, University of New Brunswick. www.unb.ca/FVRC.

Putnam, F.W. (2003). Ten-year research update review: Child sexual abuse. *Journal of the American Academy of Child and Adolescent Psychiatry, 42,* 269–78.

Raffaelli, M., Bogenschneider, K., & Flood, M.F. (1998). Parent-teen communication about sexual topics. *Journal of Family Issues, 19,* 315–333.

Weaver, A.D., Byers, E.S., Sears, H.A., Cohen, J.N., & Randall, H.S. (2002). Sexual health education at school and at home: Attitudes and experience of New Brunswick parents. *Canadian Journal of Human Sexuality, 11,* 19–32.

Weber, R.P. (1990). *Basic Content Analysis* (2nd edn). Thousand Oaks, CA: Sage.

Culture, Religion, and Curriculum: Lessons from the 'Three Books' Controversy in Surrey, BC

Damian Collins

I find that the separation of the church and the state is one of the most beautiful inventions of modern times (Pierre Pettigrew, Foreign Minister, 2005, commenting on the same-sex marriage debate in Canada).

Introduction

In April 1997 the Board of Surrey School District in British Columbia enacted a resolution declining to approve three books portraying same-sex parents. This decision, made in response to religious objections from local parents, meant that the books could not be used as part of the family life education curriculum in Kindergarten and Grade 1 classrooms within the District's 99 elementary schools. It prompted a prolonged and often heated debate in a province where schools are required by statute to 'be conducted on strictly secular and non-sectarian principles'. Concerns over the legality of the resolution were referred to the courts, with a final decision being handed down by the Supreme Court of Canada in December 2002.

This article reviews the six years of controversy that surrounded the Surrey School Board's actions, and the ways in which the issues raised were framed and resolved by the courts. It suggests that geographical categories—in particular, the distinction between public and private—are central to cultural and legal conflict over religion's place in the curricula and governance of public schools. It also employs the concept of 'culture war'—developed by Hunter (1991)—to help make sense of stakeholder positions in the 'three books' debate.

The content, purpose, and methods of public education are matters of widespread interest. Public schools have been characterized as 'the primary institutional means of reproducing community and national identity for succeeding generations' (Hunter 1991, 198), in part because they are places in which most children 'are compelled . . . [to] undergo a decade and more of group socialization' (Bocking 1995, 227). Since at least the mid-nineteenth century, they have been seen as vital tools for instilling shared values, and a common identity, in children from diverse backgrounds. However, the place of religion within public schools has been an enduring point of controversy, including in Canada (Clark 1968; Dickinson and Mackay 1989; Sweet 1997; Smith and Foster 2000). [. . .]

Conflicts such as that sparked by the Surrey School Board's books resolution go to the heart of contemporary debates about the place of religion in public education. This article contends that the public/private distinction—a concept routinely invoked in efforts to order society and space—is critical to understanding what is at stake in these debates, and the broader cultural conflict of which they are part. The claims advanced by stakeholders, and the responses of decision-making institutions such as school boards and courts, are not only cultural and constitutional, but also inherently geographical. Spatial categories and metaphors—including not only public and private, but also related concepts such as place, scale, the boundary, and jurisdiction—are central to the positions advanced and decisions made. These positions and decisions, in turn, have practical ramifications for the organization of material spaces such as the classroom.

Public and Private

An extensive body of research highlights the significance of the public/private distinction to the organization of social and governmental affairs, and to moral and political debate (Arendt 1958; Bobbio 1989; Weintraub and Kumar 1997). In particular, it occupies a central place in legal thought and rhetoric; indeed, much of the 'work' of law can be seen to involve attempts to draw 'bright lines' between spheres of public and private activity (Klare 1982; Walzer 1984). While the distinction may be expressed in abstract terms, it also provides the basis for distinguishing between two primary types of material space: that which is owned by government, typically for the use and benefit of the community at large, and that which is owned by individuals and corporations (Blomley 2005). This article contends that the public/private distinction has significant implications for religion and the spaces of public education, extending previous geographical research in which rights and property boundaries have been central matters of concern (Blomley and Bakan 1992; Delaney 2000; Blomley and Pratt 2001; Collins and Blomley 2003; Blomley 2005).

In discussions of religious liberty and freedom of conscience, the term 'private' is typically equated with the interests of individuals, families, and religious institutions, while 'public' is usually synonymous with governmental authority (hence 'church/state' terminology). Historically, religious freedom secured one of the first spheres of private autonomy, within which individuals were not accountable to the state (Habermas 1989; Mill 1859/1975). [. . .] It is generally assumed that religious freedom is secured when the authority of government to interfere in matters of faith is curtailed. [. . .]

In debates over the place of religion in public schools, notions of public and private are vehemently contested. In the view of liberal/progressive commentators (see next section), the ideal of the public school as an open, accessible, and socially unifying institution is threatened by the potential (re)introduction of religious influences deemed divisive, exclusive, and destabilizing. It is contended that if schools are to accommodate children irrespective of their varied backgrounds and particularistic ties, they must refrain from imparting religious views (but not arguments or theories based on reason, which are seen as accessible to all). Such claims resonate with the more general liberal notion that religious views may guide the development of the private self, but must not form the basis for organization of the public sphere.

A very different vision is espoused by those who advocate governmental accommodation of religious beliefs and practices. They locate state schools within a public sphere, often constituted at the local level, which encompasses religious believers—most notably religious parents, who are said to have an inherent right to bring their faith to bear in directing the education of their children, and contributing to the rules that govern school space. From this perspective it is the *exclusion* of religious viewpoints that threatens the openness and inclusiveness of the public school. Indeed, it is argued that religious claims should not be barred from any aspect of governmental decision making.

One of the most common conservative criticisms of secular public education is that it constitutes government indoctrination of a 'captive group of students . . . in beliefs and values that will lead them to defect from the teachings of their church and parents' (Baer 1998, 110). This is seen as an inappropriate intrusion by public authorities into the private sphere of faith. It is argued that in order for the (religious) home and the parent-child relationship to be accorded proper respect and protection, the state may not advance hostile or contrary viewpoints in public schools. Moreover, a host of social ills is attributed to children's indoctrination in secular humanist thought, including supposed increases in immorality, disrespect for authority, promiscuity, and drug use (Wood 1992, 120).[1] [. . .]

Culture War

The concept of culture war, developed by Hunter (1991), is a useful framework for considering the controversy raised by the Surrey School Board's resolution. [. . .] Hunter emphasizes that most major religious groupings contain both orthodox/conservative and liberal/progressive elements that contribute to public debate on cultural and political issues. As these divisions cut through denominations, they have prompted significant new avenues of co-operation:

> *At the heart of the new cultural realignment are pragmatic alliances being formed across faith traditions.* Because of common points of vision and concern, the orthodox wings of Protestantism, Catholicism, and Judaism are forming associations with each other, as are the progressive wings of each faith community—and each set of alliances takes form in opposition to the influence the other seeks to exert in public culture (Hunter 1991, 47; original emphasis).[2]

[. . .]

In broad terms, the secularization of public education that has occurred since the adoption of the Canadian Charter of Rights and Freedoms in 1982 has been championed by liberal stakeholders, and contested by conservatives.

By way of example, following a series of court orders which secularized Ontario public schools—a change vigorously opposed by many conservative religious believers—a coalition of Christian, Hindu, and Muslim parents sought to establish a constitutional right to funded parochial education. In *Bal v. Ontario (A.G.)* (1994), they contended that it was essential for their children to attend parochial schools, because they could not 'fulfil their religious obligations . . . by simply teaching their children about their religious faith in their home and at their place of worship and by sending them to a secular school during the week' (p. 701). Given that conventional religious instruction and exercises in public schools were now prohibited throughout Ontario, the applicants proposed that state funding be extended to alternative schools in which religious perspectives imbued every aspect of instruction, and children's faith was continuously encouraged and affirmed (a position advocated by the Catholic Church for over 150 years). Their claims, while ultimately unsuccessful, were little different from those advanced by orthodox stakeholders in the United States.

[. . .]

Study Background and Approach

Surrey is a large, predominantly suburban municipality within Greater Vancouver that is well known for its cultural diversity. Protestants form the single largest religious grouping in the city, which also has significant numbers of non-believers, Catholics, and Sikhs, and sizable Muslim and Hindu populations (Statistics Canada 2003). From at least 1996, tension was building within the community over whether resources dealing with homosexuality—a list of which had been compiled by GALE BC (Gay and Lesbian Educators of British Columbia)—should be included in public school classrooms. The issue came to a head when James Chamberlain, a Kindergarten–Grade 1 ('K–1') teacher in the Surrey School District, asked the School Board to approve three books from the list for use in the family life education curriculum: *Asha's Mums* (Elwin and Paulse 1990); *Belinda's Bouquet* (Newman 1991); and *One Dad, Two Dads, Brown Dad, Blue Dads* (Valentine 1994). All three portrayed (with varying degrees of emphasis) families with same-sex parents. Board approval would have made the books available for use in all K–1 classrooms in the District, subject to the discretion of individual teachers.

The Board considered Chamberlain's request at its meeting on 24 April 1997, and after considerable deliberation the trustees voted 4–2 in favour of a resolution not to approve the books (the 'three books resolution'). This almost immediately prompted litigation alleging breaches of both the Canadian Charter of Rights and Freedoms (1982) and the Province's School Act (1996). Two provisions of the Charter were particularly significant in this case: s. 2(a), which guarantees 'freedom of conscience and religion', and s. 15(1), which provides that '[e]very individual is equal before and under the law and has the right to the equal protection and equal benefit of the law without discrimination . . . '. Section 76 of the School Act, which requires public schools to 'be conducted on strictly secular and non-sectarian principles' and to inculcate 'the highest morality', while refraining from teaching any 'religious dogma or creed' was also pertinent.

The remainder of this article draws upon a textual analysis of three court decisions handed down in the case of *Chamberlain v. Surrey School District No. 36*, and associated legal documents and commentaries. This data set records, often in considerable detail, the positions of those individuals and organizations who spoke formally on the public record to oppose or support the decision of the Surrey School Board. The views presented are strongly dichotomized, reflecting the adversarial nature of the legal process, and the fact that there was no obvious middle ground in the debate: either the Board's decision would be allowed to stand, or it would be overturned.

[. . .]

In the present case, the courts of British Columbia, and ultimately the Supreme Court of Canada, were called upon to determine whether (or to what extent) religious concerns could influence the governance and curricula of BC's public schools. The decisions they handed down had consequences that extended beyond the classrooms and boardrooms of one province, however, in that they addressed constitutional and geographical themes of broad concern to the Canadian polity.

Chamberlain v. Surrey School District No. 36

The Surrey School Board's three books resolution represented a central moment in a debate which pitted two fundamentally opposed schools of thought against each other. At an institutional level, the Board's decision was supported by a conservative alliance of Catholics and evangelical Protestants, which advocated a central role for religion in school governance and curricula. It was opposed by progressive stakeholders, such as the British Columbia Civil Liberties Association (BCCLA) and EGALE Canada, a gay and lesbian rights group, which maintained that religious arguments were out of place in a public school system catering for a socially and religiously diverse population, and required by statute to operate on secular and non-sectarian principles.

The positions of these stakeholders can be elucidated with reference to their submissions to the courts. Progressive opinion emphasized the themes of pluralism, tolerance, and individualism—contending that these values formed the appropriate basis for public morality, in contradistinction to private and particularistic religious beliefs. For example, the British Columbia Civil Liberties Association (BCCLA 2002, para. 14) stated that a 'separation of church and state in the public school system' was necessary in order 'to respect and enhance the dignity of the individual'. In its view, the legislation governing BC public schools did just this by 'clearly [drawing] a bright line between the secular education that every citizen requires to be a fully contributing member of society and the individual religious beliefs that every member of society should be free to develop and practice according to his/her own conscience' (BCCLA 2002, para. 19). This interpretation underpinned the argument that 'only those values which have become part of the moral fabric of our civil society' had a place in

public schools, whereas values associated with particular religious traditions were properly confined to the private sphere (BCCLA 2002, para. 19). For this group, 'respect and tolerance for the personal characteristics of all individuals who make up our multicultural, pluralistic society' fell into the first category, in large part because they were thought to stem from the Charter, while 'moral approbation of same sex parents' fell into the second (BCCLA 2002, para. 36, 60).[3] [. . .]

A markedly different vision was articulated by the orthodox intervener, the Evangelical Fellowship and (Catholic) Archdiocese of Vancouver. It contended that religious arguments were entitled to a place in public deliberation: the notion that a public body should countenance only those moral views founded on (purportedly) non-religious grounds was considered fundamentally undemocratic. It followed from this claim that religious persons had the right to make their views on education and morality known, provided only that they did not seek to reinstitute religious instruction or denominational exercises in public schools (Evangelical Fellowship and Archdiocese of Vancouver 2000, paras. 16, 30). In this vision the public school was an integral part of a local political community that included religious believers, and did not confine religious perspectives to a purely private sphere of individual or familial concern.

The polarized opinions of progressive and orthodox interveners signalled that the courts were being called upon to resolve a classical struggle in the culture war centred on education. The central question concerned the place of religion in public education, and whether a school board could accommodate religious objections to homosexuality; or, more precisely, to books which arguably normalized same-sex parents by presenting them in a non-problematic manner. The objections presented to the courts were framed, universally, in terms of religious and 'moral' beliefs, and at no point did any of the parties seek to cast doubt upon the sincerity of those beliefs (i.e., it was never claimed that they were a convenient 'smokescreen' for homophobia). Accordingly, a great deal of the courts' attention was focused on the nature of religious freedom, and its boundaries.

The first decision in this case was delivered by Justice Saunders of the British Columbia Supreme Court (1998). [. . .] Justice Saunders ordered the Board to reconsider the three books resolution on the grounds that it contradicted s. 76 of the School Act. She found that those trustees who declined to approve the books did so in response to religiously motivated complaints from parents and others in the Surrey community, and in doing so they had failed to act in a strictly secular manner. Saunders J. also dismissed the Board's claim that s. 2(a) of the Charter provided a defence for its decision, ruling that freedom of religion included freedom from religion for non-believers and dissenters. While it was important for boards to consult with their communities, this could not lead to the coercive imposition of particular religious values upon the public education system. It followed that the public school was required to be 'a place independent of religious considerations' (para. 102).

Justice Saunders also considered the statutory requirement that BC public schools inculcate 'the highest morality'. She found that this morality was properly grounded in the values embodied in the Charter—and in particular the s. 15 right to equal treatment irrespective of sexual orientation. In addition to emphasizing Charter values, the decision stressed the provincial context for educational decision making. This was held to include 'the increasingly pluralistic nature of modern British Columbia' as well as 'the history of schools in British Columbia as being beyond overt church or religious intervention or influence' (para. 78). The former appeared to suggest that achieving consensus on religious claims

within the province was increasingly improbable, while the latter was held to preclude school board decisions significantly influenced by religious considerations.

This ruling alarmed conservative commentators. It was seen to infringe on the rights of religious parents to direct their children's upbringing, and to send a more general message that government institutions, required to operate on secular grounds, could not countenance arguments motivated by religious belief (Benson 2000; Benson and Miller 2000; Brown 2000). In a forceful response, Benson and Miller (2000) argued that '[n]othing in the Charter, democratic theory or principled pluralism requires that atheism be preferred to religiously informed moral positions in matters of public policy'. This echoed the orthodox view that the exclusion of religion from the public sphere is unjustifiably discriminatory.

The British Columbia Court of Appeal (2000) essentially adopted such reasoning in its unanimous decision to overturn the original ruling. It ruled that while s. 76 of the School Act 'precludes any religious establishment or indoctrination associated with any particular religion in the public schools . . . it cannot make religious unbelief a condition of participation in the setting of the moral agenda' (para. 31). Indeed, the Court of Appeal argued that '[s]uch a disqualification would be contrary to the fundamental freedom of conscience and religion set forth in s. 2 of the Charter, and the right to equality in s. 15. It would negate the right of all citizens to participate democratically in the education of their children . . .'. (para. 31).

This ruling turned on an understanding of the public/private distinction different from that underpinning the earlier decision. It acknowledged the practical difficulties inherent in maintaining a strict separation of religious values and public life. Noting that moral positions are derived from multiple sources, it asserted: '[t]here is no bright line between a religious and a non-religious conscience. Law may be concerned with morality but the sources of morality in conscience are outside the law's range and should be acknowledged from a respectful distance' (para. 20). Given this limitation, a clear boundary between religious belief and public schools could not be sustained. Henceforth, moral positions were to be 'accorded equal access to the public square without regard to religious influence. A religiously informed conscience should not be accorded any privilege, but neither should it be placed under a disability' (para. 28).

The Court of Appeal's decision suggested that religious and non-religious arguments were equivalent, for constitutional purposes, and that no free society could permit the former to be banished from the public sphere. It also addressed the politics of scale, offering a vision of localized decision making that was, at least in its initial expression, inclusive of all perspectives. Indeed, the Court stated that the inclusion of religious perspectives was entirely consistent with statutory requirement of 'strictly secular' schooling, as these words were 'intended to reinforce the non-denominational character of the public schools', and did not 'requir[e] religious unbelief' (para. 26).

[. . .]

This decision represented a significant setback for progressive stakeholders, who launched an appeal led by James Chamberlain. A final ruling was subsequently handed down by the Supreme Court of Canada (2002), which issued a 7–2 ruling remanding the issue of whether to approve the three books to the Surrey School Board. Chief Justice McLachlin, writing on behalf of a six-justice majority, determined that the Board had acted outside the mandate of the School Act. This ruling was in various respects more technical than those issued by the lower courts, but canvassed many of the same themes. First, it addressed the question of jurisdiction, and the scale at which decisions over curricula resources are best made. While the Board was well placed 'to know what types of families and children fall within its district and what materials will best serve their diverse needs', the majority determined that judicial review was appropriate in this case, given its human rights dimensions, and a Provincial requirement that the school curriculum promote 'norms of tolerance, respect for diversity, mutual understanding, and acceptance of all the family models found in British Columbian society' (para. 12). The Board had the right, and the duty, to consider the opinions of parents, but could not act on views that 'trumped' statutory requirements, including 'the need to show equal respect for the values of other members of the community' (para. 71).

Second, on the issue of religion's place in the public sphere, the majority essentially affirmed the position of the Court of Appeal: the requirement of strict secularism did not mean 'that religious concerns have no place in the deliberations and decisions of the Board' (para. 19). However, the Board was deemed to have erred in basing its decision *solely* on one set of religious views, while excluding all other perspectives from consideration. The requirement of secularism, the majority continued, meant 'that the school board must consider the interests of all its constituents and not permit itself to act as the proxy of a particular religious view held by some members of the community, even if that group holds the majority of seats on the board' (para. 27). Thus, the problem was not that the Board was motivated by religious views, but that it had acted 'without considering the interest of same-sex parented families and the children who belong to them in receiving equal recognition and respect in the school system' (para. 58). Had the Board reached the same decision following a genuine consideration of all viewpoints—or based it upon other, clearly secular grounds—it would presumably have withstood judicial scrutiny.

Echoing the decision of the Court of Appeal, the Supreme Court of Canada placed religious concerns firmly within the public sphere, and promised locally constituted government bodies' considerable discretion in responding to religiously motivated concerns. At the same time, it imposed conditions that offered some protection for the liberal values of secularism, pluralism, and tolerance. The majority insisted that religion not be 'left at the boardroom door'—thereby rejecting a strict divide between matters of faith and matters of public governance—at the same time as it signalled a new and arguably more ambiguous distinction. Specifically, while public decision-making bodies were free (and perhaps required) to address citizens' religious concerns, '[r]eligious views that deny equal recognition and respect to the members of a minority group cannot be used to exclude the concerns of the minority group' (para. 19). Such an approach appears to guarantee minority groups procedural, but not substantive, fairness: they have the right to be heard, but their views may still be overridden by hostile faith-based claims.

Elsewhere, the decision offered a clearer defence of liberal values, as when it was noted that '[p]arental views, however important, cannot override the imperative placed upon the British Columbia public schools to mirror the diversity of the community and teach tolerance and understanding of difference' (para. 33). This theme was expanded upon in response to the claim advanced by the Board and its supporters that use of the three books in classrooms might instill in children values different from those they were taught at home, and that such 'cognitive dissonance' could confuse 5- and 6-year-olds, and

undermine the authority of their parents. In reply, the majority determined that 'dissonance is neither avoidable nor noxious', but something that is 'part of living in a diverse society' and 'part of growing up' (para. 65). The diversity of the school community meant that pupils would inevitably encounter others from different family backgrounds, and in this sense the three books dealt with an issue that would always have been raised through children's attendance at a public school in the Surrey District. The only 'additional' message in the books, the majority determined, was tolerance—something that was 'always age-appropriate' (para. 69).

Education, by its very nature, appears to require exposure to unfamiliar and challenging concepts, and not merely the reinforcement of parental beliefs or prejudices (Lerner 2000). While the Supreme Court offered parents' religious concerns a role in school governance, it signalled that public schools could not be cleansed of issues or perspectives deemed hostile to certain beliefs or believers. As LeBel J. suggested in concurrence, school boards could not allow themselves 'to be decisively influenced by certain parents' unwillingness to countenance an opposed point of view and a different way of life' (para. 189).[4]

[. . .]

Following the Supreme Court of Canada's ruling, the Surrey School Board revisited the issue of the three books. In a June 2003 meeting, it affirmed commitments to tolerance and teaching about a variety of family models, but again refused to approve the books in question, ostensibly on the grounds that *Asha's Mums* had poor spelling, grammar, and punctuation, *Belinda's Bouquet* raised the 'risky' subject of dieting in a 'clumsy' manner, and *One Dad, Two Dads, Brown Dad, Blue Dads* 'made fun of skin colours and dealt too much with sexual orientation for its intended audience of kindergarteners' (CBC 2003). Unsurprisingly, critics responded by suggesting that the Board's reasoning was disingenuous. However, their concerns appeared to be assuaged when, two weeks later, the Board approved two different books portraying same-sex parented families for use in K–1 classes. In practical terms, this represented a victory for progressive stakeholders (albeit one that was six years in the making), while in jurisprudential terms, the legacy of *Chamberlain* was rather more mixed.

Conclusions

The terms public and private are open to multiple, and often incompatible understandings, yet the public/private distinction remains an enduring preoccupation of Western thought. In the controversy sparked by the Surrey School Board's three books resolution, the division between public and private—and the manner in which this mapped on to school space—was a central preoccupation for both organized stakeholders and the courts. Debate was strongly polarized, with one side defending a liberal-legal vision in which religious belief and the values emanating from it were uniquely private and non-political, and the other articulating a place for religious concerns in a public sphere that did not discriminate between perspectives on the basis of their conscientious or metaphysical foundations.

This article has signalled the centrality of the public/private distinction to contemporary cultural conflict, particularly in the area of public education. Indeed, it can be argued that the culture war is *about* the public/private distinction—or, more precisely, about the constitution of the public and private spheres, and the meaning of the line separating them. In the three books case, both sides articulated visions of public and private space, and advocated spatial solutions to the issue at hand. Conservative religious groups contended that the 'contentious' issue

of homosexuality was inappropriate for young pupils, and properly privatized (i.e., left 'for parents to deal with at home') so as to minimize any dissonance between the values parents wished to promote, and those inculcated in public school classrooms. By contrast, progressive stakeholders maintained that family models could not be excluded from the public sphere on the basis of objections founded on particular religious beliefs, and that *dissonance* was properly privatized.

[. . .]

In the case considered here, the Supreme Court of Canada ultimately accepted the claim of orthodox stakeholders that religious concerns have a place in public decision making, and cannot be confined to a private sphere centred on the family home. Its ruling was not an unmitigated victory for conservative opinion, however, as the Court sought to safeguard certain liberal values, and determined that dissonance between the religious and moral teachings of the home, and the values promoted in the public school, is legally unproblematic. A precedent has been set for acknowledging and acting upon faith-based positions in setting public school curricula, although variations in provincial arrangements for public education make it difficult to predict the ramifications of this ruling in classrooms outside of British Columbia. What can be said is that the three books debate provoked considerable controversy, when what was at stake was the *refusal* of a single school board to *approve* three books—albeit books whose content represented a cultural touchstone. Should religious views, whatever their purported relationship to the 'inherent dignity of the individual', come to play a major role in determining the content of an entire school library, or the nature of the provincial science curriculum, it seems reasonable to predict that the conflict will be more intense still.

Notes

1. Causal connections between secular instruction and alleged social problems are not established in any rigorous sense, but are asserted in an atmosphere of moral panic that reflects a generalized distaste for, and suspicion of, secular public culture.
2. In the Canadian context, the legalization of same-sex marriage was opposed by many conservative Protestant groups, and by the hierarchy of the Catholic Church. The initiative was supported by many liberal Protestants, including the United Church of Canada (the country's largest Protestant denomination), and by progressive Jewish congregations.
3. Hunter (1991, 154) notes that progressive concern for individual autonomy frequently generates opposition toward positions deemed 'choice restrictive' and thus 'intolerant'.
4. Some orthodox objections to secular public education betray an anti-intellectualism in which materials that expose children to concepts unfamiliar to their parents, or encourage them to engage in independent thought, are deemed objectionable and coercive.

References

Cases and Legislation Cited

Bal v. Ontario (A.G.). 1994. 21 O.R. (3d) 681 (Ont. Ct., Gen. Div.)

Canadian Charter of Rights and Freedoms. Part I of the Constitution Act, 1982, being Schedule B to the Canada Act, 1982. (U.K.), 1982, c. 11.

Chamberlain v. Surrey School District No. 36. 1998. 60 B.C.L.R. (3d) 311 (B.C.S.C.).

———. 2000. 60 B.C.L.R. (3d) 181 (B.C.C.A.).

———. 2002. 4 S.C.R. 710.

School Act R.S.B.C. 1996, c. 412.

Other Works

Arendt, H. 1958. *The Human Condition* (Chicago: University of Chicago Press).

Baer, R.A. 1998. 'Why a functional definition of religion is necessary if justice is to be achieved in public education' in *Curriculum, Religion, and Public Education: Conversations for an Enlarging Public Square*, eds J.T. Sears and J.C. Carper (New York: Teachers College Press), 105–25.

British Columbia Civil Liberties Association [BCCLA]. 2002. 'Factum of the Intervener British Columbia Civil Liberties Association in the Supreme Court of Canada (on Appeal from the Court of Appeal for the Province of British Columbia)' in *Chamberlain v. Surrey School District No. 36* Court File No. 28654.

Benn, S.I., and Gaus, G.F. 1983. 'The public and the private: Concepts and action' in *Public and Private in Social Life*, eds S.I. Benn and G.F. Gaus (London & Canberra: Croom Helm), 3–27.

Benson, I.T. 2000. 'Notes towards a (re)definition of the "secular"'. *University of British Columbia Law Review 33*, 519–49.

Benson, I.T., and Miller, B. 2000. *Court Misunderstands the Meaning of 'Secular'* (Ottawa: Centre for Cultural Renewal [Lex View]).

Blomley, N. 2005. 'Flowers in the bathtub: Boundary crossing at the public-private divide'. *Geoforum 36*, 281–96.

Blomley, N.K., and Bakan, J.C. 1992. 'Spacing out: Towards a critical geography of law'. *Osgoode Hall Law Journal 30*, 661–90.

Blomley, N.K., and Pratt, G. 2001. 'Canada and the political geographies of rights'. *The Canadian Geographer/Le Géographe Canadien 45*, 151–66.

Bobbio, N. 1989. *Democracy and Dictatorship: The Nature and Limits of State Power* (Cambridge, UK: Polity Press).

Bocking, B. 1995. 'Fundamental rites? Religion, state, education and the invention of sacred heritage in post-Christian Britain and pre-War Japan'. *Religion 25*, 227–47.

Brown, D.M. 2000. 'Freedom from or freedom for? Religion as a case study in defining the content of charter rights'. *University of British Columbia Law Review 33*, 551–615.

Canadian Broadcasting Corporation [CBC]. 2003. 'School board rejects books with gay parents for bad grammar'. CBC News Online, 13 June (available at http://www.cbc.ca/stories/2003/06/13/samesex_books030613).

Clark, L. ed. 1968. *The Manitoba School Question: Majority Rule or Minority Rights?* (Toronto: Copp Clark).

Collins, D., and Blomley, N. 2003. 'Private needs and public space: Politics, poverty and anti-panhandling by-laws in Canadian cities', in *New Perspectives on the Public-Private Divide*, ed. Law Commission of Canada (Vancouver: University of British Columbia Press), 40–67.

Delaney, D. 2000. 'Of minds and bodies and the legal-spatial constitution of sanctuary'. *Historical Geography 28*, 25–40.

Dickinson, G.M., and Mackay, A.W. 1989. *Rights, Freedoms and the Education System in Canada: Cases and Materials* (Toronto: Emond Montgomery).

Elwin, R. and Paulse, M. 1990. *Asha's Mums* (Toronto: Women's Press).

Evangelical Fellowship of Canada and Archdiocese of Vancouver. 2000. Factum of the Intervener the Evangelical Fellowship of Canada and the Archdiocese of Vancouver in the British Columbia Court of Appeal (on Appeal from the Supreme Court of British Columbia)', in *Chamberlain v. Surrey School District No. 36*. Court of Appeal File No. CA0254656.

Habermas, J. 1989. *The Structural Transformation of the Public Sphere: An Inquiry into a Category of Bourgeois Society* (Cambridge, MA: MIT Press).

Hunter, J.D. 1991. *Culture Wars: The Struggle to Define America* (New York: Basic Books).

Klare, K.E. 1982. 'The public/private distinction in labor law'. *University of Pennsylvania Law Review 130*, 1358–1422.

Lerner, L.S. 2000. 'Good and bad science in US Schools'. *Nature 407*, 287–90.

Mill, J.S. 1859/1975. *On Liberty* (New York: W.W. Norton).

Newman, L. 1991. *Belinda's Bouquet* (Boston: Alyson Wonderland).

Pettigrew, H.P. 2005. 'Reported comments', in *Who Defines Marriage: God or Government?* eds E. Thompson and K. Kleis, Edmonton Journal.

Smith, W.J., and Foster, W.F. 2000. 'Religion and education in Canada part I: the traditional framework'. *Education & Law Journal 10*, 393–447.

Statistics Canada. 2003. Community profiles: Religion statistics for Surrey, British Columbia (available at http://www.statcan.ca, accessed 01 March 2005).

Sweet, L. 1997. *The Controversial Issue of Religion in Canada's Schools* (Toronto: McClelland & Stewart).

Valentine, J. 1994. *One Dad, Two Dads, Brown Dad, Blue Dads* (Boston: Alyson Wonderland).

Walzer, M. 1984. 'Liberalism and the art of separation'. *Political Theory 12*, 315–30.

Weintraub, J., and Kumar, K., eds. 1997. *Public and Private in Thought and Practice* (Chicago: University of Chicago Press).

Wood, J.E. 1992. 'The battle over "secular humanism" in the public schools', in *Why We Still Need Public Schools: Church/State Relations, and Visions of Democracy,* ed. A. Must (New York: Prometheus Books), 119–38.

8 Media Representing Realities?

Reading Contemporary 'Bad Girls': The Transgressions and Triumphs of Madonna's 'What It Feels Like for a Girl'

Charity Marsh

Introduction

The 'bad girl' figure plays a predominant, but often ambiguous, role in popular culture. These ambiguities lie in the multiple interpretations of what it means to be 'bad': the seemingly symbiotic connection between being 'bad' and highly sexualized, the actions/behaviours for which she is labelled a 'bad girl', and a 'bad girl's' prevailing impact on the world. Turning to the United States (US) pop icon Madonna, and the 'bad girl' figures she presents in the music video and stage performances of her song, 'What it Feels Like for a Girl', I offer a response to and intervention in current debates on how to read contemporary 'bad girl' figures. Beginning with a contextual analysis of the televised *Too Much For Much* episode where the video content and whether or not the video should be banned from, or restricted to a later hour in rotation on the Canadian specialty television channel MuchMusic was initially debated, I call into question the impulse (by some feminists) to dismiss women pop stars like Madonna who transgress boundaries and challenge gender norms, in spite of their own complicity within traditional systems of power and privilege. Rather than rejecting outright the 'bad girl' figures and the controversy caused by Madonna's behaviour in these performances as simply another marketing strategy, I suggest a shift in focus toward the possibilities of an alternative interpretation of these 'bad girls', as well as a critique of reading practices which continue to be reliant upon conventional ideals of morality, heteronormative codes, and the perpetuation of power relations based on gender inequalities and binary oppositions.

Drawing on Donna Haraway's (1991) 'Cyborg Manifesto', Jennifer González's (2000) understanding of imaginary cyborgs as an empowering metaphor particularly for women, and Laura Mulvey's (1975) critique of the male gaze, I argue that in Madonna's performances of 'What It Feels Like for a Girl' she plays with the boundaries between reality and fantasy, embracing her cyborgian self as a means to critique and take on the world—'a man's world'.

As part of this process, and through her use of fantasy and the 'bad girl' trope, the audience is introduced to Madonna's 'imaginary representations of cyborgs' and more importantly, to how these imaginary cyborgs 'take over when [her] traditional bod[y] fail[s]' (González 2000, 61). By embracing the 'bad girl' and her mythical abilities to respond to the 'horrific' experiences of 'being a girl in this world', Madonna challenges the inequalities and injustices of such realities. This make-believe narrative captures the terrors, anxieties, and pleasures of resisting normative ideas and queering gender performances resulting in the transgression and transformation of what it feels like for a girl. Through a close reading of the music, images, lyrics, and characters presented in the music video and two stage performances of 'What It Feels Like for a Girl', I argue that Madonna's 'bad girls' may also be read as imaginary cyborgs who defy the male gaze and subsequently, in disrupting the gaze, negate its power.

Too Much for Much

In March 2001 Kim Cooke, then Managing Director for Warner Brothers, Deborah Powell, a representative from the organization FACT (Fathers are Capable Too), Jane Stevenson (*Toronto Sun* columnist), Kieran Grant (*Toronto Sun* music columnist), and I were invited to participate as part of an expert panel for MuchMusic's television show *Too Much For Much*, offering our interpretations of the previously unaired music video for 'What It Feels Like for a Girl'. Along with viewers, fans, and the host, George Stroumboulopoulos, we discussed, via a variety of interactive media technologies (email, websites, fax, mail, phone), the controversy surrounding the video, resulting from its content. Unlike the previous controversies concerning sex, sexuality, and cultural appropriation, Madonna's music

video for 'What It Feels Like for a Girl' (2001) was initially banned and/or censored by the US-based specialty channels MTV and VH1 because of its graphic use of violent imagery. Considering its reception in the United States, *Too Much For Much* offered viewers a chance to participate in the decision around whether or not the music video was 'too violent' or 'too graphic' to air on MuchMusic.[1]

Host George Stroumboulopoulos initiated the on-air discussion with a contextualization of Madonna's previous controversy surrounding the video for 'Justify My Love' and some reasoning for why 'What It Feels Like for a Girl' should be included as it addressed concerns related to gender. Stroumboulopoulos' introduction concluded with him looking into the camera to directly address the viewing audience, asking 'What do you think?' What followed was the debut airing of 'What It Feels Like for a Girl' on MuchMusic.

'What It Feels Like . . .'

The first thing one notices about the video is that a dance remix version of the song has replaced the original released in 2000 on Madonna's album, *Music*. The difference between the two, a ballad pop song and a pulsating dance remix, signifies to the audience a change in what the music conveys, how it affects the listener, and a new way of thinking about 'what it feels like for a girl'. Musically, the remix creates a film soundtrack sound rather than a typical pop song from the album, which has an immediate affect on the reading of the video. The idea of the remix itself is indeed a cyborgian entity in that it is a synthesis of different forms of musicality and a combining of the 'organic' song with 'technology'. But how does the change in music contribute to the viewer's interpretation of the video content? Is one seduced to listen to the song differently? What do these new readings mean for Madonna's 'proto-pop feminist anthem' (O'Brien 2003, 122)? Does the musical track—pulsating, quick tempo, heavy-bass, dance remix—heighten our reading? Does Madonna perpetuate or confront the problematic notion of a 'sisterhood' experience based on gender oppression? Is her critique of gender norms valid in spite of the pitfalls of identity politics?

Madonna employs musical discourse to produce and share her knowledge claims. The creation of knowledge claims within the realm of fantasy allows one to move beyond the confines of material reality. Fantastical places, events, bodies, stories, provide the means to reflect on and/or reinterpret lived experience provoking new readings of one's reality. Music functions well in these contexts because of its enigmatic qualities and its reception. How one determines musical meaning is a subjective process, and yet, one's interpretations are bound by experience, socialization, and learned reading practices.

Filled with explicit images of the daily harsh realities for a girl, the video portrays examples of sexual harassment, poverty, exclusion, violence, police oppression, sexism, and misogyny within a fictional (yet real) narrative. Drawing on the real and imaginary, using metaphor, symbolism, and affect, Madonna responds to these circumstances by becoming a 'bad girl'. This role play enables Madonna to enact a different kind of behaviour—behaviour read and understood as socially inappropriate for a girl/woman. Because of its inappropriate and violent nature, Madonna's actions are surprising and unexpected to both the fictional characters to whom she reacts, as well as to the real viewing audience. Through such actions, Madonna creates counter-hegemonic knowledge claims.

Within the first few frames of the video the audience is introduced to the two protagonists—Madonna and her companion, an elderly woman. The connection between the two women becomes more apparent as the narrative progresses; theirs

I read as an intergenerational relationship rather than a familial one. These women share experiences of oppression, pleasure, pain, and a desire for freedom. But it's Madonna who offers a means to achieve this state—a purely mythical state—as the two begin their journey. From the putting on of their armour—for Madonna this means the bulletproof vest, her blue coveralls, her spiked stilettos, her black leather driving gloves, her earrings, and for the elderly woman this means putting on her glasses, strapping on her leg brace, buckling up her seatbelt, and for both women the car also becomes another layer of armour—Madonna and her companion embrace their cyborgian selves. Within the narrative of the song these characters illuminate the instability of binary categories (nature/technology, young/old, pleasure/pain) and the anxieties that accompany a disregard for deeply entrenched ideologies.

At times in the video there is a reclamation of and play on particular words—language which is often used to oppress—words such as 'pussy', appearing on the front license plate of Madonna's car, only to have the back plate spell out the word 'cat'. When Madonna arrives at the senior's complex to pick up her companion, a sign above the door reads, 'Old Kuntz Guest House'. The play is on the word 'cunt' and all its embedded meanings, insults, and abjection associated with the aging female body. The significance is emphasized as the camera pauses on the sign not allowing the viewer to look away. This language politicizes the ways women are forced to negotiate the world as one's identity and value change with age. By drawing viewers' attention to these words it forces us to consider their meaning in more complex ways. Reclaiming language that is used to oppress and silence women is one way to confront and challenge patriarchal relations of power. Michel Foucault (1978) argues language can be both enabling and constraining. Here, in calling attention to the words 'pussy' and 'cunt' and manipulating and playing with words such as 'cat' and 'lady', Madonna reclaims these words and contests their signified gendered meanings.

Madonna's decision about which lyrics to include and which to omit is another significant use of language. Rather than embedding all the lyrics from the original song to convey the story, Madonna makes use of metaphorical images and musical codes. The lyrics are pared down so the listener hears only the chorus—'Do you know what it feels like for a girl. Do you know what it feels like in this world for a girl?'—and the prelude to the song, a segment of dialogue from the 1993 film *The Cement Garden*[2]: 'Girls can wear jeans and cut their hair short; wear shirts and boots, cause it's okay to be a boy. But for a boy to look like a girl is degrading. Cause you think that being a girl is degrading. But secretly, you'd love to know what it's like. Wouldn't you?'

There are two moments in the video where the prelude is heard. Actor Charlotte Gainsbourg speaks about how it is okay for girls to take on some of the conventions of being a boy, but how a boy's desire of wanting to know what it feels like to be a girl is forbidden—because being a girl is degrading. The combination of lyrics and dialogue conveys the naturalization of conventional gender categories ('being a boy'/'for a girl'), the consequences of transgressing these norms ('you think being a girl is degrading'), the desire to perform the other ('secretly you'd love to know what it's like'), and a lack of understanding or willingness to know the affect of being a girl ('in this world'). The film clip occurs consistently over 16 measures and is accompanied by more subdued music, drawing attention to the dialogue. At the conclusion of these sections there is a dramatic break in the music creating a tension that is resolved slightly on the downbeat of the next bar. Throughout the song, however, there is a continuous building of musical tension, broken only as the video comes to an end.

The sequence of events is not chronological. Prior to the images of Madonna and her companion in their preparation stages, Madonna purposefully drives into another vehicle with three men inside who, when stopped at a traffic light just prior, make sexual gestures toward the women. Following this sequence, Madonna steps out of the car holding a Taser and walks toward a man in a business suit at an automatic bank machine. In the next frame he is on the ground and Madonna walks back toward the car with fistfuls of cash in her hand dropping money without seeming to care. This 'senseless' act becomes much more meaningful in the following sequence as Madonna literally stuffs the money into a waitress' pocket at a diner. These actions comment on class struggles, and the inequity of power between men and women in the working world. Not only is Madonna taking from the rich to give to the poor, she draws attention to the ghettoization of women in low paying jobs.

As the women leave the diner, Madonna sideswipes a police car with both officers standing next to it, eating takeout. The two white male police officers stare in disbelief as Madonna pulls up alongside them, takes out a silver pistol, aims at their heads pulling the trigger twice. A stream of water hits between the officers' eyes. The music used as Madonna shoots the water gun sounds directly on the beat for emphasis, yet the sounds are playful, not foreboding. The gun can easily be read as the all-powerful phallus; however, the water is slightly more ambiguous. On one hand, the liquid may represent 'sperm' with Madonna holding the phallus and 'ejaculating' into the officers' faces. With this action she certainly disrupts conventional power relations, authority, and the law of the father. On the other hand, the gun shoots streams of water not bullets, and despite the metaphoric violence, Madonna does not kill—her actions are startling, provocative, and challenging, but not literally violent.

These outcomes challenge the naïve readings that this video is merely about retaliation; Madonna is playing with the relationship between power and unearned privilege and the fear and anxieties associated with the loss of such power.

As the police begin to chase the women, Madonna reverses into their vehicle, disabling the car by activating their air bags. The women drive off and into a parking lot where a group of boys are playing hockey—there are no girls playing here. Both implicit and explicit issues of exclusion and privilege continue throughout the video, and her ongoing critique of brotherhood and male privilege even reflect back to examples evident in childhood. Next Madonna drives the vehicle through the hockey game knocking down and running over several of the boys. At the end of the parking lot she stops, drops her fries into a garbage can and speeds off. During these moments the images of the sexual harassment, the bank machine incident, and the disruption of the hockey game, Madonna sings, 'Do you know what it feels like for a girl in this world.' The singing of the chorus stops altogether during the sequence with the police officers—a comment on the silencing effect of the law.

The next sequence is initially shot from above; the screen is filled by a red sports car with a painted firebird on the hood being fuelled by its owner at a petrol station. As the owner focuses on filling his tank, Madonna assists the elderly woman out of their wrecked car and into his car. Madonna jump starts the engine and pulls away. The gas hose is left flailing as fuel spills all over and the owner chases after the car. Madonna turns the car around, runs the owner down, speeds off but then stops, lights her Zippo, and drops it onto the trail of gas. The explosion is witnessed through reflections in the car windows.

At this moment in the song the audience is taken back in time, back to a sequence of Madonna and her companion preparing for their ride. Madonna slams the door of her motel room causing the last digit in the room number to invert revealing 666—the mark of evil, alluding to women as evil—as being in cohorts with Satan in order to deceive and lure men to their deaths. Madonna's tattoos—a smoking gun on the inside of her left forearm, a cross on the inside of her right forearm which reads 'no surrender' and the word 'loved' on the back of her neck are revealed. The elderly woman, who may look catatonic, shows signs of agency. As she watches a vehicle crash on television she squeezes her armchair in excitement, preparing herself for what she knows will come. Both times the film clip plays the audience is privileged to these preparation stages. The music plays an essential role here in letting us know that both women are fully aware. In the final segment of the video Madonna revs the engine and speeds toward a pole. The wings of the firebird on the hood rise up on impact, wrapping around the pole and seemingly taking flight. As the tension builds with the use of techniques such as sound layering, silent pauses, pushing the beat, quick image changes and heightening the pitch, the audience is finally given release as the women crash into the pole and the wings lift.

Throughout the video Madonna strategically embraces the 'bad girl' metaphor and all its symbolism as a strategy to reveal hegemonic gender norms and to challenge the perpetuation of such norms within popular discourses. Although reminiscent of other instances where women's lives must end once they have stepped outside the hegemonic gender roles, the final image can be interpreted as a smashing of tradition and freedom through flight or release. The video has a non-linear narrative emphasizing the need to break out of the norm—it is not organic. This non-sequential effect aids the viewer in understanding that much of what is going on in the narrative is 'unnatural'. Madonna is playing with the 'nature of things'. The images in the video create jarring effects because Madonna—a woman—has taken on roles and actions typically reserved for men. And although the video may seem to cry out retaliation, it provokes much more than this. In donning a conventionally aggressive masculine role which includes specific kinds of freedoms and privileges, Madonna presents the stark contrast between gendered roles. By including the elderly woman who appears catatonic along for the ride, there is a struggle to wake her from this state, to release her from an entrenched tradition. Another aspect of this jarring effect occurs at the video's conclusion when the final crash shakes the audience out of the visual trance.

Reactions

Initial reactions from panelists, audience members, and fans included adjectives such as cheeky, irreverent, extreme, violent, degrading, victimizing, self-indulgent, and evil. This language illustrates diverse reactions to the video, as well as to Madonna. As the responses continued throughout the broadcast it became evident that Madonna had once again succeeded in provoking controversy and debate concerning hegemonic ideas about women's roles in society and in popular culture. In spite of differing opinions about the content of the video, there was agreement that Madonna challenged some normative strongholds.

One of the first issues raised was the double standard imposed upon women concerning violence and sex in music videos. If a video features a male artist, or is in a genre engendering a masculine identity or feel, such as rock or hip hop, portrayals of graphic violence and explicit sexuality are questioned less, especially if the violence is perpetuated by a man and it is women who are highly sexualized as objects or commodities to be possessed. The romanticization of violence and sex is often considered an integral component of commercially successful videos for such genres and do not seem out of place or controversial. However, when a woman commits violent acts, audiences tend to respond in a different, often contemptuous manner. During *Too Much for Much*, many of these attitudes surfaced. For example, Stevenson described Madonna as self-indulgent, while another interactive viewer claimed Madonna was 'masturbating her ego again'. Comments like these are problematic in that they contribute to a discourse of morality for women, a discourse that dramatically differs for men. More importantly, these are the very ideas that Madonna calls into question within the narrative of the song and the video.

In her assessment, Powell suggested that although Madonna sings about the degradation of women in the song, she 'brings out an awareness that women are also violent' and that too often women are only seen as victims. Although her argument that women are often read as victims within larger social discourses is a legitimate concern, [. . .] Powell reads the video straight without realizing the broader context and playfulness of 'What It Feels Like for a Girl' and the character of Madonna herself.

Contrary to Powell, Grant suggested that Madonna was acting out a 'sisterhood of destruction' as a form of retaliation to protest the exclusion of women, most apparent to him during the scene where she runs over the boys playing hockey. From Grant's comments, it seems that the process of identification with some of the supporting characters plays an important role in how one interprets and responds to the actions in the video. As many theorists have argued, one's experience, socialization, and context become an essential tool in reading media. During the televised conversation I wondered about Grant's identification with the young boys playing hockey and why he chose not to identify with Madonna's character. Also there did not seem to be consensus around the idea of retaliation. For one audience member, although there were a number of meaningful and recognizable fear-inducing symbols with which he could identify (i.e., 666), he stated, 'there was nothing that made me scared to be a man.'

[. . .]

Fantasy, Responsibility, and Cyborgs

[. . .]

According to Haraway a cyborg is a 'cybernetic organism, a hybrid of machine and organism, a creature of social reality as well as a creature of fiction' (1991, 149). The cyborg embodies both reality and fantasy—it is constructed from lived realities and fantasies and thus, it can '[n]o longer [be] structured by the polarity of public and private' (1991,151). In the video for 'What It Feels Like . . . ' there are representations and the fusion of reality and fantasy as a means to call into question such categories and the power relations constituted through narrowly articulated dichotomies. The cyborg creates the potential for a disruption of dualistic categories of male/female, mind/body, culture/nature, self/other. And yet, cyborg bodies (like Madonna's body) are somewhat ambiguous; there is no one specific definition that applies to all cyborgs (nor to the many re-inventions of Madonna). [. . .] In other words, cyborgs may be used to re-interpret or transform gendered power relations, but in some moments the cyborg can also be used as a tool to restrict and limit the social, cultural, and political movements of women.

Within a capitalist framework the cyborg often becomes a symbol of increasing efficiency, productivity, and sterility. As a result the cyborg is sometimes 'more trapped by her mechanical parts than liberated by them' (González 2000, 61). In many commercial Hollywood films

cyborgs obey rather than disrupt conventional categories of femininity/masculinity. A cyborg gendered female often performs the traditional female categories—virgin/mother or whore—whose goals, despite however heroic or villainous, can only be reached through subjugation, purification, and/or death (i.e., Maria from *Metropolis* (1927), Rachael from *BladeRunner* (1991), Ripley from *Alien3* (1992), the Borg Queen from *Star Trek: First Contact* (1996), Trinity from *Matrix Revolutions* (2004), Pam from *Death Proof* (2007)). This argument could also be made around the final scene when Madonna wraps the car around the pole. With Madonna, however, it is essential to understand that symbolically Madonna *never* dies, rather she always re-invents herself. The final scene is not a death scene, rather it offers change and renewal.

In contrast, a cyborg gendered male is often understood as a powerful hero (the protagonist) or villain (the antagonist) rationally using logic, cunning, and physical aggression to achieve his ultimate goals (i.e., Luke/Darth Vadar from *Star Wars* (1977), Picard from *Star Trek: First Contact* (1996), Neo/Smith from *The Matrix Revolutions* (2004), Stuntman Mike in *Death Proof* (2007)). Here too, these signifiers can be mapped onto Madonna and her companion. They play both protagonist and antagonist, and draw on many signifiers understood as masculine.

The appropriation of the cyborgian body is also evident within the music industry, particularly when it comes to constructing/marketing a star identity in the feminized genre of pop. An example worth studying is in the March 6th 2001 issue of *Time Magazine*. On the cover there is a photo of singer Christina Aguilera with the caption, 'The Making of Christina Aguilera'. Alongside the article she is depicted as half computerized or cyborgian with the caption: 'Building a 21st century star.' The comments read: 'Behind her music—so you want to build a teen pop star? In Aguilera's case, it started with talent. But these promotional steps didn't hurt.' The captions detail how Aguilera's image was produced through Disney, online websites, and marketing gimmicks. The reader is reminded that it is the industry that creates stars, particularly young female stars like Aguilera. Aguilera is stripped of all agency; literally and figuratively she is represented as a cyborg, part human and part machine, controlled by those who hold power in the music industry, primarily men. From this perspective Aguilera is just another cog in the well-oiled music industry machine.

The discourse surrounding Madonna and her 'Queen of Pop' status is quite different from artists such as Aguilera. Madonna's agency concerning the construction of her identity is not in question. Madonna is both applauded and criticized for constructing an image founded in controversy, exoticism, sex, and cultural appropriation. Because she draws on archetypal figures to continually re-invent her image, one could argue Madonna reflects rather than resists hegemonic constructions of femininity. And yet, the female body, although 'subordinated within institutionalized systems of power and knowledge and crisscrossed by incompatible discourses, is not fully determined by those systems of meaning' (Balsamo 1996, 39). Undeniably Madonna is a highly sexualized and objectified woman and yet, she is publicly recognized as a successful, strong business-minded subjective woman who commands all aspects of her career including her sexualized and objectified image.[3] Rather than being trapped by such contradictions, Madonna performs a plurality of identities, re-conceptualizing the boundaries determining the personal and political. Similar to the cyborg, used to both reinforce and challenge gender norms, Madonna's interpretations of 'being a girl' are relevant in today's world.

[. . .]

Drowned World Tour

In her *Drowned World Tour* performance (2001) Madonna continues to address ideologies of gender using both animé and material cyborg bodies. Approximately half way through the concert another remix version of 'What It Feels . . .' begins. The focus turns to a massive screen hanging at centre stage playing a Manga *animé*. Within the animation there are numerous images of girls/women: some with super human strength, others ordinary in prom dresses; there are images of women fighting, running, chasing, being chased, being violent with each other, and being raped by a monster. At two moments the dialogue from *The Cement Garden* is played. This time however, the accompanying music is urgent, aggressive, louder, and driving the beat. The only lyrics sung by Madonna (pre-recorded) are 'for a girl' and 'in this world'. Diegetic sound effects[4] are also audible—specifically the characters' screams and moans. There are numerous moments of tension and release in the music, with the music building to a painful climax, agitated by the heightened pitch and intense drum tracks. In the final moments when one of the female characters screams out during a violent rape scenario, a male voice yells, 'Hold it everyone. We have to move the cameras.' The man/actor who is on top of the woman spurts out, 'I'm really sorry.' She replies, 'No, it's all right.' Then she jolts awake.

This explicit and violent animation is interesting because the story is being produced as a fictional performance within the already fictional animation. In other words, the audience is meant to believe that the violence, struggle, and degradation of being a girl are fictional twice removed. Revealing the apparatus and production calls attention to the reality expressed as imaginary, and more importantly, even within a non-real world, a girl's experiences are embedded within conventional gender narratives of exploitation, power, and violence.

Toward the end of the concert the song is performed again, but this time it is similar to the album version. There are three distinguishing elements: The instrumentation uses strings and additional percussion; the dialogue is omitted; and Madonna sings the lyrics in Spanish. It is essential to call into question the reconstruction of her white American body as an exoticized 'Other'. This is not the first time Madonna sings in Spanish or invented this representation of herself.

As the music plays dancers appear on the candle-lit stage, all women wearing pin-stripe suit trousers, tank tops, suspenders, black leather gloves, and sporting short hair or closely shaven heads; women simultaneously performing both masculine and feminine. The conventional signifiers exposing their femininity are high heels, makeup, their visible bodies, and gestures. This blurring of feminine and masculine is indeed cyborgian and the audience is given 24 measures of music without Madonna's presence to gaze only on these bodies. In response they too gaze at each other and out at the audience as they wait for the real object of their desire. Then a large black box (Pandora's box) rises up from below and the sides fall open to reveal Madonna inside. The dancers' masculine signifiers contrast against Madonna's femininity, emphasizing her role as both desiring subject and object of desire. For the majority of the song she remains inside the parameters of the box while the dancers tempt her out. Once she moves outside the boundaries she too begins to dance, dancing with each woman closely, expressing her own agency and desires. As she moves from person to person they gaze at her longingly. As she leaves each one, they move off the stage until Madonna is left singing alone and the stage goes dark.

Here we are reminded of how Madonna has made queer culture consumable through a heteronormative gaze—a gaze that titillates and gives space to heterosexual male fantasy. In contemporary queer culture, however, Madonna is also an important figure of resistance—she is emulated in drag, danced to in queer clubs and on the gay circuit, and represents queer women's sexual desire. Through her playful perversions Madonna (re)presents queer desire as flowing into her heteronormative practices. Madonna as 'bad girl' unsettles boundaries.

Conclusion

In the video and stage performances, Madonna embraces the 'bad girl' figure in order to disrupt and challenge gender norms. She uses her cyborgian body to 'represent that which cannot otherwise be represented' (González 2000, 59), to blur boundaries between real and imaginary, and to move in and out of ideological borders. Drawing on the realm of fantasy, Madonna contributes to an ongoing dialogue countering the naturalization of women's/girl's oppression through practices of exclusion, violence, capitalism, and exploitation. Through counter-hegemonic knowledge claims that depict both lived experience and fantasy, Madonna utilizes the tools of oppression to metaphorically disrupt the norms of 'what it feels like for a girl'. Aided by her imaginary cyborgs, Madonna defies hegemonic gender norms, displacing the female body from its prescribed position, while simultaneously problematizing the actions associated with the masculine through humour and play.

Madonna's 'bad girls' illustrate that anything from dominant society can be appropriated—anything is up for grabs. Madonna can infect anything. To blur boundaries it is imperative to be able to move freely around the contradictions of the middle without needing to resolve them. Madonna does not resolve these contradictions, she adds to them. But what then does Madonna's appropriation of the conventional do for cyborg strategies? Madonna's playful, perverted, and controversial performances call into question points of crisis for her audience and in so doing, she opens up and cultivates new possibilities. Through Madonna's performances, it is apparent that fantasy and the cyborg have become points of intervention in popular culture. Through such interventions, 'what it feels like for a girl', even a contemporary 'bad girl', is redefined.

Notes

1. For a discussion on MuchMusic outlining its mandates, as well as content and delivery style, refer to Pegley 2008.
2. The film is an adaptation of Ian McEwan's 1978 novel bearing the same title.
3. Marsh and West (2003).
4. Diegetic sound describes sound where the source is visible on screen.

References

Balsamo, A. *Technologies of the Gendered Body: Reading Cyborg Women*. Durham and London: Duke University Press, 1996.

Foucault, M. *The History of Sexuality: An Introduction*, Vol. 1. New York: Random House Inc, 1978.

González, J. 'Envisioning Cyborg Bodies: Notes From Current Research', *The Gendered Cyborg: A Reader*, G. Kirkup, L. Janes, K. Woodward and F. Hovenden, eds. London and New York: Routledge, 2000, pp. 58–73.

Haraway, D. 'A Cyborg Manifesto: Science, Technology, and Socialist-Feminism in the Late Twentieth Century', *Simians, Cyborgs, and Women: The Reinvention of Nature*. New York: Routledge, 1991, pp. 149–82.

Madonna. *Music*. CD47598. New York: Warner Brothers/Maverick, 2000.

———. *Drowned World Tour*. New York: Warner Records, 2001. [DVD]

———. *What it Feels Like for a Girl*. New York: Warner Records, 2001. [DVD single]

Marsh, C., and M. West. 'The Nature/Technology Binary Opposition Dismantled in the Music of Madonna and Björk', *Music and Technoculture*, R. Lysloff and L. Gay Jr., eds. Middletown, Connecticut: Wesleyan Press, 2003, pp. 182–203.

McEwan, Ian. *The Cement Garden*. New York: Simon and Schuster, 1978.

Mulvey, L. 'Visual Pleasure and Narrative Cinema', *Screen* 16.3 (Autumn 1975): 6–18.

O'Brien, L. 'The Second Coming', Q: *Madonna 20th Anniversary Collector's Edition*. London: Mappin House, 2003, pp. 120–25.

Pegley, K. *Coming to You Wherever You Are: MuchMusic, MTV, and Youth Identities*. Middletown: Wesleyan University Press, 2008.

Time Magazine (March 6, 2001).

Media Representations of Adolescent Pregnancy: The Problem with Choice

Anita Shaw

Introduction

Late in 2007 a movie was released that caused quite a stir, reminding me of a similar event a generation ago, the 1986 release of Madonna's music video *Papa Don't Preach*. The movie and the music video were both progressive and contentious at the time of their release and both stimulated lively public discussions about teenage sexuality, pregnancy, and motherhood.

By the spring of 2008, it seemed that most of my friends had seen the movie and were encouraging me to do the same. *Juno* had hit a nerve. Many women, it seemed, could relate. Some of them had experienced teenage pregnancy or, if they hadn't, were likely to have experienced that lesser nightmare: the pregnancy scare. And these women really admired Juno, the title character, for being smart, sassy, and in control and they appreciated the way she broke down negative stereotypes of teen moms as irresponsible, maladjusted, and selfish. Juno might have made the mistake of getting pregnant too young and in less than ideal circumstances but she was back in the driver's seat, making her own choices and doing the right thing. She was a role model. And this is where I became uncomfortable.

Why, you might ask, would a feminist scholar feel uneasy about the popularity of a young, female fictional character who exercises agency and authority over her life? Does this not represent a feminist utopia for girlhood? Ideally, perhaps it does. But this storyline is built upon fairly narrow expectations of girls and of girlhood and overlooks some of the ways that girls' agency is undermined. Because the mass media play a critical role in shaping culture, media representations of adolescent pregnancy have profound effects on pregnant and mothering teenagers.

In this paper I delineate some of the ways that Juno both challenges and reinforces stereotypes of pregnant teenagers and some possible implications of this. I compare and contrast *Juno* to an earlier and, I argue, more progressive iconic media image of adolescent pregnancy: the music video *Papa Don't Preach* by Madonna (1986). Responses to adolescent pregnancy are complex and overlapping; they differ depending on the marital status, race, class, and even the age of the girl. Consistent with the subjects of these media texts, my analysis focuses on the experiences of unmarried, white, working-class, school-aged girls, though I explore some of the ways that stigmatization of these girls is relevant in the lives of girls and women who do not identify with this group. I examine the dominant discourse as it is applied to adolescent girls in the context of their sexuality, arguing that the choices discourse sets narrow the parameters for girls' socially acceptable behaviour and stigmatizes those who venture outside those boundaries. I contend that pregnant adolescents are evaluated according to white, middle-class standards; that they have faced and continue to face structural challenges for which they are individually held responsible; and that there is a political need for feminist scholars to collaborate with young mothers in an effort to expose this ideology.

Discourse

According to Teun van Dijk, power, domination, and social inequalities are constructed, reproduced, and contested through the text and talk, or discourse, which takes place within any number of social and political institutions including, for example, medical, religious, educational, and, importantly, media institutions. The power of these dominant groups may or may not be contested and the extent to which they remain uncontested will determine to what degree their ideology is integrated into the culture, either through law or convention. When any idea or way of thinking about any subject, for example, teenage pregnancy, becomes the most commonly accepted view, it is known as the dominant, or hegemonic, form (van Dijk 2001). Users of dominant discourses limit their own contestation by setting the parameters for what can be discussed (Cohn 2007; Critcher 2003). Regardless of the issue, the mass media usually present the dominant discourse and, by contrasting it to a nonsensical position, convince most media consumers that the dominant discourse simply makes sense (Brickell 2000). As long as the dominant discourse positions adolescent pregnancy as not an option it requires a great shift in thinking to consider it an option. Motherhood is never considered a legitimate option for Juno. Once her father reminds her that she cannot even remember to give her younger sister her 'breathing meds', the thought of Juno taking care of a child seems foolhardy. Not becoming a mother, in this example through placing her baby for adoption, becomes the only outcome that makes sense to most people in the audience.

[. . .] While discourses are always subject to contestation and change, our experiences and the meanings that we make of them are mediated by and filtered through the discourses most familiar to us, usually, though not always, the culturally dominant discourses. Media representations are never value-free, they do not simply describe events but actively construct evaluative versions of events. Culture shapes media and media shapes culture. This has important social and political implications (Potter and Wetherell 1987, 6). As an example, Carmen Luke believes that 'the texts and artefacts of mainstream culture construct motherhood and childhood . . . as a powerful normalizing discipline with and against alternative and feminist constructs' (Luke 1996, 184).

'Normal' is defined by what is projected as well as by what is silenced. In her study of mainstream parenting magazines, Luke found that 'parenting magazines present only one version of motherhood . . . which largely excludes women and children of colour, single mothers, poor mothers, fathers, and non-heterosexual family formations' (1996, 184). The magazines' images and text suggest that children's well-being is highly dependent on being cared for by a married heterosexual couple within a nuclear family (Luke 1996, 183). Angela McRobbie writes about the media portrayal of the 'yummy mummies', wealthy celebrities such as Victoria Beckham whose maternity clothing comes from upscale boutiques and whose children are cared for, largely, by nannies. She argues that the 'yummy mummy' is positioned against the largely absent image of the 'pramface', that is, 'the face of impoverished, unkempt, and slovenly maternity', restigmatizing single motherhood and acting as a deterrent. According to McRobbie, 'yummy mummies' signify a new moral economy within which being poor is just one more stigma (2006).

If normal parents are white, wealthy, heterosexual, and beautiful, then every other parent is not normal. Pregnant teenagers live with the implications of this on an ongoing basis, from interpersonal to institutional encounters, from nasty comments heard on the bus to inappropriate educational requirements (Kaufman 1999). Shanti Kulkarni found that adolescent mothers are aware of and constantly respond to the stigma. She speculates that a number of the young women she interviewed stayed in abusive relationships precisely to oppose the negative stereotypes; if she is in a committed relationship, she cannot be called a slut (Kulkarni 2007, 16–17). Despite the efforts of the feminist movement, patriarchal feminine ideals remain foundational to media representations of women. These ideals remain largely uncontested and are even reinforced by our families and communities, impacting girls' and women's sense of self (2007, 20).

Kathryn Addelson argues that responsibility, as distinct from blame, takes into account all points of view, the insiders' and the outsiders'. She suggests that there is a need to consider girls' standpoint on the issue of choice: that is, the context of their decisions about sexuality, pregnancy, and motherhood. Currently, we are hearing primarily from outsiders, the we who have solutions for them (Wong and Checkland 1999, 174–75). Although women who have experienced teenage pregnancy are ideally storied to disrupt the dominant discourse, they are rarely well-situated to do so. Feminist scholarship, by virtue of academic privilege, has an important role to play in amplifying girls' voices contesting the dominant discourse through, for example, reconstructing adoption 'as a "real" choice' (Caragata 1999, 113), revealing hidden dimensions of girls' sexuality (Tolman 2005), or showing that adolescent pregnancy, rather than disrupting girls' development, can be a healthy route to adulthood (Leadbeater and Way 2001, 3–4).

Although teenage mothers are engaged in creating counter-hegemonic discourses concerning adolescent sexual and reproductive rights (O'Reilly 2007; girlmoms.com; teenmoms.page) their voices continue to be marginalized. In a search of the Canadian News Index from 1980 to 1992, Dierdre Kelly found that 3 per cent of articles about teen mothers were produced by young moms (2000, 81). When given an opportunity to speak, teen moms' narratives are often positioned in ways that serve the dominant discourse. [. . .] Van Dijk emphasizes that having the power to influence institutional texts is, itself, a '"symbolic" resource' available to only a few. Critical discourse analysts, therefore, recognizing the privileged position they occupy with their ability to contribute to the public discourse, work with and for marginalized groups to expose and remediate social inequalities (van Dijk 2001, 355).

Choices

Teenage pregnancy and parenting have always been part of the human experience but they have not always been perceived, as they are now, as crises or even as problems. While it is not immediately clear what causes public concern about teen pregnancy, it is clear that this phenomenon is not related to the numbers of adolescent pregnancies. Teenage pregnancy rates in Canada are 50 per cent lower than in the United States and have seen a decline since at least 1974 with the Canadian pregnancy rates for 15- to 19-year-olds dropping from 53.7 per 1000 in 1974 to 38.2 per 1000 in 2000 (Kelly 1996, 422; McKay 2004). Despite these declining numbers Canadian scholars assert that social stigma about teenage mothers continues to be quite prevalent (Kaufman 1999; Kelly 1996, 422; Wong and Checkland 1999, xviii–xix). So what is behind this consternation?

If culture and ideology are, indeed, inscribed on women's bodies and if women's bodies are also sites of resistance to such ideologies (Darling-Wolf 2009, 251–57), adolescent pregnancy provides a unique window into historically and culturally specific social structures. In her discussion of adolescent sexuality, pregnancy, and abortion Rosalind Petchesky writes, 'getting pregnant . . . has no intrinsic social or political meaning; it receives its meaning from the historical and political context in which it occurs and the circumstances . . . of the woman involved' (Petchesky 1990, 207). A feminist position suggests that teenage sexuality and pregnancy represent challenges to contemporary North American patriarchal constructs of gender, family, and gender-specific class and race (1990). *Papa Don't Preach* illustrates this well: the character's white, female, working-class, cultural minority identity is not challenged but, rather, underscored by her unmarried teenage pregnancy. Juno, on the other hand, is also a white working-class girl and placing her baby for adoption offers her the possibility of upward mobility while assuring her child an upper-middle-class standing. We witness shifts in the father-daughter relationships as the pregnancies in both *Juno* and *Papa Don't Preach* challenge paternal authority. The daughter in *Papa Don't Preach* appears to have successfully negotiated a more adult status than *Juno* but both fathers have been forced to relinquish some control, both in terms of the daughters' sexuality and with regards to their pregnancy outcomes.

While she acknowledges that she may be oversimplifying, Deborah Rhode writes that opposition to teen pregnancy falls into two ideological camps. Conservatives view teen pregnancy as a personal moral issue, which leads to the consideration of other moral issues, such as abortion and contraception, an attack on patriarchal family hierarchy, and, citing welfare costs, an issue of financial dependence on the state (Rhode 1993). The liberal position, which gained momentum in the 1970s, contests the conservative perspective. Liberal ideology points to health and socio-economic issues, arguing that teen pregnancy reduces the mother's academic opportunities thereby limiting her financial independence and life choices. Conservatives believe that teenagers should not be having sex, liberals believe that teenagers should not be having babies. Their proposed solutions follow logically, though both assessments of the problem are flawed (1993, 312–16).

Both the liberal and conservative discourses conflate teenage pregnancy with unplanned pregnancy and unplanned pregnancy with unwanted pregnancy. But, of course, this is not always the case. Young women become pregnant for a variety of reasons as do older women (Phoenix 1991, 87). Both discourses predict financial hardship but research regarding maternal outcomes for adolescent women is equivocal, to say the least. Recent studies suggest that the predicted dire outcomes for the women and their children have been overstated; in fact, many fare quite well. Over their lifespan, young mothers' lives tend to follow a similar pattern to those of their peers who delayed child-bearing. Class standing, rather than age at first childbirth, appears to be a primary determinant of women's life outcomes (Kelly 1999, 56–59; Phoenix 1991, 89–90). The challenges faced by adolescent mothers tend to be similar to their peers who delayed mothering, though they are often complicated by the specific stigma which is reserved for the younger mothers (Furstenberg et al. 1987, 145–46).

Despite their different approaches, conservative and liberal discourses end up converging, centring on the issue of choice, their differences simply reflected in the particular choice with which they are concerned. Conservatives consider sex outside of heterosexual marriage to be immoral and support movements such as abstinence-only sex education and chastity pledges. Liberals, who tend to be more accepting of teenage sexual activity, still consider adolescent mothering unacceptable (Rhode 1993, 312–16) and tend to support, for example, sex education that emphasizes healthy choices. It appears that liberals are able to suspend judgments about individuals' morality only to judge the outcomes of their behaviour.

Both conservative and liberal discourses are evoked in the same breath when the 'stupid slut' label is applied to pregnant and mothering adolescents as it is currently, primarily by other adolescents. The slut label is applied automatically because the young woman has had sex; she has transgressed the conservative moral code. But if it is discovered that she had sex without using contraception the 'stupid' qualifier is added because she has apparently ignored the liberal admonition to make healthy choices (Kelly 2000, 27–31).

But girls really are in a double bind. Using contraception can also result in the slut label. A girl who plans to have sex is unfeminine; according to the romance narrative, sex is supposed to 'just happen' (Beres 2009). Regardless of whether contraception is available, she could find herself in a situation where the choice is between consenting to sex or not consenting and experiencing some form of violence, sexual or otherwise (Gavey 2005). The amount of power she will have in relation to her boyfriend will depend on their age, race, and class hierarchies as well as other factors, such as each of the partners' perceived attractiveness and popularity. If the girl becomes pregnant she will likely be labelled a stupid slut because of her decision to have sex without using contraception (Kelly 2000, 25–31; Tolman 2005). If her subsequent decisions are bad she may well be coerced into making what are considered good decisions. The choices discourse becomes a vehicle for exercising even more control over people who appear unable or unwilling to make good choices, cloaking social control mechanisms in a tone of neutrality. The moral inferences are just below the surface.

The 'Good Girl Life Plan'

Kathryn Addelson's 'Good Girl Life Plan' (1994, 115; 1999, 87) outlines one dominant, possibly *the* dominant, discourse concerning contemporary expectations of North American girlhood. The 'Good Girl Life Plan' represents the projected linear expectations for white, middle-class, North American girls: that they get an education before they commit to a relationship; that they marry a man before having sex; and that they have babies and grandchildren within a heterosexual, patriarchal family structure. Although the sequential steps of the 'Good Girl Life Plan' might vary according to race and class (Addelson in Wong and Checkland 1999, 157), non-white, working-class girls' lives tend to be evaluated in comparison to this unstated standard: whatever privilege or status a girl may enjoy is compromised by her 'poor choices' or non-compliance with the plan.

Addelson's 'Career of the Unwed Mother' (1994, 118; 1999, 87) represents the possible missteps on the way to a proper future. These missteps, such as unmarried pregnancy or motherhood, which characterize bad girls and bad mothers are also, inevitably, decision points for adolescent girls. Addelson refers to these choices as 'elevators' which can lift girls back onto the 'Good Girl Life Plan'. For example, if she becomes pregnant outside marriage, a girl can correct that misstep by having an abortion or by placing her child for adoption. In this way, she can return to school or courtship and carry out the life plan according to the cultural prescription. Juno considers first abortion and then adoption in order to get back on the 'Plan'. [. . .]

An ideology of choice may seem liberating, but, in fact, girls do not always have equality of opportunity in sexual and reproductive decision making (Wong and Checkland 1999, 180–81). As Dierdre Kelly makes clear, 'The good choices discourse is particularly insidious because it works to obscure unequal power relations based on age, gender, class, and race' (2000, 61). The widely held assumption that all women have meaningful choice in matters of sexuality and reproduction, for example, elides structural inequalities and holds them individually responsible for such things as access to contraception, abortion, decent housing, quality childcare, employment, and education. The more marginalized she is, by virtue of her race, class, age, or sexuality, the less real choice she will be able to exercise, and the more stigma she will face. 'The Good Girl Life Plan' and the choices discourse support and reinforce each other, stigmatizing girls with their emphasis on individual responsibility.

Setting the parameters for what can be considered the gendered discourse of women's sexual and reproductive choice makes it difficult to see those spaces where women do not have choice or have only constrained choice. Carefully reflecting on the discourse can lead us to discover fissures therein (Plummer 1995).

Reflections

A cultural commitment to an ideology of choice with regards to issues of sexuality is reflected in media engagement with adolescent pregnancy and mothering. When the mass media portray adolescent mothers, they generally depict images of the morally defective teen mom. Two images that offer some challenge to the hegemonic discourse are *Papa Don't Preach* and *Juno*. In *Papa Don't Preach*, Madonna plays a white, Italian-American, unmarried, working-class, pregnant teenager. Her girlfriends tell her she is too young to be a mother and that she should 'give it up' for adoption. Madonna decides to keep her baby and appeals to her father for advice and support. In *Juno* the main character is a 16-year-old white, working-class high school student who also discovers that she is unintentionally pregnant. After considering an abortion, she decides to place the baby for adoption and, by searching the wanted ads, finds a wealthy, white, married, heterosexual, early middle-age couple to adopt her baby.

Conservatives have been ambivalent about these two texts. On the one hand, they applaud both young women because neither had an abortion. Agreeing with this assessment, liberals and feminists have accused both texts of promoting an anti-abortion message. On the other hand, liberals and conservatives alike have criticized the two texts for glorifying teenage mothering (Dullea 1986; Garcia 1986; Gulli 2008; Luneau 2008; Miller 2008). And, according to Rhode's breakdown, liberals would support Juno placing her baby for adoption though they would not support the girl in *Papa Don't Preach* keeping her baby.

In terms of an alternate reading, *Juno* offers some laudable moments of feminist resistance. One such moment occurs when Juno points out the sexual double standard to her boyfriend, Paulie, who faces no ostracism for being an adolescent father. Juno yells at him, 'You don't have to have the evidence under your sweater!' Another important moment comes when Juno's stepmother loses her temper with the ultrasound technician after she suggests that teenagers are ill-equipped for mothering. While this scene does acknowledge motherhood as a legitimate choice for adolescents, it implies that this is only if they can be good mothers. Unfortunately, the point is further undermined by the stepmother's use of racist language.

The scene where Juno and Paulie have intercourse presents Juno as a strong teenage girl in a committed, loving, heterosexual relationship (read: feminine) who is in charge of, and making choices about, her sexuality (read: liberated). When they both acknowledge that he has 'wanted this for a long time' (*Juno* 2007) I was left wondering whether she felt any pressure to comply with Paulie's desire for sex or any worry about what might happen if she did not. This scene reinforces another dominant narrative, that teenage pregnancy is the result of two teenagers fumbling around in the dark. This stereotype is contradicted by recent research which shows that teenage girls are less likely to be impregnated by teenage boys than they are to be impregnated by boys and men who are sometimes much older that they are (Males 1992 & 1996; Manlove et al. 2006; Taylor et al. 1999).

Although audiences were left with a sense that Juno is a powerful character, she is often portrayed as very childish: her language use and appearance are juvenile; she states that she decides against abortion because the clinic 'smelled'; she chooses the Lorings from the wanted ads because, in their photograph, 'they are beautiful'; and she explores the Lorings' bathroom in a manner typical of a young child. Even if she eventually proves herself responsible she is most certainly incapable. Ultimately, this movie promotes the choices discourse and 'The Good Girl Life Plan'. Sex is a bad choice, adoption is a good choice. Neither she nor the people around her seem to question the white, middle-class, North American expectations for her life. On at least two occasions Juno's aberrant pregnancy is contrasted to the 'typical' pregnancies of 'our moms and our teachers'; the anguish and grief most women feel about placing a child for adoption are glossed over. By the end of the movie, Juno hops on her bike with her guitar on her back, to go hang out with her boyfriend. She is absolutely unencumbered by a child and is decidedly back on 'The Good Girl Life Plan'.

Compare *Juno* to *Papa Don't Preach*

Simply *making* this video broke the rules; at the time adolescent pregnancy was not a discussion topic for general consumption. But it was timely. In the late 1970s and early 1980s in the United States and somewhat later in Canada abortion was becoming more accessible to teenagers and, for girls who carried their pregnancies to term, adoption was becoming increasingly rare (Maticka-Tynedale 2008; Moore and Rosenthal 1994; Petchesky 1990; Petrie 1998; Solinger 2005). As we have come to expect, Madonna's character is not a good girl. She says to her father, 'I'm not a baby'; she embraces her sexuality at the same time as she challenges parental authority. She acknowledges two pregnancy options, adoption and motherhood, and challenges the patriarchal script that her pregnancy is poorly timed. There is some contradiction here, though. The camera shot of the elderly couple on the ferry and her plan to marry her boyfriend could be seen as referents to 'The Good Girl Life Plan'.

Importantly, though, *Juno* explores class issues in ways that *Papa Don't Preach* does not. The Lorings class status affords them the priv-ilege of considering adopting a child and Vanessa Loring's white yuppie status marks her as a legitimate mother even after she becomes single. But I wonder, would these stories have been as compelling had the girls been black, Asian, or Aboriginal? Given the historical and ongoing devaluation of non-white mothers and non-white babies in North America, I suspect not (Kelly 2000; Roberts 2006, 446–52). Frank Furstenberg et al. (1987) point out that the obligation to make good choices appears to be premised on the belief that middle-class white girls have so much more to lose in terms of educational, career, and social opportunities by early parenting than do their non-white, working-class peers

(Kelly 2000,44–45; Luker 1996, 154). Even so, the 'Good Girl' rules apply without exception. Although choices are differentially constrained, blame is delegated to everyone, and those whose choices are most constrained are often those who experience the most stigma.

Papa Don't Preach challenged the choices discourse and offered teenage girls some new possibilities, that they could enjoy being sexual and keep their babies if they wanted. In comparison, *Juno*, while also challenging negative stereotypes of pregnant teenagers, is disappointing in terms of the narrow range of options it presents. *Juno* and *Papa Don't Preach* rely heavily on the choices discourse; both girls have apparently made some bad choices and become pregnant. The consequences they face serve as cautionary tales to other girls about the importance of making good decisions. Both scripts depict adolescent sexuality as dangerous in that sex leads to pregnancy and pregnancy is a crisis. Additionally, both texts emphasize the romance narrative. The heterosexual love interest is prominent in both stories; in *Papa Don't Preach* the young woman's relationship with her boyfriend is a significant factor in her decision to keep the baby. And, in the end, both girls get their men.

Conclusion

Adolescent pregnancy is an emotional issue; the pregnant teenage body challenges patriarchal family structure, gender roles, sexuality, and class structure. Because the mass media play a critical role in shaping culture, media images of adolescent pregnancy have profound effects on the lives of pregnant and mothering teenagers and their families. The choices discourse and 'The Good Girl Life Plan' support and reinforce each other, setting narrow parameters for girls' lives, stigmatizing those who venture outside those boundaries, and eliding structural inequalities with their emphases on individual responsibility. Any debate about choice assumes that young women have the agency required to make such choices. But, clearly, structural constraints limit girls' ability to make any choices, good or otherwise (Rhode 1993, 324). Added to this burden is the reality that 'the individual being condemned for having made bad choices is often female and poor, a member of a racialized "caste", or both, and that the standard of assessment reflects a white, middle-class ideal' (Kelly 2000, 62).

Like all discourses, the choices discourse is subject to ongoing contestation. *Juno* and *Papa Don't Preach* challenge the choices discourse, presenting a more empowering picture of adolescent pregnancy than that of deviant other. But, considering that the mass media provide insights into the dominant discourses, it appears that girls are more constrained by 'The Good Girl Life Plan' today than their mothers were in the 1980s. As young mothers, alongside feminist scholars, continue to experience incremental success in challenging the healthy choices discourse it is important to remember that simply deconstructing this ideology can be liberating. Exposing the dominant discourse opens a space for girls and women to explore alternate discourses, providing new contexts within which to place our experiences and, rather than assigning blame, consider our collective responsibilities.

References

Addelson, K.P. *Moral Passages: Toward a Collectivist Moral Theory*. New York: Routledge, 1994.

———. 'How Should We Live? Some Reflections on Procreation', *Teen Pregnancy and Parenting: Social and Ethical Issues*, J. Wong and D. Checkland, eds. Toronto: University of Toronto Press, 1999.

Beres, M.A. 'Moving Beyond 'No Means No': Understanding Heterosexual Casual Sex and Consent', *Open Boundaries: A Canadian Women's Studies Reader* 3rd edn, B. Crow and L. Gotell, eds. Toronto, Ontario: Pearson Prentice Hall, 2009.

Brickell, C. 'Heroes and Invaders: Gay and Lesbian Pride Parades and the Public/Private Distinction in New Zealand Media Accounts', *Gender, Place, and Culture*, 7.2 (2000): 163–78.

Caragata, L. 'The Construction of Teen Parenting and the Decline of Adoption', *Teen Pregnancy and Parenting: Social and Ethical Issues*, J. Wong and D. Checkland, eds. Toronto: University of Toronto Press, 1999.

Cohn, C. 'Wars, Wimps, and Women: Talking Gender and Thinking War', *The Gendered Society Reader*, M. Kimmel and A. Aronson, eds. New York: Oxford University Press, 2007.

Critcher, C. *Moral Panics and the Media*. Philadelphia: Open University Press, 2003.

Darling-Wolf, F. 'From Airbrushing to Liposuction: The Technological Reconstruction of the Female Body', *Open Boundaries: A Canadian Women's Studies Reader*, B. Crow and L. Gotell, eds. (3rd edn). Toronto, Ontario: Pearson Prentice Hall, 2009, pp. 251–56.

Dullea, G. 'Madonna's New Beat is a Hit, But Song's Message Rankles'. [Electronic version]. *New York Times*, 18 Sept 1986. www.nytimes.com/1986/09/18/nyregion/madonna-s-new-beat-is-a-hit-but-song-s-message-rankles.html?sec=health&spon=&pagewanted=all (accessed 22 October 2009).

Furstenberg, F.F., J. Brooks-Gunn, and S.P. Morgan. *Adolescent Mothers in Later Life*. New York: Cambridge University Press, 1987.

Garcia, G.D. 'People'. [Electronic version]. *Time*, 6 Oct 1986. www.time.com/time/magazine/article/0,9171,962477,00.html (accessed 22 October 2009).

Gavey, N. *Just Sex? The Cultural Scaffolding of Rape*. New York: Routledge, 2005.

Girl-moms. www.girlmoms.com [Website.] (accessed 7 June 2009).

Gulli, C. 'Suddenly Teen Pregnancy Is Cool?' [Electronic version]. *Macleans*, 17 Jan 2008. www.macleans.ca/culture/lifestyle/article.jsp?content=20080117_99497_99497 (accessed 10 June 2008).

Juno. J. Reitman, dir. Fox Searchlight Pictures, 2007. [DVD.]

Kaufman, M. 'Day-to-Day Ethical Issues in the Care of Young Parents and Their Children', *Teen Pregnancy and Parenting: Social and Ethical Issues*, J. Wong and D. Checkland, eds. Toronto: University of Toronto Press, 1999.

Kelly, D.M. 'Stigma Stories: Four Discourses about Teen Mothers, Welfare, and Poverty', *Youth and Society*, Vol. 27.4 (1996): 421–49.

————. 'A Critical Feminist Perspective on Teen Pregnancy and Parenthood', *Teen Pregnancy and Parenting: Social and Ethical Issues*, J. Wong and D. Checkland, eds. Toronto: University of Toronto Press, 1999.

————. *Pregnant with Meaning: Teen Mothers and the Politics of Inclusive Schooling*. New York: Peter Lang Publishing, 2000.

Kulkarni, S. 'Romance Narrative, Feminine Ideals, and Developmental Detours for Young Mothers', *Affilia: Journal of Women and Social Work*, 22.1 (Spring 2007): 9–22.

Leadbeater, B.J.R., and N. Way. *Growing Up Fast: Transitions to Early Adulthood of Inner-City Adolescent Mothers*. Mahwah, NJ: Lawrence Earlbaum Associates, Publishers, 2001.

Luke, C. 'Childhood and Parenting in Children's Popular Culture and Childcare Magazines', *Feminisms and Pedagogies of Everyday Life*, C. Luke, ed. Albany: State University of New York Press, 1996.

Luker, K. *Dubious Conceptions: The Politics of Teenage Pregnancy*. Cambridge: Harvard University Press, 1996.

Luneau, K. 'Babies Are the New Handbag'. [Electronic version]. *Macleans*, 17 Jan 2008. www.macleans.ca/article.jsp?content=20080117_133527_1008&page=3 (accessed 10 June 2008).

McKay, A. 'Adolescent Sexual and Reproductive Health in Canada: A Report Card in 2004', *The Canadian Journal of Human Sexuality* 13.2 (2004): 67–81.

McRobbie, A. 2006. 'Yummy Mummies Leave a Bad Taste for Young Women'. [Electronic version]. *The Guardian*, 2 March 2006. www.guardian.co.uk/world/2006/mar/02/gendercomment (accessed 24 June 2008).

Males, M.A. 'Adult Liaison in the "Epidemic" of "Teenage" Birth, Pregnancy, and Venereal Disease', *The Journal of Sex Research, 29*.4 (1992): 525–45.

————. *The Scapegoat Generation: America's War on Adolescents*. Monroe, ME: Common Courage Press, 1996.

Manlove, J., E. Terry-Humen, and E. Ikramullah. 'Young Teenagers and Older Sexual Partners: Correlates and Consequences for Males and Females', *Perspectives on Sexual and Reproductive Health*, 38.4 (2006): 197–207.

Maticka-Tynedale, E. 'Sexuality and Sexual Health of Canadian Adolescents: Yesterday, Today and Tomorrow', *Canadian Journal of Human Sexuality* 17.3 (2008): 85–95.

Miller, M. 'Teen Pregnancy Pact: Celeb Culture Cited'. [Electronic version]. *CBS News*, 20 June 2008. www.cbsnews.com/stories/2008/06/20/earlyshow/main4198453.shtml (accessed 25 June 2008).

Moore, S., and D. Rosenthal. *Sexuality in Adolescence*. New York: Routledge, 1994, p. 151.

O'Reilly, A., ed. 'Young Mothers' [Special Issue]. *Journal of the Association for Research on Mothering*, 9.1 (2007).

Papa Don't Preach. J. Foley, dir. 0 Pictures, 1986 [CD video] www.youtube.com/watch?v=LY1RNuzT4XU (accessed 28 June 2008).

Petchesky, R.P. *Abortion and Woman's Choice: The State, Sexuality, and Reproductive Freedom*, rev. edn. Boston: Northeastern University Press, 1990.

Petrie, A. *Gone to an Aunt's: Remembering Canada's Homes for Unwed Mothers*. Toronto, Ontario: McClelland and Stewart, 1998.

Phoenix, A. 'Mothers Under Twenty: Outsider and Insider Views', *Motherhood: Meanings, Practices, and Ideologies*, A. Phoenix, A. Woollet, and E. Lloyd, eds. Newbury Park: Sage Publications, 1991.

Plummer, K. Telling *Sexual Stories: Power, Change and Social Worlds*. New York: Routledge, 1995.

Potter, J., and M. Wetherell. *Discourse and Social Psychology: Beyond Attitudes and Behaviour*. Thousand Oaks, CA: Sage Publications, 1987.

Rhode, D.L. 'Adolescent Pregnancy and Public Policy', *The Politics of Pregnancy: Adolescent Sexuality and Public Policy*, A. Lawson and D.L. Rhode, eds. New Haven: Yale University Press, 1993.

Roberts, D.E. 'Punishing Drug Addicts Who Have Babies: Women of Color, Equality, and the Right of Privacy', *Theorizing Feminisms*, E. Hackett and S. Haslanger, eds. New York: Oxford University Press, 2006.

Solinger, R., ed. *Pregnancy and Power: A Short History of Reproductive Politics in America*. New York: New York University Press, 2005, pp. 210–16.

Taylor, D.J., G.F. Chavez, E.J. Adams, A. Chabra, and R.S. Shah. 'Demographic Characteristics in Adult Paternity for First Births to Adolescents Under 15 Years of Age', *Journal of Adolescent Health* 24.4 (1999): 251–58.

Teenmoms. www.geocities.com/miraclechick/teenmoms.html Accessed 21 October 2009.

Tolman, D. *Dilemmas of Desire: Teenage Girls Talk about Sexuality* (2nd edn). Cambridge: Harvard University Press, 2005.

van Dijk, T.A. 'Critical Discourse Analysis', *The Handbook of Discourse Analysis*, D. Schiffrin, D. Tannen; and H.E. Hamilton, eds. Malden, MA: Blackwell Publishers, 2001.

Wong, J., and D. Checkland, eds. *Teen Pregnancy and Parenting: Social and Ethical Issues*. Toronto: University of Toronto Press, 1999.

'The Lone Streetwalker': Missing Women and Sex Work–Related News in Mainstream Canadian Media

Shawna Ferris

This paper interrogates the ever-popular 'lone streetwalker' trope in mainstream media representations of sex workers. Such reporting simultaneously echoes and reifies traditional anti-prostitution dogma, seemingly with little regard for the effects of such dogma on the already disenfranchised disappeared and murdered women such journalism often purports to represent. Significantly, even as more serial kidnap and murder cases involving prostitute victims have become national news since the case of Vancouver's missing women made international headlines eight years ago, the same stigma-laden images continue to narrate sex work and sex workers in particularly problematic ways.

In their 2000 article, 'Images of Prostitution: The Prostitute and Print Media', Erin Gibbs Van Brunschot, Rosalind A. Sydie, and Catherine Krull discuss their study of prostitution-related news in *The Vancouver Sun*, *The Winnipeg Free Press*, *The Toronto Star*, *The Montreal Gazette*, and *The Halifax Chronicle Herald* between the years of 1981 and 1995. About this news Van Brunschot, Sydie, and Krull write,

> [T]he depiction of the street prostitute and her (or his) work remained consistent and there was often remarkable homogeneity in the media coverage irrespective of the political leanings of various newspapers. There were four themes that were most prevalent in the years under review: [neighbourhood] nuisance, child abuse, violence, and non-Western prostitution. Two other themes—drugs/organized crime and disease—were less nationally prevalent, but were regionally specific. (53)

My own survey of prostitution-related news from the years following this study reveals similar patterns. When reporters, politicians, and the police they routinely interview turn from bloody stories of mutilated bodies of sex workers in Edmonton, Saskatoon, and Halton/Hamilton, or haunting tales of human DNA from murdered women on a pig farm in Vancouver, they do not focus on the need to interrogate and take apart whore stigma.

Neither do they provide in-depth stories about the poverty and racism that push people into the survival sex trade, or the broader systemic marginalization of indigenous and other non-white populations, immigrants, and the poor in this country.

Mainstream news rarely features the concerns of politically active sex workers, let alone average 'worker-on-the-street' interviews, about their concerns in particular neighbourhoods. My own research supports Sex Professionals of Canada spokesperson Wendy Babcock's claim that the one current exception to this choking off of sex workers' voices in newspapers and television reports occurs after incidents of violence against persons involved in the sex trade. Van Brunschot, Sydie, and Krull found a similar trend: 'It is in the association of prostitution with violence that the prostitutes' own voices are most frequently reported', they write, '[However,] employing the rhetoric of "safety on the job", violent experiences are often recounted as a means of illustrating the risks prostitutes run in having to ply their trade in a covert manner' (61). Though violence against sex workers thus precipitates some media exposure for the concerns of people working in the industry, prostitutes and/or representatives from groups like the Prostitution, Alternatives, Counselling and Education (or PACE) Society of Vancouver, the Toronto-based Sex Professionals of Canada (SPOC), the Sex Workers Alliance of Toronto (SWAT), Stella of Montreal, or the Halifax-based Stepping Stone rarely appear outside of violent contexts. Instead, their bodies are photographed and filmed in predictable ways, and their comments become short excerpts in response to reports that may very well be written before these interviews take place. More often than not, the anti-prostitution opinions of police, politicians, and other citizens outside the industry precede or offset sex worker concerns. Pieces 'featuring' sex industry participants too often include photographs of missing or murdered women who are then memorialized in the words of their families and friends.

'The lone streetwalker', a prevalent image of prostitution in mainstream Canadian news-papers, television news, and the online news sites affiliated with these agencies, features a solitary, usually white woman, who appears to be working at night, seemingly unaware of the camera, but posing seductively or otherwise dis-playing her body for drivers in the cars on the street on which she stands. Despite the fact that the exchange of sexual services for remuneration is legal in Canada, the women's faces are rarely shown clearly. And while many of these women may request that their faces not appear in news reports, precious few mainstream news sources include commentary from these subjects on the ways that current legislation allows police to detain and arrest them despite their engage-ment in a legal profession. Instead, their faces veiled in darkness and their comments trun-cated or written over in a variety of ways, these women's bodies are used to signify criminality and victimization.

Significantly, the light skin of this familiar figure—show-cased primarily through the play of light on her legs or arms (she usually wears a short skirt and/or a skin-bearing top) remains a consistent feature of this image. Despite the fact that sixteen of Vancouver's murdered women, and at least five of the fifteen murdered women of Edmonton were First Nations—not to men-tion the early 1990s case in Saskatoon in which all seven murder victims were First Nations women: the hegemonic image of women at risk is uniformly white.

A number of disturbing interpretations of this over-representation of whiteness in narrations of the sex industry are available here. For exam-ple, Native groups' struggles to dissociate First Nations women from colonial representations of Native women as 'squaws', or whores, in concert with 'multicultural' Canada's hegemonic denial of the legacy of such historical embarrassments, may whitewash current images of sex workers in stories that do not address trafficking.[1] In addi-tion, predominantly white spokespeople for the sex industry, alongside the recurrent media focus on 'good' white families whose daughters have gone missing from Vancouver's Downtown Eastside, signal a continued privileging of white-ness over aboriginality and other ethnicities. Such incarnations of racist denial, alongside a currently overwhelming hegemonic romantic investment in multiculturalism, or racial equal-ity, make unthinkable, or at least unspeakable, the plight of the non-white members of the urban sex trade.

Furthermore, images of the lone streetwalker imply that the street sex trade continues, seem-ingly unaffected by increasing concerns about the 'harm' and nuisance that street-involved sex work constitutes to urban neighbourhoods or by increasing risks of violence and mounting evidence of foul play. These faceless figures continue to work alone in the dark, flagrantly disregarding 'legitimate' concerns about neigh-bourhood safety, and risking their lives in these dangerous times. While there are always those workers for whom waiting for a companion to begin work, or checking in with a buddy or drop-in centre contact before and after a trick remains at best a distant thought in relation to their need for money, or for drugs, etc., these people do not represent the majority of sex trade workers.[2] Despite the great variety of people involved in the street sex trade—let alone the rest of the industry—news sources continue to offer these faceless pictures of lone white 'working girls', as though only white women enter this industry, and as though working and simultaneously risking their lives is all they ever do. Images like these—and the stories that accompany them—rarely include street and/or survival sex workers' claims that they often work together (or during the day), taking down licence plate numbers for one another and looking after one another as much as possible.[3] Photographs like these instead imply that sex workers foolishly tempt both passing motorists *and* fate each night after dark.

[Typical of these images are those] that appeared in the November 1999 issue of the now-defunct feminist magazine *Elm Street*, in a story by reporter Daniel Wood entitled 'Vancouver's Missing Prostitutes'. [. . .] [T]hroughout Wood's article, female sex workers stand faceless, blurred, and alone against a darkened cityscape. The caption below [one] image reads, 'On Vancouver's Downtown Eastside, women sell themselves for as little as $5 to buy heroin. Who'd care if a killer were stalking them? Even after 31 went missing, no one did—until their friends and families demanded the police take action.'

While Wood's story sympathizes with and promotes the political agendas of the missing women's family and friends, his use of the melodramatic phrase 'sell themselves' instead of 'sell sex' or 'sell sexual services' evokes echoes of the fallen woman, that traditional patriarchal emblem of female sexual transgression and social failure. In this phrasing—phrasing that other reports regularly feature—Wood suggests that a woman's worth relates directly to the demands she makes on those to whom she grants sexual access to her body. Another serious oversight here is the reporter's failure to note that someone who provides a sexual service to finance a heroin addiction participates in the *survival* sex trade, a trade that other members of the sex industry also wish to eliminate.

Similar images appear periodically throughout CBC Television reporter Judy Piercey's, 1 September 2003 report for *The National* entitled 'How Police, Street Workers and Families are Dealing with the Murders of Edmonton Women'. Highlighting the ways this report mimics much of the journalism that responds to Vancouver's missing women, CBC anchor Peter Mansbridge introduces Piercey's piece as a 'story about murder [that has] a disturbing and familiar ring'. Mansbridge continues, 'Some of the victims worked in the sex trade. All had high risk lifestyles. Then they went missing.' Having thus included the far from unusual implication that sex workers, as participants in 'high risk lifestyles', put themselves in harm's way and therefore share responsibility for the violence to which they are subjected, Mansbridge turns the story over to Piercey.

The report that follows centres around the disappearance and murder of five Edmonton women who are thought to have been involved in the street sex trade. First recording her ride-along with a man who helps the joint Edmonton Police Services/RCMP task force called Project Kare record pertinent information from street sex workers to aid in the identification of bodies during murder investigations, Piercey then interviews two grieving mothers, two young sex workers, RCMP and Edmonton police supervisors, and criminologist John Lowman about police performance in the current murder cases. While images of 'lone nightwalkers' standing on curbs, or even in the street are interspersed throughout the report, faces of interviewed sex workers do not appear. Instead a series of edited clips show the women's shadows against the wall next to a concerned-looking Piercey, and foreground one woman's short skirt and bare legs as she discusses the case with the demurely dressed reporter.

Repeatedly including such juxtapositions between sex workers and others involved in these cases, Piercey's report consistently contrasts the comments of these two women with those of the mothers of murder victims and police. [. . .] In addition, though the two young white sex workers interviewed suggest that women like themselves work together to protect each other on the street, especially since these high profile murder cases, none of the 'street life' clips included here reflect this reality.

[. . .]

It is perhaps hegemonic denial of such culturally legitimizing identities that fuels journalistic portrayals of missing and/or murdered women in prostitution-related news. Figure 1 features the 2007 version of Vancouver's missing women poster. Canadian news sources routinely use pictures from this or the earlier version of this poster when reporting on the case of the 68 disappeared Vancouver women. Many of the women pictured here were dead long before Vancouver officials finally agreed to post this reward for the first time in 1999. What effect, if any, do images like these, or variations of them, have? Do they foster public concern for these disappeared people? Do they appropriately memorialize the victims of violent crime?

Sex worker activist Kyla Kaun argues that pictures like these further prejudice an already prejudicial public against sex workers. Kaun, who testified in 2005 in Vancouver before the

federal Subcommittee on Solicitation Laws (the SSLR), notes that mugshot or mugshot-like photos portray the missing women as criminals, people about whom the public is less likely to care when they are represented this way. Kaun suggests that if police and press reports on missing and murdered sex workers were to use a woman's 'grad picture or a picture of her with her children or her family, then we are going to have a different feeling about that individual than from the image we see of her being arrested' (Canada 2006: SSLR mtg 17, page 46).

Kaun's point is well taken. Most of the missing women of Vancouver had community and/or family ties to the area. Many of them are mothers, and most of the women were reported missing by friends and family members. But unlike, for example, the much-publicized (and temporary) disappearance of Lethbridge, Alberta alderwoman Dar Heatherington four years ago, reports of which routinely featured pictures of Heatherington with her family (see, for example, the professional photograph of the Alderwoman with her husband and children included in CTV's 7 May 2003 report on her disappearance—available at www.ctv.ca), the (permanently) missing women of Vancouver are regularly portrayed in the news in groups of single-person photographs, as though their disappearances only become remarkable when grouped together. In addition, they are too often included as a series of photographs from the 1998, 2004, or 2007 posters, grouped together but separated even from one another, especially in the 2007 version of the poster.

More recent reports in British Columbia have begun to address concerns like Kaun's, foregrounding many of the women's roles as mothers of children who are (or who soon will be) old enough to understand the circumstances surrounding their mothers' disappearances and/or murders. However, pictures like those included in Lori Culbert's January 2006 *Vancouver Sun*

Figure 1 The most recent incarnation of the Missing Women Task Force reward poster (April, 2007). Reprinted with permission from the RCMP.

article (see 'Children of Vancouver's Missing Women' at www.missingpeople.net/children_of_vancouver.htm), set motherhood up as one of the few 'redeeming' features of these disappeared or murdered women's existences. 'Children of Vancouver's Missing Women' includes an older photograph of disappeared woman Sarah DeVries[4] cuddled together with her young daughter, who smiles up at the camera from behind a book they are reading together. In another more recent photograph, Marnie Lee Frey's teenage daughter, Brittany, poses, smiling, with her grandparents, Lynn and Rick Frey.[5] Culbert's article describes the 75 children of Vancouver's 68 missing women as 'precious reminders of lost lives', and notes that 'the backgrounds of the missing women—some came from poverty, others from middle-class families—were as varied as the reasons that led them to drug addictions and prostitution. But despite their challenges, many of the women shared a common thread of dedication to their children.' Culbert's article goes on to discuss caregivers' concerns about the experiences and feelings of the women's children as the Pickton trial progresses, and includes comments such as the following from Janet Henry's 20-year-old daughter, Debra Chartier: 'My mom is an important part of my life even though she did have some problems and wasn't there most of the time. I don't plan to follow in her footsteps. I don't plan to be better than her either. Nobody's perfect. But I do plan to fight for her until she's found.'[6] The article also notes that 'some of the missing women's children have escaped the cycle of poverty, violence, and drugs that claimed their mothers, while others have fallen into it. Their experiences are as diverse as their mothers.' Such commentary and images work to facilitate public concern about the fate of the disappeared and murdered women of Vancouver by suggesting that, while these women—devoted mothers or

no—are lost, we must care about their fates for the sake of their children. And while the pictures included here indeed offer a more nuanced account of the women's lives, the accompanying article effectively factors the women themselves out of public interest in this case. Having 'fallen' into drug addiction and prostitution, the text implies, the missing and murdered women of Vancouver failed their children, and society must now attempt to make amends for this collective failure.

Kaun's words ring true again with the recognition that some of the more flattering photographs in the poster appear to be cropped from pictures of larger groups. And even in significant and well-intentioned initiatives such as Project Edan's in which artists create sketches to 'soften' the missing women's appearances (see 'Sketches Express Softer Side of Missing Women' at www.missingpeople.net/sketches_express_softer_side_of.htm),[7] or Vancouver artist Pamela Masik's project 'The Forgotten', featuring a series of large individual portraits of all of Vancouver's missing women (see some preliminary images from Masik's project at www.masik.ca/features/theforgotten/),[8] the women appear together, but alone. Such projects poignantly illustrate how these women's lives all too often become important only insofar as their images and life stories may be used to impart object lessons to 'good' citizens about the violent fallout from cultural, especially sexual, deviance. Nonetheless while reports like those discussed above regularly interview women who describe extensive networks of friends and business associates who look out for one another on the streets, the images accompanying these stories continue to portray solitary sex workers.

Current efforts to re-envision missing and murdered women involved in the street sex industry appear [. . .] to be gaining ground. These gains are particularly important to take note of now as, despite escalating violence against sex workers, despite the federal government's striking of the SSLR (which has since been dropped) in response to national and international public concern over this violence, despite 'Stolen Sisters', the Amnesty International report expressing grave concern over the high numbers of disappeared First Nations women in Canada, national news venues continue to tell us the same stories and to show us the same images we have come to know so well. Experiential women[9] and other advocates of decriminalization, activists who discuss institutional racism, analysts who highlight and critique the current importance of high unemployment rates (key circumstances in the lives of many survival sex workers) in sustaining a 'healthy' economy, and prostitutes who describe the violence and sexual exploitation to which police subject them do not have the ear of the media in Canada, yet.

Notes

1. This in direct contrast to nineteenth-century moralists' portrayals of white working-class prostitutes as having black, or low, 'Negro' attributes (McClintock 56).
2. While there are no statistics regarding the numbers of people who work in the sex industry, those who work closely with sex workers through their research such as Cecilia Benoit and Alison Millar, John Lowman, and Katrina Pacey (of the Vancouver-based sex worker and human rights advocate Pivot Legal Society) estimate that street-level sex work constitutes only 20 per cent of the sex trade as a whole.
3. See, for example, sex worker comments in Cecilia Benoit and Alison Millar's *Dispelling Myths and Understanding Realities*, or Pivot Legal Society's *Voices for Dignity*.
4. Sarah DeVries disappeared in 1997.
5. Marnie Lee Frey also disappeared in 1997.
6. Janet Henry disappeared in June 1997. She is among the 40 women still considered missing in the Vancouver case.
7. The US-based Project Edan (Everybody Deserves a Name) commissioned this artistic project in an effort to see the Vancouver women's 'inner spirits' more accurately portrayed in popular media.
8. Exhibition of 'The Forgotten' was planned for 2007.
9. This term describes persons who have worked or are currently working in the sex trade.

References

Amnesty International Canada. 'Stolen Sisters'. 4 Oct 2004. 15 Aug 2005. www.amnesty.ca/resource_centre/reports/view.php?load=arcview&article=1895&c=Resource+Centre+Reports.

Benoit, Cecilia, and Alison Millar. *Dispelling Myths and Understanding Realities: Working Conditions, Heath Status, and Exiting Experiences of Sex Workers*. Victoria: Prostitutes' Empowerment Education Resource Society & B.C. Health Research Foundation, 2001. http://web.uvic.ca/%7Ecbenoit/papers/DispMyths.pdf.

Canada. *Proceedings of the Subcommittee on Solicitation Laws of the Standing Committee on Justice, Human Rights, Public Safety and Emergency Preparedness*. Chair John Maloney. 15 July 2006. www.parl.gc.ca.

Culbert, Lori. 'Children of Vancouver's Missing Women'. *Vancouver Sun*. 28 Jan 2006. 26 Nov 2006. www.missingpeople.net/children_of_vancouver.htm.

———. 'Sketches Express Softer Side of Missing Women'. *Vancouver Sun*. 17 Dec 2006. www.missingpeople.net/sketches_express_softer_side_of.htm.

'How Police, Street Workers and Families are Dealing with the Murders of Edmonton Women'. Rep. Judy Piercey. *The National*. CBC Television. 1 Sept 2003. www.cbc.ca/news/background/edmonton_murders/.

Lowman, John. 'Violence and the Outlaw Status of (Street) Prostitution in Canada'. *Violence Against Women* 6.9 (2000): 987–1011.

———. 'Prostitution Law Reform in Canada'. 20 Nov 2005. mypage.uniserve.ca/~lowman/Pro-law/prolawcan.htm.

McClintock, Anne. *Imperial Leather: Race, Gender and Sexuality in the Colonial Contest*. New York: Routledge, 1995.

PACE Society: *Prostitution Alternatives, Counselling and Education*. www.pace-society.ca.

Pivot Legal Society. *Beyond Decriminalization: Sex Work, Human Rights and a New Framework for Law Reform*. Eds. Naomi Brunemeyer, Karen Mirsky, and Sean Rossiter. Vancouver: Pivot Legal Society, 2006. www.pivotlegal.org/Publications/reportsbd.htm.

Pivot Legal Society Sex Work Subcommittee. *Voices for Dignity: A Call to End the Harms Caused by Canada's Sex Trade Laws*. Vancouver: Pivot Legal Society, 2004. www.pivotlegal.org/Publications/reportsvfd.htm.

'Search Continues for Missing Alberta Alderwoman'. *CTV.ca.* 7 May 2003. www.ctv.ca/servlet/ArticleNews/print/CTVNews/1052221362044_51/?hub=TopStories&subhub=PrintStory. 27 Dec 2005.

SPOC: *Sex Professionals of Canada.* www.spoc.ca/.

Stella of Montreal. www.chezstella.org.

Stepping Stone. www.supercity.ns.ca/~stepping/index.html.

SWAT: *Sex Workers Alliance of Toronto.* www.walnet.org/csis/groups/swat/about_swat.html.

SWAV: *Sex Workers Alliance of Vancouver.* walnet.org/csis/groups/swav/index.html.

VanBrunschot, Erin Gibbs, Rosalind A. Sydie, and Catherine Krull. 'Images of Prostitution: The Prostitute and Print Media'. *Women & Criminal Justice* 10.4 (2000): 53–71.

Wood, Daniel. 'Missing: Vancouver's Missing Prostitutes'. *Elm Street.* (November 1999): 2–10.

Sex, Lies, and Videotape: The Presentation of Sex Crime in Local Television News

Kenneth Dowler

Introduction

Crimes involving sex are often misrepresented and sensationalized by popular media outlets. Ideally the news media can be a productive force in reducing myths associated with sex crimes. Media reports of sex crimes, however, evoke a number of disturbing images that are based in stereotypes and misogyny. These reports create fear and misinformation while reinforcing dominant ideologies of rape. Nevertheless, there were few studies that investigated broadcast news portrayals of sex crime. As a result, the purpose of this research was to examine the presentation of sex crime in the local broadcast media newscasts [. . .]

Despite limited research, there were a number of themes that were constantly presented by the news media, which included the image of 'sick' rapist; the overrepresentation of stranger rape; and the tendency to blame the victim. First, the media often presented the image of the rapist as 'sick' or pathologically deviant (Benedict, 1992; Carringella-MacDonald, 1998; Howitt, 1998; McCormick, 1995; Soothill & Walby, 1991). Willis (1994) contended that it was more appealing to sell sensationalized cases

that target a few 'sick men' instead of exploring structural inequality and sexism that encompasses and encourages the domination and subsequent rape of women. For instance, there was disproportionate attention given to serial rapists. As a result, these 'few' cases heightened the contrast between extraordinary cases and the 'normality' or reality of rape, which might cause the public to revert to a somewhat narrow definition of rape (Soothill, 1991).

Second, the media treated rape as being committed by strangers (Benedict, 1992; Carringella-MacDonald, 1998; Howitt, 1998; McCormick, 1995; Soothill & Walby, 1991). Soothill and Walby's (1991) study of English newspapers found three problems with press coverage of sex crimes. First, the media constructed the typical rapist as a 'sex beast' or 'fiend'. The early focus of coverage was on the police investigation and the 'excitement of the chase'. Later coverage was based on the trial where the victim was portrayed as either a 'whore or virgin'. Second, there was a narrow definition of a sex crime. For example, the media portrayed the typical sexual assault as being committed by a total stranger. Third, there was little academic information about the causes of sexual violence or sex crimes. Newspapers tended to rely on 'official' explanations of rape that maintained that sex crimes were frightening but rare.

Furthermore, in an examination of rape cases profiled in magazines during the years 1980 to 1996, Carringella-MacDonald (1998) found that by selecting stereotypical cases involving strangers or gangs, magazine coverage of rape was hegemonic and non-progressive. Essentially, acquaintance and date rape were not getting attention commensurate with their historic neglect or with their proportion of actual rapes committed. Similarly, marital rape was rarely presented in newspapers (Soothill & Grover, 1994). Conversely, some research indicated that newspaper coverage had changed to account for changing definitions of rape. For example, Los and Charmard (1997) found that there was an increase in the coverage of 'acquaintance rape'. This led to the shift toward the portrayal of rape as an ambiguous interaction that had more to do with sex than violence. As a result, the reporting was more apt to treat the complainant as a partner rather than a victim. Similarly, Cuklanz (1996) found that news stories failed to include coherent or complete depictions of sexual assault. Consequently, media coverage fitted a 'mythic framework' with its implicit traditional understandings of rape; however, coverage of rape trials was increasingly reflecting elements of a reformed understanding of rape.

Third, the media's coverage of rape was characterized by the blaming of the victim (Benedict, 1992; Carringella-MacDonald, 1998; Howitt, 1998; McCormick, 1995; Voumvakis & Ericson, 1984). Research had confirmed that this victim-blaming strategy underlies the media's treatment of female victims of rape. For example, a study of Toronto newspapers revealed that items concerning sexual attacks against women characteristically implied that female victims were at fault for placing themselves at risk by going to dangerous areas or premises (Voumvakis & Ericson, 1984). Furthermore, rape victims were portrayed as either hysterical women, promiscuous 'sluttish women', or manipulative women. The reason the media constructed these images was the focus on the defence or perpetrator's version of the events (Howitt, 1998). This was inconsistent with other research that showed that the media relied on prosecutors for many details of criminal events (Drechsel, Netteburg & Aborisade, 1980). In addition, Howitt (1998) found that acquittals of rape suspects were more likely to make the front page of a newspaper and that rape convictions were relegated toward the middle of the newspaper. In essence, the message conveyed was that rape acquittals were more important than rape convictions.

Moreover, the media sensationalized certain cases which ultimately distorted the facts of the case, which resulted in the creation of myths such as victims lying to protect their reputations (Hamlin, 1988). Similarly, Benedict (1992, p. 23) reported that the media coverage divided rape victims into two types, the 'vamp' and the 'virgin'. The 'vamp' was a rape victim defined by her looks, behaviour such as sexual enticement and loose morality, or provoking actions. The 'virgin' was a rape victim that was defined as a pure and innocent victim that was violated by a sick and perverted monster. As Benedict (1992, p. 24) explained: 'Both of these narratives are destructive to the victims of rape and to public understanding of the subject. The vamp version is destructive because it blames the victim of the crime instead of the perpetrator. The virgin is destructive because it perpetuates the idea that women can only be Madonnas or whores, paints women dishonestly, and relies on portraying the suspects as inhuman monsters.' In sum, sex crime coverage was portrayed through paternalistic and patriarchal viewpoints. Rape victims were stereotyped, minimized, ignored, or used as scapegoats for male actions that were based in sexual desire and misinterpretation, rather than male dominance and violence.

One way to understand media coverage of sexual assault is through the theory of framing, which was first introduced by Goffman (1974). Frames supply contextual cues which provide order and meaning to problems, events, and actions. Within the mainstream media, frames guide the selection, presentation, and evaluation of information, by placing the stories into familiar categories. News frames tend to simplify, prioritize, and structure the narrative flow of events (Tuchman, 1978). Essentially, framing promotes a particular interpretation by prioritizing some facts, events, or developments, while excluding other information (Entman, 1993). In this way, the media provide a frame of reference that enables the audience to comprehend a particular story or topic. Tuchman (1978) argued that news frames create and shape knowledge by ascribing ideological traits to events, individuals, and spaces which maintain the status quo. Tuchman (1978) further argued that the news media were not neutral transmitters of facts, but make decisions that define events and give them meaning, thus the news frames construct reality for their audiences.

The present study sought to build on existing literature concerning media presentations of sex crime. Through the use of content analysis and multivariate analysis, this research systematically and critically explored the presentation of sex crime within local newscasts. Of central importance was exploring the differences and/or similarities between the presentation of sex crime compared to other types of crime, such as homicide, assault, and robbery. Past literature suggested that sex crime stories were highly sensational,

stereotypical, and inaccurate (Greer, 2003). This research empirically tested these assumptions against other types of crimes. Specifically, this study explored whether sex crime stories presented more fear, outrage/sympathy, sensationalism, and/or a proactive police response.

Method

The Sample

Consecutive day sampling was used to acquire 400 (thirty-minute) episodes from four markets (100 from each market). Equal proportions of news broadcasts in the cities of Detroit, Toronto, Toledo, and Kitchener were acquired. Within each market, television stations might provide varying types and degrees of crime coverage. As a result, stations available to the researcher were taped in relatively equal proportions. Detroit had the most television channels available, which included WDIV (29 episodes), WXYZ (28), WJBK (28), and WKDB (15). Toledo stations included WNWO (32), WTOL (34), and WTVG (34). Toronto television stations included Global (48) and City-TV (52). Finally, Kitchener had only one station CKCO (100). In addition, noon (45), evening (186), and nightly (169) news broadcasts were taped.[1]

Content analysis was conducted on 400 episodes, which consisted of 1042 crime stories. A content analysis is a detailed and systematic examination of the contents of a particular body of material for the purpose of identifying patterns, themes, or biases. The focus is primarily on any verbal, visual, or behavioural form of communication. In the current study, content consisted of both visual and verbal communication in relation to news stories that presented criminal acts, criminals, victims, criminal justice agents, and issues. The focus of the current study was on quantitative content analysis, which consisted of identification, sampling, and counting specific manifest content (i.e., race, gender, type of crime) and classifying latent content into distinct categories.

Manifest coding is the coding of the visible or surface content (Neuman, 2003). In other words, quantitative content analyses involve the coding of the material in terms of predetermined and precisely defined characteristics. Latent coding or semantic analysis looks for the underlying, implicit meaning in the content of a text. Obviously, the meaning of words, phrases, or terminology is subjective in nature; as a result, some latent or semantic analysis is performed. In order to provide reliability, the researcher had strict rules on the interpretation on how the content was coded. Berg (2001, p. 243) suggested that 'researchers should offer detailed excerpts from relevant statements that serve to document the researchers' interpretations'. As a result, subjective decisions required documented excerpts from the story to provide justification and verification.

Variable Construction and Measurement

Manifest Coding

A code sheet was developed to examine manifest and latent content. There were several variables that were created within the code sheet. These variables enabled the researcher to statistically examine differences in story presentation. The first section of the code sheet identified the city, country, market, station, date, and time of newscast. The second section examined the nature of the story presentation which included type of crime(s), lead story, live story, reporting of weapon, local or national story, length of story, stage of crime, use of interviews, number of interviews, and reporting of motive.

Local or national story was the region or area in which the crime story occurred. For instance, local involved stories that occurred in the local broadcast region. [. . .] For all markets, national stories were defined as stories that originated outside of their market. Length of story was measured by timing the story from beginning to end with a stopwatch. It was coded in seconds because the majority of stories did not last for one minute.

Stage of crime was coded as pre-arrest, arrest, court, and disposition. The pre-arrest stage involved stories that did not report an arrest. The arrest stage involved stories in which an arrest had been made, but suspects had not appeared in court. The court stage involved stories in which the suspects/defendants had appeared in court (including preliminary or sentencing phase). The disposition stage involved stories in which the suspect/defendant had served his/her sentence or was currently serving his/her sentence for the crime.

Latent Coding

Reporting a Motive

Reporting of motive required a subjective appraisal by the researcher; however, it was based in precise guidelines. The reporter/anchor, interview subject, or police officer would provide a motive in the presentation. The motive was implied or suggested; it did not have to be confirmed. In many instances, the motive was not 'really' known, but was reported as 'possible' or linked to other activity such as drugs or gangs. When motive was suggested or implied, the motive was documented on the code sheet to provide verification. For example, the anchor or news reporter might suggest that the 'crime occurred because . . .' or that ' . . . is the probable cause for the crime'. Interview subjects might speculate on the reason the incident occurred, while police officers might try to explain the crime.

Emotive Presentation

Several variables were constructed to examine emotive presentation of crime stories. Stories were examined in regards to their presentation of fear, presentation of sensationalism, and presentation of outrage/sympathy. Presentation of fear involved stories in which the interview subject or reporter/anchor explicitly stated words or quotes that presented fear. Adjectives in the stories were closely examined for words and comments. For example, statements included: 'the only thing to expect is the unexpected', 'be advised', 'be more cautious', 'you never know', 'act of random violence', 'gunmen at large', '[crime] on the rise', '[suspect] on the loose', 'on the run', '[suspect] is on violent frenzy', 'is high risk to re-offend', 'fears are not calmed', 'can't sleep at night', '[It's] creepy, you don't know who's out there', 'I'm scared, worried about kids', 'It's a scary thing, I'm shaken', 'It scares me, that's crazy', 'scared, very scared, it's too close too home'.

Sensational stories involved famous persons, or individuals considered to be notable in the community, such as athletes, actors, politicians, entertainers, musicians, and prominent community members. In addition, although rare, sensational stories also included stories that appeared to be comical or humorous in some way. Sensational stories included robberies that involved strange items (such as shrimp, eyeglasses, farm tractors, liquor or booze, g-strings, pennies, kitchen sink, windows, etc.) or involved video of incident(s), dramatic arrests or takedowns, helicopter footage, victim(s) on stretchers or being attended to by paramedics, and stories that were described as 'bizarre', 'wild', 'unbelievable', and 'high drama'.

Presentations of outrage/sympathy involved crime stories that provided words, comments, or video that conveyed the message of outrage toward the crime or sympathy toward the victim.

Presentation of outrage/sympathy was measured through explicit comments made by interview subjects, news anchor/reporters, or by video displaying emotional responses such as crying, yelling, or visual dejection (such as slumping over, hands on head, head buried under hands, etc.). Although the audience might feel sympathy for a person who was victimized, only stories with a clear example of sympathy were considered. For instance, sympathy was displayed by the statements such as '[crime occurred in an] area filled with small children, it's sickening', 'it is a tragedy', '[victim] didn't deserve this', 'sad for victim and family', 'didn't deserve', 'it breaks my heart', and words employed such as 'devastated', 'sickening', 'upsetting', 'dismayed', 'grief stricken', 'emotional', 'hurt', 'mourned', 'upset', 'overwhelmed', 'shaken', 'troubling', and 'shocked'. Sympathy would also be presented by coverage of a funeral (memorial) or a visible display of crying or anguish by relatives, friends, and community members. Outrage included the use of the words: 'brutal', 'disturbing', 'horrifying', 'cold-blooded', 'savage', 'angry', 'deplorable', 'heinous', and 'gruesome'. In addition, outrage was presented in public protests against crime or suspect(s), which included yelling, fists raised in the air, or screaming at the offender/suspect. In stories that presented outrage/sympathy, the specific reason was documented on the code sheet to provide verification. Nevertheless, a limitation was the subjectivity in deciding the meaning or definition of words or quotes within the presentation of fear, sensationalism, and outrage/sympathy. Consequently, the coder recorded words and quotes onto the code sheet to be as consistent as possible and to provide the opportunity for verification.

Proactive Police Response

Finally, police response was coded as proactive or non-proactive. Proactive stories involved the police actively seeking a suspect, which was verified through adjectives describing the work by the police, providing information about a reward, police chase, actively searching in a video caption, SWAT team activity, and the police actively seeking the public's help in solving the crime.

Findings

There were 108 stories involving sex crime in the newscasts. Detroit newscasts presented 34 (31.5 per cent) sex crime stories, followed by Kitchener at 31 (28.7 per cent), Toronto at 23 (21.3 per cent), and Toledo at 20 (18.5 per cent). Sex crime could be divided into several types, which included child molestation with 42 stories, sexual assault/ rape with 54, indecent exposure with four stories, voyeurism with three stories, sex with minor with two stories, and child pornography with one story.

Table 1 presents the conditional distributions for sex crime by lead story, live story, creation of fear, outrage/sympathy, sensationalism, local/ national crime story, reporting of a firearm, reporting of a motive, interview, and stage of crime. The results indicated that lead story, live story, local/national crime story, use of interviews, and outrage/sympathy were not statistically related to sex crime stories. The presentation of sensationalism, presentation of fear, reporting of a firearm, presentation of motive, and stage of crime were statistically related to sex crime stories.

Sex crime stories were significantly related to the presentation of fear in newscasts ($\chi^2 = 19.82$, $p < .01$). For example, 26.9 per cent of sex crime stories presented fear, while only 11.6 per cent of non-sex crime stories presented fear. Closer scrutiny revealed three characteristics in the presentation of fear in sex crime stories. First, female community members were the primary interview subjects. The statements provided the impetus for the feelings of unease within the community, primarily among female residents.

The impression given was that women were not safe in their neighbourhoods or homes. Second, compared to other crimes, the police were more likely to give the public a warning or ask the public to be on alert. Third, sex offenders were portrayed as being unable or unwilling to stop

Table 1 Descriptive Characteristics of Sex Crime Stories and Non-sex Crime Stories

	SEX CRIME STORIES, %	NON-SEX CRIME STORIES, %
STORY CHARACTERISTICS		
Canadian story	50.00	44.20
American story	50.00	55.80
Large market story	52.80	59.30
Small market story	47.20	40.70
Lead story	10.20	9.30
Live story	13.00	14.30
Local story	83.30	76.80
Interview	38.00	39.10
Firearm reported**	8.30	27.70
Length of story (mean)	50.24	52.59
STAGE OF CRIME**		
Pre-arrest	30.60	52.60
Arrest	20.40	26.70
Court	36.10	16.90
Disposition	13.00	3.90
LATENT CHARACTERISTICS		
Fear presented**	26.90	11.60
Outrage/sympathy presented	23.10	27.30
Sensationalism presented**	18.50	39.10
Motive reported*	3.70	20.60
Proactive police response	45.60	33.60

*$p < .05$.
**$p < .01$.

their behaviour, which implied that they were more dangerous than other offenders.

Sex crime stories were related to the presentation of sensationalism (χ^2 = 17.57, p < .01). For instance, 18.5 per cent of sex crime stories were sensational, compared to 39.1 per cent for non-sex crime stories. For a variety of reasons, sex crime stories were less likely to be sensational. One possible reason was that crimes involving sex were newsworthy regardless of the sensational nature of the event. In other words, sex crime was inherently sensational without the use of verbs or adjectives to enhance the incident, which were employed by reporters/anchors in other types of crimes. Secondly, sex crime stories were more likely to present fear, which might preclude the use of sensationalism as a selling point for the story.

Sex crime stories were statistically related to the reporting of firearms (χ^2 = 19.07, p < .01). For example, only 8.3 per cent of sex crime stories reported a firearm(s) compared to 27.7 percent for non-sex crime stories. This finding was not surprising as many sex crime stories revolved around molestation of young children (where weapons were not employed) and cases of statutory rape in which weapons were also not employed.

Sex crime stories were significantly related to the reporting of motives (χ^2 = 18.00, p < .01). Only 3.7 per cent of sex crime stories reported a motive, while 12.3 per cent of non-sex crime stories reported a motive. Overall, motives were rarely employed in crime newscasts; however, motives were even less likely to be reported in sex crime stories. Nevertheless, the only motive that was employed for sex crimes was that the crime was related to sexual desire. For example, one female community member claimed: 'I would be hurt, I would be devastated. The most I would have on my mind is revenge because it is sad that you have to go out here and rape a teenage girl to

get satisfied' (McDaniel, 2000a). Essentially, rape was equated with sex rather than power, control, violence, and/or domination. Not one sex crime story used experts to help explain the incidents; the interviews relied primarily on the police and community members. In some cases, family members of suspects and defence lawyers were employed to attack credibility of the victim. The only time that a rape counsellor was even mentioned involved a story in which the rape crisis director's son was accused of sexual assault. The realties of rape and the effects on victims, family members, and the community were not even discussed. News reports employed sex crime stories as a means to disturb and upset viewers, not to educate or inform viewers about the reality of sex crime in contemporary society.

Stage of crime was statistically related to sex crime stories (χ^2 = 46.41, p < .01). The results indicated that 30.6 per cent of sex crime stories were reported in the pre-arrest stage, compared to 52.6 per cent of non-sex crime stories. In the arrest stage, 20.4 per cent were sex crime stories, while 26.7 per cent were non-sex crimes stories. In the court stage, 36.1 per cent were sex crime stories compared to 16.9 per cent for non-sex crime stories. In the disposition stage, 13 percent were sex crime stories, while 3.9 per cent were non-sex crime stories. Clearly, sex crime stories increased their proportion in each stage of crime when compared to other types of crimes.

[. . .]

Interestingly, when compared to homicide, robbery, and assault, sex crime stories were more likely to appear in the later stages of the criminal justice system. There were three significant dimensions of this finding that require further discussion. First, in the disposition stage, sex crimes involved the release of potentially dangerous sex offenders. One particularly virulent case involved Peter Whitmore, a convicted pedophile, whose release from prison captured the attention of both the Kitchener and Toronto media outlets. Each day stories focused on how the police were dealing with his release, community outrage, community meetings, and eventually ended with Whitmore violating parole and being arrested. Whitmore's case exemplified the debate about public notification of sex offenders and portrayed the corrections system as ineffective and inadequate.

Second, questioning the credibility of the victim was a prominent feature in sex crimes stories that appeared in the court stage. Victims were often relegated to secondary status and defence lawyers openly questioned the victims' actions or behaviours. In contrast, defence lawyers were rarely employed in other non-sex crime stories. There were three cases that highlighted this finding, which included the Ronald Archer–Michael Schmidt case, the so-called 'sex diary' scandal, and the River Rouge football scandal.

The Kitchener-Waterloo newscast provided extensive coverage of the Ronald Archer–Michael Schmidt sexual assault case. Fifty-three year old high school teacher Ronald Archer was accused and ultimately convicted of sexually abusing a former high school student named Michael Schmidt (age 18). There were ten stories that covered the trial, and throughout the story, Schmidt's (who was 14 at the time of the abuse) credibility was broadly questioned. For instance, prosecution witnesses suggested that 'he was lying', that it was an extortion attempt, the daughter of the suspect even claimed: 'Schmidt was moody, smoking drugs and worked for the family after the abuse allegedly occurred' (Hansen, 2000a). Throughout the coverage, the impetus was placed on the victim; however, the story shifted when Archer was found guilty and sentenced to four years in prison. For the first time, Archer was labelled as a 'sexual predator' and the victim's family members came forward for support. After the trial, Michael Schmidt remarked, 'sexual abuse victims, can

come forward, they can be believed . . . we finally got justice' (Hansen, 2000b).

Similarly, in Detroit newscasts, three stories involved the so-called 'sex diary scandal', in which two teenagers were accused of statutory rape of a 14-year-old girl. These stories focused on a defence claim that the 'sex diary' written by the victim was inaccurate and was further labelled as 'fiction' (Collura, 2002a). The defence lawyer claimed that the diary 'read more like a Danielle Steel novel', and further claimed that the victim engaged in sex with 22 boys and clearly had not been taken advantage of by his client (McDaniel, 2002). Furthermore, another story focused on the prosecutor who wanted the public (especially teenagers) to be aware of laws regarding the age of consent. The prosecutor suggested that maybe the law should be changed and several teenagers interviewed claimed that they could make their own decisions about sex (Collura, 2002b). Essentially, the victim was minimized, as the foci of the story was the debate about legal age of consent for sexual relations.

Correspondingly, the River Rouge High School football scandal was reported in Detroit newscasts. This case involved four black teenagers who were star football players for River Rouge High School. The victim in this case was rarely mentioned and the assumption presented was that she was 'lying' about the incident. The story was framed as controversial, as the focus was on whether the suspects should be allowed to play football. Although rape is a serious offence, the focus of one story was entirely on an important football game in which the suspects played and were described as 'heroes on the field'. The reporter claimed that there was 'overwhelming support for the boys'. Several spectators loudly supported the decision to let the 'boys' play football because 'futures were on the line' (Bell, 2000). Essentially, the victim was neglected in the story and school supporters openly questioned her credibility (even though facts were not presented).

Despite the similarities between the stories, there was one notable difference. The River Rouge case involved African American suspects. Their demeanour, appearance, and portrayals were quite different than cases involving white teenagers accused of statutory rape. The River Rouge suspects were shown in court with 'street' clothes, one boy was sleeping, one was yawning, and two boys were looking toward their feet (McDaniel, 2000b). In contrast, white suspects were shown in suits and ties, with the lawyer directly in front speaking for his clients, while the suspects looked directly at the judge (Collura, 2002a; McDaniel, 2002). The impression that the viewer might receive is that the River Rouge suspects were not taking the charges seriously, while the white suspects looked 'respectable' and serious in their demeanour. Nevertheless, both cases involved 'victim blaming' because culpability was placed on the victim rather than the suspect(s).

Discussion/Conclusion

Media pundits often suggest that 'sex sells', images of sexuality are frequently utilized to sell products and to attract audiences. There is, however, considerable debate regarding the amount of coverage that sex crime receives within the news media. In this study, sex crime accounted for approximately 10 per cent of all crime stories. Interestingly, it appeared that sex crime stories were less sensational than robbery, homicide, and assault stories. This unexpected finding might be the result of how sensationalism was measured in this study. Although measurement of sensationalism might be a limitation, an alternative explanation is rooted in how sex crimes are framed. Essentially, sex crime stories do not need to be sensational or be sensationally portrayed to entice or attract an audience. Crimes of a sexual

nature are inherently newsworthy because they are framed in ways that encourage fear, and thus, the primary frame employed in sex crime stories is fear or danger.

Fear of crime is a dominant discourse in news reports (Altheide, 2002). The media's impact on fear levels is frequently debated, with many studies claiming that the media increases fear among audience members. Interestingly, many feminists argue that women's fear of crime is enhanced by media constructions of victimization (Madriz, 1997). This may be important in understanding why females are more likely to report higher levels of fear than males (Dowler, 2003; Stanko, 1992). This discrepancy 'has led some to assume that women's higher levels of fear are linked to the horrors of rape, which may be combined with other crimes' (Carmody, 1998). Nevertheless, the portrayal of victimization can instill frightening and terrifying images for many women. These images are often based in the myths that women are in constant danger, especially by strangers and in the public arena. For example, in a study on the impact of the media on women's level of fear, female respondents reported that the media increased anxieties and fear of crime, while having little or no impact in decreasing those fears (Dobash, Schlesinger, Dobash & Weaver, 1998). Within the literature, the link between media consumption and fear of crime is not clearly established (Dowler, 2003). It is salient to note that the news media employ a 'lens of fear' (Altheide, 2002, p. 175). The 'concerns, risks, and dangers are magnified and even distorted by this lens. Caution has given way to avoidance. Rarity has been replaced by typicality. And the focus of the media attention has taken a toll on our ability to see clearly' (Altheide, 2002, p. 175). Within this study, it was clear that sex crime stories embraced this 'lens of fear' by magnifying audience concerns about victimization. This was especially true when stories contained a so-called 'innocent' victim(s), in which the audience could readily identify and have sympathy with.

Conversely, sex crime stories without the 'innocent' victim are framed in a different manner. The principal frame in these stories is victim credibility or accountability. According to Altheide (2002), in order to engage the audience, the media attempt to induce an emotional response, which can be in the form of anger, pity, sorrow, fear, or compassion. The news producer foresees and fits the proper frame around the story to elicit an expected emotional response. Consequently, the status of the victim as deserving or innocent is formed. The most deserving victims are the most helpless and innocent, as the audience feels more of an attachment (Altheide, 2002). As a result, in sex crime stories in which the credibility or culpability of the victim is questioned, the frame of fear is replaced by skepticism and victim blaming. This was similar to 'myths surrounding domestic violence. Responsibility for domestic violence was shifted away from its perpetrators, and blame was assigned to the victim' (Carmody, 1998).

In conclusion, unlike other crime stories, victim credibility was often questioned as stories unfolded. Essentially, the victim was minimized with an increase in coverage. This was an important finding, as it provided some validity to the notion that sexual assault is underreported based on the stigma that victims endure. Moreover, it appeared that fear was a vital component in the presentation of sex crime. Stories that presented fear were approximately five times more likely to be sex crime stories. The perception is that sexual predators are lurking behind every corner and no one is safe, especially women and children. Sexual assault is a serious crime that deserves media attention. The coverage, however, was not focused on practical solutions to the threat of sexual assault or even the reality of sexual assault. The primary motivation was not to inform viewers, but to scare the audience. Paradoxically, this tactic can also create high interest among viewers and ultimately higher ratings for newscasts, which in turn results in little change or variation in newscast presentation of sex crime.

Note

1. Each market was taped daily with a VCR timer. Taping of episodes in Kitchener began on 20 October 2000 and taping stopped on 2 February 2001 when 100 episodes were taped. The taping of Detroit, Toronto, and Toledo markets began on 8 October 2000 and ended on 24 December 2000 with 76, 73, and 71 episodes respectively. Some days were missed due to programs being delayed or pre-empted by election or sports coverage. In order to have an equal amount of episodes, taping resumed 9 May 2002 and ended on 7 June 2002 when each market acquired 100 episodes.

References

Altheide, D.L. (2002). *Creating fear: News and the construction of crisis.* New York: Aldine De Gruyter.

Bell, T. (News Director). (2000, October 20). UPN *Detroit action news* [Television broadcast]. Detroit, MI: WKBD.

Benedict, H. (1992). *Virgin or vamp: How the press covers sex crimes.* New York: Oxford University Press.

Berg, B.L. (2001). *Qualitative research methods for the social sciences.* Needham Heights, MA: Allyn and Bacon.

Carmody, D. (1998). Mixed messages: Images of domestic violence on reality television. In M. Fishman & G. Cavender (Eds), *Entertaining crime: Television reality programs* (pp. 159–74). New York: Aldine De Gruyter.

Carringella-MacDonald, S. (1998). The relative visibility of rape cases in national popular magazines. *Violence Against Women, 4(1),* 62–80.

Collura, D. (News Director). (2002a, May 20). *Local 4 news* [Television broadcast]. Detroit, MI: WDIV.

———. (News Director). (2002b, May 23). *Local 4 news* [Television broadcast]. Detroit, MI: WDIV.

Cuklanz, L.M. (1996). *Rape on trial: How the mass media construct legal reform and social change*. Philadelphia: University of Pennsylvania.

Dobash, R.E., Schlesinger, P., Dobash, R., & Weaver, K. (1998). Crimewatch UK: Women's interpretations of televised violence. In M. Fishman & G. Cavender (Eds), *Entertaining crime: Television reality programs* (pp. 37–58). New York: Aldine De Gruyter.

Dowler, K. (2003). Media consumption and public attitudes toward crime and justice: The relationship between fear of crime, punitive attitudes, and perceived police effectiveness. *Journal of Criminal Justice and Popular Culture, 10*(2), 109–26.

Drechsel, R., Netteburg, K., & Aborisade, B. (1980). Community size and newspaper reporting of local courts. *Journalism Quarterly, 59*(1), 71–78.

Entman, R. (1993). Framing: Towards clarification of a fractured paradigm. *Journal of Communication, 43*(4), 51–58.

Goffman, E. (1974). *Frame analysis: An essay on the organization of experience*. New York: Harper and Row.

Greer, C. (2003). Sex crime in the media: Press representations in Northern Ireland. In P. Mason (Ed.), *Criminal visions: Media representations of crime and justice* (pp. 90–115). Devon, UK: Willan.

Hamlin, J.E. (1988). Who's the victim? Women, control, and consciousness. *Women's Studies International Forum, 11*(3), 223–33.

Hansen, B. (News Director). (2000a, October 24). *News at six* [Television broadcast]. Kitchener, Ontario, Canada: CKCO.

———. (News Director). (2000b, October 27). *News at six* [Television broadcast]. Kitchener, Ontario, Canada: CKCO.

Howitt, D. (1998). *Crime, the media and the law*. New York: John Wiley and Sons.

Los, M., & Charmard, S. (1997). Selling newspapers or educating the public? Sexual violence in the media. *Canadian Journal of Criminology, 39*(3), 293–328.

Madriz, E. (1997). Images of criminals and victims: A study on women's fear and social control. *Gender and Society, 11*, 342–56.

McCormick, C. (1995). *Constructing danger: The mis/representation of crime in the news*. Halifax, Nova Scotia, Canada: Fernwood Publishing.

McDaniel, D. (News Director). (2000a, December 20). *Fox 2 news* [Television broadcast]. Detroit, MI: WJBK.

———. (News Director). (2000b, December 6). *Fox 2 news* [Television broadcast]. Detroit Ml: WJBK.

———. (News Director). (2002, May 22). *Fox 2 news* [Television broadcast]. Detroit, MI: WJBK.

Neuman, W.L. (2003). *Social research methods: Qualitative and quantitative approaches* (5th edn). Boston: Allyn and Bacon.

Soothill, K. (1991). The changing face of rape? *British Journal of Criminology, 31*(4), 383–92.

Soothill, K., & Grover, C. (1994). Marital rape in the news. *Journal of Forensic Psychiatry, 5*(3), 539–49.

Soothill, K., & Walby, S. (1991). *Sex crime in the news*. London: Routledge.

Stanko, E. (1992). The case of fearful women: Gender, personal safety and fear of crime. *Women and Criminal Justice, 4*(1), 117–35.

Tuchman, G. (1978). *Making news*. New York: The Free Press.

Voumvakis, S., & Ericson, R. (1984). *News accounts of attacks on women: A comparison of three Toronto newspapers*. Toronto, Ontario, Canada: University of Toronto.

Willis, E. (1994). Villains and victims. *Salmagundi, 101–102*, 68–78.

PART 3
Dialogue Box 3
Kiss and Tell

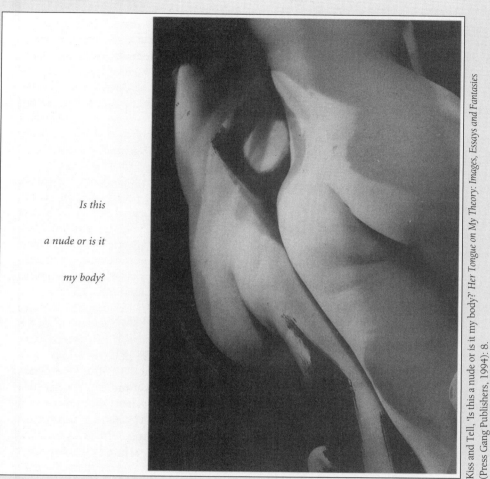

Is this

a nude or is it

my body?

Kiss and Tell, 'Is this a nude or is it my body?' *Her Tongue on My Theory: Images, Essays and Fantasies* (Press Gang Publishers, 1994): 8.

Critical Conversations: Discussion Questions

1. Health care, education, and mass media are important parts of our social structure. In what ways do they each influence our ideas about sexuality?

2. In, 'Stigma Management? The links between enacted stigma and teen pregnancy trends among gay, lesbian, and bisexual students in British Columbia', the authors position teen sexual activity as a form of 'stigma management'. What is meant by this concept? What other forms of stigma management do you notice in the chapter readings?

3. Morgan Holmes' article demonstrates the profound way that societal beliefs about gender and sexuality are used to transform our bodies. How else are our ideas of 'health' shaped by norms of gender and sexuality?

4. Youth sexuality has often been a topic of concern in Canadian society. Compare Adams' article in chapter 3 to Mitelman and Visser's account in chapter 7. What similarities, differences, and changes do you see in the concerns expressed in these articles?

5. Which topics relating to sexuality should be included in elementary, junior, and high school courses? Why?

6. What role does televised news play in constructing our norms of sexuality and gender?

Glossary

Intersex 'A general term used for a variety of conditions in which a person is born with a reproductive or sexual anatomy that doesn't seem to fit the typical definitions of female or male' (http://www.isna.org). These 'conditions' represent chromosomal and other variations of physiology that, while rare, occur throughout the human population and are not always known at birth.

LBGTQ An acronym standing for Lesbian, Bisexual, Gay, Trans-identified, and Queer, used to indicate the complexities and diversities of the community previously known simply as 'gay and lesbian'.

Sexual Health Education (SHE) Educational endeavours designed to enhance students' knowledge about sexual health issues, to help them acquire the skills necessary to avoid sexual health problems, and to contribute to the creation of an overall social environment of increased sexual health.

Social institution Important and longlasting elements of a society's social structure that enhance societal stability. Social institutions communicate and accomplish high consensus goals within a society such as child-rearing, governance, and the reproduction of labour. Widely recognized examples include the family, economy, politics, education, and religion.

Stigma A term coined by Canadian sociologist Erving Goffman (1922–82) to describe a trait, characteristic, or differentness of an individual or social group that is judged negatively by others. A stigma is a social attribution that discredits or devalues the judged individual or group.

PART IV

Mutually Constructing Knowledges: Sex, Gender, and Sexualities

Starting Points

1. How does your race and cultural background influence your sexuality?
2. What is 'homophobia'? How does homophobia affect your life?
3. Have you ever been introduced to someone and, based on their mannerisms, made an assessment of their sexual orientation that you later found to be false? Why do you think this happens?
4. Thinking about everything you've read so far in this collection, what are the three most important things you have learned about sexuality and sexualities studies?

Introduction

As you read this anthology, you may have noticed that the idea of sexuality is a bit elusive, in that sexuality tends to be defined differently depending on who is defining it. Sexuality, this basic way of describing what we do and desire in our intimate lives, means 'different' things to 'different' people at 'different' times and in 'different' places. Sexuality, then, is not just something we can think of as innate, timeless, or unchanging. Sexuality is a set of experiences that is fundamentally connected to our social context.

The connectedness between society and our notions of sexuality is demonstrated by the variety of approaches to the topic taken by the authors in this anthology. Some authors explore discourses about specific sexual behaviours (including Alan Hunt and Bruce Curtis in chapter 3). In other instances, the regulation of certain sexual identities and relationships is explored (including by Gayle Rubin in chapter 1). Still other authors examine how specific communities or subcultures respond to and develop sexual norms (including Frederick Engels in chapter 1). Of one thing we can be certain: meanings and experiences of sexuality will continue to change.

Keeping in mind this inherent changeability, what then can we take away from our study of this field? There are two themes in particular that organize the chapter selections in this final part of the collection. First, it is impossible (and quite misleading) to separate meanings and experiences of sexuality from their social context. Second, our understandings of sex, sexuality, and gender are mutually reinforcing notions. Our ideas are mutually reinforcing in that each of these experiences shape and inform the others (what we think about sex and sexualities influences what we think about gender and vice versa). As the collection concludes with these chapters, we will elaborate a bit on these themes before discussing the particular authors in this section.

As per the first theme mentioned above, inquiries into the nature, meanings, and experiences of sexualities need to be conducted with reference to the broader social context in which they occur. Indeed, sexuality, like all social processes and interactions, is necessarily connected to the organization of our society. As Juanne Nancarrow Clarke, a noted Canadian health scholar, writes ' . . . individual decision making must always be seen in the context of the social structure and of the constraints that impede the behaviours of the people placed in different locations in the social structure' (Clarke, 2008, p. 166). Following this understanding of the indivisibility of experience from social context, many sexualities studies scholars are drawn to intersectional analytical perspectives because even though we all 'have' a sexuality, we do not all consider or experience our sexuality in the same way. Think, for example, about your response to seeing a young, attractive straight couple cuddling at a restaurant. Think about your response if the cuddlers were a couple of senior citizens. Whose behaviour is more appropriate and why? The idea of intersectionality, first proposed by feminist activists and academics, refers to 'the combined effects of race, class, gender, religion, nationality, and other major social status in producing systematic advantages and disadvantages' (Lorber, 2005, p. 326). With this understanding in mind, we can see that experiences of sexuality vary—not just across time—but also across social groups within the same time period. What is more, this intersectional awareness also helps us understand the contested nature of discourses and experiences of sexuality. The intersectional realities of societies produce the dynamics that construct the meanings we have about sexual behaviours and identities. These meanings include the phenomenon of homophobia and its connection to gender norms (chapter 9), the various notions of appropriate sexuality within Canada's multicultural social groups (chapter 10), and the ways that social institutions count on and promote universal notions of sex, sexualities, and genders (chapter 11).

The second theme that runs through the articles in this concluding section is that the more we study sexualities, the more we come to realize that our understandings of sex, sexualities, and gender are experienced in intricate combination; that is, they are mutually reinforcing. In the Starting Points Questions, you were asked if you had met someone new and misread their sexuality based on their mannerisms. We form impressions about sexuality through our reading of a person's gender. Not just whether they are a man or a woman but what *kind* of man or woman they are. If their ways of speaking, moving, and interacting conform to our expectations of masculinity or femininity, we are likely to understand their sexuality as similarly normative, as heterosexual. If this new person does not conform to gender expectations, often they may be perceived as homosexual. Such assessments, whether accurate or not, speak to the power of norms of gender to organize our lives. As demonstrated throughout these final articles, standards of sex, sexuality, and gender together combine to powerfully influence our behaviours and our sense of ourselves within society.

In chapter 9, 'Homophobia and Its Implications for Everyone', the assembled authors specifically explore the organizing power of the prospect of sexual misrecognition, through the reading of norms of sex and gender, discussed above. Homophobia, classically thought of as the fear of homosexuals has been more recently reconceived as the fear of being misrecognized as, or thought to be, gay. (Kimmel, 2008).

The risk of sexual and gender misrecognition has proven to be a fearful motivator, especially among young males in North America. Phyllis Dalley and David Campbell explore the organization of heteronormative discourses and their effects on the lives and sexual identities of students at a Franco-Ontarian high school. In 'Wearing Pink as a Stand Against Bullying: Why We Need to Say More', I put forward a contextual discourse analysis of the media response to a local anti-bullying campaign organized by students in a Nova Scotia high school. I argue that mainstream media cannot be relied upon to change discriminatory attitudes about sexuality and masculinity as such media is a prominent agent in the construction of these attitudes. The role of insults in the phenomenon of homophobia is specifically explored by Tyler Brown and Kevin Alderson. In their study, Brown and Alderson investigate the relationship between participants' belief in traditional heterosexual male sexual identity and the use of homosexual insults. The authors explore the purpose of these insults in relation to group male bonding and the stigmatization of outsiders, thus complicating easy understandings of homophobia as hatred of gays. This stigmatization is also explored by Tia Dafnos. Dafnos reviews the legal proceedings related to the human rights complaint filed by Azmi Jubran against the Vancouver School Board for not protecting him against homophobic taunting and bullying throughout his high school years. In her article, Dafnos models a variety of feminist conceptions of harm and examines their utility in understanding the issues at stake in this case.

The second theme of intersectionality is further highlighted in chapter 10, 'Racialization, Immigration, and the Politics of Sexualities'. As established in the previous chapter, there are competing discourses about sexuality within our society. These discourses take shape as power, knowledge, and tradition organize our communities and identities. Competing cultural knowledge of sexual and gendered norms continues to enliven and complicate Canadians' experiences today. David Newhouse describes how Aboriginal peoples' traditional knowledges claim sexuality as an experience of magic and joy. Khosro Refale Shirpak, Eleanor Maticka-Tyndale, and Maryam Chinichian use an interview-based analysis to explore Iranian immigrants' views of sexuality. Interviewees perceived a significant divide between their values and prominent discourses and behaviours in Canada. The authors explore this divide in terms of government initiatives to bridge cultural differences as new Canadians integrate with Canadian society. These competing notions are especially provocative as our communities mix and change through marriage and other similar relationships. Susan Brigham and Catherine Baillie Abidi examine the intersections of gender, race, class, nationality, and education as they are present in the technology-aided migration of women to Atlantic Canada through online matchmaking agencies. The chapter concludes with an analysis of the confluence of homophobia and racism in the experience of visibly ethnic communities in Canadian society. In 'Double Jeopardy: Building Strong Communities to Fight Homophobia and Racism', journalist Andrea Zoe Aster explores the lives of variously racialized members of LGBT communities.

Much like the evolving field of sexualities studies itself, the anthology closes without definitive conclusions. However, the focus on the mutually reinforcing discourses of sexuality, sex and gender is continued within the selections in chapter 11, 'Sex and Gender: Boundaries, Connections, and Meanings in the Context of Change'.

Each of the concluding essays revisits or reinvigorates the issues, theories, and debates found throughout the anthology. These include the influence of Marxist, feminist, and post-structural approaches, the changing norms of sexual conduct within Canadian society over time, the influence of our prominent social institutions on these norms, the different ways in which members of different social groups, classes, and genders (the intersectional approach) experience sexuality and the general inextricability of sexuality from our larger social context. In 'Harassment Based on Sex: Protecting Social Status in the Context of Gender Hierarchy', Jennifer Berdahl reframes our understanding of sexual harassment as fundamentally connected to gender status. Gender, age, and authority are the focus of sociologist Rebecca Raby's focus group–based analysis of secondary students' attitudes toward school dress codes and appropriate self-presentation. Raby's work reveals the subtleties of these students' participation in, and resistance to, gender and sexual regulation. The intersections of gender and sexuality are also the subject of Ajnesh Prasad's article. Prasad explores the insufficiency of 'scientific' definitions of sex and gender in light of the refusal of a Vancouver women's advocacy group to train male-to-female transsexual Kimberly Nixon for crisis line work. The article demonstrates the inadequacy of contemporary conceptions of sex, gender, and sexualities in terms of accounting for transsexual experience. The last article in the collection is 'What's to Fear: Calling Homophobia into Question', by sociologist and education theorist Didi Khayatt. Khayatt's article makes use of personal anecdotes from her time as a high school teacher in Northern Ontario and Michel Foucault's conceptions of discourse and power to provoke questions about everyday understandings of sex, gender, and sexuality. As the final article in the anthology, this piece usefully brings the collection's considerations back to the familiar space of the classroom.

Our classrooms are a space where all these issues come together in unique and provocative ways every time students and educators meet. They are also the space where together, we strive to generate understandings across the powerful differences of sex, gender, sexuality, race, class, ability, and age that organize our experience and, often, keep us at a distance. At the core, the field of sexualities studies, as various and changing as it is, is about the pursuit of greater understanding about our subject across these differences. This collection, and the work of the scholars assembled within it, is offered in the service of this goal.

References

Clarke, Juanne Nancarrow. 2008. *Health, Illness, and Medicine in Canada* (5th edn). Don Mills, ON: Oxford University Press.

Kimmel, Michael. 2008. *Guyland: The Perilous World Where Boys Become Men*. New York: HarperCollins Publishers.

Lorber, Judith. 2005. *Gender Inequality: Feminist Theories and Politics*. Los Angeles, CA: Roxbury Publishing, Co.

9 Homophobia and Its Implications for Everyone

Wearing Pink as a Stand Against Bullying: Why We Need to Say More

Diane Naugler

The first day of school is often an anxious and exciting time for students and parents alike. These tensions are heightened for students entering a new school. The whole 'back to school' phenomenon is invested with many consumer, friendship, and educative possibilities. On 5 September 2007, the first day of school in Nova Scotia, Canada, a grade 9 student arrived for his first day at Central Kings Rural High School. He was wearing a pink shirt. At some point during the day the often gruelling gendered dynamics of the high school's social terrain were made specifically clear to him. As reported just over a week later in the Halifax *Chronicle Herald*, a group of older male students mocked him, threatened him, and called him 'a homosexual' (Fairclough, 2007a, p. B5).[1] I suggest that this particular incident is exemplary, but not extraordinary. North American children, especially boys, have been subjected to threats of violence by older peers for generations. These threats are a mechanism of gendered socialization that has long functioned to inculcate normative masculinity for bullies and victims alike. While there is considerable contemporary public discourse on bullying, its victims, and its perpetrators, little at all is said of the productive link between bullying and normative masculinity. As I will elaborate herein, in the discursive service of normativity, the productive link between bullying and masculinity is most 'unremarkable'.

It is no surprise that a pink T-shirt worn by a male adolescent in a small Nova Scotia town functioned as a catalyst for abuse and for bullying. The reasons for such abuse are no mystery. Within the gendered stereotypes of contemporary North American society, pink on a boy is at once shorthand for effeminacy and homosexuality, a disruption of common sense gendered attributes, and an invitation for peer group policing. Although it is tempting to view the bullies in this particular case as simply 'bad kids', I will argue that their behaviour was not anomalous. Rather, they are typical Canadian high school boys. Society has afforded them ample social capital through which to legitimate their authority (Olweus, 1993) as adolescent male gender police. [. . .] Moreover, following Michel Foucault's (2001) conception of discourses 'as practices that systematically form the objects of which they speak' (p. 49), we must consider the epistemological work of these gendered representations of bullying as not only instructive to social subjects but, simultaneously, constructive of them.

What made this fairly routine incident of bullying in a rural Nova Scotia high school remarkable was the response of two grade 12 students who witnessed the harassment. David Shepherd and Travis Price were not willing to let this bullying behaviour go unchallenged in their school. As male seniors, they rightly surmised that they could encourage others in their school to stand up to bullying. As Shepherd commented on their motivations, 'It's my last year. I've stood around too long and I wanted to do something' (Fairclough, 2007a). Both boys acknowledge having been targets of bullies in the past.[2] Within two days they organized a school-wide response. Through the encouragement of Price, Shepherd, and their friends, approximately half of the school's 830 students wore items of pink clothing to school that Friday.[3] For that day at least, these students changed the gendered rules. By refusing to explicitly or tacitly accept the bullying and intimidation of a younger student and by encouraging others not to do so, Shepherd and Price exposed the injustices of the routine tyrannies of adolescent masculinity and the fallacious association of pink with homosexuality in the contemporary discourses of North American masculinity.

The response to this incident of bullying is also remarkable in that it has been the subject of extensive media coverage, both locally and throughout the province. As I have read this coverage, I have found myself wondering why the narrowly conceived version of masculinity that is at the core of the precipitating incident of bullying is never explored in the many news items about Price and Shepherd's activism, the grassroots response, and the popularity of their campaign throughout provincial schools and beyond. Certainly, and justifiably, the feel-good story here is about 'good kids' doing 'good things'. Shepherd and Price should be commended for their concern and most especially for their actions. However, in the silence about the stereotypes of masculinity and sexuality found at the heart of such incidents, an important educative moment has been lost. Media, government, and educators do not see—or knowingly ignore—how a narrow ideology of aggressive masculinity is promulgated through a myriad of everyday bullying incidents that function through the denigrated and feminized symbol of pink.

This article offers a contextual analysis of the print media coverage of this story. [. . .] I conducted a comprehensive analysis of the reportage in the Halifax *Chronicle Herald*, the most widely circulated daily newspaper in the Atlantic region. I have limited the scope of my analysis to the 30-day period from 13 September 2007, the date of the first report in the *Chronicle Herald*, to 13 October 2007. This period provides a concise overview of the trajectory of this news story as it developed from a local interest piece to the province-wide Pink Campaign [. . .] in the paper's national edition. The findings of this analysis are considered through recent feminist and social constructionist scholarship on gender and sexuality that positions gender as an interactional (Ferguson, 2007; Pascoe, 2003, 2007) and constructed (Butler 1993, 1999; Warren 2003) identity and status.

Thus situated, I move my analysis to the question of why we need to say more about bullying. Specifically, our scholarship must resist the normalizing discursive production knowledge that only situates public and popular discussions of bullying behaviours as a problem of specific individuals or institutional contexts (Olweus, 1978;

Cullen, 1999; Xin, 2002) and therefore renders the productive connection between bullying and normative masculinity 'unremarkable'. So conceived, *unremarkability* is a discursively encouraged set of silences. I use the concept of unremarkability to describe the discursive facilitation of the social reproduction of embodied normativities (such as gender) through the production of a lack of attention to all the curious, diverse, and utterly common ways our bodies, and ourselves, are produced through these very norms.

To this end, I compare the condemnation of adolescents who would bully a young male teen for wearing a pink shirt to other examples of the institutionalized gender colour codes that situate pink as unmasculine and effeminate. In this comparison I draw on a range of sociological scholarship that queries the relationship between hegemonic masculinity (Connell, 1987) and North American sports cultures (Carlisle Duncan & Messner, 1993). Through these perspectives, I explore male-on-male adolescent bullying as an aspect of a continuum of ritualized masculine accomplishments that build gendered solidarity (Goffman, 1963) and are authorized and gain coherence through an institutionalized masculine social imaginary (Warren, 2003). In summary, the aim of this analysis is to demonstrate the sexist and homophobic discursive workings of male-on-male physical bullying as these practices continue to centrally anchor the production of normative masculinities.

What Is Missing in the Move from 'Wear Pink' to the 'Pink Campaign'

Fairclough's original September 13 news story about David Shepherd and Travis Price's response to this incident published in the Halifax *Chronicle Herald* spawned one of the paper's most successful stories of fall 2007. The *Chronicle Herald* printed an additional seven news items, two editorials, two opinion pieces, two pink-themed political cartoons, and published 15 letters to the editor on this story in a one-month period; these items were accompanied by eight photos. The news articles alone filled over 111 column inches. Additionally, *Chronicle Herald* news director Dan Leger reported that more than 200 000 people logged on to the newspaper's website to read the original and subsequent stories (Leger, 2007, A7).

From the outset however, this coverage misses the educative opportunity to acknowledge and understand why male-on-male bullying is so common in contemporary educational settings. The newspaper coverage is framed as a story about 'good kids doing good things' and subsequently develops into a story about a 'pink bandwagon' against bullying (Meek, 2007, A15; Moore, 2007, A13). The most expansive description of the bullying that precipitated the Pink Campaign is found in the opening lines of Fairclough's (2007a) original story in the *Chronicle Herald*. He writes,

> Two students at Central Kings Rural High School fought back against bullying recently, unleashing a sea of pink after a new student was harassed and threatened when he showed up wearing a pink shirt. The grade 9 student arrived for the first day of school . . . and was set upon by a group of six to ten older students who mocked him, called him a homosexual for wearing pink and threatened to beat him up. (p. B5)

Over the life of this story, this description was eventually abbreviated as, presumably, the newspaper audience became familiar with the facts. By September 30, just a little over two weeks later, the incident was simply described as ' . . . standing up against the bullying of a younger student at their school' (Hits and misses, 2007, A12). A September 28 front-page aerial photo (which ran above the fold) by Cathy Von Kintzel (2007) pictured students and staff at Bible Hill Junior High School in Truro, Nova Scotia, clad in pink standing on their sports field in formation to spell P-I-N-K. This photo was not accompanied by any story at all, indicating that, at this point in the coverage, the framing of the story has become its truth and that standing up in pink had become an action that no longer needed explanation. As newspaper readers, we learned that to stand up in pink is to stand up to bullying.

What we do not learn, indeed what our attention is explicitly turned away from in the slippage between Fairclough's description to Von Kintzel's photo, are the sexualized and gendered ideologies central to this harassment. The deployment of supposed homosexuality as a slur and the fact that both victim and aggressors were male becomes 'unremarkable' and, therefore, unexamined and unchallenged. This falling away of the dynamics and ideologies of sexuality and gender that motivate such incidents of bullying is not random or insignificant; it is illustrative of the discursive workings of normativity. It is this falling away, or unremarkability, that protects (in this instance) normative masculinity from critical consideration. In this way the 'discourses and practices that produce subjects who are "normal", live "normality", and . . . who find it hard to imagine anything different' retain hegemonic legitimacy (Adams, 1997, p. 13).

Indeed, why this incident of bullying occurred was never held up for consideration in the press coverage. Just under eight column inches, or 7.2 per cent of the *Chronicle Herald* news coverage of this story, discussed the bullying incident that sparked Price and Shepherd's activism. This minimal amount of discussion did explicitly link 'pink' to violence. For example, a September 22 story on the spread of this campaign notes, '[b]ullies picked on a new Grade 9 student at Central Kings for wearing a pink shirt on the first day of school, then "got physical" with him the next day' (Graham, 2007, p. A8). However, such descriptions do not draw on an understanding of the role of male-on-male bullying in the production of (more) normative masculinities through aggressive sexism and homophobia. There is one dismissive mention of schoolyard knowledge that pink on a male means that he's gay (Fairclough, 2007a) but this knowledge is unexamined.

Moreover, it is the taken-for-granted knowledge of this gendered stereotype of emasculated sexuality in our broader popular culture that necessarily precludes such examination. This common sense stereotype is actually used in the *Chronicle Herald's* coverage. A September 25 article about a male school bus driver's support for the campaign was headlined, 'School bus driver turns pink too', with 'turns' used here as a not so subtle play on the contemporary vernacular of 'go gay' or 'turn gay' (Medel, 2007, B2). [. . .] It is discursively significant though that the feel good story of teens doing good things did not also spawn ancillary stories about the prevalence of bullying in schools, contemporary or recalled first-person testimonials, or, most importantly, analyses of the causes and consequences of male-on-male bullying. To do so would have made remarkable the everyday violence of our two gender ideology and the gendered dynamics through which our sexualities are policed within the discursive combination of these inattentions and attentions.

As I have demonstrated, it is not lack of knowledge of the sexist and homophobic pink stereotype that leads *Chronicle Herald* reporters and editors away from an analysis of why 'fag' and 'homo' are effective and common insults among adolescent boys. The new, pink-shirt-wearing male student at Central Kings Rural High was doubtless called some version of 'fag', 'faggot', 'fairy', or 'homo'; and he was called these names because, by wearing a pink shirt, he challenged an interactional boundary of teenage boys: Don't wear pink because 'real men' don't wear pink.

Considered discursively, these homophobic insults cannot be separated from the stereotypes and stigmatization of homosexuality that is commonplace in contemporary teenaged vernacular. As gender theorist Michael S. Kimmel (2008) writes, '[j]ust about every student [today] knows that the most common put-down in middle school and high school . . . is, "That's so gay."' Kimmel sees this phrase as evidence of how, '[t]he fear of being tainted with homosexuality [homophobia]—the fear of emasculation—has morphed into a generic put-down' (Kimmel, 2008, p. 190). This discursive trajectory also reveals the lingering androcentrism of contemporary Westernized cultures. In the teenage vernacular, '"gay" is a fairly common synonym for "stupid"' (Pascoe, 2007, p. 129). The word gay can refer to inanimate objects as well as people. In this way, a masculine-focused homophobia becomes a generic gender-, behaviour-, and object-crossing insult. The media coverage offers no analysis about why such specifically gendered and sexualized bullying occurs (primarily, but not exclusively in schools). Further, there is no consideration of the distinction between bullying someone because they are gay and, as in this case, bullying someone by calling them gay. I suggest that the absence of media discussion about these issues exists because such behaviours actually reinforce gender conformity among teenage boys and work to reproduce norms of masculinity that are valued in adult society. In the following section, I examine two specific examples of media representations in which 'pinkness' functions as a constitutive outside (Khayatt, 2006) to normative masculinity.

Real Men Don't Wear Pink or Pinking the Effeminate Other

Brandon Herritt wouldn't usually be caught dead wearing pink. Pink hair, however, is a whole different matter. The Grade 6 pupil was among almost all of the 70-member student body who showed up at East St. Margaret's Elementary School in Indian Harbour on Friday morning sporting pink . . . 'I don't really feel comfortable in pink clothes', said 11-year-old Brandon, who came up with the idea of dying his hair. (Jeffrey, 2007, p. AI)

Why is 11-year-old Brandon 'uncomfortable' wearing pink? Despite loosening gender stereotypes as represented by media offerings such as the cable television show *Queer Eye for the Straight Guy* (2003–2007) and the rise of female breadwinners, norms of masculinity have exhibited a tenacious resistance to change. As Pascoe (2003) observes, '[o]ver the past several decades . . . cultural understandings of women have grown consistently more liberal as women have gained status politically and socially, but there has not been a shift of the same magnitude for men' (p. 1423). In a society that organizes itself and whose members learn to identify themselves through a binary and oppositional set of gendered relations, changes to women's roles (one side of the gender binary) necessarily effect the social relations and expectations of masculinity (Pascoe, 2003). In the context of this cultural lag, or crisis, of masculinity, the experiences and dynamics of bullying during boyhood constitute an interesting ground for the analysis of the construction of the gendered identities of the next generation of men.

How boys learn to be men and on what grounds they are encouraged to constitute their masculinity is of vital political and social significance as North American hegemonic masculinity (Connell, 1987) is constituted in part through aggressive physicality. The violent circuit of identification and recognition that runs through the interactions of teenaged masculinity in North America needs explication before we can understand this bullying incident and the grassroots response at Central Kings High School. As summarized by Xin (2002),

. . . bullying is a form of aggression in which a student or group of students physically or verbally harasses a victim without provocation (Hazler, 1992). Physical bullying includes hitting, pushing, holding, and hostile gesturing, whereas verbal bullying includes threatening, humiliating, degrading, teasing, name-calling, put-downs, sarcasm, taunting, starving, sticking out the tongue, eye-rolling, silent treatment, manipulating friendship, and ostracizing. (p. 63)

There is a clear connection between male-on-male bullying in and around schools and the production of adolescent performance and imitation of hegemonic masculinity. [. . .]

In the context of North American schools, bullying often works in combination with other interactional and institutional discourses to produce a normative masculinity

. . . that places an assertive physical presence and a sense of superiority at its core; entails conflictual relations, whether that be physical ones as found in the realms of sport, or disciplinary conflicts as found in school; and a notion of masculinity that assumes a public and aspirational place for men. (Warren, 2003, p. 9)

[. . .] That bullying is a central tactic in the acquisition of normative conceptions of masculinity is evidenced through the gendered significance of bullying activities and the gender of bullies (Ferguson, 2007). Contemporary research on bullying across disciplines and methodologies concludes that bullying is predominantly an activity used by males to police other males; that

is, 'boys are more likely to be both bullies and victims' of bullying (Xin, 2002, p. 65).[4]

In her 2007 article, Pascoe reports on her ethnographic observation of the social scene at a California high school. Throughout her observation, she encountered the ritualized use of verbal labelling of boys and behaviours as 'faggy' or 'fags' and the joking imitation of exaggerated fag traits such as lisping, bent wrists, and feigned sexual acts. Pascoe concluded that this 'fag discourse is the interactional process through which boys name and repudiate' an abject, unmasculine identity (p. 126). In her observations, she found that '[a] boy could get called a fag for exhibiting any sort of behaviour defined as non-masculine (although not necessarily behaviours aligned with femininity) . . . being stupid, incompetent, dancing, caring too much about clothing, being too emotional or expressing interest (sexual or platonic) in other guys' (p. 129). Pascoe, like Kimmel (2008), situates these put downs as examples of the routine and ritualized gender policing that occurs among adolescent males.

This bonding through homophobic repudiation is commonly observed among adolescent males in North America. As feminist author and bisexual activist Jennifer Baumgardner (2007) writes of boy culture in the 1980s and 1990s,

. . . at Fargo South High, when the popular—and, it goes without saying, 'straight'—guys, would occasionally pretend that they were rear-mounting one another as we loitered in the Commons between class bells. Their horseplay was meant to be both a dismissal of gay or anal sex and also proof that they were so straight that they could razz each other that way. My younger sister remembers that the skater boys from South High would jerk off together on the half-pipe—a masturbat-a-thon of sorts. I remember the wooden paddles at college that fraternities gave to (and applied to) new brothers each winter, part of some traditional butt-spanking ritual. Those sorts of quasi-sexual single-sex activities are ingrained in the culture of American boys coming of age. (pp. 57–58)

Baumgardner contends that these variously and simultaneously homophobic and homoerotic behaviours among boys and men are 'coming of age rituals' in contemporary North American society. As she suggests, a joking repudiation of homosexuality is a part of that ritual. The connection of these rituals to male-on-male homophobic bullying is quite clear: Bullying is a related, often more aggressive, set of behaviours that explicitly go beyond friendship groups and targets those considered 'outsiders'. In these instances, 'fag discourse' involves a specifically homophobic constitution of 'us' (those who hate fags) and 'them' (the putative fags). As one of the Central Kings bullies told Shepherd on the day of the original Pink Campaign, 'pink on a male [is] a symbol of homosexuality'; while Shepherd told the bully that such an idea was 'ridiculous', (Fairclough, 2007a, p. B5) it is an idea with significant social currency. Thus, while 'fag' may be a term applied in masculine solidarity-building camaraderie through joking relationships among male adolescent friends or peers, it is also applied in a much more menacing spirit by bullies in order to claim and perform masculine social authority at the expense of particular vulnerable 'others'. Indeed, bullying and harassment of this kind has been widely identified as an aspect of the social and educational climate endured by recent high profile school shooters in the United States (Cullen, 1999; Kimmel, 2008).

[. . .]

Of course, the narrow homophobic vision of masculinity that tactically infuses such bullying behaviours is actually quite hard to articulate in a society whose mainstream cultural institutions such as mass media, professional sports, and capitalism continue to use the colour pink on men as a commonplace sign of effeminacy and deviance. As Warren (2003) proposes, 'masculinity . . . does exist as a *social imaginary* . . . as it is instituted in social relations that [provide] masculinity with its objective sense of identity and its appearance as a recurring pattern in the social realm' (p. 11, italics in original). Masculinity appears innate and becomes *traditional* not only through the repetition of this imaginary but also through how such repetition renders its own ideological production unremarkable.

Masculinity and femininity are relationally and ideologically constructed. Through the repetition and reification of our gendered social imaginary, gendered norms gain coherence. Drawing on the work of philosopher Foucault (1978), sociologist Judith Lorber (1993) outlines the subjective consequences of this gendered dichotomy

. . . in Western societies, we see two discrete sexes and two distinguishable genders because our society is built on two classes of people, 'women' and 'men'. Once the gender category is given, the attributes of the person are also gendered: Whatever a 'woman' is has to be 'female'; whatever a 'man' is has to be 'male'. (p. 569)

In this way, as behaviours, preferences, traits, and pleasures are associated with either one or the other gender any non-normative individual characteristics become deviant or understood as transgressions. Given the patriarchal and sexualized underpinnings of this ideology, such gender crossings are particularly censored for men as they risk affiliation with the less valued others—women and homosexuals—against whom masculine privilege is contrasted (Connell 1987; Kimmel 2008).

One of the most commonly repeated gendered codes in Westernized societies is 'pink for girls, blue for boys'. As many feminist authors have indicated over the years this colour scheme instantiates and reproduces the differential socialization through which dichotomous gendered normativities are constructed (Bridges, 1993; Paoletti, 1987; Pomerleau, Bolduc, Malcuit & Cossette, 1990; Thorne, 1993; Witt, 1997). A compelling example of the commonsensical positioning of 'pink' as a female colour comes from the popular American television sitcom *Friends*.[5] In an episode first aired in 2002, one of the main plotlines revolves around science geek Ross' loss of his pink shirt that he left at an ex-girlfriend's apartment. The storyline begins with this exchange among the main characters:

Ross: (entering) Hey! Has anyone seen my shirt? It's a button down, like a, like a faded salmon?
Monica: You mean your pink shirt?
Ross: Faded salmon colour.
Monica: No, I-I haven't seen your pink shirt.
Ross: Great! Great. Then I must've left it at Mona's. I knew it.
Chandler: Well, I'm sure you can get another one at *Ann Taylor's*.

(Rosenhaus, 2002, emphasis in original)

In this excerpt, the friends tease Ross about the gendered inappropriateness of his 'pink' shirt. Specifically, this humorous exchange is constructed through reliance on the gendered cultural understanding that pink is a colour that is incompatible with normative masculinity due to its strong association with femininity.

The association of the colour pink with women and femininity is repeated later in this same episode when Ross sneaks into Mona's apartment to look for the shirt. He is interrupted in this search by the arrival of his ex-girlfriend and her date and hides behind a couch.

Mona: (entering with her date) I am so sorry I spilled wine all over your shirt.
Mona's Date: Oh, it's okay.
Mona: No, it's still wet. Y'know what? Let me get it out before it sets. Ooh, I have something you can wear. Here. (Hands him Ross' shirt.)
Mona's Date: Oh umm, I-I don't know if I want to wear a woman's shirt.
Mona: No-no that's a man's shirt.
Mona's Date: It's awfully pink. (Ross mouths, 'It's salmon!')

(Rosenhaus, 2002)

Here, the gendered underpinning of the humour of the first scene is made explicit. The pinkness of the shirt makes it a 'woman's shirt'. Necessarily unremarkable though, is the fallacy of this association. Ross can argue the point but his friends' interpretation has the discursive weight of our gendered social imaginary behind it. Moreover, through our consumption of this popular culture commodity, we are implicated in the reproduction of this sex-gender stereotype in schoolyards across North America. While adult audiences know that Ross is not 'a woman' because of his ownership of, and affection for, his 'pink' shirt, teen audiences may have a different interpretation. For a population whose 'rules' of gender are narrower and for whom 'gay' functions as a generic put down, the *Friends* plotline may well reinforce their vision of gender and sexuality-appropriate conduct. In her analysis of fag discourse among male adolescents, Pascoe (2007) contends:

The relationship between adolescent masculinity and sexuality is embedded in the spectre of the faggot. Faggots represent penetrated masculinity [which] symbolize[s] a masculinity devoid of power, which, in its contradiction, threatens both psychic and social chaos. It is precisely this spectre of penetrated masculinity that functions as a regulatory mechanism of gender for contemporary American adolescent boys. (p. 124)

Echoing Lorber (1993), a hierarchical ideology of gendered power is at the core of this conception. A faggot is not a real man because he is vulnerable and woman-like. This ideology is in no way circumscribed to public schools; North American sports culture is one of the principle arenas through which this conception is reproduced (Carlisle Duncan & Messner, 1998).

The start of the school year in North America is also the start of the National Football League (NFL) season. In our contemporary consumer culture, the start of the NFL season brings with it a feeding frenzy of marketing, including expensive new football-themed television commercials. Of particular significance to this analysis is Visa's 'When the Saints Go Marching In' commercial, which, coincidentally, ran on Canadian and US channels during the fall in 2007. This commercial has been designed to promote payWave, Visa's then-new swipe and go charge card system. The commercial is set in post-Katrina, New Orleans, a city on the mend, whose populace happily supports the 'home team' through a swell of Visa-fuelled consumer-driven fandom.

The feel-good pace of the commercial is established through the use of Louis Armstrong's rendition of 'When the Saints Go Marching In', as men, women, and children of all ages clad in New Orleans Saints merchandise play, party, and dance in the streets. Approximately halfway through this one-minute commercial, the music stops and actors' smiles turn to frowns as a thin, 30-ish white male, spotting a powder pink golf shirt and nattily knotted sweater about his shoulders offers a clerk cash to pay for a tin of tennis balls. The ensuing four seconds of silence are broken only by the clink of coins as the clerk makes change and pink-shirt-guy looks nervously around at the visibly disgruntled customers in the line behind him. As he meekly exits the store with his purchase, the music returns full force and the scene switches to a shot of a (seemingly spontaneous) street parade.

If the cash payer was dressed like everyone else, the commercial message (that Visa is better than cash) wouldn't work. Within the conventions of the television commercial there are a wide variety of visual and aural cues available to marketers to communicate the outsider status of this cash payer. It is only necessary, in order to favourably position Visa's product, to represent the cash payer as someone who might not understand the superiority and ease of the new Visa transactions. What is most interesting, however, are the gendered visual choices of the producers in distinguishing this 'other' consumer. Visa and its marketing firm use the spectre of pink as worn by a man to constitute a specifically unmasculine contrast to the masculine and community-sanctioned iconography of the New Orleans Saints and the NFL. As the preceding discussion demonstrates, this coding is a contrast instantly recognizable to Visa's target audience for this campaign: young, male NFL fans. In particular, pink remains, in the masculinist vernacular, a colour associated with weakness, effeminacy, homosexuality, and deviance.[6] As Visa and NFL viewers well know, there is just something about a guy in pink that marks him as outside the bounds of gendered belonging. In light of the discursive connections between the colour 'pink', effeminacy, and homosexuality in the contemporary masculine social imaginary the colour-coded choice of foil in this advertisement is quite deliberate.

As Quart (2003) writes of marketing aimed at youth, 'youth marketers aim to sell their products. And they do so even if it means playing kids' fears of being social outcasts' (p. 10). Thus, in Visa's 'When the Saints Go Marching In' commercial, a regular homophobic joke is infused with meanings about the constitution, performance, and recognition of a 'real' or normative man.

Conclusions

In the preface to the latest edition of his text *The Gendered Society*, Michael Kimmel (2008) links the insanity of Virginia Tech shooter Cho Seung-Hui to the litany of gendered persecutions young boys routinely endure. Kimmel notes of Cho, '[h]is was a madness of revenge, retaliation for a laundry list of injuries he had suffered at the hands of others'. The media response to the Virginia Tech shootings echoes Canadian coverage of the 1989 Montreal Massacre and the 2006 Dawson College shootings. Of such coverage Kimmel argues that, 'focusing only on the madness means we never actually examine the laundry list' (Kimmel, 2008; p. x). Instead, Kimmel advocates making remarkable the connections between such horrifying tragedies and the everyday constructions of gender as operations of power that shape not only our relationships with each other but also our sense of ourselves as gendered individuals.

Although nowhere near as tragically violent a precipitating event, the media coverage and popularization of the pink anti-bullying campaign in Nova Scotia exhibits the conventions of our societal denial of the routinely aggressive, violent, and traumatizing gendered policing of young boys. In studying this example, we can simultaneously observe the tacit societal approval of the denigration of a stereotype of homosexuality as it is ritualistically used to train boys to become normally masculine men

and our media's widespread avoidance of naming this kind of harassment. In concert with popular media, sport, and capitalist cultures that trade on this gendered imaginary, news coverage of the Pink Campaign failed to make remarkable the normalizing work of everyday male-on-male adolescent bullying and also failed to observe that this behaviour is routine rather than aberrant. Knowledge of the normalizing of this fallacious association remains unremarkable in favour of commentary on the (remarkable) spirit of these 'good kids' to stand up against bullying.

While the Pink Campaign is important and laudable, as a society, we owe it to boys to not only stand up against bullying but to expose the fallacy of the gendered and sexual stereotypes routinely used to both terrorize and broadly socialize adolescent boys. If the cultural meaning of 'real' manhood is to shift, as feminist scholars advocate that it must, now is the time to act. As Meidzian (Meidzian as cited in Kimmel, 2008) suggests, we must

> . . . protect boys 'from a culture of violence that exploits their worst tendencies by reinforcing and amplifying the atavistic values of masculine mystique'. After all, it is men who are overwhelmingly the victims of violence—just as men are overwhelmingly its perpetrators. (p. 337)

The Pink Campaign is a good start in this direction. However, its effectiveness was limited by a lack of critical discussion about the gendered dynamics of the bullying that instigated David Shepherd and Travis Price's campaign. In order to strengthen such potentially provocative initiatives we must make remarkable what it means to be a good man, why there is no such thing as a 'real' man, and offer a strong critique of a capitalist culture that links economic success to reification of a dangerous and outmoded stereotype.

Notes

1. Subsequent coverage of this story identifies these students as male (Jeffrey, 2007).
2. Not unsurprisingly, as I will demonstrate, the reports do not mention the gender composition of participants or offer perspectives from non-pink wearing students.
3. The coverage of the bullying incident and the 'Pink Campaign' deliberately does not disclose the name of the bullied student.
4. This institutionalized authority also structures the resistance and socialization of girls. Given the focus of the discourse of femininity on the ornamentation and display of women's bodies, however, girls' gendered policing tends to take the form of 'body talk' or 'fat talk' rather than physical aggression directed at others. I hope to address these issues in a subsequent article.
5. Throughout the mid- to late 1990s, this show was consistently among the highest rated prime-time television programs. It continues to garner large contemporary audiences in syndicated distribution.
6. This articulation of real men as sporting men and, therefore, the antithesis of the effeminacy represent by a pink-wearing man has also been reproduced in the online group 'I Hate Sydney [sic] Crosby'. This group's page of facebook.com features a photo of the young National Hockey League star wearing a pink flowered dress that has been transposed on an advertising image of Crosby. The group description calls Crosby 'a girl' and 'a whinning [sic] little bitch'. As of 9 April 2008, the group had 97 members.

References

Adams, M.L. (1997). *The trouble with normal: Postwar youth and the making of heterosexuality*. Toronto, ON: University of Toronto Press.

Baumgardner, J. (2007). *Look both ways: Bisexual politics*. New York: Farrar, Straus and Giroux.

Bridges, J.S. (1993). Pink or blue: Gender-stereotypic perceptions of infants as conveyed by both congratulations cards. *Psychology of Women Quarterly*, 1(2), 193–205.

Butler, J. (1993). *Bodies that matter: On the discursive limits of 'sex.'* New York: Routledge.

———. (1993). *Gender trouble*. New York: Routledge.

Carlisle Duncan, M., & Messner, M. (1998). The media image of sport and gender. In L. Wenner (Ed.), *Mediasport* (pp. 170–85). London: Routledge.

Connell, R.W. (1987). *Gender and power*. Stanford, CA: Stanford University Press.

Cullen, D. (1999), The rumor that won't go away: Jocks say Littleton killers were gay, but friends deny it. Retrieved 11 October 2007, from http://www.salon.com/news/feature/1999/04/24/rumors/index.html

Fairclough, I. (2007a, September 13). 'I wanted to do something': Central Kings students wear pink to send bullies a message. *The Chronicle Herald*, p. B5.

———. (2007b, September 13), Pink shirts legend grows: Valley students' anti-bullying success reaches CBS, Spanish newspaper. *The Chronicle Herald*, pp. A1, A10.

Ferguson, A. (2007). Making a name for yourself: Transgressive acts and gender performance. In M. Kimmel and M. Messner (Eds), *Men's lives* (7th edn, pp. 111–23). Boston, MA: Allyn and Bacon.

Foucault, M. (1978). *The history of sexuality: An introduction*. Translated by Robert Hurley. New York: Pantheon.

———. (2001). *The archaeology of knowledge*. London: Routledge.

Graham, M. (2007, September 22). Today's lesson is pink, pink, pink: Students' original action against bullying grows to school-wide protest. *The Chronicle Herald*, p. A8.

Goffman, E. (1963). *Stigma*. Englewood Cliffs, NJ: Prentice-Hall.

Hits and misses. (2007, September 30). *The Chronicle Herald*, p. A12.

Jeffery, D. (2007, September 22). 'Pink power: kids across Nova Scotia put on pink to say no to bullies, yes to peace'. *The Chronicle Herald*, pp, A1, A5.

Khayatt, D. (2006). What's to fear: Calling homophobia into question. *McGill Journal of Education*, 4(2), 133–44.

Kimmel, M.S. (2008). *The gendered society* (3rd edn). Toronto, ON: Oxford University Press.

Leger, D. (2007, October 1). From small-town Nova Scotia to the whole world. *The Chronicle Herald*, p. A7.

Lorber, J. (1993). Believing is seeing: biology as ideology. *Gender & Society*, 7(4), 568–8l.

Medel, B. (2007, September 25). School bus driver turns pink too: Retired Mountie impressed by students' anti-bullying campaign. *The Chronicle Herald*, p. B2.

Meek, J. (2007, September 15). Kids in pink save the world. *The Chronicle Herald*, p. A15.

Messner, M.A. (1993). Separating the men from the girls: The gendered language of televised sports. *Gender and Society*, 70, 121–37.

———. (1998). Radical feminist and socialist feminist men's movements in the United States. In S.P. Schacht & D.W. Ewing (Eds), *Feminism and men: Reconstructing gender relations* (pp. 67–85). New York: New York University Press.

Moore, O. (2007, October 13). Students take colourful stand against bullying. *The Globe and Mail*, p. A13.

Olweus, D. (1978). *Aggression in the schools: Bullies and whipping boys*. New York, NY: Hemisphere.

———. (1993). *Bullying at school: What we know and what we can do*. Cambridge, MA: Blackwell.

Paoletti, J.B. (1987). Clothing and gender in America: Children's fashions, l890–1920. *Signs*, 13(1), 136–43.

Pascoe, C.J. (2003). Multiple masculinities? Teenage boys talk about jocks and gender. *American Behavioral Scientist*, 46(10), 1423–38.

———. (2007). Dude, you're a fag: Adolescent masculinity and the fag discourse. In M.S. Kimmel & M.A. Messner (Eds), *Men's lives*, (7th edn; pp. 124–36). Boston: Allyn and Bacon.

Pomerleau, A., Bolduc, D., Malcuit, G., & Cossette, L. (1990). Pink or blue: Environmental gender stereotypes in the first two years of life, *Sex Roles* 22(5–6), 359–67.

Quart, A. (2003), *Branded: The buying and selling of teenagers*. New York: Basic Books.

Rosenhaus, S.E. (2002). The one with the tea leaves. Retrieved 28 October 2007, from http://livesinabox.com/friends/season8/817towtl.htm

Thorne, B. (1993). *Gender play: Girls and boys in school*. New York: Rutgers University Press.

Visa International Service Association. (2007). *Visa advertising*. Retrieved 25 November 2007, from http://usa.visa.com/personal/visa_brings_you/advertising/index.html

Von Kintzel, C. (2007, September 28). Untitled photo. *The Chronicle Herald*, p. A1.

Warren, S. (2003) Is that an action man in there? Masculinity as an imaginative act of self-creation. *Discourse: Studies in the Cultural Politics of Education*, 24(1), 3–18.

Witt, S.D. (1997). Parental influence on children's socialization to gender roles. *Adolescence*, 32, 253–57.

Xin, M. (2002). Bullying in middle school: Individual and school characteristics of victims and offenders. *School Effectiveness and School Improvement: An International Journal of Research, Policy and Practice*, 13(1), 63–89.

Sexual Identity and Heterosexual Male Students' Usage of Homosexual Insults: An Exploratory Study

Tyler L. Brown and Kevin G. Alderson

Introduction

Heterosexual men relative to heterosexual women have more hostile attitudes toward gay men (Kite & Whitely, 2003) and they often use homosexual insults to deride one another (Burn, 2000). However, only about half of the men who use homosexual insults feel strongly negative toward homosexuality (Burn, 2000). Homosexual individuals are often seen as violating gender role norms (Eliason, Donelan & Randall, 1992), resulting in disapproval by others (Rudman & Fairchild, 2004). Perhaps because of this social stigma against gender role violation, heterosexual men respond with more hostility toward feminine gay men than they do toward masculine gay men following a threat to their own masculinity (Glick, Gangl, Gibb, Klumpner & Weinberg, 2007). The excessive regularity of homosexual insults by heterosexual men may signify a reaction to culturally shaped pressures, internalized by heterosexual men, to demonstrate heterosexual masculinity (Theodore & Basow, 2000). The aim of the present study was to determine whether differences in heterosexual male sexual identity (HMSI) would influence the likelihood of heterosexual men using homosexual insults. If such differences in sexual identity are influential, certain forms of HMSI may be more reliant on homosexual insults to manage perceived threats against gender identity, suggesting a social significance for homosexual insults beyond homophobia. For this reason, we use here the term 'homosexual insult', rather than 'homophobic insult', to characterize both gendered and homosexual putdowns. This terminology avoids characterizing all such putdowns in advance as having an exclusively homophobic purpose.

Masculine Identity and the Struggle for Status

The Problem with Heterosexual Men and Homosexual Insults

Insults that imply homosexuality are perceived by some men as the worst type of insult (Preston & Stanley, 1987). Homosexual insults are often used to express sexual prejudice (D'Augelli, 1992) and serve to designate targets as outcasts (Dafnos, 2007). Possibly due to their connection with gender-role failure, homosexual insults play a pivotal role in the school bullying and victimization of both gay and heterosexual males (Kimmel & Mahler, 2003). Nevertheless, many homosexual insults within male discourse appear jovial and seem to facilitate 'male bonding' (Silverschanz, Cortina, Konik & Magley, 2008, p. 187). Armstrong (2006) proposes that certain insults, including homosexual terms, are only possible between equals, signifying inclusion. The interpretation of homosexual insults is complex in that such insults can be associated with both inclusion and exclusion, i.e., they can signify both acceptance and rejection depending on the context of use and the sexual identity of the user and target.

Heterosexual Men and Sexual Identity

Sexual identity represents the sense of self a person establishes through giving meaning to their sexual lives in relation to the culturally available categories of self-identification (Frankel, 2004). One conceptualization of sexual identity encompasses four components: (a) biological sex: as reflected in physical anatomy; (b) gender identity: the conviction of being male or female (or ambivalent); (c) sexual orientation: degree of physical and affectional attraction to opposite-sex or same-sex partners, and (d) gender ideology: cultural expectation for masculine or feminine behaviour based on biological sex (Shively & De Cecco, 1977).

[. . .]

Hegemonic Masculinity and Identity-motivated Behaviour

If heteronormativity does develop naturally, it should be unnecessary for heterosexual men to prove their HMSI because its appearance would be inevitable and effortless. If one considers the fourth component of sexual identity in Shively and De Cecco's (1977) conceptualization, i.e., gender ideology, it seems plausible that it may not be heterosexual men that are believed to develop naturally but rather 'good' men developing naturally into what our culture wants them to be: masculine. If a man views himself as being less masculine than his culturally shaped understanding of gender ideology says he ought to be, he must work hard to cultivate the appropriate gender-role in order to confirm his HMSI (Kimmel, 1997). This introduction of a value judgment into sexual identity, through gender ideology, illustrates how sexual identity interacts with cultural pressures to produce stress over a gendered self. Consequently, men's response to this stress may perpetuate the problem of 'hegemonic masculinity'.

'Hegemony' is a sociological term used to describe the dominance of one group over another. In the case of hegemonic masculinity, traditional masculine qualities are given a place of honour while traditional feminine qualities are devalued (Connell, 1995). Masculine over-conformity occurs when men look to rigidly oversubscribe to masculine qualities with the aim of proving their manhood. Such a burden of proof leads men into a never-ending cycle of masculine testimony that is experienced indefinably as a relentless and debilitating trial (Kimmel, 1997).

To prove masculinity this way is to collapse the distinction between 'sufficiently' masculine and 'absolutely' masculine, setting the stage for what Eisler and Skidmore (1987) call 'masculine gender role stress'. According to Eisler and Skidmore, masculine gender role stress may occur if a man judges himself unable to cope with the traditional demands of the male role or if a man is required to act in a traditionally feminine way.

Homosexual insults may act as a quick way to alleviate this stress by both verbally demonstrating the speaker's personal allegiance to a gender ideology that supports hegemonic masculinity and by defending sexual identity. According to Plummer (1999), this method of stress reduction and identity defence is first taken up in boyhood and adolescence.

Boyhood and Adolescent Homosexual Insults

Rather than referring to sexuality, boyhood homosexual insults refer to boys who fail to meet the gendered demands of the male peer group (Plummer, 1999). Boys become fearful of these terms because of their status-discrediting potential. During the teenage years, homosexual insults take on a sexual nuance; however, the original meaning associated with gender-role failure and the fear related to it remain active within an adolescent's pattern of awareness (Plummer, 1999).

Boyhood homosexual insults place all men at risk of being positioned outside of the male peer group and thus receiving an outcaste identity. This outcast identity may best be illustrated through the 'spectre of the faggot' (Pascoe, 2005, p. 329) which occupies a symbolic space outside the boundaries of heterosexual masculinity and serves to shape and discipline adolescent men. The 'faggot' is not simply a man who is gay but instead a man removed from his masculinity and left defenceless in a world of more powerful men who are at liberty to dominate him. Men painstakingly strive to avoid this fluid identity by theoretically transferring it to other men via homosexual insults (Pascoe, 2005).

Antecedents to 'Faggot' Identity Avoidance

According to Lock and Kleis (1998), men, in contrast to women, are more vulnerable to gender-role anxiety, which may lead to an increased need to defend against threats to gender identity (Burke, 1996). Childhood violation of traditional gender-roles has been linked with self-reported anxiety for both gay and heterosexual men but not for women (Lippa, 2008). [. . .] Gender identity as a possible means to sexual opportunity gives heterosexual men a strong reason to feel anxious about their masculinity. [. . .] Some homosexual insults may be interpreted as a reaction to culturally shaped pressures placed on heterosexual men, and internalized through gender ideology, to demonstrate heterosexual masculinity with the aim of being sexually desirable to heterosexual women. To compete with other men who share the same opposite-sex sexual interest, men must evoke as many masculine qualities as possible, leaving them pressured toward masculine absolutism in order to achieve sexual ends (Dupré, 2001).

The Present Study

The purpose of the present study was to determine whether differences in HMSI (as measured by magnitude of sexual orientation, masculine gender role, and gender ideology) would influence the likelihood of heterosexual men to use homosexual insults. Specifically, this study aimed to establish whether men who are higher in the different components of HMSI would be more likely to use homosexual insults than men who are lower or moderate in these same components.

The ten hypotheses for this study (Table 1) reflect two categories of homosexual insults: 'non-sexual homosexual insults' (relating to gender and independent of sexual orientation) and 'sexualized homosexual insults' (relating to and dependent on sexual orientation).

Hypotheses 1–6 represent primary hypotheses in line with the literature discussed above while hypotheses 7–10 represent secondary hypotheses of interest related to demographic variables.

[. . .]

Table 1 Primary and Secondary Hypotheses

HYPOTHESIS	DESCRIPTION
1	Men with high opposite-sex sexual orientation scores will be more likely to use non-sexual homosexual insults (i.e., insults relating more to gender and independent of a man's sexual orientation) than men with low and moderate opposite-sex sexual orientation scores.
2	Men with high opposite-sex sexual orientation scores will *not* be more likely to use sexualized homosexual insults (i.e., insults that are dependent on a man's sexual orientation) than men with low and moderate opposite-sex sexual orientation scores.
3	Men high in masculine gender-role will be more likely to use non-sexual homosexual insults than men low and moderate in masculine gender-role.
4	Men high in masculine gender-role will be more likely to use sexualized homosexual insults than men low and moderate in masculine gender-role.
5	Men high in gender ideology will be more likely to use non-sexual homosexual insults than men low and moderate in gender ideology.*
6	Men high in gender ideology will be more likely to use sexualized homosexual insults than men low and moderate in gender ideology.
7	Men who are presently younger than 21 will use more non-sexual and sexualized homosexual insults than men who are presently older than 21.
8	Men who have one year or less of full-time post-secondary education will be more likely to use both non-sexual and sexualized homosexual insults compared to men who have more than two years of full-time post-secondary education.
9	Men from religions that are part of the Abrahamic traditions (i.e., Judaism, Christianity, and Islam) will use more non-sexual and sexualized homosexual insults compared to men not from those traditions.
10	Men who are Caucasian will be more likely to use non-sexual and sexualized homosexual insults than men who are Non-Caucasian.

* High gender ideology refers to a high investment in or adherence to traditional gender ideologies. Low and moderate gender ideology refers to a low and moderate investment in or adherence to traditional gender ideologies.

We expect that men higher in sexual identity components will be more reliant on homosexual insults to comply with cultural pressures to be masculine and defend against stress. This is because such men are more representative of hegemonic masculinity and can therefore use homosexual insults to make their representativeness more salient. In contrast, men who are low and moderate in sexual identity components are less representative of hegemonic masculinity and are therefore less likely to gain validation from it. Instead, these men may look for alternative ways to manage role pressures (e.g., by promoting diversity).

Methods

Participants

In total, 111 male undergraduate students at the University of Calgary participated in the study. Each received half a bonus credit that could be applied to any psychology course in which they were currently registered. Participants read and signed a consent form before filling out the research instruments and all were debriefed after completing the questionnaires. Data from 11 participants were not included in the analyses either because of missing responses or because, given the focus of the study on heterosexual males, their replies

Table 2 Selected Demographic Characteristics of Participants

AGE	
Mean	20.8
Median	20.0
Range	18–38
ETHNICITY	
White/Caucasian	52
Aboriginal	0
Southeast Asian	25
South Asian (Indian or Pakistani)	9
Arab/Middle Eastern	3
Hispanic	1
Black	2
Mixed Race	6
Other (please specify):	2
EDUCATION (HIGHEST LEVEL COMPLETED)	
Masters Degree	1
Bachelaureate Degree	3
Three Years Post-secondary	36
Two Years Post-secondary	16
One Year Post-secondary	30
High School Graduate	14
RELIGION	
Protestant	11
Catholic	13
Christian – Unspecified	20
Jewish	1
Mormon	2
Muslim	6
Hindu	1
Buddhist	5
Native	0
Spiritual, no label	7
Atheist	15
Agnostic	10
Other	8

to the question on sexual orientation identified them as other than 'predominantly' or 'exclusively heterosexual' (i.e., bisexual or homosexual). All participants were required to be at least 18 years of age due to the sexual nature of the study. The total sample for the purposes of the statistical analyses was thus 100 heterosexual male undergraduates (mean age 20.8 years) from diverse ethnic and religious backgrounds (Table 2).

Measures

The research instruments used in the study were as follows:

The Kinsey Scale (Kinsey et al., 1948): This Likert scale offers seven distinct categories of sexual orientation, ranging from 0 ('exclusively heterosexual') to 6 ('exclusively homosexual') with varying degrees of bisexuality in between. Since the present study focused on heterosexual males, this scale was used for screening purposes only.

The Sexuality Questionnaire (Alderson, Orzeck, Davis, and Boyes, 2010): This questionnaire sought to represent the six components of sexual orientation previously identified by Alderson et al. as: (a) sexual attraction, (b) sexual fantasies, (c) sexual preferences, (d) propensity to fall in love, (e) being in love romantically, and (f) sexual partners. Participants in the present study were assessed separately on opposite-sex and same-sex interest for each of the six components using a Likert scale that ranged from 0 (no interest), 1 (unsure), 2 (low), 3 (moderate), to 4 (high interest). The possible score range was 0–24 for opposite-sex interests and 0–24 for same-sex interests (coding of the responses for statistical analyses is described below). Gender role, defined as the 'extent to which you see yourself as behaving in traditionally masculine and/or feminine ways' (Alderson et al., 2010, p. 1) was measured using this single statement, addressed separately based on masculine and feminine gender role interests. The possible score range was from 0 (zero or no interest) to 4 (high interest) (coding of the responses for statistical analyses is described below). Overall, the Sexuality Questionnaire offers high internal consistency, with a reliability of alpha = .85 for the complete scale, alpha = .94 for same-sex items, and alpha = .84 for opposite-sex items.

Demographic questionnaire: In addition to the previously presented information on age and ethnic and religious background (Table 2), this questionnaire included two items that measured masculine and feminine gender-role in a slightly different way than in the Sexuality Questionnaire above. Responses were gathered using a Likert scale ranging from 0 ('no traditional masculine/feminine behaviour') to 4 ('high traditional masculine/feminine behaviour') with

interval values of 1 ('unsure'), 2 ('low'), and 3 ('moderate').

Non-Standardized Homosexual Insult Usage Questionnaire: This 22-item questionnaire (Table 3) was developed by the first author to represent participants' usages of homosexual insults. The questionnaire sought to represent 'non-sexual homosexual insults' (i.e., insults directed at male gender role behaviour that does not meet traditionally masculine standards, including the presumed gender role behaviour of gay men but not their sexuality) and 'sexualized homosexual insults' (i.e., insults that are directed at gay men's sexuality). The Homosexual Insult Usage Questionnaire offers high internal consistency, with a reliability of alpha = .95 for the non-sexual joking homosexual insult items, alpha = .87 for the non-sexual pressuring homosexual insult items, and alpha = .87 for the sexualized homosexual insults.

Table 3 Homosexual Insult Usage Questionnaire

#	QUESTION
1	How often in pre-pubescence (ages 6–12) did you use the word(s) 'fag' or 'faggot' as a generic insult (i.e., an insult you would use towards any male, regardless of his sexual orientation)?*
2	How often in adolescence (ages 13–17) did you use the word(s) 'fag' or 'faggot' as a generic insult?*
3	How often in the past year did you use the word(s) 'fag' or 'faggot' as a generic insult?*
4	While around friends how often do you use the word(s) 'fag' or 'faggot' as a generic insult for males outside of your group of friends?*
5	How often do you use the word(s) 'fag' or 'faggot' as a generic insult to describe male celebrities or famous persons (i.e. actors, athletes, or musicians) you otherwise do not know personally?*
6	How likely are you to use the word(s) 'fag' or 'faggot' as a specific insult (i.e. an insult dependent on a man's sexual orientation) towards a man who is gay, either behind his back or to his face?**
7	How likely are you to use the word(s) 'fag' or 'faggot' as a generic insult towards a straight man, either behind his back or to his face, who is obviously attempting to 'show off' or appear overly-masculine/macho?**
8	How often do you use the word(s) 'fag' or 'faggot' to express personal contempt or disgust for men who are gay?*
9	How often do you use the word(s) 'fag' or 'faggot' as a generic insult towards another man even though, to the best of your knowledge, the man is straight?*
10	How likely are you to call another man, with whom you are having a serious disagreement, a 'fag' or 'faggot', either behind his back later or to his face during the disagreement?**

#	QUESTION
11	How often do you use the word(s) 'fag' or 'faggot' with the aim of implying that the man in question is not a 'real man' or in some way is unmasculine?*
12	How often do you call another man a 'fag' or 'faggot', in the generic sense, with the intention of 'challenging' him or having him 'prove' himself?*
13	Do you consider male homosexuality 'unmanly' or otherwise counter to masculinity? [*yes*, *no*, or *neutral*]
14	How often do you use the word(s) 'fag' or 'faggot' as a generic insult, to refer to your male friends, in a way that might be considered harmless and basically humorous?*
15	Approximately, how many times a day would you say you use the word(s) 'fag' or 'faggot'? [*0*, *1–2*, *3–5*, *6–10*, or *more than 10 times/day*]
16	When reflecting on the use of the word(s) 'fag' or 'faggot' as a generic insult do you consider this [generic] usage homophobic? [*yes*, *no*, or *undecided*]
17	How often do you use the word(s) 'fag' or 'faggot' as a generic insult for men who exhibit situational weakness or incompetence? For example, how often do you call a man a 'fag' for being unable to operate a particular piece of equipment or complete a task?*
18	How often do you use the word(s) 'fag' or 'faggot' as a generic insult to pressure another man into conforming to your expectations?*
19	How often do you generically call another man a 'fag' or 'faggot' for having an opinion (i.e. political, moral, or preferential) that differs from your own?*
20	How likely is it that you would call two straight men who appear to have a close and caring emotional relationship with one another 'fags' or 'faggots', in the generic sense, either behind their backs or to their faces?**
21	How likely are you to call a straight man a 'fag' or 'faggot', either behind his back or to his face, if he were to express emotional tenderness or to act otherwise 'feminine'?**
22	If you were to call a straight man a 'fag' or 'faggot' would you seriously be suggesting that you really and truly believe the man is gay? [*yes*, *no*, *undecided*, or *I would not call another man a 'fag' or 'faggot.'*]

*7 pt. scale reply: "never", "very rarely (once or twice a year)", "rarely (once or twice every 6 months)", "occasionally (once or twice a month)", "frequently (once or twice a week)", "very frequently (almost daily)", or "daily".
**6 pt. scale reply: "definitely unlikely" (0%), "very unlikely" (10%), "possible" (50%), "likely" (75%), "very likely" (90%), or "definitely likely" (100%).

Procedures

Participants were provided with a stapled questionnaire that included all of the instruments mentioned above. The first page consisted of the Kinsey Scale, followed by the Sexuality Questionnaire and demographic questionnaire, followed by the Non-Standardized Homosexual Insult Usage Questionnaire. All participants received the same questionnaire package with the same questions in exactly the same order.

[. . .]

Statistical Analyses

Responses on the questionnaire were entered into the SPSS version 16 computer software program. A formula in SPSS was written to compute the sexual orientation scores based on the data collected by the sexuality questionnaire, the gender-role scores, and the gender ideology scores.

Sexual orientation scores were calculated by adding up the opposite-sex scores and then subtracting the same-sex scores on all six factors, thereby creating a range of scores from −24 to +24. To ensure that all of the numbers had a positive valence, 24 was added to each sexual orientation score. The resulting possible score range was 0 (representing the highest level of same-sex interest) to 48 (representing the highest level of opposite-sex interest). Participants with a sexual orientation score between 42 and 48 were coded as being high in opposite-sex interest while sexual orientation scores between 0 and 41 were coded low to moderate in opposite-sex interest.

Gender-role scores were calculated by subtracting the participants' self-reported feminine gender-role score from their self-reported masculine gender-role score. Six was then added to this number to create a possible range of 1–10. This provided a gender-role difference score with 1 being the most feminine and 10 being the most masculine. Men who scored between 9 and 10 were considered high in masculine gender-role, while men who scored between 1 and 8 were considered low and moderate in masculine gender-role.

Gender ideology scores were calculated based on item 13 in the homosexual insult questionnaire that asked, 'Do you consider male homosexuality "unmanly" or otherwise counter to masculinity?' Men who replied 'yes' (3) were coded as having a high adherence to traditional gender ideologies and those who replied 'neutral' (2) or 'no' (1) were coded as having moderate or low adherence to traditional gender ideologies, respectively. High gender ideology in this sense means having a high adherence to a traditional understanding of what makes a suitably masculine man and where homosexuality fits in relation to this expectation.

[. . .]

Results

Factor Analysis for the Homosexual Insult Usage Questionnaire

Factor analysis was done on responses to the 19 questions retained in the homosexual insult usage questionnaire in order to identify and group items that were measuring the same construct. We were aware at the outset that a sample of 100 was less than desirable for such an analysis (see Discussion) but chose to do so because of the exploratory nature of the study and the novel items in the questionnaire. Inter-item correlations were computed (Pearson product moment correlation) and the resulting correlation matrix was subjected to a factor analysis with varimax rotation of all the variables in the homosexual insult questionnaire. Principal component analysis appeared to be an appropriate way to describe structure, giving unit weight to each variable. Initially, the distributions were examined for each variable to ensure that the particular data set was suitable for factor analysis.

The analysis determined that three factors provided the best fit out of the remaining items and accounted for 71.23 per cent of the variance. The three factors and their Coefficient alpha estimates of internal reliability were: Factor A, non-sexual joking homosexual insult items (alpha = .95); Factor B, non-sexual pressuring homosexual insult items (alpha = .87); and Factor C, sexualized homophobic insult items (alpha = .87) (Table 4).

Factor A included items that assessed the use of homosexual insults around friends and towards friends in a non-sexual jovial manner, hence the label 'non-sexual joking homosexual insults'. The item numbers that made up this factor were: 2, 3, 4, 5, 7, 9, 10, and 14.

Factor B included the items using homosexual insults in a more aggressive way to pressure another man into accepting one's own way

Table 4 Item Groupings from Factor Analysis of Homosexual Insult Characterizations

ITEM	FACTOR A
2	Frequency of using 'fag' or 'faggot' as a generic insult in adolescence
3	Frequency of using 'fag' or 'faggot' as a generic insult over the past year
4	Frequency of using 'fag' or 'faggot' as a generic insult for non-friends around friends
5	Frequency of using 'fag' or 'faggot' as a generic insult for famous people
7	Frequency of using 'fag' or 'faggot' as a generic insult for men 'showing off'
9	Frequency of using 'fag' or 'faggot' as a generic insult for men you know are straight
10	Frequency of calling another man a 'fag' or 'faggot' during a disagreement
14	Frequency of using 'fag' or 'faggot' humorously as a generic insult for male friends

ITEM	FACTOR B
11	Frequency of using 'fag' or 'faggot' to imply someone else is not really a man
12	Frequency of using 'fag' or 'faggot' generically to challenge another man
17	Frequency of using 'fag' or 'faggot' to imply another man is weak
18	Frequency of using 'fag' or 'faggot' as a generic insult to pressure other men
19	Frequency of using 'fag' or 'faggot' for men who think differently than oneself
20	Frequency of using 'fag' or 'faggot' for straight men who are emotionally close/caring

ITEM	FACTOR C
6	Frequency of using 'fag' or 'faggot' specifically to refer to men who are gay
8	Frequency of using 'fag' or 'faggot' to express contempt/disgust for men who are gay
21	Frequency of using 'fag' or 'faggot' to describe a straight man acting feminine

of thinking about the world. Like non-sexual joking homosexual insults, this use was also independent of sexual orientation, and was therefore labelled 'non-sexual pressuring homosexual insults'. The item numbers that made up this factor were: 11, 12, 17, 18, 19, and 20.

Factor C included the items that focused on homosexual insults directed toward the sexuality of gay men with an intent to express contempt and rebuke intimacy between men, hence the label 'sexualized homosexual insults'. The items that made up this factor include: 6, 8, and 21.

Participants' Perceptions of Male Homosexuality and Insults and Their Scores on Related Measures of Sexual Orientation, Gender Role, and Gender Ideology

Perceptions

Participants' responses to two questions intentionally excluded from the foregoing factor analysis provide insights into their perceptions of male homosexuality and the nature of homosexual insults. Item 13 in Table 3 asked: 'Do you consider male homosexuality 'unmanly' or otherwise counter to masculinity?' The responses were: 'yes' (33%), 'no' (44%), and 'undecided' (23%); over half either considered male homosexuality counter to masculinity or were at least undecided about its relation to masculinity. Item 22 in Table 3 asked: 'If you were to call a straight man a "fag" or "faggot" would you seriously be suggesting that you really and truly believe the man is gay?' The responses were: 'yes' (0%), 'no' (77%), and 'undecided' (2%) with 21 per cent choosing the fourth option 'I would not call another man a "fag" or "faggot"'. This finding is consistent with the factor analysis in that participants clearly recognized gendered insults (non-sexual homosexual insults) as distinct from insults about sexuality (sexualized homosexual insults).

Likelihood of Heterosexual Male Participants Using Homosexual Insults: Analysis and Statistics

In order to determine whether differences in heterosexual male sexual identity (HMSI) influenced the likelihood of heterosexual men using homosexual insults, nine one-way ANOVAs were performed with 'low/moderate' and 'high' scores for sexual orientation, masculine gender-role, and gender ideology as predictor variables and non-sexual joking insults, non-sexual pressuring insults, and sexualized homosexual insults as criterion variables (i.e., Factors A–C in Table 4). The findings reported in Table 5 provide a basis for the hypothesis testing that follows.

A brief example will serve here as an introduction to Table 5. The first row of the table shows that men with low/moderate opposite-sex sexual interest had lower mean scores ($M = 1.26$) for likelihood of non-sexual joking homosexual insults (Factor A) than did participants with higher opposite-sex sexual interest ($M = 2.10$). This difference was significant, $F(1, 98) = 6.765$, $p = .011$. Significant differences in this respect were not found for use of non-sexual pressuring

homosexual insults (Factor B) or use of sexualized homosexual insults (Factor C).

[. . .]

Testing of Primary Hypotheses

Opposite-sex Sexual Interest

Hypothesis 1 proposed that higher opposite-sex sexual interest would correlate with a greater likelihood of non-sexual homosexual insult usage. As noted above, this hypothesis was supported for non-sexual joking homosexual insults (Factor A) in that men with higher opposite-sex sexual interest scores were significantly more likely to use such insults ($M = 2.10$) compared to men with low/moderate opposite-sex sexual interest scores ($M = 1.26$). However no such difference was found for non-sexual pressuring homosexual insults (Factor B) ($p = .423$).

Hypothesis 2 proposed that higher opposite-sex interest would not correlate with a higher likelihood of sexualized homosexual insult usage. This hypothesis was supported (Table 5). Men with high opposite-sex sexual orientation scores were not significantly more likely to use sexualized homosexual insults (Factor C) ($M = .97$) than were men with low/moderate opposite sex sexual interest ($M = .58$) ($p = .119$).

Masculine Gender Role

Hypothesis 3 proposed that higher masculine gender-role would correlate with higher likelihood of non-sexual homosexual insult usage. This hypothesis was supported (Table 5). Men with high masculine gender-role were significantly more likely to use non-sexual joking homosexual insults ($M = 2.29$) than men with low/moderate masculine gender role scores ($M = 1.53$) ($p = .006$) and that was also the case for non-sexual pressuring homosexual insults ($p = .010$).

Hypothesis 4 proposed that higher masculine gender-role would correlate with higher likelihood of sexualized homosexual insult usage. This hypothesis

Table 5 Descriptive Statistics for the Three-Factor Homosexual Insult Characterization

OPPOSITE-SEX SEXUAL ORIENTATION

	LOW/MODERATE			HIGH					
	M	*SD*	*N*	*M*	*SD*	*N*	*F*	*df*	*p*
Factor A*	1.26	1.49	22	2.10	1.31	78	6.765	1,98	0.011
Factor B	0.70	1.24	22	0.89	0.93	78	0.647	1,98	0.423
Factor C	0.58	0.90	22	0.97	1.06	78	2.476	1,98	0.119

MASCULINE GENDER ROLE

	LOW/MODERATE			HIGH					
	M	*SD*	*N*	*M*	*SD*	*N*	*F*	*df*	*p*
Factor A	1.53	1.25	49	2.29	1.43	51	7.852	1,98	0.006
Factor B	0.59	0.80	49	1.10	1.11	51	6.865	1,98	0.010
Factor C	0.60	0.77	49	1.16	1.18	51	7.606	1,98	0.007

GENDER IDEOLOGY

	LOW/MODERATE			HIGH					
	M	*SD*	*N*	*M*	*SD*	*N*	*F*	*df*	*p*
Factor A	1.75	1.34	67	2.26	1.44	33	3.007	1,98	0.086
Factor B	0.62	0.80	67	1.31	1.20	33	11.67	1,98	0.001
Factor C	0.53	0.63	67	1.60	1.31	33	30.91	1,98	0.000

ETHNICITY

	CAUCASIAN			NON-CAUCASIAN					
	M	*SD*	*N*	*M*	*SD*	*N*	*F*	*df*	*p*
Factor A	1.64	1.42	52	2.22	1.30	48	4.569	1,98	0.035
Factor B	0.67	0.98	52	1.05	1.00	48	3.705	1,98	0.057
Factor C	0.76	1.02	52	1.02	1.06	48	1.467	1,98	0.229

*Factor A = non-sexual joking homosexual insults; Factor B = non-sexual pressuring homosexual insults; Factor C = sexualized homosexual insults.
Note: To achieve a common insult usage scale for the factor analysis, thirteen questionnaire items scored as 0 to 6 were compressed to fit the 0 to 5 format, i.e., scores of 6 were included with scores of 5 (see Methods).

was supported (Table 5). Men higher in masculine gender-role were significantly more likely to use sexualized homosexual insults (M = 1.15) than men low/moderate in masculine gender role scores (M = 0.60) (p = .007).

Gender Role Ideology

Hypothesis 5 proposed that higher adherence to traditional gender ideologies would correlate with higher likelihood of non-sexual homosex-ual insult usage. This hypothesis was partially supported. It was not supported for non-sexual joking homosexual insults (p = .086) but it was supported for non-sexual pressuring homosexual insults (Table 5) in that men with high gender ideology scores were significantly more likely to use non-sexual pressuring insults (M = 1.32) compared to men with low/moderate gender ideology (M = 0.62, SD = 0.80) (p = .001).

Hypothesis 6 proposed that higher adherence to traditional gender ideologies would correlate with higher likelihood of sexualized homosexual insult usage. This hypothesis was supported (Table 5). Men high in gender ideology were significantly more likely to use sexualized homosexual insults ($M = 1.60$) compared to men with low/moderate gender ideology ($M = 0.53$) ($p < .000$).

Testing of Secondary Hypotheses

Effects of Age

Hypothesis 7 proposed that younger age would correlate with greater likelihood of both non-sexualized and sexualized homosexual insult usage. This hypothesis was not supported. Men who were younger than 21 were not significantly more likely to use non-sexual joking homosexual insults ($M = 1.97$, $SD = 1.50$) than men who were older than 21 ($M = 1.82$, $SD = 1.19$), $F(1, 98) = 0.326$, $p = .569$. Men younger than 21 were also not significantly more likely to use non-sexual pressuring homosexual insults ($M = 0.95$, $SD = 1.12$) than men who were older than 21 ($M = 0.69$, $SD = 0.75$), $F(1, 98) = 1.624$, $p = .206$ nor were they significantly more likely to use sexualized homosexual insults ($M = 0.94$, $SD = 1.14$) than men who are older than 21 ($M = 0.79$, $SD = 0.86$), $F(1, 98) = 0.516$, $p = .474$.

Post-secondary Education

Hypothesis 8 proposed that less post-secondary education would correlate with increased likelihood of both non-sexualized and sexualized homosexual insult usage. This hypothesis was not supported. Men with one year of full-time post-secondary education or less were not significantly more likely to use more non-sexual joking insults ($M = 2.00$, $SD = 1.52$) than men with two years or more of full-time post-secondary education ($M = 1.85$, $SD = 1.28$), $F(1, 98) = 0.294$, $p = .589$. Similarly, men with one year of full-time

post-secondary education or less were not significantly more likely to use non-sexual pressuring homosexual insults ($M = 1.02$, $SD = 1.22$) than men with two years or more of full-time post-secondary education ($M = 0.72$, $SD = 0.79$), $F(1, 98) = 2.189$, $p = .142$, nor were they significantly more likely to use sexualized homosexual insults ($M = 1.00$, $SD = 1.16$) than men with two years or more of full-time post-secondary education ($M = 0.79$, $SD = 0.94$), $F(1, 98) = 0.963$, $p = .329$.

Religious Affiliation

Hypothesis 9 proposed that Abrahamic religious affiliation would correlate with increased likelihood of both non-sexualized and sexualized homosexual insult usage. This hypothesis was not supported. Men from religions that are part of the Abrahamic tradition were not significantly more likely to use non-sexual joking homosexual insults ($M = 2.01$, $SD = 1.49$) than men who were not from religions that are part of the Abrahamic tradition ($M = 1.85$, $SD = 1.27$), $F(1, 97) = 0.376$, $p = .541$. Similarly, men from religions that are part of the Abrahamic tradition were not significantly more likely to use non-sexual pressuring insults ($M = 0.94$, $SD = 1.09$) than men who were not from religions that are part of the Abrahamic tradition ($M = 0.77$, $SD = 0.89$), $F(1, 97) = 0.775$, $p = .381$, nor were they significantly more likely to use sexualized homosexual insults ($M = 1.02$, $SD = 1.19$) than men who were not from religions that are part of the Abrahamic tradition ($M = 0.75$, $SD = 0.82$), $F(1, 97) = 1.657$, $p = .201$.

Caucasian versus Non-Caucasian Ethnicity

Hypothesis 10 proposed that Caucasian ethnicity would correlate with increased likelihood of both non-sexualized and sexualized homosexual insult usage. This hypothesis was not supported. In contrast, a significant finding was found in regards to ethnicity and non-sexual joking homosexual insults. Non-Caucasian men were significantly more likely to use non-sexual homosexual joking insults ($M = 2.22$, $SD = 1.30$) than Caucasian men ($M = 1.64$, $SD = 1.42$), $F (1, 98) = 4.57$, $p = .035$. Caucasian men were not significantly more likely to use non-sexual pressuring homosexual insults ($M = 0.67$, $SD = 0.98$) than non-Caucasian men ($M = 1.05$, $SD = 1.00$), $F (1, 98) = 3.705$, $p = .57$ nor were they significantly more likely to use sexualized homosexual insults ($M = 0.76$, $SD = 1.02$) than non-Caucasian men ($M = 1.02$, $SD = 1.06$), $F (1, 98) = 1.456$, $p = .229$.

Discussion

A scale newly designed to assess the usage of homosexual insults by heterosexual men was employed on university students to test 10 hypotheses about the relationship of such usage to participants' scores on opposite-sex sexual orientation, masculine gender-role, and adherence to traditional gender ideologies, and to other demographic variables. The hypotheses were predicated on two categories of insult: non-sexual homosexual insults (i.e., insults directed at male gender role behaviour that does not meet stereotypical expectations, including the presumed gender role behaviour of gay men), and sexualized homosexual insults (i.e., insults directed at gay men's sexuality). Factor analysis yielded three categories consistent with these conceptualizations: (a) non-sexual joking homosexual insults, (b) non-sexual pressuring homosexual insults, and (c) sexualized homosexual insults. The relationship between different aspects of male heterosexual sexual identity (HMSI) and usage of such insults is a primary focus of this discussion.

Opposite-sex Sexual Orientation

Given the apparent abundance of homosexual insults in heterosexual male discourse, the relationship of participants' scores on an opposite-sex sexual orientation scale to insult usage was of interest. As previously noted, the use of homosexual insults may foster male peer group inclusion (Armstrong, 2006) and such group inclusion may serve as an indicator of greater masculinity to heterosexual women (Miller et al., 2000) which, in turn, could increase men's chances of sexual experience, a further validation of male group approval (Kimmel, 1997). These kinds of outcomes might well provide an incentive for continued use of homosexual insults, particularly among men with higher opposite-sex sexual orientation. We hypothesized such a relationship for non-sexual homosexual insults but found it only for non-sexual joking homosexual insults but not for non-sexual pressuring homosexual insults. As expected, there was no effect for sexualized homosexual insults.

Men may well learn which types of insults are either unattractive to women (e.g., sexualized homosexual insults) or ineffective in increasing women's perception of their stature within their peer group (e.g., non-sexual pressuring insults) and react accordingly. The way women respond to certain patterns of male discourse may reinforce gendered and sexualized teasing. The present findings should provide a stimulus for future research on women's perceptions of men who use homophobic or gendered insults.

Masculine Gender-role

In this study, masculine gender role scores of 9 or 10 on a 10-point scale were considered 'high', and the remainder moderate to low, in relation to their stereotypical masculine behaviours. As hypothesized, males with high scores were more likely to use all three categories of homosexual insult compared to men with lower scores. In all three cases, their likelihood of using such insults was well below the midpoint of the insult usage scale, but the differences were nevertheless statistically significant and may reflect the rationale for the hypotheses. Perhaps highly masculine men have greater status in their male peer group and/or they are more representative of traditional expectations and hence more comfortable in employing gendered insults to subtly or not so subtly cue a patriarchal power structure that both works to their benefit and is already in place. The resulting gendered power and inequality reflected, in particular, in the use of sexualized homosexual insult may also signal a person's need to distance themselves from stigmatized others based on a fear of receiving similar stigmatization (Sigelman, Howell, Cornell, Cutright & Dewey, 1991). It has been generally believed that those who violate traditional sexual orientation norms also violate traditional gender-role norms (Schneider, 2004). This leads to the mistaken assumption that all men who are gay are also feminine. Men with high masculine gender-role scores may use specific patterns of sexualized discourse (including homosexual insults) to secure the advantages associated with gendered power and to avoid the 'stigmatization' of being labelled feminine.

Future research should look at the relationship between masculine gender-role stress and homosexual taunting. It is important to establish empirically whether or not masculine gender role stress influences the likelihood that a man will use a gendered insult. Given the serious and sometimes violent outcomes associated with homosexual taunting, more research is required to understand the deep-seated social significance of these powerfully versatile and potentially volatile forms of homosexual insult.

Adherence to Traditional Gender Ideologies

Consistent with the report by Burn (1996) that males with more traditional gender ideologies are less accepting of homosexuality in general, we found, consistent with our hypotheses, that men with higher adherence to traditional gender ideologies were more likely than men with low/moderate adherence to use non-sexual pressuring homosexual insults and sexualized homosexual insults. However, there was no such difference in the use of non-sexual joking insults. One explanation for these findings is that men higher in gender ideology may be more seriously against male homosexuality as a legitimate style of manhood but do not treat non-sexual joking homosexual insults as a joking matter. Pressuring or sexualized homosexual insults might thus be seen as a method of aggressive persuasion or manipulation toward a particular gender ideology.

Ethnic Background

Among the demographic factors of age, educational status, religion, and ethnicity, only ethnic background showed any relationship to use of homosexual insults and in that case only in the usage of non-sexual joking homosexual insults. Our finding that non-Caucasian men were significantly more likely to use non-sexual joking insults than Caucasian men (but not pressuring or sexualized homosexual insults) is important because it highlights Pascoe's (2005) observation that 'researchers who look at the intersection of sexuality and masculinity need to attend to the ways in which racialized identities may affect how "fag" is deployed and what it means in various social situations' (p. 342).

To the extent that different ethnic groups may hold different ideas about what they consider masculine, it could be that masculinity rather than sexual orientation is the defining feature of most or even all homosexual insults. In that regard, our finding that non-Caucasian men were significantly more likely to use non-sexual joking insults may not necessarily indicate that these men were using insults about sexual orientation, per se, but rather that our homosexual insult questionnaire may have highlighted behaviours considered more non-masculine by non-Caucasian than Caucasian men. This is not to imply that such insults do not have an undeniable impact on gay men whose presumed 'masculinity' is being questioned. Research on the various ideologies that constitute masculinity for different ethnic groups could inform efforts to develop protective factors for young gay and heterosexual males of various ethnic backgrounds who are regularly victimized by homosexual taunting.

Limitations

Comrey and Lee (1992) have proposed that the recommended sample size for a factor analysis should be a minimum of 200 participants. Due to the difficulty in recruiting a larger sample size within the study's time constraints, statistical analysis was performed on 100 participants. While the three factor solution was informative, future studies on this topic that use factor analysis should incorporate larger numbers. Although our original aim was to compare men's scores on the predictor variables in three groups, i.e., low, moderate, and high, the low and moderate groups tended to be small, making it necessary to combine the low and moderate groups to compare to the high group. This was a particular problem with the sexual orientation score groups. Even after grouping men who were low and moderate on sexual orientation scores, the group was small ($n = 22$) compared to the high group ($n = 78$).

The gender ideology predictor variable was based on a single question in the homosexual insult questionnaire. This was item 13 that read as follows: 'Do you consider male homosexuality "unmanly" or otherwise counter to masculinity?' Gender ideology, as a component of sexual identity, is supposed to capture a person's understanding of what a gendered person is to be like (Shively & De Cecco, 1977). Someone high in gender ideology would have highly traditional beliefs concerning gender ideology, while someone low or moderate in gender ideology would have low or moderate traditional beliefs about gender ideology. Item 13 does not fully represent gender ideology as well as it could be represented, as it simply asks about one domain of gender ideology: homosexuality and masculinity. In the future, it would be preferable to capture gender ideology in a more complete way, perhaps by defining gender ideology for participants and then asking them to self-report on their beliefs regarding the way a man or woman should be.

References

Alderson, K.G., Orzeck, T.L., Davis, S., & Boyes, M. (2010). *Sexual orientation: Defining and measuring it.* Manuscript in preparation.

Armstrong, J.D. (2006), Homophobic slang as coercive discourse among college students. In H. Luria, D.M. Seymour, & T. Smoke (Eds), *Language and linguistics in context* (pp. 219–25). Hillsdale, NJ: Lawrence Erlbaum.

Burke, P. (1996). *Gender shock.* New York, NY: Anchor.

Burn, S.M. (1996). *The social psychology of gender.* New York, NY: McGraw-Hill.

———. (2000). Heterosexuals' use of 'fag' and 'queer' to deride one another: A contributor to heterosexism and stigma. *Journal of Homosexuality, 40,* 1–11.

Comrey, A.L., & Lee, H.B. (1992): *A first course in factor analysis.* (2nd edn), Hillsdale, NJ: Lawrence Erlbaum.

Connell, R.W. (1995). *Masculinities.* Los Angeles, CA: University of California Press.

Dafnos, T. (2007). What does being gay have to do with it? A feminist analysis of the Jubran case. *Canadian Journal of Criminology and Criminal Justice, 49,* 561–85.

D'Augelli, A.R. (1992). Lesbian and gay male undergraduates' experiences of harassment and fear on campus. *Journal of Interpersonal Violence, 7,* 383–95.

Dupré, J. (2001). *Human nature and the limits of science.* New York, NY: Oxford University Press.

Eisler, R.M., & Skidmore, J.R. (1987). Masculine gender role stress: Scale development and component factors in the appraisal of stressful situations. *Behavior Modification, 11,* 123–36.

Eliason, M., Donelan, C., & Randall, C. (1992). Lesbian stereotypes. *Health Care for Women International, 13,* 131–44.

Frankel, L. (2004). An appeal for additional research about the development of heterosexual male sexual identity. *Journal of Psychology & Human Sexuality, 16*, 1–16.

Glick, P., Gangl, C., Gibb, S., Klumpner, S., & Weinberg, E. (2007). Defensive reaction to masculinity threat: More negative affect toward effeminate (but not masculine) gay men. *Sex Roles, 57*, 55–59.

Kimmel, M.S. (1997). Masculinity as homophobia: Fear, shame and silence in the construction of gender identity. In M. Gergen & S. Davis (Eds), *Toward a new psychology of gender* (pp. 223–42). New York, NY: Taylor & Frances/Routledge.

Kimmel, M.S., & Mahler, M. (2003). Adolescent masculinity, homophobia, and violence: Random school shootings, 1982–2001. *The American Behavioral Scientist, 46*, 1439–57.

Kinsey, A.C., Pomeroy W.B., & Martin C.E. (1948). *Sexual behavior in the human male*. Philadelphia, PA: W.B. Saunders.

Kite, M.E., & Whitely, B.F. (2003). Do heterosexual women and men differ in their attitudes toward homosexuality? A conceptual and methodological analysis. In L.D. Garnets & D.C. Kimmel (Eds), *Psychological perspectives on lesbian, gay, and bisexual experience second edition.* (pp. 165–87). New York, NY: Columbia University Press.

Lippa, R. A. (2008). The relation between childhood gender nonconformity and adult masculinity-femininity and anxiety in heterosexual and homosexual men and women. *Sex Roles, 59*, 684–93.

Lock, J., & Kleis, B. (1998). Origins of homophobia in males: Psychosexual vulnerabilities and defence development. *American Journal of Psychotherapy, 52*, 426–36.

Miller, L.R., Bilimoria R.N., & Pattni, N. (2000). Do women want 'new men': Cultural influences on sex-role stereotypes. *Psychology, Evolution, & Gender, 2*, 127–50.

Pascoe, C.J. (2005). 'Dude, you're a fag': Adolescent masculinity and the fag discourse. *Sexualities, 8*, 329–45.

Plummer, D.C. (1999). *One of the boys: Masculinity, homophobia, and modern manhood.* New York, NY: Haworth Press.

Preston, K., & Stanley, K. (1987). 'What's the worst thing . . .?' Gender-directed insults. *Sex Roles, 17*, 209–19.

Rudman, L.A., & Fairchild, K. (2004). Reactions to counterstereotypic behavior: The role of backlash in cultural stereotype maintenance. *Journal of Personality and Social Psychology, 87*, 157–76.

Schneider, D.J. (2004). *The psychology of stereotyping.* New York, NY: Guilford Press.

Shively, M.G., & De Cecco, J.P. (1977). Components of sexual identity. *Journal of Homosexuality, 3*, 41–48.

Sigelman, C.K., Howell, J.L., Cornell, D.P., Cutright, J.D., & Dewey, J.C. (1991). Courtesy stigma: The social implications of association with a gay person. *The Journal of Social Psychology, 13*, 45–56.

Silverschanz, P., Cortina, L.M., Konik, J., & Magley, V.J. (2008). Slurs, snubs, and queer jokes: Incidence and impact of heterosexist harassment in academia. *Sex Roles, 58*, 179–91.

Theodore, P.S., & Basow, S.A. (2000). Heterosexual masculinity and homophobia: A reaction to the self. *Journal of Homosexuality, 40*, 31–48.

What Does Being Gay Have to Do With It? A Feminist Analysis of the *Jubran* Case (Canada)

Tia Dafnos

Introduction

When a student calls another student a 'homo', is it schoolyard name-calling or homophobic harassment? This kind of behaviour is common in the school experiences of many young people and if overheard, a teacher might simply reprimand the offending student. Although pervasive, homophobic taunting is rarely dealt with by school authorities as seriously as derogatory behaviour toward other aspects of identity like race, ethnicity, or religion. Just replace 'homo' with an offensive

term along these lines and imagine the reaction. Azmi Jubran was subjected to homophobic harassment throughout high school even after reporting it to school officials. In 1996, he filed a human rights complaint against the school board alleging discrimination on the grounds of sexual orientation.

The *Jubran* case is the first in Canada to deal with the issue of school responsibility for peer-to-peer harassment. In addition, and importantly, it makes a significant contribution to the jurisprudence in the realm of sexual orientation harassment and discrimination. [. . .] The first part of this paper summarizes the case and its progression through the legal system, and discusses the legal framework for establishing discrimination. A detailed feminist analysis of the decisions follows, focusing on the relevance of sexual orientation identity in the case. The third part of the paper looks critically at how harm—a key element in harassment and discrimination cases—was addressed, including the courts' use of various incarnations of the 'reasonable person' test. Three different feminist conceptions of harm that may address the issue of homophobia more appropriately are examined. Finally, the implications of the *Jubran* decision on the issue of school liability for student behaviour are briefly discussed.

[. . .]

The *Jubran* Case

Azmi Jubran endured bullying and name-calling by other students throughout his high school experience at Handsworth Secondary School in Vancouver, British Columbia. It began in grade 8 and continued until he graduated from grade 12. The majority of the harassment involved homophobic epithets—he was called 'homo', 'faggot', and 'gay', among other things. Physical harassment sometimes accompanied the epithets as he was pushed, shoved, spit on, and had things thrown at him. These incidents happened in the schoolyard, hallways, and in classrooms when teachers were not present (*Jubran v. Board of Trustees* at para. 8–75). In 1996, when he was in grade 10, Jubran filed a complaint with the British Columbia Human Rights Commission against the Vancouver School Board. His claim alleged that the School Board had violated the British Columbia Human Rights Code (BCHRC) (1996) by discriminating against him on the grounds of sexual orientation. Section 8(b) of the BCHRC prohibits the denial of, or discrimination regarding

any accommodation, service or facility customarily available to the public . . . because of the race, colour, ancestry, place of origin, religion, marital status, family status, physical or mental disability, sex or sexual orientation of that person or class of persons.

Jubran argued that the school had failed to provide him with an environment free from discrimination because the harassment continued even after he reported incidents making school authorities aware of the situation. In response, the School Board argued that it could not be held responsible for failing to eliminate such behaviour among students, and that the Tribunal did not have the power to make judgments about how suitable the efforts of the school were (*Jubran v. Board of Trustees* at para. 5). The Tribunal decided that the School Board was responsible for student behaviour that violated the BCHRC and awarded Jubran $4000 in compensation. The School Board appealed the decision and the British Columbia Superior Court overturned the Tribunal's ruling. The case then went to the BC Court of Appeal, which struck down the lower court's ruling and reinstated that of the Tribunal. In October 2005, the Supreme Court of Canada refused leave to appeal to the School Board. The decision of the BC Court of Appeal thus stands as the final one in this case. The three decisions dealt with two key legal issues:

1. What constitutes discrimination based on sexual orientation? Specifically, did Jubran experience discrimination on these grounds?
2. Can a School Board be held responsible for the conduct of students that contravenes human rights legislation?

The question of whether the harassment Jubran faced constituted discrimination was pivotal in this case, as it formed the basis for the Court of Appeal's decision to overturn the lower court. [. . .] What became a central point of contention was that Jubran did not self-identify as homosexual. Additionally, his peers claimed that they did not perceive him as such. This issue of the relevance of sexual orientation identity will form the bulk of the analysis that follows because of its importance as a threshold leading to the second legal issue of school liability.

Legal Framework for Discrimination

As responsibility for education falls under provincial jurisdiction, schools are governed by provincial human rights legislation, that is, human rights codes. The first element to establish in the case was whether the behaviour of the other students constituted harassment. Richard (1996) defines harassment as unwanted or unwelcome behaviour that makes one feel unsafe or uncomfortable. Because the term 'harassment' is not defined in the BCHRC, the Tribunal looked to other provincial codes for guidance. Like Richard's definition, the codes generally include concepts of 'unwelcome' abusive conduct or comments, and the idea that it occurs over a period of time.[1] After hearing evidence about the nature of the conduct that occurred throughout his high school years, the Tribunal decided that Jubran was subjected to behaviour that constituted harassment based on sexual orientation (*Jubran v. Board of Trustees* at para. 101).

Although sexual orientation is a prohibited ground under the BCHRC, it does not have the same status as sexual harassment in establishing prima facie discrimination. [. . .] Jubran had to show that the harassment he experienced led to differential treatment based on sexual orientation. In human rights law, the emphasis is on the *effect* of discriminatory behaviour, not the intent or motive of the harasser/discriminator (*Ontario Human Rights Commission v. Simpsons-Sears*). This evolves from the purpose of human rights legislation to ameliorate discriminatory conditions rather than to assign blame and administer punishment. [. . .] In the following sections, the interlinked issues regarding the relevance of Jubran's sexuality and the harm caused by the homophobic harassment will be examined. The decisions of the Tribunal and courts on these issues will be analyzed from a critical feminist perspective. As there is no one feminist perspective, the critique will attempt to acknowledge various approaches.

The Relevance of Sexual Orientation Identity

The Purpose of Human Rights Legislation

The issue of the relevance of Jubran's sexuality and the students' perception of it was a matter of the proper interpretation of human rights law. The Tribunal ruled that Jubran was eligible to make the claim of discrimination on the grounds of sexual orientation, stating '[w]hether or not Mr. Jubran self-identifies as a homosexual, he is nevertheless entitled to the protection of the Code'. It found that Jubran was the target of harassment based on the prohibited ground of sexual orientation because of the nature of the harassment (*Jubran v. Board of Trustees* at para. 100–101). Following *Ontario Human Rights Commission v. Simpsons-Sears*, the Tribunal reasoned that both Jubran's sexuality, and the perceptions of the other students were irrelevant, as 'it is the effect of the conduct' that is of issue in determining the occurrence of discrimination (*Jubran v. Board of Trustees* at para. 97). It stated that '[t]he evidence is clear that the harassment negatively affected Mr. Jubran's school experience, and caused him to contemplate suicide' (para. 99). This was sufficient to qualify the conduct as discrimination without needing proof of the harassers' intent.

The decision of the BC Superior Court took a completely different approach, focusing on the intent or perceptions of the harassing students. Justice Stewart ruled that Jubran was not entitled to make a claim under section 8 of the BCHRC because 'Jubran is not a homosexual and the students who attacked him did not believe he was a homosexual' (*Board of School Trustees of School District No. 44 v. Jubran* at para. 11). His judgment centred on the wording of section 8, specifically: 'because of the . . . sex or sexual orientation *of that person or class of persons*' [his emphasis] (para. 13). He interpreted this as a limiting phrase, restricting protection to a particular group of people. He looked to Supreme Court of Canada rulings to reason that while human rights legislation should have a broad and liberal interpretation, courts should 'not let the application of legislation such as section 8 of the Human Rights Code slip the anchor of the words chosen by the legislature' (para. 13).[2] He quashed the Tribunal's decision and ordered that the case not be reheard again. Justice Stewart interpreted 'sexual orientation' to mean homosexuality. [. . .] As the Court of Appeal later stated, 'nothing about those words requires that a person have a particular sexual orientation or identify himself as homosexual' (para. 51). [. . .] It cited the Supreme Court, which said that 'it is inappropriate to rely solely on a strictly grammatical analysis, particularly with respect to . . . legislation which is constitutional or quasi-constitutional in nature' and its recognition that 'all statutes, whether or not they are constitutional in nature, must be interpreted contextually . . .' (para. 31).[3]

[. . .]

Furthermore, as MacDougall (2004) argues, the decision of the Superior Court also ignored the hostility that non-heterosexual youth face in society, and the dilemma of self-identifying in a public setting, such as in a court. By preventing individuals who are unwilling to self-identify in public from bringing forward claims of discrimination, the court has the ability to use its judicial powers to maintain a heterosexist society. As demonstrated by Stewart J.'s ruling, a narrow interpretation of human rights legislation would disallow claims preventing the identification and amelioration of discriminatory situations.

In contrast, a broad or liberal interpretation of human rights statutes—such as that taken by the Court of Appeal—opens the door for other analyses of harm, allowing for the consideration of homophobia as a context. The Court of Appeal looked to the purposes of the BCHRC (1996), as set out in section 3, which states,

The purposes of this Code are . . .
a. to foster a society . . . in which there are no impediments to full and free participation . . . ,
b. to promote a climate of understanding and mutual respect where all are equal in dignity and rights,
c. to prevent discrimination prohibited by this Code,
d. to identify and eliminate persistent patterns of inequality associated with discrimination prohibited by this Code,
e. to provide a means of redress. . . .

It decided that Jubran's complaint fell within these objectives, in particular those regarding the elimination of persistent patterns of inequality and protecting human dignity and equality. Within the context of these objectives, it is possible to raise the issue of homophobia rather than simply focus on the individual case.

The Harm of Homophobic Harassment

Poisoned Environment

In discrimination jurisprudence, one way that harassment can cause harm is by creating a 'poisoned' environment.[4] The harassing conduct 'demeans, humiliates or upsets' the victim, causing the environment to become 'psychologically and/or emotionally intolerable' (Georgas 2001: 58). This poisoned environment prevents the victim from enjoying the full benefit of a service or opportunity, thus amounting to discrimination (Georgas 2001: 41). For harassment to be discrimination, it must have had the *effect* of causing *harm* to the victim. The concept of harm is therefore essential in linking harassment to discrimination. In finding that the harassment of Jubran constituted discrimination, the Tribunal wrote, 'The evidence is clear that the harassment negatively affected Mr. Jubran's school experience, and caused him to contemplate suicide' (*Jubran v. Board of Trustees* at para. 99). We can infer the 'poisoned' environment reasoning from this statement—the harassment created a psychologically or emotionally negative setting that affected Jubran's ability to fully enjoy and participate in his education experience. Although this principle fits Jubran's situation, it is interesting that none of the decisions in the case explicitly referred to it. This may indicate a reluctance to view homophobia as a systemic problem by dealing with the case as an isolated incident.[5] To declare it as a poisoned environment would indicate a widespread problem in the school and raise the possibility that other people in the environment could have been affected. The school administration had addressed Jubran's situation as a private, or isolated, matter by offering him counselling services, and by disciplining some of the perpetrators on an individual basis. Fineran (2002) argues that treating sexual harassment (including homophobic harassment), as an individual problem does not consider the students who could have witnessed the harassment and the effect it could have on them. [. . .] Lacking was some direction toward addressing homophobia and heterosexism in the school community through proactive measures such as curriculum initiatives.

As noted, one of the major feminist criticisms of using the legal system is that claims must be tailored to fit under the legal framework. Often this means that feminist analyses must be left out, thus weakening the wider goals of exposing inequality and the domination of patriarchy. We can see this in the assessment of harm in this case. Under the legal framework, Jubran was harmed because he was not allowed to enjoy the full benefit of the educational environment/ system, *not* because the homophobic harassment attacked (his) sexuality and created a power inequality between him and his peers based on heterosexism. Feminists have developed new notions of harm that address these goals more closely. To varying degrees, these conceptions can be reconciled with the existing legal structure as represented by the decisions of the judiciary in the *Jubran* case. Conversely, Jubran may not have the benefit of protection under all these feminist definitions of harm.

The Harm of Sexual Shame

Drucilla Cornell (1995) begins from the premise that sexual orientation harassment be incorporated into sexual harassment provisions. This is based on her conception of people as what she calls 'sexuate' beings—that sexuality is who we are. Her definition of sexual harassment includes three possible manifestations, the most important for the purpose of this paper is the following:

> The creation and perpetuation of a work environment, which enforces sexual

shame by reducing individuals to project- ed stereotypes or objectified fantasies of their 'sex' so as to undermine the primary good of their self-respect (170).[6]

The concept of sexual shame rests on her adop- tion of the Rawlsian argument that everyone in a just society should be guaranteed self-respect as a primary good. Cornell argues that this self- respect lies in our ability to *be* a sexuate being. To be denied self-respect 'closets sexuality and by doing so, cuts some of us off from the equivalent chance of becoming a person' (185). The harm is this inability to be oneself (i.e., with self-respect), which occurs when one is 'projected as a stereo- type' that is negatively perceived (207). Targets of harassment become 'projected as a stereotypes' when homophobic epithets are used against them.

From the language used by the Tribunal (*Jubran v. Board of Trustees*), Cornell's idea of shame as relating to self-respect may not be so much of a stretch. The following excerpts seem to reflect this (with emphasis added),

'. . . the epithets . . . were designed to *shame*' (para. 95);

'. . . the words used were hurtful and insulting, and *demeaning*' (para. 98); and

'The harassment was an unwanted *intrusion* upon his dignity' (para. 98).

Finally, in justifying the monetary remedy, the Tri- bunal provided that the compensation was 'for the injury to his dignity, feelings and *self respect*' (para. 232). Similarly, the idea of projecting stereotypes is reflected in the Court of Appeal's statement that the harassment of Jubran projected to him 'the negative perceptions, myths and stereotypes attributed to homosexuals' (*North Vancouver School District No. 44 v. Jubran*, 2005 at para. 47).

[. . .]

Jubran would be eligible to make a claim under Cornell's framework because the nega- tive stereotypes associated with homosexuality were projected onto him, imputed by the homo- phobic epithets. He would have experienced sexual shame because he became defined by an imposed sex(uality) stereotype. This denied him self-respect because it restricted his ability to be free in his own sex. Essentially, it is Cornell's (re)definition of sex that would allow Jubran to make the claim. Because sex, gender, and sexuality are not differentiated, a claimant would not need to self-identify—it is irrelevant. What is of issue is that a person was denied self-respect because of the negative stereotypes emerging through the harassment. The focus is on the harassing conduct, not on the individual making the claim.

The Harm of Words

The students who harassed Jubran claimed that the terms they used 'were simply . . . another form of insult' along the lines of 'dork' or 'geek'. One student said that they are 'part of the high school vocabulary' (*Jubran v. Board of Trust- ees* at paras. 37, 44). The Tribunal and both courts often referred to the use of the words as 'name-calling'. The question is raised: If these were simply words, what is the harm? Accord- ing to Judith Butler (1997), words have the power to injure. Certain words have the ability to construct a power relationship between the speaker and the target. The speaker of the word is citing it, 'making linguistic community with a history of speakers'. It has the potential to injure because it has built up force through the accumulation of actions and vocalizations over time (51–52). The relationship between homophobia and violence—physical, emotional, verbal, and psychological—has a long history.

In particular, there is a very real association between words and physical violence (Perry 2000). In Jubran's case, this may be illustrated by the fact that physical harassment was often accompanied by homophobic epithets. The power of words such as 'fag' or 'homo' to harm comes from how they have taken on negative connotations through the history of homophobia, but also from the way that they designate their target as being outside the norm. This understanding emerges in the Tribunal's decision, which accepted the argument that the harassing behaviour had 'at its basis *a sense of his difference* which was described frequently in homophobic terms' [emphasis added] (*Jubran v. Board of Trustees* at para. 96). The use of these words can be seen as an act or performance that is able to establish a power difference between speaker and target.

Following Butler's conception of the ability of words to injure, it does not seem relevant whether or not Jubran self-identified as homosexual. While the degree of harm could likely be greater for someone who *did* identify, the meaning and force of those words can still have an impact on someone who does not. The reason that these words have the ability to injure is because everyone understands their denotations—the speaker, the target, and witnesses. This is how it can effectively construct or reinforce power differences between the speaker as heterosexual and 'normal' and the target as homosexual and 'abnormal'.

While Butler's arguments show that words themselves have the potential to cause harm, it removes responsibility from the speaker. She discusses the ambiguity of moral blameworthiness when someone 'cites' a word, but is not fully responsible for the history that gives it the power to injure (1997: 50). In a sense, this can be reconciled with the purpose of human rights legislation in that it does not assign blame, but only remedies discriminatory situations.

The Harm of Visibility and Homophobia: The Homophobic Environment

Gail Mason (2002) rejects Cornell's concept of sexual shame as problematic because it assumes that everyone targeted by homophobic harassment 'automatically' experiences sexual shame in the same way. Instead, she argues that the only thing that a target can be certain of is the knowledge that the harassers view his/her sexual preference 'in a negative or stereotyped light' (617). Mason expands on the idea of the poisoned environment, but specifically as a *homophobic* one where the target's fear of the homophobia of others is harmful in itself. Harm occurs because the target 'feels "trapped" by the visibility of their homosexuality' which is rendered visible by the harassment. Being 'named' as gay or lesbian creates the possibility of 'unwelcome effects' (619). As Mason points out, to be named as heterosexual would not be seen as negative or elicit negative responses.[7]

The question of whether Jubran's case would be successful under Mason's framework may be trickier to answer. On the surface, it appears that homosexual identity is central to experiencing the fear of being 'outed' through naming. Mason talks about the proverbial closet as a tool of 'self-regulation' and as a way of resisting unwanted scrutiny of one's sexual preferences (2002: 618). The idea of visibility seems to be inextricably linked to actual identity—how can something that does not exist be visible? It could be that the fear is that a falsehood could be seen as 'truth'—one would not want to have a negative image whether or not it was 'true'. But this veers into the terrain of libel, slander, and defamation. Arguably, if a person is heterosexual, he/she can still be subject to unwanted homophobic conduct as Jubran was. As Black (2003) argues, a person who does not identify as a member of a vilified group can still be harmed because certain stereotypes are imputed to them. The conceptions of Butler and Cornell support this position. However, Mason's arguments seem to imply that the harm caused to Jubran would not be as severe as for someone who did identify as homosexual. [. . .] It seems then that under Mason's framework, a claimant would have to self-identify as homosexual, because the degree of harm of the harassment is directly linked to it. It is interesting that this approach parallels that taken by the Superior Court.

While Mason's definition may rule Jubran out, the harm of a homophobic environment could allow homosexual students who are not the direct targets of harassment to bring a claim forward. Lovell writes that when 'a queer student witnesses a classmate harassing another classmate due to his or her sexual orientation, she can discern the harasser's opinion about homosexuality. This may lead the student to avoid contact with peers to avoid discovery' (1998: 628). The harm to students can be just as significant whether or not they are the direct targets of the harassment. What they have in common is their sexual orientation identity, which makes the harm possible.

The feminist conceptions of harm discussed provide ways of thinking about the effects of harassment that allow for an analysis of systemic homophobia. They address homophobia and the harassing behaviour as harmful, rather than focus solely on the victim's emotional or psychological response to the harassment, which is at the centre of the poisoned environment approach. [. . .] Mason's approach, which is the most individualistic of the feminist conceptions discussed, is also the one under which the eligibility of Jubran's claim might be uncertain. Individualistic approaches rely on an assessment of the victim's reaction to harassment. In the legal system, 'reasonableness' is the standard of evaluation used to assess the reaction.

Assessing Harm: The 'Reasonable Person'

To establish that an environment was indeed poisoned by the harassment, courts invoke a reasonable person test. Often, this takes the form of a 'modified objective' or 'reasonable victim' test as the reasonable person is placed in the victim's position to determine whether the circumstances would be perceived as a poisoned environment (Georgas 2001: 58). The concept of reasonableness is highly contested in feminist theory and criticism. Historically, the perspective of the reasonable person has been that of a white, middle to upper class, heterosexual male. The 'objective' assessment therefore tends to maintain oppressive conditions.

[. . .]

Applying the reasonable victim test in Jubran's case would have to take the perspective of a high school student. Georgas argues that this may lessen the likelihood that a school board would be held liable because of the 'diminished capacity' of the harassers—as youth—to understand the consequences of their actions. This is flawed reasoning, because he initially ignores that the test would take the *victim's* perspective, not that of the offending students. He suggests that an 'adult standard' would be more effective (2001: 62). On the contrary, adults would probably be more likely to dismiss a situation like Jubran's as youthful bullying or 'nasty name-calling'[8]— not discrimination. Labelling such behaviour as name-calling or teasing implies that as a 'normal' part of school experience, one should (reasonably) expect and endure it to a degree. As Stein (1999) argues, however, bullying itself is a form of harassment because it deprives victims of a right to education and to feel safe. The willingness to believe that the students were not aware of the effect or meaning of the words, and that their use of homophobic terms was along the lines of 'dork' or 'geek', is clearly contradicted by their circulation in class of an illustration of Jubran holding hands with a male student. Evidently, homophobia did inform their behaviour. The argument that youth are not aware of the effect of such behaviour because of their age or lack of life experience infantilizes them. Furthermore, even if this claim were accepted, it ignores the fact that the victim is also a youth and that the harassment could therefore have a *greater* impact. A frequently cited American study by the American Association of University Women (1993) found that 86 per cent of students reported that they would be 'very upset' if called gay or lesbian by their peers. The researchers noted that no other form of harassment elicited such a strong response.

[. . .]

The Superior Court also used the concept of reasonableness, but in terms of legislative interpretation. Justice Stewart stated that the Tribunal's decision to allow Jubran's claim under section 8 was 'unreasonable' (*Board of School Trustees of School District No. 44 v. Jubran* at para. 12). Although he did not discuss reasonableness in much detail, Justice Stewart was relying on the old standard in determining that a reasonable person would not have read section 8 in such a broad manner as to include Jubran. Instead, his narrow reading is 'reasonable'. Firstly, it interprets sexual orientation as homosexuality; secondly, it ignores the wider context of homophobia and how it contributes to harm. Because heterosexuality is the norm for this 'reasonable person', it is invisible—thus any reference to sexual orientation is associated with something outside the norm, that is, homosexuality. The second element of his interpretation reflects a refusal or inability to acknowledge or recognize oppression from a privileged position.

[. . .]

The reasonable person test is a common tool used by the courts in cases to determine whether harassment amounted to discrimination. The decisions in the *Jubran* case provide illustrations of the various criticisms of this tool. As discussed, the common standard of reasonableness reflects a privileged viewpoint. It can discount the context for harm that is shaped by experiences outside of this dominant perspective. At the same time, an individualized approach can also be problematic because it places the focus on the individual rather than on the behaviour or environment. The final decision of the Court of Appeal in the case is significant, however, because it held the School Board responsible for the discrimination. While the conceptualization and assessment of harm in the case centred on Jubran, the result is that it may pressure schools to deal with homophobia as the source of the problem.

The Responsibility of Schools

The second key legal issue in which the *Jubran* case sets a precedent deals with school liability for the conduct of students, which potentially contributes toward the goal of eliminating systemic inequalities. While it is beyond the scope of this paper to fully analyze this aspect of the *Jubran* case, it is necessary to briefly discuss it as it relates to the wider goal of addressing homophobia in schools.

In *Ross v. New Brunswick School District No. 15*, the Supreme Court ruled that schools have a responsibility to provide a 'positive' environment for all. The Supreme Court has also hinted that schools have a duty to be proactive, stating that 'schools are meant to develop civic virtue and responsible citizenship, to educate in an environment free of bias, prejudice and intolerance . . .' (*Trinity Western University vs. British Columbia College of Teachers* at para. 13). Drawing on these rulings, the Tribunal concluded that the School Board had a responsibility to provide an educational environment free from discriminatory harassment. The Deputy Chief Commissioner argued that the School Board did not take action to deal with homophobia in the schools, and that the disciplinary measures taken with individual students did not end the discrimination. Although resources on homophobia were available, the School Board had not taken advantage of them. The Tribunal ruled that the School Board had not accommodated Jubran in providing a discrimination-free environment to the point of undue hardship, and thus it did not have a bona fide justification for violating section 8 of the Code. The Superior Court did not deal with this issue, precluded by the decision that Jubran was ineligible to make the claim in the first place. This demonstrates how judicial interpretation in this ruling—through a narrow reading of the legislation—carried the power to maintain the existing heterosexist environment by not holding the School Board responsible for dealing with homophobia. In contrast, the Court of Appeal upheld the Tribunal's decision and reasoning, stating that a discrimination-free environment is 'mandated by the special position educational institutions occupy in fostering the values of our society and by the Code . . .' (*North Vancouver School District No. 44 v. Jubran* at para 92).

Fineran (2002) maintains that school authorities should be proactive in identifying and reporting incidents of harassment. This would take the burden away from students. As the Tribunal heard, school authorities were concerned that students might retaliate against Jubran for reporting the incidents. The School Board had argued that it could not be held responsible for failing to eliminate discrimination by its students. However, as Fineran (2002) points out, schools have the ability to intervene and provide clear consequences for perpetrators. Also, providing education and training contributes toward improving the school environment as

a whole (Fineran 2002). School authorities decided that dealing with individual students 'on an incident-by-incident basis was more effective than "preaching at the masses at an assembly"' because it was believed that the students to whom the 'preaching' would be directed would probably not attend or listen (*Jubran v. Board of Trustees* at para. 142). The failure of the courts to specifically address the issue of harm as arising from a poisoned environment reflects a similar position—that the harassing behaviour affected Jubran solely and directly without impact on the school surroundings. This reflects a refusal to acknowledge oppressive behaviours as part of a wider problem by rationalizing them as isolated incidents (Matsuda 1993). Furthermore, when school authorities treat homosexuality as taboo by not discussing it openly, gay and lesbian students do not have anything to counterbalance pervasive negative stereotypes (MacDougall 2000, cited in Black 2003: 51). Isolation can lead to academic problems, irregular attendance, drug abuse, or suicide (Lovell 1998). The final *Jubran* decision essentially places a duty on schools to actively ensure a discrimination-free environment. This is a positive step toward eliminating homophobia as well as other forms of oppression from the school environment, which can benefit society as a whole.

[. . .]

Conclusion

The Jubran case produced new jurisprudence in two areas of discrimination law. The decision of the BC Court of Appeal means that the sexual orientation identity of a complainant is not relevant to claims of discrimination on that ground. Secondly, school boards can be held liable for the discriminatory behaviour of its students. From a feminist perspective, although the outcome of the case is positive with the Court of Appeal's decision, the process demonstrates some of the problems with using the legal system as a means towards eliminating oppression in society.

Azmi Jubran argued that the harassment he faced was discriminatory because it affected his ability to fully participate and enjoy his school experience. His sexual orientation became a pivotal issue as it formed the basis for the Superior Court's decision to overturn the Tribunal. [. . .] The narrow versus broad interpretations of human rights legislation by each court contrasted the ability of the judiciary to, on the one hand, maintain heterosexist conditions and, on the other, take a progressive approach by allowing for a contextual understanding of homophobia. The dilemma of undermining some feminist goals/values to achieve others under a legal framework is evident in the conceptualization of harm in the case. While the language of the Tribunal implied a poisoned environment, its failure to specifically use that term could be interpreted as a reluctance to acknowledge homophobia as a wider problem in the school by focusing on Jubran as an isolated case. Feminist conceptions of harm such as Cornell's 'sexual shame' and Butler's 'harm of words' focus on the harassment itself as problematic instead of the victim's reaction to it. Both of these approaches are reflected in some elements of the Tribunal and Court of Appeal decisions. Although Mason's discussion of visibility and naming specifically takes homophobia

as harmful in itself, it could exclude Jubran from eligibility. However, queer students who witnessed the harassment could be harmed and therefore make a claim. The reasonable person test used to assess harm is problematic because of its ability to reinforce dominant values and perceptions. This was most clearly illustrated by Justice Stewart's 'reasonable' narrow interpretation. [. . .] An individualized approach is also problematic because it relies on the victim to construct and prove the harm. Holding the School Board responsible in this case creates a precedent that may encourage schools to deal with homophobia as a root problem to avoid legal claims. However, the relatively low monetary remedies awarded in human rights cases and the many barriers to bringing a claim forward may temper their zeal.

There must be an effort to deal with homophobia in schools from the ground level. Although progressive feminist conceptions of harm can be reconciled within the existing legal framework, the system will continue to deal with homophobia on a case-by-case basis rather than addressing it as systemic oppression. Schools should be proactive in dealing with homophobia rather than waiting for a court order to institute programs and policies. It needs to be seen as a critical endeavour for which governments should make funding available. Only through recognition of homophobia as a systemic problem can real social change happen.

Notes

1. The Tribunal cited the human rights codes of Manitoba, Ontario, Newfoundland, and Yukon as examples.
2. Referring to *University of British Columbia v. Berg*, [1993] 2 S.C.R. 353.
3. Citing L'Heureux-Dubé J. in *Quebec (Commission des droits de la personne et des droits de la jeunesse) v. Montréal (City)*, [2000] 1 S.C.R. 665.
4. Described as a 'hostile' environment in the American context.
5. See Matsuda (1993).
6. The other two manifestations of sexual harassment are 'unilaterally imposed sexual requirements in the context of unequal power' or 'employment-related retaliation against a subordinate employee or, in the case of a university, a student, for a consensually mutually desired sexual relationship'.
7. It is possible to view this exposure to unequal, i.e., differential treatment as discriminatory under an equality framework.
8. As Justice Ryan referred to it in her alternative opinion (*North Vancouver School District No. 44 v. Jubran*, 2005 at para. 121).

References

American Association of University Women Educational Foundation. (1993). *Holistic Hallways: AAUW Survey on Sexual Harassment in America's Schools* (Research Report 923012). Washington, DC: Harris/Scholastic Research.

Black, William. (2003). Grading human rights in the schoolyard: *Jubran v. Board of Trustees*. *University of British Columbia Law Review 36:* 45–55.

Butler, Judith. (1997). *Excitable Speech: A Politic.* New York: Routledge.

Cornell, Drucilla. (1995). *The Imaginary Domain: Abortion, Pornography and Sexual Harassment.* New York: Routledge.

Fineran, Susan. (2002). Sexual harassment between same-sex peers: Intersection of mental health, homophobia, and sexual violence in schools. *Social Work 47:* 65–74.

Georgas, William. (2001). Student-on-student harassment: A new paradigm for Canadian human rights legislation. *Dalhousie Journal of Legal Studies 10:* 36–73.

Lovell, Amy. (1998). Other students always used to say 'look at the dykes': Protecting students from peer sexual orientation harassment. *California Law Review 86:* 617–64.

MacDougall, Bruce. (2004). The legally queer child. *McGill Law Journal 49:* 1057–91.

Mason, Gail. (2002). Harm, harassment and sexuality. *Melbourne University Law Review 26:* 596–623.

Matsuda, Mari. (1993). Public response to racist speech: Considering the victim's story. In Mari Matsuda and Kimberle W. Crenshaw (Eds), *Words that Wound: Critical Race Theory, Assaultive Speech, and the First Amendment.* Boulder, CO: Westview.

Perry, B.D. (2000). Traumatized children: How childhood trauma influences brain development. *Journal of the California Alliance for the Mentally Ill, 11*(1): 48–51.

Richard, Chantal. (1996). Surviving student to student harassment: Legal remedies and prevention programmes. *Dalhousie Law Journal 19:* 169–97.

Stein, Nan. (1999). *Classrooms and Courtrooms: Facing Sexual Harassment in K–12 Schools.* New York: Teachers College Press.

Cases Cited

Board of School Trustees of School District No. 44 (North Vancouver) v. Jubran (2003), 9 B.C.L.R. (4th) 338.

Janzen v. Platy Enterprises Ltd., [1989] 1 S.C.R. 1252.

Jubran v. Board of Trustees, 2002 B.C.H.R.T. 10.

North Vancouver School District No. 44 v. Jubran, (2005) CHRR Doc. 05-166, 2005 BCCA 201.

Ontario Human Rights Commission v. Simpsons-Sears, [1985] 2 S.C.R. 536.

Ross v. New Brunswick School District 15, [1996] 1 S.C.R. 825.

Legislation Cited

British Columbia Human Rights Code, RSBC 1996, c. 210.

Constructing and Contesting Discourses of Heteronormativity: An Ethnographic Study of Youth in a Francophone High School in Canada

Phyllis Dalley and Mark David Campbell

Using ethnographic data of youth interactions in a Francophone high school in Ontario, Canada, this article explores the possibilities and impossibilities of establishing queer discursive spaces at the school, given the heterosexual hegemony that prevailed.

Heterosexual hegemony, it has been argued, is reproduced in schools through two silencing processes: systematic exclusion, which operates by 'ignoring or denying the presence of lesbian, gay, and bisexual people' (Friend, 1993, p. 212), and systematic inclusion: 'When discussions regarding homosexuality do occur, they are consistently placed in a negative context. This results in the systematic inclusion in conversations about homosexuality only as pathology, only in regard to sexual behaviour and/or framed as dangerous' (Friend, 1993, p. 215). As Foucault (1990) has argued about sexuality generally, silencing is achieved through the careful and continual production and monitoring—by the self and by others—of speech acts. This process requires the construction of heterosexuality as 'normal' human sexuality through explication of the abnormal. In other words, the silencing of homosexuality is predicated on the construction of a heterosexual/homosexual binary. [. . .] Likewise, they are materialized through an everyday 'performativity' or straightness, queerness, maleness, and femaleness:

> To say that 'gender/sexual identity/desire is performative' does not mean the same as 'it is performed'. Indeed, if 'performed' is interpreted in its everyday sense to mean a kind of deliberate play-acting, it is obviously unsatisfactory: most of us, most of the time, are not aware of performing anything in this highly self-conscious way. What we are doing, however, is materializing gender/sexual identity/desire by repeating, consciously or not, the acts that conventionally signify 'femininity' or 'butchness' or 'flirting'. (Cameron & Kulick, 2003, p. 150)

Thus, deciphering how insurgent sexualities are effectively silenced within institutions entails studying the everyday performances and uses of language that constitute, and also resist, norms of sexual and gender identities.

This article explores these issues using data from a three-year ethnographic study of language and identity in a Franco-Ontarian high school that we shall call 'Champlain'.[1] Official school discourses regularly promote the importance of respecting differences, following the 'Vive la différence' ideology that was popular in the 1960s, when Francophone schools like Champlain were founded. As a minority language school, Champlain is a linguistically and culturally complex space. At the school, the main language of instruction is French, but in the broader environment surrounding the school, the predominant language is English (in the province of Ontario, Francophones account for 4.7 per cent of the total population, and only 1.5 per cent of the population in the city where the school was located [Statistiques Canada, 2005]). Most Champlain students are French/English bilinguals. At the time of this study, the only exceptions were monolingual Francophones arriving from the Francophone provinces of Quebec or New Brunswick, and Somalian/French bilinguals from Somalia.

As members of a larger research team, we draw here on our close observations of teenage students as they interacted with their peers at school events and in the corridors and classrooms of the school. This article focuses on discourse of heteronormativity. We use the term 'heteronormativity' to refer to the insistence that 'humanity and heterosexuality are synonymous' (Warner, 1993, p. xxii). 'Heteronormative discourses', then, are linguistic and/or cultural practices which construct and circulate heterosexual representations, practices, and identities as *the* natural or normal discourses of humanity. Our article examines the ways in which discourses of heteronormativity were reproduced as well as contested at Champlain in students' interactions within three domains: the general student population, a friendship network of five socially marginalized female students, and the lives of two gay male students. The analysis indicates that the heteronormative discourses prevalent among the student population had a silencing effect on the gay-identified male students but, paradoxically created space for some straight-identified female students to 'play-act' lesbianism as a counter-hegemonic discourse. [. . .] Our interest here is in the ways student construct, contest, and struggle with discourses of heteronormativity in the classrooms and throughout the schools.

[. . .]

In the current study, taking an ethnographic approach (Gans, 1999; Thomas, 1993) made it possible to examine youth interactions (primarily with each other but also with their teachers and with us as researcher) in the school environment. This was significant because it allowed us to focus on the students' actual socio-discursive interactions at school, instead of just their self-reported experiences of school after graduating. [. . .] This focus on discourse meant that we could take into account not only what was said but also what was not said, and thus trace some of the heteronormative silencing practices that became evident. Related to this is the fact that our investigation was long term, which meant that the same youth could be observed over time and across a range of situations and interaction types.

[. . .]

Method

Our long-term, first-hand observations of student struggles with heteronormativity were conducted in the context of a larger ethnographic study of ethnolinguistic identity and schooling[2] (Heller, Dalley, Ibrahim & Campbell, 1994; Heller & collaborators, 1999). The larger study involved a team of bilingual researchers (including the authors of this article[3]) collecting data in the following ways: observing and audiotaping classroom sessions over a four-year period; conducting audiotaped interviews with 46 students and eight parents; accompanying 15 students as they went about their lives in school and, where possible, outside of school; observing, audiotaping, and sometimes videotaping informal discussions among several friendship networks; obtaining video-recordings (produced by the school's student technology committee) of extracurricular activities; and taking detailed ethnographic notes of all observations and interactions with students and school staff. In this article, we discuss data gathered from observations of all-school, whole-class, and small in-class group situations as well as of informal friendship network discussions.[4] We focus on one female friendship network in particular, the marginalized 'Nerds' (and their interactions with the dominant 'Populaires'), as well as on two gay boys, Bernard and Zadun.[5]

The data are presented in three sections, which mirror student positionings in relation to the dominant heteronormative discourses of the school. The first section sets the broad context by exploring how these discourses were co-constructed as dominant across a number of sites in the school; the next section looks at how the Nerds openly challenged heteronormativity from their peripheral position; and the third section focuses on how Bernard and Zadun struggled with, and against, the dominant heteronormative discourses and their silencing effects. It is important to note that our knowledge of lesbian students at the school is limited to second-hand reports, while our knowledge of lesbian teachers is non-existent. The limited space allocated here to lesbian perspectives thus reflects the limited space they seemed to occupy at the school.

It should also be noted that we use the terms 'lesbian' and 'gay' to signify same-sex attraction and coupling because that is how the students in the study used them. Though 'queer' was not a commonly used term at Champlain, we borrow Sumara and Davis' (1999, p. 192) definition of queer as 'a marker representing interpretive work that refuses . . . the cultural rewards afforded those whose public performances of self are contained within that narrow band of behaviours considered proper to a heterosexual identity'.

Constructing Heteronormative Discourse at School

At Champlain, boys and girls controlled different public discursive spaces. Multicultural lunches and fashion shows were the domain of female students and general assemblies that of male students. The lunches positioned women as cooks at the service of others and the fashion shows constructed idealized forms of female beauty (skinny but not bust-less, preferably white skinned, blond haired, and blue eyed) and femininity/masculinity. In these fashion shows, females were ambiguously presented as alluring yet virtuous whereas males were presented as virile and commanding. The environment at Champlain can be characterized by Cameron and Kulick's (2003, p. 31) observation that for 'good boys' and 'bad boys' alike, interest in sex is considered 'normal and legitimate', while for girls, such interest marks one as a rebellious 'bad girl'. Normalcy was also constructed within a heterosexual/homosexual binary in which homosexuality was always deviant, as the following example shows.

At the fashion shows, expressions of homosexuality were strictly excluded. Indeed, when two boys decided to walk down the catwalk together during a rehearsal, the girls responsible for the show stopped the proceedings to insist upon the seriousness of the activity at hand and on the need for all to follow directions. The boys' whispers and laughter suggested that presenting themselves as a same-sex couple was a way to ridicule the girls and their work, since homosexuality was clearly considered an absurdity.

The most legitimate student-controlled discursive spaces in this school were the assemblies, which were organized by the male dominated student council.[6]

Here, when a female character was needed in a skit, male students in drag were used. These boys were received with much laughter, and there was no question that they were playing female roles and not those of transvestites or transgendered males. The only direct reference to homosexuality that we observed within this

space was negatively associated with pedophilia. In that instance, the part of Michael Jackson was play-acted as a homosexual pedophile gyrating around a group of sleeping boys. Even in slightly less public spaces such as classrooms and hallways, the dominant heteronormative discourse overtly constructed all sexual activity outside of male/female relations as deviant or dangerous. As the following two examples illustrate, this occurred through exclusion as well as negative inclusion.

During an English class,[7] three boys were reading aloud to the class a section of Arthur Miller's play *Death of a Salesman*. One male character calls another 'Baby'. The reading stopped and a boy exclaimed, 'Baby! What are they? What's going on here?' Another snorted and replied, 'I don't know.' (Co-author) Mark explained to the students that the two men were brothers, and that in the 1950s, when the play was published, 'baby' was used in a similar way to 'boy' or 'man' today. Apparently accepting this explanation, the boys resumed reading. The possibility of a homosexual relationship seemed to be sufficient reason for these students to resist the prescribed task of reading.

In another class, students referred to feminists and gays as 'special interest groups' which threaten freedom of expression. The male English teacher responded by taking this point further, saying that special interest groups were responsible for threats to Canadian unity and a lack of national identity. He added that 'many people question whether there should even be a Gay Pride Day' and suggested that the question should be put to a national referendum. The teacher's comments were aligned with Canada's right-wing movement, which argues that so-called 'special interest groups'—gays, feminists, native organizations, and unions—'stand in opposition to the interests of "one big family"' (Laycock, 2002, p. 162), and as such threaten

Canadian national unity. (In this view, minority groups are seen to control the development of social policies that ignore the interests of the taxpaying majority.) The salient point here is that such comments by students and teachers reinforce discourses of heteronormativity by intimating that heterosexuals can, and perhaps should, have the right to limit the freedom of expression of queer and feminist Canadians.

As Foucault (1990) has argued, processes of normalization depend on the construction of a normal/abnormal binary in which the abnormal is set up as a point of reference for the normal. Students in our study took up and reproduced this categorization in their conversations about human sexuality, where themes of penetration and power often came to the forefront. As an example, during small-group work in a drama class, a male student, Sami, relayed an incident he said he had read in the newspaper: 'Sixty-two year old men broke themselves in a Hoover . . . Their wives had been dead for, like, 10 years and they broke themselves in . . . a Hoover vacuum cleaner! I don't know what they did . . . but think about it. You're 62 years old, your wife's been dead for 10 years, and you pull out the vacuum cleaner.'

As explicit as the general discourse on sexuality was, however, there remained little opportunity to present homosexuality as a legitimate possibility. Indeed, what was left unsaid reveals the perceived menace that homosexuality poses to heteronormative discourses: it is permissible to talk about sex with vacuum cleaners, but the danger of homosexuality is so imminent that it must be silenced. In fact, we observed a remarkably consistent discursive pattern among the students at this school: the subject of homosexuality was repeatedly silenced through exclusion.

At one point during the above conversation about male sex with vacuum cleaners, one boy mentioned the name of another boy in the school. A girl responded with, 'Oh, he's a faggot, he's such a fag.' The other boys did not respond to her comment, neither opposing nor agreeing with her characterization of the boy mentioned. They remained silent for a few seconds, then one boy reintroduced the task at hand and they returned to writing their play. Furthermore, whenever someone was referred to as 'gay', a student, most frequently a male student, could take the opportunity to assert his heterosexuality while distancing himself from the deviant Other by using such phrases as: 'those people', 'special interest groups', 'fags', and 'George Michael is a fudge packer anyways'.[8] An even more extreme distancing move occurred when a teacher attempted to include a positive mention of homosexuality in the curriculum (in our observation, such attempts were rare).

Following an in-class viewing of a video of John Steinbeck's *Of Mice and Men*, the teacher, Mr Choquette, told the class that Steinbeck was gay. A male student, Leo, announced to the class that he would kill his son if he turned out gay. Since dominant discourses of heteronormativity associate having children with heterosexuality, Leo was able to publicly assert his own heterosexuality while at the same time condemning the homosexuality of others. A few students in the class raised a slight protest at Leo's suggestions of violence against a specific yet fictitious son, but no one in the room objected to violence against homosexual people in general and the topic was dropped.

As the above examples demonstrate, violating their constructed gender roles or questioning heteronormativity were generally regarded by students as dangers to be avoided at all costs. Such reactions seem to be manifestations of the menace which homosexuality poses to male privilege:

> Homosexuality is perceived as a challenge to traditional gender-roles, and is therefore, considered by some people to be a

threat to the established order—gay men divesting themselves of male privilege by loving other men and lesbians co-opting male privilege by loving other women. (Schneider, 1997, p. 18)

Through the use of silence as well as language, in numerous instances (mostly male) students constructed their own sexual practices—actual or imagined—as normal, by referencing homosexuality as abnormal.

Taking Up 'Lesbian' Positionings to Challenge Discourses of Heteronormativity

Five female friends were brought together by their perceived marginalization at Champlain and at previous schools, and by their shared interest in creative and intellectual pursuits such as literature and poetry. Calling themselves 'the Nerds', Carole, Lisa, Ellen, Mélanie, and Suzanne believed their differences, which were respected within the group, to be the source of their marginalization: they did not conform to linguistic, identity, and fashion norms dominant at the school. Contrary to other groups, this group did not share a unified code of dress, musical preference, or cultural and linguistic trajectory.[9] Although all tried at one time or another to conform—Carole, for example, auditioned for the fashion show—their attempts were rejected time and again.

In response to their marginalization and the image of femaleness that prevailed at the school, the Nerds created their own discursive space which was overtly lesbian and sexually aggressive. In this way, they not only played on and accentuated their own marginalization, but also contested taken-for-granted norms associated with heterosexuality and femaleness. As we shall see, it became clear that these girls did

not seriously consider themselves lesbians, even though they took up lesbian personas in public domains.

[. . .]

The Nerds shared most of their physical space—in-school hangouts and classrooms—with a mixed male-female group known to other students as 'les Populaires' (the Popular Ones). This latter group had the most direct control over the dominant student discourse: the boys were on student council and organized student assemblies and both male and female members participated in the fashion show. For the most part, it was in moments of 'co-presence' (Giddens, 1986) with the Populaires (whom the Nerds considered superficial) that the Nerds would appropriate 'lesbian' positionings and role-play the parts of same-sex lovers. This involved exaggerated displays, well within earshot of the Populaires, of making passes at one another and having mock lovers' quarrels, in which they would say things like 'Charlene is angry because I haven't been satisfying her sexual needs lately'. These displays suggested that it was the heteronormativity materialized by the Populaires that the Nerds were specifically contesting. In doing so, they were constructing a Populaire/Nerd binary that paralleled the heterosexual/homosexual, good girl/bad girl, normal/abnormal binaries of the school's dominant discourses.

Despite the pleasure they took in publicly presenting lesbian personas, it seemed clear that none of the Nerds actually self-identified as lesbian (or bisexual). Carole, for example, wrote the following in a letter to (co-author) Phyllis: 'I am hopelessly straight as a board, although I do enjoy giving the opposite impression, just part of my shock appeal I suppose.' The Nerds seemed to enjoy challenging taken-for-granted assumptions about sexuality.

At times the Nerds created violent fantasies concerning their treatment of each other, with these discussions usually taking the form of a threat/counter-threat repartee. These episodes would only end when one Nerd had managed to induce disgust in another. For example, in one class Mélanie and Lisa were writing threatening notes to one another. The writing stopped when Mélanie exclaimed that Lisa had threatened to stick a vacuum hose to her clitoris and drag her across a carpet. This received the desired reaction from another girl, Debbie, who sat with the Nerds in class and in the hallways from time to time: 'You guys! How can you talk about things like that. You are hurting me, look, I'm crossing my legs.' The Nerds seemed proud of the various ways they had conjured up to verbally abuse each other about sexual matters—as one Nerd, Carole, put it, 'I enjoy corrupting unjaded minds.'

[. . .]

The Nerds spoke openly about homosexuality in class, not as 'a running joke', but as a serious attempt to introduce the possibility of homosexuality into class discussions. For example, during a whole-class discussion of a televised version of Tom Stoppard's play *Rosencrantz and Guildenstern are Dead*, the Nerds proposed that the actors were homosexuals: 'Did you notice there are no girls in the play? . . . Did you see the way Rosencrantz looked at Alfred [a male actor playing a female role]?' However, these girls did not succeed in breaking the conversational cycle described earlier. Following the above comment, a male student replied, 'Let's move on.' The teacher sidestepped the issue of homosexuality; focusing instead on the absence of females, he stated that historically, women were not allowed on stage so adolescent men were hired to play the female parts. The fact that this was a recently televised version of the play was not taken up. With the possibility of discussing transsexuality or homosexuality being effectively silenced, the class discussion continued down a different path.

[. . .]

The Nerds' relentless questioning of the heterosexual norm also paralleled the dominant student discourse at this school in important ways: it dealt with issues of sexual power in explicit ways, objectified women's bodies, and, at times, treated same sex attraction as deviant. This seems to confirm that 'identifying oneself within the heterosexual/homosexual binary always places one within and reproduces heteronormative discourses' (Grace et al., 2004). This binary apparently either precludes, or includes as homosexual, both bisexual and transgender, two identity categories the Nerds could have claimed but did not.

These young women did open up the possibility for two gay students to express this aspect of their identity (as we shall see in the next section), even though this expression rarely reached beyond the social circle created by the Nerds— and even this circle did not seem to be safe for a lesbian student. Carole told (co-author) Phyllis about how Joanne had 'come out' as a lesbian to her. After her 'outing', Joanne quickly transferred to a school in the city's gay neighbourhood, apparently because of the numerous difficulties she faced at Champlain as a result of heteronormativity.

Regardless of the constant marginalization of their persons and of their ideas, the Nerds finished high school in the belief that they had 'won the war' against the popular students. At graduation, all of the Nerds received awards for academic excellence.

As Lisa wrote in a letter to Phyllis: 'I deeply enjoyed going up to the podium five times for awards as I watched their faces.' After graduation, Lisa received her first invitation to a Populaires party, which she gladly refused.

As Foucault (1990) indicates, there is always the possibility of resistance. Indeed, the dominant discourse depends on that resistance to continually reaffirm its position and define the boundaries between the legitimate and the illegitimate. In this section we have seen how, by introducing the social category 'homosexual' into class and hallway discussions, and by playacting lesbianism, a group of marginalized girls contested the heteronormative discourses at the school. In so doing, the Nerds co-constructed binaries which not only disrupted but also reinforced dominant discourses. Indeed, the existence of a predefined heterosexual/homosexual binary seemed to at once create the possibility for resistance and define the terms of that resistance.

Struggling with Heteronormative Discourses from Gay Male Positionings

We will now turn our attention towards Champlain students who identified themselves as gay to co-author Mark. Queer space per se existed only as a negative reference point in overwhelmingly heteronormative discourses, within which the construction of gay ranged from the immoral to the avant-garde. In fact, we found no evidence of gay male students forming friendship groups, nor of male students performing gay personas similar to that of the Nerds. Rather, the data we have shows how two male students were positioned as outsiders within the school with respect to their gay identity.

Bernard, a gay white student, came from the neighbouring Francophone province of Quebec, and Zadun, a gay black student, came from Somalia as a refugee. Although Bernard and Zadun had very different histories and occupied different social and cultural environments within and outside of the school, their experiences as gay students in the school were strikingly similar: both guarded their sexual identity and adopted strategies to survive in the school's heteronormative milieu.

Bernard successfully used his ability to 'pass' as a survival strategy (Friend, 1993). Other students assumed he was heterosexual: 'My nickname [at Champlain] was "Sexy", it was kind of stupid, no one knew I was gay.' This 'passing' did not alleviate his sense of loneliness and alienation. 'As a gay high school student I would love to find others, but I haven't got any', he explained. Given this impossibility, he created a distinction between his gay persona and his student persona.

Following his departure from the school, Bernard explained the difficulty of living a fragmented identity: 'I wasn't out [as gay] there. I had to be a grade 11 or 12 kid there and I was going back with my boyfriend, who was nine years older than me, trying to adjust myself.'

Zadun felt the need to separate his gay life not only from his school life but also from his community life. He was especially concerned that people in the Somalian community might find out about his sexual identity. He explained, 'Cause this is my private life, there's gonna be a lot of difference between your old life and your new life as soon as you tell them [other Somalian students] you are gay.' Even though he suspected that some of his close friends were also gay, they never raised the subject of their sexual identity: 'We don't know that we [each other] are [gay] but we know that we are different from them [other Somalian boys].'

Aware of the possible consequences of being openly gay, these students learned to survive through ambiguity or the performance of multiple personas. For Bernard, the consequences of being 'out' in school ranged from infamy and ostracization to a sort of trendy or counter-celebrity status. As he explains, when it became known in school that he was gay:

I got bashed, I don't mean physically but I had some real bad comments. . . .

And then it was totally the opposite side of being abused, it was like almost a cool thing to hang around with a gay guy. At the beginning I thought it was quite funny somehow, but then it hurt me. You [the other students] just had to say 'I know someone who is gay' and it was a big deal. 'You know Bernard?' 'Who.' 'Ya, you know the faggot.' 'Ah.' 'That's Bernard.'

His use of the word 'faggot'—a pejorative term commonly used by students in elementary and secondary schools to emphasize their contempt for students judged as different (Louganis & Marcus, 1995; Mondimore, 1996; Schneider, 1997)—reveals the pain of rejection inscribed in the treatment that Bernard endured. Indeed, the notoriety gained from 'hanging out with a gay guy' points to the construction of an exotic Other rather than to acceptance of difference or positive inclusion. Furthermore, when Bernard decided to bring a young man from another school to the spring formal as his date, one girl in his class told him, 'But you can't, you're supposed to bring a girl!' It was therefore 'cool' to hang around a gay guy, but performing gayness was still disallowed. Thus, straight students maintained their right to define the acceptable and the unacceptable while positioning themselves as open to difference.

In Zadun's case the situation was compounded by his fear of repercussions in each of the three domains identified by Grace and Wells (2001, p. 141): 'Queer youth fear or face prejudice, discrimination, violent behaviour, and language assaults in three key spaces: the family, the school and the community.' Zadun explained why he did not want it known that he self-identified as gay:

The reason is first of all we are not accepted being gays [in the Somalian community]

and second they will find out, one of my family. They [his family, all of whom live in Somalia] will reject me, that will be the end of my life. They are going to kill me, my brothers.

The consequences of heteronormativity, as Ryan and Futterman (1997), Sears (1997), and Snider (1996) point out, are often accentuated in situations of multiple minorities (gendered, linguistic, ethnic, racial). Sears (1997) notes, for example, that: 'to maintain comfortability in the black community, particularly in those places that cultivate black culture and black solidarity, many have felt a need to downplay their homosexuality.' As a result, Wilson (1996, p. 313) observes, 'the positive bicultural [or tri-cultural] adaptation that sexual and racial identity development models prize is simply not available to most of us'.

Friend (1993) suggests that simply having an openly gay teacher can lessen a gay student's solitude. At Champlain, however, gay students did not seem to get support from either gay or straight teachers. Bernard, for example, tells of seeing one of his teachers at a downtown gay bar: 'I know he's gay, but we never talk about it.' As the following example illustrates, (apparently) straight students participated actively in the silencing which isolated gay students from peers, teachers, and support staff who were also gay.

One day during lunch, a male student, Leo, questioned a teacher, Mr Choquette about his sexuality. (As mentioned in the previous section, during a class discussion Mr Choquette had stated that Steinbeck was gay.) Leo explained to Mr Choquette that there was a rumour among the students that he (the teacher) was gay. Leo said he had 'defended' Mr Choquette's reputation so now he had the right to know. Although Mr Choquette objected vigorously at this invasion into his personal life, Leo was insistent and eventually Mr Choquette denied being gay.

Co-author Mark was present during this discussion. Later the same day, this teacher confided to Mark that if he had continued to refuse to answer Leo, that would have confirmed the rumours and he would have been labelled a 'fag'. In confiding to Mark, Mr Choquette expressed the anger and frustration that he felt, as a gay man, about working in 'this fucking school', and said he was thinking of leaving the school. Similar to a case reported by Middleton (1998), the power of heteronormativity at Champlain seemed to place the authority of straight students above that of teachers suspected of homosexuality.

At the end of grade 12, Bernard, Mélanie (one of the Nerds), and Bernard's male prom date went to the spring prom as a threesome. As for Zadun, two of his Somalian friends who were no longer at the school revealed their gay identity to him and he took them. After graduation, Zadun also spent more time at the gay bars downtown, often the only social space in which youth can explore their sexual orientation (Ryan & Futterman, 1997) when queer youth support groups[10] are non-existent. Unfortunately, as a Francophone living in a predominantly English-speaking city, no such group was immediately accessible to Zadun. The last Mark heard of him, Zadun planned to leave the local Somalian community and move to Montreal, where his linguistic identity would not be marked and he could readily interact with other Francophones who share his racial and sexual identities.

At Champlain, lesbian students were invisible. While Bernard was 'out' at school, he was constructed as an exotic Other and his performance of gayness was tightly constrained by other students. Indeed, the 'acceptance' of his difference seemed to translate into a form of surveillance or silencing within the heteronormative discourses of the school. Zadun felt that he could not be openly gay at school, not only because of that institution's heteronormative discourses,

but also because being out there would entail being out in his Somalian community, a possibility this student could not fathom. Silencing is clearly a multilayered process in which teachers, students, and communities participate, and whose effects are at once similar and different for individual students.

Conclusion

It would be absurd to attribute the heteronormative discourses so prevalent in this particular high school to the fact that it happens to be Franco-Ontarian. At the same time, we suggest that it is the very nature of our research site—a predominantly French-language high school in a predominantly English-speaking province of Canada—that made it possible to investigate how students construct and resist those discourses. In a school preoccupied with the definition of what and who counts as French, actions which raise other issues or identities are highly marked. Perhaps in this context, presenting queer identities was considered so threatening because it interrupted the construction of a student body that was unified by being not only French but also heterosexual.

As our article has shown, virtually any move by an individual student or teacher to introduce a queer perspective into classroom discussions was systematically negated, meeting with rejection (exclusion) or negative inclusion by teachers and students alike. Yet at the same time, lesbianism offered a discourse of resistance to five straight girls, the Nerds. The Nerds also put the straight/gay binary into question: in maintaining both straight *and* queer personas, they posited the possibility of a dynamic and complementary heterosexual/homosexual identity. While adopting this fluid yet counter-hegemonic sexual persona made it possible for these girls to challenge constraining gender roles by being assertive and outspoken about socio-sexual matters, such social benefits did not seem to be available to a female friend who self-identified as a lesbian. Gay males also struggled with and against the silencing effects of the heteronormative discourses of the school. Without the protection of a heterosexual persona, however, they could not safely materialize their sexual identities at school. There, they developed strategies to remain hidden, relegating the expression/exploration of their sexual identities to safer zones outside of school.

The Quebec Ministry of Education has stipulated that high schools must 'help students to realize their full potential, to handle everyday life situations, to learn to learn, to feed their self-esteem, to preserve their interests and integrity and to become good citizens' (our translation), ('aider les élèves à se réaliser pleinement, à se débrouiller dans le quotidien, à apprendre à apprendre, à nourrir leur estime de soi, à conserver des intérêts et leur intégrité et à devenir de bons citoyens') (Ministère de l'Éducation et de la Formation, 1998, p. 1). In line with Ministry guidelines, changes were put into place at Champlain to better meet the self-realization, integrity, and learning needs of a multiracial school population (see also Grace & Wells, 2001). Indeed,

> . . . [W]hile Champlain is still thought of as an *oasis culturel*, a Francophone island in an Anglophone sea, its motto, 'Unity in diversity', has come to refer mainly to a polyglot, multicultural student body, joined together by their mutual affinity with French. (Heller et al., 1999, p. 72)

Our ethnographic analysis has shown that this high school could hardly be considered an oasis of diversity where many young girls and all queer youth are concerned.

Yet at the time of this study, there was virtually no evidence that school administrators or teachers had begun to address—or even to recognize—the heteronormative discourses that pervaded the school and the potentially damaging effects of these discourses on youth. While we can make no claims about the ways in which, or the degree to which, the sorts of heteronormative discourses so prevalent at Champlain might be circulating within other (high) schools in other regions, our study strongly suggest that these questions do need to be asked, at the very least within those educational institutions where the notion of 'Vive la différence' or inclusion is valued.

Notes

1. The name of the school and the names of students and teachers have been replaced with pseudonyms to protect the identity of participants.
2. The larger research project from which the data analyzed in this article derive, was funded by the Social Sciences and Humanities Research Council of Canada. Its principal investigator was Monica Heller.
3. Mark is a Spanish/English bilingual and Phyllis is a French/English bilingual.
4. Throughout the article, student talk placed in quotation marks represent quotes taken from ethnographic notes, not from recorded materials. Data in this article are presented in the language used by the students: English. French was not used in discussions about homosexuality. While our data do not allow for a full analysis of this phenomenon, it may be due to a lack of French vocabulary on the topic, to

the generalized use of English in out-of-class socialization, and, in some cases, to co-author Mark's limited command of the French language.
5. Co-author Phyllis developed a privileged relationship with the Nerds: when she left the larger study in its final year in order to pursue her doctoral field work, she and the Nerds exchanged letters, which became part of our database. Likewise, co-author Mark maintained contact with both Bernard and Zadun for a short time after the study; the knowledge our article presents of their post–high school trajectory came from that continued contact.
6. Assemblies took place during class time and were mandatory for all students, whereas lunches and fashion shows took place outside of class time and were optional.
7. Champlain offered two levels of English classes: one for students with limited English language proficiency (French

monolinguals and Somalian/French bilinguals) and the other for students with native-like proficiency (French/English bilinguals). All English classes mentioned in this article were of the latter type, so in these classes English was the only language of communication.

8. George Michael is a British pop star with a wide fan base in North America. 'Fudge packing' is a derogatory term for anal intercourse.

9. To briefly illustrate, Lisa was a weight lifter who dressed like a 'rocker', Carole and Mélanie wore black clothes and heavy makeup generally associated with 'punks'. Ellen was a practising evangelical Christian, and Suzanne claimed a multicultural (Native, Francophone, Anglophone, and Black) identity and was exploring matriarchal Celtic religions.

10. See Grace and Wells (2001) for a discussion of such groups in Alberta, Canada.

References

Cameron, D., & Kulick, D. (2003). *Language and sexuality*. Cambridge, England: Cambridge University Press.

Dalley, P., & Campbell, M. (2003). Être gai, lesbienne ou bisexuel(le) a l'école [Being gay, lesbian, or bisexual at school]. In N. Labrie & S.A. Lamoureux (Eds), *L'Éducation de la langue française en Ontario; Enjeux et processus sociaux* (pp. 203–22). Sudbury, ON: Prise de parole.

Foucault, M. (1972). *The archaeology of knowledge* (1st American edn). New York: Pantheon.

————. (1990). *The history of sexuality* (Vintage Books edn). New York: Random House.

Friend, R.A. (1993). Choices not closets: Heterosexism and homophobia in schools. In L. Weiss & M. Fine (Eds), *Beyond silenced voices: Class, race and gender in the United States* (pp. 209–35). New York: State University of New York Press.

Gamson, J. (2000). Sexualities, queer theory, and qualitative research. In N.K. Denzin & Y.S. Lincoln (Eds), *Handbook of qualitative research* (2nd edn, pp. 347–65). Thousand Oaks, CA; Sage.

Gans, H.J. (1999). *Participant observation in the era of 'ethnography'*. Thousand Oaks, CA: Sage.

Giddens, A. (1986). *The constitution of society: Outline of the theory of structuration*. Berkeley: University of California Press.

Grace, A.P., & Benson, F.J. (2000). Using autobiographical queer life narratives of teachers to connect personal, political and pedagogical spaces. *International Journal of Inclusive Education*, 4. 89–109.

Grace, A.P., Hill, R.J., Johnson, C.W., & Lewis, J.B. (2004). In other words: Queer voices/Dissident subjectivities impelling social change. *International Journal of Qualitative Studies in Education, 17*, 301–24.

Grace, A.P., & Wells, K. (2001). Getting an education in Edmonton, Alberta: The case of queer youth. *Toquere, Journal of the Canadian Lesbian and Gay Studies Association*, 3, 137–51.

Heller, M., with the collaboration of M. Campbell, P. Dalley, and T. Goldstein. (1999). *Linguistic minorities and modernity: A sociolinguistic ethnography*. New York: Longman.

Heller, M., Dalley, P., Ibrahim, A., & Campbell, M. (1994, May). *L'Espace francophone en milieu minoritaire et les inégalités internes* [Francophone space in minority contexts and internal inequalities]. Paper presented at the Association Canadienne-Française pour l'advancement des sciences conference, Montreal, Canada.

Laycock, D.H. (2002). *The new right and democracy in Canada: Understanding reform and the Canadian alliance*. Don Mills, ON: Oxford University Press.

Louganis, G., & Marcus, E. (1995). *Breaking the surface*. New York: Random House.

Middleton, S. (1998). *Disciplining sexuality: Foucault, life histories, and education*. New York: Teachers College Press.

Ministere de l'Éducation et de la Formation. (1998). Les écoles secondaires de l'Ontario [Secondary schools in Ontario]. Retrieved 3 November 2005, from http://www.edu.gov.on.ca/fre/document/discussi/oss.html#1

Mondimore, F.M. (1996). *A natural history of homosexuality*. Baltimore: Johns Hopkins University Press.

Ryan, C., & Futterman, D. (1997). *Lesbian and gay youth: Care and counseling*. Philadelphia: Hanley & Belfus.

Schneider, M.S. (1997). *Pride and prejudice: Working with lesbian, gay, and bisexual youth*. Toronto: Central Toronto Youth Services.

Sears, J.T. (1997). Black-gay or gay-black: Choosing identities and identifying choices. In G. Unks (Ed.), *Educational practice and theory for lesbian, gay and bisexual adolescents* (pp. 135–58). New York: Routledge.

Snider, K. (1996). Race and sexual orientation: The (im)possibility of these intersections in educational policy. *Harvard Educational Review, 66*, 294.

Statistiques Canada. (2005). Le Canada en statistiques. Retrieved 12 May 2005, from http://www40.statcan.ca

Sumara, D., & Davis, B. (1999). Interrupting heteronormativity: Toward a queer curriculum theory. *Curriculum Inquiry, 29*, 191–208.

Thomas, J. (1993). *Doing critical ethnography*. Newbury Park, CA: Sage.

Warner, M. (1993). *Fear of a queer planet: Queer politics and social theory*. Minneapolis: University of Minnesota Press.

Wilson, A. (1996). How we find ourselves: Identity development and two-spirit people. *Harvard Educational Review, 66*, 303–17.

10 Racialization, Immigration, and the Politics of Sexualities

Magic and Joy: Traditional Aboriginal Views of Human Sexuality

David Newhouse

It's rare that I get to talk about so intimate and personal a topic in public. Sex and sexuality, and maleness and masculinity, are not normally the topics that I explore in so open a forum. These issues are also not issues which are discussed with such frankness within most Aboriginal communities. There is increasing pressure to do so as our people heal from the difficulties of the recent past.

I grew up on the Six Nations of the Grand River community about 100 kilometres from [Toronto]. My ancestors came to what is now Canada after fighting on the side of the British in the Revolutionary War of 1776. It was a question of either move or be killed, and so, like most people, we chose to move. We have lived in this part of the country since 1784 and have lived in the middle part of this continent for close to a thousand years.

We lived here before many of your ancestors came here. In fact, we had one of the oldest functioning systems of government for more than 400 years when Columbus arrived in this part of the world, searching for that mysterious and elusive link to India. I tell you this history not to make you feel guilty, but to ground what I want to say in this place.

I also want to remind you that we were not Christians, and hence we did not have a Christian morality with respect to sex and sexuality, so I don't tackle these questions from this perspective.

I grew up in the Handsome Lake tradition of the Iroquoian Longhouse. Handsome Lake was a Seneca prophet who brought the good news of the Gawio in the latter part of the 18th century. The Gawio or Code of Handsome Lake is the fundamental document detailing good moral behaviour within Iroquoian society. Handsome Lake was influenced by the Quakers, and his Code is a mixture of Quakerism and the old way, a mixture of Iroquoian and Quaker views, if you will. It has remained the guiding document within traditional Iroquoian peoples' lives for the past 200 years.

I am telling you this because it is difficult, after a few hundred years of contact between Aboriginal peoples of this continent and the newcomers to this land, to uncover what would be traditional views of sexuality. There is a lot of borrowing and absorption that has occurred.

These are confusing times for all of us with respect to sexuality. Over the past few decades, we have seen the development of personal identities built upon sexuality and since Freud, in the West, we have seen sex move to the centre of human existence and come to be seen as a prime motivator for much of human behaviour. Within the Aboriginal communities of North America, the changes have also been immense. Many communities have seen a move away from traditional views as the centre of everyday life. Over the past two decades, there has been a movement to bring traditional ideas back into the centre of everyday contemporary Aboriginal life. And over this same period, male sexuality has been under scrutiny as never before. It's hard to know what the new rules will be.

For four years in the early part of this decade [the 1990s], I served as the Chair of the Joint National Committee on Aboriginal AIDS Education and Prevention (JNC). One of the tasks that we set out to undertake was to examine contemporary Aboriginal attitudes toward sex. The government officials were quite concerned at that time because they believed that Aboriginal people were having too much sex (I must admit that they didn't say this directly, but couched their comments in concern about the high birth rate and higher-than-mainstream incidence of STDs), and that HIV would move like wildfire through the communities.

I was struck by a remarkable similarity between these comments and comments that I had read in two historical sources: Amerigo Vespucci and Fernandez de Oviedo, both early historians of the Americas. Vespucci wrote, 'they

have as many wives as they desire; they live in promiscuity without regard to blood relations; mothers lie with sons, brothers with sisters; they satisfy their desires as they occur to their libidos as beasts do'.[1] De Oviedo made similar comments in 'Historia general y natural de las Indias Occidentales'. The same comments were made in most historical sources that I investigated. Throughout the last 500 years, Europeans, and priests in particular, constantly complained about the sexual habits and mores of Indian people that they encountered. They were completely taken aback by what they described as 'wanton sex of all sorts'; people did it with no shame, no guilt, and no sense of indecency. Not only did we do it often, we did it wrong. Consider the reaction to the sex in *Dances with Wolves* and *Black Robe*, two of the most popular movies about Indians over the past decade. Women were not supposed to be the initiator of sex nor were they supposed to be on top!

A few years ago, one of the first contemporary examinations of Aboriginal peoples' attitudes toward sex was conducted by researchers at the University of Toronto as part of a healthy lifestyle project conducted jointly with the Chiefs of Ontario office. It asked 658 Aboriginal people across Ontario, among other things, their attitudes toward sex. I was quite struck by one particular result: 57 per cent of the sample described sex as 'magical'. Most respondents said that sex was enjoyable, pleasurable, and some even went so far as to say spiritual. This report would surely have caused much consternation and gnashing of teeth among European priests and government officials.

It seemed to me that there was something to be investigated: after all, almost 500 years of reports complaining of a consistent pattern of behaviour would appear to me to be strong empirical evidence that my ancestors were doing something that irked the Europeans. It is this something that I want to talk about. Is there something that we, living in the end of the twentieth century, can learn from traditional Aboriginal views of sex and sexuality?

I began to investigate to see what I could find out about sex and sexuality, about the relationships between male and female, and the wide variations on the theme of relationships that are possible among human beings. First of all, I learned that sex was considered a gift to humans and that it was to be considered pleasurable. One of the Anishnabe teachings tells of the way in which sex is introduced into the world. Men and women lived separately for a long time. The Creator, in his efforts to increase the population of humans, made sex pleasurable so that men and women would desire it, and hence, through acting upon their desire, increase the population. Sex was to be an act of pleasure.

In addition, I learned that sexuality was spirituality, that having sex was to touch the life force within us, and that to touch the life force meant to touch Creation. The same force that animates our spirit also animates our sexuality.

Traditional Aboriginal societies also supported clear definitions of and boundaries between roles for men and women. Men's roles were prescribed as falling within the public sphere; women's roles fell primarily in the private or domestic sphere. We should understand that different did not translate into unequal or inferior or superior. They were simply different, and as a result, men and women could be expected to behave in different fashions. The fulfillment of the duties and obligations of these roles, for both men and women, was regarded as important for the proper functioning of society.

Traditional societies were, appearances to the contrary, highly structured and moral societies. By morality, I mean that traditional societies were concerned about maintaining relationships between things. It was important to ensure that these relationships were recognized and honoured and respected. There was or is a great emphasis upon the notions of balance and harmony. Within the realm of sex and sexuality, there were strict moral codes that defined sexual behaviour. These moral codes focused on the proper relationship between people, rather than on the prohibition of certain types of behaviour.

Within traditional societies, we also see a more easy acceptance of the diversity of people and relationships within the world. Consequently, we see in traditional times a more easy acceptance of same-sex relationships in many forms. Among the Navajo of Arizona, Colorado, and New Mexico, we find a social group of people whom they called *nadles*, and whom we today might call homosexual. The Navajo seemed to understand that all men were not necessarily erotically attracted to women, and to have created a role within their society for them. In fact, within the Navajo cosmology, nadles are essential for the creation of wealth and some assurance of success, as well as essential for the continued survival of the universe.

Among the Mojave, we see a similar pattern for both women and men. Men who assumed cross-gender roles were called *alyha*, and women, *hwame*. Both could engage in relationships with members of the same sex. Again, both classes of people were well accepted into Mojave society: hwames were considered lucky in gambling and had the potential to become powerful medicine men. Alyhas were often sought as wives of chiefs. Mojaves believed that 'from the beginning of the world, it was meant that there should be homosexuals'.

So here we have, at least from both anthropological and oral records, a view of sex and sexuality that is, I think, somewhat different from that which is prevalent in much of contemporary Western society. Here we see sex and sexuality as a gift from the creator, to be enjoyed and meant to bring pleasure. This contrasts with the dominant view in the Christian-influenced West of sex as an uncontrollable passion that, unless controlled, will harm, if not destroy, the individual and society. And while there was not a uniform acceptance of a wide range of sexualities among traditional societies, there was at least a recognition and incorporation of these differences into traditional Aboriginal social worlds. I found my investigation to be difficult. It was difficult for elders to talk about sex and sexuality in the explicit terms that we do today. While there is an implicit acceptance of sexuality, it is often not discussed in public, and more importantly, not conceived of as something separate from the other characteristics of the individual. Often, when I asked about sexuality, they asked, 'do you mean sex?', and I had to say both 'yes' and 'no'.

And so I was forced to rethink my ideas and to look at this whole area from a very different perspective. What I was led to was an understanding not of sexuality in and of itself, but an understanding of the relationship between sexuality and the individual. In traditional thought, the world is seen as connected, and everything is seen as connected to everything else, and more importantly, in relation to everything. The proper maintenance of that relationship was as important as the thing itself. I had to think about my own relationship to my own sexuality and to my own behaviour.

Traditional Aboriginal societies also believed that sexuality was powerful. It was awakened at puberty, and in many societies, there was a series of rites and rituals for both boys and girls which were designed to instill within the individual an understanding of the nature of this power and the way in which this power was to be harnessed and used. These rites taught men their duties and obligations as men, and more importantly, their duties and obligations as sexual beings.

They were not to use their sexuality to cause harm to others, and were to respect its power.

You can see the framework which is beginning to be built: sexuality is a gift, a powerful gift that is to be respected. While the expression of sexuality through sex is pleasurable, it also comes with a set of duties and obligations that govern its expression.

We want to move on then to another central idea in traditional Aboriginal thought: the idea of balance. Human beings, in most Aboriginal conceptions, are thought of as consisting of four parts: a physical body; an intellect or mind; a set of emotions; and a spirit. A healthy human is one in which these four parts are attended to and for whom these parts are in balance. The idea is that no one part of the human should dominate; we should attempt to develop each of the four areas.

Using this idea then, the notion of sexuality doesn't just have a physical component, it has three other aspects that need to be tended to: intellectual, emotional, and spiritual. So you can begin to see the puzzlement at the question that I posed to elders. It is impossible to isolate the aspects of sexuality and discuss them separately. I need to consider sexuality within the whole of the human being, not just the physical aspect of it, and I need to be cognizant that this should be a balanced approach. There are those who teach that sexuality is the spiritual, and that the spiritual is what keeps us connected to our mind, our body, and to others through our emotions.

We must move on then to another fundamental idea: respect. It sits at the centre of traditional thought. This notion requires me to consider the relationship between not just my own self and my sexuality, but also to conduct that relationship in a respectful way, that is, acknowledging its power within me and ensuring that it does not overwhelm me. The idea of respect also requires me to conduct the relationship between me and others with respect to my sexuality in a respectful manner, that is, to acknowledge the power of our sexualities and not use it to overwhelm others.

Northrop Frye, the noted literary critic, said that to understand the literature of the West, you must understand the Bible and its themes. In order to understand a culture, I think that it's important to understand its religion. I think that we can all agree that the West, and in particular North American society, has strong roots in Christianity. We can, I believe, still see the influence of Christian ideas on sexuality.

Western society has a tortured relationship with sexuality and sex. Indeed, there is a constant and longstanding battle between spirit and body. The body, in much Christian thought, is just a temporary vessel for the spirit as it passes through this world. Experiencing the pleasures of the body is seen somehow as a detraction from the real business of life: the development of the spirit in preparation for its reward in another world. For Aboriginal people, the spirit can only properly develop if you feel the pain and pleasure of the body. One needs to experience both in order to know the meaning of balance.

The story of Adam and Eve exemplifies the tortured relationship of the West. It begins to associate the terms 'shame' and 'sin' and 'dirt' with sex and sexuality. The West also recognizes the power of sex, and since Freud, has given the development of sexuality a central place in the psychological development of the individual. It is, however, the link of sexuality with sin, and particularly the link of women's sexuality with sin, that is problematic for some Aboriginal people, especially those who are not Christian.

There is no concept of sin within traditional Aboriginal spiritual thought. When we go against the teachings, we are seen not to have understood them and are provided with an opportunity to learn and to try again. This is not to say that there was no punishment and that the society had infinite patience. It did not. When it came, the punishment could be severe and range from milder forms to shunning, banishment, or death.

You can begin, I hope, to see the problem that faces many contemporary Aboriginal people. There is a large movement afoot these days to make traditional Aboriginal teachings the centre of contemporary Aboriginal life. As contemporary Aboriginal men, we are caught between these two conflicting views of sexuality: one, that it is a sin, an uncontrollable passion, and the other, that it is spiritual and a gift from a Creator. There is an incredible distance between these views, not unlike the conflict that exists within many people in the West about their own sexuality. Balancing the two views makes it difficult to behave in a consistent fashion, especially when ideas about the proper behaviour of men are changing so much.

I grew up in a traditional Longhouse household in the Six Nations community. I did not learn the things there that I have talked about. It has been hard to uncover them. I grew up learning about sex and sexuality from those around me. I learned to hide and deny my own sexual nature. I learned these lessons from those around me. I felt shame at my first sexual experiences, and I learned to regard my own sexuality as shameful and dirty. Sex was something that one did in the dark. I learned to be afraid of the power of my sexuality.

Like many men of my generation, we have become more and more uneasy with the way in which men's sexuality has been defined and portrayed. My work with the JNC and in HIV/AIDS has given me an opportunity to think about the views and teachings of my ancestors, and to try to interpret them for these times. The test of the truth of the teachings is whether or not they can provide some guidelines for living today.

Today, we live in a largely secular world dominated by reason. The traditional Aboriginal world was a spiritual world. Yet, I believe that we can draw some lessons from that world that would be applicable to our times.

First of all, I think that we should recognize the sexual aspect of our nature, and more importantly, recognize this aspect of ourselves as a positive attribute. Second, I think that we should recognize it as a powerful gift that demands that we respect its power. Third, I think that we need to use this powerful gift with respect for others and for ourselves. These then are the things that I learned from my investigations. I hope that they can be helpful to you. They have been helpful to me in regaining the magic.

Note

1. Amerigo Vespucci, in Gruner, Aphrodisiacus, p. 117.

References

Fernandez de Oviedo y Valdes, Gonzalo. (1959). Historia general y natural de las Indias. Madrid: Ediciones Atlas.

Myers, T., Calzavra, L.M., Cockerill, R., Marshall, V.W., & Bullock, S.L. with the First Nations Steering Committee.

(1993). Ontario First Nations AIDS and Healthy Lifestyle Survey. Ottawa: Canadian Public Health Association.

Iranian Immigrants' Perceptions of Sexuality in Canada: A Symbolic Interactionist Approach

Khosro Refale Shirpak, Eleanor Maticka-Tyndale, and Maryam Chinichian

Introduction

Global migrations have figured prominently in the formation of the Canadian social and cultural landscape with that landscape becoming increasingly diversified as the heritage countries of the majority of immigrants shift from Europe (90 per cent prior to 1961) to Asia and the Middle East (60 per cent beginning in the 1990s) (Statistics Canada, 2006). These newer immigrants bring to Canada ways of thinking about sexual relationships rooted in understandings of human nature and social order that are often profoundly different from those that have set the foundations of Canadian culture and institutions (Aswad & Bilge, 1996; Barot, Bradley & Fenton, 1999; Beckett & Macey, 2001), posing a new acculturative challenge to immigrants and Canadian society alike.

Iran is a non-Arab country in the Middle East that has contributed growing numbers of immigrants to the Canadian population. Among the countries of the Middle East, Iran is one that has established coherence between Islamic teachings and laws (*Shari'a*) and state laws and government policies (Moghadam, 1992; Shahidian, 1999). Thus, Iranian immigrants come from a country where Islamic world views and normative systems are not only learned as part of religious teachings, but permeate the laws and policies that govern their lives. This is particularly salient to the area of norms, roles, and expectations related to sexuality since this is an area where Islamic countries such as Iran may be seen as standing in stark contrast to countries like Canada (Shirpak et al., 2007). At the root of these contrasts are beliefs related to sexual drive and desire, the role of family in the lives of individuals, and the positioning of patriarchy.

The question addressed in this paper is how Iranian immigrants understand and interpret (i.e., make sense of) Canadian sexuality, including the meanings they ascribe to what they see and experience while living in Canada. The analysis is set within the framework of Symbolic Interaction Theory and is based on interviews with 20 adult immigrants from Iran living in Ontario.

Contextual Frames

Iranian Context

Sexual interest and drive are presented in Muslim teachings as natural and necessary parts of the human condition. Their rightful expression, however, is restricted to marriage. Sexual relationships between unmarried partners are referred to as *illegitimate* and violate article 638 of the Iranian criminal code (Validi, 2004).

Sexual drive and desire are considered easily aroused and difficult for individuals to control. External mechanisms of control such as codes regulating dress and cross-gender interaction are used to avoid or control desire. It is believed that exposure of the body—especially a woman's body—either through the absence of covering or through tight covering, can lead to sexual thoughts, fantasies, arousal, and interest, and it is inappropriate to have such thoughts or interests other than for one's spouse. Thus, public dress is modest using various forms of loose, full-body covering. Gender segregation, another external mechanism of control, predates Islam (Keddie, 1991; Nashat & Tucker, 1999), but is now practised and supported by Islamic teachings and laws (*Shari'a*). Children become accustomed to segregation since it begins in the primary level and continues, in some form, through all levels of schooling. Beaches, swimming pools, and schools have separate areas (or times) designated for men and women. Male-female interaction is discouraged, except with *maharem* (people of the opposite sex with whom marriage is religiously and legally forbidden such as parents and siblings), with public segregation required by law. If, for example, a woman and man are together in public, members of the law enforcement task force may require them to show documentation that proves they are relatives. With the exception of *maharem*, conversation across gender lines is restricted to 'serious' topics with casual socializing, laughing, or 'kidding around' considered inappropriate (Nikzad, 2004).

In no country are culture, norms, and behaviour patterns static and immutable, and it is often the young who challenge established codes and expectations. This is evident in Iran in the actions of some urban young people who defy the restrictions on cross-gender interactions, meeting in cafes, parks, or other social places or even becoming involved in sexual contacts (Mohammadi et al., 2006), despite the potential for arrest. More modern families tolerate the cross-gender relationships of their children, even if they may wish they followed tradition more closely (Azadarmaki, Zand & Khazaie, 2000).

As in most Muslim countries, the family and its well-being is privileged over individual needs or desires (Ahmadi, 2003a, 2003b; Azadarmaki & Bahar, 2006; Shahidian, 1999) and the socialization of children is designed to ensure they understand and observe this priority. One's identity and, especially for most women, one's economic and social survival are tied to marriage and the family. Children are expected to maintain strong emotional bonds to the family, to observe its rules, and, even as adults, to remain in close contact with family members (Azadarmaki & Bahar, 2006). The parental role prescribes that parents know about and exert influence over their children's daily activities.

[. . .] In a nationwide study that surveyed 3540 respondents, Mohseni and Pourreza (2003) found that a majority agreed that parents should have a role in the friendship-making process of their children. The bond between parents and children is expected to remain strong throughout life (Azadarmaki & Bahar, 2006; Mohseni & Pourreza, 2003). Thus, even in adulthood it is common to consult family members and to consider what is best for the family (sometimes even more than what is best for oneself) when making important decisions, such as in marriage or career choices.

In Iran, maintaining the family unit is privileged in both law and custom (Farkhojasteh, 2003), albeit with different responsibilities and rights allocated to men and women. The male-dominant family continues to be supported through Iran's legal and social system and religious teachings, with fathers and husbands being the head of both family and marital partnerships and women having more limited rights than men. Azadarmaki and Bahar (2006) found that in 61.6 per cent of Iranian families the father is the main decision maker. [. . .]

While these laws and customs set the basic framework for gender and sexual relations in Iran, there is considerable variation in how they are followed. In the experience of the authors, marital relationships in Iran vary widely. In some, husbands and wives respect and treat each other as equals. Other couples, however, follow traditional teachings more strictly and reject egalitarian relationship and courtship styles. There is also considerable variation in dress as seen on the streets of urban centres such as Tehran, including women wearing the full black *chador* and women wearing various colours of loose-fitting, albeit stylish, long pants and long sleeve tops with a *rosary*, or head scarf covering their hair (Qarooni, 2006). Modern urban Iranians consider themselves 'fashion conscious'

within the requirements set by law for public appearance. Finally, some Iranian youth frequently challenge traditional restrictions in that they sometimes meet, dress, and engage in other activities that are formally forbidden.

Canadian Context

Canada is increasingly characterized by a variety of sexual lifestyle choices and prioritization of self-fulfillment and self-actualization. Leonard (2003) points out that 'sexual matters in the West have been progressively secularized such that they are left to individuals subject to adulthood, free consent, and privacy' (p. 70). In Canada, initiation into intimate and sexual relationships typically occurs during the teenage years, well before marriage (Barrett et al., 2004; Gillis, 2005; Maticka-Tyndale, 2001). The delay of marriage into the late twenties or thirties often results in men and women moving through several intimate and sexual relationships prior to marriage (Marcil-Gratton, 1998; Maticka-Tyndale, 2001). While a double standard still prevails, with men and women experiencing and expressing sexual power differently (Fraser, 2000; Kahn, O'Leary, Kruelwitz & Lamm, 1980; Tolman, 1994; 2002), diversity in forms of sexual pleasuring, focus on personal pleasure, individual choice and rights are components of contemporary scripts of sexual relationships for both men and women (Byers, 2005; Giddens, 1992). An exaggerated, and largely false, image of North American sexual culture is exported around the globe in movies and television shows which, in the latter twentieth and early twenty-first century typically portray struggling and troubled marriages and parent-child relationships, independent youth, and young adults without meaningful ties to their families, maritally unfaithful couples, and sexually adventurous singles. These are the public images of North American (including Canadian) relationships, family and sexuality that are most readily, publicly, accessible both inside and outside of North America.

Iranian Immigrants

Research on Iranian immigrants to Sweden (Ahmadi, 2003a; 2003b; Darvishpour, 2002), Norway (Predelli, 2004), the United States (Hojat, Shapurian, Nayerahmadi et al., 1999; Ghaffarian, 1998), and Canada (Shahidian, 1999; Moghissi, 1999) provides insights into their response to the encounter between Iranian/Islamic and contemporary secularized scripts. Each study documented tensions in parent-child and in marital relationships related to gender and sexuality. The latter were ascribed to women embracing more individualistic ways of thinking about their sexuality and exercising new-found powers available to them in the individual rights orientation of their host countries. These posed difficulties for marital relationships founded on ways of thinking that privileged maintenance of the relationship (Ahmadi 2003a; 2003b; Shahidian, 1999).

[. . .]

Theoretical Framework

This research study was informed by Blumer's (1969) symbolic interactionist approach to understanding human actions. The symbolic interactionist approach views individuals as pragmatic actors who live in both a physical (or factual) world and a symbolic (or interpretive) world. Symbolic interactionism focuses attention on the symbolic world formed by the individual in interaction with the environment and, in particular, on how people ascribe meanings and values to the world in which they live. People actively engage in the interpretation and creation of symbols as a way of making sense of, assigning meanings to, and communicating about their daily lives and the world in which they live. To symbolic interactionists, it is these ascribed meanings, values, and interpretations that have a dominant influence on our way of thinking and being in the world. Communication is built on a set of common symbols and interpretations including both language and non-verbal communication. The latter is evidenced, for example, in forms of dress, body positioning, facial expressions, language tone, and actions. For people to communicate effectively they must share common meanings and interpretations of the symbols they use. Roles—e.g., gender roles, sexual roles, family roles (husband, wife, parent, son, daughter)—are part of the symbol system that people create. As integrated sets of social norms or societal expectations about how one should or should not behave, roles form unconscious guidelines for behaviour. Roles, and the cultures of which they are a part, however, are not static and fixed, but dynamic and subject to change. If a person experiences difficulty in a role, as when role expectations are unclear or are different from what was anticipated, or when an individual is transitioning into or out of a role, role strain occurs.

In analyzing the experience and actions of people who are faced with a new social world, as is the case for Iranian immigrants to Canada, symbolic interactionism calls the researcher's attention to the symbolic meanings of particular actions and experiences in both the old world and the new; to role requirements and the potential for different meanings, costs and rewards associated with role performance; and to potentials for role strain, its source, experience, and resolution. These dynamics will be examined from the perspectives of Iranians' interpretations of sexuality in Canada.

Methodology

Symbolic interactionism calls for a qualitative methodology (Blumer, 1969; Denzin, 2001) that permits research participants to reflect on and explain the meanings they attribute to observations or experiences. In this study, in-depth interviews were used for this purpose.

The Sample

Adult (i.e., > 18 years of age), heterosexually married men and women who immigrated to Canada from Iran and were living in a mid-sized Canadian city, were asked to participate in in-depth interviews. Participants were recruited through personal contacts of the co-investigators, through an Iranian woman who works with new immigrants, and through snowball sampling with those interviewed referring others to the study. The sample consisted of 10 men and 10 women. Sixteen identified as Muslim and four as Baha'i. Interviews were conducted between May and July 2005.

The Procedure

Interviews were conducted in Farsi by two of the co-investigators. Based on prior work in this community (Maticka-Tyndale, Shirpak & Chinichian, 2007) the researchers knew that interviewing on sexual matters required that interviewers be of the same sex as participants and that they preferably come from a health background. For Iranians, speaking about sexual matters is something that is acceptable with health professionals, but not necessarily with others. The interviewers were both Iranian immigrants to Canada, one a male physician and the other a female midwife with an MA in anthropology. Both had experience in in-depth interviewing from other research projects.

Participants received an information package including a consent form and letter describing the project and interview. After providing consent for the interview, participants were asked about problems and concerns that Iranian immigrants living in Canada have with respect to sexuality, their views of sex education both for children and for adults like themselves, and any concerns they had with respect to the sexuality of their children. Participants were not asked directly about their views of the sexuality of Canadians; however, participants framed their personal concerns and views within the context of a comparison with what they interpreted as a Canadian way of living and dealing with sexuality and marital and parent-child relationships.

Ethics

The research procedures were reviewed and cleared by the Ethics Review Board of the University of Windsor. Prior to beginning the interview, each respondent was informed about the purpose of the study and the background and interests of the researchers. They were fully informed of their rights as participants and the steps taken to maintain confidentiality. Consent was obtained to tape-record interviews. They were given the opportunity to ask questions of the interviewers at the close of the interview.

Data Handling

All interviews were transcribed and translated to English prior to analysis. To ensure accuracy of translation, transcripts were translated by one of the co-investigators and then checked against the original tape by a second co-investigator. Co-investigators also regularly cross-checked each other's coding and interpretation of data.

Analysis Procedures

Thematic analysis was used to explore how study participants interpreted and understood

Canadian sexuality and marital and parent-child relationships. Comparisons were made by age, gender, religion, and time in Canada. To compare the views of younger and older participants, those below the sample median of 42.5 years for women and 38.5 years for men (referred to as younger) were compared to those above the median (referred to as older). Quotations are identified by gender and whether participants were younger or older. Time in Canada is not noted with quotations since there were no differences evident based on this factor.

Results

Participants

Participants included 10 married females (8 Muslims and 2 Baha'is) and 10 married males (8 Muslims and 2 Baha'is) ranging in age from 22 to 53 years for women (median 42.5) and 29 to 67 years for men (median 38.5). Participants had been married between 2.5 and 36 years (medians 19 for women and 10.5 for men). The majority were well educated, with a median of 15 years for women (range 5–16) and 17 for men (range 5–20). All had left Iran since the 1979 Islamic revolution, with the time in Canada ranging from 8 months to 18 years with a median of 7 years for women and 4.75 years for men. The number of children varied from none to 3 and children's ages ranged from 2 to 33 years old.

Themes and Sub-themes

Using the symbolic interactionist approach, the theme chosen as the initial departure point for analysis was Iranian immigrants' interpretation and understanding of the symbols of Canadian sexuality and sexual relationships. Participants drew on a diversity of experiential sources for their observations, including personal conversations,

visual observations in the course of daily activities, rumours or unsubstantiated commentary, and media discourse and depictions. The following themes and sub-themes emerged from the data:

1. Meanings which Iranian immigrants attached to adult Canadians' sexuality and sexual relationships based on
   - Observations of women's dress style in Canada
   - Information related to women's freedom and rights in Canada
   - Observations of interpersonal relationships between unmarried men and women
   - Observation of parent-child relationships
2. Immigrants' perceptions of adolescents' sexuality
   - Observations and rumours of adolescent sexual activity
   - Experience with school-based sex education
3. Experiences they had in interactions with Canadians related to sexuality and the meanings they ascribed to these.

Meanings Ascribed to Canadian Sexuality and Sexual Relationships

Most participants spoke positively and, at times, enviously of the apparent ease with which Canadian men and women interacted with each other and, in particular, of the knowledge they believed that Canadians had on sexual matters and their ability to speak together about these. As one young woman reflected,

> Most (Canadian) couples here have been friends for four or five years before marriage. I think these people will have fewer problems. People who know each other before marriage are more successful . . . (Female, youngest)

However, participants felt that the 'Canadian ways' would not 'work' for them. They repeatedly spoke of how their own understandings of sexuality and cross-gender relationships led them to conclude that if they took up wholly 'Canadian ways', their marital and familial relationships would be jeopardized. Some spoke of what they saw as incompatibilities between Canadian and Iranian ways, making it very difficult for them to integrate the two. An older female commented on this difficulty.

> Iranian families who want to be Canadians go away from their culture and turn into 'foreigners' and even behave in an exaggerated way. These families behave like they are overdoing Canadians' lifestyle. (Female, older)

The Symbolic Nature of Dress

Iranians come from a culture where public exposure of parts of the body other than hands, feet, and face is considered immodest and signalling sexual interest. Men and women, regardless of age and religion ascribed the symbolism of seduction and sexual availability to the dress of Canadian women.

> Almost all revealing clothes have been designed for women. It has no reason but that they [women] want to satisfy and attract men. (Female, younger)

> Here in Canada women dress in a revealing way and their body is visible. Some Iranian men's minds might become preoccupied with that. The way men dress [in Canada] is not different from Iran. Women are different. (Male, older)

The women we interviewed were fearful that their husbands would be enticed to pursue liaisons with Canadian women whose way of dressing, in their view, might be interpreted by men as expressing an interest and availability for sexual liaisons. Men confirmed the fears of women, commenting that they saw Canadian women's dress as seductive.

> Canadian women are used to wearing revealing dress and it seduces men. (Male, youngest)

> Canadian women are used to wearing revealing dress and it might attract men. . . . But men are more concerned about their women than women for their men. In Iran we say to our wives that you must not wear a short sleeve shirt, or you'd better observe the Islamic dressing code (Hejab) and wear a scarf. (Male, younger)

Women's Rights and Freedoms

Iranian men interpreted the freedom that women had in Canada to make their own decisions related, for example, to work, social relationships, recreation, dress, and where and with whom they would go, as potentially jeopardizing the stability of Iranian families. Their understandings of family, and especially marital relationships, were founded on family and gender role practices, codes, and laws that they had experienced and observed since childhood in their home country. They reflected on how these differed and the difficulties they had in finding a way to integrate what was possible in Canada with what they understood as essential to maintaining a strong family. They viewed women's right to petition for divorce on an equal footing with men, the availability of state support for single mothers, and the potential for state intervention into marital affairs (e.g., in response to accusations of abuse or denial of rights) as encouraging women to walk out of the marital relationship.

Iranian women who have come to Canada feel more independence than they do in Iran. They say 'I can get divorce' with strong confidence; a statement that they couldn't easily make in Iran. They are supported by the government here in Canada and it is why they raise divorce issue easily. It is not just a claim. Some women really do it. They can do it because they have financial support here in Canada after divorce. (Male, older)

Iranian women might leave their husband because of more freedom here in Canada. They might find someone whom they think is a better match with them and want to be with him. Iranian men are worried about these things. (Male, younger)

Men are worried about women's rights and freedoms here. They are concerned about the misuse—by claiming divorce—of this freedom by their wives. (Male, oldest)

As evident in these quotations, the status of women in Canada was seen as especially challenging by men. Coming from a male-dominant social system they wondered how women could be kept in an unhappy marriage if they had the right to leave, could access financial support in the form of welfare and mother's allowance, and could readily experience the freedom to make their own decisions without consultation with husbands or other family members.

Non-marital Interactions and Friendships

In Iran, private cross-gender interactions of two *namahram* (people of the opposite sex who can religiously and legally marry with each other) in private are religiously discouraged and any social

relationships of such people might be seen as a signal that there is a sexual liaison. With religious teachings, folk wisdom, and law all supporting a common set of beliefs and interpretations, it is not surprising that our participants had difficulty viewing social relationships across gender lines as non-sexual, casual, or non-threatening, particularly in their meaning for women.

. . . our marital relationship will be destroyed if we try to be like Canadians. For example, Canadian men don't care if other men, in a party for instance, flirt with their wives. It is absolutely unbearable and unacceptable for us. If we let these things happen and if we try to be Canadian, mutual respect [between husband and wife] will be broken. We cannot let other men flirt with our wives just because it is acceptable in Canadian society. (Male, older)

Canadian divorce rates and knowledge of the existence of extramarital affairs were interpreted as indicating that Canadians readily and easily formed extramarital liaisons, left their marital relationships with little thought or provocation and, essentially, cared little about their marriage.

. . . Canadians' relationships are incomparable to Iranians. Canadian couples have no commitment and no emotion about each other. They are with somebody today and with somebody else the next day. I have witnessed it myself among Canadian couples. I know Canadian married men who have girlfriends. Canadian women do the same. . . . Canadian men say, 'OK, if I don't get satisfaction with my wife I will go with my girlfriend.' Their wives have the same idea. But Iranians try to keep their marital relationship in any condition. If the problem is their sexual relationship,

I think, Iranians will try to make it better. They try to modify their relationship and make it better in a way that helps their marital life. (Male, older)

What is relevant, from a symbolic interactionist perspective, is not the factual validity or basis of these interpretations, but the meanings ascribed to the purported 'evidence' or 'facts', which in this case was that Canadian men and woman put little effort into their marital relationship.

Parent-child Relationships

There was considerable diversity in how participants viewed parent-child relationships in Canadian families. Some saw little difference in Canadian compared to Iranian parenting, with both paying close attention to the activities of their children and having definite rules and expectations of their children, even to the point of more restrictions and protections of girls as compared to boys.

I think their [Canadians'] concerns about their children are like us. Some Iranians let their children to stay in their friends' house overnight but some Canadians don't. It is a rule for girls [not to stay at a friend's overnight] but boys are permitted to stay. So I think, like Iranians, girls are different from boys in Canadians' point of view. (Female, older)

I know some Canadian families who are similar to us, who formally propose to their prospective bride's family for marriage. They get permission of their prospective bride's family before marriage. (Female, older)

Others, however, relayed quite different observations of Canadian parent-child relationships. They spoke of Canadian parents who allowed their adolescent children to make their own decisions and spend time away from home (for example, overnight at a friend's house). To some of our participants, these observations symbolized that Canadian parents cared less about their children or about remaining close to their children than did Iranians.

. . . Canadians are not worried about their children. They kick their 16- or 17-year-old children out of home and let them do whatever they want. But we like to be with our children until death. (Male, older)

. . . Canadians feel free with these things. They don't care if their 16-year-old daughter doesn't come back home at night. It is important for us as Iranian. (Male, older)

Our participants expressed surprise and concern that Canadian institutions such as schools, the health care system and the police supported children's independence from parental authority. Some parents struggled with how they could properly supervise and guide their children without the co-operation of Canadian institutions and laws.

When my younger daughter was 18, I went to her school and asked about one of her scores in math. Her teacher said that her score was decreased because she was absent two times. When I asked her teacher about the dates of her absence, she said she couldn't tell me because in her opinion my daughter was old enough to decide on her own and I had no right to ask about my daughter's personal information. I said to her 'I am supporting her financially and she is still my daughter. She is not a Canadian girl and I am not a Canadian mother.' But she didn't understand me. (Female, older)

Adolescence and Sexuality

The sexual activity of adolescents was often raised as a concern in interviews. Virginity prior to marriage is highly valued in Iran. The future, especially of a young woman who becomes sexually active prior to marriage, is cause for concern.

Observations and Rumours about Canadian Youth

The independence afforded to Canadian youth and what appeared to be a willingness of Canadian parents to allow their teenage children to go unsupervised, to stay out late, and to socialize across gender lines were all seen as contributing to early sexual activity among Canadian youth. The potential for the same among Iranian teenagers was of grave concern to the participants in our study. Perhaps because of the attention given in the media to the sexual activity of young teens, our participants fairly consistently believed that Canadian teens were sexually active from a very young age and that their parents were either unconcerned about this or had no way of influencing or controlling their children.

> Iranians like their children to wait to begin sex until after marriage or at least not to have sex at a younger age. For example, they don't want their children to have sex at 14. (Female, youngest)

> Our concerns about our children will be different at different ages for sure. In puberty our concern is about sexual relationships. When they get older we are worried if they start their sexual relationship. How can we find if they did? For girls we are worried about pregnancy and for boys for diseases. (Female, older)

Sex Education and Adolescent Sexuality

[. . .]

Iran does not have a formal system of broadly based sex education for either youth or adults (Mohammadi et al., 2006). School-based sex education in lower grades is believed to encourage or contribute to sexual activity among youth and to expose children to materials that are only appropriate for adults (Poraboli, 2000). In recent years several educational programs regarding maturation and its related bodily and emotional changes have begun to be offered in secondary schools in Iran. However, because of the strong belief that sexual matters are private between husband and wife, and the concern that sexual information and materials might incite young people to become sexually active, the educational materials speak only euphemistically of sexual and relationship issues, without mention of specifics or details (Amado, 2003; Greene, Rasekh, Amen, Chaya & Dye, 2002; Shirpak, Chinichian & Maticka-Tyndale, 2005).

Although they criticized and were sorry about the lack of sex education in their adolescence in Iran and acknowledged the constructive role of such education in adulthood and marital relationships, some interviewees were worried about the presence of sex education in the first years of school as one of the probable causes for the early initiation into sexual activity of Canadian youth. Given the stronger expectations of purity and virginity for girls, concern was expressed primarily about daughters.

> If Iranians have daughters they are concerned about their daughters' virginity in their adolescence. The vast majority of Iranians think in the same way. I am one of them. It is not a big deal for Canadians. If a Canadian young girl is virgin she will be humiliated by her friends and will be

stigmatized that she has a problem. This is our concern about our children in schools and we are really worried about it. Here they teach children about sex from primary school. Maybe my way of thinking is old fashioned but I think it is not appropriate to teach these things in primary school . . . Some children the age of 8 or 9 are sexually active. I think it is because of watching some movies and reading some books and being exposed to sex education classes in school. (Male, older)

Families should bring up their children so rational and wise that they postpone their sexual relationship for 10 years until they are completely mature. Or they should move to a place they can control their children . . . I want to come back to Iran if I have a 12-year-old daughter until she will be grown up enough. Here in Canada you can say nothing to your 15-year-old daughter. If you push her to do something that you want she yells at you and runs away with a Canadian boy to California. (Male, younger)

On the other hand, some others, despite their concerns about their children's exposure to sex education in early childhood, considered this education to be necessary and helpful.

If these educations start earlier, children will be more curious. I don't like that my child is exposed to these education too soon. I am worried, even from now, that if my child will be born here s/he will be involved with these issues too soon. But after all, they're better to be educated than kept uninformed. So, for educating children, they can teach them only general things and don't go to the details. If they just talk about general subjects it would be OK to teach children in younger age, for example, eight.

If this education starts later, it has consequences. It is better for children to have information before they want to start having sex. (Female, younger, no child)

They are not ready enough. They are not ready for digesting these things. Having knowledge about their body does not mean necessarily that they are ready for a sexual relationship and sexual intercourse. I am not saying to leave them uninformed and let them gather information by themselves and directly from their experience. Let them get older and at least have some information about other parts of their body, know where their bladder and kidneys are and then teach them about those things. . . . If they are not taught until later they could face problems; they don't know how to deal with. (Female, older, mother)

Sexual Meanings and Misunderstandings: Examples from Health Care

Our participants also spoke of instances where they felt that they were being judged from a Canadian standpoint, resulting in what they considered to be inappropriate meanings being ascribed to their actions. These were typically in encounters with professionals. One woman in her early twenties reported an instance when her physician expressed surprise that she had never had a Pap test.

In the very first visit my doctor asked me how many times I have had Pap test in Iran. When I told her I have never had Pap test in Iran, she was surprised and recorded that. I don't know if she knew anything about the belief in Iran that a virgin girl cannot have a Pap test. (Female, younger)

In Iran, a Pap test is not only considered unnecessary until a woman is sexually active, but is also seen as compromising her virginity. She explained this to her physician, but felt that she was viewed as unusual, exceptional, and perhaps even irrational because of her refusal of the Pap test. In her own culture, she would not have had to discuss her virginity, let alone explain why she did not want a Pap test.

In a second interview, a recently married woman described an instance where she sought advice from a health care provider about how to improve her sexual relationship with her husband. She complained about pain during urination and explained that she thought this might be related to sexual activity.

I wanted to know if my problem (burning during urination) is because of a virus that transferred from my husband or it is simply because of his behaviour during sex that hurts me. I was not good in English language . . . and I couldn't communicate with my doctor freely and say my problem in a way that I usually did in Iran. (Female, youngest)

Her unfamiliarity with how to speak about sexual matters led her to describe her sexual encounters with her husband as 'violent' and 'hurting'. Misinterpreting what the woman was saying as a report of sexual abuse, the health provider contacted the police, who then contacted her husband.

. . . The day after, I found that police warned my husband about his violent behaviour toward me. He was crying when he explained that the police called. He kept asking me what he did to me that I complained to police. . . . I just wanted to know what I should do for my physical problem. . . .

What the woman wanted was advice on sexual intercourse and an explanation or treatment for her pain. She was acting from within the framework of her culture where the role of health care providers is to provide advice about sexual problems, and where a health provider would know that a newly married woman was unlikely to know much about sexual practices. However, to her Canadian health provider her comments were interpreted as signalling the probability of sexual violence or abuse in her marital relationship, a valid reason for contacting the police.

Discussion

The degree to which one's own 'ways of being' are entrenched in a sense of normality and propriety and the ways of others are seen as strange or deviant is repeatedly illustrated in this research. For the Iranians in our study, the actions of Canadians were interpreted and assigned meanings from within an Iranian cultural framework. Although religion and culture are closely intertwined in many societies, and religion is enshrined in law and policy in Iran, our participants identified their views as rooted in Iranian culture rather than in Islamic or Baha'i belief systems or teachings. They also felt that their own actions and words were likewise interpreted and assigned meanings by representatives of the educational or health care system from within a Canadian cultural framework. In both cases, this produced a considerable gap in understanding, both reflected and entrenched in misinformation about each others' ways of being and relating to sexuality.

The privileging of family and maintenance of a marriage over the needs, desires, and preferences of individuals was foundational to the interpretations and concerns expressed by Iranians. The greater focus in Canada on the rights of the individual was interpreted as indicating that Canadians value themselves over and above their value for family and marriage—opposite to Iranian values. The value placed on independence and the rights of individuals, the acceptance of a broad range of styles of dress and casual cross-gender interactions for people of all ages and marital statuses, interpreted from within their own beliefs about gender, sexuality, and relationships, were each seen as potentially threatening to Iranian marriages and as contributing to high divorce rates. We note that while concerns were expressed by both men and women, they expressed different concerns. For women, the focus was on men being drawn away from the marriage by 'seductive' Canadian women. This concern is similar to that of women in Iran who, in a study of women's needs in the area of sexuality education, expressed concern over not being able to satisfy their husbands' sexual needs or desires and their husbands consequently looking for it somewhere else (Shirpak, 2006). Men focused on the social systems that made it possible for women to leave an 'unhappy marriage'.

The differences between what our participants valued and what they believed was valued in Canada was further demonstrated to them in their interactions with Canadian institutions. Schools demonstrated respect for the privacy and rights of older teenagers to choose whether or not to share information with their parents by refusing to release information to parents. Health care providers erred on the side of protecting the health and well-being of their female patients, recommending what are considered standard and necessary preventive procedures and reporting suspected spousal abuse to the police. Their

actions, however, were different from Iranian cultural norms. For the school officials and health providers, these actions reflected respect for and protection of individual rights and well-being. To our participants they were in contrast to the prescribed parental roles, sexual norms, and both marital and health provider–patient relationships of their own culture. They were interpreted by our participants as evidence that their values were neither understood nor respected by Canadians.

While some of our participants saw benefits to the way Canadians approach marriage and friendships between the sexes, they likewise produced considerable anxiety about how living in Canada would influence their own relationships. These concerns cut across all age groups and did not appear to abate as immigrants were in Canada for longer time periods. For example, the very same young woman who was quoted earlier as speaking positively of Canadian couples being friends for several years prior to marriage, compared this to what she knew of Iranian couples.

> . . . I know many (Iranian) couples who got married and had a good relationship for more than 8 or 10 years but after living in Canada for one year, they got divorced. The reason for their divorce was that the wife was informed about her rights and realized that here in Canada they (women) have more rights. (Female, youngest)

[. . .]

Based on research among Muslim immigrants to Western countries, it appears that our participants' fears that their marriages could not survive in Canada are well grounded. Hojat et al. (1999) noted that divorce rates among Iranian immigrants in the United States were more than six times higher than in Iran. According to Darvishpour (2002), Iranians have the second highest divorce rate among immigrant groups in Sweden. Research with Muslim immigrants to other 'Western' countries reports similar experiences with acculturative stresses and divorce rates (e.g., Buijs, 1993; Frederick & Akhtar, 2005; Ghaffarian, 1998; Hanassab & Tidwell, 1996; Hendrickx, Lodewijckx, van Royen & Denekens, 2002; Kelson & Delaet, 1999; Killoran, 1998; Phalet & Hagendoorn, 1996). Further, considerable research on the children of immigrants has documented their tendency to acclimatize to and accept the 'Western ways', creating tension between children and parents (Hall, 1992; Talbani & Hassanali, 2000).

Limitations

In considering the results of this study, readers are reminded that this was a small sample of only heterosexual Iranian immigrants living in coupled relationships (married), drawn in one city in Canada. The views focus a great deal on maintaining relationships and concerns about how the differences in Canadian and Iranian ways might influence relationships. Such views might be quite different if divorcees or single men and women had been included in the sample. [. . .] [W]e might expect the symbolic/interpretive reality with respect to sexuality and relationships to be different for divorcees, and particularly divorced women. Similarly, those who are not yet married might interpret the freedom to form friendships and to interact in a sociable way across gender lines quite differently than those who are married. These further insights must be left to future research with more diverse samples.

A second potential limitation is the use of Iranian interviewers. The advantages and disadvantages to insider versus outsider researchers, particularly when using qualitative methods, have been discussed extensively in the literature (Christensen & Dahl, 1997; Fine, 1994; Humphrey, 2007; Labaree, 2002). The advantage

of Iranian interviewers included the ability to conduct interviews in Farsi, which interviewees expressed as a benefit; and to analyze the interviews in the original language and verify the retention of meaning when quotations for the research were translated to English. Participants expressed comfort in being interviewed by those who understood their culture and several commented that they could not speak of these matters with people outside their culture. The fact that interviewers were both health professionals was consistent with Iranian cultural norms that permitted open discussion of sexual matters with health professionals and the religious belief that health professionals but not others may be trusted as confidants (*mahram*). The disadvantages of insider interviewers include the possibility that interviewees provided only culturally acceptable responses and that, because of the shared culture, interviewers assumed a shared meaning and understanding rather than probing to confirm one. However, similar disadvantages exist with outsider interviewers. An acquiescence bias—i.e., participants say what they believe an interviewer wants to hear—and insufficient knowledge about a culture to know where to probe more deeply have also been noted as problems with outsider interviewers. By combining skilled, experienced insider interviewers with analyses and in-depth discussions among insiders and outsiders we feel we have balanced the advantages and disadvantages of the two approaches. [. . .]

Conclusions

Much has been written of cross-cultural misunderstandings with differences in meanings ascribed to common daily events (e.g., dress, physical closeness between strangers in public places, facial expressions, body language, codes of politeness, interpersonal interactions) both the source of humour and of serious consideration related to lost business opportunities or political alliances. For immigrants, as well as for citizens of countries that receive immigrants, differences in interpretations of daily events may create more longstanding tensions and strains in developing inclusive, mutually respectful relationships across communities. They create barriers to recognizing the commonalities of experience of husbands, wives, and parents who in both Canada and Iran focus on maintaining quality relationships within their marriages and families. Instead, differences in interpretation perpetuate stereotypes and lead to ongoing suspicion and misunderstanding that maintain and widen the distance between people. Discordance between the meanings and interpretations of symbols impacts on social interactions among Iranians and Canadians and on the use of professional services by Iranians (Maticka-Tyndale, Shirpak & Chinichian, 2007). For a country such as Canada, whose approach to immigration and nation building is founded on a principle of multiculturalism, it can be argued that understanding and communication across cultural divides is essential to living the principle of multiculturalism and for the delivery of quality services to its entire population. Strides have been made to provide culturally appropriate sexual health services and to acknowledge cultural diversity in much sex education programming. This ranges from making cultural interpreters available in the health provider–patient encounter as is done, for example, by Toronto Public Health, to involving representatives of cultural minorities in developing sexual health programming, as is done, for example, with representatives of the Muslim community in London, Ontario's programming related to sexual and family violence. What this study demonstrates is that the recognition of cultural diversities and the inclusion of people from different cultures in programming and service provision is essential in a multicultural context.

References

Ahmadi, N. (2003a). Migration challenges views of sexuality. *Ethnic and Racial Studies, 26*, 684–706.

———. (2003b). Rocking sexualities: Iranian migrants' view of sexuality. *Archives of Sexual Behavior, 32*, 317–26.

Amado, L.E. (2003). *Sexual and Bodily Rights as Human Rights in the Middle East and North Africa: A Workshop Report.* Istanbul, Turkey: Women for Women's Human Rights (WWHR)—New Ways.

Aswad, B., & Bilge B. (Eds.). (1996). *Family and Gender among American Muslims: Issues facing Middle Eastern immigrants and their descendents.* Philadelphia, PA: Temple University Press.

Azadarmaki, T., & Bahar, M. (2006). Families in Iran: Changes, challenges and future. *Journal of Comparative Family Studies, 37*, 589–608.

Azadarmaki, T., Zand, M., & Khazaie, T. (2000). Barasiye tahavolat-e-ejtemaie va farhangi dar tool-e se nasl khnevade-ye Tehrani [Study of socio-cultural changes in three generations of Tehrani families]. *Nameh-ye olum-e ejtemai, 16*, 3–29.

Barrett, M., King, A., Levy, J., Maticka-Tyndale, E., Fraser, J., & McKay, A.. (2004). Sexuality in Canada. Revised. In R. Francoeur, *International Encyclopedia of Sexuality*, vol. 1, (pp. 126–191). New York, NY: Continuum Publishers. (Updated and revised from 1997).

Barot, R., Bradley, H., & Fenton, S. (Eds). (1999). *Ethnicity, Gender and Social Change.* London, UK: Macmillan Press.

Beckett, C., & Macey, M. (2001). Race, gender and sexuality: The oppression of multiculturalism. *Women's Studies International Forum, 24*, 309–19.

Blumer, H., (1969). *Symbolic Interactionism: Perspective and Method.* Englewood Cliffs, NJ: Prentice-Hall.

Buijs, G. (1993). *Migrant Women: Crossing Boundaries and Changing Identities.* Oxford, UK: Berg Publishers.

Byers, S.E. (2005). Relationship satisfaction and sexual satisfaction: A longitudinal study of individuals in long-term relationships. *Journal of Sex Research. 42*, 113–18.

Christensen, D.H., & Dahl, C.M. (1997). Rethinking research dichotomies. *Family and Consumer Sciences Research Journal, 25*, 269–85.

Darvishpour, M. (2002). Immigrant women challenge the role of men: How to changing power relationship within Iranian families in Sweden intensifies family conflicts after immigration. *Journal of Comparative Family Study, 33*, 271–96.

Denzin, N. (2001). *Interpretive Interactionism.* Thousand Oaks, CA: Sage Publications.

Farkhojasteh, H. (2003). *Ketab-e Iran (Khanevadeh)* [Iran's Book (Family)]. Tehran, Iran: Markaz-e Motaleate Farhangi-beinolmelali.

Fine, M. (1994). Working the hyphens: Reinventing self and other in qualitative research. In N.K. Denzin & Y.S. Lincoln (Eds.), *Handbook of Qualitative Research* (pp. 70–82). Thousand Oaks, CA: Sage.

Fraser, J. (2000). *Women's Stories of Power: Exploring reclamation and subversion of heterosexual sex*. Unpublished doctoral dissertation, University of Windsor, Ontario.

Frederick, Y.H., & Akhtar, S. (2005). Immigration sex: the transport of affection and sensuality across culture. *The American Journal of Psychoanalysis, 65*, 179–88.

Ghaffarian, S. (1998). The acculturation of Iranian immigrants in the United States and the implications for mental health. *The Journal of Social Psychology, 138*, 645–54.

Giddens, A. (1992). *The Transformation of Intimacy: Sexuality, Love and Eroticism in Modern Societies*. Cambridge, UK: Polity Press.

Gillis, R. (2005). *Examining the National Longitudinal Survey of Children and Youth: A Profile of Canadian Adolescent Sexuality*. Unpublished Master's thesis. University of Windsor, Ontario.

Greene, M.E., Rasekh, Z., Amen, K., Chaya, N., & Dye, J. (2002). In This Generation—Sexual & Reproductive Health Policies for a Youthful World. Population Action International, Washington, DC. Retrieved 20 December 2007, from http://www.populationaction.org/Publications/Reports/In_This_Generation/English.pdf

Hall, S. (1992). The question of cultural identity. In S. Hall, D. Held, & T. McGrew (Eds.), *Modernity and Its Future* (pp. 273–325). Cambridge, UK: Polity Press.

Hanassab, S., & Tidwell, R. (1996). Sex roles and sexual attitudes of young Iranian women: Implications for cross-cultural counseling. *Social Behavior and Personality, 24*, 185–94.

Hendrickx, K., Lodewijckx, E., van Royen, P., & Denekens, J. (2002). Sexual behaviour of second generation Moroccan immigrants balancing between traditional attitudes and safe sex. *Patient Education and Counseling, 47*, 89–94.

Hojat, M., Shapurian, R., Nayerahmadi, H., Farzaneh, M., Foroughi, D., Parsi, M., et al. (1999). Premarital sexual, child rearing, and family attitudes of Iranian men and women in the United States and in Iran. *The Journal of Psychology, 133*, 19–31.

Humphrey, C. (2007). Insider-outsider, activating the hyphen. *Action Research, 5*, 11–26.

Kahn, A., O'Leary, J., Kruelwitz, H., & Lamm, H. (1980). Equity and equality: Male and female means to a just end. *Basic and Applied Social Psychology, 1*, 173–97.

Keddie, N.R. (1991). Introduction: Deciphering Middle Eastern women's history. In N.R. Keddie & B. Baron (Eds.), *Women in Middle-Eastern History: Shifting Boundaries in Sex and Gender* (pp. 1–22). New Haven, CT: Yale University Press.

Kelson, G., & Delaet, E. (1999). *Gender and Immigration*. London, UK: Macmillan Press.

Killoran, M. (1998). Good Muslims and bad Muslims: Good women and feminists: New identities in northern Cyprus (or, the condom story). *Ethos, 26*, 183–203.

Labaree, R.V. (2002). The risk of 'going observationalist': Negotiating the hidden dilemmas of being an insider participant observer. *Qualitative research, 2*, 97–122.

Leonard, K. (2003). *Muslims in the United States: The state of research*. Albany, NY: The University of New York Press.

Marcil-Gratton, N. (1998). Growing up with mom and dad? The intricate family life courses of Canadian children. Statistics Canada/HRDC Publication No. 89-566-XIE. Ottawa, ON: Minister of Industry.

Maticka-Tyndale, E. (2001). Sexual health and Canadian youth: How do we measure up? *The Canadian Journal of Human Sexuality, 10*, 1–17.

Maticka-Tyndale, E., Shirpak, K.R., & Chinichian, M. (2007). Providing for the sexual health needs of Canadian immigrants: The experience of immigrants from Iran. *Canadian Journal of Public Health, 98*, 183–86.

Moghadam, V. (1992). Patriarchy and the politics of gender in modernizing societies: Iran, Pakistan and Afghanistan. *International Sociology, 7*, 35–53.

Moghissi, H. (1999). Away from home: Iranian women, displacement cultural resistance and change. *Journal of Comparative Family Study, 30*, 207–17.

Mohammadi, M.R., Mohammad, K., Farahani F.K.A., Alikhani, S., Zare M., Tehrani, E.R., Ramezankhani A., & Alaeddini F. (2006). Reproductive knowledge, attitudes and behavior among adolescent males in Tehran, Iran. *International Family Planning Perspectives, 32*, 35–44.

Mohseni, M., and Pourreza, A. (2003). *Ezdevaj va khanevade dar Iran* [Marriage and family in Iran]. Tehran: Arvan.

Nashat, G., & Tucker, E. (1999). *Women in the Middle East and North Africa: Restoring women to history*. Bloomington, IN: Indiana University Press.

Nikzad, A. (2004) Ravabet-e- zan va mard az didgah-e-Islam [Man and woman relationship from Islamic point of view]. *Ketabe Zanan, 7*, 117–51.

Qarooni, N. (2006). Iran uncovered—Tehran women make their own statement, in color (2006, September 5). *The Star-Ledger the Voice of New Jersey* [New Jersey], p. 001.

Phalet, K., & Hagendoorn, L. (1996). Personal adjustment to acculturative transitions: The Turkish experience. *International Journal of Psychology, 31*, 131–44.

Poraboli, M., (2000). *Baresi moaleman-e shahr-e Kerman nesbat be amozeshe jensi va baresi nazarate anan dar mored-e nokat-e mored-e lozoom dar amoozesh-e jensi be nojavanan* [Attitude of city of Kerman teachers toward sex education and its content to adolescents]. Masters' dissertation, Kerman University of Medical Sciences, 2000.

Predelli, L.N. (2004). Interpreting gender in Islam: A case study of immigrant Muslim women in Oslo, Norway. *Gender and Society, 18*, 473–93.

Shahidian, H. (1999). Gender and sexuality among immigrant Iranians in Canada. *Sexualities, 2*, 189–215.

Shirpak, K.R. (2006). *Tadvin-e Barnameh-ye Amoozeshe Behdasht-e Jensi va Sanjesh-e Tasir-e an bar Taghire Raftar-e Zanan Morajeh-e Konandeh be Vahedha-ye Tanzim-e Khanevadeh-ye Marakez-e Behdashti Shahre Tehran.* [Developing and Testing a Sex Education Program for the Female Clients of the Family Planning Unit of Health Centers in Tehran]. Ph.D. dissertation, Tehran University of Medical Sciences, 2006.

Shirpak, K.R., Ardebili, H.E., Mohammad, K., Maticka-Tyndale, E., Chinichian, M., Ramenzankhani, A., & Fotouhi, A. (2007). Developing and testing a sex education program for the female clients of the health centers in Iran. *Sex Education, 7,* 333–49.

Shirpak, R.K., & Chinichian, M. (2001). KAP Study on Sexual Health in Getting Married Couples. Poster session presented at the 10th International Congress of Epidemiology. Jhansi, India.

Shirpak, R.K., Chinichian, M., & Maticka-Tyndale, E. (2005). Providing Sexual Health Services to Immigrants from Muslim Countries. Guelph Sexuality Conference. June 13–15. Guelph, Ontario.

Talbani, A., & Hassanali, P. (2000). Adolescent females between tradition and modernity: Socialization in South Asian immigrant culture. *Journal of Adolescence, 23,* 615–27.

Tolman, T.L. (1994). Doing desire: Adolescent girl's struggles for/with sexuality. *Gender and Society, 8,* 324–42.

———. (2002). *Dilemmas of Desire.* Cambridge, MA: Harvard University Press.

Validi, M.S. (2004). *Hoghoghe Jazaye Ekhtesasi* (Exclusive Criminal law). Tehran, Iran: Amir Kabir Institution.

International Female Migration to Atlantic Canada through Internet Mediated Matchmaking Agencies

Susan M. Brigham and Catherine Baillie Abidi

I find what I need. Magic. First man I write. I find very quickly. Like magic I find him.

(Russian woman – Natasha)

My friends couldn't believe it. 'Why would she want you? You are old and she is young' . . . They could not believe that there was a woman on the other side of the world in Russia who was interested in me!

(Canadian man – Jack)

Some men see the woman as a sense of possession because they have invested a lot of money into the relationship. . . . I just say to them 'you can't purchase a person'.

(Immigrant Service Provider – Bea)

Introduction

The practice of international female migration through Internet mediated matchmaking agencies or so-called 'mail-order bride marriages' is a poorly understood and inadequately considered aspect of women's migration to Canada despite the fact that it has been growing internationally, particularly since the advent of the Internet (Lacroix and Brigham 2006; Kojima 2001; Perez 2003; Simons 2001; Vergara, 2000). These relationships are defined as a 'transaction between a [Canadian] man and a woman from . . . countries [of the South], usually brokered by an agent, who is part of the mail-order bride industry, via catalogues or the Internet' (Philippine Women Centre of BC and the Status of Women Canada Policy Research 2000, 1). Louise Langevin and Marie-Claire Belleau (2000) assert that one of the main objectives of such relationships is to enable women to immigrate to Canada.

The purposes of this paper are to examine some of the complexities inherent in international female migration through Internet mediated matchmaking agencies and understand the ways in which policy (for example, immigration policy) has an impact on migrant women in Canada. To do this we draw on data from a qualitative study conducted in Atlantic

Canada. We centre our discussion around the transcripts and notes of in-depth interviews with one Russian woman and one Canadian man, both of whom used an international Internet matchmaking agency to meet one another. We also draw on interview data from four immigrant service providers in Atlantic Canada. In this paper, we begin with a discussion of the theory of post-colonial feminism as it pertains to our study. We then provide background on the prevalence of the phenomenon of Internet mediated matchmaking, policy, and legislation, followed by a discussion and critical analysis of power, a dominant theme arising in our data. Finally, we conclude with recommendations related to a) settlement, support, education, and legislation and b) research.

Theoretical Framework

We draw on insights from post-colonial feminism in order to better understand the complex ways in which the experiences of migrant women are impacted by class, gender, race, culture and language, nationality, geographic origin and residence, level of education, previous work and cross-cultural experience, familial/kinship roles, and so on.

[. . .]

Our theoretical assumptions are multifaceted to ensure a holistic analysis of the experiences of this particular group of migrant women. Firstly, we recognize that women are not a homogenous group (that is, they are divided by class, race, ethnicity, citizenship, geographical location, level of education, etc.). We also recognize that women migrants have varying degrees of social and cultural capital, which has an impact on their migration experience (Riano and Baghdadi 2007). Finally, we recognize that the politics of difference result in unequal social relations

locally, nationally, and internationally (Dhruvarajan and Vickers 2002; Razack 2002).

We are critical of the conception of a composite, singular 'migrant woman'. [. . .] In the literature, we found feminist analyses that consistently attempt to homogenize women who migrate to Western countries through Internet mediated matchmaking agencies. For example Langevin and Belleau (2000), Donna Hughes (1999), and Vanessa Vergara (2000) discuss women who develop relationships with men from Western countries through Internet based matchmaking agencies as either trafficked, naïve, passive, suffering false consciousness, and coerced solely by their desperate circumstances (Lacroix and Brigham 2006) or all of the above. By categorizing migrant women in binary opposition to men and/or to other women, such as women from Western Europe, Canada, the United States, or Australia, we ignore the intricacies and effects of interlocking systems of oppression in which we are all embedded.

In the next section, we explore how patriarchal capitalism as it is enacted through such complex organized practices as Canada's immigration policy shapes the experiences of migrant women at the intersecting sites of power. We look briefly at the historical background and then current policy and legislation in juxtaposition to the narratives of our research participants.

Background

Historically, the means and methods of marriage have often included the intervention of a matchmaker (Kojima 2001; Langevin and Belleau 2000; Simons 2001). In the North American context, the first accounts of women immigrating for the purpose of marriage were the *filles du Roi* in French settlements in Canada during the mid-seventeenth century, when French women travelled to New France with the intention to marry a French man (Langevin and Belleau 2000).

In the United States (US) during the nineteenth century, men from China, Japan, and the Philippines immigrated to Hawaii and the West Coast to work on sugar cane plantations and farms. Restrictive immigration laws combined with anti-miscegenation policies prohibiting relations (marriage) between Asian men and white women contributed to a 'picture bride' system. The 'picture bride' system involved an exchange of photographs between men living in the US and women from Asia. It developed in the early 1900s and led to the migration of several thousand Asian women to the US (Perez 2003). The main distinctions between the international Internet matchmaking agencies, the *filles du Roi*, and the 'picture bride' matchmaking system are the nationalities of the individuals involved in the relationships (Langevin and Belleau 2000; Simons 2001) as well as the obvious role of modern communication technology, namely the Internet. [. . .] Although there is limited information in the literature about the prevalence of international Internet matchmaking that result in marriage, there is even less information about informal relationships that evolve through international Internet matchmaking agencies.

Little is known about the international Internet matchmaking industry in Canada (Lacroix and Brigham 2006). Of the little research that exists about the experiences of migrant women and the relevant policies, the literature is almost exclusively focused on the experiences of women from the Philippines (Philippine Women Centre of BC and the Status of Women Canada Policy Research 2000). According to the Philippine Women Centre of British Colombia, 3500 women from the Philippines have entered Canada on 'spousal' or 'fiancée' visas; however this figure does not reveal how many of these women have met their partners/spouses through an Internet matchmaking agency (Philippine Women Centre of BC and the Status of Women

Canada Policy Research, 2000). Our immigrant service provider informants state that the women they have worked with who developed relationships through international Internet matchmaking agencies in Nova Scotia are largely from Eastern Europe (particularly Russia), Latin America, the Philippines, and the Caribbean; on average they are in their mid-twenties; and they are often highly educated individuals.

Policy and Legislation

At the international level, there is little policy or legislation dedicated to the issue of marriage migration. The main international body of law that is referred to in the literature in connection to the international Internet matchmaking industry is the Palermo Convention (United Nations Office on Drugs and Crime 2006). This body of law, to which Canada is a signatory, focuses on the recruitment, migration, and exploitation of persons and is not exclusively focused on intercultural marriages (United Nations Office on Drugs and Crime 2006).

The Philippines, Australia, and the United States are among the few countries to enact specific legislation pertaining to the international Internet matchmaking industry. The Philippines passed the *Republic Act 6955* called the 'Anti-Mail Order Bride Law' in 1990, which sought to protect Filipino women from being exploited in their quest for economic security (Hughes 1999). Australia has introduced policy to limit the number of foreign partner sponsorships (Rossiter 2005). Australia also provides residency to migrant women even if their marriages to Australian nationals fail (Philippine Women Centre of BC and the Status of Women Canada Policy Research 2000). The United States has three areas of legislation that specifically regulate the international Internet matchmaking industry (Simons 2001).

The K-1: Fiancée Visa and the CR-1: Conditional Resident Visa provide opportunities for US citizens to apply to support the immigration of a fiancé or spouse (Simons 2001). [. . .] The third piece of legislation in the US is the Violence Against Women Act (VAWA) of 1994 which has a component that seeks to protect migrant women if they are experiencing domestic violence (Simons 2001).

There is no specific legal framework that regulates the international Internet matchmaking industry in Canada (Langevin and Belleau 2000). Citizenship and Immigration Canada policies restrict the migration of minors; restrict sponsorship from Canadians who have committed violent crimes; and require that a relationship must have existed for at least one year for Internet relationships/marriages to be considered for approval (Citizenship and Immigration Canada 2007). Although the government created new legislation in 2008 restricting the number of partners a Canadian can sponsor within a certain time frame, Bella, one of our service provider informants, suggests this change in legislation has more to do with curbing migration than supporting women. Unlike legislation in the US and Australia, women migrating to Canada have few options to apply for immigration status without the sponsorship of their partner/spouse (Langevin and Belleau 2000; Philippine Women Centre of BC and the Status of Women Canada Policy Research 2000). Women who come to Canada via the international Internet matchmaking industry require spousal sponsorship in order to stay in Canada. Bea recalls several clients who wanted advice on the question: 'This is my sponsor, how long do I have to stay with him?' In other cases, Bea's clients experience difficulty accessing health care because they were not officially sponsored and were in Canada on visitor visas (visitors do not have access to national health care). This lack of access to health care is also a concern

for those whose visas have expired (for example, when their partners do not apply for an extension before the expiration of a visa). Those whose visas have expired are deemed to be contravening the Immigration Act for being 'out of status' and can be deported. Threat of deportation may be used by the Canadian partner to keep the non-Canadian visitor isolated.

Methodology

We employed a qualitative research methodology, which involved in-depth interviews with an immigrant woman (Natasha) who migrated to Canada via an Internet mediated matchmaking agency, a Canadian man (Jack) who formed a relationship with Natasha through an Internet mediated matchmaking agency, and immigrant service providers at women's centres and immigrant settlement agencies who were not directly connected to the aforementioned participants. Each interview lasted between one and two hours. Half of the interviews were conducted by both researchers and half by the first author alone. Some of the interviews were audio-taped; however, where some participants opted not to be audio-taped we took interview notes only. Although interpretation services were offered, the interviews were all conducted in English as preferred by the participants. All participants were assured of their confidentiality. All names of participants are pseudonyms.

By focusing on one couple (Natasha and Jack) we are able to tease out dimensions of diversity such as class, ethnicity, citizenship, geographical location, and level of education. We do not claim that Natasha represents all women who migrate through Internet mediated relationships, although some of her experiences in Canada may be similar to those of other women who migrate in this way or women who migrate on visitor visas in general. Similarly, we do not claim that

Jack represents other men seeking a relationship through Internet mediated matchmaking agencies. We do acknowledge, however, that their relationship fits some of the descriptions of other couples that form relationships through Internet mediated matchmaking agencies, in that she is younger than he, is more highly educated, and is seeking a better standard of living than she can find in her country of origin.

Natasha is in her mid-thirties. She has a child from her former marriage. The child lives with family in Russia. Jack is in his early fifties and is also divorced with a child. Natasha and Jack have known one another for approximately one year. They are not married. Natasha is a graduate student in Russia and is currently unemployed. She is in Canada on a visitor visa. Jack is employed as a salesman in a company.

Women who migrate to Canada through Internet mediated relationships are a particular heterogeneous group of migrants who have received limited scholarly attention but whose lives have very much been impacted by globalization processes, particularly with the rise of the Internet. This group of women is often referred to in popular culture as 'mail-order brides'. However, we feel the term 'mail-order bride' is both highly ambiguous and problematic as it has been used to construct some women in certain ways such as coming from low socio-economic backgrounds, having low levels of education, being young, 'traditional', and 'feminine', and according to Langevin and Belleau (2000) having a penchant for tall, white, blue-eyed men.

In this paper we simply use the term migrant women to refer to the specific group of women in our research who are/were citizens of countries other than Canada, who may or may not have established legally recognized or registered marriages with Canadian men but who have developed relationships with Canadian men through Internet based matchmaking agencies and have come to Canada.

Having provided the historical and contemporary scene pertaining to international Internet matchmaking we next draw on the narratives of our research participants to highlight the ways in which the theme of power was taken up in relation to their experiences and understandings of the international Internet matchmaking phenomenon.

Discussion

POWER

It all boils down to power.

(Sophie, immigrant service provider)

In the data a recurring theme we identified was around issues of power. We had no specific interview questions that included the word 'power' yet it was a word that arose frequently. The term 'power' was taken up by our research participants in different ways. For some of our research participants power is defined as a complicated network embedded in relations and exercised through immigration policies, immigrant service provider agencies, etc. For others, it was defined simply as such that when someone has it, other persons do not and are disadvantaged. For example, both Sophie and Bella compare so-called present day 'mail-order brides' with 'war brides' (women who immigrated to Canada to marry Canadian military men during World Wars I and II). Both service providers feel that unlike the latter, the former lack 'equal power in the relationship'. Bella elaborates: '[A war bride] had the power to reverse the position. [She could say,] "You can live with me in England."' In this way colonial power is invoked by those from the British motherland, a power that cannot be claimed by a woman from the South. Bella agrees with Sophie's suggestion that the term '"Mail-Order Bride" only goes with two nationalities, Russian and the Philippines [sic]'. Bella then distinguishes Russian women from Filipino women based on various levels of power that certain women are assumed to have, presumably because of their class and savvy. She states,

> The women from the Philippines are usually coming from a poor family . . . Russian women are really smart enough to learn the human rights as defined in Canada. They can easily present themselves [to authorities] as abused. At the same time they cannot be compared with women from the Philippines. Two different levels.

For Bella, women migrating from England during the world wars and present day Russia are set apart from the 'ever poor Filipina'. While a distinction is made between nationalities of migrant women as suggested in the above quotations, when discussing them in contrast to white Canadian men both Sophie and Bella tend to group women from the South as a singular disempowered group. This supposedly unified group of migrant women is formed in opposition to men, particularly white Canadian men who are also assumed to be a unified homogeneous group. In contrast to the migrant women, white Canadian men are described as 'more powerful' based on their gender, their assumed economic privilege, their geographical location, their language and culture. Sophie comments: 'Men have power. They can do whatever they want with a [migrant] woman. They can get away with more.' She adds:

> [Because] the man offers an opportunity for a woman to migrate [and] it is hard to get to Canada any other way, the man demands an extra mile of whatever they want because they have invested in them.

The man has money. There's no balance [or] equality between them [man and the woman]. They own them. Are we going back to slavery?

Bella also emphasizes the power imbalance. She describes a migrant woman this way: '[The migrant woman is] scared. How does she know any better? She doesn't speak English. She doesn't have information. If there is more equal power distribution, but it is unbalanced.'

Natasha and Jack both talk about the ways in which Natasha's right to be in Canada is dependent upon Jack as is her access to health care and transportation. For example, Jack suggests that the decision about when and if Natasha would come to Canada rested primarily with him. He explains: '[At first] I was concerned I was taking her away from her family and her friends. . . . And I thought maybe it would be better just to leave her in Russia and not go through the process. Then . . . I said, "OK, I'd bring her to Canada."'

As her sponsor Jack elaborates on his critical role in Natasha's migration process:

> [Citizenship and Immigration] has to have a letter of invitation from me to give to her. They have to have a letter from my employment to say I have a job. Have to have a letter of my income to show I can support her financially if she came over here. All that just for her to come as a visitor and you have to pay every time 75 dollars. As soon as she got the visa I called the travel agent and got her a ticket.

In this way Natasha's dependence on Jack for her visit to Canada is evident as he, the sponsor, abides by the immigration laws, although the decision to take up Jack's offer ultimately rests with Natasha. On the topic of sponsorship, Bea, an immigrant service provider, explains that the reliance on the Canadian partner contributes to a power discrepancy within the interpersonal relationship. She states that should a man choose to sponsor his partner, 'he is responsible for [his partner] for three years. But maybe he does not want to sponsor her. If she is sponsored she will have all the rights of a permanent resident. If he does not sponsor her he has more power. He holds that power over her.'

Jack and Natasha both discussed the issue of sponsorship and the insecurity of Natasha's present visitor status. Here Jack explains the difficulty and precariousness of Natasha's sponsorship application:

> We have to apply for visitor visa and everything [each time]. It has been a single visa where she can come once and go back . . . we have to wait [every time we apply]. It all depends on the visa officer in Moscow . . . The immigration officer said it is better to keep bringing her back under a visitor visa until she can remain . . . CIC [Citizenship and Immigration] can always say no and try again.

Natasha has similar concerns about her status. She states, 'For me, better [get married] in Canada . . . Because I think about documents. I don't think about [wedding] party. I always think about documents for me.'

Analysis

When analyzing the ways in which power is exercised in Internet mediated relationships, many of our immigrant service provider participants described a conceptualization of power which maintains a 'victimhood dogma' (Chow 1993, 68) of migrant women, particularly women from the South. According to most of the immigrant

service providers, women who look for Internet mediated relationships are largely passive, ill-informed, dependent, and desperate. These migrant women are either blameless victims of economic restructuring or they are blamed for their desire to become involved with men outside of their countries and migrate to pursue economic security.

The comments of the immigrant service providers, particularly in regard to the ways in which they discuss power and how it is invested, ignores the directionality of the power relationships between/within hemispheres, nation states, genders, classes, and individuals. This reductive notion of power is bolstered by the ways in which some of the service providers reduce the material and historical heterogeneities of the lives of migrant women, with some distinctions between Russian and Filipino, and a monolithic notion of male domination. This assumes a 'stable, ahistorical something that apparently oppresses most if not all the women in these countries' (Mohanty 2003, 19). [. . .] Moreover, it excludes other conceptions of gender and deflects a critical analysis of the interlocking systems of oppression.

Our research participant, Natasha, discusses power and in doing so challenges and also confirms some of the service providers' perceptions. Her views offer a more dynamic understanding of operations of power. [. . .] She resists the fixed images imposed on her as a migrant woman and in this way we are reminded that sexuality is located with matrices of power, produced within discursive and institutional historical practices (Foucault 1990). For example, in contrast to the notion of a woman desperate, ill-informed, and poor, Natasha describes herself as a healthy, fit, attractive, middle-class woman with a high level of education, a graduate student in Russia, with a network of support, motivated by a desire for a new relationship and a change in country of residence. She describes her life in Russia as 'not a good life' partly because she is a divorced single mother. She also underscores the problems of unemployment, ageism, a lack of 'good looking' men, and men's promiscuity.

Her decision to use an Internet mediated matchmaking agency was a choice she made with her 'eyes wide open'. It provided her options, which she could take or leave. Her position in Canada while precarious as a visitor is far from what she would describe as slave-like. She sees her life in Canada not so much as an escape from dreadful circumstances but as a place where she can be with the person with whom she is in love. She indicates that her life in Canada cannot be easily described as better or worse than in Russia. [. . .]

Natasha explains her view of Canada and how it has changed: 'For people in my country, Canada like star, like impossible go to Canada. You cannot go. [Compared with] different countries, we always think, Oh, Canada is very good, the United States very good, but I stay here [in Canada], and I see not all good'.

She elucidates that Canada's health care system, quality of food especially for babies, and state support for families are not as good as they are in Russia. She also declares Canadian women pay little attention to their appearance and cleanliness and that of their family members. She further highlights her present lack of money, support, close friendships and family, interactions with other Russian speakers, and access to English language classes, Natasha feels the isolation of living in a rural area of Atlantic Canada. She says,

> I never say I am upset I am in Canada. For me very difficult. But I try stop thinking about [it] . . . Difficult I am alone and because no one come. Nobody come. Nobody speak. I have no friends. No women walk with babies. This big problem. I try to

forget about this problem. Um, I miss about this relation maybe all my life . . . I think maybe later I can have a relations. Perhaps later maybe I can have relations with the woman cut my hair. Nice woman, young woman . . . I try but it is difficult.

For Natasha the difficulties experienced in Atlantic Canada stem largely from her immigration status, her lack of a support network and limited resources (financial and otherwise). The research participants in this study highlight contextual issues in their identification and articulation of power. They underscore ambiguities and contradictions in their perceptions of the representations of Internet mediated relationships and the people involved in them. While the data force us to question the ethno/Western-centric, sexist, and racist representations, they also point to political implications of power. We discuss those in our conclusion.

Conclusion

Power, as was highlighted by the research participants, is a valuable concept on which to focus. An analysis of power helps us recognize this complicated, misrepresented sector of women's migration. Through this focus we are forced to be attentive to the many and varied ways power is invested in our lives, in our social spaces, our societal structures and institutions, and in our 'infinitesimal mechanisms' (Foucault 1980, 99). Even though each relationship involves unique challenges and experiences, it is apparent that there is a general lack of awareness of the complexity of issues facing this particular group of migrant women in Canada and a dearth of research on the topic in Atlantic Canada. Some of the issues as indicated in our findings are that migrant women may find themselves in precarious situations due to a multiplicity of factors including legislation that is inadequate for protecting some migrant women, lack of status or sponsorship, lack of language competency, and lack of awareness of their basic rights and freedoms. We summarize our findings and make recommendations within these two categories: a) settlement, support, education, and legislation, and b) research.

Settlement, Support, Education and Legislation

Our findings indicate that multiple barriers exist for this specific group of immigrant women to access settlement and support services. The barriers range from the lack of status (and therefore limited access to assistance from settlement agencies), limited access to information and support (such as legal and language support), and the negative societal perceptions (including those of immigrant settlement workers) of migrant women. Migrant women (and others) who are in Canada on visitor visas cannot access immigrant services (with the exception of employment services if the visitor has a work permit). The barriers are further intensified for women migrating to rural areas.

Canada's legislation related to migrant women is weak. Isolation, lack of a support network, and dependency on their Canadian partners contributes to the settlement and support challenges of migrant women. The isolation they may experience in combination with the precariousness of their immigration status can cut this group of immigrant women off from essential services and affect their adjustment in a new cultural environment in multiple ways. Without access to services and learning opportunities such as language training, orientation programs, health care, employment, or peer support, migrant women who come to Canada via the international Internet matchmaking industry can experience a level of vulnerability that exceeds that of other immigrant women.

Current policy has evolved from colonialist discourse reflecting ethnocentric and patriarchal ideologies. The legal framework that exists in Canada has enhanced the level of vulnerability of migrants who come to Canada (Langevin and Belleau 2000). Women migrating to Canada through international Internet matchmaking have few options to apply for immigration status without the sponsorship of their partner/spouse, unlike in the US and Australia where legislation provides some forms of protection for migrant women.

We recommend that women (and men) be given access to clear information about their rights in Canada, pertaining to immigration law regarding sponsorship and visitor visas; family law (marital, divorce, child welfare law), criminal law, and civil law. They require information and access to language training resources, skills training, and other resources available for immigrants, such as business start-up loans. This information must be made accessible (translated in many languages) through ethnic/cultural/religious groups, web sites, embassies, points of entry and on the Internet (Canadian Law and Modern Day Foreign Brides 2007). As Jack states,

> [There should be some way that they inform immigrants about any kind of opportunity] like some kind of immigrant portal, online or something where they can go and read it in their language what's available for them showing them what they can do and how they can contribute back to Canada, because if they can get a loan to start a business [and] then offer employment, they can give back to the country that accepted them.

Local immigrant settlement agencies need to increase and enhance services for this population of women, by advertising their services in many places and in multiple languages and providing easy access to contact information, as well as to translators and attorneys. Further, it is critical to work in creative ways to raise consciousness and awareness of the barriers experienced by this multifaceted group of women so as to challenge societal attitudes and perceptions and existing legislation. We recommend that in the long term, policy analysis and further research as to how policy can be transformed be undertaken.

Research

Due to the lack of research that exists to help us understand the power relations at the micro, meso, and macro levels that affect the complex experiences of this particular heterogeneous group of migrant women, it is imperative that activists, feminists, advocates, adult educators, researchers, and others who focus on social justice find ways to work with, open up safe spaces for dialogue with, and above all hear the range of migrant women's voices. This requires vigilance against reproducing hierarchies. It requires persistent and careful attention to the specificities of women's experiences, and a tireless critiquing of the concept and construction of 'migrant women'.

This also entails critically analyzing the complex reality between power and relations and understanding power beyond negative terms, as Foucault (1979, 294) demands: 'We must cease once and for all to describe the effects of power in negative terms: it "excludes", it "represses", it

"censors", it "abstracts", it "masks", it "conceals".' Canada has a global reputation for being a hospitable multicultural society, yet Canadian legislation and services do not protect or support many women migrating via the international Internet matchmaking industry. In Atlantic Canada, the buzzwords around attraction and retention of immigrants are 'welcome', 'welcoming communities', and 'welcoming environment' (Province of New Brunswick 2009; Province of Newfoundland and Labrador 2009; Province of Nova Scotia 2005; Province of Prince Edward Island 2009) but what do those words mean? All of us have a moral responsibility to assess this concept, to be critical of the ubiquitous pleasant sounding words 'welcoming' and 'community' to discover how power courses through them. We need to find the radical counter-hegemonic significance in them so that making newcomers 'welcome' in the Atlantic Canadian 'community' does not begin and end with pinning a Canadian flag pin on a migrant's lapel. Welcoming requires questioning taken-for-granted assumptions and taking political action in solidarity with one another so as to ensure that the human rights of all are met. It requires keeping Edward Said's statement in mind: 'No one can deny the persisting continuities of long traditions, sustained habitations, national languages, and cultural geographies, but there seems no reason except fear and prejudice to keep insisting on their separation and distinctiveness, as if that was all human life was about. Survival, in fact, is about connections between things' (Said 1993, 336).

References

Canadian Law and Modern Day Foreign Brides, 2007. A Project of Changing Together . . . a Centre for Immigrant Women and Legal Resource Centre of Alberta, Ltd. Available at: www.lawforeignbrides.ca

Chow, R. *Writing Diaspora*. Bloomington: Indiana University Press, 1993.

Citizenship and Immigration Canada. Canada's New Government Strengthens Protection for Victims of Human Trafficking, 2007. Retrieved 24 February 2008, from www.cic.gc.ca/english/department/media/releases/2007/2007-06-19.asp

Dhruvarajan, V., and J. Vickers. *Gender, Race and Nation: A Global Perspective*. Toronto: University of Toronto, 2002.

Foucault, M. *Discipline and Punish*. New York: Vintage Books, 1979.

———. *Power and Knowledge*. New York: Pantheon Books, 1980.

————. *The History of Sexuality, vol. 1*. New York: Vintage Books, 1990.

Hughes, D. *Pimps and Predators on the Internet: Globalizing the Sexual Exploitation of Women and Children*. Rhode Island, USA: Coalition Against Trafficking in Women, 1999.

Kojima, Y. 'In the Business of Cultural Reproduction: Theoretical Implications of the Mail-order Bride Phenomenon', *Women's International Forum 24.2* (2001): 199–210.

Lacroix, M., and S. Brigham. 'Mail Order Brides'—Transnational Relationships and Local Homeplace: Some Critical Issues'. Paper presented at Violence Against Women: Diversifying Social Responses. Montreal, Quebec. Oct. 22–24, 2006.

Langevin, L., and M-C. Belleau. *Trafficking in Women in Canada: a Critical Analysis of the Legal Framework Governing Immigrant Live-in Caregivers and Mail-order Brides*. Ottawa: Status of Women Canada, 2000.

Mohanty, C. *Feminism Without Borders: Decolonizing Theory, Practicing Solidarity*. Durham: Duke University Press, 2003.

Perez, B. 'Woman Warrior Meets Mail-Order Bride: Finding An Asian American Voice in the Women's Movement', *Berkeley Women's Law Journal 18* (2003): 211–36.

Philippine Women Centre of BC and the Status of Women Canada Policy Research. *Canada: the New Frontier for Filipino Mail-Order Brides*. Ottawa: Status of Women, 2000.

Province of New Brunswick. *Population Growth Secretariat. Immigration*, 2009. Available at: www.gnb.ca/lmmigration/index-e.asp

Province of Newfoundland and Labrador. *Settlement and Integration*, 2009. Available at: www.hrle.gov.nl.ca/hrle/income-support/immigration/english/settlement.htm

Province of Nova Scotia. *Nova Scotia's Immigration Strategy*, 2005. Nova Scotia: Author. Available at: www.novascotiaimmigration.com/en-page7.aspx

Province of Prince Edward Island. *Immigration*, 2009. Available at: www.gov.pe.ca/immigration/

Razack, S. 'When Place Becomes Race', *Race, Space and the Law: Unmapping a White Settler Society*, S. Razack, ed. Toronto: Between the Lines, 2002.

Riano, Y., and N. Baghdadi. 'Understanding the Labour Market Participation of Skilled Immigrant Women in Switzerland: the Interplay of Class, Ethnicity, and Gender', *International Migration and Integration 8* (2007): 163–83.

Rossiter, M.J. 'Slavic Brides in Rural Alberta', *Journal of International Migration and Integration 6* (2005): 493–512.

Said, E. *Culture and Imperialism*. London: Chatto & Windus, 1993.

Simons, L.A. 'Marriage, Migration, and Markets: International Matchmaking and International Feminism'. Unpublished dissertation, University of Denver, June 2001.

United Nations Office on Drugs and Crime. *Toolkit to Combat Trafficking in Persons*. New York: United Nations, 2006.

Vergara, V. 'Abusive Mail-Order Bride Marriages and the Thirteenth Amendment', *Northwestern University Law Review 94.4* (2000): 1547–99.

Double Jeopardy: Building Strong Communities to Fight Homophobia and Racism

Andrea Zoe Aster

Frank Brawn is gay. He knew that by age six. Now, more than five decades later, and married with children, he's certain about one more thing—he will never come out as a gay man, not to his wife and grown children, and certainly not to the Eastern European Muslim community, within which he is a prominent figure. And though it's a source of crushing anguish, Brawn (a pseudonym he uses) knows he will never act, even secretly, upon his desire.

'I've had opportunities to have a gay relationship, but I've always managed not to', says Brawn, who suffers from debilitating depression and is seeing a psychologist for the first time. 'Perhaps instead, I will write a memoir to be published after my death. It will be helpful for the medical community to have insight into the torment I go through.'

Brawn's story is stark, and sadly, it's not unique. Being homosexual in a heterosexual world is difficult enough. But it's even harder for gay, lesbian, bisexual, and transgendered (LGBT) people from minority ethnic communities. For them, the key challenge is dodging a double-edged sword of systemic homophobia and racism—racism that may even exist within the LGBT community itself, which is largely white and middle class. Unfortunately, advocates agree, it's a myth that racial tolerance flows more easily within the LGBT community.

What's more, while many members of the LGBT community risk estrangement from family when coming out, white people find alternative havens more readily. In Toronto, to feel a sense of instant community, any university-aged white male can simply take a short stroll down Toronto's Church Street on a Saturday night.

'If a white person is kicked out of their family, they still have a connection with a Canada that reflects who they are; they don't lose connection with their identity', says Silvana Bazet, a Toronto-based psychotherapist in private practice who works with many LGBT people of colour including those in South Asian and Latin American communities.

But what if you're, say, a Nigerian lesbian? For many minority LGBTs, the stakes are higher if they lose family support, says Bazet. Not only is there racism within the queer community; but also, tight-knit minority communities offer a collective buffer against societal racism, and that's not something to be traded away lightly.

That buffer is especially precious within Canada's African community, says Notisha Massaquoi, a member of the Toronto-based social forum Gays and Lesbians of African Descent, and program director of Women's Health in Women's Hands, a community health network in Toronto.

'Preserving a sense of community can be a much stronger impulse than the individual desire to be out', says Massaquoi. 'That need to preserve your family is especially amplified in Canadian communities. Sometimes, all you have here is a small group of Nigerians, and it's not worth it for many LGBTs to alienate them, especially if they have no other family here.' In fact, so critical is this insight that Massaquoi cautions health care professionals to avoid encouraging minority LGBTs, especially Africans, to come out, even if that seems contrary to conventional practice.

'As mental health professionals, we're taught to look at the mental anguish caused by staying silent about sexual orientation', says Massaquoi. 'The goal, always, is to get to the point of disclosure, working with clients to tell their family, and if they're rejected, working to find support elsewhere. But to understand African clients, you can't push them because you can't provide them with the support they need. You're asking them to risk the loss of their family, but what are you going to replace it with?'

Indeed, that insight hits home for many minority communities. Brawn, for example, has made a few timid trips to meetings with Salaam Toronto, a community network for queer Muslims. But after only five meetings, he decided Salaam couldn't become a satisfactory replacement for his own community. He has found it difficult to find other, older gay Muslims with whom to connect.

'It's not common for Muslim men over 45 to come out', says Brawn. Religious pressures are simply too constricting. 'Homosexuality is strictly prohibited by the Koran. You go to hell if you're gay. It's that kind of interpretation'.

Bleak as that may be, many experts are quick to defend minority communities against at least one rampant stereotype—that ethnic minority communities are more homophobic, says Stacia Stewart, diversity coordinator for Ottawa-based EGALE, a support group for under-represented gays and lesbians.

Indeed, especially in the African-American lesbian community, it's common that a family's loyalty often prevents alienation, not the opposite, as is the stereotype, according to a 2003 study by Sara Bridges and colleagues in the *Journal of Multicultural Counseling and Development*. 'The misperception that African communities are more homophobic results from this mainstream push to construct them as primitive', says Massaquoi.

Bazet agrees. 'I often hear more horrifying stories coming out of white communities.' But some minority families of LGBTs generate their own myths. If their child does come out, 'the easiest thing for them to do is blame this decadent Western culture,' says Bazet. 'They say "We never should have come here", as if LGBTs didn't exist in our home countries. For example, in Latin America, LGBT communities have been organizing since the 1960s.'

Part of this misunderstanding comes from the fact that in many ethnic minority communities, sex isn't discussed openly with parents, even if you're heterosexual, says Massaquoi. 'That discussion hasn't happened, so a person may not consider themselves officially "out" in the Western sense. Many minority communities don't have labels for same-sex behaviour. If you'd ask certain [women of colour] if they're lesbian, they might say no because they believe lesbians act and look a certain way within a Western context, and they don't match up.'

Faced with an extraordinary raft of pressures, from both within and outside their communities, what are minority LGBTs doing to cope?

'It's especially important for minorities to see themselves reflected in public spaces', says Massaquoi. 'And if you have the privilege of being out, it's important to be vocal. There's a lot of mystery surrounding the African gay community. The whole mainstream doesn't know it exists.'

There are also an increasingly diverse number of organizations for minority LGBTs, offering both online and community support. For example, Rauda Morcos is making pioneering efforts as the voice for Palestinian lesbians in Israel. As co-founder of Haifabased Aswat, she was recently in Toronto as part of a North American fundraising tour. The group's efforts include an online chat room and political-education material for communities. The group also holds regular meetings where members face the challenge of forging a new vocabulary to describe LGBT identity. This is a challenge for many minorities. There is no word for 'lesbian' in most Asian languages, says Bridges' study.

'The first time I said the word "lesbian", I had to use English because there is no word in Arabic,' says Morcos. 'In a society that doesn't allow questioning of sexual identity, we had no model to refer to.'

Outside the minority LGBT community, health care professionals need to become more sensitive to the unique concerns of this population. Doctor and Bazet are taking a step in this direction by offering what may be the only workshop in Canada to train professionals who work with lesbian and bisexual women of colour.

Though minority LGBTs face challenges, some of which are more easily overcome than others, most agree that visibility and joint efforts among non-mainstream communities are a vital coping strategy. 'We're increasingly seeing queer people of colour getting together to face common challenges,' says Stewart at EGALE. 'It's not impossible to find and build community.'

11 Sex and Gender: Boundaries, Connections, and Meanings in the Context of Change

Harassment Based on Sex: Protecting Social Status in the Context of Gender Hierarchy

Jennifer L. Berdahl

Most people think sexual harassment is about sexual desire. Policy and research have focused on behaviours of a sexual nature: a boss who pressures a subordinate into sexual activity, a coworker who repeatedly asks another out on a date, or an environment rife with sexual jokes and materials. This focus has created the widespread assumption that sexual harassers are motivated by a desire for sexual expression and gratification. It has also led to a considerable amount of controversy. Heated debates have taken place over how realistic, or even desirable, it is to regulate sexual expression at work (Schultz, 1998). Sexual harassment is the frequent fodder of jokes, and the idea that it is a problem worthy of attention and sanction is often dismissed.

[. . .]

This paper offers a different view of sexual harassment. I argue that the primary motive underlying all harassment is a desire to protect one's social status when it seems threatened, a desire held by men and women alike. Harassment generally is repeated or persistent treatment that pressures, provokes, frightens, intimidates, humiliates, or demeans a person (Adams & Bray, 1992; Brodsky, 1976; Einarsen, 2000). I argue that sexual harassment should be viewed as harassment that is based on sex—as behaviour that derogates, demeans, or humiliates an individual based on that individual's sex—and that sexual harassers derogate others based on sex to protect or enhance their own sex-based social status, and are motivated and able to do so by a social context that pervasively and fundamentally stratifies social status by sex.

This perspective provides a unified theory of sex-based harassment that both encompasses the variety of forms currently recognized in the literature and suggests others. It identifies a more basic motive than sexual expression or male dominance for sex-based harassment, as well as a more basic conceptualization of sex-based harassment than sexual comments and come-ons. It focuses attention on the social structure that encourages individuals to define and protect their status based on sex, and on behaviours that derogate individuals based on sex generally, from sexual behaviours to sex-based insults, exclusion, and sabotage. Importantly, this perspective expands the focus of sexual harassment research and policy beyond male harassers and female targets to consider why women might harass others based on sex, why men might be harassed based on sex, and what these different forms of harassment might look like.

I review how sexual harassers came to be viewed as individuals driven by sexual motives, as men driven by a desire to protect male dominance, or both. I explain why these views are problematic and propose that sexual harassers are driven by a desire to protect and enhance their social status in the context of gender hierarchy.

I discuss what factors are likely to predict this desire and which events are likely to trigger it, and I then consider the different forms harassment may take when men harass men, men harass women, women harass men, and women harass women. The paper ends with a discussion of the theory's implications for future research.

From Sexual Desire to Male Dominance: Prior Views of What Motivates Sexual Harassers

Sexual harassment largely has been conceptualized as sexual behaviour directed at women by men at work. In the late 1970s, quid pro quo sexual harassment, defined as the loss or denial of a job-related benefit (e.g., a promotion, salary increase, or the job itself) for refusing to co-operate sexually, was judged to be a form of sex discrimination (*Williams v. Saxbe*, 1976). The ruling was based on a case of a male boss who sexually coerced his female subordinate, a case resembling other cases to reach the courts at the time (e.g., *Barnes v. Costle*, 1977; *Corne v. Bausch & Lomb*, 1975; *Heelan v.*

Johns-Manville Corporation, 1978; *Miller v. Bank of America*, 1979). In the 1980s, sexual behaviours that were not accompanied by tangible or economic job outcomes but created a hostile or abusive work environment for one sex were judged to be sex discrimination.[. . .] Theorists argued that persistent sexual attention, repeated requests for dates, and sexual comments, jokes, and materials create an abusive work environment for women by invoking the broader socio-cultural context of sexual exploitation and oppression of women by men (Farley, 1978; MacKinnon, 1979; Nieva & Gutek, 1981).

The Motive of Sexual Desire

Legal and social theories of sexual harassment initially viewed it as sexually motivated. [. . .] Proponents of the natural/biological approach view harassment as the expression of natural sexual urges that are expressed more by men than by women because, proponents argue, men are inherently more sexually aggressive and promiscuous than women (cf., Studd & Gattiker, 1991). Proponents of the sex roles approach view sexual harassment as 'socio-sexual behaviour' gone wrong, guided by sex roles that assign men the role of sexual agent and women the role of sexual object (Gutek, 1985; Gutek & Morasch, 1982; Nieva & Gutek, 1981). Proponents of the power approach view sexual harassment as the use of power to extract sexual compliance. According to this perspective, mostly men harass mostly women because men have more power than women (Bargh, Raymond, Pryor & Strack, 1995; Cleveland & Kerst, 1993; Equal Employment Opportunity Commission, 1980; Evans, 1978; Farley, 1978; MacKinnon, 1979; Schultz, 1998; Zalk, 1990). Implicit in this reasoning is the assumption that harassers use their power to sexually coerce others because they desire them sexually.

Viewing sexual harassment as motivated by sexual desire is problematic. It has generated tremendous controversy that has undermined the ability to understand the harassment as a form of sex discrimination and to eradicate it in the workplace. Some forms of sexual expression at work may be benign or even pleasant, and many workplace romances become long and lasting relationships. Therefore, there has been resistance to the idea that socio-sexual behaviour at work generally is a bad thing and that attempts to police it are good. Viewing sexual harassment as sexual expression has led to the (largely unfounded) fear that benign expressions of sexual interest may result in lawsuits, demotions, or unwarranted firings. Furthermore, this view of sexual harassment has been convincingly accused of hurting the fight against sex discrimination by promoting policies that ban sexual behaviour at work, which, in turn, implicitly encourage employers to keep the sexes separate (and therefore unequal) in order to avoid sexual issues from arising (Schultz, 1998). [. . .]

More important, viewing sexual harassment as motivated by sexual desire is inconsistent with much of what we now know about sexual harassment. The most common form of sexual harassment is gender harassment, which involves sexual and sexist comments, jokes, and materials that alienate and demean victims based on sex rather than solicit sexual relations with them (e.g., Fitzgerald, Drasgow, Hulin, Gelfand & Magley, 1997; Fitzgerald, Magley, Drasgow & Waldo, 1999; Franke, 1997; Schultz, 1998; Waldo, Berdahl & Fitzgerald, 1998). Examples of gender harassment include displaying offensive pornography, leaving soiled condoms in someone's locker, making sexually obscene comments or gestures, and insulting someone's sexual abilities or orientation.

[. . .]

The Motive of Male Dominance

Some have suggested that a desire in men to dominate women drives sexual harassment generally, a view that has been championed by legal theorists. [. . .] Consistent with this view, men who endorse male dominance and female subordinance are more likely to say they would sexually exploit a woman if given the chance, and to actually do so (Pryor, 1987; Pryor, La Vite & Stoller, 1993). Also consistent with this view is the fact that women who challenge male dominance are not only more likely to be targeted for gender harassment (Maass et al., 2003) but for sexual approach forms of harassment as well (Berdahl, in press).

This view of sexual harassment is limiting and problematic as well, though. It implies that only men are motivated to sexually harass, but the little evidence that exists on whether women sexually harass others suggests they do (Magley, Waldo, Drasgow & Fitzgerald, 1999; US Merit Systems Protection Board, 1995; Waldo et al., 1998). Furthermore, viewing sexual harassers as men who want to dominate women reinforces the negative stereotype of men as 'bad but bold'. This stereotype is strongly associated with societal male dominance (Glick & Fiske, 2001; Glick et al., 2004) and is likely to reinforce it by suggesting that women need 'good' men to protect them from 'bad' ones, or that men are bad in general and therefore men and women should be segregated to protect women from men and men from themselves around women (cf. Schultz, 1998). In short, this view is not only limiting but potentially damaging to the cause of sex desegregation and equality at work.

Reenvisioning Harassment Based on Sex: The Motive of Social Status

Instead of viewing sexual harassment as inherently driven by sexual desire, a desire in men to dominate women, or both, I suggest it is fundamentally motivated by the basic desire, present in everyone, to protect or enhance one's social status against threat. Sexual harassment occurs because the motive for social status takes shape in a context of gender hierarchy. The fact that social status is stratified by sex motivates and enables individuals to defend their status based on sex by derogating others' status based on sex. A man may be motivated to protect his status relative to a woman, but not necessarily on the grand scale of wanting to keep women subordinate to men generally. Rather, *both* men and women are motivated to protect their sex-based social standing as individuals, along with the benefits derived from it, and may do so by derogating a woman or a man based on sex.

This view of sexual harassment, henceforth referred to as sex-based harassment (SBH) to deemphasize its sexual nature, is developed below. I begin with a discussion of what SBH is and then articulate a motivational theory of SBH as driven by the basic human motive for social status. I consider what drives individuals to protect or enhance their social status based on sex and what kind of threats are likely to trigger a desire to do so with SBH. I conclude this section with a discussion of who is likely to be targeted for SBH and the forms it may take when it is directed at women by men, at men by men, at men by women, and at women by women.

SBH

I define SBH as behaviour that derogates, demeans, or humiliates an individual based on that individual's sex. SBH may involve acts, comments, or materials that derogate an individual in sex-based ways, such as sexually objectifying and subordinating women. It may also involve seemingly sex-neutral acts, such as repeated provocation, silencing, exclusion, or sabotage, that are experienced by an individual because of sex. SBH casts an individual in a demeaning role or light by portraying that individual as unworthy, inferior, servile, or a means to an end based on that individual's sex.

To determine whether an episode of harassment was based on sex, it is instructive to ask if the behaviour served to derogate an individual in sex-based ways or if an individual of the other sex would have experienced it. If the act itself involved a sex-specific derogation or would not have been experienced by an individual of the other sex, it was harassment based on sex. This does not mean that all individuals of that sex had to experience the harassment. Only some individuals may be singled out for harassment based on their sex, such as an outspoken woman who is sabotaged by her coworkers but whose demure female colleagues or outspoken male ones are not. If a soft-spoken male is demeaned by coworkers in the same organization, the double standard is *even* clearer in establishing harassment based on sex (cf. Ely & Meyerson, 2000; Sturm, 2001).

A critical component of harassment is power (cf. Brodsky, 1976; Cleveland & Kerst, 1993). Power is relative control over outcomes through the capacity to withdraw rewards or introduce punishments (Dépret & Fiske, 1993; Keltner, Gruenfeld & Anderson, 2003). Harassment requires a difference in actual or perceived power between the harasser and the target of harassment that leaves the target little recourse for self-defence or retaliation (Brodsky, 1976; Einarsen, 2000). A harasser may control a target with organizational or economic power, physical intimidation or might, or social norms that define the terms of social inclusion and respect. The latter is a less visible form of power because it takes place against the backdrop of everyday social assumptions and practices, but this does not mean it is less threatening or effective

(Fiske & Berdahl, in press). Harassers can use organizational, economic, physical, or social power to harass (e.g., Cleveland & Kerst, 1993; Farley, 1978; MacKinnon, 1979), which explains why organizational subordinates can, and do, harass their superiors (Benson & Thomson, 1982; DeSouza & Fansler, 2003; Grauerholz, 1989; McKinney, 1992).

SBH can also be a cumulative experience. An individual may be targeted by a variety of sources for social slights and harms that seem minor by themselves but add up to have significant impact when repeated often enough. It may be even more damaging when harassment is experienced in this way because it means the harassment is more pervasive and difficult to escape, more normative and difficult to demonstrate as wrong, and may come from multiple sources, making it more difficult to identify a particular wrongdoer. Several of the examples I give later of sex-based derogations may not amount to harassment by themselves, but would if done repeatedly.

The Desire to Protect or Enhance Sex-Based Status

I suggest that the primary motive underlying all forms of harassment is the desire to protect or enhance social status when it seems threatened. The need to belong—to receive social acceptance, approval, and admiration—is a basic human motive (e.g., Baumeister & Leary, 1995; Fiske, 2004; Hogan & Hogan, 1991). [. . .] Our lives are replete with reminders of the importance of this status, from advertisements selling products to help us achieve it to everyday social comparisons assessing the relative status of individuals. No wonder individuals are motivated to achieve high social status: its many benefits include an increased chance and quality of survival, more influence and control over others (French & Raven, 1959), and a host of other physical,

psychological, social, and economic rewards (Keltner et al., 2003; Mirowsky & Ross, 2003; Morin, 2002; Sartorius, 2003).

While social status is a core social motive, sex is a core social organizer. More than any other social characteristic, sex is used as a basis to differentiate individuals, to assign social roles, and to accord status (Fiske, Haslam & Fiske, 1991; Stangor, Lynch, Duan & Glas, 1992; van Knippenberg, van Twuyver & Pepels, 1994). The primary distinction made is male versus female, with male carrying higher status (Connell, 1987). Distinctions are also made within sex. Men are compared to other men to assess the degree to which they meet masculine ideals, and women are compared to other women to assess the degree to which they meet feminine ones. Masculine and feminine ideals are defined by prescriptive stereotypes that include physical, psychological, and social characteristics (Fiske & Stevens, 1993).

[. . .]

I propose that all forms of SBH stem from the harasser's desire to protect or enhance his or her own sex-based social status when it seems threatened. [. . .] Gender hierarchy is both an intergroup and an intragroup phenomenon: sex-based distinctions are made between as well as within the sexes. At one time or another, and to varying degrees of intensity, all individuals are motivated to defend their sex-based status and the benefits it yields when this status seems threatened, and all individuals are capable of doing so by derogating another based on sex.

I now consider what may strengthen or weaken a desire in individuals to defend sex-based status. [. . .]

Gender hierarchy
A social system that emphasizes sex differences and assigns higher status to one sex creates incentives to define and defend social status in terms of sex.

Socio-cultural systems marked by male dominance are ubiquitous. [. . .] Subsystems, like organizations, tend to mirror the intergroup power relations in their embedding contexts (Alderfer & Smith, 1982). Status is likely to be stratified by sex in organizations in ways similar to the socio-cultural context in which they operate. Subsystems may amplify or dampen the stratification of men and women in their embedding environments, however. Some organizations may emphasize sex differences even more than the societies in which they operate by valorizing male dominance and privilege (e.g., some fraternities, sports teams, police and fire departments, political bodies, or corporate boards), whereas other organizations may de-emphasize sex differences and focus on treating people as individuals.

The more an organization differentiates the status of men and women, the stronger the incentives will be to meet sex-based ideals in that organization. Masculine and feminine ideals will differ somewhat by context (Connell, 1987), as when being a 'real' man means being courageous and strong on a firefighting squad but being creative and intelligent on a team of scientists. There is much consistency in sex-based ideals across contexts, however (Bergen & Williams, 1991; Buss, 1989; Connell, 1995; Eagly, 1987; Fiske, Cuddy, Glick & Xu, 2002; Williams & Best, 1990). Competence and dominance generally are desired in men more than women, whereas deference and warmth generally are desired in women more than men (Bern, 1974; Cuddy, Fiske & Glick, 2004; Fiske et al., 2002, Prentice & Carranza, 2002).

Position in gender hierarchy

Gender hierarchy may provide everyone incentives to protect his or her sex-based status when it seems threatened, but it provides stronger incentives for some than for others. Because sharper distinctions are made between men based on their achievement of masculine ideals than between women based on their achievement of feminine ones, and because meeting masculine ideals is associated with more benefits for men than meeting feminine ideals is for women (Connell, 1987), men should be more motivated than women to defend their sex-based status against threat.

Within sex, the status of extreme individuals is not likely to change as easily as the status of average individuals. By definition, most people are 'average' in meeting ideals for their sex. Small differences in meeting these ideals should therefore be used to distinguish between average individuals. This is consistent with the idea that those in the middle of the pack in terms of status vie for it more vigorously than those at the top and the bottom (Owens & Sutton, 2001). 'Average' men have much to gain from being seen as more masculine and much to lose from being seen as less masculine, whereas men who have clearly proven themselves as men or who have no hope of doing so are probably more impervious to threats to their sex-based identity. Similarly, 'average' women have more to gain from being seen as more ideal and more to lose from being seen as less ideal than do women who unquestionably accomplish or fail feminine standards. In short, individuals whose sex-based status is average, and therefore more negotiable and tenuous, should be more strongly motivated to protect it against threat.

Beliefs about gender hierarchy

Holding constant an individual's sex-based status, the more an individual endorses beliefs that justify gender hierarchy, the more that individual will define his or her own and others' social status in terms defined by this hierarchy and the more that individual will want to defend his or her status accordingly. To some extent, all individuals endorse beliefs that justify gender hierarchy, given its ubiquity and the pervasiveness of beliefs that support it. Consistent with self-interest, men are more likely than women to support altitudes that favour male dominance (e.g., Pratto et al. 2000; Sidanius, Pratto & Bobo, 1994; Twenge, 1997). Women also endorse beliefs that reinforce male dominance, however, consistent with the general tendency of low-status groups to experience and perpetuate false consciousness or beliefs and behaviours that justify their subordinance (Jost & Banaji, 1994). Therefore, both men and women are motivated to protect their status in terms defined by male dominance, although men should be more strongly motivated than women to do so. There are also within-sex differences in these beliefs that should predict the likelihood to defend sex-based status. Men and women with particularly sexist attitudes should be more strongly motivated than their same-sex counterparts to protect their status based on sex.

Threats to Sex-Based Status

We have considered what predicts a desire to protect sex-based status. What triggers this desire? Branscombe, Ellemers, Spears, and Doosje's (1999) typology of social identity threats is useful for analyzing the forms that threats to sex-based status may take. These include (1) distinctiveness threats, which blur distinctions between the sexes, (2) acceptance threats, which challenge an individual's status as a good or prototypical member of his or her sex, (3) category threats, which categorize an individual in a sex-based group against his or her will and (4) derogation threats, which threaten the value of an individual's sex group. [. . .] I suggest that all four types of threat can trigger a desire in men *and* in women to defend their sex-based status. The forms these threats may take, and the defences they are likely to trigger, are discussed below. The threats are grouped by

whether they challenge distinctions between the sexes (distinctiveness threats) or emphasize them (acceptance, category, and derogation threats).

Threats that Challenge Group Distinctions

Distinctiveness threats are unique among the four types of threats because they challenge the very notion of different groups. Blurring the distinctions that are usually made between men and women suggests these distinctions, and the benefits associated with them, are illusory and illegitimate. Distinctiveness threats involve women performing roles or displaying characteristics traditionally associated with men, or vice versa. Examples include women who perform 'men's' jobs or are outspoken and assertive, and men who perform 'women's' jobs or wear dresses and date men. Individuals who feel threatened when distinctions between men and women are blurred will try to reassert these boundaries by emphasizing the veracity or value of sex differences. This might include acts of SBH, such as repeated statements about what men and women can and should do, and socially rejecting or humiliating individuals who violate these prescriptions.

Consistent with this, women in male-dominated occupations are more likely than other women to be sexually harassed (Berdahl, in press; Fitzgerald, Dragow, Hulin, Gelfand & Magley, 1997; Glomb, Munson, Hulin, Bergman & Drasgow, 1999; Gruber, 1998), and women in these occupations who display characteristics considered more appropriate for men than for women are especially likely to be harassed. Case examples include a female police officer and bodybuilder who was subjected to sexually explicit noises and materials and who found vibrators, a urinal device, and a soiled condom and sanitary napkin in her mailbox at work (*Sanchez v. Miami Beach*, 1989) and a woman in a male-dominated accounting office who was denied partnership despite her exceptional performance because she needed to learn to 'walk more femininely, talk more femininely, dress more femininely, wear make-up, have her hair styled, and wear jewellery' (*Price Waterhouse v. Hopkins*, 1989). Computer experiments show that women who express an intention to pursue a male-dominated career and the belief that men and women are equal are more likely than women who express traditional career goals and beliefs to be sent offensive pornography from men (Dall'Ara & Maass, 1999; Maass et al., 2003).

[. . .]

Men who pose distinctiveness threats are also harassed. Male nurses are frequently targets of bullying (Erikson & Einarsen, 2004), and men in male-dominated jobs are harassed when they are perceived to be too feminine, or not masculine enough, by their supervisors or coworkers (Berdahl, Magley & Waldo, 1996; Berdahl & Moore, 2006; Waldo et al., 1998). For example, men who leave work to care for their children, wear earrings, or refuse to discuss sexual exploits with women have been called 'pussy', 'fag', and 'girlie-man'; incessantly taunted and teased; and subjected to sexually humiliating acts, such as simulated sodomy and threatened rape (cf. Axam & Zalesne, 1999; Berdahl et al., 1996; *Dillon v. Frank.* 1992; *Doe v. City of Belleville*, 1997; Franke, 1997; MacKinnon, 1997).

[. . .]

Looking at SBH as a response to threats induced by blurred distinctions between men and women illuminates its role as a basic form of sex discrimination. In this light, SBH clearly can be seen as a punitive means of 'doing gender': defining, enacting, and enforcing masculinity in men and femininity in women with everyday social practices (cf. Burgess & Borgida, 1999; Ely & Meyerson, 2000; Padavic & Reskin, 2002; Ridgeway, 1997; West & Zimmerman, 1987). As Franke puts it, sexual harassment is sex discrim-ination 'not because it is sexual,

and not becausemen do it to women, but precisely because it . . . perpetuates, enforces, and polices a set of gender norms that seek to feminize women and masculinize men' (1997: 696). SBH, thus, is one of many negative social repercussions faced by individuals who violate sex roles (for examples of other repercussions, see Gill, 2004; Heilman, Wallen, Fuchs & Tamkins, 2004; Herek, 1993; Rudman & Fairchild, 2004; Thomas-Hunt & Phillips, 2004).

Threats that Emphasize Group Distinctions

Rather than blurring distinctions between men and women, acceptance, category, and derogation threats draw on them. Acceptance threats challenge an individual's status as a good or prototypical member of his or her sex: a man's masculinity (e.g., his virility, courage, or competence) or a woman's femininity (e.g., her purity, attractiveness, or warmth). Such challenges would not be threatening if distinctions between men and women were not considered meaningful or legitimate. Acceptance threats trigger a desire to prove one is a typical and worthy member of one's group (Branscombe et al., 1999). [. . .] Category threats associate an individual with a sex-based group against his or her will. Individuals tend to experience more threat when associated with a low-status group than a high-status group, so in most contexts both men and women will likely experience a category threat when associated with women (e.g., when a man or a woman is called 'bitch') than when associated with men (e.g., when a woman or a man is said to 'have balls'). Category threats trigger a desire to disidentify from the group with which one has been unwillingly associated (Branscombe et al., 1999; Steele, 1997; Steele & Aronson, 1995), which may involve derogating the group or, in most cases, women. Finally, derogation threats devalue the status of an individual's sex group and are threatening to the extent one identifies with that group (Branscombe et al., 1999; Maass et al., 2003). Derogation threats trigger a desire to defend one's group or to distance oneself from it, which may involve putting down the other sex or demeaning other members of one's own sex.

[. . .]

We have considered what motivates a desire to protect sex-based status and what triggers this desire and SBH. We now consider who is likely to be targeted for SBH and what it may look like when men harass women, when men harass men, when women harass men, and when women harass women.

Targets of Harassment

If SBH stems from a desire to protect sex-based status when it seems threatened, targets of harassment will be chosen to achieve this goal. *Individuals who pose the threat* to the harasser's status in the first place are likely targets, since the threat will be most satisfactorily quelled if its source is. Individuals who blur distinctions between the sexes, challenge someone's achievement of sex-based ideals, categorize someone in a sex-based group against his or her will, or threaten the value of someone's sex-based group are therefore likely to be targeted for SBH. *Individuals who are less powerful* than the harasser are also likely targets (Blumenthal, 1998; Bourgeois & Perkins, 2003; Lester et al., 1986). If the person posing the threat is more powerful than the person threatened, the latter may target another who is less powerful for harassment (e.g., O'Leary-Kelly et al., 2000). For example, if a boss threatens a subordinate's status, the subordinate may pick on a coworker instead of the boss to try to restore a sense of status.

Because harassers are likely to target the source of the threat and men are more strongly motivated than women to protect their sex-based status, individuals who threaten men's status are

especially likely to be targeted for SBH. Because harassers are likely to target less powerful individuals and because men, on average, are more powerful than women, men more than women will harass and women more than men will be harassed (Berdahl et al., 1996; Cleveland & Kerst, 1993; Fiske & Stevens, 1993). Combined, this means the most likely form of SBH should be men harassing women, especially women who challenge men's status. The second most likely form of harassment should be men harassing other men, especially men who challenge their status. The relative prevalence of these forms is supported by prior research. When women harass, they should mainly target other women, especially those who challenge their status. The least likely form of harassment should be women harassing men. When a woman harasses a man, she typically will target a man who challenges her status. We now consider these different harassment scenarios and how they reinforce gender hierarchy in the workplace.

Male-to-female Harassment

The harassment of women by men needs little introduction [. . . however,] it requires interpretation from the perspective of a sex-based status motivation. A man wishing to protect or enhance his status relative to a woman may do so by derogating her as a woman. Hostile environment harassment that includes sexist jokes, comments, and put-downs derogates women, reminds them of their low status relative to men, and reminds men of their high status relative to women. This can even take the form of 'not man enough' harassment against women who are told they are not tough enough, or are too sensitive, for the job (Berdahl & Moore, 2006). In a male-dominated environment, a man may harass a woman coworker in these ways because she poses a distinctiveness threat to his sex-based status. By undermining her, he may restore his sense of status as a man who can do the job better than a woman and may enhance his status among other men, if they view his behaviour as manly and stand to benefit from it (Connell, 1987). When groups of men perpetrate this type of harassment against women, they can gain courage, legitimacy, and cohesion by closing ranks and acting together (Farley, 1978).

Sexual advance forms of harassment may serve a similar purpose of enhancing a man's status by derogating a woman's. By sexually objectifying or dominating her, the man may increase his sense of masculinity by being heterosexually dominant (Franke, 1997). By being sexually objectified and dominated, the woman is relegated to the low status of being a means to a man's sexual ends. Like hostile environment harassment, bystanders are affected by this type of harassment (Bowes-Sperry & O'Leary-Kelly, 2005; Glomb et al., 1997). It yields dividends for all men and subordinates all women by reinforcing male dominance (Connell, 1987).

Male-to-male Harassment

If a man wishes to protect or enhance his status relative to another man, he may do so by derogating the other man's status as a man. He can 'prove' he is manlier than the other man by outperforming him on a masculine ideal, such as virility, courage, athletic ability, or intelligence. [. . .] He can also prove he is manlier by emasculating the other man. When such competition and challenge turns to sabotage, threatening insults, and sexual or other forms of derision that undermine the target specifically as a man, it is SBH (MacKinnon, 1997).

Competing with other men in sex-specific ways defined by gender hierarchy has the effect of reinforcing status distinctions within and between the sexes. It enforces the notion that 'manly' characteristics are most relevant for evaluating men, but not women, who are omitted

from candidacy in the competition. Women may be used in the competition between men as status symbols (e.g., a man who 'scores' a more attractive woman has higher status) or as a derogatory reference group to which the male target of harassment is likened (Connell, 1987, 1995; Franke, 1997; Harry, 1992), furthering the view of men as subjects and women as objects for attainment or derision.

Female-to-male Harassment

The harassment of men by women has received little theoretical attention. Primarily, it has been envisioned as the mirror image of the prototype of harassment against women by men: unwanted heterosexual attention. As research has shown, however, sexual attention from women generally is not appraised by men as threatening or bothersome and is unlikely to be experienced by men as harassment (Berdahl, in press; Berdahl et al., 1996; Malovich & Stake, 1990). Power discrepancies between men and women mean that women are less likely to threaten men than men are to threaten women, but this does not mean it never happens. [. . .]

If a woman wishes to protect or enhance her sex-based status relative to a man, she may do so by derogating him as a man. This might take the form of deriding men as a group, but this is likely to pack relatively little punch in most contexts. [. . .] Comments that suggest a man does not measure up to other men are likely to be more threatening to a man than are comments suggesting he does not measure up to women. Women may find it more effective, in attempting to knock a man down in status, to compare him to other men and suggest he comes up short. This could involve a direct comparison, such as suggesting he is less courageous, competent, or virile than other men, or an implicit comparison, such as suggesting he is not courageous, competent, or virile enough. Likening him to women is another way to demote his status, although perhaps less likely from women, who would disparage themselves in the process. Such comparisons draw on sex-specific characteristics to evaluate the man and are thus based on sex; to the degree they succeed in hurting him, they are harassing.

More sexual forms of harassment from women toward men are likely to be rare for three reasons (see Fiske & Stevens, 1993). First, for many men, 'unwanted' sexual attention from a woman is a foreign concept. Men evaluate heterosexual attention, even unwanted attention, as a neutral to positive experience (e.g., Berdahl et al., 1996; Waldo et al., 1998). Second, being forceful is contrary to the female sex role and is therefore likely to incur negative consequences for women and deter them from such behaviour (e.g., Berdahl, in press; Rudman, 1998). Third, it is physically more difficult for women to be sexually aggressive against men than the other way around, further undermining its likelihood and threat. [. . .] When a woman *does* overpower a man sexually, *against his will*, it is likely to be experienced as quite threatening by the man. A man who is sexually dominated is likely to experience a substantial threat to his masculinity, defined in terms of heterosexual dominance (e.g., Connell, 1995; Franke, 1997; Gutek, 1985). As such, sexually dominating a man is a potent way to demote his status as a man.

Female-to-female Harassment

Harassment between women has received the least attention of all, [. . .] although experimental research suggests women are prone to discriminate against other women (Biernat & Fuegen, 2001; Rudman, 1998). If sex harassment is targeted at less powerful individuals who threaten the harasser's sex-based status, other women are likely to be the primary targets of harassment by women. Harassment between women should be similar to harassment between men, in the sense

that it involves a woman trying to derogate the other woman in sex-based terms. The style of harassment will differ, however, because ideals for men and women differ.

A woman who feels her sex-based status is threatened may try to outperform another woman in feminine ideals, such as beauty, sexual desirability, warmth, and mothering. Again, ideals will be specific to the particular context (Alvesson & Billing, 1997; Prentice & Miller, 2002), but much commonality exists across contexts (e.g., Connell, 1987; Williams & Best, 1990). When a woman tries to demote another woman's status by calling her ugly, a bad mother, a bitch, a slut, or a bull dyke, for example, she undermines that woman in sex-specific ways. Likening a woman to a man should be less insulting than likening a man to a woman, but it still suggests a woman has failed feminine ideals and carries the threat of social rejection. A woman may also attempt to enhance her status relative to another woman by winning the approval of higher-status men. Like other forms of SBH, competing with other women in sex-specific ways has the effect of reinforcing status distinctions within and between the sexes. It enforces the notion that 'feminine' characteristics are most relevant for evaluating women, but not men. When this competition turns to active sabotage, insults, and other forms of undermining designed to demote the target as a woman, it becomes SBH.

[. . .]

Conclusions

SBH, broadly conceptualized, is behaviour that derogates, demeans, or humiliates an individual based on that individual's sex. [. . .] An important implication of this view of SBH is that it is contextually defined. Whether an act derogates another based on sex depends on the history and the social context of the behaviour, power differences between the individuals involved (physical, organizational, and social inequalities), and the target's experience of fear or powerlessness. This means that a priori classifications of certain behaviours as SBH are not possible. What may be harassing to some may be fun or flattering to others, depending on the context in which it occurs, the relationship between those involved, and the way it was delivered and received. Future studies should assess the degree to which a potentially harassing behaviour derogated a recipient before concluding it was harassing and to what degree (cf. Berdahl, in press; Berdahl & Moore, 2006; Einarsen, 2000). This will help avoid classifying experiences as harassing that were not and will help prevent making erroneous estimates of the prevalence and severity of harassment.

Defining SBH in this way may raise the concern that it will become diluted and taken less seriously. I believe just the opposite is the case. Definitions that rely on sexual behaviours or motives pose a much bigger threat to the perceived legitimacy of sexual harassment as a form of sex discrimination. Construing SBH as sexual in nature has caused behaviours that are sexual but not harassing to be wrongfully classified as harassment—for example, consensual or desired sexual attention—and behaviours that are harassing and based on sex but not sexual to be overlooked—for example, 'not man enough' harassment between men (Schultz, 2003).[1] A focus on sexual behaviours has generated confusion and controversy about sexual harassment as a form of discrimination and has led to policies that focus on policing sexual behaviour at work rather than on acts that perpetuate sexual inequality (cf. Schultz, 1998; Williams, Giuffre & Dellinger, 1999). Viewing SBH as behaviour that derogates an individual's status based on sex offers an improved understanding of harassment as discrimination.

[. . .]

This perspective of SBH considers why women, not just men, may be motivated to commit SBH, what this harassment might look like, and how it might differ from harassment committed by men. Earlier views of harassers as motivated by sexual desire allowed for women to harass others in sexual ways, but more recent views of harassers as men motivated to protect male dominance have not left room for understanding why women might harass others based on sex. The current perspective proposes that women and men share the same underlying motive that gives rise to SBH: a desire to protect their social status when it is threatened. How this status is obtained, threatened, and protected differs by sex, however, because status and ideals differ by sex.

[. . .]

The premise of this theory can be applied to study harassment that is based on social distinctions other than sex. This theory locates the basic motivation for harassment in the motive for social status, the terms and conditions of which are in large part defined by sex. Sex may be the primary distinction made between individuals (Fiske et al., 1991; Stangor et al., 1992; van Knippenberg et al., 1994), but other distinctions are made as well, including ethnic, national, socio-economic, and age. To the degree a social characteristic is used to define status, individuals will be motivated to protect and enhance their status based on that characteristic and will be able to do so by derogating another's. SBH has probably received the most attention because of the primacy of sex as a category and the resulting pervasiveness of SBH. Future research could broaden our understanding of harassment generally by studying how it serves to derogate individuals based on social characteristics used to define status, thereby reinforcing social hierarchies and the status quo.

Note

1. 'Not man enough' harassment took especially long to recognize as a form of sex discrimination because it does not fit the original prototype of sexual harassment. Some courts said harassment between men was not actionable because individuals could not discriminate against their own sex (e.g., *Goluszek v. H.P. Smith*, 1998). Others claimed that such cases were actionable only when harassers were homosexual (e.g., *McWilliams v. Fairfax County Bd. of Supervisors*, 1996). Other courts concluded that 'not man enough' harassment was actionable only if sexual in content (e.g., *Doe v. City of Belleville*, 1997).

References

Adams, A., & Bray, F. 1992. Holding out against workplace harassment and bullying. *Personnel Management*, 24(10): 48–52.

Alderfer, C.P., & Smith, K.K. 1982. Studying intergroup relations embedded in organizations. *Administrative Science Quarterly*, 27: 35–65.

Alvesson, M., & Billing, Y.D. 1997. *Understanding gender and organizations*. London: Sage.

Axam, H.S., & Zalesne, D. 1999. Simulated sodomy and other forms of heterosexual 'horseplay': Same sex sexual harassment, workplace gender hierarchies, and the myth of the gender monolith before and after *Oncale*. *Yale Journal of Law and feminism*, 11(1): 155–243.

Barnes v. Costle. 561 F.2d 983 (D.C. Cir. 1977).

Bargh, J.A., Raymond, P., Pryor, J.B., & Strack. F. 1995. Attractiveness of the underling: An automatic power sex association and its consequences for sexual harassment and aggression. *Journal of Personality and Social Psychology*, 68: 768–81.

Baumeister, R.P., & Leary, M.R. 1995. The need to belong: Desire for interpersonal attachments as a fundamental human motivation. *Psychological Bulletin*, 117: 497–529.

Benson, D.J., & Thomson, G.E. 1982. Sexual harassment on a university campus: The confluence of authority relations, sexual interest and gender stratification. *Social Problems*, 29: 236–51.

Bern, S.L. 1974. The measurement of psychological androgyny. *Journal of Consulting and Clinical Psychology*, 42: 155–62.

Berdahl, J.L. In press. The sexual harassment of uppity women. *Journal of Applied Psychology*.

Berdahl, J.L., Magley, V.J., & Waldo, C.R. 1996. The sexual harassment of men: Exploring the concept with theory and data. *Psychology of Women Quarterly*, 20: 527–47.

Berdahl, J.L., & Moore, C. 2006. Workplace harassment: Double-jeopardy for minority women. *Journal of Applied Psychology*, 91, 426–36.

Bergen, D.J., & Williams, J.E. 1991. Sex stereotypes in the United States revisited: 1972–1988. *Sex Roles*, 24: 413–23.

Biernat, M., & Fuegen, K. 2001. Shifting standards and the evaluation of competence: Complexity in gender-based judgment and decision making. *Journal of Social Issues*, 57: 707–24.

Blumenthal, J.A. 1998. The reasonable woman standard: A meta-analytic review of gender differences in perceptions of sexual harassment. *Law and Human Behavior*, 22(1); 33–57.

Bourgeois, M.J., & Perkins, J. 2003. A test of evolutionary and sociocultural explanations of reactions to sexual harassment. *Sex Roles*, 49: 343–51.

Bowes-Sperry, L., & O'Leary-Kelly, A.M. 2005. To act or not to act: The dilemma faced by sexual harassment observers. *Academy of Management Review*, 30: 288–307.

Branscombe, N.R., Ellemers, N., Spears, R., & Doosje, B. 1999. The context and content of social identity threat. In N. Ellemers, R. Spears & B. Doosje (Eds), *Social identity: Context, commitment, content*: 35–58. Oxford: Blackwell.

Brodsky, C.M. 1976. *The harassed worker*. Toronto: Lexington Books.

Burgess, D., & Borgida, E. 1999. Who women are, who women should be: Descriptive and prescriptive gender stereotyping in sex discrimination. *Psychology, Public Policy, and the Law*, 5: 665–92.

Buss, D.M. 1989. Sex differences in human mate preferences: Evolutionary hypotheses tested in 37 cultures. *Behavioural and Brain Sciences*, 12(1): 1–49.

Cleveland, J.N., & Kerst, M.E. 1993. Sexual harassment and perceptions of power: An under-articulated relationship. *Journal of Vocational Behavior*, 42: 49–67.

Connell, R.W. 1987. *Gender and power*. Stanford, CA: Stanford University Press.

———. 1995. *Masculinities*. Berkeley: University of California Press.

Corne v. Bausch & Lomb, 390 F. Supp. 161. (1975).

Cuddy, A.J.C., Fiske, S.T., & Glick, P. 2004. When professionals become mothers, warmth doesn't cut the ice. *Journal of Social Issues*, 60: 701–18.

Dall'Ara, E., & Maass, A. 1999. Studying sexual harassment in the laboratory: Are egalitarian women at higher risk? *Sex Roles*, 41: 681–704.

Dépret, E.P., & Fiske, S.T. 1993. Social cognition and power: Some cognitive consequences of social structure as a source of control deprivation, In G. Weary, P. Gleicher & K. Marsh (Eds), *Control motivation and social cognition*: 176–202. New York: Springer-Verlag.

DeSouza, E., & Fansler, A.G. 2003. Contrapower sexual harassment: A survey of students and faculty members. *Sex Roles*, 48: 519–42.

Dillon v. Frank, No. 90-2290, WL 5436 (6th Cir. 1992).

Doe v. City of Belleville, 119 F.3d 563, 566-67 (7th Cir. 1997).

Eagly, A.H. 1987. *Sex differences in social behavior: A social-role analysis*. Hillsdale, NJ: Lawrence Earlbaum Associates.

Einarsen, S. 2000. Harassment and bullying at work: A review of the Scandinavian approach. *Aggression and Violent Behavior*, 5(4): 379–401.

Ely, R.J., & Meyerson, D.E. 2000. Theories of gender in organizations: A new approach to organizational analysis and change. *Research in Organizational Behavior*, 22: 103–51.

Equal Employment Opportunity Commission. 1980. Guidelines on discrimination because of sex (Sect. 1604.11). *Federal Register*, 45: 74 676–77.

Erikson, W., & Einarsen, S. 2004. Gender minority as a risk factor of exposure to bullying at work: The case of male assistant nurses. *European Journal of Work and Organizational Psychology*, 13: 473–92.

Evans, L.J. 1978. Sexual harassment: Women's hidden occupational hazard. In J. Chapman & M. Gates (Eds), *The victimization of women*: 203–23. Beverly Hills, CA: Sage.

Farley, L. 1978. *Sexual shakedown: The sexual harassment of women on the job*. New York: McGraw-Hill.

Fiske, A.P., Haslam, N., & Fiske, S.T. 1991. Confusing one person with another: What errors reveal about the elementary forms of social relations. *Journal of Personality and Social Psychology*, 60: 656–74.

Fiske, S.T. 2004. *Social beings: A core motives approach to social psychology*. New York: Wiley.

Fiske, S.T., & Berdahl. J.L. In press. Social power. In A, Kruglanski & E.T. Higgins (Eds), *Social psychology: A handbook of basic principles* (2nd edn). New York: Guilford Press.

Fiske, S.T., Cuddy, A.J.C., Glick, P., & Xu, J. 2002. A model of (often mixed) stereotype content: Competence and warmth respectively follow from perceived status and competition. *Journal of Personality and Social Psychology*, 82: 878–902.

Fiske, S.T., & Stevens, L.E. 1993. What's so special about sex? Gender stereotyping and discrimination. In S. Oskamp & M. Costanzo (Eds), *Gender issues in contemporary society*: 173–96. Newbury Park, CA: Sage.

Fitzgerald, L.F., Drasgow, P., Hulin, C.L., Gelfand, M. J., & Magley, V.J., 1997. Antecedents and consequences of sexual harassment in organizations: A test of an integrated model. *Journal of Applied Psychology*, 82: 578–89.

Fitzgerald, L.F., Magley, V.J., Drasgow, F., & Waldo, C.R. 1999. Measuring sexual harassment in the military: The Sexual Experiences Questionnaire (SEQ—DoD). *Military Psychology*, 11: 243–63.

Franke, K.M. 1997. What's wrong with sexual harassment? *Stanford Law Review*, 49: 691–772.

French, J., & Raven, B. 1959. The bases of social power. In D. Cartwright (Ed.), *Studies in social power*: 150–65. Ann Arbor: Institute for Social Research.

Gill, M.J. 2004. When information does not deter stereotyping: Prescriptive stereotyping can foster bias under conditions that deter descriptive stereotyping. *Journal of Experimental Social Psychology*, 40: 619–32.

Glick, P., & Fiske, S.T. 2001. Ambivalent sexism. *Advances in Experimental Social Psychology*, 33: 115–88.

Glick, P., Lameiras, M., Fiske, S.T., Eckes, T., Masser, B., Volpato, C., Manganelli, A.M., Pek, J.C.X., Huang, L., Sakalli-Uguru, N., Castro, Y.R., D'Avila Pereira, M.L., Willemsen, T.M., Brunner, A., Six-Materna, I., & Wells, R. 2004. Bad but bold: Ambivalent attitudes toward men predict gender inequality in 16 nations. *Journal of Personality and Social Psychology*, 86: 713–28.

Glomb, T.M., Munson, L.J., Hulin, C.L., Bergman, M.E., & Drasgow, F. 1999, Structural equation models of sexual harassment: Longitudinal explorations and cross-sectional generalizations. *Journal of Applied Psychology*, 84: 14–28.

Glomb, T.M., Richman, W.L., Hulin, C.L., Drasgow, F., Schneider, K.T., & Fitzgerald, L.F, 1997. Ambient sexual harassment: An integrated model of antecedents and consequences. *Organizational Behavior and Human Decision Processes*, 71: 309–28.

Goluszek v. H.P. Smith, 697 F. Supp 1452, 1455-57 (N.D. Ill.19BB).

Grauerholz, E. 1989. Sexual harassment of women professors by students: Exploring the dynamics of power, authority, and gender in a university setting. *Sex Roles*, 21: 789–801.

Gruber, T.E. 1998. The impact of male work environments and organizational policies on women's experiences of sexual harassment. *Gender and Society*, 12(3): 301–20.

Gutek, B.A. 1985. *Sex and the workplace: The impact of sexual behavior and harassment on women, men, and organizations*. San Francisco: Jossey-Bass.

Gutek, B.A., & Morasch, B. 1982. Sex-ratios, sex-role spillover, and sexual harassment of women at work. *Journal of Social Issues*, 38: 55–74.

Harry, J. 1992. Conceptualizing anti-gay violence. In G.M. Herek & K.T, Berrill (Eds), *Hate crimes: Confronting violence against lesbians and gay men*: 113–22. Newbury Park, CA: Sage.

Heelan v. Johns-Manvme Corporation, 451 F. Supp. 1382 (1978).

Heilman, M.E., Wallen, A.S., Fuchs, D., & Tamkins, M.M. 2004. Penalties for success: Reactions to women who succeed at male gender-typed tasks. *Journal of Applied Psychology*, 89: 416–27.

Herek, G.M. 1993. On heterosexual masculinity: Some psychical consequences of the social construction of gender and sexuality. In L.D. Garnets & D.C. Kimmel (Eds), *Psychological perspectives on lesbian and gay male experiences. Between men—between women: Lesbian and gay studies*: 316–30. New York: Columbia University Press.

Hogan, R., & Hogan, J. 1991. Personality and status. In D.G. Gilbert & J.J. Connolly (Eds), *Personality, social skills, and psychopathology: An individual differences approach*: 137–54. New York: Plenum Press.

Jost, J.T., & Banaji, M.R. 1994. The role of stereotyping in system-justification and the production of false consciousness. *British Journal of Social Psychology*, 33(1): 1–27.

Keltner, D.O., Gruenfeld, D.H., & Anderson, C. 2003. Power, approach, and inhibition. *Psychological Review*, 110: 265–84.

Lester, D., Banta, B., Barton. J., Elian, N., et al. 1986. Judgments about sexual harassment: Effects of the power of the harasser. *Perceptual and Motor Skills*, 63: 990.

Maass, A., Cadinu, M., Guarnieri, G., & Grasselli, A. 2003. Sexual harassment under social identity threat: The computer harassment paradigm. *Journal of Personality and Social Psychology*, 85: 853–80.

McKinney, K. 1992. Contrapower sexual harassment: The effects of student and type of behavior on faculty perceptions. *Sex Roles*, 27: 627–643.

MacKinnon, C.A. 1979. *Sexual harassment of working women*. New Haven, CT: Yale University Press.

———. 1997. *Oncale Amicus Brief for the U.S. Supreme Court*. Amici Curiae.

McWilliams v. Fairfax County Bd. of Supervisors, 72 F.3d 1191. 1193 (4th Cir. 1996).

Magley, V.J., Waldo, C.R., Drasgow, P., & Fitzgerald, L.F. 1999. The impact of sexual harassment on military personnel: Is it the same for men and women? *Military Psychology*, 11(3): 283–302.

Malovich, N.J., & Stake, J.E. 1990. Sexual harassment on campus: Individual differences in attitudes and beliefs. *Psychology of Women Quarterly*. 14(1): 63–81.

Mansfield, P.K., Koch, P.B., Henderson, J., Vicary, J.R., Cohn, M., & Young, E.W. 1991. The job climate for women in traditionally male blue-collar occupations. *Sex Roles*, 25: 63–79.

Miller v. Bank of America, 600 F.2d 211 (9th Cir. 1979).

Mirowsky, J., & Ross, C.E. 2003. *Education, social status, and health*. Hawthorne. NY: Aldine de Gruyter.

Morin, P. 2002. Rank and salutogenesis: A quantitative and empirical study of self-rated health and perceived social status. *Dissertation Abstracts International: Section B: The Sciences and Engineering*, 63(6-B): 306–9.

Nieva, V.P., & Gutek, B.A. 1981. *Women and work: A psychological perspective*. New York: Praeger.

O'Leary-Kelly, A.M., Paetzold, R.L., & Griffin, R.W. 2000. Sexual harassment as aggressive behavior: An actor-based perspective. *Academy of Management Review*, 25: 372–88.

Owens, D.A., & Sutton, R.I. 2001. Status contests in meetings: Negotiating the informal order. In M.E. Turner (Ed.), *Groups at work: Theory and research*: 299–316. Mahwah, NJ: Lawrence Erlbaum Associates.

Padavic, I., & Reskin, B. 2002. *Women and men at work*. Thousand Oaks. CA: Pine Forge Press.

Pratto, P., Liu, J.H., Levin, S., Sidanius, J., Shih, M., Bachrach, H., & Hegarty, P. 2000. Social dominance orientation and the legitimization of inequality across cultures. *Journal of Cross Cultural Psychology*, 31: 369–409.

Prentice, D., & Miller, D.T. 2002. The emergence of home-grown stereotypes. *American Psychologist*, 57: 352–59.

Prentice, D.A., & Carranza, E. 2002. What women and men should be, shouldn't be, are allowed to be, and don't have to be: The contents of prescriptive gender stereotypes. *Psychology of Women Quarterly*, 26: 269–81.

Price Waterhouse v. Hopkins, 490 U. S. 228 (1989).

Pryor, J.B. 1987. Sexual harassment proclivities in men. *Sex Roles*, 17, 269–90.

Pryor, J.B., La Vite, C., & Stoller, J. 1993. A social psychological analysis of sexual harassment: The person/situation interaction. *Journal of Vocational Behavior*, 42: 68–83.

Ridgeway, C.L. 1997. Interaction and the conservation of gender inequality: Considering employment. *American Sociological Review*, 62: 218–35.

Rudman, L.A. 1998. Self-promotion as a risk factor for women: The costs and benefits of counter-stereotypical impression management. *Journal of Personality and Social Psychology*, 74, 629–45.

Rudman, L.A., & Fairchild, K. 2004. Reactions to counter-stereotype behavior: The role of backlash in cultural stereotype maintenance. *Journal of Personality and Social Psychology*, 87: 157–76.

Sanchez v. Miami Beach, 720 p, Supp. 974, 977 n.9 (S.D. Fla, 1989).

Sartorius, N. 2003. Social capital and mental health. *Current Opinion in Psychiatry*, 16(Supplement): 8101–5.

Schneider, K.T., Swan, S., & Fitzgerald, L.F. 1997. Job-related and psychological effects of sexual harassment in the workplace: Empirical evidence from two organizations. *Journal of Applied Psychology*, 82: 401–15.

Schultz, V. 1998. Reconceptualizing sexual harassment. *Yale Law Journal*, 107, 1683–1796.

———. 2003. The sanitized workplace. *Yale Law Journal*, 112, 2061–2193.

Sidanius, J., Pratto, P., & Bobo, L. 1994. Social dominance orientation and the political psychology of gender: A case of invariance? *Journal of Personality and Social Psychology*, 67, 998–1011.

Stangor, C., Lynch, L., Duan, C., & Glas, B. 1992. Categorization of individuals on the basis of multiple social features. *Journal of Personality and Social Psychology*, 62: 207–18.

Steele, C.M. 1997. A threat in the air: How stereotypes shape intellectual identity and performance. *American Psychologist*, 52: 613–29.

Steele, C.M., & Aronson, J. 1995. Stereotype threat and the intellectual test performance of African Americans. *Journal of Personality and Social Psychology*, 69: 797–811.

Studd, M.V., & Gattiker, U.E. 1991. The evolutionary psychology of sexual harassment in organizations. *Ethology and Sociobiology*, 12(4): 249–90.

Sturm, S. 2001. Second generation employment discrimination: A structural approach. *Columbia Law Review*, 101: 458–568.

Tang, D.S., & Hayes, S.M. 1997. Theories of sexual harassment, In W. O'Donohue (Ed.), *Sexual harassment: Theory, research, and treatment*: 99–111. New York: Praeger.

Thomas-Hunt, M.C., & Phillips, K.W. 2004. When what you know is not enough: Expertise and gender dynamics in task groups. *Personality and Social Psychology Bulletin*, 30, 1585–98.

Twenge, J.M. 1997. Attitudes toward women, 1970–1995: A meta-analysis. *Psychology of Women Quarterly*, 21: 35–51.

US Merit Systems Protection Board. 1981. *Sexual harassment in the federal workplace: Is it a problem?* Washington, DC: US Government Printing Office.

———. 1988. *Sexual harassment in the federal government: An update*. Washington, DC: US Government Printing Office.

———. 1995, *Sexual harassment in the federal workplace: Trends, progress, continuing challenges*. Washington, DC: US Government Printing Office.

van Knippenberg, A., van Twuyver, M., & Pepels, J. 1994. Factors affecting social categorization processes in memory. *British Journal of Social Psychology*, 33: 419–31.

Waldo, C.R., Berdahl J.L., & Fitzgerald, L.J. 1998. Are men sexually harassed? If so, by whom? *Law and Human Behavior*, 22(1), 59–79.

West, C., & Zimmerman, D.H. 1987. Doing gender. *Gender and Society*, 1: 125–51.

Williams v. Saxbe, 413 F. Supp. 654 (1976).

Williams, C.L., Giuffre, P.A., & Dellinger, K. 1999. Sexuality in the workplace: Organizational control, sexual harassment, and the pursuit of pleasure. *Annual Review of Sociology*, 25: 73–93.

Williams, J.E., & Best, D.L. 1990. *Sex and psyche: Gender and self viewed cross culturally. Cross-cultural research and methodology series*, vol. 13, Thousand Oaks, CA: Sage.

Zalk, S.R. 1990. Men in the academy: A psychological profile of harassment. In M. Paludi (Ed.), *Ivory power: Sexual harassment on campus*: 141–75. Albany: State University of New York Press.

'Tank Tops Are OK But I Don't Want to See Her Thong': Girls' Engagements with Secondary School Dress Codes

Rebecca Raby

Halter-tops, tube-tops, one shoulder tops . . . muscle shirts, see-through or mesh tops (unless underneath a shirt) aren't to be worn. Blouses, shirts, or tops that reveal bare backs, midriffs, undergarments, or that have spaghetti straps or revealing necklines are not to be worn in Trent's classes, hallways, class activities, or on field trips.

—Trent Secondary

A common feature of schools across North America is a code of conduct or a set of rules outlining the expectations for student behaviour and consequences for rule infractions. Most codes of conduct also include a dress code, like the one cited above, that describes unacceptable dress, frequently citing short skirts, revealing tops, ripped or torn clothing, heavy chains, and so forth. Such dress codes are commonly justified through explanations that dress code violations are distracting to others, not fitting the desired image of a school, and disrespectful toward oneself and others (Raby, 2005). The details of dress codes do shift, however, as school administrators respond to trends in popular fashion, as reflected in rules banning midriff tops now making way for new concerns with girls revealing cleavage. These dress codes also reflect broader social concerns about young people's dress as illustrated in recent examples of young women being asked to cover up on Southwest Airlines (Tarrant, 2007) and several American towns banning young men from wearing low-slung pants that reveal their underwear. Of course, dress codes are also gendered. Dress codes participate in a broader, ongoing cultural concern with forms of female dress (and sexuality), defining what is acceptable (Pomerantz, 2007). They consequently normalize certain forms of girlhood, problematize others, and suggest girls' responsibility for the school's moral climate.

This article draws on data collected through focus groups with secondary students within a southern region of Ontario, Canada, in which young people were asked about their school rules and what they think of them. Within these focus groups, dress codes received particular attention, especially from the female participants, with discussion concentrated on girls' clothing. These young women had a nuanced analysis of dress codes, although in most groups there were also striking moments when they condemned girls who dress like 'sluts'. This article thus concentrates on the female participants' negotiation of dress codes, for within such commentaries these young women both contest and reproduce institutional and peer regulation of girls' dress.

This article [...] examine[s] my female respondents' casual, public, and complex discussions of their school dress codes, discussions which flag current challenges in negotiating girlhood as girls navigate the fine line between attractive and provocative. I also consider how these statements are embedded within educational structures, especially the rules and the actions of teachers, wider social patterns of fashion and media, and peer cultures. These focus-group conversations disrupt an easy interpretation of girls as either embracing or condemning bodily displays. They also illustrate young women actively, and sometimes critically, constructing gender.

Literature

Within North America, several distinct and conflicting strands of popular commentary currently frame discussions of young women and their clothing. First, various scholars and popular writers have explored the gendered, sexual double standard, which has stigmatized girls who are deemed to be sluts. *Slut!*, by Leora Tanenbaum (1999) and *Fast Girls* by Emily White (2002), both written for non-academic audiences, discuss

how certain girls are labelled slut by their peers and the devastating consequences. Their research found that within white, suburban America this powerful term is applied to girls who develop sooner than others, are isolated, fail to conform, and who have experienced sexual abuse at some point in their lives (White, 2002).

At the same time, other recent, popular texts present quite a different picture, which suggests a moral panic around girls' provocative dress (Pomerantz, 2006). For instance, Ariel Levy (2005) cited pole-dancing classes, midriff tops, *Charlie's Angels*, porn stars, and *Girls Gone Wild* video collections to argue that girls and women actively participate in a sexualized North American culture in which female raunch is now celebrated in the false belief that it is a liberating and powerful progression of feminism. Rather than stigma, sluttiness in high school brings stardom; girls learn that to get attention from boys they need to perform themselves as sexy. Yet, this is not really sexual empowerment or liberation, Levy argued, but instead it is absorption into a consumerist, sexist culture.

[. . .]

Whether girls marginalize others through the label of slut, embrace a sexualized culture, or rally against it through embracing modesty, girls' dress is the focus of significant commentary, evaluation, and regulation (Duits & van Zoonen, 2006). Such commentary often references girls' socialization or their internalization of culture (Christensen & Prout, 2005). For example, by categorizing others as sluts, girls are seen to draw on the culturally embedded language of patriarchy, using it to compete with one another. Chambers, van Loon, and Tinknell (2004) suggested that when their female respondents policed other girls' reputations by using terms like slut or *slag* (the British equivalent), they 'thus colluded with dominant sexual models by internalizing sexist comments also offered by boys they encountered' (p. 408). In her discussion of the stigma of slut, Tanenbaum (1999) similarly argued that girls reproduce and reinforce the sexual double standard to exercise power over other women. [. . .]

These positions acknowledge the structural environments within which young men and women learn about gender and sexuality and recognize girls' participation in the production of peer and wider culture. They rightly point to the misogyny and inequality that is perpetuated by girls. Yet, sometimes such representations of slut-bashing can imply that boys and men more actively create social space and their own dominant positions while girls uncritically reproduce their own subordination. For example, Brown's recognition of competition between girls is important for identifying the role of power in girls' relationships, but ultimately this competition is seen to perpetuate boys' reality. What of girls' agency, analysis, and the complexity of power relations within their lives? Are girls only considered to have agency when they embrace modesty, as Shalit (2007) seemed to imply?

A recent body of research on girls has emerged that draws on feminist post-structuralism (Butler, 1990) and the new sociology of childhood (James & Prout, 1990). This work has been particularly noteworthy for examining how girls, as social agents, negotiate social structures and discourses that reproduce girls' marginality (Baxter, 2002). Such positions recognize that gender is not fixed into two clear categories of masculinity and femininity but that instead gender is fluid and intersected by a number of other identities, including class, sexuality, age, race, ethnicity, and so on, providing for a range of masculinities and femininities. This complication of femininity and gendered power relations among girls and young women is seen, for example, in Baxter's own research and in the

works of Davies (1989), Hey (1997), Reay (2001), Renold (2005), and Pomerantz (2007). These authors identify how girls negotiate competing and often contradictory discourses as active, social agents who participate in the construction of the social world around them (Davies, 1989; James & Prout, 1990) and who can concomitantly invest in, play with, and critique dominant representations of femininity (Bettis & Adams, 2003; Russel & Tyler, 2002).

As will become evident below, young women debate clothing rules, break dress codes, speak up against sexual double standards even while reproducing them (Kitzinger, 1995) and yet also rail against other girls' revealing dress. Such multiple meanings, contradiction, and resistance all need attention. [. . .] I illustrate that girls must (and do) actively negotiate such contradictory messages of girlhood (Tolman, 2002) and locate their forming selves within and against them, through challenge and reproduction.

Method

It is required that schools in this study's region have a dress code. These dress codes differ to some extent between schools but generally include no gang-related, ripped, or torn clothing; no winter jackets, non-religious headgear or hoods; no beachwear or other distracting clothing; no clothing promoting hatred, advertising tobacco, alcohol, or drugs; and no jewellery, such as spiked bracelets, dog collars, or heavy chains that could be used as a weapon. It is quite common in this region for school rules to specifically state that provocative clothing is not allowed, occasionally even citing specific items of girls' clothing. Dress code details are often framed in terms of respect for others and self-respect in which certain activities, such as doing drugs or wearing provocative clothing, are considered to indicate a lack of self-respect (Raby, 2005).

This article draws on eight focus groups, two from the summer of 2004 and six from 2005, with a diverse range of young people in a southern region of Ontario, Canada, made up of small cities and farmland. Focus groups were conducted with local groups of secondary students located through word of mouth and direct requests to community organizations. Participants in the focus groups were usually those who showed up for a drop-in program, were interested in the topic, and who remembered their parental consent forms. Often they were friends. [. . .]

The focus groups lasted about an hour and a half and ranged in size from 3 to an unwieldy 14. Participants received a small honorarium. Questions addressed not only dress codes but also school rules in general, asking if they are fair, if they are fairly applied, which rules they would change, what recourse they have if they feel they have been unfairly accused of breaking a rule, and whether students should participate in creating school rules. Participants had the opportunity to provide private, written comments at the end of their focus group, although few added anything new. As a form of member checking, they were also all sent a summary report and an invitation for comments once the focus groups were completed, but none were forthcoming.

This analysis concentrates on parts of the focus groups where the students addressed dress codes. Such conversations included debates about the relative merits of uniforms and discussion of rules against hats, gang wear, and provocative writing or images on T-shirts. They also addressed revealing dress, discussion that tended to be quite involved and dominated by the girls. It is important to acknowledge, however, that although the focus here is on girls' comments, these comments were usually made in the presence of boys and sometimes in response to boys' comments (which are also included where present). [. . .]

Critical Engagements with Appropriate Dress

Many participants were critical of certain features of their dress codes that focused on appropriate dress, their application, and fellow participants' defence of them. They also narrated instances when their critique resulted in comments to school staff or openly resistant actions, including rule breaking (Raby & Domitrek, 2007). Together these engagements suggest that these young women held detailed knowledge of the rules, keenly observed their application, and were sufficiently concerned about injustices that they were sometimes willing to act on them.

All participants demonstrated extensive awareness of what the specific school rules were. Girls, in particular, were acutely aware of the fine details of the dress codes. In response to these rules, they were frequently inclined to debate the rules' exact details, rather than accepting or rejecting them altogether.

I:	And the spaghetti strap thing too, you think, you should be able to wear tank tops?
Barb:	Well maybe not spaghetti straps but like /
Betty:	Yeah, that's kinda acceptable.
Emilia:	Yeah, like a one-finger [strap] sort of thing, not like some little thing you can snap off [chuckling and agreement from group].
Betty:	It's not a big deal. (Focus Group 4)[1]

Such comments illustrated the importance of dress details and that the girls recognized a fine line between acceptable and unacceptable clothing. When critical of these details, the girls most commonly referred to practical needs and occasionally to self-expression.

Practical needs, based on temperature or efficient negotiation of the day, came up frequently to criticize many school rules, though this strategy may have hidden other, unspoken intentions behind revealing dress. Notably, girls commonly referenced practicality by arguing that tank tops, spaghetti straps, short skirts, and muscle shirts should be acceptable when it is hot out rather than mentioning a desire to look good, to be sexy, or to experience pleasure in dress. Extending this emphasis on practicality, some participants also suggested that rules against revealing dress, and their enforcement, unfairly target girls.

Catherine:	That's like, the spaghetti strap rule is like kind of unfortunate because it's like, for boys it's not a problem, and it's just like, 'Sorry I am a female like and it's hot and I would like to wear a spaghetti strap tank top', but it's like 'No, no you must not expose skin', which is kind of ridiculous 'cause /
Janice:	You are not even showing anything, just your arm [laughs].
Catherine:	Yeah, you're really not; it is just your body; it's like 'Oh no the human body!' (Focus Group 1)

Although Catherine and Janice quite typically drew on practical bodily need (being warm) and the naturalized human body to explain their dress choices, they also used humour to point out both the gendered nature of such rules and institutional discomfort with bodies.

[. . .]

Participants similarly criticized boys for seeming to prefer to go out with girls who wear sleazy clothes and the fashion industry for shaping girls' dress. For example, Patricia (Focus Group 1) stated, 'But you know what's really wrong though, that all the girls' clothes are made

to be a slut', and others in Focus Group 4 were critical of the adoration of fashion star Paris Hilton. In Focus Group 3, the students critically evaluated concerns with provocative clothing by recognizing that cultural norms are contextual:

I:	Why is it a problem to see underwear or thongs or pubic hair or whatever?
Carrie:	It's different in different parts of the world, but like in Canada it's considered indecent, I dunno why. In Europe, it's not like . . . 'bad'. [Talking over each other] there's porn advertised on the lampposts!
//	
Tina:	Yeah, I dunno what it is I think if everyone just kinda goes 'I don't want to see that'. Like a kinda collective thing. (Focus Group 3)

In these examples, we see the participants identifying and criticizing broader cultural patterns that extend beyond the specific school rules and yet impact on questions of dress. They make sense of multiple registers of culture.

[. . .]

There were also a number of instances in which their critique was linked to action. Participants in Focus Group 1 resisted the rules through breaking them, for instance, by wearing short shirts or bandanas and hoping that the principal would not see them. Girls in Focus Group 5 not only noticed that a bigger girl was more likely to find her dress regulated but also were openly critical with administration to address such hypocrisy. Occasionally, there is even evidence of more overt resistance, though notably the following example involves boys' dress.[2] In the lesbian, gay, bisexual, transgender, two-spirited, and queer and questioning

(LGBTQ) focus group, participants discussed an occasion when a boy was suspended for wearing a skirt to school. In this school, which is well-known for its arts programs, a number of boys came to the school wearing skirts in response. Allison recognized this as a form of solidarity and resistance:

> So I mean a lot of the students will stick together. They're like 'hey, wait a second, something's not right' you know. And they do good things like that, where they're like 'hey, let's do something about it'. (Focus Group 8)

More individually, Nicole (Focus Group 3) unsuccessfully challenged her administration when she was asked to change her home-made, shredded outfit on the basis that it was not revealing, and Sammie (Focus Group 7) successfully fought back on religious grounds when her principal asked her to remove her head scarf. None of these forms of challenge were about the acceptability of revealing dress in itself, however. Indeed, on this question these young women were quite conservative.

Reproduction and the Location of Self

[. . .]

The language of the dress codes in themselves (Raby, 2005), sex education curricula (van Vliet & Raby, 2008), some elements of popular media (Levy, 2005), and parents and teachers (Chambers et al., 2004; Renold, 2005) all reinforce the language of respectability and reputation. Many comments within the focus groups reflect such popular talk and anxiety about young women's provocative dress. Even dress codes themselves produce reference points for students in their regulation of other girls' dress.

An example of this arises in girls' use of the language of self-respect.

I: What does that mean, 'something degrading to themselves'?
Crystal: Uh, whorish.
[Laughing]
Allison: Basically, 'I have no self-respect, I'm going to flaunt myself in the hope of feeling loved'. (Focus Group 1)
**
Liz: You don't respect yourself then you're not respecting anyone else. (Focus Group 6)

Liz's statement, in particular, is an almost verbatim reproduction of local, institutional language of dress codes, which commonly refer to self-respect. Through the language of self-respect, schools participate directly in the production of both gendered and sexualized identities. This emphasis on self-respect disciplines and individualizes bodies. Thus, if students who wear provocative dress are considered to lack self-respect, then responsibility for their marginalization is their own, rather than located in the social control of female sexuality or slut-bashing from others. These young women in turn reproduce such wider structures in their own commentaries, suggesting merit to the literature that suggests that girls are socialized into patriarchy. Several groups also cited the importance of appropriate dress in an educational environment and the preparation of students for future work, explanations cited within codes of conduct.

Barbara: Why would you need to attract that kind of attention at school? I mean like who—like who are you there to impress when you're there for, like . . . education? (Focus Group 4)

In this sense, schools participate directly in the production of both gendered and sexualized identities (Kehily, 2004).

As well as embracing the language of the rules, the girls frequently embraced their sentiment. Despite disputes with minor dress code details, most group participants at some point lamented girls' revealing dress.

Nicole: For me it's disturbing. Like 'great, you're wearing a thong, show it to your boyfriend, show it to someone who cares'. (Focus Group 3)

**

Janice: But if you are walking around with a tank top that just covers your boobs then, you know you should probably put a [sweater] on [everyone laughs]. I would kind of be disgusted if I saw you [Marc says 'yeah'] and probably make fun of you behind your back. (Focus Group 1)

Dress codes were valued for the very reason that they regulate girls' clothing and bodily exposure. During analysis, these moments stood out as frequently quite hostile toward girls who were seen to wear revealing clothing. In five different groups, such hostility was evident through the choices of language: certain clothing was described as whorish, slutty, disgusting, disturbing, and wrong. Such sleaziness was explained as resulting from girls' desires to get boyfriends, their attempts to be cool and trendy, and their fashion incompetence. These comments also extended beyond the school:

[In reaction to a girl wearing a very short skirt on Canada Day]

Catherine: I thought it was a belt—I like literally shouted out 'whoa, whoa'.

Janice: But she left and changed, she went back home and changed 'cause everyone was waiting for her to come out. (Focus Group 1)

Despite such peer regulation, many focus-group participants felt the need for formal dress codes, to not only control the behaviour of other girls but also to help young women avoid either sexual or peer harassment:

Bee: 'Cause [the rules are] preventing that.
I: Preventing what?
Bee: They're trying to keep you safe.
//

Liz: What it is, is that, if you wear something like, ok well, if she's wearing something and her boobs are showing, other girls are gonna be calling her names like a slut or a whore. (Focus Group 6)

Overall, girls' dress was dominantly framed by these participants as individually problematic and inviting harassment.

As illustrated, these young women participate, sometimes quite wholeheartedly, in regulating dress: They seemed eager to discuss the dress codes, to frequently concur with the spirit of them, and to even enjoy criticizing other girls' revealing dress choices. Although this section is framed around the girls' acceptance of the rules and their reproduction of a narrow regulation of other girls' clothing, it is not intended to suggest that these girls passively reproduce a patriarchal framework.
[. . .]

From this position, girls draw on regulating, gendered discourses not only to jockey for power but also to define themselves and to indicate their skill in recognizing the safe side of the fine line between attractive and unacceptable. Indeed, these conversations seemed to include a degree of pleasure in this recognition. In these conversations, the girls could show their skill in deploying gendered discourses to locate themselves and 'displace practices that do not concur with their collectively defined femininity' (Kehily, 2004, p. 209). Nicole (Focus Group 3), for example, supported her own reputation with her peers and the researcher after criticizing the details of school dress codes by making it clear that she is not saying that anything goes: 'Oh man, on dress codes I just totally thought of this example. I actually think I have to agree now there should be some sort of dress code.' She proceeded to provide examples of a girl exposing a thong and another wearing extremely low-riding pants. Othering secures belonging (Hey, 1997), particularly within a context of fear, for example, of failing in the face of a challenging bodily standard, or of erring oneself on the side of revealing too much. Othering is thus one strategy (among others) to illustrate one's own social, gender, and fashion competence. If we consider young people's construction of self in peer groups and we recognize that this construction is related to that of others (Tanenbaum, 1999), then positioning other girls as sluts helps to prevent the label from being attached to themselves. One other focus group moment hit home this othering process. In Focus Group 4, several girls talked about rules which they follow:

Marjory: I don't wear, like, skanky clothing or . . . I wear appropriate clothing.

Betty: I follow the dress code, but that's just the way I dress, so it's not like I'm doing it intentionally or anything.

Marjory defines her own dress as appropriate in contrast to skanky clothing, thus defining herself as normal. Betty gestures toward the familiarity of a habitus that matches her school's.

Emphasis on a forced gaze was a recurring othering strategy evident in these focus groups. In their evaluation of other girls' revealing dress, respondents commented that they felt that there was nowhere else to look:

Marjory: I like the dress code ones' a lot' cause I don't appreciate the girls wearing like . . . [group agreeing] the midriff and the thong. I don't like seeing that. (Focus Group 4)

**

Lana: I don't feel like staring at someone's butt. (Focus Group 4)

**

Nicole: This girl that was in my tech class in Grade 9. We all sat on stools and she'd sit in front of me and she'd pull her thong out of her pants, so you could see it when she sat down. I'm just like [look of surprise]. And then I'd ask her 'could you not do that', and she's like 'look somewhere else!' It's like 'where else do you look?' [chuckles] There! (Focus Group 3)

These findings suggest that bodily displays are meant for someone else, specifically boys (who are consequently distracted). This positioning locates the speaker as straight, as invested in the regulation of displays of femininity and the female body and as focused on other things, including school. Orenstein (1994) argued that as girls come of age they learn to suppress their sexuality and convert it into disgust, projecting that disgust onto others.

Certainly, my focus-group participants expressed disgust and similarly divided themselves from others, in this case in response to quite specific performances of gender and sexuality through clothing. This response can be interpreted as an illustration of gender performance and self-constitution, as well as the perpetuation of gender inequality (Brown, 2003; Hey, 1997).

Girls' regulation of other girls' self-presentations was most evident in their use of terms such as slut and 'whorish'. Such regulation reproduces gender inequalities by narrowing ideas of acceptable female sexuality and policing anything considered excess. Such comment may also reflect more complex meanings than direct peer gender regulation, however, when we account for the multiple uses of terms such as slut or slag (Kitzinger, 1995).

[. . .]

Some researchers suggest that such a powerful sexuality is being embraced when girls dress provocatively (White, 2002) or enjoy the freedom, challenge, and/or individuality that can come with embracing the term slut (Tanenbaum, 1999). We have seen that a few comments from the girls come close to this position, Allison's temporary celebration of a miniskirt or Nicole's reference to individuality and freedom of expression, but these are at the same time undermined through discourses of self-respect and chaste femininity or hidden behind discourses of practicality. Levy (2005) suggested that the power of provocative dress is an empty form of power as it fulfills a consumerist and patriarchal script; yet, such an analysis continues to problematize

girls' and women's bodies and choices (Duits & van Zoonen, 2006). Kitzinger's (1995) typology complicates our understanding of the word slag, suggesting that it is sometimes used as a substitute for talk about gendered inequalities and reminding us that provocative dress can have multiple meanings, including ones associated with power. What seems most evident in these focus groups, however, is a missing discourse of desire (Tolman, 2002) where there is little if any room for girls to openly speak of themselves as sexual beings.

Discussion

There are several analytic points arising from this investigation that I wish to emphasize. The first is to foreground the challenging fine line girls negotiate between what is acceptable, expected, and attractive and what is seen to go too far. This distinction is a challenge because it is constantly in flux, based on specific contexts, changing fashions, girls' own changing ages, and definitions of taste that vary by culture and class. It is also a challenge because the stakes are so high. Being considered attractive and desirable can bring a girl popularity and acceptance, whereas being considered overly sexual or sleazy can bring hostility and ostracism (Tanenbaum, 1999). These findings belie Levy's (2005) argument that girls are currently embracing raunch culture and instead resonate with arguments that suggest that a sexual double standard remains and that girls risk their reputations with each other, with boys, and even with school staff when they err on the side of being too revealing. It is telling that as part of the girls' need to position themselves as safely acceptable, girls' desire seems largely absent, despite these girls' direct attacks on blatant sexism from both teachers and peers.

Furthermore, to most of these students, normative gender and heterosexuality were reproduced and considered mutually consti-tutive, both when critiquing and supporting the rules; being feminine is about attraction to boys, and masculine boys are attracted to girls. Boys and girls wear different kinds of clothing and it is, for the most part, girls' clothing that is problematic for being revealing and distracting. Interestingly, the sexual nature of the clothing per se received less comment, either positive or negative, than concern with what was revealed and how such exposure affects others. Many par-ticipants were uncomfortable with girls' sexual bodies or exposed flesh within the classroom. For the most part, boys' (hetero)sexuality was only relevant when respondents were concerned that boys were distracted by girls' provocative clothing, a position holding girls responsible for boys' sexual desires (Duits & van Zoonen, 2006).

Finally, these processes are not clear-cut. These young women reproduced sexual double standards but also challenged them. Like adults, they were frequently contradictory in their com-ments. Certain forms of sexism were condemned and yet sexism was accepted and reproduced. Skimpy clothing was contextualized and explained, and yet certain girls were deemed sleazy. There was some attempt to discuss boys' presentation of self and regulation of dress, but for the most part, boys could not also be sluts. Clearly, challenges are at the same time repro-ductive of the status quo. It is therefore difficult to describe these girls as merely reproducing the patriarchal structures that surround them, nor as easily embracing their own sexual agency.

Conclusion

[. . .]

Some limitations to this research indicate future avenues to pursue. Although focus groups pro-vide an excellent forum for learning about public talk and meaning-making among peers, they do not capture more private views (Mitchell, 1999). Although respondents had the opportunity to provide private written comments, individual interviews may have allowed for more confi-dential material to arise. Similarly, a study more directly concentrated on the topic of dress codes, rather than school rules in general, would pro-vide for more detailed discussion and consequent analysis. For example, a robust analysis of dress codes ideally addresses intersections of class and race, yet neither was sufficiently addressed in the focus groups to warrant conclusions.

Class is arguably an important factor within the regulation of girls' dress. This variable has been examined within school rules (Raby, 2005) and between girls (Hey, 1997; McRobbie, 1978), with slut seen as more likely to be applied to working-class girls (Tanenbaum, 1999). Victor (2004) discussed the racist and classist over-tones of the term slut as it is used by lower-class American teenage girls as a sweeping term used to denigrate others. Robinson (1992) similarly found that Australian teachers felt that accept-able behaviour for young women 'stemmed from middle class values that had little relevance for girls from working-class backgrounds' (p. 81). Working-class girls' challenge to the image of a good girl was seen by the teachers as problematic. Unfortunately, although some potential class dif-ferences between focus groups and participants were evident within my data, available informa-tion was not sufficient for a conclusive analysis. Furthermore, class arose rarely in participants' comments. Some clothes were described as trashy, and class was thought to affect fashion:

Betty: Well [girls who wear skimpy clothes] just don't get that not all fashions are good. [Yeahs from group.] You know, there's a rea-son only rich people can afford these things. (Focus Group 4)

Another respondent felt that uniforms would prevent wealthier students from harassing poorer ones. These comments suggest that working-class girls are more vulnerable to such challenges to reputation, underscoring the need for more research.

Similarly, these focus groups produced little on culture and race. In the United States, Victor (2004) and White (2002) found that white girls were called sluts if they had sex with black men. In an ethnographic study of girls in Vancouver, Pomerantz (2006) noted that hoochie was a racialized replacement for skank (aka slut) in reference to Hispanic girls. Yet, White (2002) argued that the condemnation of sluts does not occur in the same way within groups of Black or Latino girls where girlfriends do not abandon friends who are labelled sluts, and there is more room to talk about liking sex. Allusions to race occasionally arose in my almost-entirely-white focus groups when discussing the 'stupid' style of boys wearing baggy pants, a style associated with hip-hop and skater cultures. Focus Group 3 discussed cultural differences. Yet, other than this there was silence. Interestingly, one of the groups that was least inclined to discuss and denigrate girls' revealing dress was the group of new immigrant youth.

The importance of age also requires further study. In research on younger girls, this fine line between attractive and sleazy is evident, although it seems to be negotiated a little differently. In Renold's (2005) study of junior school girls, she found the girls to be much more open about their desire to look sexy, and even tarty, although they recognized that one doesn't want to look too tarty. Within my focus groups, age was raised in two groups, with the suggestion that it is in middle school that there is more pressure to dress provocatively to be cool, whereas it is in the older grades of secondary school that those who dress provocatively are criticized.

Others' work on girls' policing of each others' reputations has argued that interventions need to occur. Tanenbaum (1999) contended that young women need positive, supportive spaces for females to address common issues. She believed that such an opportunity would dissipate the intensity of competition and slut policing. Hird and Jackson (2001) argued that young women and men need access to feminist discourses rather than trying to deal with these issues with an insufficient, individualized vocabulary. Kitzinger (1995) also noted the need for a vocabulary beyond slut or slag to talk about reputation, exploitation, and sexuality. Finally, Tolman (2002) argued that we need to recognize girls as desiring subjects.

[. . .] Ultimately, of course, much wider change is needed to imagine a society wherein girls' sexuality is acceptable, where girls are able to negotiate sexual and gender relations from a location of power, and where the deep, normative, gendered inequalities that we see reflected in the data for this article are displaced.

Notes

1. The transcription code '/' indicates interruption by the next speaker.

2. There were also a few instances of overt homophobia. For example, it was mockingly suggested in Focus Group 6 that any boy wearing tight clothing must be gay.

References

Baxter, J. (2002). A juggling act: A feminist post-structural analysis of girls' and boys' talk in the secondary classroom. *Gender and Education*, 14, 5–19.

Bettis, P.J., & Adams, N.G. (2003). The power of the preps and a cheerleading equity policy. *Sociology of Education*, 76, 128–42.

Brown, L.M. (2003). *Girl-fighting: Betrayal and rejection among girls*. New York: New York University Press.

Butler, J. (1990). *Gender trouble: Feminism and the subversion of identity*. New York: Routledge.

———. (2004). *Undoing gender*. New York: Routledge.

Chambers, D., van Loon, J., & Tincknell, E. (2004). Teachers' views of teenage sexual morality. *British Journal of Sociology of Education*, 25, 563–76.

Christensen, P., & Prout, A. (2005). Anthropological and sociological perspectives on the study of children. In S. Greene & D. Hogan (Eds), *Researching children's experience: Methods and approaches* (pp. 42–60). London: Sage.

Davies, B. (1989). *Frogs and snails and feminist tales: Preschool children and gender*. Sydney, Australia: Allen and Unwin.

Duits, L., & van Zoonen, L. (2006). Disciplining girls' bodies in the European multicultural society. *European Journal of Women's Studies*, 13, 103–17.

Hey, V. (1997). *Company she keeps: An ethnography of girls friendships*. Buckingham, UK: Open University Press.

Hird, M.J., & Jackson, S. (2001). Where 'angels' and 'wusses' fear to tread: Sexual coercion in adolescent dating relationships. *Journal of Sociology*, 37, 27–43.

James, A., & Prout, A. (1990). *Constructing and reconstructing childhood: Contemporary issues in the sociological study of childhood*. Bassingstoke, UK: Falmer Press.

Kehily, M.J. (2004). Gender and sexuality: Continuities and change for girls in school. In A. Harris (Ed.), *All about the girl: Culture, power and identity* (pp. 205–18). New York: Routledge.

Kitzinger, J. (1995). 'I'm sexually attractive but I'm powerful': Young women negotiating sexual reputation. *Women's Studies International Forum*, 18, 187–96.

Kitzinger, J., & Barbour, R.S. (1999), Introduction: The challenge and promise of focus groups. In R.S. Barbour & J. Kitzinger (Eds.), *Developing focus group research: Politics, theory and practice* (pp. 1–20). London: Sage.

Levy, A. (2005). *Female chauvinist pigs: Women and the rise of raunch culture*. New York: Free Press.

McRobbie, A. (1978). Working class girls and the culture of feminism. In C.C.S. Women's Studies Group (Ed.), *Women take issue: Aspects of women's subordination* (pp. 96–108). London: Hutchinson.

Mitchell, L. (1999). Combining focus groups and interviews: Telling how it is; telling how it feels. In R.S. Barbour & J. Kitzinger (Eds), *Developing focus group research: Politics, theory and practice* (pp. 36–46), London: Sage.

Orenstein, P. (1994). *School girls: Young women, self-esteem, and the confidence gap*. New York: Anchor Books.

Pomerantz, S. (2006). 'Did you see what she was wearing?' The power and politics of schoolgirl style. In Y. Jiwani, C. Mitchell & C. Steenbergen (Eds), *Girlhood: Redefining the limits* (pp. 173–90), Montreal, Quebec, Canada: Black Rose Books.

———. (2007). Cleavage in a tank top: Bodily prohibition and the discourses of school dress codes. *Alberta Journal of Educational Research*, 53, 373–86.

Raby, R. (2005). Polite, well-dressed and on time: Secondary school conduct codes and the production of docile citizens. *Canadian Review of Sociology and Anthropology*, 42, 71–92.

Raby, R., & Domitrek, J. (2007). Slippery as fish, but already caught? Secondary students' engagement with school rules. *Canadian Journal of Education*, 30, 931–58.

Reay, D. (2001). 'Spice girls', 'nice girls', 'girlies', and 'tomboys': Gender discourses, girls' cultures and femininities in the primary classroom. *Gender and Education*, 13, 153–66.

Renold, E. (2005), *Girls, boys and junior sexualities: Exploring children's gender and sexual relations in the primary school*. London: Routledge-Falmer.

Robinson, K.H. (1992). Class-room discipline: Power, resistance and gender. A look at teacher perspectives, *Gender & Education*, 4(3), 273–88.

Russel, R., & Tyler, M. (2002). Thank heaven for little girls: 'girl heaven' and the commercial context of feminine childhood. *Sociology*, 36, 619–37.

Shalit, W. (2007). *Girls gone mild: Young women reclaim self-respect and find it's not bad to be good*. New York: Random House.

Tanenbaum, L. (1999). *Sluts! Growing up female with a bad reputation*. New York: Seven Stories Press.

Tarrant, S. (2008). The great cover-up: Can high necklines cure low morals? *Bitch Magazine*, 38, 60–65.

Tolman, D. (2002). *Dilemmas of desire*. London: Harvard University Press.

van Vliet, J., & Raby, R. (2008). Too little, too late: The right to comprehensive sexual health education in childhood and adolescence, In T. O'Neill & D. Zinga (Eds), *Children's rights: Theories, policies and interventions* (pp. 245–70). Toronto, ON: University of Toronto Press,

Victor, J. (2004). Sluts and wiggers: A study of the effects of derogatory labeling. *Deviant Behaviour*, 25, 67–85.

White, E. (2002). *Fast girls: Teenage tribes and the myth of the slut*. New York: Scribner.

Reconsidering the Socio-Scientific Enterprise of Sexual Difference: The Case of Kimberly Nixon

Ajnesh Prasad

When I first viewed *Boys Don't Cry* (1999), I was struck by conflicting sentiments. On the one hand, I lauded the fact that issues pertaining to the experiences of a particular sexual minority group were finally making their way into popular culture. Hillary Swank's portrayal of the life, rape, and murder of Brandon Teena, vividly illustrated the lived reality of a female-to-male trans man. On the other hand, I could not help but ponder what impact Teena's legacy would have—and perhaps, more importantly, should have—on feminist and queer theorizing. At the crux of my inquiry rested the question: Was Brandon Teena reifying or transcending the male/female binary?

In this paper, I use the Kimberly Nixon case to consider the impact transsexuals have on the conventional socio-sexual paradigm. Nixon was prohibited from working at the Vancouver Rape Relief Centre—a women's only organization—after it was made known that she is a male-to-female trans woman. As a result, there was a complaint lodged with the British Columbia Human Rights Tribunal (BCHRT), and two judicial cases were taken before the provincial court. Central to each of these proceedings was the question of the corporeal ontology of MTF transsexuals.

This analysis is primarily rooted in understanding that 'sex' and 'sex differences' have been intricately constructed through science *and other* cultural discourses. I provide a brief but critical account of how sex differences have been construed since the Enlightenment. Thereafter, I use the Nixon case to elucidate the fallaciousness of the nature/culture and male/female binaries and rethink the culturally marked, scientifically pre-scribed ideology of sexual difference.

Constructing Sexual Difference

Since the Enlightenment, social relations in the West have pivoted on a paradigm of sex dichotomy (Laqueur, 1990). Cohesive with liberal democratic theory and dictated by modern science (Schiebinger, 1989: 244), sex dichotomy has become crystallized in language and pervades every institution signified by human authority. Its ideological fixation has proved so hegemonic that sexual difference is commonly experienced as part of ontology rather than epistemology, as part of nature instead of culture. Even many prominent feminist scholars have relied upon the two-sex model to endorse the project for gender egalitarianism (Firestone, 1970; Chodorow, 1978; Gilligan, 1982; Dworkin, 1981; MacKinnon, 1987).

The sex dichotomy hinges on laws of gender, which have been succinctly abridged by Harold Garfinkel in his 1967 seminal text *Studies in Ethnomethodology*. These laws conclude that:

1. There are two genders, and everyone is/has one.

2. Gender is lifelong, invariant, and unchangeable.

3. Exceptions to two genders are jokes or abnormalities.

4. Genitals (penis, vagina) are the essential sign of gender.

5. The categories are created by nature, and membership in a gender category is assigned by nature.

In short, Garfinkel concludes that sex dimorphism is dictated by the presumption of genitalia; often understood to be immutable, stable, and above all 'pre-social'. Indeed, since the mid-eighteenth century Western civilization has been witness to an epistemic shift; a transition from the understanding that all individuals are 'positioned on a single axis of "sex"' (Hird, 2004: 18) to the rigid inference that two distinct sexes produce two essentialized genders. This epistemic shift, undergirded in the *natural* sciences, negated the question of cultural agency in creating categories of 'male' and 'female'.

During this period there was a socio-political agenda supported by Cartesian and other classical liberal values which actively discredited previous appreciation for the one-sex continuum, denied alternative assertions for sex diversity, and strategically brought into mainstream focus what one scholar refers to as 'The Triumph of Complementarity' (Schiebinger, 1989: 214–44). Refuting the one-sex model of the human body that existed from antiquity to the Enlightenment was quintessential in cultivating a rationale that permitted, if not encouraged, the subordination of women while remaining consistent to the emerging creed of universal, inalienable, and equal rights (Shilling, 1993: 44). In other words, providing scientific explanations for sex differences rooted in the natural world effectively eschewed demands for the rectification of social, political, and economic injustices that emanated from being female without 'self-constitution' (Scheman, 1997: 350).

Moreover, the ontology of sex post-Enlightenment became a segment of a much broader endeavour. It relied on transcendental reason of the monadic subject to demarcate categorical truths from corporeal experiences.[1] Within this schema, science became posited into the privileged realm of nature, severed from cultural variables of subjectivity, interpretation, and nuance, and ultimately became mystified as the repository possessing factual answers to all questions human. Those who challenged science, and in this case ontological sex, were either dismissed, labelled 'uppity', or persecuted.

In recent years, academics from within and outside the feminist community have attempted to configure how and why we understand sex and the sex dichotomy. Historians Londa Schiebinger (1989) and Thomas Laqueur (1990) each provide a genealogy of sex construction in the past few centuries. Anthropologist Emily Martin (1991) examines the reification of orthodox gender roles in research concerning the sperm and the egg, and sociologist Alan Petersen (1998) cites how sex differences are perpetuated in a seminal anatomy text. What is amplified by each of these scholars is the idea that the scientific understanding of sex differences is a corollary not of the Archimedean model of disembodied knowledge but rather of specific cultural manifestations. As such, the corporeal can never be defined solely within the domain of nature, as even nature's very parameters—that is, what constitutes nature—have been circumscribed by cultural precepts.

This analysis shares an intricate nexus with power, righteousness, and the politics of imperialism. Several post-colonial theorists, including Edward Said (1978), have noted the methodical and, at times, discursive registers through which the racialized Other is produced at the interface of sexuality discourses. Ann Stoler (2002) has taken this examination further in her critique of Foucault. Borrowing from the thesis-claim put forth by Anne McClintock (1995), among others, Stoler describes how during Western imperialism the governance of sexual relations was central in classifying the colonizer and the colonized into spheres of 'distinct human kinds while policing the domestic recesses of imperial rule' (145). This move was both strategic and calculated, and resulted in two occurrences worth mentioning here. Positioning the colonizer and the colonized into *distinct human kinds* on the one hand engendered 'corporeal malediction' (Fanon, 2000: 258) on the psyche of latter, and on the other hand, played a seminal role in implementing colonial policies through the logistical enactment of the discourse, 'white men saving brown women from brown men' (Spivak, 1988: 296). In short, the intersection between the enabling paradigms of racism and sexuality that underlies the imperialist project, manifested as a crucial technology of colonial rule (Stoler, 2002; Yuval-Davis, 1997).

During the eighteenth and nineteenth centuries, distinguishing one race of individuals from another—which would serve as the justification for imperialist conquest—was supported by *evidence* from scientific disciplines. This evidence, however, was encumbered by the fact that naturalists were unable to develop a universal criterion from which to categorize races into neat taxonomies. As John Haller Jr, explains,

> [t]o visually identify differences is one thing, but to determine a method for measurement and an index for tracing affinities among various races is far more vexatious undertaking. (1971: 3)

By the nineteenth century, anatomic measurement emerged as the preferential, albeit, essentialist source for the study of racial difference—interestingly, analogous physical traits were employed to champion the case for sexual difference.

Since the decolonization and civil rights movement, many of the premises of racial difference have been debunked. Indeed, it has been commonly accepted that '[s]tudies which purport to demonstrate the genetic basis for this or that behavioural characteristic observed among persons who make up popularly defined races are essentially non-scientific and should be labelled as such' (Marshall, 1993: 125). While racial difference has been adamantly repudiated, and the nexus between ontology and race similarly dismantled, differences relating to sex have unfortunately only gone reinforced.

This is perhaps because, in addition to being derivative of epistemological and political transformations, sexual difference is functional to the socio-sexual paradigm of heteronormativity. As one scholar notes, '[h]eteronormativity, the hegemonic discursive and non-discursive normative idealization of heterosexuality, played a leading role in establishing and then maintaining sex complementarity' (Hird, 2004: 27). It is precisely heteronormativity and its institutionalization through patriarchal marriage that sustains dominant ideals of 'family values', which privileges and vigorously demands for 'two biological parents' with a 'stable relationship to male authority' (Stacey, 1996: 69). Within this framework, often described as the 'sexual contract' (Pateman, 1988), sex differences are reproduced whereby men and women *naturally* undertake distinct, however, complementary roles. Women are relegated to the private economy fulfilling domestic responsibilities, while men occupy the public sphere where decisions of popular morality, social norms, and public policy are debated and subsequently validated.

For sex complementarity—and thus, heteronormativity, family values and the patriarchal marriage—to stay intact, two strict equations that conflate biological sex with cultural gender must be maintained. These equations are structured by the laws of gender described earlier and pivot on genital determinism. They can be read as follows:

Penis $\rightarrow$ Male $\rightarrow$ Masculinity

Vagina $\rightarrow$ Female $\rightarrow$ Femininity

Sex complementarity's stability is inherently dependent on society's adherence to these equations; divergence from them is, as a result, portrayed as aberration. What requires acknowledgement here is that resistance to these equations in fact poses substantial challenges to the entire scientific enterprise that attempts to decipher and instill sex differences. Indeed, such challenges vividly disclose that 'bodies are not static slaves to their biology' (Fausto-Sterling, 2004: 31). Kimberly Nixon, a transsexual woman, is central to this resistance campaign.

Contextualizing Kimberly Nixon

Kimberly Nixon was born a biologically read male in 1957. At an early age, it was clear to Nixon that her gender identity was not congruent with her *naturally* assigned genitalia. After years of living as a woman, in 1990 Nixon underwent sex reassignment surgery, and had her birth certificate altered to indicate her sex as being female.

In 1995, Nixon began training as a peer counsellor at the Vancouver Rape Relief Centre—a non-profit organization that provides services to women who encounter male violence. While attending a training session, Nixon acknowledged that she was a post-operative transsexual woman. On the spot, a representative at the centre terminated Nixon's training, concluding that Nixon had not always been a woman, and thus, had not been subject to those experiences—presumed monolithic—associated with being a woman. Nixon, subsequently, retained the services of barbara findlay, a legal and gay rights advocate, and filed a complaint with the BCHRT. In 2000, prior to the BCHRT releasing its decision, the rape centre went to provincial court—*Vancouver Rape Relief v. B.C. Human Rights*—in an attempt to eschew the tribunal's authority. The case was ultimately dismissed. Two years later, the BCHRT ordered the rape centre to compensate Nixon $7500 for injury to her dignity. In response, the rape centre filed a second case. In *Vancouver Rape Relief Society v. Nixon et al.*, the rape centre made a successful petition to overturn the verdict of the BCHRT (findlay, 2003; Boyle, 2004).

Both cases initiated by the rape centre, invoked notions of ontological sexual difference. They contended that being born with male genitalia involuntarily consigned Nixon to certain privileges and experiences not delineated to those individuals born female. They failed to consider how identification with the opposite gender may have precluded Nixon from taking advantage of privileges designed to benefit men. In short, by denying a transitioned transsexual woman from working at their institution, the rape centre's argument relied upon socio-scientific knowledge concerning sex articulated in the post-Enlightenment, which renders innate differences between males and females.

Nixon's Implications

Why is it important for feminists to scrutinize the Nixon case? What value, if any, does it hold for feminist theory and practice?

Nixon's legal claim affectively 'denaturalize[s] and resignifie[s] bodily categories' (Butler, 1990: xii). It challenges the core of the traditional socio-scientific understanding of sex, as described by Garfinkel. Some may argue that by undergoing sex reassignment surgery, Nixon simply moved from one end of the sex continuum to the other, thereby fortifying it. However, by attesting that her gender identity did not reflect her genitalia, Nixon refutes biological determinism and provokes disorder and anxiety to a cultural ideology that is reliant so heavily on a priori scientific and metaphysical claims. She exemplifies that *natural* genitalia do not have ontological meaning. Accordingly, Nixon becomes part of the feminist revolution, resisting masculinity and patriarchy, while simultaneously embodying 'a subject of differentiation—of sexual contradictions' (Krisreva qtd. in Hekman, 1991: 56).

In other words, Nixon affirms the claim that the scientific production of knowledge is congenitally affixed to the regulatory measures defined by cultural forces. Science, although it purports to do otherwise, cannot think or act outside of culture (Schiebinger, 1999). The dichotomies that science fabricates—nature/culture, male/female—are each part of a more conceptual political project that sustains the subordination of women through their relegation into devalued social spheres.

Science asserts that the dichotomies it supports are salient and pre-social. Nixon as a post-operative transsexual woman belies this claim. Her body, like other classified human aberrations, becomes the site of ambiguity for science. For this reason, when transsexuality was becoming more widely acknowledged in the modern West, the medical establishment rushed to discover its causes (Brown and

Rounsley, 1996: 22). After several endeavours to understand this condition, the psychiatry discipline entered transsexuality as a psychosexual disorder into the *Diagnostic Statistical Manual III* (Whittle, 1996: 197).

Patricia Elliot (2004) examines how the Kimberly Nixon case has divided members of the Canadian feminist community. From Elliot's argument, it is apparent that what has been neglected from feminist debate concerning this case is substantive dialogue on how science has created our understanding of what it means to be a woman, or man. If sex is a cultural manifestation, and the nature/culture binary is likewise a myth, then there is definitely great potential for alliance between trans and non-trans feminists. At a minimum, Nixon uses jurisprudence to illustrate the need for feminist scholars to engage with and critique the hard sciences, and reconsider their position on exclusion.

Note

1. During this period it was deemed that unlike men, women lacked the faculties to ascertain transcendental reason because '[t]he conditions of women's embodiment were ruled by natural cycles associated with pregnancy, childbirth and menstruation' (Shilling, 1993: 43).

References

Boyle, Christine. 'The Anti-Discrimination Norm in Human Rights and *Charter* Law: *Nixon v. Vancouver Rape Relief*'. *The University of British Columbia Law Review* 37(1) (2004): 31–72.

Brown, Mildred L. and Chloe A. Rounsley. *True Selves: Understanding Transsexualism—For Families, Friends, Coworkers, and Helping Professionals*. San Francisco: Jossey-Bass Publishers. 1996.

Butler, Judith. *Gender Troubles: Gender and the Subversion of Identity*. London: Routledge, 1990.

Chodorow, Nancy J. *The Reproduction of Mothering: Psychoanalysis and the Sociology of Gender*. Berkeley: University of California Press, 1978.

Dworkin, Andrea. *Pornography: Men Possessing Women*. New York: Perigee, 1981.

Elliot, Patricia. 'Who Gets to Be Woman? Feminist Politics and the Question of Trans-inclusion'. *Atlantis: A Women's Studies Journal* 29(1) (2004): 13–20.

Fanon, Frantz. 'The Facts of Blackness'. *Theories of Race and Racism: A Reader*. Eds Les Back and John Solomos. New York: Routledge, 2000. 257–66.

Fausto-Sterling, Anne. 'Refashioning Race: DNA and the Policies of Health Care'. *Differences: A Journal of Feminist Cultural Studies* 15(3) (2004): 1–37.

findlay, barbara. 'Real Women: *Kimberly Nixon v. Vancouver Rape Relief*'. The University of British Columbia Law Review 36(1) (2003): 57–76.

Firestone, Shulasmith. *The Dialectic of Sex: The Case of Feminist Revolution*. London: J. Cape, 1970.

Garfinkel, Harold. *Studies in Ethnomethodology*. Cambridge: Polity Press, 1967.

Gilligan, Carol. *In a Different Voice: Psychological Theory and Women's Development*. Cambridge: Harvard University Press, 1982.

Haller, John S. Jr. *Outcasts from Evolution: Scientific Attitudes of Racial Inferiority, 1859–1900*. Urbana: University of Illinois Press, 1971.

Hekman, Susan. 'Reconstituting the Subject: Feminism Modernism, and Postmodernism'. *Hypatia: A Journal of Feminist Philosophy* 6(2) (1991): 44–63.

Hird, Myra J. *Sex, Gender and Science*. Basingstoke: Palgrave, 2004.

Laqueur, Thomas W. *Making Sex: Body and Gender From the Greeks to Freud*. Cambridge: Harvard University Press, 1990.

MacKinnon, Catherine. *Feminist Unmodified: Discourses on Life and Law*. Cambridge: Harvard University Press, 1987.

Martin, Emily. 'The Egg and the Sperm: How Science Has Constructed a Romance Based on Stereotypical Male-Female Roles'. *Signs: Journal of Women in Culture and Society* 16(3) (1991), 485–501.

McClintock, Anne. *Imperial Leather: Race, Gender and Sexuality in Colonial Contest*. New York: Routledge, 1995.

Marshall, Gloria A. 'Racial Classifications: Popular and Scientific'. *The 'Racial' Economy of Science: Toward a Democratic Future*. Ed. Sandra Harding. Bloomington: Indiana University Press, 1993. 116–27.

Pateman, Carole. *The Sexual Contract*. Stanford: Stanford University Press, 1988.

Petersen, Alan. 'Sexing the Body: Presentations of Sex Differences in Gray's *Anatomy*, 1858 to the Present'. *Body and Society* 4(1) (1998),1–15.

Said, Edward. *Orientalism*. New York: Pantheon Books, 1978.

Scheman, Naomi. 'Though This Be Method, Yet There *Is* Madness in It: Paranoia and Liberal Epistemology'.

Feminist Social Thought, A Reader. Ed. Diana T. Meyers. New York: Routledge, 1997, 342–67.

Schiebinger, Londa. *Has Feminism Changed Science?* Cambridge: Harvard University Press, 1999.

———. *The Mind Has No Sex? Women in the Origins of Modern Science*. Cambridge: Harvard University Press, 1989.

Shilling, Chris. *The Body and Social Theory*. London, Sage, 1993.

Spivak, Gayatri C. 'Can the Subaltern Speak?' *Marxism and the Interpretation of Culture*. Eds Cary Nelson and Lawrence Grossberg. Urbana: University of Illinois Press, 1988. 271–313.

Stacey, Judith. *In the Name of the Family: Rethinking Family Values in the Postmodern Age*. Boston: Beacon Press, 1996.

Stoler, Ann L. *Carnal Knowledge and Imperial Power; Race and the Intimate in Colonial Rule*. Berkeley: University of California Press, 2002.

Vancouver Rape Relief v. B.C. Human Rights, [2000] BCSC 889.

Vancouver Rape Relief Society v. Nixon et al., [2003] BCSC 1936W.

Whittle, Stephen. 'Gender Fucking or Fucking Gender? Current Cultural Contributions to Theories of Gender Blending'. *Blending Genders: Social Aspects of Cross-Dressing and Sex-Changing*. Eds. Richard Ekins and Dave King. New York: Routledge, 1996.

Yuval-Davis, Nira. *Gender and Nation*. New York, Sage, 1997.

What's to Fear: Calling Homophobia into Question

Didi Khayatt

Over 30 years ago, when I started teaching secondary school in a small town in Northern Ontario, I was assigned a general level, grade 11, French-as-a-second-language class to teach in the last period of every Friday afternoon. French was a compulsory course in that era of Pierre Trudeau—a fact that could partially explain the students' antipathy for the subject. On one particular Friday, the students were especially apathetic about working on their French, pleading tiredness, boredom, and disinterest in the subject. I had a very difficult time keeping them working. They tried to find excuses to leave the classroom, to speak to their neighbour, and

generally to disrupt my attempts to force them to exercise their French language. One young man, a student who was 19 and who was doing badly in every one of his courses, shot his hand up wanting to be recognized. I acknowledged his request for attention and he immediately asked if he could go to the bathroom. He had made this same request—and been granted it—at least twice already. I answered 'no' rather emphatically. He then whispered in a voice he made sure reached me: 'She's in a bad mood because she probably did not get fucked last night.'

This anecdote clearly articulates Foucault's notion of power as exercised or negotiated: I am the teacher with institutionalized authority, and I am female. He is a student with little institutional authority and he is male. He has a certain social power and one way to play it out is to reduce me to a sexual subject. It also indicates, however, an intuitive knowledge of how gender and sexuality interact. How did he learn about the interplay of gender and sexuality? How did he think he could get away with challenging the institutional authority of a teacher? 'Sexuality', said Foucault, 'is a means through which power is exercised' (quoted in Kritzman, 1988, pp. 113, 122).

The social power invested in masculinity has long been analyzed by feminists (see for instance, Walkerdine, 1990; Arnot, 2002; Grumet, 1988). More recently, as I continue to retell the anecdote, always with some amount of disbelief, the question became, not what compelled (indeed, allowed) him to confront the authority of a (female) teacher, but more: what is the connection between his ability to evoke sexuality and established gender domination? A great deal has been written about hegemonic masculinity in the last decade, the best of which disrupts mainstream adherence to a notion of 'true masculinity' that, as Connell (1995) reminds us, 'is almost always thought to proceed from men's bodies—to be inherent in a man's body or to express something about a male body' (p. 45). We currently recognize that there are multiple expressions of masculinity, because, in the words of Connell:

> [T]o the extent the term can be briefly defined at all, is simultaneously a place in gender relations, the practice through which men and women engage that place in gender, and the effects of these practices in bodily experience, personality and culture. (1995, p. 71)

Despite numerous studies that have looked at, referred to, and reported on research about masculinity and have recognized its multiplicities and complexities, mainstream expressions of masculinity continue to put forth a notion of the term that is 'generic', that is the binary opposite to femininity, and that is essentialized. It is precisely this view of masculinity that I will deal with in this paper: a version of an essentialized hegemonic conception of the term. The most salient reason for continuing to work with a normative and essentialized understanding of masculinity is that most students in both elementary and secondary schools believe that it is the *only* form of masculinity and that anything that deviates from this one expression of masculinity is, in the words of youngsters in the school hallways and playground: 'gay'.

Two unrelated reasons forced me to look at the interplay between gender and sexuality: the first happened when writing a chapter (Khayatt, 1992) about lesbian teachers trying to manage their sexuality by passing as heterosexual. The question occurred to me that it was not their sexuality they needed to alter so much as their gender in order for students and staff to perceive them as 'straight'. Since then, and because of the work of a number of scholars (Butler, 1990; Sedgwick, 1990), I realized that the act of passing is one that relies on performativity of gender: for a lesbian, for instance, to pass as straight means dressing and acting as straight; and for a gay man to pass as straight, he must dress and act as straight. The second reason that compelled me to look at the connection between gender and sexuality occurred when I realized that the sexual acts engaged in between partners are essentially the same regardless of the sex/gender of the partners. So what is it that makes lesbians, gay men, transgendered/transsexual people threatening in mainstream society? What is the fear and loathing often engendered by queers? I suggest, in this paper, that it is not so much the sex acts that people practice as how some sexual practices disrupt what is hegemonically expected of each gender.

A number of other reasons over the years lead me to note to what extent queers[1] seem to pose a threat to mainstream and hegemonic notions of gender, but in particular to masculinity. For instance, it has seemed imperative in North American mainstream media to distance masculinity from gayness. Why else is 'Western'[2] science currently obsessed with finding a 'gay gene' (see *The Globe and Mail*, 1995, p. A12 or *The Toronto Star*, 1996, p. B2), with attempting to measure fingers to reflect hetero or homo sexuality (*G&M*, 2000),[3] or intentionally overlooking incidents of homoerotic behaviour in animals?[4] [. . .] Furthermore, we now know that physicians surgically reshape the genitalia of those babies who are born ambiguously constituted. Yet it is not merely a matter of sexuality, since those boys at school who get bashed either verbally or physically are not those who are necessarily gay, but those who *look* gay.[5] [. . .]

Schools both reinforce and, at the same time, reflect mainstream normative genders and sexualities. Schools teach intentionally (through the curriculum) and unintentionally, through values promoted by teachers, administration, boards, and parents, a taken-for-granted normative sexuality and concomitant expectations of gender behaviour. Many scholars working within education have suggested that schools reproduce gender conformity, and by extension, sexual conventionality for both boys and girls. For instance, David Denborough, discussing specifically what is expected for males (1996), states that 'sexuality for many young men [in schools] becomes a key area to prove one's masculinity and source of power' (p. 5). Chris McLean also believes that 'Boys quickly learn [at school] that one of the most important signifiers of masculinity is having a sexual relationship with a woman' (p. 29). In a more recent article, Amy Wallis and Jo VanEvery (2000) take the argument even further and claim:

We do not believe that (hetero)sexuality is *only* about gender, but we find it difficult in theory and in practice to completely separate the two. Key processes which constitute both sexuality and gender include naturalization, particularly through notions of the complementarity of masculinities and femininities, with clear effects on the intelligibility of homosexualities. (Emphases in original, p. 410)

Furthermore, Jill Blackmore et al. (1996) refer to Mac an Ghaill's contention that the cultural elements that constitute 'the dominant modes of heterosexual subjectivity informing male students' learning to act like men in schools describes them as "contradictory" forms of compulsory heterosexuality, misogyny and homophobia' (p. 210).

Whether it is sexism, racism, classism, or ableism, we are frequently talking about discrimination, often systemic, sometimes harsh and hateful, always hurtful and demeaning. While 'heterosexism' is an omission, a pervasive yet systemic assumption that precludes any expression of sexuality that does not conform with heteronormativity, homophobia is about hatred and fear. Wayne Dynes (1985, p. 66) writes in his *Homolexis* that homophobia: 'connotes irrational fear of homosexual acts, persons, or sentiments'.[6] Clearly we are not just referring to 'discrimination', which, appalling as it is, indicates at 'best' legal injustice and at worst, hatefulness and humiliation. We are, in the case of homosexuality, discussing a 'phobia', a term that Peter Redman, drawing on the work of Freud and of Laplanche and Pontalis, reminds us is derived from 'psychoanalytic theory in which phobias are understood as the product of "anxiety hysteria": an extreme fear of an object or situation characterized by avoidance strategies, in which anxiety arising from conflict in the inner-world of the psyche is displaced on to an external object or situation, which then stands in for the original' (p. 485).

My questions for this paper are: what is to fear and why fear and not simply loathing? Why 'anxiety' rather than plain hatred? What is it that mainstream society cannot bear about homosexuality, or any expression of resistance to heteronormativity? And, what makes schools particularly hostile to teaching or tolerating deviance from set notions of essentialized and normative sexuality?

[. . .]

In this paper, therefore, I will attempt to elaborate sociologically on mainstream elision between gay male sexuality and femininity, and how this is played out in our schools in North America. I am arguing that it is precisely this elision of gay male sexuality with 'femininity' that renders schools sites where a hegemonic masculinity disavows any deviation from heteronormativity.

In a recent issue of *Saturday Night* (Bauer, 2003) the subtitle for an article entitled 'Gender Bender' is, 'if your little boy wants to be a little girl . . . Dr. Kenneth Zucker will treat him'. The reader is quickly informed of the new diagnosis of 'childhood gender identity disorder' or GID. The article states that Dr. Zucker heads the Child and Adolescent GID Clinic in Toronto, the only full-time North American centre devoted exclusively to the diagnosis and treatment of child and adolescent GID. As readers, we are also given to understand that anxious parents from all across Canada 'come to Dr. Zucker's office accompanied by their children—mostly boys—who either believe themselves to be, or desperately wish to be, the opposite gender' (p. 61). His detractors believe that Zucker is capitalizing on a cultural fear of 'sissies' particularly since most of his attention is on male children. Zucker himself is convinced that 'letting nature

run its course raises the odds that these children will seek out gender-reassignment (sex change) surgery later in life—an enormously complicated procedure that may provide patients with the desired parts, but hardly assures their happiness' (p. 61). Zucker maintains that children suffer from their gender dysphoria, that they are harassed and bullied in school because they are perceived as sissies, that they are ostracized, and that this condition often leads to homosexuality: 'According to Dr. Zucker about 75 per cent of children with GID report a homosexual orientation by late adolescence' (p. 61).

Throughout the article about Zucker's work, there is a collapsing of gender and sexuality, in some cases as a causal relationship, in other instances one term seems to stand for the other. Furthermore, the article does not show any understanding that 'masculinity' can have multiple expressions, and that these are contextually reliant. That gender and sexuality are related, not to say fundamentally interconnected, is the premise of this paper, but it is precisely the tension between gender and sexuality that I intend to explore within the context of education.

Although schools are not the only place that children learn about gender, they do play a significant role in the development and reinforcement of gender performativity. From a very young age, as shown by Karen Bailey (1993) in her book *The girls are the ones with the pointy nails*, children are aware that there should be a difference between girls' and boys' behaviour, looks, likes, and abilities. Adolescents are even more inclined to conform to normative, even if multiple expressions of gender. (See, for instance, McLean, 1996; Marino & Pallotta-Chiarolli, 2001; Epstein & Johnson, 1998; Hilton, 2001.) Furthermore, it is not only children and adolescents who engage in gender displays in schools, but, as both Connell (1995) and Francis and Skelton (2001) demonstrate in their study of men teachers and masculinity in British schools, there is no denying that, for the most part, 'a successful construction of [normative] masculinity also requires individual male teachers to demonstrate their own heterosexual identity' (p. 488).

Although this connection between gender and sexuality is not new as I demonstrated above, I became interested in the interplay between those two concepts during the time I was working on attempting to disrupt the sexual categories by which Euro-North-American scholars assume the unproblematic transposition of sexual categories, such as 'gay', 'lesbian', 'bisexual', and 'transgendered'. There have been a number of volumes that recount looking for gays and lesbians, bisexuals, transgendered people in various nations around the globe (see Penelope & Valentine, 1990; GLQ; Herdt, 1997), some of which recognize differences in conceptualizations of such terms. The tendency, however, is to see the development of the concept of sexual identities as parallel to those assumed by the authors, and when these do not correspond, they are presumed lacking in terms of a developmental linearity. By that I mean that frequently when conceptualizations of gender/sexuality categories occur in various areas of the world, they are measured hierarchically against a Euro-North-American understanding of sexual identities and are often found wanting. They are often perceived as a primitive instance that will eventually develop into identity categories similar to those found in North America. It is this very tendency that led me to research how gender/sexuality practices are articulated, understood, and played out in Egypt.[7]

This study, and what I had to read in connection with it, disrupted my understanding of sexuality. Where I previously thought I was looking to trouble categories of sexuality as these are articulated in current Euro-North-American scholarship, I came to realize that any study of sexuality that proceeded without a thorough examination

and a fundamental reconceptualization of how gender operates in conjunction with sexuality in a particular culture is incomplete in its analysis.

At the time of my research, my understanding of the consummate relation between gender and sexuality came as a result of two separate incidents. The first was my reading that sexual relations between two men in Egypt is not in itself denounced culturally and socially.[8] It is the sexually passive partner who is condemned as a '*khawal*', a word that approximates the term 'faggot'. The second instance that allowed me to rethink some of my assumptions was when I interviewed some women who mentioned the connection between gender and sexuality within the context of what is appropriate sexually for women in Egypt. I did not particularly want to hear what they had to say because it concerned the issue of cliterodectomy, and yet I could not deny the importance of what they were saying. Several of my interviewees mentioned that one of the reasons a woman may desire another one is if her clitoris was not cut off. Cliterodectomy (*khitan al-banar*) or *Tahara*, as it is colloquially known in Egypt, means purification or cleanliness. Farha Ghannam (1997), in a monograph on reproductive health in Egypt, elaborates:

> [cliterodectomy] reduces the burden of sexual practices for the husband, beautifies and purifies the female body, and maintains the dignity of the woman who should not humiliate herself by demanding sexual attention. The circumcision is also part of the process of defining gender identities. Removing the clitoris is perceived as essential to inscribe the (female) identity on her body. It is argued that, if the clitoris is not removed, it will grow and become a penis. Women will be like men. Several circumcized women insisted that they saw the 'penises' of uncircumcized

women. Thus, the female identity is partially formed through shaping the body in a way that exaggerates the biological features that differentiate women from men and suppress or remove 'natural' features that are believed to resemble the male body. (pp. 9–10)

Unless she is 'circumcized' a woman would not be able to find a husband, hence the prevalence of the custom despite its illegality.

Homoerotic practices, in the Middle East are condemned officially, yet deemed necessary because of segregation of the sexes. As Dunne (1990, p. 64) observes:

'The crime is not homosexuality, but the public exposure of conventionally unacceptable, if nonetheless widespread, behaviour, in effect a failure of a social strategy of concealment.' When homoerotic practices do occur, a Middle Eastern man's masculinity is not imperilled should he penetrate, but his ('passive') partner's masculinity is jeopardized in the act of being penetrated. Oberhelman, quoting Rowson, observes that boys, being not yet men, could be penetrated without losing their potential manliness, 'so long as they did not register pleasure in the act, which would suggest a pathology liable to continue into adulthood' (1997, p. 70).

This reflects a concept of masculinity that considers penetration as a dominant act and being penetrated as subordination. It would apply to men with either women or other men. The distinction between 'penetrator' and 'penetrated' seen in homoerotic practices between two men in the Middle East suggests that masculinity is defined in terms of gender: who is dominant in this intercourse?

Conversely, in Euro-North-American homoerotic sexuality, both partners are condemned regardless of who is on top because the very penetration of a man imperils his masculinity.

Masculinity, in this culture *is* impenetrability.[9] Clearly, impenetrability is not the only factor that defines notions of masculinity in Euro-North-American contexts, but it can and does act as a metaphor for how masculinity is played out, particularly for young males in high school, but also for adult men who perceive masculinity only in its normative articulation. For instance, in a study of Norwegian gay men, Middelthon (2002) argues that they both desire and fear, even dread, the act of being penetrated anally. The author, questioning this fear, quotes a young man in her study who was able to articulate this dread:

If I am to do it [be anally penetrated]—it is terribly humiliating—then I would have to have a possibility to fuck [take] him afterwards—one example of this [he gives the interviewer a glance of apology], is that if I did not do so I would feel like a cunt [fitte] afterwards—if I had fucked [taken] him too—that would have restored or repaired the humiliation. (p. 193)

Clearly, it is not *what actually happens* between two men that is at stake, but what is *imagined* as happening between two men that may cast aspersions on their masculinity: both are imagined as penetrated. It should be mentioned, however, that not all gay cultures are included in this analysis, because mainstream representations of gay men do not include such gay subcultures as skinheads, leathermen, or other hypermasculine images that may exist.

I suggest that because gender is perceived as an essentialist bi-polar category with masculinity as impenetrable and femininity as penetrable, the phallic penetration of a man by another man, orally, but especially anally, renders both of them 'feminized', that is, potentially capable of being penetrated. This would constitute a profound disruption to the social order that presumes that masculinity and femininity are separate categories, that they are mutually exclusive of each other and, at best, socially complement each other, but more importantly, that masculinity is imbued with social power in relation to femininity. I am not suggesting that other social factors, such as race and class, do not affect power relations, but rather pointing to a particular domination based on gender as articulated through sexuality. A Foucaudian discursive analysis that allows categories of gender and/or sexuality to be conceived as unsettled, fluid, shifting, and with permeable boundaries is threatening precisely because it destabilizes essential notions of masculinity as impenetrable. Mainstream interpretation of the diversity of sexualities and genders relies on and demands solid categories that are separate and distinct from the essential binary notion of gender.

This paper was written with the express intention of troubling hegemonic notions of gender and sexuality as these are played out within the context of the education system in Canada. But what have we learned from the analysis above? For one, attempting to deal in schools with the subject of sexuality alone cannot work as long as this notion is not tied with an analysis of hegemonic masculinity and, by extension, femininity. Secondly, as long as in schools we are teaching boys about 'tolerance' toward 'homosexuality' without ever broaching the subject of what exactly is threatening about 'queer' sexuality, without making the connection between the anxiety of being penetrated and their fear of having their masculinity questioned or being perceived as 'feminized', we are maintaining the status quo. Thirdly, because there are school principals who are women, and because many of the issues in education that deal with gender have been recognized, it is often felt that we have dealt with gender and now should go on to a more 'difficult' topic, that of sexuality. I propose that schools should deal with gender *in conjunction* with sexuality, to show the connection and thus dispel or even just trouble the fear, the 'homophobia'. I suggest that what allowed the young man in my initial story to challenge the teacher's authority by drawing on gender/sexuality, to say that what I really needed is a 'good fuck' was that he intuitively saw me as penetrable, and himself implicitly as impenetrable and therefore somehow beyond the purview of institutional influence.

In conclusion, I think that, as long as masculinity is privileged, as long as there are systemic and personal advantages to being a man, and as long as essentialist notions of male homosexuality are conceived as a 'feminized masculinity', there is little hope that libratory work will successfully change attitudes toward sexual orientation.

Notes

1. I am using 'queer' as an umbrella term to denote all sexualities that are not heteronormative.
2. By putting quotation marks around 'Western', I am signalling my understanding that the 'West' is not monolithic. Having said that, the term stands in contradistinction to 'Middle East', another problematic word that flattens the diversity of that area.
3. The article maintained that you can tell if someone is gay by the shape of the fingers of a hand. The need to make a *physical* distinction between gay and straight men points based on the shape of fingers to a necessity for the media to distance straight masculinity from gay masculinity: not only are gay men different in sexuality, but they are also different physically, goes the argument. Furthermore, the

article creates a binary between straight and gay masculinity, hinting that the latter are tainted or not quite the real thing.

4. See *The Globe and Mail:* Study confirms existence of gay gene in men. October 31, 1995, p. Al2; *The Globe and Mail:* Brains of gay, straight men show differences. Thursday, November 17, 1994, p. A6; *The Toronto* Star: Birth Order Linked to homosexuality. Tuesday, January 16,1996, p. B2. Regarding the size of fingers, see *The Globe and Mail,* Can fingers point to sexual preference? Thursday, March 30, 2000. And finally, see the Spring issue (Number 101) of *Equinox,* pp. 24–35.

5. See recent account of the young teenager who killed himself in Vancouver because he was harassed at school.

6. Kenneth Plummer (1975, p. 103), in his *Sexual Stigma: An Interactionist Account* (p. 103) writes that 'Other writers have recently begun to characterize this phenomenon [homophobia] with such names as "dread of homosexuality" (Hoffman, 1968), "homophobia" (Smith, 1971; Weinberg, 1973), "homoerotophobia" (Churchill, 1967) and "anti-homosexualism" (Hacker, 1971). The term that has emerged in mainstream writing is "homophobia" which, as Dynes reminds us, was made widespread by George Weinberg and others' (p. 66).

7. See Khayatt, M. Didi, 1992.

8. Although, religiously, sex between two men is an abomination.

9. I want to thank Gretchen Phillips for this word. Private conversation in Toronto, November, 1999.

References

Arnot, M. (2002). *Reproducing gender? Essays on educational theory and feminist politics.* London; New York: Routledge/Falmer.

Bailey, K.R. (1993). *The girls are the ones with the pointy nails: An exploration of children's conceptions of gender.* London, ON: The Althouse Press.

Bauer, G. (2003, Feb. 21), Gender bender: If your little boy wants to be a little girl . . . *Saturday Night,* pp. 60–64.

Blackmore, J., with Kenway, J., Willis, S., & Rennie, L. (1996). Putting up with the put down? 'Girls, boys, power and sexual harassment. In L. Laskey & C. Beavis (Eds), *Schooling and sexualities: Teaching for a positive sexuality* (pp. 201–20). Victoria, Australia: Deakin Centre for Education and Change, Deakin University.

Butler, J. (1990). *Gender trouble: Feminism and the subversion of identity.* New York: Routledge.

———. (1993). *Bodies that matter: On the discursive limits of 'sex'.* New York, London: Routledge.

Connell, R.W. (1995). *Masculinities,* Berkeley/Los Angeles: University of California Press.

Denborough, D. (1996). Power and partnership? Challenging the sexual construction of schooling. In L. Laskey & C. Beavis (Eds), *Schooling and sexualities: Teaching for a positive sexuality* (pp. 1–10), Victoria, Australia: Deakin Centre for Education and Change, Deakin University.

Dynes, W. (1985). *Homolexis: A historical and cultural lexicon of homosexuality.* New York: Gai Saber Monograph No.4.

Epstein, D., & Johnson, R. (1998). *Schooling sexualities.* Buckingham, Philadelphia: Open University Press.

Francis, R., & Skelton, C. (2001). Men teachers and the construction of heterosexual masculinity in the classroom. *Sex Education,* 1(1), 9–21.

Ghannam, E. (1997). Fertile, plump, and strong: The social construction of the female body in low-income Cairo, *Reproductive Health,* 3, 9–10.

GLQ: *A Journal of Lesbian and Gay Studies,* 5(4).

Grumet, M.R. (1988). *Bitter milk: Women and teaching.* Amherst: University of Massachusetts Press.

Herdt, O. (1997). *Same sex different cultures: Exploring gay and lesbian lives.* Boulder, CO: Westview Press.

Hilton, G.L.S. (2001), Sex education—the issues when working with boys. *Sex Education,* 1(1), 31–41.

Khayatt, M.D, (1992). *Lesbian teachers: An invisible presence.* Albany, NY: State University of New York Press.

Kritzman, L (Ed.). *Michel Foucault: Politics, philosophy, culture, interviews and other writings 1977–1984.* New York: Routledge.

McLean, C. (1996). Men, masculinity and heterosexuality. In L. Laskey & C. Beavis (Eds). *Schooling and sexualities: Teaching for a positive sexuality* (pp. 25–36). Victoria, Australia: Deakin Centre for Education and Change, Deakin University.

Middelthon, A.-L., & Being, A. (2002, May). Penetrated: Erotic inhibitions, improvizations and transformations. *Sexualities,* 5(2), 181–200.

Oberhelman, S.M. (1997). Hierarchies of gender, ideology, and power in ancient and medieval greek and arabic dream literature. In J.W. Write, Jr. & E.K. Rowson (Eds), *Homoeroticism in classical arabic literature.* New York: Columbia University Press.

Penelope, J., & Valentine, S. (1990). *Finding the lesbians: Personal accounts from around the world.* Freedom, CA: The Freedom Press.

Plummer, K. (1975). *Sexual stigma: An interactionist account.* London: Routledge and Kegan Paul.

Sedgwick, E.K. (1990). *Epistemology of the closet.* Berkeley/Los Angeles: University of California Press.

Walkerdine, V. (1990). *Schoolgirl fictions.* London; New York: Verso.

Wallis, A., & VanEvery, J. (2000, Nov.). Sexuality in the primary school. *Sexualities,* 3(4), 409–23.

PART IV
Dialogue Box 4
Trust the Web: It Gets Better

Ivor Tossell

It Gets Better just gets bigger.

In late September, rattled by the suicides of a series of gay teens, author and advice columnist Dan Savage had a thought: 'I wish I could've talked to him for five minutes; I wish I could've told him that it gets better.'

It didn't take him long to realize that, in fact, he could. He set up a YouTube channel and posted a video in which both he and his long-term boyfriend, sitting behind a table in a café, discussed their experiences of growing up, and how much better life became after they'd run the gauntlet of high school. Then they invited everyone to do the same.

In the month since then, what started as a personal plea from an advice columnist has become a full-blown political movement.

A remarkable thing is happening here. Online phenomena are often derided as flashes in the pan that rattle around online without having real-world impact. But here, a viral video project has enabled a political conversation at the highest levels—and in a country that sorely needs it.

At last count, *It Gets Better* had attracted more than 3000 entries. Mr Savage's video was followed by thousands of others, from women and men, from the transgendered and the straight. An episcopal clergyman from Richmond, VA, telling young people that God loves them 'just the way they are'. A city councillor in Fort Worth, TX, tearfully describing how his cowboy father came to accept him. Ontario Premier Dalton McGuinty taking to Twitter to urge citizens to 'stand up against bullying and support our gay children'.

US Secretary of State Hillary Clinton made her own video.

Finally, five weeks after Dan Savage sat down in a restaurant, President Barack Obama himself sat down in front of a video camera and delivered a three-minute appeal. 'I don't know what it's like to be picked on for being gay', he said. 'But I do know what it's like to grow up feeling that sometimes you don't belong. It's tough.'

Even by the loose standards of things-that-go-viral, this is noteworthy. It is not terrifically easy to get the president of the United States to contribute to your viral video project. The man is busy. He has some unfinished business with the global economy; he's trying to keep his party from being thrashed in next month's elections, and he probably spends at least some time fiddling with the launch codes. Yet there he was.

The fact that this project has gone from grassroots (or as grassroots as you can be if, like Mr Savage, you're an enormously popular relationship-advice columnist) to something the Oval Office deems politically expedient is extraordinary.

First, it's a testament to the project's universality. Put aside the question of homophobia for a moment. Who hasn't, at some point, wanted to deliver a message-in-a-bottle to their younger selves? Who hasn't wanted the reassurance that the trial of adolescence will eventually end? (Never mind youth being wasted on the young: The years that are the hardest are the ones that drag on the longest.)

One of the most refreshing things about the project is how unmanipulative it is. There's plenty of emotion in tales of harassment, repression, redemption, and accept-ance. But, by definition, this is a bunch of people talking about how happy they are now. That's the kind of sentiment it's easy to get behind.

More importantly, the project arrived at the right moment in North American life. *It Gets Better* comes at a time when homophobia—like many forms of nativism and xenophobia—is enjoying a period of acceptance in the United States.

The US media still give credibility to the kind of people who put the word 'gay' in quotation marks. America is so great, so wild-eyed, that it's not just debating gay marriage; it's simultaneously asking itself whether it's all right to be gay at all. Voices that comfortable urban liberals, gay and straight, once wrote off as hopeless fringe elements are coming to dominate US politics.

Just two weeks ago, the Tea Party–backed Republican candidate for governor in New York, a nasty piece of work named Carl Paladino, delivered a major speech urging that children not be 'brainwashed into thinking that homosexuality is a . . . valid and successful option'. Mr Paladino was pressed into backpedalling, but the fact remains: This is where their national conversation is at these days.

This is the moment at which *It Gets Better* has entered the stage. And that might be why a project whose audience was meant to be a group of voiceless, at-risk youth has instead found itself on the national agenda, giving leaders a framework for action. It's become a bridge between the experiences of citizens and the national dialogue, from a teen's darkened bedroom to the legislature.

It also shows us that online activism doesn't always stay online. When a ground-swell of citizens embraces a cause, it gives leaders an opportunity to jump on the bandwagon and provides them with a time, and a reason, to speak out. It's a frame-work for taking a stand, and that stand comes none too soon.

Critical Conversations: Discussion Questions

1. How would you describe homophobia? How does homophobia affect you? [Editor's Note: If you answered Starting Points question 2, pay attention to how your answers to these questions may have changed from your responses before you read the chapters in this section. Which articles would you say most influenced these changes?]

2. All the authors in this section have demon-strated the complex ways notions of sexuality are implicated in (are a part of) other aspects of our identity (for example, gender, ethnicity, employment status, age group, citizenship). How do these perspectives encourage you to change what you thought sexuality was before you read this book?

3. What differences do you see between Sandy Welsh's analysis of harassment in chapter 2 and Jennifer Berdahl's theory of sex-based harassment in chapter 11? Which approach makes the most sense to you and why?

4. Didi Khayatt wants us to think about the subtle, and not so subtle, ways sexual norms are used to keep people in line/in their place. Does her discussion remind you of any of the arguments of other authors in this collection? Which ones? Explain.

5. At the end of Part I you were asked about the relationship between sex and gender. Considering the scholarship you have now read, do you think that there is a necessary relationship between sex, gender, and sexuality? How do you explain the persistence of this conception?

Glossary

Homophobia Coined by George Weinberg (1972), homophobia originally referred to the psychological fear of homosexuals. The use of this term has since been expanded and complicated to include the idea of homophobia as the fear of being misrecognized as gay or homosexual. Contemporary considerations of homophobia, such as from R.W. Connell (1995), consider its influence in the construction of normative notions of masculinity.

Social constructionism A general term applied to social theories that emphasize the social created aspects of social life. Specifically, these theories emphasize the perspective that society is actively and creatively constructed by humans rather than simply a set of given or taken-for-granted arrangements. Our social worlds are created through the ongoing processes of interpretation by individuals and groups.

Credits

Mary Louise Adams, '"Why Can't I Be Normal?"': Sex Advice for Teens'. From *The Trouble with Normal: Postwar Youth and the Making of Heterosexuality*. Published by the University of Toronto Press. Copyright ©1997. pp. 83–106.

Andrea Zoe Aster, 'Double Jeopardy: Building Strong Communities to Fight Homophobia and Racism,' *Cross Currents* (2004/05): http://camh.net/Publication/Cross_Currents/Winter_2004-05/doublejeopardy_crcu0405.html. Published by the Centre for Addiction and Mental Health. As accessed June 28, 2010. Pp. 1–2.

Jennifer L. Berdahl, 'Harassment Based on Sex: Protecting Social Status in the Context of Gender Heirarchy,' *Academy of Management Review*, 32, 2 (2007): 641–58.

Melanie Beres, '"It Just Happens" Negotiating Casual Heterosexual Sex.' From *The Gendered Society Reader*: Canadian Edition. Published by Oxford University Press. Copyright © 2008.pp. 370–81.

Susan Brigham and Catherine Baillie Abidi, 'International Female Migration to Atlantic Canada through Internet Mediated Match-Making Agencies,' *Atlantis* 34, 1 (2009): 159–68.

Tyler L. Brown and Kevin G. Alderson, 'Sexual Identity and Heterosexual Male Students' Usage of Homosexual Insults: An Exploratory Study,' *The Canadian Journal of Human Sexuality*, 19, 1-2 (2010): 27–42.

E. Sandra Byers, Heather A. Sears, Susan D. Voyer, Jennifer L. Thurlow, Jacqueline N. Cohen and Angela D. Weaver, 'An Adolescent Perspective on Sexual Health Education at School and at Home: I. High School Students,' *The Canadian Journal of Human Sexuality*, 12, 1 (2003) 1–17.

Martin Cannon, 'The Regulation of First Nations Sexuality,' *The Canadian Journal of Native Studies* 18, 1 (1998): 1–18.

Richard Carpiano, 'Passive Medicalization: The Case of Viagra and Erectile Dysfunction,' *Sociological Spectrum*, 21, 3 (2001): 441–50.

Damian Collins, 'Culture, Religion and Curriculum: Lessons from the 'Three Books' Controversy in Surrey, BC,' *The Canadian Geographer* 50, 3 (2006): 342–357.

Tia Dafnos, 'What Does Being Gay Have to Do with It? A Feminist Analysis of the Jubran Case,' *Canadian Journal of Criminology and Criminal Justice* 49, 5 (2007): 561–85. doi:10.3138?cjccj.49.5.561

Phyllis Dalley and Mark David Campbell, 'Constructing and Contesting Discourses of Heteronormativity: An Ethnographic Study of Youth in a Francophone High School in Canada,' *Journal of Language, Identity, and Education* 5, 1 (2006): 11–29.

Simone de Beauvoir, 'The Data of Biology'. From *The Second Sex*, translated by Constance Border and Sheila Malovany-Chevallier, translation copyright © 2009 by Constance Border and Sheila Malovany-Chevallier. Used by permisison of Alfred A. Knopf, a division of Random House, Inc. Pp. 3–37.

Velma Demerson, from *Incorrigble*. Published by Wilfrid Laurier University Press. Copyright © 2004. Pp. 31–49.

Keith Dowler, 'Sex. Lies, and Videotape: The Presentation of Sex Crime in Local Television News," *Journal of Criminal Justice*, 34 (2006) 383–92.

OmiSoore Dryden, 'Canadians Denied: A Queer Diasporic Analysis of the Canadian Blood Donor,' *Atlantis*, 34, 2 (2010): 77–84.

Friedrich Engels, 'The Monogamous Family'. From *Origins of the Family, Private Property, and the State*. Published by Marx/Engels Internet Archive (marxists.org). Copyright © 2000. Pp. 2–18.

Shawna Ferris, '"The Lone Streetwalker" Missing Women and Sex Work Related News,' *West Coast Line*, 41, 1 (2007): 14–24.

Michel Foucault, 'The Repressive Hypothesis'. From *The History of Sexuality: An Introduction, Volume 1*. Published by Vintage Books, A Division of Random House, Inc. Copyright © 1990. Pp. 17–35.

Andre P. Grace and Kristopher Wells, 'The Marc Hall Prom Predicament: Queer Individual Rights v. Institutional Church Rights in Canadian Public Education,' *Canadian Journal of Education*, 28, 3 (2005): 237–70.

Adam Isaiah Green, 'Until Death Do Us Part? The Impact of Differential Access to Marriage on a Sample of Urban Men,' *Sociological Perspectives* 49, 2 (2006): 163–89.

Cailey Hartwick, Serge Desmarais, and Karl Hennig, 'Characteristics of male and female victims of sexual coercion,' *The Canadian Journal of Human Sexuality*, 16, 1-2 (2007) p. 31–44.

Morgan Holmes, 'Minding the Gaps: Intersex and (Reproductive) Spaces in Disability Studies and Bioethics,' *Bioethical Inquiry* 5, 2-3 (2008): 169–81. doi 10.1007/s11673-007-9073-2

Alan Hunt and Bruce Curtis, 'A genealogy of the genital kiss: oral sex in the twentieth century,' *Canadian Journal of Human Sexuality* 15, 2 (2006): 69–84.

Mahida Didi Khayatt, 'What's to Fear: Calling Homophobia into 'Question,' *McGill Journal of Education* 41, 2 (2006): 133–44.

Gary Kinsman, 'The Historical Emergence of Homosexualities and Heterosexualities: Social Relations, Sexual Rule and Sexual Resistance,' 2nd revised edition. From *The Regulation of Desire: Homo and Hetero Sexualities*. Published by Black Rose Books. Copyright © 1996. Pp.23–47.

Celine Le Bourdais, Evelyne Lapierre-Adamcyk, 'Changes in Conjugal Life in Canada: Is Cohabitation Progressively Replacing Marriage?' *Journal of Marriage and Family*, 66, 4 (2004): 929–42.

Charity Marsh, 'Reading Contemporary "Bad Girls": The Transgressions and Triumphs of Madonna's "What it Feels Like for a Girl"', *Atlantis* 34, 1 (2009): 111–20.

Jennifer Matthews, *The Whistler Guys Study* (2007). www.whistlerguysstudy.com/ as accessed January 6, 2011.

Steven Maynard, '"Horrible temptations": Sex, Men, and Working-class Male Youth in Urban Ontario, 1890-1935.' Canadian Historical Review, 06 (1997) pp.1–28. http://home.wanadoo.nl/ipce/library_two/pdf/horr_temp.pdf

Stephanie Mitelman and Jo Visser, 'Trends in Adolescent Sexuality: A Look at Canadian Youth'. Canadian Principal. 13, 3: 21–4. http://www.cdnprincipals.org/vol13 no 3 Trends in Adolescent Sexuality.pdf

Todd G. Morrison, Travis A. Ryan, Lisa Fox, Daragh T. McDermott and Melanie A. Morrison, 'Canadian University Students' Perceptions of the Practices that Constitute "Normal" Sexuality for Men and Women'. *Canadian Journal of Human Sexuality* 17, 4 (2008) p. 161–71.

Viviane Namaste, "Making the Lives of Transsexual People Visible: Addressing the Politics of Social Erasure". From *Sex Change, Social Change: Reflections on Identity, Institutions, and Imperialism*, 2nd edition. Published by The Women's Press. Copyright © 2011. Pp. 1–10. Reprinted by permission of Women's Press.

Diane Naugler, 'Wearing Pink as a Stand Against Bullying: Why We Need to Say More'. *Journal of Homosexuality* 57, 3 (2010): 347–63.

David Newhouse, 'Magic and Joy: Traditional Aboriginal Views of Human Sexuality'. *The Canadian Journal of Human Sexuality* 7, 2 (Summer 1998): 183–87.

Ajnesh Prasad, "Reconsidering the Socio-Scientific Enterprise of Sexual Difference: The Case of Kimberly Nixon". *Canadian Woman Studies* 24, 2/3 (2005) p. 80–4.

Rebecca Raby, '"Tank Tops Are OK but I Don't Want to See Her Thong": Girls' Engagements With Secondary School Dress Codes,' *Youth & Society* 41, 3 (2010): 333–56.

Gayle Rubin, 'Thinking Sex: Notes for a Radical Theory of the Politics of Sexuality'. From *Devisionats*. Copyright © 2012. Duke University Press. All rights reserved. Reprinted by permission of the publisher. www.dukeupress.edu. Pp. 137–81.

Elizabeth M. Saewyc, Coleen S. Poon, Yuko Homma and Carol L. Skay, 'Stigma Management? The Links Between Enacted Stigma and Teen Pregnancy Trends Among Gay, Lesbian and Bisexual Students in British Columbia. *Canadian Journal of Human Sexuality* 17, 3 (2008): 123–39.

SIECCAN (Sex Information and Education Council of Canada, 'Sexual Health Education in the Schools: Questions & Answers, 3rd edition,' *The Canadian Journal of Human Sexuality* 18, 1-2 (2009): 47–60.

Anita Shaw, 'Media Representations of Adolescent Pregnancy,' *Atlantis*, 34, 2 (2010): 55–64.

Khosro Refale Shirpak, Eleanor Maticka-Tyndale and Maryam Chinichian, 'Iranian Immigrants' Perceptions of Sexuality in Canada: A Symbolic Interactionist Approach'. *Canadian Journal of Human Sexuality* 16, 3/4 (2007) 113–28.

Ivor Tossell, 'Trust the Web: It Gets Better,' The Globe and Mail October 26, 2010. http://www.theglobeandmail.com/news/technology/personal-tech/ivor-tossell/trust-the-web-it-gets-better/article1772920/ CTVglobemedia Publishing Inc. as accessed December 2, 2010. Pp. 1–4.

Jessie M. Tzeng. "Ethnically Heterogamous Marriages: The Case of Asian Canadians'. *Journal of Comparative Family Studies* 31, 3 (2000) 321–37.

Mariana Valverde, 'Bisexuality: Coping with Sexual Boundaries'. From *Sex, Power and Pleasure*. Published by The Women's Press. Copyright © 1985. Pp. 109–20. Reprinted by permission of Women's Press.

Mariana Valverde. 'A New Entity in the History of Sexuality: The Respectable Same-Sex Couple'. *Feminist Studies* 32, 1 (2006): 155–62.

Sandy Welsh, 'Gender and Sexual Harassment'. *Annual Review of Sociology* 25 (1999): 169–90.